Microsoft® Access 2000 Development

Stephen Forte
Tom Howe
James Ralston

Unleashed

Microsoft® Access 2000 Development Unleashed

Copyright ©1999 by Sams Publishing

International Standard Book Number: 0-672-31291-3

Library of Congress Catalog Card Number: 98-85915

Printed in the United States of America

First Printing: June 1999

00   99   4   3   2   1

Trademarks

Warning and Disclaimer

EXECUTIVE EDITOR
Rosemarie Graham

ACQUISITIONS EDITOR
Rosemarie Graham

DEVELOPMENT EDITORS
Marla Reece-Hall
Robyn Thomas

MANAGING EDITOR
Jodi Jensen

PROJECT EDITOR
Heather Talbot

COPY EDITOR
Linda Morris

INDEXER
Diane Brenner

PROOFREADER
Mike Henry

TECHNICAL EDITORS
Mark Duvall
Bruce Handley
David Juth
Eeraj Qaisar

SOFTWARE DEVELOPMENT SPECIALIST
Andrea Duvall

INTERIOR DESIGNER
Gary Adair

COVER DESIGNER
Aren Howell

COPY WRITER
Eric Borgert

LAYOUT TECHNICIAN
Cyndi Davis-Hubler

Contents at a Glance

Table of Contents

5   THE MICROSOFT JET DATABASE ENGINE 4.0   99

PART II DATA ACCESS 119

6   INTRODUCTION TO ACTIVEX DATA OBJECTS 121

About the Authors

Stephen Forte runs the New York City consulting firm, The Aurora Development Group (`www.auroradev.com`), which specializes in Microsoft Database and Web technology. He has authored and coauthored several books, including *Microsoft Jet Database Programmers Guide* (Microsoft Press) and *Access 97 Unleashed Second Edition* (Sams Publishing). He has written several magazine articles and is a contributing editor of *Access/VB Advisor*. Stephen also serves as president of the NYC Access and VB Developers group (`www.nycaccessvb.com`) and travels around the world speaking at Microsoft Developer Conferences.

Tom Howe graduated from Northwestern School of Law in 1982 and has been a practicing attorney ever since. Having tired of the practice of law, which has changed very little over the centuries, he decided to join the most dynamic profession in the world—software development. So now, except for a few trials a year (mostly to keep insurance companies in line), he spends almost all his time developing software and speaking at developer conferences.

Tom is president of Control Center Computing, Inc., a software company and Microsoft Solution Provider that develops applications for law firms and government offices.

He specializes in application development using Microsoft Access, Visual Basic, Outlook, Exchange, and SQL Server. Tom is a regular speaker at Tech*Ed, Advisor, Informant, and other developer conferences around the world.

Tom also is a Visual Basic Instructor for Application Developers Training Company and has produced Outlook development videos for Keystone Learning Systems.

Tom lives in Lake Oswego, Oregon, with his wife, Suzanne, and four kids: Josie, Andy, Sarah, and Mychal; and their slothful dog, Leo.

James Ralston is the president and CEO of The Oasis Group, Ltd., a Microsoft Certified Solution Provider that develops desktop and client/server solutions for major corporations and has applications running in a dozen countries around the world. He is also president and executive director of Triana Solutions, LLC (Seeing New Worlds First™), a provider of enterprise-scale compliance systems for banks and financial institutions. James speaks at conferences around the United States and writes magazine articles on client/server development topics. James has also developed and delivered training to thousands of users and developers at Fortune 500 companies. James contributed to *Peter Norton's Guide to Visual Basic 6.0* (Sams Publishing) and *Teach Yourself Visual Basic 6.0* (Osborne Press).

Dedication

I dedicate this book to my parents, who taught me the value of hard work.
—Steve

To my son, Mychal, who always asks to play basketball at just the right time.
—Tom

To my son, J.P., for teaching me to believe in joy.
—James

Acknowledgments

Stephen Forte

Without the support, patience, love, and homemade chicken soup of my wife Karen, none of this would have been possible.

I especially would like to thank Al Cadalzo for his hard work, friendship, support, feedback, and continued loyalty.

I would like to thank Kevin Collins for all that he has done to help me and this book.

Some people may not even know it, but without them, I would have never had a successful writing career or have stuck with writing at all. They are: Lori Ash for her thoughtfulness, Brad Jones for taking a chance on me, Sarah Walker for believing in me early on, Kelly Marshall for her encouragement, Richard Campbell for keeping me honest, and Melody Hendricks for keeping me on the right track. I would also like to thank Ken Getz and Paul Litwin for their support, professionalism, continued friendship, and inspiration.

There are several people at Microsoft that I would like to thank as well. All the members of the Jet team in particular, most especially Kevin Collins, Conor Cunningham, Debra Dove, and Beth Scott. I would like to thank the Access team in general for making such a great product. On the Access team, Dave Gainer in particular deserves a medal for his patience with me. In addition I would like to thank Jim Sturms, Bret Tanzer, Kevin Mineweaser, and Richard Dickinson. Other Microsoft people that deserve some thanks are Mike Gilbert, Alyssa Henry, and Tod Nielsen for his advice over two years ago on genesis of Chapter 27.

Thanks to Tom Howe, for great chapters, friendship, support, and great legal advice (even if I don't always follow it!).

I would like to thank all the good people at Sams, Marla Reece-Hall who kept it all together, and Rosemarie Graham for making it all happen. I would like to thank Brad Kingsley for not only writing Chapter 24, but for his patience and support. Brad is the only person who could have brought Chapter 24 to life! Tom Howe and James Ralston were awesome coauthors.

I would like to thank the members of the NYC Access and VB Developers group for their support and feedback. Lastly, I would like to thank Professor David Burner for teaching me the importance of good writing.

Tom Howe

Many thanks to Tom and Kathy Grant of Grant & Associates in Portland, Oregon, for writing Chapter 2, "Planning the Development Process." Access developer books generally do not cover this most important topic. Thanks also to Tom and Kathy for translating their years of project management experience into writing so the rest of us can benefit.

A special thanks to Alex Feinberg of Odessy Consulting of New York City for writing Chapter 8, "Advanced Form Design." All the authors are grateful for his immense experience with Microsoft database technologies.

A book needs technical expertise. A special thanks to Mark Hammer of Access Advantage in Portland, Oregon; Wayne Callaghan of Cal Group of Companies in Irvine, California; and Tom and Kathy Grant of Grant & Associates in Portland, Oregon, for technical review of many chapters. These highly skilled and technically expert individuals gave tremendous insight and valuable ideas.

Thanks to Lisa MacQueen and Lynn Swanson for countless hours of editing, usually under ridiculous deadlines. Their contributions made technically difficult material readable and easy to understand.

Last, but most important, thanks to my family: Suzanne, Josie, Andy, Sarah, and Mychal who share my enthusiasm for world travel and long bicycle rides.

James Ralston

I could not have survived the long hours and late nights it took to write this book without the constant support of my wife, Karen. Also, Charles McMahon, senior developer at The Oasis Group, Ltd. was indispensable in this effort. Without his skill and dedication, the company could not have functioned so well while I dedicated so much of my time to exploring Access 2000 and writing about it.

The opportunity to coauthor this book was presented to me by my good friend Steve Forte. Steve has been a never-ending source of encouragement and support in recent years and to him I owe a great deal of thanks and a debt I may never be able to repay. I am also indebted to my other coauthor, Tom Howe, for all his work on some of the thornier topics covered in these pages.

I owe a great deal of thanks to Klaus Sommer, Gino Composto, Marco Oglivie, and Yogi Ghelani for the faith they placed in me and the opportunities they presented to me over the years. Thanks also go to Bob Dively for taking the time to informally review some of my ideas and for being available to kick them around.

Rosemarie Graham was as patient and helpful an editor as I could ever have hoped for and the technical editors were a pleasure to work with. I am thankful for that.

Everyone at Microsoft who helped out with questions during the early betas deserves my thanks. These include, but are not limited to: Kevin Collins, Dave Gainer, James Sturms, Micheal Kaplan, and Conor Cunningham.

Finally, thank you for purchasing this book and I hope you are able to put it to good use on exciting projects!

Tell Us What You Think!

As the reader of this book, *you* are our most important critic and commentator. We value your opinion and want to know what we're doing right, what we could do better, what areas you'd like to see us publish in, and any other words of wisdom you're willing to pass our way.

As an Associate Publisher for Sams Publishing, I welcome your comments. You can fax, email, or write me directly to let me know what you did or didn't like about this book— as well as what we can do to make our books stronger.

Please note that I cannot help you with technical problems related to the topic of this book, and that due to the high volume of mail I receive, I might not be able to reply to every message.

When you write, please be sure to include this book's title and author as well as your name and phone or fax number. I will carefully review your comments and share them with the authors and editors who worked on the book.

Fax: 317-581-4770

Email: mstephens@mcp.com

Mail: Michael Stephens
            Associate Publisher
            Sams Publishing
            201 West 103rd Street
            Indianapolis, IN 46290 USA

Introduction

- Why Read This Book?
- What You Can Learn from This Book
- Conventions Used in This Book

Why Read This Book?

I am currently sitting in the Barnes and Noble bookstore on West 68th Street in Manhattan in the computer books section. I just went to the shelf to buy a good book on UML and it took me about an hour to decide which one was right for me. I was inspired to sit down, power up my laptop, and write this introduction. Chances are you are standing in the bookstore like me, with a million things to do and reading through the table of contents and introductions of Access books trying to determine whether you should add this book to the large collection of developer books you already own. (My wife has decided to use start using computer books as extra tables when we have company.) With so many Access books out there, it is hard to make the right choice. This book is different from the typical Access books sitting right next to it on the bookshelf. Some of the reasons are

- **This book is written by Access developers for Access developers.** So many computer books these days are written by professional trainers and writers. The three authors who wrote this book have the same job as you—to make Access solutions for their users. We share our real-world experience and knowledge through this book. We focus on the aspects of developing with Access that you will need to use, rather than listing every property of every dialog box. Whether you're a professional Access developer, you've been using Access for a while, you're coming over from VB or another development environment to connect to databases, or you're checking out Microsoft Access as a front-end to SQL Server, Oracle, or Sybase, this book is for *you*.

- **This book is the *only* Access book to have extensive coverage of working with Oracle.** Other computer books totally forget that Oracle is the leading database server product and totally ignore such a large aspect of Access development. I remember the first time I had to make an Access front-end to Oracle, I was totally disappointed to find that there was absolutely no literature on the topic. Sad to say that years later, this was still true…until now. With James Ralston's experience with Oracle comes a complete chapter on using Access with Oracle. We did not forget SQL Server: We devoted two whole chapters to SQL Server and have many parts of other chapters focusing on using SQL Server.

- **We have the best coverage of using Access on the Internet.** With the Internet changing the face of development, it is surprising that most books still treat the Internet as an afterthought at the end of the book. These chapters treat the Internet as what it is, the next development platform. I have been working with Access on the Internet since Access 95 and have created many Web sites for customers powered by Access. I bring this real-world experience to you, mostly so that you do not have to make the same stupid mistakes that I did at first! We also brought in a Windows 2000/Windows NT expert to show you how to build a Web server from scratch, or develop on Windows 95 with Personal Web Server. Our coverage dives into XML, ASP, DAPs, Office Web Components, and all the latest development trends. In addition, we had people from Microsoft review these chapters not only for accuracy, but to make sure that they will be current by the time that you read them.

- **We do not ignore the design, planning, and "human" side of Access development.** Most studies show that the coding, table design, maintenance, and so on is only about 55 percent of a software project. So most computer books ignore the other side of development—the design side. Tom Howe is not only an Access developer, he is a professional lawyer with his own practice. With this legal and academic background, Tom is in a unique position to talk about the "human" side of software development, the importance of design, writing specifications, and project plans.

- **This book has been completely rewritten from the ground up—a completely fresh approach to the latest version of the product by experienced developers.** Tom, James, and I have been working closely with Microsoft and the Access Development team all through the beta development cycle. Few other books can make both those claims. We also tested all the code examples on the full *Release* version of Office 2000 that you have, not like some other books that are rushed to the market.

What You Can Learn from This Book

Part I of this book, "Database Design Unleashed," shows you important concepts from a perspective of experience. These chapters will help you rethink your current design and planning skills to include business object modeling and the latest Jet engine capabilities.

In Part II, "Data Access," you will find out everything that you really need to know about using the new data access method: ActiveX Data Objects (ADO). We show you how to make the transition from DAO to ADO and show you the parts of ADO that you will need to use and work with on a daily basis.

In Part III, "User Interfaces Unleashed," we all know that using Access effectively requires the use of forms and reports. This section shows you ways to program your application's interface with powerful technologies, such as ActiveX controls and components.

In Part IV, "VBA Unleashed," you will see the importance of the powerful programming environment behind Access: Visual Basic for Applications (VBA). You will learn invaluable techniques and have ready-to-run sample code right on the CD-ROM to plug into your applications.

In Part V, "Access Client/Server," you will learn how to use Access in a client/server environment. There is a new type of Access project devoted to client/server development called "Access Data Projects" and chapters on Oracle development as well.

In Part VI, "Interoperability," you will learn how to use Access with other products, including Microsoft Office. In addition, a whole chapter will try to answer the question "Which tool to use, Access or VB?"

In Part VII, "Multiuser Issues," you will learn about the exciting new row-level locking, replication, and security enhancements. Since so many of our Access applications are multiuser, this is one of the most important chapters.

In Part VIII, "Web Publishing with Access 2000," we explore the aspects of using Access 2000 on the Internet. Since Access 2000 has embraced the Internet, we decided to really drill down into the topic with coverage on how to create dynamic Web sites powered by Access 2000 and a review of the new tools in Office 2000 that make Internet development easier.

Appendix A, "References for Further Reading," directs you to books and online sites where you'll find valuable information to supplement what you learn in this book.

This book started one rainy morning in a London laundromat with Tom and I cranking out code and an outline. We wanted to give something to the Access developer community that you can use, but something that came from our personal experiences. We then recruited James, who is equally dedicated to that vision. The result is in your hands, let us know what you think. We did it for you.

Thanks for reading.

Stephen Forte

New York, May 1999

Conventions Used in This Book

The following conventions are used in this book:

- Code lines, commands, statements, variables, and any text you type or see on the screen appears in a `computer` typeface.

- Placeholders in syntax descriptions appear in an *`italic computer`* typeface. Replace the placeholder with the actual filename, parameter, or whatever element it represents.

- *Italics* highlight technical terms when they first appear in the text and are being defined.

- A special icon ➥ is used before a line of code that is really a continuation of the preceding line. Sometimes a line of code is too long to fit as a single line in the book, given the book's limited margin width. If you see ➥ before a line of code, remember that you should interpret that "line" as part of the line immediately before it.

- As a part of the *Unleashed* series, this book also contains Notes, Tips, and Cautions to help you spot important or useful information more quickly. Some of these are helpful shortcuts to help you work more efficiently.

Database Design Unleashed

PART I

What's New for Developers in Access 2000

CHAPTER 1

There is an old saying that from a tiny acorn, a mighty oak tree grows. If this could be said of a software product, it would never be more apt than for Microsoft Access. Those of us who remember Access 1.0 remember an application with a file size limit of 128MB, no transaction capability, no real programming capability, static toolbars, a lack of referential integrity, and agonizingly slow performance. Yet, it was a knockout at the time with its simple user interface construction tools, dynasets, and query builder. With almost every update, Access has grown into an ever-more powerful and useful productivity tool and development platform.

Access Users and Developers have welcomed constant improvements in the underlying database engine, now at release 4.0. With these releases we have gotten transactional processing, referential integrity, replication capabilities, better concurrency management, more speed, and greater stability. We have also graduated from simple macros to Access VB to full-blown VBA with a development environment almost identical to Visual Studio 6.0. The interface tools have improved also. Third-party tools and ActiveX controls expanded the design options available to developers. With Access 95 and 97, developers gained the ability to create multiple instances of forms. Access 97 also enabled developers to use Access' Active Server Pages, thereby extending the reach of Access to the Internet.

Over the years, the number of improvements in Microsoft Access number in the hundreds. Today, the improvements in Access 2000 are truly astonishing. The differences between Access 2000 and the previous version might be almost as great as the differences between the original version and Access 97. There can be no doubt that the millions of dedicated Access users and developers will find this new version to be an exciting and liberating tool; there can also be no doubt that millions more will take up Access with the zeal of converts in the months and years to come.

New User Interface

The first thing you will notice about Access 2000 is the new interface. Microsoft has attempted to unify the GUIs for its applications and Access is no exception. The Database window has an Outlook-style group bar on the left side for the developer to choose his collection. This change is not just a cosmetic face-lift though. It affords you the ability to create logical, custom groupings with shortcuts to the actual objects. For example, you could create an "Orders and Sales" group and in it create a shortcut to the queries, forms, reports, pages, macros and modules related to orders and sales. This eliminates the need for long searches among all the objects. This convenient feature is illustrated in Figure 1.1.

FIGURE 1.1

*Everything related
to orders and
sales is in one
convenient place.*

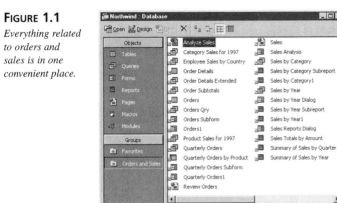

More subtly, but just as important, the menus throughout Access 2000 display only the
most-frequently used commands. A double click on the menu or a single click on the
pull-down character will display the rest, as shown in Figure 1.2. This really helps cut
down on the congestion on the screen. For Access, with all its different and ever-
changing menus and toolbars, it should be seen as a relief from option overload.

FIGURE 1.2

*Collapsing menus
can help cut the
clutter.*

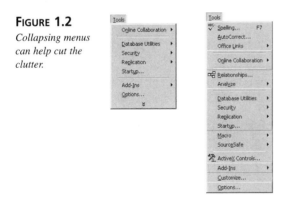

Wizards for creating objects and editing objects are also permanently positioned in their
relevant containers, ready for you to use at any time. This contextual availability will
save developers time.

A long-standing feature of Windows, the clipboard, has had its functionality enhanced
within Office 2000. Now you can copy multiple selections to the clipboard and then
selectively paste them into a document. This could make it much easier to rearrange a
function or reset object properties.

Changes to the VBE

Another major cosmetic change is the layout of the Visual Basic Environment (VBE).
Rather than simply opening a module as if it were a text document, Access 2000 has a
separate, rich workspace for writing, debugging, and running your Access 2000 projects.
Access's development environment has finally caught up with the other Office family
members and now provides the same Integrated Development Environment (IDE). If you
have ever worked with the VBA of Office 97 or with Visual Basic, the new Access 2000
VBE, shown in Figure 1.3, will be familiar.

With its dockable toolbars and windows, you can arrange the working area any way you
like. In one window, you can see the code you are writing; in another, you can review an
object's properties. A third window can display the forms, reports, modules, and classes
of your database. In yet another window, tools such as the Immediate window or the
Locals window (they are separate windows in this version) are ready to help you debug
your code.

Unlike VB, all the modules you create in this separate, integrated environment are stored
within the .MDB file with all the other objects in your database. However, you can easily
import and export *.bas, *.cls and *.frm files to and from your Access 2000 application.

FIGURE 1.3

*The environment
is now highly cus-
tomizable.*

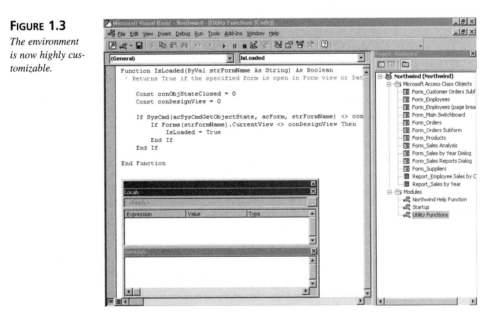

Data Access Pages

The development capabilities of Access have also been extended with a new object, Data Access Pages (DAPs). DAPs enable you to create Web pages that are bound to your data like a bound form or report. Simply put on some special controls, set a few properties, save them to the intra- or Internet, and other users can view them and interact with them through their browsers. DAPs can also contain grouped data (Grouped Data Access Pages). Grouped DAPs can enable users to drill down through their data interactively from their browsers. There may be no faster way to share data and interface functionality with users than DAPs. This could be a viable alternative to distributing MDEs.

The DAPs in Figure 1.4 use HTML intrinsics and COM components for their functionality. They also have a rich object model and support Visual Basic Scripting Edition, JavaScript and Office 2000 Web components, so Web development skills learned previously can be transferred to Access 2000 very easily.

FIGURE 1.4

The data and functionality can be viewed in the application or with a browser.

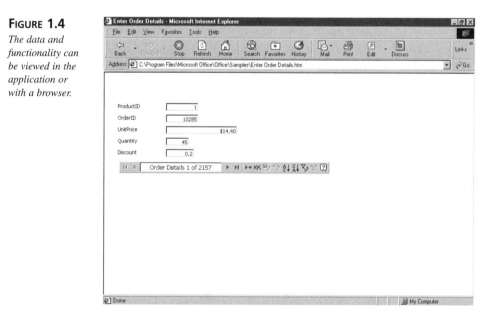

Subdatasheets

Access has provided another user interface feature that is sure to get a lot of usage—subdatasheets. With almost no work on your part, you can create an editable, hierarchical view of your data that expands by simply clicking on a small plus sign. These views can be had anywhere you can have a Datasheet view. This three-dimensional view is sure to find plenty of uses and might make a fast, simple replacement for the tree control.

Name AutoCorrect

Another really helpful feature of Access 2000 is the Name AutoCorrect feature. In previous versions of Access, you had to be careful about changing an object's name because Access would not recognize the new name unless you updated everything that depended on that name. Access 2000 will handle this arduous task automatically for you, so if you find that a field name would make more sense if it were called something else, you can rename it at any time and your application will continue to work.

ADO Is the Default Data Access Method

Behind the scenes, Access has changed its default data access method. Rather than the familiar but memory-intensive Data Access Object (DAO), Access now employs Active Data Objects (ADO) to retrieve and manage data. The benefits of ADO are many: a simpler interface, a flat hierarchy, consistent techniques and interfaces between similar data sources, the ability to get and manage data from data stores other than traditional RDBMS, and the promise of greater performance and extended features. Though still supported in Access 2000, DAO will no longer be extended by Microsoft, so if you have not had a chance to work with ADO yet, Chapters 6, "Introduction to ActiveX Data Objects," and 7, "Advanced ADO," cover the topic extensively.

Along with ADO are the OLE DB providers that provide consistent interfaces to an ever-wider variety of data sources under the standards of Microsoft's Universal Data Access initiative. The settings for the OLE DB providers can also be written into a Universal Data Link file (UDL) that makes controlling data sources (and changing them) a simple matter.

Online Collaboration

Online collaboration could be a boon to developers who work together over a distance. By starting a meeting, Access developers can communicate with one another over a list server about their project and use features like the white board to effectively express their ideas.

Access as a Front-End to SQL Server

Without a doubt, the most exciting new feature of Access 2000, and one that is dealt with extensively in this book, is the new Microsoft Access Project (*.adp). The Access Project is the coming of age for Access. Whereas Access was always a remote database operating under the confines of a file server environment and was limited in the amount of data its native Jet engine could manage and the number of users it could serve, a Microsoft Access Project has no such constraints because it is a true front end to SQL Server and Microsoft Data Engine databases.

Because of the support for OLE DB, Access 2000 can completely bypass Jet and interoperate directly with other database engines. When creating a new database in Access 2000, the developer has the option of creating a Project and choosing the Microsoft Data Engine (MSDE), which comes with Office 2000, SQL Server 6.5 or SQL Server 7.0. These are all capable of handling thousands of users and terabytes of data for mission-critical applications. Access is a development/administrative environment for SQL Server and the final application becomes a true client/server client.

The Access Project does not contain any data, tables, or queries. It is directly connected to the back-end and can create, view, and modify the database's tables, stored procedures, views, and database diagrams. This is radically different from earlier versions of Access. Although many developers and users attached tables from SQL Server and Oracle, their queries were performed locally. (Querying an attached table causes data to be transferred to the desktop for processing.) Some developers created pass-through queries so the server would do most of the work, but this is quite different all together. An attached table could not be modified, and the server's views or stored procedures called through a pass-through query or through code might have required separate administrative tools to create and maintain them. These limitations caused delays in a project and involved additional people when it might not have been necessary. Access Projects enable the developer to create the entire client/server project alone and with one tool.

Microsoft is dedicated to the success and wide acceptance of this new feature. To this end, they have changed Access data types to conform to SQL Server, updated the SQL syntax to conform more closely to ANSI standards, and updated the wizards and the tools to support the new client/server architecture. They have also created new tools to create and manage the server-side objects from the Design view of the client. Other common administrative tasks, such as security, backup, and replication, can also be managed from Access 2000.

Summary

A new interface, a new Visual Basic environment, Active Data Objects as the default data access system, Data Access Pages to reach the Web, online collaboration and a true client/server capability are just a few of the many new features and improvements that come with Access 2000. It is hard to imagine a more powerful, flexible, and easy to use database tool.

Planning the Development Process

CHAPTER 2

The other chapters in this book cover all the powerful development features that Access 2000 has to offer. But, even after you master the material and become the best database developer in town, the successful completion of your project is still at risk unless you understand the importance of a professional development process. Having great strength in implementing technology without having a good repeatable process or a well-functioning team, can result in an unsatisfactory completion of the your project.

This chapter presents some key issues and activities related to the team and the development process. Our goal is to help you improve your project success by creating your own effective development process based on proven methods. To cover these issues fully could easily consume the entire book. References to other sources for more detail and further study are included in the appendix.

A successful development process focuses on four key phases of the project: the Requirements, Architecture, Development Planning, and finally the actual Construction phase. During the Requirements phase, you'll be gathering and analyzing the real needs of the users. The Architecture phase is where you will choose the top-level design, technologies, and development tools that will best satisfy them. During the Development Planning phase you will complete a development plan that describes how it will be implemented, how many developers will be needed, and how much it will cost. The final development phase is the construction of the application.

Figure 2.1 depicts the four phases of the development process from gathering requirements through construction of the application. It also shows some of the software releases created during the construction phase. This chapter details each of these areas.

FIGURE 2.1

The development process.

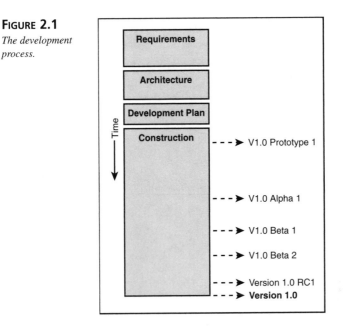

Gathering Requirements

Gathering and analyzing requirements is the single most important activity in delivering a successful application. Conversely, many project failures result from inadequate or incorrect requirements.

Why Are Requirements So Important?

Well-researched and analyzed requirements will reduce the number of unanticipated changes that lead to rework later. The software industry has found that the cost to make a requirements change to an application goes up by a factor of between five and ten at every major step in the development process. For example, if the customer notices a problem in the requirements, which is solved during the requirements phase, the change might take one hour. If the problem isn't noticed until after the feature has been implemented, it could take ten hours to correct. If the feature has already been integrated and tested with the rest of the application, the problem will take closer to fifty hours to correct. If the problem isn't noticed until after the application has been deployed, it will probably take closer to 100 hours to resolve.

Why so long? First of all, the requirements need to be updated. Design and code must be analyzed to assess where changes are needed. These changes must then be made, and the various modules, queries, forms, and reports must be tested. The application itself must be retested to ensure that the changes did what was anticipated and did not create new problems. Finally, the revised application must be redeployed to each of the end-users.

Of course, these factors are software-industry averages, not absolutes. Depending on the changes made, costs may be more or less expensive than these averages. If the error causes damage to your customer's business, for example, the cost could be astronomical.

Finding the Real Problem

Begin the requirements-gathering process with the "perceived scope" of the application. Your customer undoubtedly has a problem he or she believes can be solved with a software application. The customer's perception of the problem may or may not be correct.

> **NOTE**
>
> An Employee Expense Reporting example will be used throughout this chapter to illustrate concepts of the development process.

For example, the customer may want a system for employees to enter and print expense reports. After some analysis, you may find that the real need is to automate the entry, distribution, approval, and processing of the entire expense-report process. Ferreting out differences like this is one of the challenges. Sometimes, the customer is thinking of a solution that is too small to solve the problem. Other times, the customer is thinking of a solution that is too big and complex. To understand how the application interacts with other related parts of the business, it's vital that you expand the scope of the requirements-gathering process beyond the expected project scope.

Investigation

To find the problem that really needs to be solved and to accurately determine the requirements, you have to put on a trench coat and become a business-process detective. These are a few tips for your sleuthing:

- Never rely on any one person for key information about how the current process works.

- Many business processes include the official way it's supposed to be done, and the way it's really done (the way that works). You need to understand both.

- Keep an open mind and listen carefully. Put aside your (and the clients') first vision of the problem and the solution until they are verified through interviews and analysis.

- Table 2.1 includes examples of many types of requirements to look for during your investigation.

The first step in your investigation is to identify all the stakeholders. A stakeholder is a person, group, or department with an interest in the process or the application. Managers, supervisors, and lead employees responsible for every key department involved in the process are stakeholders. Finally, the users of the current process are always stakeholders who, presumably, will become users of the new application you're developing. Some of these groups of stakeholders will be so large that you will need to limit the list by including just a few to represent the group. As the investigation proceeds, you may discover additional stakeholders to include. An additional benefit of involving stakeholders in gathering requirements is that involvement increases their feelings of ownership in the new system. You will see greater cooperation and acceptance during application deployment.

Let's continue with our expense report example. You'll want to interview a few representative users, perhaps one who rarely has any expenses, a second who travels constantly, and one or two average users. Then interview one or two people in the payroll department who process those printed expense forms and receipts every month.

Now, the real investigation begins. Interview every stakeholder. Ask lots of questions, listen well, and take copious notes. Ask how the current process works and what they like and dislike about it. Ask them how they wish it worked.

From these notes you can put together an accurate picture of the current process and business rules. Analyze the current process and document any error-prone, slow, or redundant steps. Remember to document all the likes, dislikes, wishes, and dreams you heard during the interviews.

Process Diagrams

Process diagrams are a terrific way to describe how a business process works. The diagram shown in Figure 2.2 illustrates the expense report example. These diagrams show the interactions among the key individuals, groups, or departments involved in a process. Individual steps or activities in the process progress from left to right and are represented by rectangles. These steps process inputs from the left and produce outputs to the right. Vertical arrows into a process represent any internal business rules or external regulations or constraints. Diamonds represent decisions made within the process.

Because the horizontal axis of the diagram represents time, any delays and time-consuming activities are easily identified. After diagramming and analyzing the current process and the needs of the stakeholders, a second process diagram can be drawn to represent the revised process.

Process diagrams, such as the one shown in Figure 2.2, are fairly straightforward to create and easy for stakeholders to understand. After they see the diagrams drawn out, many stakeholders will be shocked at the complexity and convolution of their current processes. If you begin your Process diagrams as early as possible, you can revise them during stakeholder interviews. process diagrams are excellent tools to help structure and guide these interviews. Each stakeholder interviewed will further clarify and detail the overall process.

You may find it useful to create a hierarchy of process diagrams. The one top-level diagram will describe the big picture, whose process steps will be rather large in scope. Subprocesses can then be detailed on their own process diagrams. This hierarchical approach often simplifies the diagrams and makes them easier to understand.

2

PLANNING THE
DEVELOPMENT
PROCESS

FIGURE 2.2

An example of a process diagram of a travel and expense report.

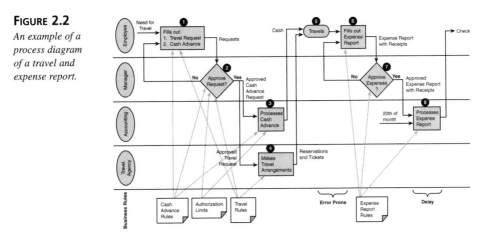

Identify the Scope of the Project

Work with the customer to determine the appropriate scope for the application. Remember, this should be a long-term scope, not just centered on this phase of the project.

In the expense report example, the developers and decision-makers came to an agreement on the project scope. They agreed that the application should eventually automate the cash-advance, travel requests, and the entire expense-reporting process from the employee's creation of a travel request to the receipt in Accounting of the balance due/owed request. They decided to ignore the accounting systems and the actual travel-booking process. These are all outside the scope of the application.

Writing Down Requirements

Written requirements are one of the best methods of communication between the developer and customer. This practice reduces misunderstandings. The writing need not result in a formal, unwieldy document. There are many effective ways to communicate requirements: sample reports, forms, process diagrams, or drawings. There is no magic to writing requirements. The most important measure is that the customer can read and understand them.

Ask the following questions about each requirement:

- Does it describe what is needed, rather than how to implement it?
- Can it be verified after implementation?
- Is it unambiguous?
- Does it completely describe the need?
- Is it consistent with the other requirements?

Table 2.1 shows examples of many kinds of requirements you should consider using. These requirements will serve as part of the work contract. Save a permanent copy of this version of the requirements documentation and ask the customer to sign it. This baseline document is now the basis for proceeding with the application development. From this point forward, you must carefully consider how requirements changes will impact the planned budget and schedule. Remember to revise the budget, schedule, and any related requirements or design documentation when changes are made.

> **TIP**
>
> Create a database of all the requirements. For each requirement, include an identification number, type, description, date, source, benefit, how to verify the requirement after implementation, priority and more.

TABLE 2.1 REQUIREMENT TYPES

Type of Requirements	Description	Example
Functional	These requirements describe functions or features that are needed, plus the business rules that apply.	The user shall be able to set the priority of the customer to: Critical High Medium Low

continues

TABLE 2.1   CONTINUED

Type of Requirements	Description	Example
Performance	Performance requirements include: • Speed • Response time • Capacity • Database size	The inventory database shall support up to 20 users across the corporate LAN with a mean order status response time of 200ms.
Security	Security requirements limit usage and access to application features and data.	All users must log in to the application. Every user will be a member of only one of the following security groups: User Administrator Manager
Scalability	Scalability concerns the capability to expand the quantity of data, users, sites, or frequency of data collection.	The application must support the current 50 users and an additional 50 added over the next two years.
Extensibility	Extensibility requirements detail the capability to add features to the application in future releases.	The application shall be designed and implemented to allow addition of customer invoicing.
Configurability	Configurability is the measure of how easily software parameters can be modified by the customer without requiring the development team to make the changes.	The Administrators shall have the capability to update the insurance rates annually.

Type of Requirements	Description	Example
Compatibility	Compatibility is the ability to be installed and operational in various hardware/ software environments, and to interact with other software applications.	The software product shall be installed on Win95, Win98, and Win NT 4.0 Workstation with a minimum of 8MB memory and 200MB hard drive available.
Availability	Availability is the measure of how many hours, or what percentage of time a software product is available to perform the work for which it was developed.	The database administrator shall reserve from 10:00 to 11:00 p.m. for backup and maintenance of the backend database.
Usability	Usability, or ease of use, is the measure of how well-trained users are able to use the system.	The application will include online Help that will cover 90% of the features.
Ease of Learning	Ease of learning is the measure of how easily and quickly users are able to learn to use the system.	One day of training shall be sufficient for users to become proficient before initial use of the application.

2

PLANNING THE
DEVELOPMENT
PROCESS

Architecture

After analyzing the written requirements, you can choose the appropriate architecture, technologies, and development tools. Should the client application be based on Excel, Access, or VB? Or should it be Web-based and use ASP and XML? Is two-tier acceptable, or would n-tier be more appropriate? Will the backend be a Jet/MDB, SQL/MSDE, SQL Server or Oracle? These are important questions that will each have a large impact on the final product. An accurate budget or schedule cannot be produced until these decisions are made.

Development Planning

With the requirements and architecture decided, consider the best way to construct the application. Should all features and functionality be implemented in one comprehensive version 1.0 release, or should you defer some of the features for later versions? Whatever method you choose, you will need a roadmap with a budget and schedule before proceeding.

You may have created a preliminary project plan to get the necessary approvals to get this far in the project. That preliminary version was based on the anticipated requirements and scope and included only rough estimates of schedule and budget. If you had a preliminary project plan, this is the time to revise it. If not, this is time to write one. With the Requirements phase complete, you now have enough information to create an accurate task list, resource list, schedule, and budget.

> **TIP**
>
> Developers should always track their actual time. The best way to improve estimating skills is to compare your original estimates with the actual time required.

Delivery Strategy

Avoid the urge to include every idea and cool feature into one huge release. It's almost always better to plan on several incremental releases.

Let's go back to the example of the expense report. Meetings were held with the developers and decision-makers during which the possible scope, schedules, and budgets were discussed. It was agreed that the Version 1.0 should focus on automating the creation, approval, distribution, and status-checking of expense reports. This will be followed by Version 2.0 that will automate the creation, approval, distribution, and status checking of travel and cash advance request process. Figure 2.3 shows the top-level development process steps and an example of possible releases. Figure 2.4 is a revised process diagram that shows which process steps are targeted by these two versions currently included in this delivery strategy.

FIGURE 2.3

A delivery strategy example.

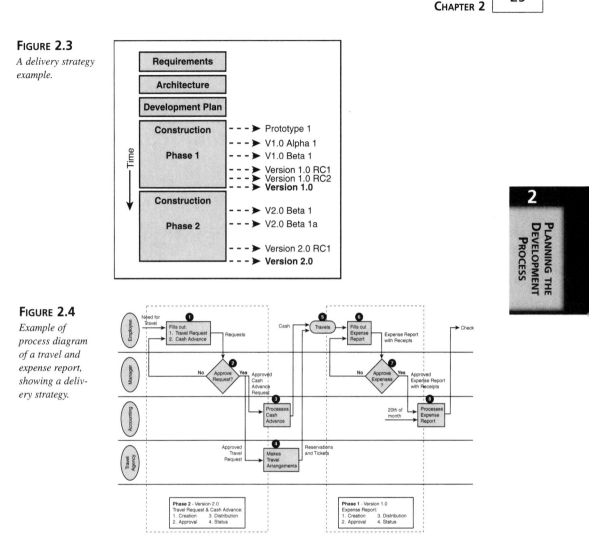

FIGURE 2.4

Example of process diagram of a travel and expense report, showing a delivery strategy.

Style

Professional applications always have a consistent look and operation. If some forms use a Cancel button to exit and others use a Quit button, the users will quickly get confused, and training and support costs will increase. If one developer likes the look of each field in its own sunken box with data in bold type, while another designs forms with labels with bold type and flat text boxes, the application will simply look thrown together. Make these decisions early in the development process and have all the developers follow them before each decides to do his or her own thing.

Here are some types of style issues to cover in your standard:

- Form layout (for example, how you arrange controls on the form, form size, and proportions)
- Field grouping (for example, sunken frames versus simple lines)
- Use of colors, fonts, font size, and bold/italic typestyle for fields and labels
- Button names and behaviors (for example, Cancel, Close, or Quit?)
- Indication to user whether forms are read-only or can be edited
- Dialog wording (for example, terse or verbose)

> **TIP**
>
> Rather than spend a lot of time writing an official-looking document, just create an MDB with a set of forms and reports that includes examples of all the common uses of controls. This can be a growing, evolving example of your preferred, user-interface styles. Better yet, include the code behind the forms to handle navigation and other common functionalities. These forms will serve as your standard templates.

Standards

Without standardization between developers, applications become very difficult to maintain and reuse.

Rule #1: Standards make a big difference.

Rule #2: The standard itself makes little difference.

Translation: Consistency between developers is the primary goal of standardization. Whether everyone does it the "best" way is a secondary benefit.

> **CAUTION**
>
> Don't waste a lot of time arguing about what's best—just pick a good method, get everyone to use it, and stick with it.

The most common types of standards are naming and coding. These standards make reading and reviewing the code much easier. They also greatly simplify maintenance tasks later on.

Naming Standards

The following example uses a data-type, prefix-naming standard, and it's fairly obvious what the developer is doing.

```
dblLodgingTotal = Double(intNights) * dblRate
```

However, with the next example, who knows? The developer probably doesn't know either.

```
x = Text7 * Text12
```

These are key parts of most naming standards:

- Object prefixes (for example, txt, cbo, lst...)
- Data-type prefixes (for example, sgl, int, str...)
- Standard base names (for example, use Acct or Account)
- Standard abbreviations (for example, stat = status)

2

PLANNING THE
DEVELOPMENT
PROCESS

Coding Standards

The following are examples of the issues you may want to cover in your coding standard:

- Comment header blocks
- Comments in code
- Indentation
- Size of subs and functions (for example, maximum of 60 lines)
- Use of "Option Explicit"

TIP

Several naming standards are published and available for Access/VBA/Office/VB development. The two most common are the Reddick and Leszynski naming conventions. One advantage of these common standards is that new developers hired by your company may already be familiar with the standard. Also, books, technical articles, and conference materials tend to follow these naming conventions. Pick one and use it consistently.

Construction

Several techniques are available to you for improving your team's effectiveness during the Construction phase of the project. This section discusses how to divide the tasks between developers and review the detailed design and implementation as you go. It will also encourage you to test thoroughly and track all defects found along the way.

Divide and Conquer: Construction Logistics

There are many ways to approach the Construction phase. You could start by implementing the most difficult or risky parts, begin implementing the easy parts first, or do the forms first and finish with the reports. Although these are all valid approaches, many developers have found more success by starting with a foundation and then building upon it. This foundation usually consists of the table design, a simple first-cut at the "core" forms, and all the widely used class modules and functions. The goal is to establish a basic functioning core that each of the developers can build upon. For the forms, you want to spend the time necessary to design and build one or two as solidly as possible. These can be used as design templates for subsequent forms.

> **TIP**
>
> This is the time to make an investment in creating reusable components. The initial effort to carefully develop and test them once will be quickly paid back with every reuse.

It's important that the development team work closely together while building the foundation. This is when the most important design decisions are worked out, and all the interfaces are defined. After this foundation is complete, it's much easier for the developers to work independently or to divide into smaller teams.

There are two effective ways to divide the implementation among teams: by Access objects or by application objects. When assigning by Access objects, one team focuses on the forms, another on the reports, and perhaps a third coding business rules and providing support routines. If you are using a more object-oriented architecture, the teams could be assigned by application objects. For example, one team would develop the Expense Report objects (class modules, tables, forms, reports) and a second team would develop the Approval objects (class modules, tables, forms, reports).

Figure 2.5 shows the process that each team follows during the Construction phase. These five steps are described as follows.

This same process is followed at several levels in the development process. At a high level, this diagram describes how the overall application construction takes place over a period of several months progressing from the detailed design to the final application testing. At a much lower level, it also describes how an individual developer might spend an afternoon developing a newly requested feature.

FIGURE 2.5

Steps in the Construction phase.

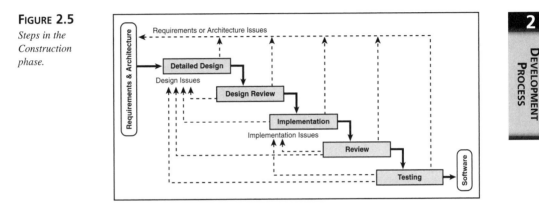

Throughout the Construction phase of a project, there are usually several software releases. These often include a prototype to confirm the graphical user interface (GUI) design; several alpha releases to solicit early-user feedback; one or two beta releases to allow users to test the application in real, day-to-day operations; and finally the official Version 1.0 release distributed to all the users.

Builds and Releases

As the complexity of the application and the project increases, it will become more and more important to track carefully the various builds and releases of your application. Periodically, create a build (see the following sidebar) by integrating the most recent changes and additions from each developer. By doing this every day or two during development, every developer has access to the latest modifications. See Table 2.2 for an example of the releases that may be produced during development.

A BUILD

A build is a new version of the application. This usually includes the front-end MDB and all the related DLLs, EXEs, and back-end data files. Many builds will be created throughout the development process for internal use by the development team. Only a few of these are actually given to any of the users. The example in Table 2.2 shows a project with 178 builds, but only sixteen releases (see definition of *release* that follows).

A RELEASE

A *release* is a build that is deployed outside the development team. This is usually distributed to one or more of the end users.

TABLE 2.2   RELEASE EXAMPLE

Release	Build
Prototype 1	
Prototype 2	
V1.0 Alpha 1	12
V1.0 Alpha 2	27
V1.0 Beta 1	42
V1.0 Beta 2	56
Version 1.0 RC1	88
Version 1.0 RC2	89
Version 1.0	89
Version 1.1 RC1	93
Version 1.1	93
Version 1.2 RC1	97
Version 1.2 RC2	98
Version 1.2	98
Version 2.0	135
Version 3.0	178

> **NOTE**
>
> Don't be concerned with the number of builds. A large number of builds is not a sign of poor development. It is a sign of careful development.

Creating a new build (see Figure 2.6) starts by collecting and integrating the changes and additions from all the developers. Sometimes, integration is as easy as importing a new report into the front-end MDB. More often than not, adding a new form or module to the application will require some changes to one or more calling forms to provide a way to use the new functionality. This may require two of the developers to sit down together to successfully integrate their changes. After everyone's changes and additions are integrated into the current build, you can update the release/build name displayed by the application.

FIGURE 2.6

Creating a build.

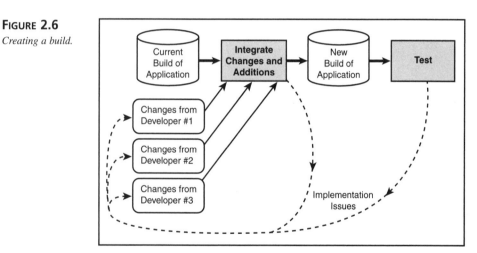

> **TIP**
>
> Include the current release name and build number on the application's start-up form and also on your "about" form opened from the Help menu. This makes it easy to determine in which release a defect is found. For example: "Version 1.0 Build 89 — 2/24/2000".

This is also an ideal time to make an archival copy of the entire build. This copy should include the front-end and back-end MDBs as well as any other files that are being changed from build to build. It is advisable to save a backup of the build offsite, because substantial resources and time have been invested in the project.

Integration testing should be done after every new build is created to ensure that the various parts work together as planned. After the build is proven to work acceptably well, it is important that the entire development team upgrades. Put a copy of the updated files in a shared folder so that all the developers and testers can access the latest build. If possible, take advantage of the features of a version-control tool such as Microsoft Visual SourceSafe to help create and track the builds you make. It will also reduce problems that can occur when changes are made by multiple developers.

> **CAUTION**
>
> If Visual SourceSafe is not used, then the archival procedures are even more important.

Several kinds of releases are made at various points throughout the development process. See the examples in Table 2.2 and Figure 2.8. During the concept or requirements phases, it is often useful to create one or more prototype releases for users to evaluate visually the proposed GUI. Later on, when a few of the key features of the application are working, you may find that demonstrating or giving to one or two users an Alpha release in order to get their early feedback can be very helpful to reduce risks. When the application is nearly feature-complete, releasing one or more Beta versions for users to test and really put to use will improve the quality of the final product. Most of these releases are done for every major version release (big changes) and minor revision (smaller changes). It's also useful to create one or more Release Candidates (RC1, RC2, and so on) for user and deployment testing prior to creating the official Version release for widespread distribution.

To create a release, take a successful build and make an installation package. This may be as simple as zipping up the front-end MDB or as complex as using the Office 2000 Developer's Edition installation tool to create a professional installation script. In either case, the release should be tested on several representative PCs to verify that it will work cleanly. See Figure 2.7.

Figure 2.7

Creating a release.

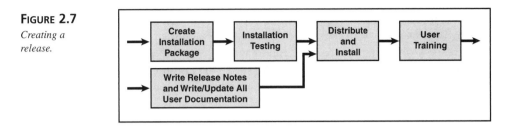

After testing is completed successfully, distribute the release to users for installation. Include a short Release Notes document with each release. At a minimum, list any new features, changes, and known problems. Even if the users never look at this Release Notes document, it's great for developers to refer to so they can remember what changed from release to release. Don't forget to update your user documentation whenever the application is revised. Out-of-date documentation is worse than no documentation at all.

Figure 2.8

A build and release cycle example.

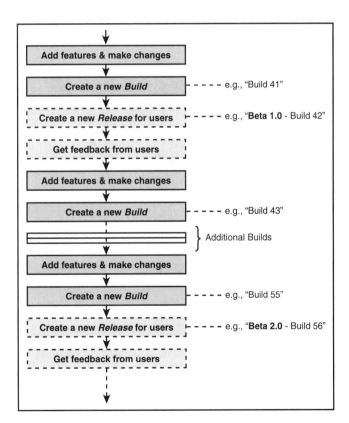

Many builds and an occasional release will be created throughout the life of the project. Figure 2.8 is an example of the cycle in which Builds and Releases are created. Every build offers an opportunity for all developers and testers, and perhaps even users, to test the application and to submit problems and ideas to the rest of the team. These are often called defects or issues. Depending on their priority relative to continuing development, these defects may be addressed by developers in time for an upcoming build or may be deferred until later.

Detailed Design

Although it's fairly obvious how to implement many of the features or tasks in an application, there are some (perhaps five to twenty percent) that require more thought. Common examples include class modules, form navigation, tough algorithms, and unusual automation techniques. The design for those features or tasks should be documented somehow. Leave some record of your design decisions and how you implemented them. You and others will find this record a great help later, when changes or additions need to be made. Hold one or more design reviews until the design is ironed out.

TIP

A great way to document non-trivial algorithms is to include pseudo-code comments in the sub or function. Pseudo-code is simplified VBA code included as comments to describe the overall process you are implementing in the following code. The exact syntax is unimportant; you are simply describing in general terms the algorithm that is implemented in VBA. The following example shows the use of pseudo-code in a sub header.

```
Public Sub ProcessAllUpdates()
   ' Comments  : Get the updated mail from the MAPI Inbox,
   '       unattatch it and update the current database.
   ' Parameters : <none>
   ' Returns  : <none>
   ' Created  : Tuesday, July 27, 1999 11:44 PM by Joe Developer
   ' Pseudo Code:
   ' ----------------------------------------------------------
   ' Sub ProcessUpdates()
   '    UpdateCount = 0
   '    UnattatchAllUpdates()
   '    Open a recordset from tblDownloadReceivedResults
   '    For each <Update file> in Recordset
   '      ProcessOneUpdate()
   '      If Successful Then
   '        Delete Update file
   '        Increment(UpdateCount)
   '    Next
   ' ----------------------------------------------------------
```

Design Review

Design reviews simply involve asking someone else to go over the design problem and your proposed solution. These reviews may range from an informal "Hey Stephanie, will you look at this for me?" to a formal meeting with a presentation and review by several team members. In the process of explaining the design to someone else, you will often see an additional problem you neglected or an even better solution. Another developer will often find something you've overlooked. This is an ideal time to find design problems—before you invest extensive time coding and testing the application.

Implementation

Implementation is the one step of the development process that clients, users, and inexperienced developers think of when they visualize how software is developed. This is when the forms and reports are built, and the code gets written. Most of the other chapters of this book discuss the challenges you face here.

Implementation Review

Implementation (or code) reviews are similar to design reviews, except that you're reviewing your implementation of the design. You will usually find it beneficial to review the implementation of each of the forms, reports, and queries, as well as all the code. Like the design reviews, just by explaining what you did and how it works, you will invariably notice something you missed. Someone else looking at your work will often see something you have overlooked dozens of times. You or your reviewer may find a problem with your implementation, design, architecture, or perhaps with the requirements. Remember that the earlier in the development process that problems are found, the easier and cheaper it is to fix them.

Code reviews are also beneficial as a way to train developers. To this end, ask senior developers to review code written by newer, or less experienced, team members. Another valuable benefit is that developers get a better understanding each other's areas of the application.

> **TIP**
>
> Consistent use of coding and naming standards will make code reviews much easier and quicker. This also helps to avoid lengthy debates and arguments between developers over whose style and naming is better.

> **TIP**
>
> If you're a single developer (Hey, no jokes! We mean: if you're not on a multi-developer team), find a partner and review each other's code. The time and energy will quickly pay off for both of you. User Groups can be a huge benefit here.

Testing

There are several kinds of testing to perform throughout the development process: unit, application, configuration, and installation testing.

Unit Testing

Before you begin implementation of a feature or object, spend some time deciding how you're going to test it. When you're finished implementing it, run your tests to verify that it works as intended and is ready for integration into the rest of the application. A good rule of thumb is to allocate about 20 percent of your total development time to testing each feature or object. For example, if it took you seven hours of detailed design time to develop the algorithm and three hours to code and debug it, start with a guesstimate of two hours to test it.

If you're testing a subroutine, function, or class module, test all the input parameters by trying the range of expected and unexpected values. When testing a new form, make sure that every control is tested. Check, among other things, data validation, locked fields, tab order, inserting new records, style consistency, and form navigation.

Application Testing

Application (or system) testing is done on the overall application after all the features have been integrated. There are several purposes for performing application testing. The most important is to confirm that all the requirements have been met. The second purpose is to determine how ready for release the application is.

The following are some examples of the kinds of tests you need to perform:

- Test the behavior when tables are empty.
- Test with different video resolutions.
- Test with the Windows display settings font size set to both Small Fonts and Large Fonts.
- Test with a couple of different Windows display color schemes.
- Test printing to several different printers (particularly the brand and model the users have).

- Test with the Windows taskbar Auto Hide option turned on and off.
- Test that "What's this?" help, ToolTips, and status bar text match their associated fields.
- Test the tab order on each form.
- Verify that all keyboard shortcuts are unique on each form.
- Test the use of default keys (Enter and Esc) on all forms.
- Test style consistency between all forms and reports (Style Standard).

Installation and Configuration Testing

PCs in the real world are seldom like the developers' machines. They have different software installed with different amounts of memory, and they use strange printers and even stranger video cards. In other words, PCs in the real world make the developer's life interesting. This variety of configurations affects how easily an application can be nstalled, as well as how successfully the application will operate after installation. If possible, test on the worst-case environments. For larger projects, consider using a company that specializes in this kind of testing. Many offer labs brimming with equipment and software, both new and old.

> **TIP**
>
> Test the installation and operation on a "clean" PC as well as a "dirty" one. Clean PCs only have an operating system and required software installed on a newly formatted disk (just like a brand new computer). A dirty PC is one on which multiple versions of many applications have been installed over a period of time. Testing on both kinds of PCs is the best way to find unexpected dependencies on DLLs, registry settings, templates, and other supporting files. Disk-imaging software can be very useful in quickly re-creating various configurations for testing purposes.

> **CAUTION**
>
> Don't expect testing to catch all defects. Most applications are far too complex to test every possible data value and execution path combination. This is why the earlier efforts such as requirements gathering, planning, design reviews, and implementation reviews are so critical. They are the first and best lines of defense in eliminating defects. It is much easier to prevent defects through careful design than to find and eradicate defects later.

Defect Tracking

A defect is any bug, flaw, error, or problem related to an application. It may be a defect in a document, a tool, or in the implementation of the application. Defects may be found at any time in the development process, and they should all be reported.

Any of the following activities may expose defects:

- Design and Implementation Reviews—Defects discovered during reviews range from disregarding standards to design errors.
- Document Reviews—During these reviews, many types of potential defects can be discovered. The requirements document may be missing or contain inadequate requirements. The design documentation may not address all the requirements, or one or more of them may be wrong.
- Testing—Coding defects are the most common type of defect discovered during testing. Also, documentation defects can be found because the tests should be developed based on the documentation.
- Customer Support/Help Desk—During Beta testing or after deployment, defects reported by the customer will come in through the developer or staff who supports the released product. Any enhancement ideas should also be included in the defect-tracking system to assure they will not be forgotten.
- Error Handler—If you are using automated error reporting, such as described in Chapter 13 "Professional Error Handling," possible defects can be received by email or obtained from the error log at the customer's site.

No matter what the source of the possible defect or who reports it, it must be documented. Collect all defects in one place. Defects scattered through various memos, scraps of paper, and email may be lost or forgotten. You can use a commercially available defect-tracking tool, create your own Access database or log defects in a three-ring notebook.

However you document the defects, you will need a process to ensure that possible defects are addressed. Note that "addressed" does not necessarily mean that it's "fixed." You may decide not to fix some defects based on their frequency or severity.

Put every defect through the same process from discovery to final resolution.

1. As soon as possible after a defect is discovered, enter the details into your tracking system. Table 2.3 shows a list of suggested information to collect. Tables 2.4 through 2.8 are used to further describe some of the defect information.
2. The development team periodically reviews all unaddressed defects assigning a priority to each. This decision is based on the severity, frequency, and reproducibility of each defect. It is then assigned to one of the developers for resolution.

3. The developer either fixes the defect or determines that it isn't a problem and updates the resolution description and status. If it's fixed the resolution status is changed to "fixed."

4. If possible, a different team member verifies all fixed defects, and the resolution status is updated to "verified."

TABLE 2.3   DEFECT INFORMATION

Data Field	Description
Unique identifier	Using sequential numbers will work. If multiple people enter defects, make sure that they are all are unique.
Description of defect	Describe the behavior of the potential defect, including error codes and steps to repeat the problem.
Found by	Name of person reporting defect.
Found when	Date and time of discovery.
Expected results	What had been expected to happen?
Found where	Create a list of documents and software items to report defects against (for example, requirements document, architecture document, form name, report name, module name).
Version	Document the version of the document or MDB (for example, Beta 2.1 of software, Build 36, the 6/29/1999 version of the Requirements Document, and so on).
Software and hardware	List any pertinent configuration information configuration such as display resolution and color depth, amount of memory, available disk space, operating system, other currently executing software, and so on.
Severity	How big a problem is this defect? See Table 2.4.
Frequency	How often is the defect encountered? See Table 2.5.
Reproducibility	How easily can the defect be reproduced? See Table 2.6.
Priority	How important is it to fix this defect? See Table 2.7.
Assigned to	Which developer is going to address this?
Resolution Status	What is the status of the defect? See Table 2.8.
Resolution Description	How was it "Fixed"? Why was it "Deferred" or "Not a Problem"?

TABLE 2.4   SEVERITY OF DEFECT

Severity	Criteria
Critical	There is a loss of functionality, or data is lost.
Serious	A feature does not work as expected, or there is a loss of usability.
Medium	Causes a non-critical aspect of the application to fail with no data loss.
Low	A cosmetic problem or an enhancement request.

TABLE 2.5   FREQUENCY OF OCCURRENCE

Frequency	Criteria
Common	A user could easily encounter the defect with normal use at least once per use. (For example, when closing the main form.)
Occasional	The user is unlikely to encounter the defect every time he or she uses the product, but will probably encounter it sometime. (For example, only when users print a two-page invoice.)
Seldom	A small fraction of the users will ever encounter this defect. (For example, only with a certain video card.)

TABLE 2.6   REPRODUCIBILITY OF DEFECT

Reproducibility	Description
Always	Can always reproduce defect.
Intermittent	Can usually reproduce defect, but not always.
Once	Observed defect once, no further testing for repeatability performed.
Non-repeatable	Observed defect once, unable to repeat it.

TABLE 2.7   PRIORITY OF DEFECT REPAIR

Priority	Description
Critical	Must be fixed.
High	Should be fixed if at all possible.
Medium	Fix if time is available.
Postpone	Don't bother fixing it at this time.

TABLE 2.8 RESOLUTION OF DEFECT

Resolution	Description
Unaddressed	New and not reviewed yet.
Not a Problem	Works as designed.
Deferred	Will not fix it at this time.
Fixed	Problem has been fixed and is awaiting verification.
Verified	Fix has been tested, and the defect is resolved.

TIP

You can improve your development process by looking for the root cause of defects. By determining how and where the defect was introduced, you may learn ways to avoid similar problems in the future. Common root causes are design errors, coding errors, missing requirements, ambiguous requirements, or developer- or customer-training deficiencies.

Version Control

There are many reasons to implement some form of version control in your development process. Whenever the development team includes more than one developer, several challenges arise. At first version control seems straightforward enough. Simply keep the "master" MDB on a server and carefully assign the object creation and maintenance to different developers. Easy, right? Sorry, as hard as you try to prevent it, it's guaranteed that, eventually two developers will make simultaneous changes to the same object. Perhaps they will both open a form at the same time, and one will add a field while the other is fixing a function. First one and then the other will save their changes back to the "master" MDB. The second one to save will win—overwriting the changes the first developer had just saved. With any luck, the first developer will retest his work and notice that his change has disappeared; otherwise, the problem will simply show up again later. There's no work like rework! However, this kind of problem is solved by monitoring and controlling who is allowed to make changes to an object.

Another reason to implement version control is to identify and re-create a prior working version. There will be times when you will need to verify that a problem exists in an earlier version. Restoring a prior version is also useful when planned changes don't work as expected, and you want to undo them. These problems apply to development teams of any size.

There are several techniques and tools that can address these version-control problems. Probably, the best solution is to purchase a commercial tool designed for the job. The most popular is Microsoft's Visual SourceSafe because it is tightly integrated with Microsoft Access 2000. You can also implement several methods to satisfy many of the version-control challenges.

To address the multideveloper issue, you could implement a shared list of objects that are in the "master" database. This could be a text document or an Access table where developers can see if an object is available before logging the time they check out an object and check it back in. The danger here, of course, is that you must rely on every developer to be disciplined about following the procedure.

The version-history problem can be solved by periodically archiving a copy of all the relevant application files to a new subdirectory or zip file. Make sure you give the subdirectory or zip file an understandable name that indicates the release, build, and date. You can even get clever and automate this process from within Access 2000.

CAUTION

Access is different from many other development tools because it saves all its objects in a single MDB file. Many of the commercial version-control tools will only track individual files. This limitation forces developers to check in and out the entire MDB! Pretty useless, huh? Make sure any tool you evaluate has support for Microsoft Access at the object level.

Summary

This chapter discussed a wide range of issues to help you plan and improve your development process. Always invest the time needed to gather and understand the user's real requirements. Plan your development approach and write a project plan to focus your development effort on meeting the requirements, budget, and schedule. Hold design and implementation reviews and track every build, version, and defect throughout the development process.

By including these concepts in your development process, you can count on the successful completion of projects that come your way.

Database Design and Normalization

CHAPTER 3

As you develop an Access application, you must always remember that every application that you create is a database. To develop smarter, faster, more efficient database applications, you need to understand the concept of database normalization, the topic of discussion in this chapter. Although you might have already learned all about database normalization in school or in a training class, you still have to take a look at the relational theory in its relationship to Microsoft Access.

Relational Database Management Systems (RDBMS)

You will hear a lot about Relational Database Management Systems (RDBMS) in the books and magazine articles that you read. You might wonder how Access fits into the RDBMS model. The RDBMS model was pioneered by Dr. E.F. Codd at IBM in 1970. The goal of the RDBMS rules was to leave front-end applications unaffected by changes in the data model. RDBMS products use common data elements such as a CustomerID to connect rows that were related in two different tables and use those fields in a join. There are 13 rules to which a product must conform to be called a Relational Database Management System. Some critics of Microsoft Access say that Access does not conform to these rules, however, I believe that Access conforms rather nicely and can correctly be called a RDBMS. Let's take a look at the 13 Relational Rules and how they relate to Microsoft Access.

Dr. Codd's Relational Rules

Microsoft Access conforms to all 13 of Dr. Codd's Relational Rules. The 13 rules are displayed in Table 3.1 with the rule name, description, and a comment on how it applies to Microsoft Access.

TABLE 3.1 DR. CODD'S RELATIONAL RULES

Dr. Codd's Rule	Name of Rule	Description	Microsoft Access Comment
Rule 0	The Foundation Principle	Any RDBMS must be able to manage databases entirely through its relational capabilities. If a database system depends on a	Access was the first Windows desktop database on the market to follow this rule. Access does not use record numbers

Dr. Codd's Rule	Name of Rule	Description	Microsoft Access Comment
		record-by-record data manipulation tool, it is not truly relational.	as some other desktop systems use.
Rule 1	Information	All data in a relational database is represented explicitly as values in tables. Data cannot be stored in any other way.	Access stores its data in the Microsoft Jet database engine as tables.
Rule 2	Guaranteed Access	Every data element must be accessible logically through the use of a combination of its primary key value, table name, and column name.	Access supports this rule by using Primary Keys. If you do not create a Primary key in your table, Access asks you to do so.
Rule 3	Missing Information	Null values are supported explicitly. Nulls represent missing or inapplicable information.	Access supports Nulls for missing information. Access can also prevent Nulls with required fields.
Rule 4	System Catalog	The database description or "catalog" at the logical level as tabular values. The relational language (SQL) must be able to act on the	This catalog resides in the Microsoft Jet database engine. You can use ADO's OpenSchema to query the system

3

DATABASE DESIGN AND NORMALIZATION

continues

TABLE 3.1 CONTINUED

Dr. Codd's Rule	Name of Rule	Description	Microsoft Access Comment
		database design in the same manner in which it acts on data stored in the structure.	catalog. (See Chapter 5, "The Microsoft Jet Database Engine 4.0.) SQL DDL gives you the ability to create tables and indices, and so on.
Rule 5	Comprehensive Language	An RDBMS must support a clearly defined data-manipulation language (SQL) that comprehensively supports data manipulation and definition, view definition, integrity constraints, transactional boundaries, and authorization.	Access (Jet) fully supports SQL for both data manipulation, view creation (Select Queries), integrity constraints (Relationships and CREATE CONSTRAINT).
Rule 6	View Updatability	All views that can be updated by the system. In a true RDBMS, most (although not all) views would be updatable.	Access was the first desktop database that allowed updatable queries.
Rule 7	Set Level Updates	An RDBMS must do more than just be able to retrieve data sets. It has	Access supports this with Action Queries.

		to be capable of inserting, updating, and deleting data as a relational set.	
Rule 8	Physical Data Independence	Data must be physically independent of the application program. The underlying RDBMS program or "optimizer" should be able to track physical changes in the data. For instance, an RDBMS's application programs should not have to change when an index is added to or deleted from a table.	Access gives you the ability to change the database objects without having to alter the rest of Access. Jet has a logical storage engine.
Rule 9	Logical Data Independence	Whenever possible, applications software must be independent of changes made to the base tables. For example, no code should be rewritten when tables are combined into a view.	When you create a query in Access, you can just as easily bind a form or report to that as if it were a table.
Rule 10	Integrity Independence	Data integrity must be definable in a relational language and stored in the catalog. Data-integrity constraints can be built into	Although Microsoft has not documented how the Jet database engine stores its integrity, you can create

3

DATABASE DESIGN AND NORMALIZATION

continues

TABLE 3.1   CONTINUED

Dr. Codd's Rule	Name of Rule	Description	Microsoft Access Comment
		applications. However, this approach is foreign to the relational model. In the relational model, the integrity should be inherent in the database design.	integrity rules via SQL. Jet does store this information in the database design as part of the catalog.
Rule 11	Distribution Independence	RDBMS capabilities will not be limited due to the distribution of its components in separate databases.	Because the Jet engine stores its data integrity rules at the engine level, other components of the engine do not affect the integrity rules.
Rule 12	Nonsubversion	If an RDBMS has a single-record-at-a-time language, that language cannot be used to bypass the integrity rules or constraints of the relational language. Thus, not only must an RDBMS be governed by relational rules, but these rules must be primary laws.	Access allows you to use DAO and ADO to manipulate one record at a time via updateable recordsets. You cannot violate integrity rules with these data manipulation devices.

A relational database management system has many advantages over other systems, especially in the design process. RDBMS use the relational design theory to create their database design models and is the focus of the next section of this chapter.

The Relational Design Theory

The relational design theory developed by Dr. Codd to build on the Relational Rules consists of these categories, which I will focus on in this section:

- Tables and uniqueness
- Foreign keys and domains
- Relationships
- Data normalization
- Integrity rules

The Benefits of Using the Relational Model

Using the relational design theory, you gain the benefits of years of research into the best way to manage data. Some of the benefits you can achieve by normalizing that database are

- Data integrity is insured at all times
- Data storage is efficient
- Your database application has tremendous room for growth
- Your database behaves predictably because it conforms to these well-tested rules
- Because you follow these rules, other database designers can understand your model much more easily
- The relationships window becomes self-documenting
- Database schema changes are easy to implement

Tables and Uniqueness

When you create database applications, each table represents an entity or process in the real world. You have tables to track people, events, financial transactions, and physical items like products. The relational theory says you must store all data in a table (Rule 1). That table consists of unique rows and columns (Rule 2). The way to guarantee uniqueness for each rule is to set a primary key for each row.

A primary key is a field or group of fields (called a composite key) that is a unique identifier for that row. A primary key has to be unique, or it would violate Rule 2. Access allows you to designate a field as a primary key by setting it as a Key value in table design view. Access will then check to see if the data in that field is unique and does not allow duplicates. Sometimes it can be hard to come up with a unique value for each row while following the business rules in your application. For example, you might be creating a contact management system to use to track your contacts as shown in Figure 3.1.

FIGURE 3.1

A sample non-normalized table.

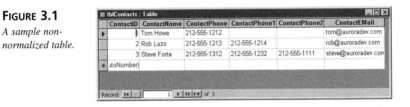

As you develop your contact management system, you might select either Name, Phone, or Email as the key. (These are commonly referred to as "candidate keys.") A common rule of database design is to keep the key as simple as possible and choose the key that will be the most unique and least likely to change. A person's name might change due to marriage, divorce, and so on, and phone numbers or email addresses will change all the time. A good key would be a Social Security number, but what if your contact lives outside the United States? In this situation, Access allows you to create an AutoNumber field to use as a primary key. An AutoNumber is a self-generating numeric value that will automatically increment each time you enter in a record. There are two types of AutoNumbers:

- Integer Values.
- ReplicationID or GUID (used in Replication). For more information, see Chapter 22, "Replication and JRO."

> **NOTE**
>
> There are a few ways to manipulate a Jet AutoNumber that were not allowed in prior versions of Access. You now have the ability to set the AutoNumber increment value, reset the starting seed, and start counting backwards. See Chapter 5 for more information. Although an AutoNumber's increment values can be controlled, always remember that the AutoNumber is not a record number.

Foreign Keys and Domains

A primary key becomes very important when you want to use that key in another table, as shown in Figure 3.2.

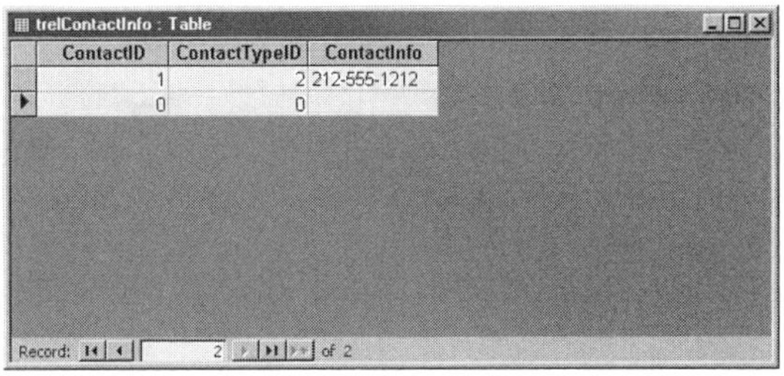

FIGURE 3.2

A table with two foreign keys.

ContactID	ContactTypeID	ContactInfo
1	2	212-555-1212
0	0	

As shown in Figure 3.2, you can store another table's primary key value to represent the record in the other table. This is called a *foreign key* and will be the basis of forming relationships as described in the next section. As you can see in Figure 3.2, the trelContactInfo stores two foreign keys, ContactID and ContactTypeID. ContactID is the primary key of the tblContact table and the ContactTypeID is the primary key of the tlkpContactType table.

When you use foreign keys, they will always be in the same domain. *Domains* are pools of values from which your columns are drawn. A good example is StudentID. Its domain is all the valid Social Security numbers available to the system.

Relationships

When you define primary keys and foreign keys, you are dealing with relationships. Relationships are rules that are supported on the engine level (see Codd's Rule 4). Access supports three different types of relationships:

- One-to-one relationships
- One-to-many relationships
- Many-to-many relationships

To set relationships in Microsoft Access, press the "relationships" button on the main menu or Tools, Relationships to bring up the relationships designer.

One-to-One Relationships

Two tables are engaged in a one-to-one relationship if, for each row in one table, there is at most one table in the related table.

Figure 3.3 shows an example of a one-to-one relationship. One-to-one relationships are the least common types of relationships because most of the time you can include the related information in one table. For security reasons, however, you might choose to break out information into two tables. Also, complex financial transactions contain a lot of one-to-one relationships.

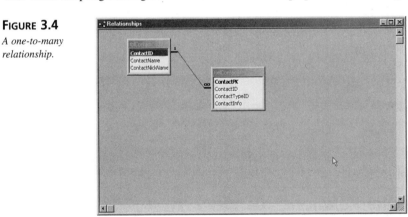

One-to-Many Relationships

The most common type of relationship, a one-to-many relationship, occurs when one table has zero or many related "child" records in another table. An example is Customer to Order, or Contact to ContactInfo as shown in Figure 3.4. Sometimes the "One" side of the relationship is what is called a "lookup" table. Lookup tables usually consists of strictly cross-reference information; for example, a table of states or ZIP Codes. It is wise when adopting naming conventions to use the "tlkp" prefix for a lookup table.

Many-to-Many Relationships

A relationship is described as many-to-many when, for each row in the first table, there can be many rows in the second table, and for each row in the second table, there can be many rows in the first table. Many-to-many relationships between two tables can not be represented in Access, so the only way to do it is via a "linking" table that contains the primary keys of both tables as foreign keys.

Figure 3.5 shows a many-to-many relationship between tblContact and tlkpContactType through the linking table trelContactInfo. The contact table contains all the contacts in your database. The contact type table contains all the types of contact info that you can have: Fax, Email, Phone, and Pager. The linking table contains a reference to a Fax or Phone and the contact, so when the contact adds a new type of communication (like a Web address) to the list, you can add "Web Address" to the lookup table (tlkpContactType) and add the linking record to the trelContactInfo. This is the most flexible way to build a contact management system because you will not have blank "Phone2" fields, nor will you have to add new fields when you add another communication type to the list. When using a linking table it is best to adopt a "trel" naming convention.

FIGURE 3.5

A many-to-many relationship.

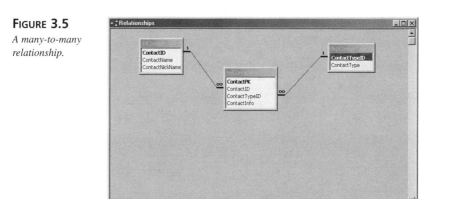

Subdatasheets

With Access 2000, there is a new way, called subdatasheets, to view your related data in table datasheet view. Subdatasheets, like the one shown in Figure 3.6, are an "expanded" view of the related data. Subdatasheets will automatically read your relationships and show the related tables. This is not always the most desirable way to view your related data, as is the case with the many-to-many relationship shown in Figure 3.6.

FIGURE **3.6**

*An Access 2000
subdatasheet.*

To optimize the view of the subdatasheet, you can create a query that joins the data in related tables to view the descriptions, not the foreign keys. Then open the table in design view and look at the table properties as shown in Figure 3.7. In the subdatasheet box, choose the name of the query that you just created. You might also need to set the Link Child and Master properties if Access does not recognize them for you automatically.

FIGURE **3.7**

*Subdatasheet
properties.*

TABLE 3.2   SUBDATASHEET PROPERTIES

Property Name	Description
Subdatasheet Name	The name of the query or related query that will fill your sub-datasheet.
Link Child Fields	The field in the child table (or query) that needs to be linked to the field in the current table.
Link Master Fields	The field in the current that needs to be linked to the field in the child table or query.
Subdatasheet Height	The height in inches of the subdatasheet.
Subdatasheet Expanded	A yes/no value to determine if the subdatasheet is to be expanded by default when you open the table.

Data Normalization

The process of designing your database according to the set of rules devised by Dr. Codd is called Data Normalization. Dr. Codd has six levels of normalization; I will focus on the main three that will affect your database design decisions:

- First Normal Form
- Second Normal Form
- Third Normal Form

First Normal Form

First Normal Form states that all columns in your table must have atomic values. In other words, each field can only contain one value, not a list of values or any repeating groups of data. Many flat file "databases" store data in this fashion, which makes searching quite difficult.

Figure 3.8 show an example of a table that is not in First Normal Form because an array of values is stored in the ContactInfo column. Figure 3.9 is an example of the same table in First Normal Form because there is no repeating information in any columns.

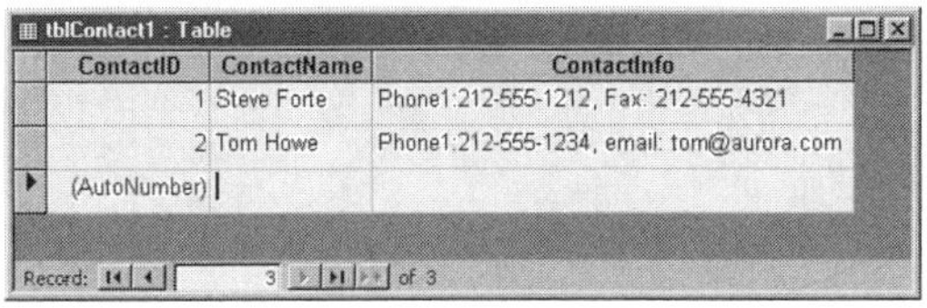

FIGURE 3.8

A table not in First Normal Form.

ContactID	ContactName	ContactInfo
1	Steve Forte	Phone1:212-555-1212, Fax: 212-555-4321
2	Tom Howe	Phone1:212-555-1234, email: tom@aurora.com
(AutoNumber)		

Record: 3 of 3

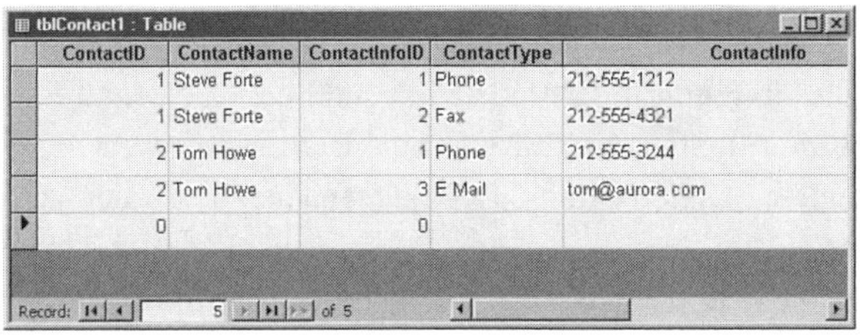

FIGURE 3.9

A table in First Normal Form, but not Second Normal Form.

ContactID	ContactName	ContactInfoID	ContactType	ContactInfo
1	Steve Forte	1	Phone	212-555-1212
1	Steve Forte	2	Fax	212-555-4321
2	Tom Howe	1	Phone	212-555-3244
2	Tom Howe	3	E Mail	tom@aurora.com
0		0		

Record: 5 of 5

Second Normal Form

Although the table shown in Figure 3.9 is in First Normal Form, it is not in Second Normal Form. A table in Second Normal Form is one that is in First Normal Form and in which every non-key field is fully dependent on the entire primary key. In other words, can some information be stored in a different table and referenced by a lookup. Take a look at the table in Figure 3.9. The primary key is a composite of ContactID, ContactInfoID, and ContactInfo. Is ContactName dependent on the parts of the key: ContactInfoID and ContactInfo? It is not because it is dependent only on the ContactID field of the primary key. To put this table in Second Normal Form, break out the Customer information into a separate lookup table and set a one-to-many relationship between the two tables, as shown in Figure 3.10. These tables are now in Second Normal Form.

FIGURE 3.10

A Table in Second Normal Form, but not Third Normal Form.

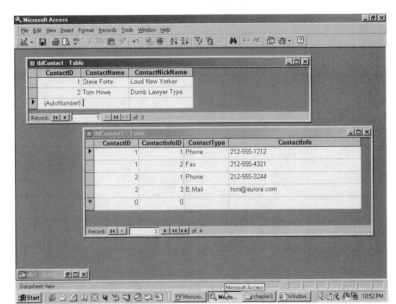

Third Normal Form

Although the tables in Figure 3.10 are in First and Second Normal Forms, they are not in Third Normal Form. A table is in Third Normal Form when every non-key column is mutually independent. A good example of a dependency is a calculated field. (You are better off not storing any calculated fields and only displaying the result as part of a query.) In Figure 3.10, the second table stores the ContactInfoID and the ContactType (description) fields in the same table. Since you know the value of ContactType from ContactInfoID, the table is not in Third Normal Form.

To achieve Third Normal Form, break out the ContactInfo into a third table and create a one-to-many relationship between Contact Info and the Contact Details, as shown in Figure 3.11.

FIGURE **3.11**

*Tables in Third
Normal Form.*

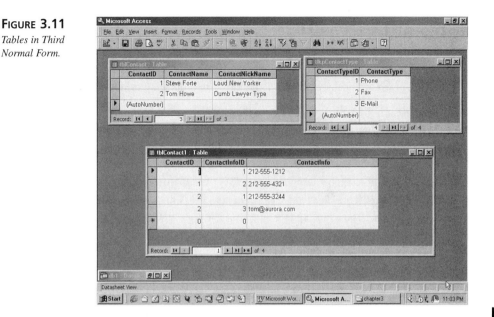

Real-World Benefits of Normalization

In the preceding example you gained a lot by normalizing the original table shown in
Figure 3.8. The original table defined the contact types in an array of values, making
searching for the contents of a Fax field only almost impossible. In addition, when a contact's phone changes, or gets a new form of communication like an email address, editing
the data is difficult and easily botched. First Normal Form drastically improved the situation and gave us more flexibility over keeping track of people's phones, faxes, and
emails, and so on.

In the table in Figure 3.9, which is in First Normal Form but not Second, the Contact
data is difficult to manage because the information is repeated many times. If you have
10 phone numbers in the database and store the name 10 times, it is not only a waste of
disk space, but difficult and time-consuming to update all 10 entries if the person's name
changes. Keeping them all in sync will be quite a chore.

The tables in Figure 3.10, although in First and Second Normal Forms, since all columns
are dependent on the entire key, are not in Third Normal Form. By moving the data and
obtain Third Normal From, you gain more flexibility in your data model because you can
now manage the Contact Types in another table.

3

DATABASE DESIGN
AND
NORMALIZATION

Data Integrity Rules

When normalizing a set of tables, you should also consider data integrity rules. Most of the rules that you set up will be determined by the relationships you defined. In addition, you can set cascade update and cascade deletes when defining relationships.

Setting a cascading update ensures that when you update the primary key value of the "One" table, the change will be reflected in all the "Many" tables. For example, say you have a Lookup table for States. New York is in this table with a primary key of NY and a description of New York. Imagine that New York City broke away and formed its own state. (Don't laugh, it almost happened in 1789!) When you change your NY value to NY1 (or something more descriptive), the values of NY in all the child tables will be changed to NY1. If cascading updates was not set, you would be required to add a record to the lookup table for NY1, update all the records in the child table, and then delete the NY record from the lookup table.

Setting a cascading delete ensures that when you delete a record from a "one" table, you will also delete all records from the "many" table. This can be both very good and very bad. If you delete a customer and cascading deletes was set, all the "many" invoices will be deleted. If you do not have deletes set, the deletion will not be allowed in the "one" table until you delete all the records in the "many" table, to avoid leaving any orphans.

Summary

Since Access is a relational database system as defined by Dr. Codd, you can take advantage of the relational design model. As you can see, by using these data modeling techniques, you gain a lot of flexibility and can standardize your approach to your design so other developers will easily understand it. In this chapter we covered the concepts of relational databases and how to structure your data model according to Dr. Codd's database normalization rules.

Advanced Queries

CHAPTER 4

The workhorses of an Access database are its queries. Queries come in a variety of forms and types. You can save them in the database, like a table, or they can run only in memory. You can build them by writing a Structured Query Language statement (SQL) or you can build them by using a graphical user interface called the QBE grid. A query might present data straight from the database, or it might perform some groupings and other calculations on the data before it shows a result to you. An Access query might know exactly what it is supposed to do when it runs, or it can ask questions beforehand. Queries can also update data, create new records, delete records, and even change the structure of the database. Queries in Access can work with data that resides in an MDB file, other data sources linked to Access, and even client/server databases such as Oracle and Microsoft SQL Server. They are the fastest and most reliable way to interact with your data in any meaningful way in a relational database.

This chapter will explore some of the advanced variations on this powerful tool.

Understanding Queries in Access 2000

A carefully constructed Access database and the query abilities it provides can solve some of your simplest everyday data management needs. It can also solve some of your most complex problems because a relational structure breaks data into logical groupings. This makes it possible to build meaningful connections between related items efficiently. With a relational database, you can get the view of your data that you want and need.

Take your telephone bill as an example. Every month your telephone company sends you a bill detailing all the calls you have made. The bill has the date and time you called, the phone number you called, the length of time you spoke, some kind of unit charge, and a total cost for the call. That is a lot of information, but the telephone bill by itself cannot easily answer some basic questions. It would be very useful to be able to cross-reference that telephone bill with your address book. If you could do that, you would have the ability to find out exactly who you called, when you called that person, and how much money you spent talking to him or her. You might be able to know how much you spent calling everyone at a particular client or how much to bill clients for each of your projects.

It might seem that this kind of data manipulation could be done with something other than a relational database. But with a properly designed relational database, this kind of data manipulation is extremely easy, reliable, and fast.

Creating Advanced Queries

Queries are objects, just like tables and forms, and as such they reside inside the query container of the Database window (shortcuts to them can reside in custom group containers created by the developer). Creating and building queries requires the setting of a variety of properties that govern the way the query will behave when it executes. You can start with the query object itself.

You can view all the saved queries by clicking on the Queries object in the Groups Window of the Database container. Right-clicking on any individual query object displays its properties dialog sheet as shown in Figure 4.1.

FIGURE 4.1

The Properties window of this query displays the object's properties.

Using the Query Object

Like any other Access database object, you can use a name up to 255 characters long, and all the naming conventions for other Access database objects apply to queries. The Properties window also shows the selected query's type. You can also see a description of the query. This is a very important property and a conscientious database designer should take advantage of this as often as possible. A good description will help you understand what the query was trying to do should you have to revisit it later. Other developers will also find the description property useful when they need to work on your query. The Properties window also provides a creation date and a modified date, which Access updates automatically. By default, the owner of the object is the person who created it. This has some implications for security. (For an in-depth treatment of security issues, read Chapter 23, "Security.") At the bottom of the window are two check boxes. The Hidden check box allows you to not display this object to the users through the Database window. This can help keep others from inadvertently changing your work.

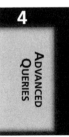

4

ADVANCED QUERIES

The replication object tells Access whether or not this object is subject to the replication scheme you might have set up for your database. When an object is replicable, it is subject to modification by another, presumably more current, version of itself through replication. For more on replication, please see Chapter 22, "Replication and JRO."

> **NOTE**
>
> Another way to keep users from seeing your query, or another object, is to begin its name with the letters *USYS*, as in USYS_myquery. You can view these objects when working on the database by choosing to view system objects from the Tools, Options dialog box.

> **CAUTION**
>
> Microsoft also hides objects prefixed with *MSYS*. You should never allow users to tamper with these system tables because they could corrupt the database. Developers should also avoid using them because Microsoft does not promise to maintain them from one version to another. Be sure system tables are hidden before giving the database back to your users.

Understanding Query Properties

Because a query behaves according to how its properties are set, it's important to understand exactly what those properties are and how they operate. So before examining the advanced query possibilities, let's have a quick review of a basic query and the terms you will use while designing more advanced forms of queries.

Understanding the QBE Grid

Access makes it easy to create queries by allowing you to compose them graphically in the QBE grid (see Figure 4.2). All data sources, whether they are native tables, linked tables, or even other select queries, can be brought into the QBE grid and manipulated in exactly the same way. In the QBE grid, the relationships between the tables (tables and queries look the same in the QBE grid), the sorting and grouping instructions, and the criteria all have a place in the interfce.

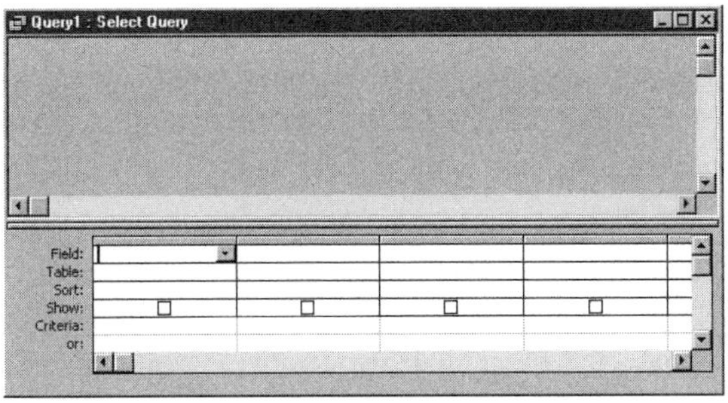

FIGURE 4.2

The QBE grid is divided into two basic sections:the table pane on top and the query grid on the bottom.

Right-click anywhere in the table pane window to display the shortcut menu and choose Properties from the menu to view the properties of the query. The following is a list of all the properties for the query:

- **Description:** This is the same property available at the object level.

- **Output All Fields:** Setting this field to Yes is the same as clicking the Show option of every field in the query. This also makes all the fields in the query available to other queries, forms, and reports.

- **Top Value:** If you want to see only the five highest-priced products, you can set this property. It will also work with percentages. The property offers you the option of choosing the top 5, 10, 25, or 100 records or the top 5% or 25%, but you can set this option any way you like. The field affected by this property is the leftmost sorted field. If you have three fields from left to right ([product name], [unit cost], and [retail price]), and you want to view the five most expensive products based on their [retail price], you have to sort [retail price] in descending order. If you also sort the [unit cost] field, the top five items presented will be based on the [unit cost] field. If no fields are sorted, you will get the first five records presented without sorting.

- **Unique Values**: This enables you to get a representative list of values in a field. If you have the Orders table, and you need to see which products have been ordered, you can use the property to distill the few dozen products out of the hundreds of orders you might have.

- **Unique Records**: This is similar to the Unique Values property, except that it works on multiple fields. The result of the combination of these fields must be unique.

- **Run Permissions:** When securing a database, you need to be able to lock your tables so users cannot edit them in ways you cannot control. However, you still need authorized users to work with those tables and the data contained within them. By setting Run Permissions, you can allow a user to execute a query as if he

4

ADVANCED
QUERIES

had the permission set of an owner of the tables. With this property, users can delete or update data in a controlled fashion in a secured database, even if their permission settings would not normally allow them to do so. Without this property, it is difficult to secure the data in a database and still allow users to perform actions against the data.

- **Source Database:** The default setting is the current database. This default setting also applies to data attached from another Access database. The property setting would contain a path and filename if the data were contained in another database to which there was no attachment.

- **Source Connect Str:** This property contains the name of the application that created the external source database. The Source Database and Source Connect Str properties work together to enable Access to use unattached external data.

- **Record Locks**: In a multiuser system, this property determines how the query will handle contention issues. A contention issue occurs when two or more users try to change the same record. There are three options for this property: No Locks, All Records, and Edited Record. These locking options affect only the records affected by this query, not all the records of the source tables. If the No Locks option is selected, it is possible for a user to make changes to a record while other users are working on that same record. The first user to write his changes to disk is the presumed winner. Access warns the other users that they are working with a record someone else has changed. Each one must make a decision as to how to handle the issue. Their choices are to abandon their own changes, to overwrite the changes of the other user, or to copy the changes to the Clipboard and decide what to do after that. If you choose the All Records option, other users will not be able to edit the records controlled by this query until the first user releases them. Edited Record affects only the record edited by the user while it he is editing it.

- **Recordset Type:** This allows you to determine whether the recordset type used by a form or report is a Dynaset, Dynaset (Inconsistent Updates), or a Snapshot. The Dynaset structure normally allows you to update the *many* side of a relationship. The Dynaset (Inconsistent Updates) setting allows you to update both sides of the relationship. It's important to note that there can be serious implications for referential integrity by using the Dynaset (Inconsistent Updates) option. It is best to use it only when the relationship has referential integrity and cascading updates enforced, and only after extensive testing. Snapshots do not allow the users to edit the data, but they execute more quickly than a dynaset. There are performance and editing implications with each of these choices.

- **ODBC Timeout:** If the query is going to run over the network, this property tells the query how long to wait for a result before it gives up. The unit of measurement is in seconds, with a default of 60 seconds. Although you can change this number, other variables still affect performance. Network traffic and the level of caching on the server can change response time from day to day. So setting this number requires some trial and error. It's important not to set the time too long because the user could be left waiting for a response when the server is actually down.

- **Filter:** This is a great development tool for beginners. It's something like an automatic criteria writer. If a user runs a query and then needs to limit the result set further, he can select values in the result set and use the filter buttons to fill this property with the equivalent of the criteria. He can do all this without having to know the syntax of the criteria section of the QBE grid.

- **Order By:** Similar to Filter, Order By allows a beginner to execute a query, and change the way the query is sorted by simply selecting a value in the result set. The instruction for that sorting is recorded in this property.

- **Max Records:** Entering a number value in Max Records limits the number of records returned by a query, regardless of how many records might satisfy the criteria of the query. If a query normally returns 500 records, and this property is set to 17, the query will return only the first 17 records. There is no way to get the additional records without resetting this property.

- **Subdatasheet Name** (NEW): This property is new to Access 2000. It allows you to create queries that have a drill-down capability. If you have a query that displays total sales by product, you can set this property to a table or query containing the actual order details. When the query runs, you'll see the summary of total sales by product, and a switch to click in order to see the details that made that summary number.

- **Link Child Fields** (NEW): This is the field on the subdatasheet, preferably a key, that matches a field on the main query.

- **Link Master Fields** (NEW): This is a field in the main query, preferably a key, that matches a field on the subdatasheet. This field must show in the query result in order for the subdatasheet to work.

- **Subdatasheet Height** (NEW): A measurement in inches for the height of the subdatasheet when it is displayed.

- **Subdatasheet Expanded** (NEW): If set to Yes, the detail in the subdatasheet will be displayed when the query is opened. If set to No, the user will need to click a switch to drill down to the detail of the subdatasheet.

4

ADVANCED QUERIES

> **NOTE**
>
> Although it is possible to update data through a subdatasheet, as of this writing, the query does not automatically reflect that change in the main data sheet's calculations without being restarted.

> **NOTE**
>
> The time range for ODBC Timeout is measured in seconds with its default setting of 60 seconds. However, setting the property to zero does not make the query constantly check for a response; it actually turns the Timeout feature off, so no timeout error will occur.

Understanding the Table Pane

All the tables or queries involved in a query are represented in the top pane of the window, the table pane. They appear as small windows with their field names listed inside. If you place a query in the table pane, only the fields that have been marked to show in that query's result set will appear. A line between the tables represents their relationship. The relationships you have established in the Relationships window will appear here automatically. This is the AutoJoin feature, and it allows Access to assume a relationship between fields with exactly the same names and the same or compatible data types. AutoJoin will create an ad hoc query between them. It might be that two fields with the same name are not really related, so be sure to check all the relationships in your query before you use it. You can disable AutoJoin through the Tools, Options dialog box. The Enable AutoJoin option is located on the Tables/Queries tab.

> **NOTE**
>
> Creating a relationship in a query, or allowing Access to assume that relationship, has no effect outside of that query. For the best and most reliable performance, establish your relationships in the Relationships window of the database object. That way they can be used in the execution plans, and referential integrity and cascading updates and deletes can be established if necessary.

Placing a Table or Query in the Table Pane

Putting a table or query into the table pane is simple. When you first create the query and go to the Query Design view, Access will prompt you to select the tables or queries you want to use. The dialog box has three tabs, one for tables, one for queries, and one for both. If you need to add a table or query after you have disposed of the dialog box, you can use Query, Show Table to retrieve the dialog box. You can also use the Add Table button on the toolbar to add more tables later.

The upper part of the Query window, the table pane, is actually quite large, so you can expand your tables by clicking and dragging their representations. If your query involves lots of tables, it is possible to scroll around in this window and see the other tables clearly. You can also use this space to put less-important tables, such as reference tables, off to the side and reduce clutter.

Establishing Relationships in the Table Pane

If you have not established a relationship between the tables through the Relationships window at the database level, you can still establish an ad hoc relationship within the query. To do this, click on a field name in one of the table representations and drag it to its related field in another table representation. This action draws a join line between those two fields and they will now act as related fields in this query.

The join line may also have some characters attached to it such as an infinity symbol and the numeral 1. These characters tell you some information about the nature of the relationship between the fields and are displayed when you create the relationship at the database level. If you established the relationship at the database level, the relationship is one-to-one, one-to-many, or many-to-one. The join line will represent this by displaying a 1 near the table of the *one* side of the relationship and an infinity sign on the *many* side of the relationship. Each character may appear on both sides of the relationship. The existence of the characters does not mean that there is actually one record on one side and several related records on the other in every case. It only describes the potential of the data relationship. These characters can help you decide what to do with a query.

Like all other objects, the join line has properties, too. Most objects show their properties windows by using a right-click to expose a shortcut menu and then you can select the Properties menu item to see the properties window. The join line's properties window appears when the user double-clicks the line. You can also choose View, Join Properties if the relationship was established at the database level. This is shown in Figure 4.3.

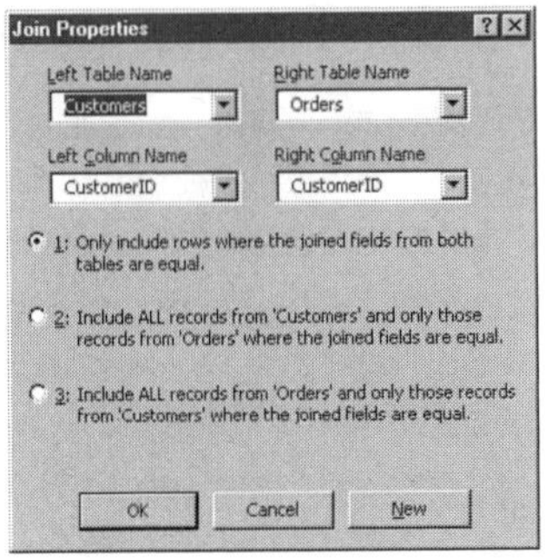

FIGURE 4.3

You can open the Properties window of the join by double-clicking on the join line.

The Properties window for the join line is quite different from the properties windows of other objects. This one has four drop-down boxes: two for table names and two for field names and three mutually exclusive selections. These selections declare what kind of relationship this is. The three options are

- **Inner Join:** This is the default selection. A straight line between two fields represents this type of relationship. The result set for a query with a relationship based on an inner join will be all the records where the two related fields are the same. In other words, if a query contained customers and orders, and they are joined on their CustomerID fields, the result would show only customers who had placed orders and only orders connected to customers in the Customers table.

- **Left Outer Join**: The line representing this relationship would have an arrow at one end. This type of relationship allows one side of the relationship to dominate. The dominating side of the relationship is pointing at the subordinate side of the relationship. That means a query of Customers and Orders where the relationship was a left outer join (the join line pointed at the Orders table) would show all customers whether or not they had placed orders. However, it would not show the orders that did not have matching customers.

- **Right Outer Join:** The line representing this relationship would also have an arrow at one end. This type of relationship also allows one side of the relationship to dominate. The dominating side of the relationship is pointing at the subordinate side of the relationship. A query of Customers and Orders where the relationship was a right outer join (the join line pointed at the Customers table) would have a result set showing all orders, whether or not they were placed by known customers. However, it would not show the customers who did not have orders.

The drop-down boxes in the dialog box allow you to determine which table and fields will be considered left and right. This is new to Access 2000. The left and right side of a relationship used to be subject to change depending upon how you built the query.

Referential integrity would necessitate the use of only a right or left outer join in most cases. It is likely that you could have customers without orders, but you should not have orders without customers at the same time. If you can achieve unmatched return records when running a left outer join and a right outer join against the same relationship, you need to check your data integrity. Records on the subordinate side of a relationship that do not have a match on the dominant side of the relations are *orphaned records*. Orphaned records are usually invisible to the normal operation of the database, but they can cause statistical discrepancies in situations where the subordinate table is queried without the dominant table being involved. In other words, your reports on orders by products might not agree with a report showing orders by customers.

It is important to not let the terms *left* and *right* confuse you. In the QBE grid, it is possible for the *left* join to point right and for the *right* join to point left. It's especially confusing now that you have control over which is left and which is right. The important thing to remember is that the dominant side will display all its records even if they don't match the subordinate side.

Another option in the dialog box is to enable you to create another relationship through the dialog box. Clicking the new button will open a dialog box that allows you to set an ad hoc relationship between the existing tables.

The following figures show the different result sets obtained by a query against the Customers table and the Orders table. The inner join result is shown in Figure 4.4 and its SQL statement is shown in Listing 4.1.

FIGURE 4.4

The ten customers with the fewest orders on an inner join.

Company Name	CountOfOrderl
Centro comercial Moctezuma	1
Lazy K Kountry Store	2
GROSELLA-Restaurante	2
Bólido Comidas preparadas	3
Laughing Bacchus Wine Cellars	3
The Cracker Box	3
North/South	3
Trail's Head Gourmet Provisioners	3
France restauration	3
Consolidated Holdings	3

Record: 1 of 10

4

ADVANCED QUERIES

LISTING 4.1 THE SQL STATEMENT FOR THE QUERY IN FIGURE 4.4

```
SELECT TOP 10 Customers.CompanyName, Count(Orders.OrderID)
AS CountOfOrderID
FROM Customers INNER JOIN Orders
ON Customers.CustomerID = Orders.CustomerID
GROUP BY Customers.CompanyName
ORDER BY Count(Orders.OrderID);
```

This query shows a count of orders for each customer and has an inner join, so the only records displayed are the ones represented on both sides of the relationship.

Contrast these results with ones in Figure 4.5 and Listing 4.2.

LISTING 4.2 THE SQL STATEMENT FOR THE QUERY IN FIGURE 4.5

```
SELECT TOP 10 Customers.CompanyName,
Count(Orders.OrderID) AS CountOfOrderID
FROM Customers
LEFT JOIN Orders ON Customers.CustomerID = Orders.CustomerID
GROUP BY Customers.CompanyName
ORDER BY Count(Orders.OrderID);
```

Figure 4.4 shows a reassuring picture; everything seems to be in order, but the query result is not truly accurate. An outer join, as seen in the result of Figure 4.5, shows that there are two customers who have not ordered anything at all, and they would not have appeared in a query with an inner join. Because the field you are displaying from the Orders side is calculated (count), the result shows as zero. Normally, the representation for a missing record on the subordinate side would be Null.

An unmatched query is just an outer join where the criteria are set to Null on the foreign key. Without setting the foreign key's criteria to Null, you might not notice the few blank fields among all the other records. Figure 4.6 uses Listing 4.3 to create an example of this.

The query displays 2 records instead of 10 or 12 when the Null criteria is not applied against the foreign key.

FIGURE 4.6

Customers without orders.

LISTING 4.3 THE SQL STATEMENT FOR THE QUERY IN FIGURE 4.6

```
SELECT Customers.CompanyName, Orders.OrderID
FROM Customers
LEFT JOIN Orders ON Customers.CustomerID = Orders.CustomerID
WHERE (((Orders.OrderID) Is Null));
```

In short, it's not enough to have the right tables and the right fields related to each other, you have to have the right type of relationship to ensure that you have an accurate result set. Two queries with the same tables and the same related fields could yield vastly different results if the type of relationship is different. The SQL statements behind the two queries in Listings 4.4 and 4.5 are different by only one word. (See Figures 4.7 and 4.8.) If the Northwind example had an orphaned order record, another SQL statement could display it by changing the word *Left* to *Inner* (Inner could also be thought of and entered as Right). Again, a completely different result set, just by changing one word in the relationship.

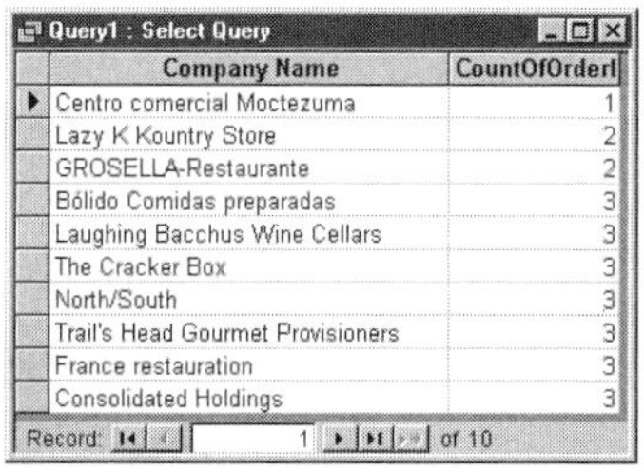

FIGURE 4.7

SQL for inner join.

LISTING 4.4 THE SQL STATEMENT FOR THE QUERY IN FIGURE 4.7

```
SELECT TOP 10 Customers.CompanyName, Count(Orders.OrderID)
AS CountOfOrderID
FROM Customers
INNER JOIN Orders ON Customers.CustomerID = Orders.CustomerID
GROUP BY Customers.CompanyName
ORDER BY Count(Orders.OrderID);
```

4

ADVANCED QUERIES

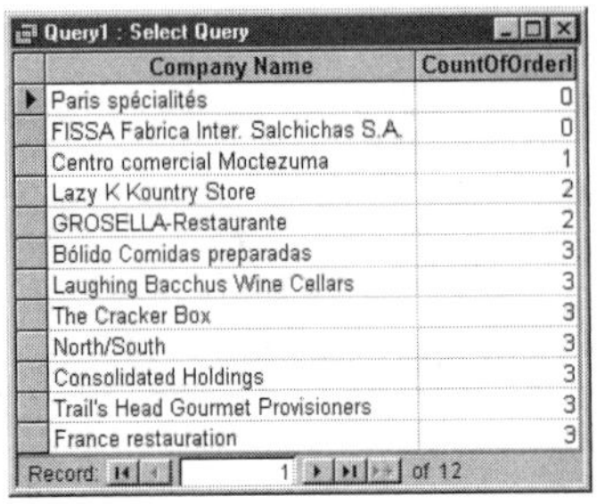

FIGURE **4.8**

SQL for outer join.

LISTING **4.5**   THE SQL STATEMENT FOR THE QUERY IN FIGURE 4.8; IT SHOWS 12 RECORDS DESPITE THE TOP 10 REQUEST BECAUSE OF THE TIE BETWEEN THE VALUES

```
SELECT TOP 10 Customers.CompanyName,
Count(Orders.OrderID) AS CountOfOrderID
FROM Customers
LEFT JOIN Orders ON Customers.CustomerID = Orders.CustomerID
GROUP BY Customers.CompanyName
ORDER BY Count(Orders.OrderID);
```

> **TIP**
>
> It's easier to select a diagonal join line than one that is vertical or horizontal. Nudging the table representations, or scrolling through their fields, might make it easier to select the join line.

Understanding the Query Grid

The lower half of the window is the query grid. Here you are able to list the fields to be presented, the sorting order, grouping information, calculations, configuration of a crosstab, and update and append information and criteria to choose the records affected by the query. This is where you will do most of your work on a query.

Placing Fields into the Query Grid

Place fields into the query grid by one of several means:

- **Double-Click:** Double-clicking on the field name in the table representation will move it into the first available position in the query grid.
- **Click and Drag:** You can place fields by clicking and dragging them to any column position in the query grid.

- **Control-Click**: Selecting one field, holding down the Ctrl key on the keyboard, and clicking on other fields in the same table will allow you to bring them to the query grid as a group.

- **Double-Click the Table Title Bar:** Double-clicking on the table title bar will select all the fields in the table. Drag the selection to the query grid. You can also use the Control-click technique to exclude some fields from the selection.

- **The Asterisk:** The first entry in the table representation is the asterisk. Double-clicking or clicking and dragging this to the query grid will create a single entry in the query grid, but all the fields from that table appear in the query's result set.

- **Select the Fields in the Query Grid:** The first row of the query grid determines which field is used. Positioning your insertion point in this row will enable you to choose the field. Be aware that it is possible to choose a field from the wrong table if you are not careful. Another row of the query grid, Table Name, can make this technique easier to use.

The second row of the QBE grid used to be optional, but in Access 2000, it is on permanent display. The Table row shows the query designer which table the field came from. This is very useful when you have similar field names in more than one table. You can also use this row to quickly change the source table for any field in the QBE grid.

Establishing Sort Order, Displaying Results, and Selection Criteria for a Query

The Sort row allows you to determine how the query sorts its result rows. For any particular field you can select Ascending, Descending, or Not Sorted. When more than one field is chosen for sorting, the sort order is controlled left to right.

The fourth row controls whether or not a field displays in the result set. A field can still affect the result of query, even if it does not appear in the result set. The result set must display at least one field for the query to execute.

The fifth row and all the following rows are for criteria. The criteria rows contain the values used to select qualifying rows into the recordset. They can also contain SQL statements, although this is not a preferred technique because that SQL statement must execute for each record in the query's possible result set before the overall result can be displayed. Using subqueries can usually achieve the same effect.

4

ADVANCED
QUERIES

> **TIP**
>
> You can add fields more than once to the QBE grid, turn off their Show option, and control the sorting of the result set without changing the order of the fields.

Another row is available in the QBE Grid if needed:the Total row. This row can be accessed by clicking the Totals button on the toolbar or by choosing View, Totals from the menu. When the Totals feature is activated, the nature of the query changes quite a bit. These aggregate queries allow you to get very creative with the result set. Using the Totals row is discussed in detail in the next section of this chapter.

Mastering Totals Queries

Usually, the result set of a query presents so much information to the user that it is not useful. To correct that, Access queries enable you to create summaries of your data with Totals queries.

To create a summary of customers and their purchases, you can create a new query in the Northwind database included with Access 2000. When finished, this query will list each customer and each product purchased as a list of unique combinations.

To start this query, bring the Customers table, the Orders table, the Order Details table, and the Products table into the table pane.

Bring the CompanyName field to the query grid from the Customers table. Bring the ProductName field to the query grid from the Products table. Sort the query by CompanyName and ProductName. Run the query by clicking on the red exclamation mark on the toolbar or by choosing Query, Run. If you look carefully at Figure 4.9, you'll see the result set lists some customers more than once for each product. The SQL statement for Figure 4.9 can be seen in Listing 4.6.

LISTING 4.6   THE SQL STATEMENT FOR THE QUERY IN FIGURE 4.9

```
SELECT Customers.CompanyName, Products.ProductName
FROM Products
INNER JOIN ((Customers INNER JOIN Orders
ON Customers.CustomerID = Orders.CustomerID)
INNER JOIN [Order Details]
ON Orders.OrderID = [Order Details].OrderID)
ON Products.ProductID = [Order Details].ProductID
ORDER BY Customers.CompanyName, Products.ProductName;
```

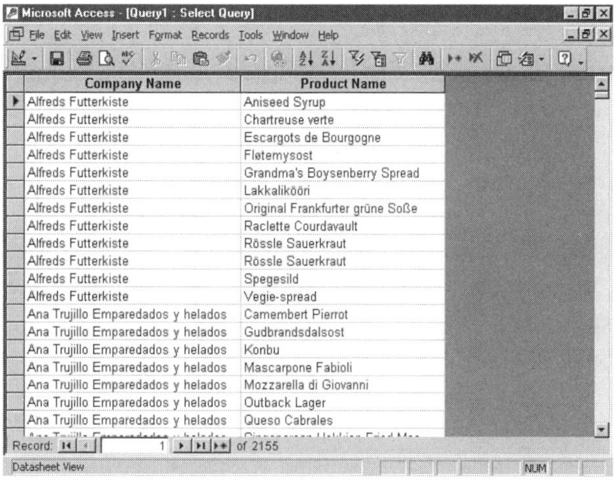

FIGURE 4.9

Some customers appear more than once for the same product because they have made more than one order of that product.

Return to the Design view of the query and click the Totals button on the toolbar or choose View, Totals. The Totals line appears in the query grid with the Group By option chosen for both fields. This means that the query will squeeze the recordset to display only one representation of each combination of values between CompanyName and ProductName. Run the query again, and you'll see that a customer's name and a product never repeat. This has also removed several hundred records from the recordset.

You can select as many as 10 fields to use with Group By, but be aware that Group By causes additional processing and every unnecessary field slows your query and adds additional rows to the result set. Only use Group By with those fields necessary for your desired result. You cannot use [tablename].* in a Group By field.

This Totals feature is very powerful and has many other capabilities. There are 12 options available to you when you choose to invoke totals in your query. Nine of these options are aggregate functions, which means they perform calculations against data in a field. You'll take a look at each of them.

TIP

None of the aggregate functions count Null values in their calculations. If you want the aggregate functions to consider these Null values, you must convert the Nulls to zeros by running an update query or by using an
IIF(IsNull([*fieldnamereference*]),0,[*fieldnamereference*]) to present the aggregate query with a zero value.

4

ADVANCED
QUERIES

The Count Aggregate Function

In order to see how many orders each customer has placed, you need to change the query. Change the ProductName field to the OrderID of the Orders table, and set its Total setting to the Count aggregate function. Delete the Order Detail table and the Products table from the table pane. When running an aggregate query, it's critical that nothing extraneous is in the query. Almost anything in the QBE grid can influence the result of an aggregate function. If you don't delete these tables, although not used in the query grid, they will cause the query to count every item ordered instead of every order. See Figure 4.10 and Listing 4.7.

FIGURE 4.10

Customer order count.

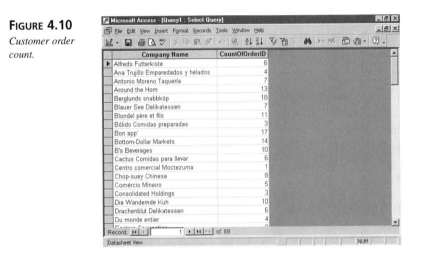

In Figure 4.10, notice that there is no need to state a sort order. A simple aggregate query will sort itself by its grouping field. The sort order is determined by the order of the Group By fields from left to right, unless otherwise specified.

LISTING 4.7   THE SQL STATEMENT FOR THE QUERY IN FIGURE 4.10

```
SELECT Customers.CompanyName, Count(Orders.OrderID) AS CountOfOrderID
FROM Customers
INNER JOIN Orders ON Customers.CustomerID = Orders.CustomerID
GROUP BY Customers.CompanyName;
```

The Average Aggregate Function

To see an average unit price by product category, create a query of just the Products table. Put the Category ID and the UnitPrice fields into the query grid, make the query a totals query, and set the Totals option for the unit price field to Avg. (see Figure 4.11 and Listing 4.8).

FIGURE 4.11

Average aggregate query as seen from the QBE grid.

Category	AvgOfUnitPrice
▶ Beverages	$37.98
Condiments	$23.06
Confections	$25.16
Dairy Products	$28.73
Grains/Cereals	$20.25
Meat/Poultry	$54.01
Produce	$32.37
Seafood	$20.68

Record: ⏮ ◀ 1 ▶ ⏭ ▶*

LISTING 4.8   THE SQL STATEMENT FOR THE QUERY IN FIGURE 4.11

```
SELECT Products.CategoryID, Avg(Products.UnitPrice) AS AvgOfUnitPrice
FROM Products
GROUP BY Products.CategoryID;
```

The Avg. aggregate function operates on all the Number, Date/Time, Currency, and AutoNumber fields within a grouping and yields the average for the values in that group.

The Minimum and Maximum Aggregate Functions

The Min/Max functions can be very useful for presenting the maximum value in a field. One good use for them is to present something like the last order date for each customer. To do this, create a query with the Customers table and Orders table, joined by CustomerID. Bring the CompanyName and the OrderDate into the query grid. Make the query a total query and set the OrderDate field's aggregate function to Max. The result will be the most recent order date for each customer. The reverse of this, the Min function, will give the earliest order date on record for each customer. You can even display them side-by-side by repeating the OrderDate field and selecting Min for one and Max for the other.

4

ADVANCED QUERIES

The First and Last Aggregate Functions

At first glance, the First and Last functions might seem like the Min and Max, but they are completely different. Min and Max actually evaluate the data presented. First and Last simply take the first or last item presented to the query, sometimes with surprising and unexpected results. Good advice is to use the First and Last functions with caution, and preferably against a presorted temporary table. Using the First and Last functions against an unsorted table, or one sorted in a way unrelated to your desires, will yield arbitrary results. This is because the order of presentation means everything to First and Last, and relevance to the other fields of data means nothing.

You will use the First and Last functions to give a list of each category's highest-priced product. This list will have the CategoryName, the ProductName, and the UnitPrice. To do this, you need to make a new query based on the Categories table and the Products table. Put the CategoryName field from the Categories table into the QBE grid, and then put the ProductName and UnitPrice fields from the Products table into the QBE grid. Sort in ascending order on CategoryName and in descending order on UnitPrice.

From the Query menu, select Make Table and call the soon-to-be-created table *Categories and Products Sorted by Price*. Run the query. This should make a table with about 77 new records. Now you can make a query using the First and Last functions.

Create another query and bring the Categories and Products Sorted by Price table into the table pane. Bring all its fields into the query grid. Make the query a totals query and set the aggregate function for the ProductName to First, and then set the aggregate function for UnitPrice to First. Run the query and you will see the most expensive product for each category. If you change the First functions to Last, you will see the least expensive product for each category. Setting one of the fields to First and the other to Last shows how First and Last can grab data from different rows in your recordset, but present them as if they were part of the same record. Try this same kind of query against the original table and you will see just how dependent upon presorting the First and Last functions really are. You must have the records sorted either deliberately (as we did in our temporary table) or through a table's indexes for the First or Last function to be effective. In this particular example, the First or Last function used on UnitPrice could have been replaced with Min or Max, but First or Last would have to be used to get the ProductName.

The Standard Deviation and Variance Aggregate Functions

Standard deviation (StDev) and Variance (Var) calculate on the values of a field. Simply create a new query with the grouping that you want. Select the appropriate field and set its aggregate function to StDev or Var. Standard Deviation and Variance employ a sampling method that uses a denominator of $(n-1)$, where n is equal to the number of records in the result set. For statistical analysis, this method is preferred.

Two more total options that are not aggregate functions are Expression and Where.

The Expression Function

Expression allows you to present a calculation in your result, but that calculation must contain an aggregate function. Use this feature when you want to present the results of multiple functions in your query. An example of an expression might look something like Figure 4.12 (see Listing 4.9 for the SQL):

FIGURE 4.12

A result set with an expression.

Category Name	CountOfProductName	Expression Example
Beverages	12	478.5375
Condiments	12	290.5875
Confections	13	343.434
Dairy Products	10	301.665
Grains/Cereals	7	148.8375
Meat/Poultry	6	340.242
Produce	5	169.9425
Seafood	12	260.5995

Record: 1 of 8

LISTING 4.9   THE SQL STATEMENT FOR THE QUERY IN FIGURE 4.12

```
SELECT Categories.CategoryName,
Count(Products.ProductName) AS CountOfProductName,
Sum([UnitPrice])*1.05 AS [Expression Example]
FROM Categories
INNER JOIN Products ON Categories.CategoryID = Products.CategoryID
GROUP BY Categories.CategoryName;
```

In this example, you are taking a count of the products and then increasing the average price of the category by 5%. To do this, you set the total property of the calculated field to Expression and then write a formula that uses an aggregate function. If your expression lacks one of the aggregate functions, you will receive an error message and the query will not run.

The Where Clause

Applying criteria to the aggregate query is done by either expressly using the Where statement, or by simply entering criteria into the QBE grid as you would in a typical Select query. However, there are differences between these approaches and your choice can affect the way the query behaves. When the Where statement is used, the query evaluates the criteria first, including or excluding records before the grouping takes place. If

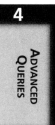

4

ADVANCED
QUERIES

you enter criteria into another field without using `Where`, those criteria will be evaluated after the grouping has been completed. Criteria expressed without a `Where` statement will be preceded by `Having` in SQL.

The implications for this are simple, but very important. If you want to exclude foreign sales from an aggregate query, do so with a `Where`. If you also want to see only results where the counts in that aggregate query are greater than 1,000, express that in the field performing the count aggregation. The criteria for excluding foreign sales would be entered in the query grid of the ShipCountry field of the Orders table, and would be expressed in SQL as a `Having` clause. `Having` clauses are useful for exercising criteria against finished calculations. Examples of the `Having` clause can be reviewed in Figure 4.13 and Listing 4.10.

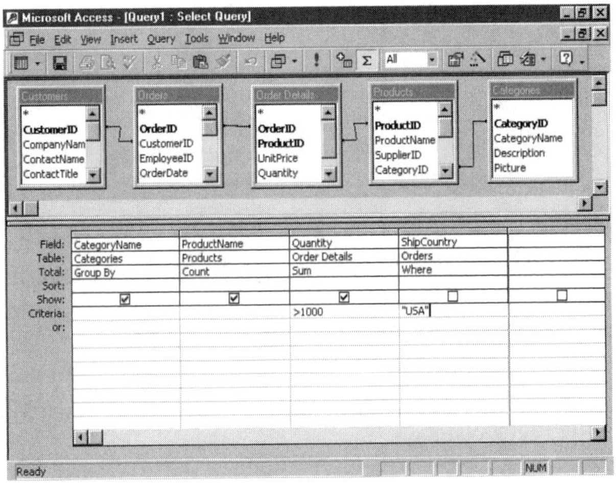

FIGURE 4.13

A query with a `Where` *clause and a* `Having` *clause as seen from the QBE grid.*

LISTING 4.10   THE SQL STATEMENT FOR THE QUERY IN FIGURE 4.13

```
SELECT Categories.CategoryName,
Count(Products.ProductName) AS CountOfProductName,
Sum([Order Details].Quantity) AS SumOfQuantity
FROM (Categories
INNER JOIN Products ON Categories.CategoryID = Products.CategoryID)
INNER JOIN ((Customers
INNER JOIN Orders ON Customers.CustomerID = Orders.CustomerID)
INNER JOIN [Order Details] ON Orders.OrderID = [Order Details].OrderID)
ON Products.ProductID = [Order Details].ProductID
WHERE (((Orders.ShipCountry)="USA"))
GROUP BY Categories.CategoryName
HAVING (((Sum([Order Details].Quantity))>1000));
```

> **TIP**
>
> An easy way to remember the execution order of Where and Having is to check the SQL string created with every query. The Having clause always follows the Group By.

Using Crosstab Queries

The crosstab query and the aggregate query are closely related and the crosstab query provides for some great analytical capabilities. In a typical select query, the fields appear across the top of the result set and the values list below them as individual records. In an aggregate query, the fields also list across the top of the result set, but the data are summarized as you move down through the rows of the result set. A crosstab allows you to take the summaries of the aggregate query and transform them so that the result values from one of your groupings is distributed across the top of the result set. The matrix formed between the left column and the top of the result set fills with calculations of your choice. The result looks very much like a pivot table.

A simple crosstab is made of at least three things: a field each for Row Headings, Column Headings, and Value. A crosstab query can use any result set produced by a select query.

To make a crosstabulation of customers' purchases by different categories, you'll need to have the following tables: Customers, Categories, Products, Orders, and Order Details. Choose the CompanyName from the Customers table, the CategoryName field from the Categories table, and the Quantity field from the Order Details table.

The query is still a select query until you choose Query, Crosstab from the menu. When you convert the query to a crosstab query, a new row appears for you in the query grid as seen in Figure 4.14 and Listing 4.11. This row allows you to designate which fields belong to which aspects of the crosstab. Set the CompanyName as the Row Heading, the CategoryName as the Column Heading (this is what will run across the top of the result set), the Quantity as the Value, and its Group By to Sum. When this query runs, Access automatically creates a sum for each intersection of customer and product.

4

ADVANCED
QUERIES

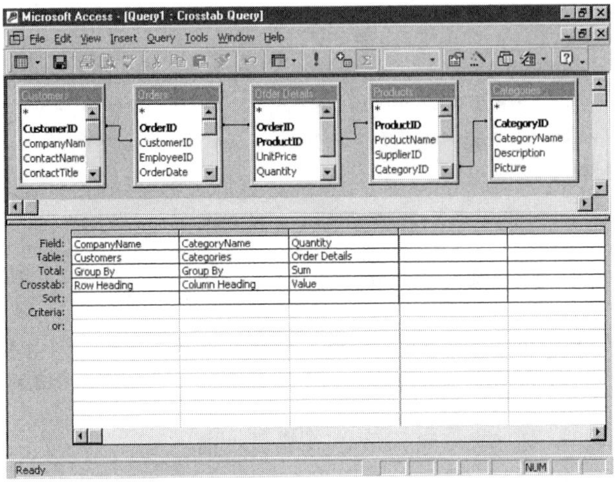

FIGURE 4.14

The crosstab query as seen from the QBE grid.

LISTING 4.11   THE SQL STATEMENT FOR THE QUERY IN FIGURE 4.14

```
TRANSFORM Sum([Order Details].Quantity) AS SumOfQuantity
SELECT Customers.CompanyName
FROM Categories
INNER JOIN (Products INNER JOIN ((Customers INNER JOIN Orders
ON Customers.CustomerID = Orders.CustomerID)
INNER JOIN [Order Details] ON Orders.OrderID = [Order Details].OrderID)
ON Products.ProductID = [Order Details].ProductID)
ON Categories.CategoryID = Products.CategoryID
GROUP BY Customers.CompanyName
PIVOT Categories.CategoryName;
```

It is possible in an Access crosstab to have more than one field set as a Row Heading, but there can only be one Column Heading and one Value. This would give you a hierarchical view of your data with increasing detail as you read it left to right. You can add Country and Region to your crosstab and set them as Row Headings to see how this works.

You can also use your own calculations as the Value of the crosstab. Change the Quantity field to the following expression:

```
Expr1:IIf(Sum([Quantity])>=50,"High","Low")
```

This code uses an aggregate function to change the display of the value in a crosstab query.

Set this field's total property to Expression.

When you run the crosstab, you'll see the result of the IIf() in the matrix. The expressions you create in a crosstab must be compatible with expressions you would write for any other aggregate query.

Just as a crosstab query can present the result of a formula as its value, it can also present the result of an expression as its row or column headings. The query below (as shown in Figures 4.15 and 4.16 and as explained by the SQL in Listing 4.12) uses an expression to break the dates into quarters for the column headings. The pivot clause contains the following expression:

```
"Q" & CStr(DatePart("Q",[OrderDate]))
```

FIGURE 4.15

A modified crosstab query as seen from the QBE grid.

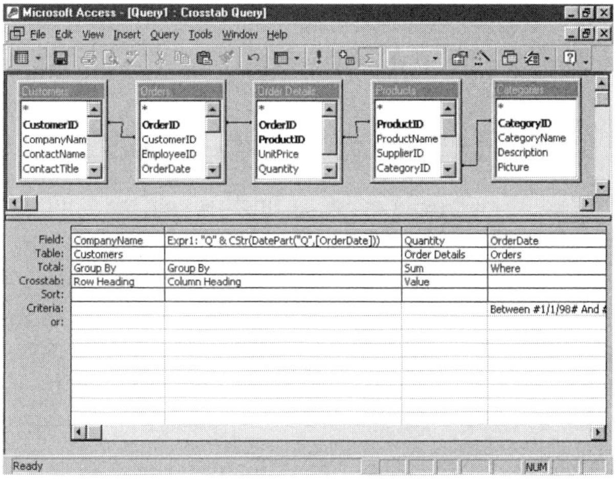

FIGURE 4.16

A modified crosstab query result set.

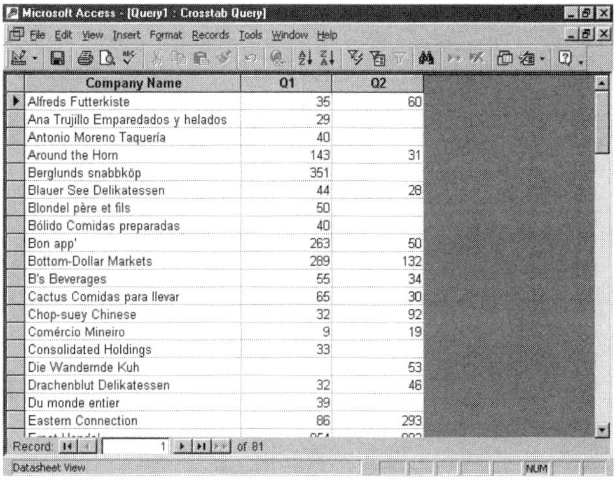

LISTING 4.12   THE SQL STATEMENT FOR THE QUERY IN FIGURES 4.15 AND 4.16

```
TRANSFORM Sum([Order Details].Quantity) AS SumOfQuantity
SELECT Customers.CompanyName
FROM (Categories INNER JOIN Products
ON Categories.CategoryID = Products.CategoryID)
INNER JOIN ((Customers INNER JOIN Orders
ON Customers.CustomerID = Orders.CustomerID)
INNER JOIN [Order Details] ON Orders.OrderID = [Order Details].OrderID)
ON Products.ProductID = [Order Details].ProductID
WHERE (((Orders.OrderDate) Between #1/1/98# And #12/31/98#))
GROUP BY Customers.CompanyName
PIVOT "Q" & CStr(DatePart("Q",[OrderDate]));
```

In order for a crosstab query to show changes in the underlying data, it must be closed and reopened because it is not a restartable query.

Using Parameter Queries

Parameter queries are not a type of query as much as they are a query that takes advantage of its ability to accept guidance from the user. All queries can request information before they run. You've probably created a query and by mistake entered an unrecognized field name or value. When you tried to run the query, it prompted you to identify this piece of information before it would continue. If this has happened to you, you've created a parameterized query. You'll make some parameters queries here, but we'll control what's happening.

A query on the Customers table with just the CompanyName, ContactName, and Phone will make for a fine example as you can see in Figure 4.17 and the SQL as shown in Listing 4.13.

LISTING 4.13   THE SQL STATEMENT FOR THE QUERY IN FIGURE 4.17

```
SELECT Customers.CompanyName, Customers.ContactName, Customers.Phone
FROM Customers;
ORDER BY Customers.ContactName;
```

When you run this query, you will get a list of all the customers, each of the contacts, and all the telephone numbers. However, it is possible to enter a value for the criteria to retrieve the contacts at just a particular customer. Figure 4.18 and Listing 4.14 illustrate this.

FIGURE 4.17

The basis for a simple parameter query.

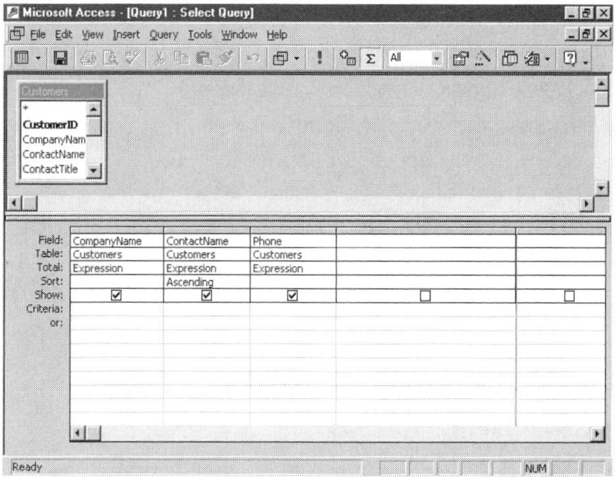

FIGURE 4.18

A query with simple criteria as seen from the QBE grid.

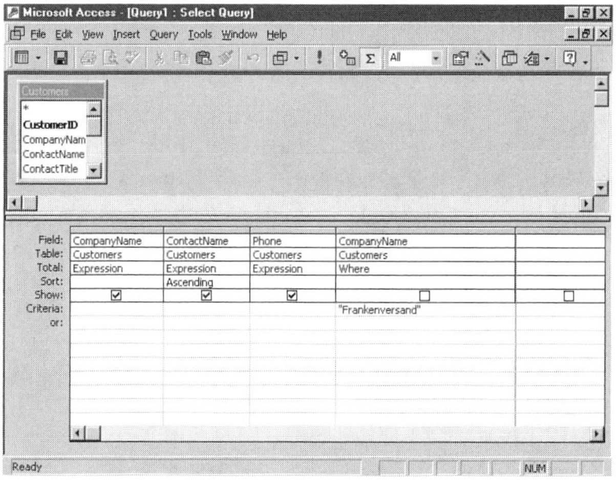

LISTING 4.14   THE SQL STATEMENT FOR THE QUERY IN FIGURE 4.18

```
SELECT Customers.CompanyName, Customers.ContactName, Customers.Phone
FROM Customers
WHERE (((Customers.CompanyName)="Frankenversand"))
ORDER BY Customers.ContactName;
```

4

ADVANCED
QUERIES

That works fine for now, but it's tedious to modify the criteria and run it each time. It's also impractical if you want your application to serve people who might not be familiar with Access's QBE grid. Instead, you can create a parameter for this query and allow it to act as a crude interface for the user. By using a parameter query, criteria are changed and the users do not have to tamper with the query's design.

Creating Parameters for a Query in the QBE Grid

In the QBE grid, a parameter can be created by selecting Query, Parameters from the menu. The dialog box allows you to list the parameters you want to set. Although it is possible to create parameter queries without using the dialog box, the dialog box allows you to control the order of the parameter presentation and the data type for each parameter. After you have listed the parameters in the dialog box, you can repeat those parameters in the query grid in the appropriate places. The parameter in the query grid must exactly match the parameter in the dialog box. If the parameter exists only in the dialog box, the query will prompt the user for information, but it will now know how to apply it to the query.

In a query of Customers, Orders, Order Details, and Products, show the CustomerID, CompanyName, OrderID, OrderDate, ProductName, UnitPrice, Quantity, and Discount fields. Sort the query by the OrderDate in descending order and by the ProductName in ascending order. Select Query, Parameters. Enter the first parameter as `Customer ID` with a data type of text. On the first line of the criteria section for the CustomerID field, enter `[Customer ID]`. This tells the query that it will accept a text parameter called `Customer ID` and apply it as a criterion against the CustomerID field in the query. The parameter query is shown in Figure 4.19 and its SQL statement is shown in Listing 4.15.

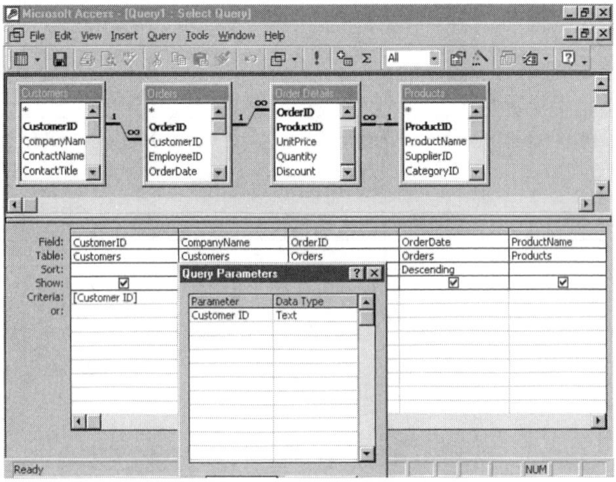

FIGURE 4.19

A parameterized query as seen from the QBE grid.

LISTING 4.15 THE SQL STATEMENT FOR THE PARAMETER QUERY IN FIGURE 4.19

```
PARAMETERS [Customer ID] Text;
SELECT Customers.CompanyName, Orders.OrderID, Orders.OrderDate,
Products.ProductName, [Order Details].UnitPrice,
[Order Details].Quantity, [Order Details].Discount
FROM Products
INNER JOIN ((Customers INNER JOIN Orders
ON Customers.CustomerID = Orders.CustomerID)
INNER JOIN [Order Details] ON Orders.OrderID = [Order Details].OrderID)
ON Products.ProductID = [Order Details].ProductID
WHERE (((Customers.CompanyName)=[Customer ID]))
ORDER BY Orders.OrderDate DESC , Products.ProductName;
```

Execute the query and enter Quick in response to the parameter prompt. The result set will give you all the matching records, those with a CustomerID of Quick.

The parameter can also be a phrase of up to 255 characters in length. This allows you to ask your users for criteria in a way they might better understand, or in a way they might simply find polite. Change the parameter and its representation to Please enter a client code.

Now the parameter query uses this phrase as the prompt to the user.

Creating Parameters for a Query Using Code

Parameter queries can run in your application in another way—through code. The parameters make up a collection in a query object where you can address them through query execution in VBA code. This provides for several advantages. In a user interface, you can collect all the parameters from a form, thereby controlling their data types and validity, and then submit them all at once to a parameter query. This allows the user to review everything he is submitting at once, and allows him to make modifications before getting the recordset. In a normal execution of a parameter query, the user is unable to go backward through the parameters. After a user has provided a value to a prompt, he can only go forward or cancel the query.

Using the QBE Grid Versus Code to Create Query Parameters

Often, developers execute a SQL statement from code. Many times this is perfectly fine, but there are some disadvantages. First, the SQL statement might not be understandable or accessible to other, less-skilled developers who might have to maintain the application in the future. This can lead to a corrupted application. Using the parameter query allows other developers, with the appropriate security permissions, of course, to modify the query using the QBE grid, which could be considered the common denominator for queries among Access users and developers. Most important is the fact that in most cases, the parameterized query is the fastest and most reliable way to execute a query with changing criteria or characteristics. The reason for this is that Access compiles query objects, so Jet has already created an execution plan for it. In short, the SQL string in the code is not optimized, and the parameterized query may be optimized. When the parameterized query is properly executed from code, the user is not prompted for any information.

Executing a Parameterized Query from Code

The following is how a parameterized query could execute from code. Listing 4.16 accepts a query name and a single parameter, and then uses those two arguments to open the named query and count its records. The return value is the number of records in the recordset. You can execute this by running the function from the debug window or from an event on a form.

LISTING 4.16   A FUNCTION TO EXECUTE A PARAMETER QUERY FROM CODE

```
Function RunParamQuery(QryName As String, CustID As String)
'This function will run a parameterized query that
'takes the customer's ID number as an argument
'Arguments:
'    QryName - Name of the parameterized query object
'    CustID - String identifying the customer
'From "Microsoft Access 2000 Development Unleashed" (SAMS)
'By:Forte, Howe, Ralston
Dim db As Database
Dim qrydef As QueryDef
Dim rs As Recordset
Set db = CurrentDb()
Set qrydef = db.QueryDefs(QryName)
'Here's where the parameter is assigned by name.
qrydef("Customer ID") = CustID
Set rs = qrydef.OpenRecordset()
RunParamQuery = rs.RecordCount
rs.Close
End Function
```

Executing a Query Using a Parameter Collection

Listing 4.17 takes advantage of the parameter collection in queries. By using the ParamArray keyword in the function's arguments, you can use it with different parameter

queries regardless of how many parameters they might require. The function loops
through the `ParamArgs()` array and assigns the parameters in the order they were given.
To use this, execute it from the Debug window. The result of the function is a count of
records. If you execute the function more than once, you'll come to appreciate the speed
of parameterized queries.

LISTING 4.17   A FUNCTION FOR RUNNING PARAMETER QUERIES WITH A VARYING NUMBER
OF PARAMETERS

```
Function OpenParamQuery(QryName, _
   ParamArray ParamArgs() As Variant) As Long
'From "Microsoft Access 2000 Development Unleashed" (SAMS)
'By:Forte, Howe, Ralston
'Arguments
'     QryName - Name of the parameterized query to run
'     ParamArgs - A varying list of values to plug into the
'        parameters of the query.  They must be submitted
'        in the same order that the query expects to find
'        them.
Dim db As Database
Dim qry As QueryDef
Dim i As Integer
Dim rs As Recordset
Dim rscount As Long
On Error GoTo OpenParamQuery_Error
Set db = CurrentDb()
Set qry = db.QueryDefs(QryName)
'Move through all the supplied parameters and assign them by index
For i = 0 To UBound(ParamArgs())
qry.Parameters(i) = ParamArgs(i)
Next
Set rs = qry.OpenRecordset(dbOpenSnapshot)
OpenParamQuery = rs.RecordCount
OpenParamQuery_Exit:
Set qry = Nothing
rs.Close
Exit Function
OpenParamQuery_Error:
OpenParamQuery = 0
GoTo OpenParamQuery_Exit
End Function
```

4

**ADVANCED
QUERIES**

> **NOTE**
>
> If you parameterize a nested query, there is still only one parameter collection.

Understanding Pass-Through Queries

Access is capable of linking tables from other data sources and querying them as if they were native data tables. But Access is also capable of sending queries to other databases and letting them process their data themselves and returning only the result set.

The main reasons to take advantage of pass-through queries is performance and network load. When you attach a table from a client/server database, such as SQL Server or Oracle, and query those tables, the server has no idea what you want from it. Even if the server could see the Access SQL statement, it could not interpret the statement because it is a different dialect of SQL than the servers use. The server's only recourse is to send mounds of data down to the desktop and let Jet figure it all out. On large databases, this can be very taxing on the network and it is not a productive use of the server either. Instead, you can meet the server halfway by using a pass-through query.

A pass-through query is one of the SQL-specific queries, which means you have to write it in SQL. In fact, you have to write in the SQL dialect of your server. Many of the things you might take advantage of in Access, such as custom functions in your application, are not available to you in a pass-through. However, the increase in speed and the decrease in network load will more than make up for these losses.

Creating a Pass-Through Query

A pass-through query is created just as any other query, except that you do not add any tables to it. After it is created, select Query, SQL Specific, Pass Through. This changes the Query view to the SQL window. There are only two properties important to running a pass-through Query:the SQL statement itself and the connection string. The SQL statement contains the instructions for the server in the correct SQL syntax understood by the server. The connection string contains the information your query needs to contact the server and represent you to it.

The following is an example of a possible connection string:

```
ODBC;
DRIVER=SQL SERVER;
```

```
SERVER=Access2000UnleashedServer;
UID=sa;
DATABASE=PUBS;
TRUSTED_CONNECTION=YES
```

`ODBC` (Open Database Connectivity) is the prefix for the connection string. It will always precede connection strings to SQL Server, Oracle, Informix, and Sybase databases. Each ODBC data source uses a driver to interpret ODBC instructions. The name usually resembles the name of the server software. The `Server` is the actual address where the database resides. `UID` (User ID) tells the server who you are. The password can also be stored in the connection string, but that is not advisable. Within each server, there can be many databases. The `Database` clause points your query to the correct one. A `Trusted Connection` allows you to get to the server if you have a permission profile that the `Server` trusts.

If you are not sure how the connection string should read, contact the database administrator or copy the connection string out of an attached table. From the Clipboard, paste it into the connection string property of your query and edit it down to the clauses shown earlier.

After the properties have been set, you can enter a SQL statement in the syntax of the server you are querying. The following is a simple SQL statement to SQL Server and its result can be viewed in Figure 4.20:

```
Select * from Authors Where State ='CA'
```

au_id	au_lname	au_fname	phone	address	city
172-32-1176	White	Johnson	408 496-7223	10932 Bigge Rd	Menlo Park
213-46-8915	Green	Marjorie	415 986-7020	309 63rd St. #4	Oakland
238-95-7766	Carson	Cheryl	415 548-7723	589 Darwin Ln.	Berkeley
267-41-2394	O'Leary	Michael	408 286-2428	22 Cleveland Av	San Jose
274-80-9391	Straight	Dean	415 834-2919	5420 College Av	Oakland
409-56-7008	Bennet	Abraham	415 658-9932	6223 Bateman S	Berkeley
427-17-2319	Dull	Ann	415 836-7128	3410 Blonde St.	Palo Alto
472-27-2349	Gringlesby	Burt	707 938-6445	PO Box 792	Covelo
486-29-1786	Locksley	Charlene	415 585-4620	18 Broadway Av	San Francisc
672-71-3249	Yokomoto	Akiko	415 935-4228	3 Silver Ct.	Walnut Creek
724-08-9931	Stringer	Dirk	415 843-2991	5420 Telegraph	Oakland
724-80-9391	MacFeather	Stearns	415 354-7128	44 Upland Hts.	Oakland
756-30-7391	Karsen	Livia	415 534-9219	5720 McAuley S	Oakland
846-92-7186	Hunter	Sheryl	415 836-7128	3410 Blonde St.	Palo Alto
893-72-1158	McBadden	Heather	707 448-4982	301 Putnam	Vacaville

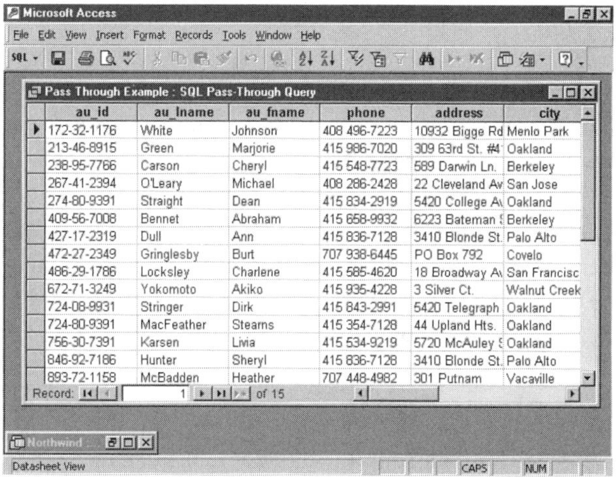

FIGURE 4.20
The result set of a SQL pass-through query.

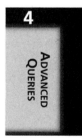

Now only the result set comes over the network because the server did all the work. The next step is to create views and stored procedures on the server. These stored procedures can run from a pass-through by calling them by name and passing in any parameters they might require. The added advantage of this approach is that the server can rely on its own optimization abilities and execution plans to provide still better performance.

Understanding Data Definition Queries

Besides having the ability to manipulate data contained in tables, Access queries also have the ability to build, alter, and delete Access tables in ways that can give your applications the ability to work intelligently with data. These data definition queries can operate against Jet tables, but not against non-Jet tables. If you need to perform data definition functions on non-Jet tables, DAO might work. If you need to perform data definition functions against SQL Server tables or Oracle tables, you can take advantage of similar capabilities in their SQL languages. Execute their data definition SQL statements from a pass-through query in Access.

> **CAUTION**
>
> Data definition queries permanently alter the number, structures, and properties of your tables, indexes, and relationships. Before working with them, back up your work and debug them in a copy of your project.

Data definition queries have a basic scheme that, when understood, makes them easier to use. They start with the verb (`Create Table`, `Alter Table`, or `Drop Table`) followed by the table name. After the table name keyword comes the field definition section, in parentheses. Next is the field name affected, its data type, and then the field size in parentheses. The field definition section can be as long as is needed. After any particular field definition, a constraint clause can set indexes, keys, and foreign keys or can limit the fields to NOT NULL. The constraint clause is optional.

Creating a New Table

A logical starting place for data definition queries is the `Create Table` statement. As its name implies, it will create a table, but the capabilities don't end there. Though you can create a query with a `Make Table` query by way of the QBE grid, you are unable to define field size, field constraints, indexes, and relationships with that query construct. By using the data definition statements in a SQL-specific query, you can create or alter a table as if you had gone into the Design view of the table object and made the alterations.

The syntax for a simple `Create Table` statement is as follows:

```
Create Table tablename (field1 datatype(size),field2 datatype(size),...);
```

> **NOTE**
>
> Tables must be closed when the data definition queries are run against them.

To create a table with two text fields of 15 characters in length, you can use the following statement:

```
CREATE TABLE TestTable (FirstName TEXT(15), LastName TEXT(15));
```

When this query executes and you refresh the database container, you will see the new table. In the Design view you will also see that the fields' length properties are set to 15 characters. Had a traditional `Make Table` query created this table, the fields would have been 255 characters in length. The size is an optional part of the statement. Without it, the fields would have been 255 characters long. It's a good practice to use the size part of the statement whenever possible.

Altering a Table

After you create a table, it is possible to continue to alter the table using the data definition queries. The following `Alter Table` statement will add a field to the table. The basic `Alter Table` statement has the following syntax:

```
ALTER TABLE tablename ADD
fieldname1 datatype(size),
fieldname2 datatype(size);
```

To change your table by adding two new fields, you can issue the following statement:

```
Alter Table TestTable Add
Phone Text (10),
Fax Text (10),
Cellular Text (10);
```

The fields created could be defined further by using the constraints clauses. Constraint clauses will be dealt with as a separate topic. New to Access 2000 is the ability to add more than one field at a time. However, it is still necessary to issue separate `Drop` statements in order to remove the fields from the table definition.

4

ADVANCED
QUERIES

```
Alter Table TestTable drop Phone;
```

And

```
Alter Table TestTable drop Fax;
```

And

```
Alter Table TestTable drop Cellular;
```

Creating an Index

It might be necessary to create an index on a table after you create, import, or link it. The `Create Index` statement allows you to do just that.

The basic syntax is as follows:

```
CREATE [UNIQUE] INDEX indexname
ON tablename (fieldname1 ASC/DESC, fieldname2 ASC/DESC...)
[WITH Primary/Disallow Null/Ignore Null]
```

If the index should contain only unique values, use the `UNIQUE` reserved word. The optional `WITH` clause enables you to enforce validation rules. Your index can prohibit Null values by using `Disallow Null`. The `Ignore Null` option would allow records with Null values in the indexed field, but exclude them from the index. When the `PRIMARY` reserved word is used, it can take the place of the unique reserved word.

The following statement will create an index in your new table:

```
Create Index LastName on TestTable (LastName) with primary;
```

Notice that the syntax is slightly different for `CREATE INDEX`. The field name precedes the table name in this case.

Check the design of the table to confirm that the primary key index was created on the LastName field.

> ### TIP
>
> Indexes are possible on tables linked to an ODBC data source if that source does not already have an index. In this case, your indexes are not on the server; they reside in Access as a dynamic cross-reference of data fields. The server is unaware of these pseudo-indexes and you do not need to have special permissions to create them. To make them, you use the same SQL syntax you would for a native table. Use pseudo-indexes when the ODBC source does not have its own index and the users need to update the data.

Removing a Table

To remove a table from the database or to remove an index from a table, issue a DROP TABLE or DROP INDEX statement.

```
DROP TABLE tablename/[indexname ON tablename]
```

The following statement will remove the table, and all its data, from the database:

```
DROP TABLE TestTable
```

Defining Field Properties

The constraints clause allows you to define other properties of the fields. These properties fall into two categories: keys and relationships. The constraints clause appears in the field section of the data definition statement. There is no punctuation in the clause, so only the order matters.

When defining keys the syntax is as follows:

```
CONSTRAINT constraintname PRIMARY KEY/UNIQUE/NOT NULL
```

When defining relationships for your table of field, the syntax of the constraint clause is a little different:

```
CONSTRAINT relationshipname REFERENCES othertablename(relatedfieldname)
```

The relationships you established by using the CONSTRAINT clause must be between fields of the same or compatible data types.

The data definition statement in Listing 4.18 creates a table with a Long data type EmployeeID field as the primary key. It also creates a relationship between that field and the EmployeeID field in the Employees table. The statement creates a FirstName, LastName, and Phone fields at the same time.

LISTING 4.18   USING CONSTRAINTS WHEN CREATING THE FIELDS

```
CREATE TABLE TestTable
(EmployeeID Long CONSTRAINT myFieldConstraint
PRIMARY KEY Constraint myRelations references Employees(EmployeeID),
FirstName TEXT,
LastName TEXT,
Phone TEXT)
```

After executing the data definition query, open the Relationships window and add the TestTable to it. Access recognizes the relationship between Employees and TestTable automatically.

4

ADVANCED
QUERIES

Optimizing Queries

The following are some things a developer can do to ensure that his queries perform well:

- Index the joined fields on both sides of a relationship. This applies to non-Jet tables, too.

- When there is more than one field joined between two tables, use the fields in the query grid in the same order they appear on their tables.

- Create an index for fields you will use for sorting. Only sort on non-indexed fields when necessary.

- Make sure you are using the appropriate data type and size for all data fields. The field should be smallest size available for your data.

- Do not overload the QBE grid. Use only the fields necessary for the result set.

- Do not put calculated fields in a nested query. Instead, perform calculations at the end of the sequence of queries or on the form or report whenever possible.

- Be conservative in the use of Group By fields. Group By fields are very taxing and can impede performance. If the grouped fields have indexes, try to use them in the same order as they appear in the table.

- Totals queries with joins might perform better if they are broken into two queries. The first query performs the join, and then the grouping query uses the first query's result set.

- Placing criteria on one side of the relationship instead of the other might also affect performance. Usually, a query with criteria on the One side of a relationship is faster, but experimentation might yield a different result.

- Forms and reports will always run faster when based on a table. When possible, create a table from a result set for your forms and reports.

- Crosstab queries run faster when they don't have calculations on the column headings. Though the calculations are sometimes necessary for summation purposes, avoid doing them for strictly cosmetic reasons.

- Use parameter queries through code instead of SQL strings in code. Because parameter queries are compiled objects and have an execution plan, they will usually run faster than their equivalent SQL string.

- Take advantage of Access 2000's client/server capabilities whenever possible.

Summary

Access 2000 delivers the same powerful query abilities as the earlier versions of Access. It also delivers some other wonderful new features, such as a new join properties dialog box, subdatasheets, and easier creation of pass-through queries. Along with a faster version of the Jet engine, queries will continue to be substantial tools for developers. This chapter covered topics that are more advanced than a simple discussion of criteria statements and action queries. By studying the topics and using the queries discussed in this chapter, a developer can harness the power of queries in ways that make his database more useful than ever before.

The Microsoft Jet Database Engine 4.0

CHAPTER 5

Microsoft Access 2000 is a sophisticated front end to the Microsoft Jet Database Engine 4.0. Whether you know it or not, Jet handles your entire database needs in the MDB file. When you are accessing a MDB file via DAO or ADO, you are also using Microsoft Jet. It stores your data tables, indices, and queries, and it runs all your queries via its query engine. Jet is a very powerful, fully functional, relational database that is multithreaded.

The History of Microsoft Jet

Today, Microsoft Jet ships as the database engine in over 30 Microsoft products besides Access, including Project, Money, Team Manager, and even educational kids' games like Computer Tutor. Jet has completely dominated the desktop database market because each release provides innovative new technology. Let's take a walk down memory lane and examine the history of Microsoft Jet.

Jet 1.0

Microsoft Jet had its origins over ten years ago when the Access project started at Microsoft. When Access 1.0 shipped in 1992, Jet 1.0 entered the desktop database market. Jet 1.0 delivered many of the expected desktop database features like data definition, querying, security, and indexing; however, Jet was a desktop database engine pioneer by supplying many brand new features like: updatable queries, heterogeneous data joins, and the capability to write a query based on another query. These features led Microsoft Access to become the most popular desktop database engine around.

Jet 1.1

The success of Microsoft Access took everyone by surprise, even Microsoft. In May 1993, Microsoft released Access 1.1 and Visual Basic 3.0, each of which came with Jet 1.1. This release of Jet gave developers many new features like improved ODBC connectivity and new ODBC drivers. Gone were the days of coding directly to the ODBC API, and accessing ODBC data became something that everyone could do. Jet 1.1 also allowed users to easily attach (link, back then!) to external data, especially the newly acquired Microsoft FoxPro data format. DAO DDLs were improved, and Jet's maximum database size was increased from 128 MB to 1.1 GB.

Jet 2.0

Jet 2.0 shipped with the very popular Version 2.0 of Microsoft Access in April 1994. With Version 2.0, Jet really matured into a modern database engine by including features such as engine-level enforcement of validation rules and referential integrity. Rushmore technology, borrowed from FOX, was added to Jet to increase performance. Jet SQL and DAO were also beefed up. It was also more ANSI-compliant than prior versions of Jet.

Jet 2.5

In October 1994, Microsoft released the Microsoft Access 2.0 service pack and the ODBC Desktop Drivers Pack 2.0. Jet 2.5 was born. Jet 2.5 now used VBA as its expression service, and Jet also greatly improved its support for ODBC data sources. Also Jet 2.5 improved its handling of multiuser applications.

Jet 3.0

When Microsoft released Access 95 in late 1995, Microsoft Jet entered the 32-bit world. Jet was now a 32-bit database engine that supported database replication and more enhanced ODBC and DAO features. Jet 3.0 was an extremely fast database engine.

Jet 3.5

Office 97, released in January 1997, introduced the world to Jet 3.5. Jet 3.5 was the completion of the work done in converting Jet to 32-bit. Performance was the number-one improvement with Jet 3.5. Jet 3.5 also provided new data cashing capabilities, improved page locking, query enhancements, ODBCDirect, and the programmatic purging of write commands to disk, among others. Replication was extended to include partial replicas, and external data support increased with support for HTML and Exchange data.

Jet 3.51

A very much overlooked service pack release of Jet 3.5, Jet 3.51 was released in mid-1997 on the Web. Jet 3.51 included a new way to compact and repair a MDB file with an "Enhanced Compact." The repair option was rolled up into a greatly improved compact process. Jet 3.5 also fixed some low-level multiuser bugs, but most importantly, it shipped with the JetCOMP.exe utility for compact/repair using the new enhanced compact feature.

Jet 4.0

In June 1999, Microsoft released Jet 4.0 with Office 2000. Jet 4.0 is the release that developers have waiting for. Jet 4.0 has more developer-related features included than all prior versions of the product combined! Most of these features came directly from developer requests compiled over the years. With version 4.0, Microsoft has really pulled out the big guns, including some incredible features like:

- A New Native OLE DB Provider
- Row-Level Locking
- Full Unicode Support

- Enhanced Data Types
- Enhanced AutoNumber Capabilities
- Searchable Memo Fields
- Multiuser Improvements
- Replication Enhancements
- New SQL Grammar (with more ANSI 92 compliance)

After you look at all these new features and build applications around them, you will find it hard to imagine what life was like before you had them!

Future Versions of Microsoft Jet

In early 1998, there were some rumors that Microsoft Jet was entering its final phases and would soon go the way of the dodo bird. Microsoft did supply a "desktop" version of SQL Server 7.0 with Office 2000 and an Access project type that does not include Jet (ADPs—see Chapter 15, "Introducing Access Data Projects and the Visual Tools") as an alternative to Jet. With ADO 2.0 and Universal Data Access, Microsoft has introduced OLE DB as the data access method of choice to client/server data. (For more on OLE DB and ADO see Chapters 6, "Introduction to ActiveX Data Objects," and 7, "Advanced ADO.") ADO 2.0/OLE DB talks to the data source directly via OLE DB. Because Microsoft wanted to take advantage of OLE DB for client/server data in Access 2000 with ADPs, people surmised that Jet was dead.

Microsoft has responded to those allegations at Tech*Ed and other conferences. Jet is still strongly supported by Microsoft and will continue to be.

Using the New Jet 4.0 Features in Your Applications

The remainder of this chapter will cover the advanced features of the Microsoft Jet database Engine 4.0. All the code examples that are provided here will work fine in Access 2000, and with some slight modification, will work in Visual Basic 5 or 6.

Native OLE DB Provider

In case you have not been told yet, Microsoft's data access strategy now revolves around ActiveX Data Objects (ADO). (For more on ADO see Chapters 6, "Introduction to ActiveX Data Objects," and 7, "Advanced ADO.") ADO works on the concept of universal data access that uses native providers to communicate with data sources. ADO 1.0

shipped with a generic provider for ODBC, so if you used Jet with ADO, you had to go though the ODBC layer (like walking through mud). Jet 4.0 ships with a native OLE DB provider code-named JOLT 4.0. This enables you to use ADO as your data access methodology with Jet. All Jet's functionality is exposed through JOLT, including some features that will only be available with JOLT. You will see more on JOLT throughout this book.

Row Level Locking

Yes, you did read this correctly! Jet 4.0 supports row level locking! Now, you can increase concurrency in your application by locking a row at a time instead of a data page at a time (which is now 4K-. See the next section on UNICODE). Row level locking can dramatically increase the performance of your high-volume, highly transactional database applications. In some tests, row level locking allowed six times the throughput as page locking! There will be no programmatic support for row level locking in DAO, only in ADO and Access. The net benefit of row level locking is that page-locking conflicts will become a thing of the past! For more on row level locking, see Chapter 21, "Multiuser Issues/File Server/Locking."

Full Unicode Support

Jet 4.0 stores all character data (all Text & Memo fields in Access) in Unicode. This enables you to switch the language/character set of your application with the greatest of ease. Now when you convert to other languages/alphabets, you will have 100% data fidelity after conversion.

What Is Unicode?

Today, many different overlapping standards exist around the world for text character encoding. With so many different character sets for code pages, the process of building a single international code base is extremely difficult. About ten years ago, Apple and Xerox got together and started to form a new character set standard. In 1991, Apple, Xerox, and others founded the Unicode Consortium. Its membership now includes such companies as Microsoft, Apple, AT&T, Compaq, Digital, Ecological Linguistics, Hewlett-Packard, IBM, Lotus, NeXT, Novell, Reuters, and many others.

In the early 1990s, the International Standards Organizations (ISO) started working on a similar standard in conjunction with the Unicode Consortium. Unicode 1.1 and ISO 10646, both published in 1993, are identical code-for-code.

Unicode uses a fixed-width 16-bit character-encoding scheme to represent all text characters from all languages except Chinese. Unicode solves the problem of the large number of language code pages and allows mixing and sharing data between multiple languages without corruption.

> **NOTE**
>
> For more on Unicode, see *The Unicode Standard, Second Edition*, ISBN 0-201-48348-9, from Addison-Wesley. This almost 1,000-page book includes the complete Unicode 2.0 specification.

Unicode Support in Jet 4.0

To accommodate Unicode in Jet 4.0, the data-page size was increased to 4KB. Having a 4KB data-page size allowed the database size limitation of an MDB file to increase from 1.07GB to 2.14GB. Because Unicode stores data in larger data pages, some databases with a lot of textual data may increase in size, however, Jet 4.0 provides Unicode Compression. The Unicode Compression option is also available from the Access Table Designer as shown in Figure 5.1.

> **NOTE**
>
> By default index compression will be on, and if you are converting an application from a previous file format, all character data types will have Unicode Compression turned on. However, if the database is already in a Jet 4.0 file format, the property must be passed to enable Unicode Compression. Unicode Compression is not available on Memo data types that are larger than 4KB and have other rows on the page.

To define a column that will use compression using SQL, use the new WITH COMPRESSION flag when creating a table with DDL:

```
CREATE TABLE MyTable (MyCompressedField CHARACTER(255) WITH COMPRESSION)
```

This SQL code is only available via VBA Code and ADO. You can execute the above SQL Statement against the current ADO connection of the VBA project as shown in Listing 5.1.

FIGURE 5.1

The Access Table Designer with Unicode Compression.

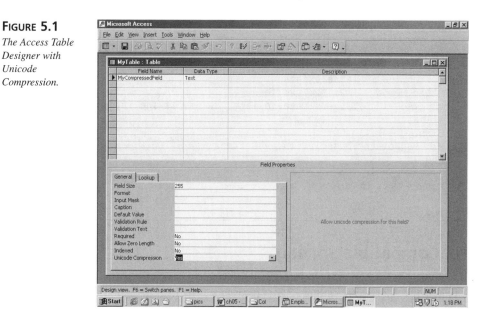

LISTING 5.1   CREATING A UNICODE COMPRESSED FIELD IN VBA

```
Private Sub cmdUnicode_Click()
'This code will create a table called MyTable
'and a Unicode Compressed Field called MyCompressedField
'This code can only run via ADO in VBA
'This is not supported in DAO
'From "Microsoft Access 2000 Development Unleashed" (SAMS)
'By: Forte, Howe, Ralston

Dim strSQL As String

On Error GoTo Proc_Err

strSQL = "CREATE TABLE MyTable " & _
    "(MyCompressedField CHARACTER(255) WITH COMPRESSION)"

'Execute the SQL Statement against the
'current database connection
'Similar to Currentdb.execute
CurrentProject.Connection.Execute strSQL

'Success
MsgBox "Table Created OK", vbInformation

Proc_Exit:
    Exit Sub
```

continues

LISTING 5.1   CONTINUED

```
Proc_Err:
    'Determine if table exists
    If Err.Number = -2147217900 Then
        MsgBox "MyTable already exists, delete it and try again", _
vbCritical
    Else
        MsgBox Err.Description, vbCritical
    End If

    Resume Proc_Exit

End Sub
```

NT Compatible Sorting

Implementing Unicode with Jet 4.0 enabled Jet to use a sorting mechanism that is based on the native Microsoft Windows NT sorting functionality. This new sorting mechanism is also used by Jet when running on Windows 95/98. On Windows 95/98, it is possible to properly sort all the languages available on Windows NT, instead of just the system default language that Windows 95 supports in its ANSI sorting. This enables you to develop international applications faster and more easily because there is now consistency in sorting across operating systems.

> **NOTE**
>
> Because Microsoft SQL Server 7.0 and Visual Basic 6 use the same sorting functionality, there now exists a great cross-product consistency.

Jet Data Types

Table 5.1 is an overview of the Microsoft Jet data types. Jet 4.0 data types have been enhanced to interpolate better with SQL Server. Jet data types were made closer to SQL Server date types to make it easier to upsize Jet databases to SQL Server databases and simpler to replicate Jet to SQL Server. Jet data type names are not always the same as in Access. Access will translate the name for you.

TABLE 5.1 OVERVIEW OF JET 4.0 DATA TYPES

Jet Data Type	Access Name	Notes
Character	Text	Maximum length remains 255 characters. Unicode support now makes this maximum length viable for all languages.
		Supported synonyms are Char, Varchar, Character Varying, Nchar, National Character, National Char, Nvarchar, National Character Varying, and National Char Varying.
		The use of the Text keyword without an accompanying length specification has been changed. It is now a synonym for Memo. This better aligns the use of the Microsoft Jet Text keyword with its use in Microsoft SQL Server.
		You can continue to use the Text keyword with a length specification, for example, TEXT (100) to define a fixed length character data column.
		Examples to further illustrate the use of the Text data type keyword:
		CREATE TABLE t1 (c1 TEXT) is equivalent to CREATE TABLE t1 (c1 MEMO) and aligns with the SQL Server definition and syntax for TEXT.
		CREATE TABLE t1 (c1 TEXT (100)) is equivalent to CREATE TABLE t1 (c1 CHAR (100)) and will provide backward compatibility for most existing Microsoft Jet applications.
LongText	Memo	Maximum length (in bytes) is now approximately 2.14GB. This would be approximately 1.07 billion characters.
		Supported synonyms are Text, NText, Memo, LongChar, and Note.
Binary	OLE Object	Maximum length remains 255 characters.
		Supported synonyms are Varbinary, Binary Varying, and Bit Varying.
LongBinary	OLE Object	Maximum length is now approximately 2.14GB.

continues

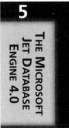

TABLE 5.1 CONTINUED

Jet Data Type	Access Name	Notes
DateTime	DateTime	The synonym `Timestamp` is no longer supported, as the corresponding SQL Server `Timestamp` does not correlate directly to the `DateTime` data type.
Single	Single	Supported synonyms are `Real`, `Float4`, and `IEEESingle`.
Double	Double	Supported synonyms are `Float`, `Double Precision`, `Float8`, and `IEEEDouble`.
		The synonym `Numeric` is no longer supported for the `Double` data type. The keyword `Numeric` is now used to define a column as an exact numeric data type corresponding to the SQL Server `Decimal` or `Numeric` data types.
Byte	Byte	The synonym is `Tinyint`.
Integer	Integer	Supported synonyms are `Smallint`, `Integer2`, and `Short`.
LongInteger	LongInteger	Supported synonyms are `Int`, `Integer`, and `Counter`.
		The synonym `AutoIncrement` is no longer. See the section on Auto-Increment Columns for more information.
Currency	Currency	The synonym is `Money`.
		Data accessed via ODBC that is typed as `SQL_DECIMAL` or `SQL_NUMERIC` (for example, SQL Server Decimal or Numeric columns) is no longer mapped to Microsoft Jet Currency.
Boolean	Boolean	Supported synonyms are `Bit`, `Logical`, `Logical1`, and `YesNo`.
GUID	ReplicationID	The synonym is `UniqueIdentifier`.
Decimal	--	The `Decimal` data type is new for Microsoft Jet 4.0.
		It is an exact numeric data type that holds values from 1028–1 through –1028–1. You can define both precision (1–28) and scale (0–defined precision). The default precision and scale are 18 and 0, respectively.

Jet Data Type	Access Name	Notes
		Supported synonyms are Dec and Numeric.
		Data accessed via ODBC that is typed as SQL_DECIMAL or SQL_NUMERIC will now be mapped to Microsoft Jet Decimal, instead of Currency.
		Note that this data type is not supported via DAO. It is supported only in ADO.

Enhanced AutoNumber Capabilities

Jet 4.0 gives you full control over your AutoNumber fields. You now have the capability to set a starting point and interval of the counter. You can set the AutoNumber field to start at 1000 and increment by 100. This functionality is only exposed via SQL DDL through ADO/JOLT. The net benefit of the new AutoNumber is that primary key sequencing can be more easily controlled. To create a table called MyCoolCounter table with an AutoNumber to start at 1000 and increment by 100 on the CoolCounter field, use this SQL syntax:

```
CREATE TABLE MyCoolCounter (CoolCounter IDENTITY (1000, 100), myTextField
CHAR)
```

In addition to being able to set the starting and increment values when you create the table, you can modify them at any time using the ALTER TABLE SQL statement. To change MyCoolCounter to use a new starting point of 5000 and increment by 10, use this syntax:

```
ALTER TABLE MyCoolCounter ALTER COLUMN CoolCounter IDENTITY (5000,10)
```

You can always find the last inserted value by using the SELECT @@IDENTITY SQL statement. The behavior of compact will be modified for users that take advantage of increments that are in values other than one. If the increment is a value other than one, Jet's compact will not reset the next value to the maximum value in the table.

By default, as in the previous versions of Jet, users will not be able to edit the Counter data types. However, administrators will be able to grant security to users that will allow them to update the Counter data type.

5

THE MICROSOFT
JET DATABASE
ENGINE 4.0

Searchable Memo Fields

In previous versions of Access/Jet, MEMO columns could not be indexed. With Jet 4.0 indexes on MEMO columns are now supported for the first 255 characters of data in a MEMO column. When wildcard (*) searches are performed, only the index is used. Although this performs well, it limits the search to just the first 255 characters of data. Be careful when searching on memo fields because you may not get accurate results if your search criteria are located after the first 255 characters.

Connection Control/Passive Shutdown

Other multiuser features include a new User List which will enumerate all the users in your database via ADO, just as the LDBView tool did. Lastly, Connection Control will empower you to deny access to a database. Although you cannot "kick out" another current user, you can prevent a new user from entering the database. This feature and the User List functionality enable you to passively shut down the database and then, when all other users are out, reopen the database exclusively. The code in Listing 5.2 demonstrates how to use the User List functionality with the passive shutdown.

LISTING 5.2   USING THE USER ROSTER IN ADO

```
Sub UserRoster()
Dim conn As ADODB.Connection
Dim rst As ADODB.Recordset

Set conn = New ADODB.Connection


With conn
    .Provider = "Microsoft.Jet.OLEDB.4.0"
    .ConnectionString = "data source=" & Application.CurrentProject.Path.
& "\employee_2k.mdb"
    .Open
    'Set up a connection where no new user
    'can log on, curent users will remain in
    .Properties("Jet OLEDB:Connection Control") = 1
End With
Set rst = conn.OpenSchema(adSchemaProviderSpecific, , _
"{947bb102-5d43-11d1-bdbf-00c04fb92675}")

Do Until rst.EOF
    Debug.Print rst!COMPUTER_NAME
    Debug.Print rst!LOGIN_NAME
    Debug.Print rst!CONNECTED
    Debug.Print rst!SUSPECTED_STATE
```

```
     rst.MoveNext
Loop

End Sub
```

We open an ADO connection to our database and then set the Jet `OLEDB:Connection Control` property to 1. As long as the connection object has scope, anyone new will be prevented from entering the database either pragmatically or via Microsoft Access 2000. Listing 5.2 also opens a user roster as an ADO recordset. To open a user roster, we use the OpenSchema method of the connection object and pass in the rather long GUID for ADO to know to give us the User Roster. The method will return a recordset filed with the computer name, login name (via Jet Security or Admin for no security), Connected field to indicate whether the user is actually still connected, and Suspected_State to determine whether the database is suspect of being corrupted.

New SQL Grammar

Many SQL extensions were added to Jet 4.0 to support new functionality and to conform more closely to ANSI 92 SQL. An added benefit is that most of the SQL extensions make it easier to write SQL statements that interoperate between Jet and SQL Server. Some of the new SQL enhancements include extensions for:

- Security
- Definition of Views and Procedures
- Parameter Calling
- Transactions
- Create/Alter Table DDL

Security

Through new SQL syntax, Jet 4.0 supports the definition of database security. The net effect is easier programmatic security maintenance. You can now use SQL to meet your security needs instead of using DAO or ADO. The listings below show the SQL extensions for Jet 4.0 security with users and groups:

```
CREATE/ADD/ALTER/DROP USER/GROUP

GRANT/REVOKE
```

Security can be applied to the following objects: CONTAINER, INDEX, QUERY, and TABLE. The code in Listing 5.3 shows you how to create a group called SuperGroup with full permissions on the tblCustomers table. Next, the code will revoke SuperGroup's permission to delete from tblCustomers. The code then adds a user, Steve, with a password of Batman, and finally adds Steve to the SuperGroup group.

Database Design Unleashed

LISTING 5.3   USING SECURITY WITH JET 4.0

```
Private Sub cmdSecurity_Click()
'This procedure will open an MDB file with
'a security file specified and add users and groups
'This code can only run via ADO in VBA
'This is not supported in DAO
'From "Microsoft Access 2000 Development Unleashed" (SAMS)
'By: Forte, Howe, Ralston

Dim conn As ADODB.Connection

On Error GoTo Proc_Err

Set conn = New ADODB.Connection


'Set up a connection to the database
'using ADO and specifying the System database in the
'connection string
With conn
    .Provider = "Microsoft.Jet.OLEDB.4.0"
    .ConnectionString = "data source=c:\employees.mdb" & _
        ";Jet OLEDB:System database=" & _
        "c:\program files\microsoft office\office\system.mdw"
    .Open
End With

'Execute the SQL Statements
conn.Execute "CREATE GROUP SuperGroup"
conn.Execute "GRANT SELECT, DELETE, INSERT, " & _
        "UPDATE ON tblCustomers TO SuperGroup"
conn.Execute "REVOKE DELETE ON tblCustomers From SuperGroup"
conn.Execute "CREATE USER Steve Batman"
conn.Execute "ADD USER Steve to SuperGroup"

Proc_Exit:
    Exit Sub

Proc_Err:
    MsgBox Err.Description, vbCritical
    Resume Proc_Exit

End Sub
```

Jet 4.0 SQL security enhancements have also been modified to create or change a database password like this:

```
ALTER DATABASE PASSWORD NewPass OldPass
```

Definition of Views and Procedures

Jet 4.0 allows you to define a stored query as either a VIEW or PROCEDURE. A VIEW is defined as all non-parameterized, row-returning queries. PROCEDURES are all non-DDL non-UNION actions and parameterized queries. You can create VIEWS and PROCEDURES via ADO, or the new Jet 4.0 SQL syntax: CREATE VIEW and CREATE PROCEDURE. The new syntax is more compatible with ANSI 92 and makes Jet 4.0 VIEWS and PROCEDURES more portable to other ANSI 92 SQL databases like SQL Server. The following SQL code creates a VIEW and a PROCEDURE.

```
CREATE VIEW qryAllCustomers AS SELECT * FROM tblCustomers
     CREATE PROCEDURE qryAllCustomers_DEL AS DELETE *FROM tblCustomer
```

Parameter Calling

Jet 4.0 from ADO now supports the capability to supply parameters in a call list, which is similar to executing a parameterized SQL Server stored procedure. The saved query, qryParameterQuery has two parameters: EmployeeID and DepID as shown from its SQL:

```
PARAMETERS [EmployeeID] Long, [DepID] Long;
SELECT Employees.EmployeeID, Employees.[First Name],
     Employees.[Last Name], Employees.Phone, Employees.[Dept ID]
FROM Employees
WHERE (((Employees.EmployeeID)=[EmployeeID])
AND ((Employees.[Dept ID])=[DepID]));"
```

Supplying the parameters and executing the parameterized query is now very easy with the EXEC syntax:

```
EXEC qryParameterQuery 1, 4179
```

This SQL code supplies the EmployeeId=1 and the DepID=4179. You must supply the parameters in the same order that is in your SQL Code. The code in Listing 5.4 shows how to open an ADO recordset based on the query qryParameterQuery.

LISTING 5.4   OPENING A PARAMETER QUERY IN ADO

```
Private Sub cmdPramQuery_Click()
'This procedure will open a parameter
'query using the new EXEC syntax
'This code can only run via ADO in VBA
'This is not supported in DAO
'From "Microsoft Access 2000 Development Unleashed" (SAMS)
'By: Forte, Howe, Ralston

Dim rst As ADODB.Recordset
```

continues

5

THE MICROSOFT
JET DATABASE
ENGINE 4.0

LISTING 5.4 CONTINUED

```
On Error GoTo Proc_Err

Set rst = New ADODB.Recordset

'Open the recordset based on the
'executed parameter query
rst.Open "Exec qryParameterQuery 1, 4179", CurrentProject.Connection

'Display the results
MsgBox rst![First Name]

Proc_Exit:
    Exit Sub

Proc_Err:
    MsgBox Err.Description, vbCritical
    Resume Proc_Exit


End Sub
```

Transactions

Jet 4.0 SQL now supports transactions. In Jet SQL you must explicitly start a transaction with this SQL:

```
BEGIN TRANSACTION
```

To commit a transaction or roll it back use the following respectively:

```
ROLLBACK
```

```
ROLLBACK TRANSACTION
```

The code in Listing 5.5 shows how to edit a record and delete records all in one transaction. Note that you have to start a transaction on a separate line from the one on which you execute the SQL statements.

LISTING 5.5 USING TRANSACTIONS IN JET 4.0 SQL

```
Sub Jet40Transaction()

Dim conn As ADODB.Connection
Set conn = New ADODB.Connection

With conn
```

```
    .Provider = "Microsoft.Jet.OLEDB.4.0"
    .ConnectionString = "data source=" & Application.CurrentProject.Path.
& "\employee_2k.mdb"
    .Open
End With

conn.Execute "BEGIN TRANSACTION"
conn.Execute "UPDATE Employees SET Employees.Phone = " & _
      Chr(39) & "2129560615" & Chr(39) & _
"WHERE (((Employees.EmployeeID)=1))"
conn.Execute "DELETE" & vbNewLine & _
    "From Tasks" & vbNewLine & _
    "WHERE (((Tasks.[Emp ID])=1));"
conn.Execute "COMMIT TRANSACTION"


End Sub
```

Create Table DDL

In Microsoft Jet 4.0, CREATE TABLE is much more powerful. The most interesting feature
of Jet 4.0 SQL Extensions is the new CHECK CONSTRAINTS option. This feature enables
business rules to span more than one table! You can use SQL to look up information in
several tables and then use that information to enforce certain conditions on your newly
inserted record. Let's say that you have a Customers Table and a Credit Limit table. You
can have Jet enforce a business rule so that the newly inserted record can only be accepted if it has a value less then the credit limit. You would define the constraint via SQL
when you create the table:

```
CHECK (<SQL Condition>)
```

The following code creates a table with a constraint on the CREDITLIMIT field:

```
CREATE TABLE Customers (CustId IDENTITY (100, 10),
CFrstNm VARCHAR(10), CLstNm VARCHAR(15), CustomerLimit DOUBLE,
 CHECK (CustomerLimit <= (SELECT SUM (CreditLimit) FROM CreditLimit)));
```

The code in Listing 5.6 shows you how to create the Credit Limit table, how to insert a
value, how to create the Customer table with the Constraint on the CustomerLimit table,
and then how to try to insert rows. The first record will be accepted into the table, but the
second will not be allowed because the customer is over the credit limit.

5

THE MICROSOFT
JET DATABASE
ENGINE 4.0

LISTING 5.6   USING THE CONSTRAINTS

```
Private Sub cmdCreateConstraint_Click()
'This procedure will create 2 tables with
'one table having a constraint based on another table
'This code can only run via ADO in VBA
'This is not supported in DAO
'From "Microsoft Access 2000 Development Unleashed" (SAMS)
'By: Forte, Howe, Ralston

Dim conn As ADODB.Connection

On Error GoTo Proc_Err

Set conn = CurrentProject.Connection

'Create the table that we will lookup the credit limit
conn.Execute "CREATE TABLE CreditLimit (CreditLimit DOUBLE);"
'Insert the Credit Limit
conn.Execute "INSERT INTO CreditLimit VALUES (100);"
'Create the Customer Table With the Constraint
conn.Execute "CREATE TABLE Customers (CustId IDENTITY (100, " & _
    "10), CFrstNm VARCHAR(10), CLstNm VARCHAR(15), " & _
    "CustomerLimit DOUBLE, CHECK (CustomerLimit <= " & _
    "(SELECT SUM (CreditLimit) FROM CreditLimit)));"

'Do a successful insert
conn.Execute "INSERT INTO Customers (CLstNm, CFrstNm, CustomerLimit)" & _
    "VALUES ('Collins', 'Kevin', 100);"

'Will bomb on this line since the credit limit violates the rule
conn.Execute "INSERT INTO Customers (CLstNm, CFrstNm, CustomerLimit)" & _
    "VALUES ('Forte', 'Stephen', 101);"

Proc_Exit:
    Exit Sub

Proc_Err:
    MsgBox Err.Description, vbCritical
    Resume Proc_Exit

End Sub
```

When you create a constraint on a field, Jet will not allow you to enter in a value in that field that violates the rule. Figure 5.2 shows you the error message produced by the last line of the code in Listing 5.6.

FIGURE 5.2

Error message when you violate a custom constraint.

Summary

As you can see, Jet 4.0 is chock full of new features. Although you might not be able to take advantage of them all directly from Microsoft Access 2000, you can write a little bit of code and then create some very powerful additions to your Access applications.

Data Access

IN THIS PART

Introduction to ActiveX Data Objects

CHAPTER 6

IN THIS CHAPTER

With the release of Office 2000, ActiveX Data Objects (ADO) has finally entered the mainstream. In Office 2000, ADO replaces DAO and ODBCDirect as the data access method of choice for both Jet and client/server data. Now there is only one data access method and object model to learn and use. It has been a long and bumpy ride to reach this data access nirvana.

History of Data Access

You will now take a look at the road to ADO. By looking at the history of data access you can see the benefit that you get from ADO.

Proprietary APIs

Back before Microsoft was in the data access game, the only way to access data programmatically was through proprietary APIs. This forced you to learn a different API for each database system that you wanted to write to. Needless to say, this was not very convenient, nor was it any fun.

Open Database Connectivity (ODBC)

A few years ago, Microsoft offered the Open Database Connectivity (ODBC) specification. ODBC was a generic programmatic API that enabled you to write to any database that had an ODBC driver. Writing to the databases required you to learn the ODBC API; however, now you now only had to learn one API for all the databases that you wanted to use. The ODBC API was not easy to use; however, it was a great first step in the data access problem of too many APIs. As you know, ODBC quickly became the data access standard.

Microsoft Jet/Data Access Objects (DAO)

When Microsoft Access 1.0 shipped with Microsoft Jet and Data Access Objects (DAO), data access became much easier. DAO provided a native data access object model for Jet. In addition, Jet was able to easily communicate with via ODBC to many ODBC-compatible data sources, and Jet could also communicate with other desktop databases. The Microsoft Jet Engine was used by millions to access different databases under one data access object model.

Remote Data Objects (RDO) and ODBCDirect

With the release of Visual Basic 4.0 Enterprise Edition, Microsoft released the new object model of ODBC data sources, Remote Data Objects (RDO). A thin wrapper around the ODBC API, RDO offered an object model to access ODBC data bypassing the Jet Engine. This eliminated the Jet communication layer and increased speed. While RDO did offer superior data access, programmers (including the authors of this book!) were not happy to have to learn and master two data access object models. Most programmers were already very comfortable with DAO and never learned RDO. Microsoft responded with ODBCDirect, an extension to the DAO object model that used RDO to access external data without using the Jet Engine. Now there were four ways to access data: the ODBC API, DAO, RDO, or ODBCDirect. Clearly the proliferation of objects models from Redmond now reached a critical mass, and something had to be done. Enter Microsoft's Universal Data Access initiative.

Microsoft's Universal Data Access Initiative

With so many data access methodologies out there, Microsoft decided to create a new standard in its Universal Data Access initiative. OLE DB is the first implementation of that new initiative. An open specification designed to build on the success of ODBC, OLE DB is an open standard for accessing all kinds of data. ODBC was created to access relational databases, while OLE DB was designed for the relational and non-relational information sources, such as mail stores, text and graphical data for the Web, directory services, and IMS and VSAM data stored in the mainframe. Where ODBC communicated via ODBC drivers, OLE DB communicates to data stores via data providers. OLE DB enables you to learn one object model for all your databases and even use that object model for non-relational data stores. OLE DB is a great improvement over ODBC because it can talk to many different data stores. TO provide backward compatibility, OLE DB shipped with a provider for ODBC. Today, in addition to the OLE DB Provider for ODBC, there exist providers for Jet, SQL Server, Oracle, NT 5 Active Directory, and many more.

Figure 6.1 shows Microsoft Universal Data Access technology as it exists today. OLE DB's main object model for data access is called ActiveX Data Objects (ADO). As you can see, either directly or via ADO, OLE DB can access database, non-relational, and mainframe data through one interface.

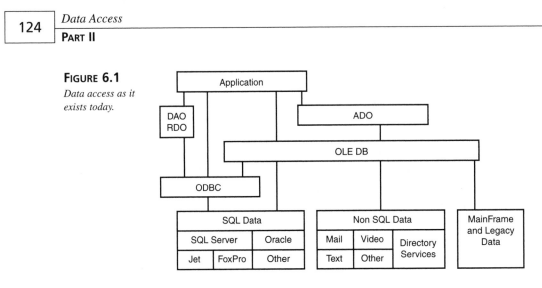

FIGURE 6.1

Data access as it exists today.

ActiveX Data Objects (ADO)

ActiveX Data Objects (ADO) is the object model that you can use to get at OLE DB data. ADO has been around for a while and with version 2.0, ADO matured into the pre-ferred data access methodology from Microsoft. Let's take a quick look at ADO's history.

ADO 1.0

When ADO was first released in late 1996, it was primarily used to access data via script in Active Server Page-based Web applications. ADO only exposed the very basic client/server data access functionality. At that time, ADO was a subset of the popular object models DAO and RDO. Developers used the only OLE DB provider available, a generic OLE DB provider for ODBC data sources.

ADO 1.5

In the Fall of 1997, Microsoft released ADO 1.5 with the Microsoft Data Access Components 1.0 (MDAC) and IIS 4.0. ADO 1.5 introduced, among other things, Remote Data Services (RDS) and support for disconnected recordsets. The first OLE DB provider to surface was a beta copy of the OLE DB provider for Jet (the Access engine) called JOLT.

ADO 2.0

With the release of MDAC 2.0 in the summer of 1998, ADO entered its third major release with ADO 2.0. ADO 2.0 is almost a superset of RDO 2.0 and DAO 3.5, with some additional cool features. ADO 2.0 also shipped with a few OLE DB providers ready for prime time, including providers for: Jet, SQL Server, and Oracle. Some of the new features in ADO 2.0 we have seen before in RDO and DAO, including asynchronous operations and re synching via client cursors. ADO also included some new innovative techniques like

- Microsoft Data Links
- Recordset Persistence
- Creatable Recordsets
- OLAP Recordsets

We will look at these technologies in the Chapter 7, "Advanced ADO."

ADO 2.1

ADO 2.1 shipped with SQL Server 7.0, Office 2000 and Internet Explorer 5.0. ADO 2.1 consists of all the ADO 2.0 features, including two new object models to help us out with DDL and replication. Included with ADO 2.1 are

- ADO —For DDL operations and Security (ADOx)
- JRO (Jet Replication Objects)— For replication features and compact/repair of Jet databases

---

CAUTION

Do not use the version of ADO that shipped with SQL Server 7.0 to perform any operations involving Access or the Jet engine; it has known bugs in it, and not all the features discussed here and in other chapters will work correctly, if at all. Make sure that you use the version of ADO supplied with Office 2000 or NT 2000.

ADOx works best with JOLT, however, it is being extended to SQL Server and other providers. JRO is Jet-specific extensions to ADO, mostly used to support Jet replication. We will be looking at ADOx in the next chapter and JRO in Chapter 22, "Replication and JRO."

TIP

Like everything in our industry, ADO and OLE DB are a work in progress. With things changing so fast, it is hard to keep up. As Microsoft releases versions of ADO out of sync with releases of Office and this book, check out the OLE DB/ADO Web site for more information and late-breaking details. The Web site is filled with code samples and technical white papers. It is shown in Figure 6.2 and located at `http://www.microsoft.com/data`.

FIGURE 6.2

The ADO/OLE DB Web site.

The ADO Object Model

The ADO object model is very simple and flat. While DAO and RDO were very hierarchical, ADO is not. This flat object model is shown in Figure 6.3.

The ADO object model consists of seven objects listed here:

- `Connection`
- `Recordset`
- `Command`
- `Parameter`
- `Field`
- `Property`
- `Error`

FIGURE 6.3
The ADO object model.

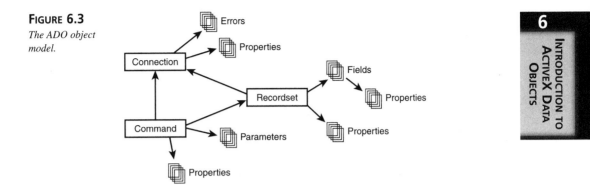

Because ADO is a COM-based object library, it should be very familiar to you how to create ADO objects. For example, you can create an ADO connection object like this:

```
Dim conn As ADODB.Connection
Set conn= New ADODB.Connection
```

After you have created your object, you can then set its properties and execute its methods, which is the focus of the rest of the chapter.

Connection Object

The Connection object represents a physical connection to your database or data provider. You can open a connection by telling the Connection object what provider to use and then specify a connection string. This code is shown in Listing 6.1 and is located in the chapter06.mdb file on the CD-ROM accompanying this book.

LISTING 6.1 CONNECTING TO AN ACCESS DATABASE VIA ADO AND A Connection OBJECT

```
Sub ConnectToDatabase()
'This procedure will establish a connection
'to a Access database using the
'OLE DB Provider for Jet
'From "Microsoft Access 2000 Development Unleashed" (SAMS)
'By: Forte, Howe, Ralston

Dim conn As ADODB.Connection

On Error GoTo Proc_Err
'Create the connection object
Set conn = New ADODB.Connection
```

continues

LISTING 6.1   CONTINUED

```
With conn
    'Set the Provider property
    'This tells ADO to use JOLT
    .Provider = "Microsoft.Jet.OLEDB.4.0"
    'Specify the path in the connection string
    'As you will see in later chapters, you
    'can also specify security information here too
    .ConnectionString = "data source=c:\northwind.mdb"
    'This determines the database open mode
    'You can specify readonly and exclusive here
        'by using .Mode=adModeRead
    .Mode = adModeReadWrite
    'Use the open method
    .Open
End With

MsgBox "Connected via " & conn.Provider & _
        " OLE DB Provider!", vbInformation

Proc_Exit:
    Exit Sub

Proc_Err:
    MsgBox Err.Description, vbCritical
    Resume Proc_Exit
End Sub
```

Listing 6.1 makes use of some of the Connection object's properties. We made use of

- Provider
- ConnectionString
- Mode

Provider is a string that represents the unique ProgID of your OLE DB provider. Here we use "Microsoft.Jet.OLEDB.4.0" to represent the OLE DB provider for Jet 4.0. The connection string is how you specify the path to the database and any other connection information like the location of workgroup file and security information. (See Chapter 23 on security for more information.) Last, we explicitly set the Mode property to an ADO constant adModeReadWrite. This enables us to open the database in Read/Write mode. You can also specify to open a database exclusively as read-only here.

Opening a Connection Within Microsoft Access 2000

When using ADO in your Access 2000 application, specifying a connection to the same database is shortened. Because Access uses a global `Connection` object itself, like the `CurrentDB` in older DAO versions, you can specify a `Connection` objection off the `CurrentProject.Connection` object like so:

```
Dim conn As ADODB.Connection
Set conn = CurrentProject.Connection
```

Executing a SQL Statement off a `Connection` Object

When you are using a `Connection` object, you can execute SQL statements off the current `Connection` object. This is very similar to executing a SQL statement off a database object in DAO. Listing 6.2 shows how to execute a SQL statement off a `Connection` object. Our SQL statement will update all rows in the Customers table where `Region=` `"BC"` to have region now equal to `"YK"`. Notice how you can find out how many records were affected by supplying a variable to the `Execute` method and then checking the value of that variable.

LISTING 6.2 EXECUTING A SQL STATEMENT AGAINST A CONNECTION

```
Sub ConnExecute()
'This procedure will establish a connection
'to a Access database using the
'OLE DB Provider for Jet, then execute a command
'From "Microsoft Access 2000 Development Unleashed" (SAMS)
'By: Forte, Howe, Ralston

Dim conn As ADODB.Connection
Dim strSQL As String
Dim lngRecordsAffected As Long

On Error GoTo Proc_Err
'Create the connection object
Set conn = New ADODB.Connection

With conn
    'Set the Provider property
    .Provider = "Microsoft.Jet.OLEDB.4.0"
    'Specify the path in the connection string
    .ConnectionString = "data source=C:\northwind.mdb"
    .Mode = adModeReadWrite
    .Open
End With
```

continues

6

INTRODUCTION TO
ACTIVEX DATA
OBJECTS

LISTING 6.2 CONTINUED

```
'SQL Statement
strSQL = "UPDATE Customers SET Customers.Region = " & _
        Chr(39) & "YK" & Chr(39) & vbNewLine & _
            "WHERE (((Customers.Region)=" & _
                Chr(39) & "BC" & Chr(39) & "));"

conn.Execute strSQL, lngRecordsAffected

MsgBox lngRecordsAffected & " Records Updated!", vbInformation

Proc_Exit:
    Exit Sub

Proc_Err:
    MsgBox Err.Description, vbCritical
    Resume Proc_Exit
End Sub
```

ADO Recordset Object

A `Recordset` object is a programmatic collection of data from a database table or query/SQL statement. A recordset will have fields filled with data for each row in the underlying table or query. To open a recordset you have to use this syntax:

```
Recordsetobject.Open "Statement", _
        ActiveConnection, CursorType, LockType, Options
```

Table 6.1 defines each option.

TABLE 6.1 ADO RECORDSET OPEN PARAMETERS

Argument	*Required*	*Notes*	*Default*
Statement	Yes	A table name, query name or valid SQL statement.	—
ActiveConnection	Yes	A valid Connection object or valid connection string.	—
Cursor Type	No	adOpenDynamic— Capability to view changes in recordset, even changes by other users.	adOpenForwardOnly
		adOpenForwardOnly— Forward only non-scrollable recordset.	

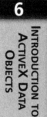

Argument	Required	Notes	Default
		adOpenKeyset—No capability to see other people's changes in recordset; ability to see change made by the current user.	
		adOpenStatic—No capability to see changes in recordset.	
Lock Type	No	adLockBatchOptimistic— Lock records in a batch.	adLockReadOnly
		adLockOptimistic— Optimistic locking.	
		adLockPessimistic— Pessimistic locking.	
		adLockReadOnly—Read only.	
Options	No	adCmdFile—Opening a persisted recordset on disk.	adCmdUnknown
		adCmdStoredProc—A SQL Server stored procedure or Access query.	
		adCmdTable—Do a Select * From a table.	
		adCmdTableDirect—Open a table directly. (Like db OpenTable in DAO.)	
		adCmdText—A SQL statement.	
		adCmdUnknown—Unknown, ADO will have to figure it out for you.	

Listing 6.3 shows you how to open a recordset based on the Customers table. We establish a connection based on the current database, and open a recordset with a forward-only, read-only cursor. We also use `adCmdTableDirect`, which will tell ADO to open the table directly.

LISTING 6.3   OPENING AN ADO RECORDSET

```
Sub OpenRecordset()
'This procedure will open a recordset
'in the current database based on the
'Customer table and print out the records
'From "Microsoft Access 2000 Development Unleashed" (SAMS)
'By: Forte, Howe, Ralston

Dim conn As ADODB.Connection
Dim rst As ADODB.Recordset

On Error GoTo Proc_Err

'Establish the connection
Set conn = CurrentProject.Connection

'Create a new recordset object
Set rst = New ADODB.Recordset

'Open the recordset
rst.Open "Customers", _
    conn, adOpenForwardOnly, adLockReadOnly, adCmdTableDirect

'Loop through the recordset
Do Until rst.EOF
    Debug.Print rst!CompanyName
    rst.MoveNext
Loop

'Close and destroy the recordset
rst.Close
Set rst = Nothing

Proc_Exit:
    Exit Sub

Proc_Err:
    MsgBox Err.Description, vbCritical
    Resume Proc_Exit

End Sub
```

Introduction to ActiveX Data Objects

CHAPTER 6

133

6

INTRODUCTION TO
ACTIVEX DATA
OBJECTS

In Listing 6.3, we are using an explicit `Connection` object based off the current connection as shown here:

```
'Open the recordset
rst.Open "Customers", _
    conn, adOpenForwardOnly, adLockReadOnly, adCmdTableDirect
```

Inside of Access 2000 only, you can use the `CurrentProject.Connection` as shown here:

```
'Open the recordset
rst.Open "Customers", _
    CurrentProject.Connection, _
        adOpenForwardOnly, adLockReadOnly, adCmdTableDirect
```

Additionally, you can supply all the connection information as a string and open the connection dynamically without a `Connection` object as shown here:

```
'Open the recordset
rst.Open "Customers", "provider=Microsoft.Jet.OLEDB.4.0; " & _
    "data source C:\northwind.mdb", _
        adOpenForwardOnly, adLockReadOnly, adCmdTableDirect
```

In addition to opening a table, you can also open a recordset based on a SQL statement. An example is shown here:

```
rst.Open "Select * From Customers Where CustomerID= ALFKI", _
    CurrentProject.Connection, _
        adOpenForwardOnly, adLockReadOnly, adCmdTableDirect
```

As you know, one of the most powerful features of Microsoft Jet is its capability to work with external data so efficiently. To open an external data source, you will have to alter your connection string. The data source has to point to the external file (text file, DBF file, Excel, and so on) and you must set the "Extended Properties" property to the name of the ISAM that you are accessing. The next code snippet example demonstrates how Jet can access an Excel 8.0 spreadsheet with ADO. In the following example we open a recordset based on the data in "Sheet1" of the Customers.xls file:

```
Dim conn As ADODB.connection
Set conn = New ADODB.connection

With conn
    .Provider = "Provider=Microsoft.Jet.OLEDB.4.0"
    .ConnectionString = "Data Source=C:\excel\Customers.xls;" & _
            "Extended Properties=Excel 8.0;"
    .Open
End With
Dim rst As ADODB.Recordset
Set rst = New ADODB.Recordset
rst.Open "Sheet1$", conn, _
    adOpenDynamic, adLockOptimistic, adCmdTableDirect
```

Using a Recordset with Command and Parameter Objects

A `Command` object represents a specific command that you intend to execute against a data source via its provider. An action query is an example of a command. You can also use a `Command` in conjunction with a `Parameter` object to execute Access parameter queries or SQL Server Stored Procedures. A `Parameter` object maps to a parameter or argument associated with your `Command` object.

We are going to look at how to execute an Access stored parameter query. This query is available in the chapter06.mdb file on the CD-ROM under the name is qryCustOrders_Prm. The query's SQL is shown here:

```
PARAMETERS OrderID Long;
SELECT Orders.*
FROM Orders AS Orders
WHERE (((Orders.OrderID)=[OrderID]));
```

In the Access query grid, we defined our query and created a parameter for our query by using the Query, Parameters menu option and defining our parameters as shown in Figure 6.4.

FIGURE 6.4

The Query Parameters dialog.

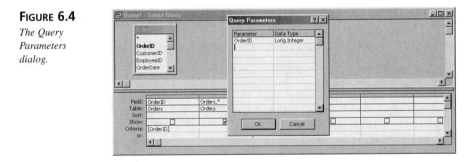

Here we create a `Command` object and tell it what `Connection` object you are going to use and what type of command it is. We tell it to use the `Connection` object that we just created and then point to the qryCustOrders_Prm query in our Access database. You can use the same connectionless options for a recordset with a `Command` object.

```
Dim cmd as ADODB.Command
Set cmd = New ADODB.Command

With cmd
    .ActiveConnection = conn
    .CommandText = "qryCustOrders_Prm"
    .CommandType = adCmdStoredProc
End With
```

Introduction to ActiveX Data Objects

CHAPTER 6

135

6

INTRODUCTION TO
ACTIVEX DATA
OBJECTS

We set the `CommandType` property to adCmdStoredProc because ADO/JOLT treats stored queries as procedures. Another type of `CommandType` is adCmdTable, used with older versions of Jet.

> **NOTE**
>
> When converting an application from Jet 3.51 to Jet 4.0 in Access 2000 or VB6, be aware of the differences in how the two methods work. With Jet 3.51, you have to specify a `CommandType` as an `adCmdTable`, with Jet 4.0, you would have to use adCmdStoredProc.

To set the parameter information, all you have to do is set four properties: `Name`, `Type`, `Value`, and `Direction`. Specify the `Name` of the parameter, and its datatype as it is named in your stored Jet query. You also need to specify the `Direction` property, which informs ADO whether the parameter is an input, output, or return value. Lastly, set the value of the parameter, based on what the user specified in your application. Then append the parameter to the `Command` object's parameter collection.

> **NOTE**
>
> When using command objects, Jet only supports input parameters. SQL Server and other database servers can support output parameters from stored procedures, so do not try to declare an output parameter.

```
With prm
    .Name = "OrderID"
    .Value = 10248
    .Type = adInteger
    .Direction = adParamInput
End With
cmd.Parameters.Append prm
```

Now use the `Execute` method of the `Command` object to create a `Recordset` object. You can use the data from the recordset to fill in text boxes on a VB Form or perform a calculation. To get the data from the executed command, you must set the `Recordset` to an executed command as shown here.

```
Set rst = cmd.Execute
```

Listing 6.4 pulls all these examples together and opens a recordset based off an executed command.

LISTING 6.4 EXECUTING A COMMAND

```
Sub OpenRecordsetviaCommand()
'This procedure will open a recordset
'in the current database based on
'an executed command object
'The command will map to the qryCustOrders_Prm
'query in this database
'From "Microsoft Access 2000 Development Unleashed" (SAMS)
'By: Forte, Howe, Ralston

Dim conn As ADODB.Connection
Dim rst As ADODB.Recordset
Dim cmd As ADODB.Command
Dim prm As ADODB.Parameter

On Error GoTo Proc_Err

'Establish the connection
Set conn = CurrentProject.Connection

Set cmd = New ADODB.Command

With cmd
    .ActiveConnection = conn
    .CommandText = "qryCustOrders_Prm"
    .CommandType = adCmdStoredProc
End With

Set prm = New ADODB.Parameter

With prm
    .Name = "OrderID"
    .Value = 10248
    .Type = adInteger
    .Direction = adParamInput
End With
cmd.Parameters.Append prm

Set rst = cmd.Execute

'Loop through the recordset
Do Until rst.EOF
    Debug.Print rst!OrderDate
    rst.MoveNext
Loop
```

```
'Close and destroy the recordset
rst.Close
Set rst = Nothing
Set cmd = Nothing
Set prm = Nothing
Set conn = Nothing

Proc_Exit:
    Exit Sub

Proc_Err:
    MsgBox Err.Description, vbCritical
    Resume Proc_Exit

End Sub
```

Executing an Action Query via a Command

You can execute saved Access action queries via a `Command` object. We have a query in our chapter06.mdb file called `qryUpdateTitle` that will update each employee title in our Customers table from Account Manager to Account Executive. The SQL of that query is shown here:

```
UPDATE Customers SET Customers.ContactTitle = "Account Executive"
WHERE (((Customers.ContactTitle)="Accounting Manager"));
```

To run the query programmatically via ADO, you must create a `Command` object, hook it up to a `Connection` object and execute it. Listing 6.5 demonstrates how to accomplish this.

LISTING 6.5   EXECUTING AN ACCESS ACTION QUERY VIA ADO

```
Running an Action Query Via a Command object
Sub ActionQueryCmd()
'This procedure will execute an
'Access action query via a command object
'and print out the properties of the recordset
'From "Microsoft Access 2000 Development Unleashed" (SAMS)
'By: Forte, Howe, Ralston
Dim cmd As ADODB.Command
Dim lngRecordsAffected As Long

On Error GoTo Proc_Err

Set cmd = New ADODB.Command
Dim rst As ADODB.Recordset
```

continues

LISTING 6.5   CONTINUED

```
With cmd
    'Connect to current database
    .ActiveConnection = CurrentProject.Connection
    'The Name of the query in Access
    .CommandText = "qryUpdateTitle"
    'Set this to adCmdStoredProc, Jet classifies
    'Saved Queries as Procedures for commands
    .CommandType = adCmdStoredProc
    'Run the Query
    .Execute , lngRecordsAffected
End With

MsgBox lngRecordsAffected & " records were updated!", _
        vbInformation
Proc_Exit:
    Exit Sub

Proc_Err:
    MsgBox Err.Description
    Resume Proc_Exit


End Sub
```

Field and Property Objects

The `Field` and `Property` objects are great objects for finding out information about your table or recordset. The `Field` object represents each field column in your recordset. The `Property` object represents each property of whatever object you are querying. You can iterate through each field in your recordset or property in your object variable via the `For...Each` syntax as shown in Listing 6.6.

LISTING 6.6   WORKING WITH Field AND Property VIA ADO

```
Sub FieldandProperty()
'This procedure will print out all the
'fields of a recordset and their values
'and print out the properties of the recordset
'From "Microsoft Access 2000 Development Unleashed" (SAMS)
'By: Forte, Howe, Ralston
Dim rst As ADODB.Recordset
Dim fld As ADODB.Field
Dim prp As ADODB.Property

On Error GoTo Proc_Err

Set rst = New ADODB.Recordset
```

Introduction to ActiveX Data Objects

CHAPTER 6

139

6

INTRODUCTION TO
ACTIVEX DATA
OBJECTS

```
'Open the recordset based on the customers table
rst.Open "Customers", CurrentProject.Connection

'Print out each field name and value
Debug.Print "Table Fields:"
For Each fld In rst.Fields
    Debug.Print fld.Name & ": " & fld.Value
Next fld

'Print out the properties of the table
Debug.Print
Debug.Print "Table Properties:"
For Each prp In rst.Properties
    Debug.Print prp.Name
Next prp

rst.Close
Set rst = Nothing

Proc_Exit:
    Exit Sub

Proc_Err:
    MsgBox Err.Description
    Resume Proc_Err

End Sub
```

The Error Object

When writing code, you sometimes introduce bugs; or system changes, beyond your control, render your code invalid. (Like a LAN administrator moving a back end MDB file without alerting you!) The ADO `Connection` object has a collection of `Error` objects that will represent each error that occurred. The `Error` object has a few properties that you will be concerned with. These properties are summarized in Table 6.2.

TABLE 6.2   THE MAJOR PROPERTIES OF THE `Error` OBJECT

Property	Comment
Description	A description of the error.
Number	The ADO error number.
Native Error	The provider's error number.
SQL State	This is a provider-specific error code. For Jet this will map to DAO's old error number.
Source	The source of the error. In our case, it will be the Jet engine.

Because any given error in your code can generate many ADO errors, you can iterate through the Connection's error collection and then query these properties. If you have code in your application that depends on an old DAO error number, you will have to use the SQLState property for backward compatibility. SQLState will return the old DAO error code for you. You can iterate though the error collection using the Error object as shown in Listing 6.7. The result of the code in Listing 6.7 is shown in Figure 6.5.

FIGURE 6.5

An error message making use of the Error *object.*

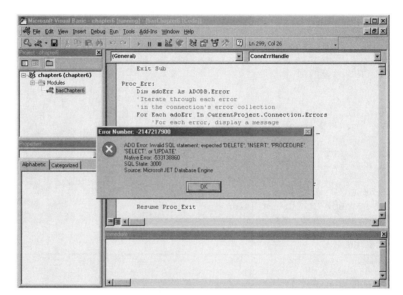

LISTING 6.7 USING THE ADO Error OBJECT

```
Sub ConnErrHandle()
'This procedure will force an error
'and use the Error object to get
'some meaningful information about the error
'From "Microsoft Access 2000 Development Unleashed" (SAMS)
'By: Forte, Howe, Ralston
Dim conn As ADODB.Connection
Dim rst As ADODB.Recordset

On Error GoTo Proc_Err
Set conn = CurrentProject.Connection
Set rst = New ADODB.Recordset

'Force an error, will just to Proc_Err
rst.Open "badTable", conn

Proc_Exit:
    Exit Sub
```

```
Proc_Err:
    Dim adoErr As ADODB.Error
    'Iterate through each error
    'in the connection's error collection
    For Each adoErr In conn.Errors
        'For each error, display a message
        MsgBox "ADO Error: " & adoErr.Description & _
                vbNewLine & "Native Error: " & _
                    adoErr.NativeError & _
                vbNewLine & "SQL State: " & _
                    adoErr.SQLState & _
                vbNewLine & "Source: " & _
                    adoErr.Source, vbCritical, _
                    "Error Number: " & adoErr.Number
    Next adoErr

    Resume Proc_Exit

End Sub
```

Moving from DAO to ADO

Our introduction to ADO has shown that there are many similarities between Data Access Objects (DAO) and ADO. Throughout this entire book, you will be given advice on how to use ADO compared to DAO. This section is intended to prepare you for the initial conversion process and to compare the two object models.

Converting from Prior Versions of Access

When converting prior version of an Access database to Access 2000, you should note that ADO is the new default data access methodology. This may cause some confusion when creating an object that has the same name in DAO and ADO like "recordset." If you have some code like this in Access 2000:

```
Dim db As Database
Dim rst as Recordset
```

Access 2000 will assume that the rst variable will be an ADO recordset, not a DAO recordset, because ADO is referenced before DAO in your VBA References by default. Prior to converting your Access 97, 95, or other database, you should prefix all your DAO objects with the type library name: DAO. The code should be rewritten like this:

```
Dim db as DAO.Database
Dim rst as DAO.Recordset
```

This will leave zero room for failure when converting for your DAO object variables.

Should I Convert to ADO?

When starting a new Access 2000 application, the choice is easy. use ADO. What about applications that you are converting to Access 2000? The move to ADO should be considered when choosing to convert to Access 2000. You will want to convert to ADO as soon as possible to take advantage of the new features that are not available in DAO. In addition, Microsoft has announced that it is phasing out DAO; so in a future version of Access, DAO may not be supported directly. Because ADO is the way of the future, you should take ADO very seriously. Do you have the time? Money? The major consideration should be your skill level and budget.

Reading through the chapters in this book and the ADO documentation on the Microsoft Web site (`http://www.micrsoft.com/data`) should prepare you for learning ADO. The next section outlines a typical conversion plan.

Learning ADO and converting your application's code from DAO to ADO should be part of the conversion budget. Converting to Access 2000 will require more developer hours than a typical conversion. Following the conventions outlined here can save you much time, money, and aggravation. This section alone can more than pay for the price of the book. (Feel free to share the wealth with Sams and the authors!)

A Conversion Guideline

This section outlines how you should approach converting an application from DAO to ADO. Remember, back up your work religiously!

1. Start in Access 97. If your application is in a version of Access prior to Access 97, convert it to Access 97 first.

2. Do a cost analysis. Do an analysis of your database to determine how many procedures are using DAO. Then list each procedure in an Excel spreadsheet and estimate how long it will take to convert each procedure.

3. Install ADO 2.1 on your machine from Microsoft's Web site.

4. In Access 97, begin by converting the procedures that do not communicate with other procedures first. When you are done with one procedure, test and retest. Then move on to the next procedure. This may take days or even weeks, depending on how large your database is.

5. Do not delete your old procedures; rename them `ProcedureName_DAO`, adding the `_DAO` to the end of the procedure, so you can quickly rename the ADO procedure (use `_ADO`) and substitute the DAO procedure in your testing.

Introduction to ActiveX Data Objects

CHAPTER 6

143

6

INTRODUCTION TO
ACTIVEX DATA
OBJECTS

6. After you convert the code that exists in more isolated procedures, start looking at the code in larger and more complex procedures. Do not get caught up in fixing other things in this procedure, save that enhancement for a later time. Change only the DAO code. Use the same testing methodology as mentioned in step 5.

7. After you convert all the code, test an old DAO copy of the application side-by-side with the new one. Then have another developer test your application.

8. Develop routines that will enable users to easily undo anything that they have done. This way, if your application is causing data errors, users can revert back to the state they were in before they started running your code.

9. Have user "beta" testing of your application in daily work. Choose a few reliable users to test your ADO version. Do not delete the old working DAO copy; provide an icon to it just in case there are errors so severe that they interfere with productivity.

10. After you are satisfied that the users have tested your application thoroughly, convert your application to Access 2000 and repeat numbers 7–9.

MAKING SURE THAT YOUR USERS ARE ACTUALLY TESTING!

In order to know that your users actually are testing the application enough, you can incorporate a technique that we use at The Aurora Development Group. We do not want to be blamed for bugs that a user could have found when testing, so we implement a very detailed audit trail in our beta test applications. At the start of each procedure, even simple ones like a Close button, we log all the information into a database. This will give us an indication as to how many times a user has entered a particular procedure, or even run a certain report. Then, we do an analysis of these numbers and ask the users to test certain parts of the application based on what was low in usage. With this procedure, we can be sure that the users have tested everything before we convert the beta application to a production system.

When Not to Convert to ADO

Smaller projects with little or no budget should not be converted to ADO. As you can see, there are a lot of steps involved in the testing process. If the users cannot budget the time to test, do not convert. DAO will work fine in Access 2000. Actually DAO 3.6 has some bug fixes in it, so your DAO code should run better in Access 2000 than Access 97 without modifying it at all.

There are a few parity issues with ADO. As you read throughout this book, you will discover there are a few things in ADO that DAO currently just does better, like some DDL operations and security. If your application heavily relies on these techniques, you may not want to convert, or at least have a hybrid DAO/ADO application.

The ADO Object Model Compared to DAO

DAO has a huge object model with over 50 objects. ADO is small and has only 7. Where did everything go? You will see in this section how to compare DAO and ADO in data access. Chapter 22, "Replication and JRO," and Chapter 7, "Advanced ADO," discuss this issue. Table 6.3 summarizes the most common objects for data access in DAO and shows their ADO equivalent.

TABLE 6.3 DAO TO ADO DATA ACCESS REFERENCE

DAO Object	*ADO Object*
DBEngine	None
Workspace	None
Database	Connection
Recordset	Recordset
Field	Field
QueryDef	Command
Parameter	Parameter
Error	Error

Summary

ActiveX Data Objects is the wave of the future! Microsoft has made available an OLE DB Provider for Access and is very committed to moving you from DAO to ADO. Proof of this is that ADO is the default database access method when you start a new Access 2000 project. This chapter gave you a good enough introduction to ADO to get you started. Future chapters include more in-depth coverage of ADO.

Advanced ADO

Now that you have seen how to use ADO and viewed it side by side with DAO, take a look at some of the features of ADO that will help you develop Access 2000 applications.

Using the OLE DB Provider for Jet in Access 2000

When you use ADO in your Access application, you will probably be using the OLE DB Provider for Jet. (Using the OLE DB Provider for SQL Server is discussed in Chapter 15.) This provider will let you talk to Access MDB files directly. The capability to talk directly to the data source of your choice, via a provider, is a giant step for ADO. To use the OLE DB Provider for Jet, you have to supply the provider name and full path to the database as part of the connection string. To keep things more readable, ADO has a `Provider` property that you can set to the use Jet's Provider. Jet's Provider's unique `CLASSID` to use in the connection string is: `Microsoft.Jet.OLEDB.4.0`. The following is an example of how to open a connection to a Microsoft Access database using the Jet OLE DB provider:

```
Dim conn As ADODB.Connection
Set conn = New ADODB.Connection

With conn
    .Provider = "Microsoft.Jet.OLEDB.4.0"
    .ConnectionString = "data source= C:\databases\sample.mdb"
    .Open
End With
```

If you must specify other connection information like a database password or workgroup file, append it to the connection string preceded by a semicolon. Table 7.1 lists the available provider-specific connection properties that can be used in the connection string. Other provider specific connection properties that are in the connection's properties collection are ignored.

TABLE 7.1   THE MICROSOFT JET OLE DB PROVIDER SPECIFIC CONNECTION PROPERTY
STRINGS

Name	Description
Jet OLEDB:Registry Path	Path to the registry key to use for Jet information. This does not include the HKEY_LOCAL_MACHINE tag. This value can be changed to a secondary location to store registry values for a particular application that are not shared with other applications that use Jet on the machine.
	For example, the setting for Access 2000 is SOFT-WARE\Microsoft\Office\9.0\Access\Jet\4.0\Engines
Jet OLEDB:System database	Location of the Jet system database to use for authenticating users. This overrides the value set in the registry or the corresponding systemdb registry key used when Jet OLEDB:Registry Path is used. This can include the path to the file.
Jet OLEDB:Database Password	Password used to open the database. This differs from the user password in that the database password is per file, whereas a user password is per user. For more information, see Chapter 21, "Multiuser Issues/File Server/Locking."
Jet OLEDB:Engine Type	An enumeration defining the storage engine currently in use to access this database.
Jet OLEDB:Database Locking Mode	Scheme to be used when locking the database. For more information see Chapter 21 on multiuser issues. Note that a database can only be open in one mode at a time. The first user to open the database gets determines the locking mode used while the database is open.
Jet OLEDB:Global Partial Bulk Ops	This property determines the behavior of Jet when SQL DML bulk operations fail. It can be overridden on a per-rowset basis by setting the Jet OLEDB:Partial Bulk Ops property.
Jet OLEDB:Global Bulk Transactions	Determines whether SQL bulk operations are transacted. This property determines the default for all operations in the current connection.

In addition to the properties listed in the table above, the Microsoft Jet database engine exposes a number of settable options that will dictate how the engine will behave. These options often have a direct impact on performance. By default, when the Jet engine is initialized, it uses the values set in the registry under the \HKEY_LOCAL_MACHINES\Software\Microsoft\Jet key. At runtime, it is possible to temporarily override these settings. In ADO, these values are set as part of the connection string. The connection string constants are shown in Table 7.2.

TABLE 7.2 ADO CONNECTION STRING OPTIONS

DAO	*ADO*
Constant	**Property**
dbPageTimeout	Jet OLEDB:Page Timeout
dbSharedAsyncDelay	Jet OLEDB:Shared Async Delay
dbExclusiveAsyncDelay	Jet OLEDB:Exclusive Async Delay
dbLockRetry	Jet OLEDB:Lock Retry
dbUserCommitSync	Jet OLEDB:User Commit Sync
dbImplicitCommitSync	Jet OLEDB:Implicit Commit Sync
dbMaxBufferSize	Jet OLEDB:Max Buffer Size
dbMaxLocksPerFile	Jet OLEDB:Max Locks Per File
dbLockDelay	Jet OLEDB:Lock Delay
dbRecycleLVs	Jet OLEDB:Recycle Long-Valued Pages
dbFlushTransactionTimeout	Jet OLEDB:Flush Transaction Timeout

The following code example opens a secured database, specifying a database password and workgroup file:

```
Dim conn As ADODB.Connection
Set conn = New ADODB.Connection

With conn
    .Provider = "Microsoft.Jet.OLEDB.4.0"
    .ConnectionString = "data source= C:\databases\sample.mdb" & _
    ";Jet OLEDB:Database Password=supersecret " & _
            ";Jet OLEDB:System database=" & _
    "c:\windows\system\system.mdw"
    .Open
End With
```

CurrentProject.Connection

When you want to access the current database via ADO code, Access 2000 provides a shortcut. It provides a global reference to an ADO Connection object via CurrentProject.Connection. Using this syntax, you can easily assign a Connection object to the current database. CurrentProject.Connection is only available in Access 2000 VBA code. The following code shows you how to use CurrentProject.Connection:

```
Dim conn As ADODB.Connection
Set conn = CurrentProject.Connection
```

CurrentProject.Connection can also save time if you want to open a recordset. You can use ADO's capability to dynamically create a connection via a recordset's open method:

```
Dim rst As ADODB.Recordset
Set rst = New ADODB.Recordset
rst.Open "Customers", CurrentProject.Connection
```

7

ADVANCED ADO

CAUTION

Be careful using CurrentProject.Connection because it is not portable to any development environment other than Access 2000. If you plan on reusing your code in an application other than Access (like Visual Basic), you must use the long syntax for creating a connection.

Using Microsoft Data Links to Connect to a Database

Now that ADO is the primary way to access data, Microsoft realizes that developers need a standardized way to persist, load, and manage OLE DB connection information, much like the old ODBC driver manager and administrator did for ODBC. Microsoft Universal Data Links (UDL) give you this capability. UDLs give you the opportunity to save connection information to an UDL file and then enable you to open a connection object in ADO based on the information saved in the UDL file. This will come in handy if you want to test a database connection at a different site without changing any code.

The Microsoft Universal Data Links consist of

- A Graphical User Interface to Create an OLE DB Connection
- Automation Interface

Before you can use a UDL in your VB or VBA application, you must first create one. Creating one is simple. Just enter Explorer and then click File, New and select Microsoft Data Link as shown in Figure 7.1.

FIGURE 7.1

Creating a new UDL file.

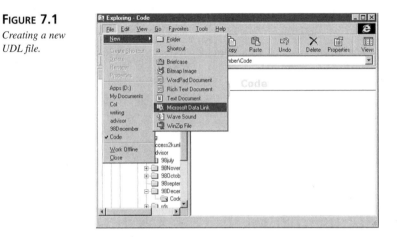

After you create the UDL file, double-click it to edit it. The first screen shown in Figure 7.2 lists all the OLE DB Providers installed on your system. Choose the provider that you want to use and click Next to go to the Connection tab of the UDL dialog. This tab will let you set your provider-specific connection information as shown in Figure 7.3. Here you are using the OLE DB Provider for Jet so you have to provide the database path, user id, and password. (If you are using the OLE DB Provider for SQL Server, you will have to specify the server and database name.) he next tab called Advanced is used to set provider-specific properties that are usually set for you by default like `CommandTimeout`. The last page All summarizes all the connection properties for you.

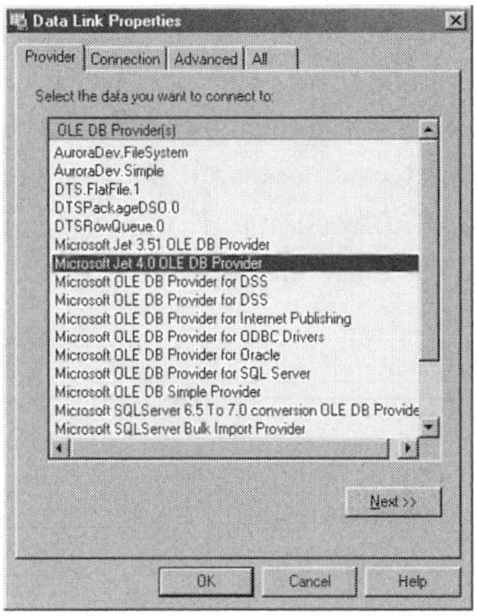

FIGURE 7.2

Choosing an OLE DB Provider.

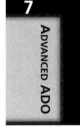

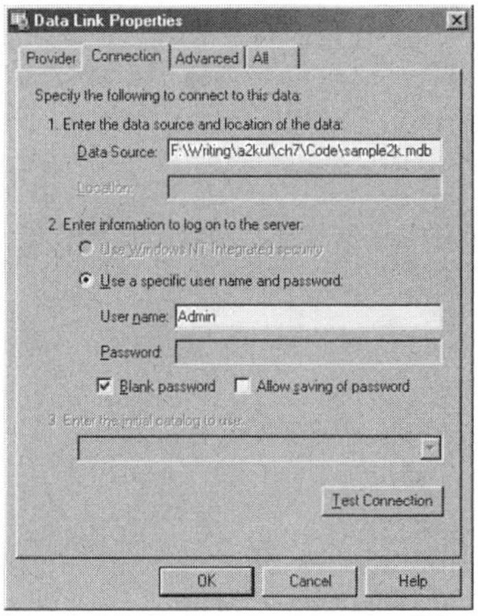

FIGURE 7.3

Entering the connection information.

Now that your UDL file is created, you can use it from your VBA code to open a connection object in ADO. The syntax is simple, just create a connection object as you normally would and use the open method. Just use the File Name identifier in your connection string and point to the UDL file as shown here:

```
Dim conn As ADODB.Connection
Set conn = New ADODB.Connection

conn.Open "File Name=c:\chapter7.udl;"
```

The code in Listing 7.1, available on the chapter07.mdb file on the CD-ROM accompanying this book, shows you how to open a Connection object based on a UDL file located in the application's directory to the Northwind database. You connect to the database and fill a list box with the contents of the Customers table. What is great about this code is that if you want to use the SQL Server 7.0 version of Northwind, all you have to do is change the UDL file's properties and then re-run the code.

LISTING 7.1 USING UDLs IN YOUR VBA CODE

```
Private Sub OpenViaLink()
'This is procedure that will use an
'ADO connection object that gets its
'Connection information from a
'Microsoft UDL File
'The procedure will then open a recordset
'From "Microsoft Access 2000 Development Unleashed" (SAMS)
'By: Forte, Howe, Ralston

Dim conn As ADODB.Connection
Dim rst As ADODB.Recordset

On Error GoTo Proc_Err

Set conn = New ADODB.Connection
'Open the connection via the
'UDL file. This will allow you to
'dynamically change the database
'by changing the UDL
conn.Open "File Name=c:\chapter7.udl;"

Set rst = New ADODB.Recordset
'Open the connection based on a SQL Statement
rst.Open "Select * From Customers", conn

'Loop through the recordset
'And print out the values
Do Until rst.EOF
    Debug.Print rst!CompanyName
    rst.MoveNext
Loop

'Clean up
rst.Close
conn.Close

Set rst = Nothing
Set conn = Nothing
```

```
Proc_Exit:
    Exit Sub

Proc_Err:
    MsgBox Err.Description
    Resume Proc_Exit

End Sub
```

Managing Data Links

There are two ways to manage UDL files. The first is via their rich user interface. Windows Control Panel has a Microsoft Data Links icon that will let you manage your data links in a favorite location as shown in Figure 7.4. This will list all the UDL files in whatever folder you indicate. An easier way is to use Windows Explorer and open the UDL file directly.

FIGURE 7.4

Managing data links.

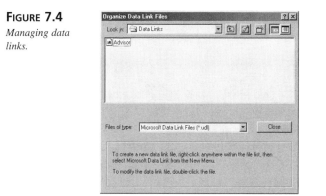

Programmatic Managing of UDLs

Because UDLs expose their own Automation Interface, you can manage and control UDLs programmatically. To use UDLs in your VBA code, set a reference to the type library called Microsoft OLE DB Service Component 1.0 Type Library (as shown in Figure 7.5).

After you have reference to the library set, you can start managing UDLs. In addition, you can prompt a user at runtime for OLE DB connection information via the UDL Dialogs. This can come in handy in prototype applications or product demos to users who are familiar with Microsoft Data Links. You can do this with the PromptNew method of the DataLinks object. The code in Listing 7.2 prompts a user for OLE DB connection information via the UDL dialog and then connects to the database and opens a recordset.

FIGURE 7.5

Setting a reference to the called Microsoft OLE DB Service Component 1.0 Type Library.

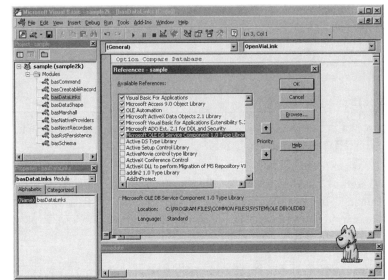

LISTING 7.2 PROGRAMMATIC UDLs

```
Private Sub OpenUDLDialog()
'Procedure that will use the
'UDL Automation Interface to
'Create a connection object
'From "Microsoft Access 2000 Development Unleashed" (SAMS)
'By: Forte, Howe, Ralston

Dim strConnect As String
Dim rst As ADODB.Recordset
'The Microsoft UDL Reference
Dim udl As MSDASC.DataLinks

On Error GoTo Proc_Err

'Create the Data Link Object
Set udl = New MSDASC.DataLinks

'Set the connection object to the
'Prompt a new Data Link dialog
strConnect = udl.PromptNew

Set rst = New ADODB.Recordset
'Open a recordset based on what
'the user has entered in the
'Data Link dialog
rst.Open "Select * From Customers", strConnect
```

```
'Display the first record
MsgBox rst!CompanyName

Proc_Exit:
    Exit Sub

Proc_Err:
    MsgBox Err.Description
    Resume Proc_Exit

End Sub
```

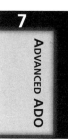

Accessing Nonrelational Data with ADO

In addition to using Microsoft Access to communicate with non-relational data like Excel, as shown in Chapter 6, ADO has some advanced features that enable you to work with non-relational data with ease. You will look at

- The Jet User Roster
- Creatable Recordsets
- Data Shaping

The Jet User Roster

The OLE DB Provider for Microsoft Jet will enable you to open a recordset filled with the names of the current users logged into the database that you specify in the connection. This replaces the need to use the LDBView utility that shipped with prior versions of Jet. The code in Listing 7.3 shows you how to open a recordset filled with all the current users in the database. Listing 7.3 will use the OpenSchema method of the Connection object with a JET/JOLT specific parameter. Notice that ADO does not support any constants for you. You have to supply the very ugly GUID value: "{947bb102-5d43-11d1-bdbf-00c04fb92675}"). Hopefully in future ADO will provide a constant for you to use.

LISTING 7.3 USING THE USER ROSTER

```
Sub UserRoster()
'Procedure that will use the
'User Roster feature or Jet 4.0
'to connect to a database and check
'to see who is in the database
'From "Microsoft Access 2000 Development Unleashed" (SAMS)
'By: Forte, Howe, Ralston

Dim conn As ADODB.Connection
Dim rst As ADODB.Recordset

On Error GoTo Proc_Err

Set conn = New ADODB.Connection

'Open the back-end database
With conn
    .Provider = "Microsoft.Jet.OLEDB.4.0"
    .ConnectionString = "data source=f:\employee.mdb"
    .Open
End With

'Create the recordset based on the
'Number of users in the database
Set rst = conn.OpenSchema(adSchemaProviderSpecific, , _
"{947bb102-5d43-11d1-bdbf-00c04fb92675}")

'For each user print out the computer name
'and other information
Do Until rst.EOF
    Debug.Print rst!COMPUTER_NAME
    Debug.Print rst!LOGIN_NAME
    Debug.Print rst!CONNECTED
    Debug.Print rst!SUSPECTED_STATE

    rst.MoveNext
Loop

Proc_Exit:
    Exit Sub

Proc_Err:
    MsgBox Err.Description
    Resume Proc_Exit

End Sub
```

Creatable Recordsets

ADO gives you the opportunity to create recordsets "out of thin air." You now can use the `Fields.Append` method and the `AddNew` method to add fields and data to your recordset. This is a great technique for creating procedures that will grab information from non-relational data locations, such as a file directory, and then return a recordset to the calling procedure. Using ADO, your application can always deal with recordsets, and your applications are easier to code. The following example shows you how to create a recordset filled with file names in a given directory. If you wrap this code in a class module, you can use it in many applications. For example, I use it to read all the ZIP files on FTP server's directory and iterate through them to create a download page. The advantage of this technique over the NT Active Directory OLE DB Provider is that it is available now and will run under Windows 95. Listing 7.4 demonstrates how to open a recordset based on a listing of file name in a directory.

LISTING 7.4   CREATING A RECORDSET FROM NONRELATIONAL DATA

```
Sub CreatableRst_Files(strPath As String)
'This is an example of creating a recordset
'from Non-relational data
'Creates a recordset of file names And Extensions
'From "Microsoft Access 2000 Development Unleashed" (SAMS)
'By: Forte, Howe, Ralston

Dim rst As ADODB.Recordset

On Error GoTo Proc_Err

Set rst = New ADODB.Recordset

With rst
    'Do local work
    .CursorLocation = adUseClient

    'Add a field here
    .Fields.Append "FileName", adVarChar, 255, adFldRowID
    .Fields.Append "Extension", adChar, 3, adFldFixed

    'Open the rst
    .Open , , adOpenStatic, adLockBatchOptimistic

    'Make sure there is an \ in the path
    If Right(strPath, 1) <> "\" Then strPath = strPath & "\"

    'Get a list of all files in the DIR and then add then to
    'the recordset
    strPath = Dir(strPath & "*.*", vbNormal)
```

continues

LISTING 7.4   CONTINUED

```
        ' Don't include the . and .. entries
        Do While strPath > ""

            'Add the record to the rst here
            .AddNew Array("FileName", "Extension"), _
            Array(strPath, Right(strPath, 3))

            strPath = Dir
        Loop

    .MoveFirst

    'Print out the files
    Do Until .EOF
        Debug.Print !FileName
        rst.MoveNext
    Loop

End With

Proc_Exit:
    Exit Sub

Proc_Err:
    MsgBox Err.Description
    Resume Proc_Exit
End Sub
```

Data Shaping

The ability to view your data in a hierarchical fashion is very easy with ADO. You can use a new ADO feature called Data Shaping to view parent and child records in just one recordset. You can use the MSDataShape OLE DB Provider to create relationship-based hierarchies and grouping hierarchies. Creating these types of hierarchical recordsets can ease the development burden for hierarchical data. For example, in Figure 7.6, you can see a group hierarchy of all customers' orders in Northwind viewed in the new Microsoft Hierarchical FlexGrid (an OLAP version of the popular FlexGrid). This control is provided with the Office 2000, Developer Edition, or Visual Basic 6. (Our figures and listings here are in VB 6 using an Access database as the data source.) Notice the plus sign at each record. This gives you the opportunity to expand and collapse each record to view its detail as shown in Figure 7.7. Before the MSDataShape OLE DB Provider, a lot of code was needed to get a grid to behave like this.

FIGURE 7.6

*An MSDataShape
OLE DB Provider
recordset in VB.*

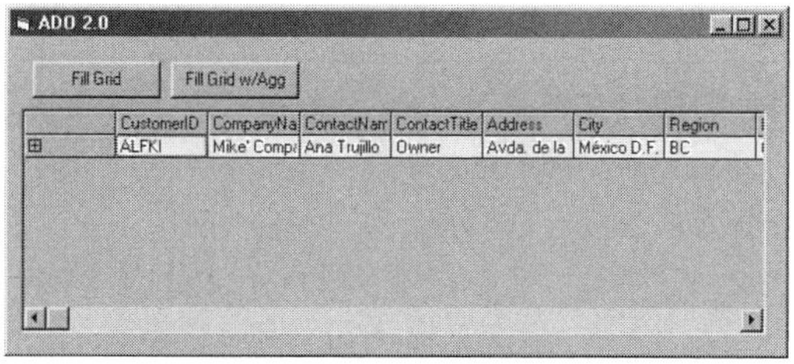

FIGURE 7.7

*A GroupBy
recordset in VB.*

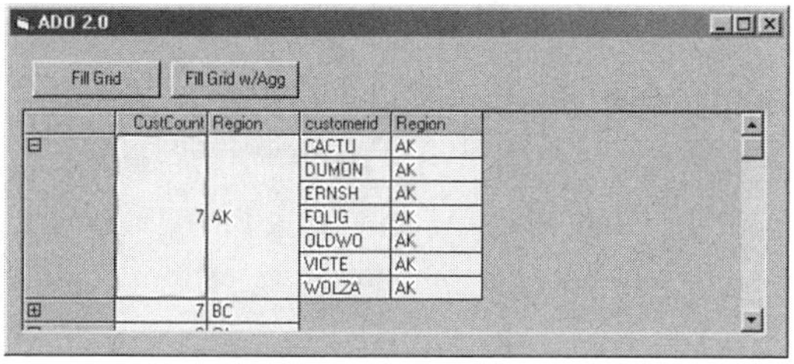

LISTING 7.5 CREATING A DATA-SHAPED RECORDSET AND FILLING THE MSHFLEXGRID IN VB 6

```
Sub CubeGroupHierarchy()
'Fill the MSFLEXGRID Control
'From "Microsoft Access 2000 Development Unleashed" (SAMS)
'By: Forte, Howe, Ralston

'Code to fill the recordset
Dim rst As ADODB.Recordset
Dim strConnect As String

Set rst = New ADODB.Recordset

'Set up the connection properties
'Tell ADO to use the OLE DB Provider for Data Shaping
'Then plug in your native OLE DB provider for the
'data source of your choice
strConnect = "Provider=MSDataShape"& _
        ";data provider=Microsoft.Jet.OLEDB.4.0" & _
    ";data source=" & App.Path & "\sample.mdb"

'Pass in the Data Shape SQL
rst.Source = "shape {Select customerid,  " & _
        "Region from Customers} rst1 " & _
    "COMPUTE COUNT (rst1.customerid) AS CustCount, rst1 By Region "

rst.ActiveConnection = strConnect
```

continues

LISTING 7.5   CONTINUED

```
rst.Open , , adOpenStatic, adLockBatchOptimistic

'Show the RST
Set frmADO.MSHFlexGrid1.Recordset = rst

End Sub
```

As you can see from the code example, you have to use special Data Shaping related SQL syntax. For a complete listing of how to use this syntax, check out the MSDN books online that ship with Visual Basic 6/Office Developer 2000 or the great ADO documentation on the Web at http://www.microsoft.com/data

You can also take this code for Data Shaping and bring the data into Microsoft Excel. The code in Listing 7.6 shows you how to take the prior example and dump the data into an Excel Spreadsheet.

LISTING 7.6   USING DATA SHAPING WITH MICROSOFT EXCEL

```
Sub CUBRelation()
'Usign OLAP with Microsoft Excel
'From "Microsoft Access 2000 Development Unleashed" (SAMS)
'By: Forte, Howe, Ralston

Dim rst As ADODB.Recordset
Dim strConnect As String

Set rst = New ADODB.Recordset

'Set up the connection properties
'Tell ADO to use the OLE DB Provider for Data Shaping
'Then plug in your native OLE DB provider for the
'data source of your choice
strConnect = "Provider=MSDataShape" & _
      ";data provider=Microsoft.Jet.OLEDB.4.0" & _
    ";data source=C:\ sample.mdb"

'Pass in the Data Shape SQL
rst.Source = "shape {Select * from customers where Customerid='ALFKI'}"&_
      " Append " & _
    "({Select * From Orders} As rsOrders " & _
      "RELATE customerid to customerid)"

rst.ActiveConnection = strConnect

rst.Open , , adOpenStatic, adLockBatchOptimistic
```

```
    'Show thew RST
    ShowRSTinExcel rst

End Sub

Sub ShowRSTinExcel(rst As ADODB.Recordset, _
        Optional blnSKipClear As Boolean = False)

Dim rstChild As ADODB.Recordset
Dim col As ADODB.Field
Dim intCurrentColumn As Integer
Dim intCurrentRow As Integer


If Not blnSKipClear Then
    'Clear out the cells
    Cells.Select
    Selection.ClearContents
End If

Do Until rst.EOF
    intCurrentColumn = intCurrentColumn + 1
    If Not blnSKipClear Then
        intCurrentRow = 1
    Else
        intCurrentRow = 2
    End If


    For Each col In rst.Fields
     If col.Type <> adChapter Then

        Cells(intCurrentColumn, intCurrentRow) = _
            col.Name & ": " & col.Value

     Else
        Set rstChild = col.Value
        ShowRSTinExcel rstChild, True
     End If

     intCurrentRow = intCurrentRow + 1
    Next

   rst.MoveNext
Loop

Cells(1, 1).Select

End Sub
```

Advanced Data Manipulation with ADO

The last chapter showed you how to open up recordsets filled with data and execute Command objects. This section will show you some additional tips and tricks with ADO. We will look at

- Modifying data in a recordset
- Persisted recordsets

Modifying Data in a Recordset

To modify data in a recordset, all you have to do is move to that record and start editing it. When you move to the next record or call the Update method, your changes will be saved. This represents an important change from DAO where you had to use the Edit method first then explicitly call the Update method. The code in Listing 7.7 shows how to edit data.

LISTING 7.7   EDITING RECORDS

```
Sub Editrecords()
'Procedure that edit data
'From "Microsoft Access 2000 Development Unleashed" (SAMS)
'By: Forte, Howe, Ralston

Dim rst As ADODB.Recordset
Dim strSQL As String

On Error GoTo Proc_Err

'Create the recordset object
Set rst = New ADODB.Recordset

'Write the SQL Statement to return the row that you want
strSQL = "Select * From Customers Where CustomerID='Anton'"

'Open the recordset with a keyset Cursor
rst.Open strSQL, CurrentProject.Connection, _
        adOpenKeyset, adLockOptimistic

'Update the Row
rst!CompanyName = "New Name"
'Use the Update Method or "MoveNext"
rst.Update
```

```
Proc_Exit:
    Exit Sub

Proc_Err:
    MsgBox Err.Description
    Resume Proc_Exit
End Sub
```

> **TIP**
>
> It is faster to open a recordset based on a SQL statement that restricts the primary key than it is to open the whole table and then search for the record that you want.

> **CAUTION**
>
> Because the changes that you make to the recordset are committed without an Update method by moving to the next record, be very careful when editing data.

Adding a Record

Adding a record is almost the same as editing one. You have to open a recordset and then use the AddNew method. The same rules apply with Update as with an Edit. After you add the record, you will be on the current record. Listing 7.8 shows an example of adding a record to a table.

LISTING 7.8   ADDING A RECORD TO A TABLE

```
Sub Addrecords()
'Procedure that will add records
'to connect to a database and check
'to see who is in the database
'From "Microsoft Access 2000 Development Unleashed" (SAMS)
'By: Forte, Howe, Ralston

Dim rst As ADODB.Recordset

On Error GoTo Proc_Err

'Create the recordset object
Set rst = New ADODB.Recordset
```

continues

LISTING 7.8   CONTINUED

```
With rst

'Open the table directly
    .Open "Authors", CurrentProject.Connection, _
        adOpenDynamic, adLockOptimistic, adCmdTableDirect
    'Still needs an AddNew
    .AddNew
    !AuthorFirstName = "Mike"
    !AuthorLastName = "Smith"
    .Update
    'After an Add, we are at the new record
    MsgBox "New Author ID: " & !AuthorID

End With

Proc_Exit:
    Exit Sub

Proc_Err:
    MsgBox Err.Description
    Resume Proc_Exit
End Sub
```

You may have noticed that you opened the table with a constant adCmdTableDirect. If you use this constant with an adOpenDynaset cursor type and Optimistic locking, you will map to the old DAO equivalent dbOpenTable. Table 7.3 shows you all the possible options for ADO cursor/lock types and their DAO equivalent.

TABLE 7.3   COMBINATIONS FOR ACCESS IN ADO

Cursor Type	Lock Type/Options	DAO Equivalent
adOpenForwardOnly	adLockReadOnly	dbOpenSnapShot, dbForwardOnly
adOpenKeySet	adLockReadOnly	No DAO Match
adOpenKeySet	adLockPessimistic	dbOpenDynaset
adOpenKeySet	adLockOptimistic	dbOpenDynaset
adOpenKeySet	adLockBatchOptimistic	dbOpenDynaset
adOpenStatic	adLockReadOnly	dbOpenDynaset
adOpenDynamic	adLockOptimistic, adCmdTableDirect	dbOpenTable

Persisted Recordsets

For those of you who have to support disconnected users, the notion of recordset persistence is just an awesome gift from Redmond. Now you have the capability to save a recordset to disk and then work with it from your VB or VBA application. Then later, you can resync it to the database. To accomplish this, open an ADO recordset with the `adLockBatchOptimistic` lock type specified and using a `client` cursor. Then use the save method of the `recordset` object. You have to specify a file name and save format type. ADO gives you as options:

- adPersistADTG
- adPersistXML

If you chose to save to the `adPersistADTG` or `adPersistXML` format, you can easily open it up later in ADO. Listing 7.9 shows you how to open a recordset, change a record, save the recordset to file, reopen it, and resync it with the database.

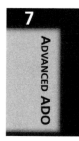

LISTING 7.9 SAVING A RECORDSET TO DISK, OPENING IT AGAIN, AND RESYNCING WITH THE ORIGINAL DATABASE

```
Sub RstPersistence_Save()

'This example will show you how to
'take a recordset, disconnect it from the database,
'store it on disk and then sync it to the db
'The resync happens in RstPersistence_Open
'From "Microsoft Access 2000 Development Unleashed" (SAMS)
'By: Forte, Howe, Ralston

Dim strSQL As String
Dim strMsg As String
Dim strNewValue As String
Dim conn As ADODB.Connection
Dim rst As ADODB.Recordset

On Error GoTo Proc_Err

strSQL = "Select * From Customers Where CustomerID='ALFKI'"

Set conn = New ADODB.Connection
With conn
    .Provider = "Microsoft.Jet.OLEDB.4.0"
    .ConnectionString = "data source=c:\sample.mdb"
    .Open
End With
```

continues

LISTING 7.9   CONTINUED

```
Set rst = New ADODB.Recordset

'Must use a client cursor with the operation
rst.CursorLocation = adUseClient
rst.Open strSQL, _
    conn, adOpenStatic, adLockBatchOptimistic

'Ask the user to change the record, but
'show the user the current data
strMsg = "Please Enter in a new CompanyName for: " & _
    rst!CompanyName & vbNewLine & _
    "This CustomerID=" & rst!CustomerID

'Get the New Name
strNewValue = InputBox(strMsg)

'Change a record only on client and save to disk
'This does NOT make the change to the database
rst.Update "CompanyName", strNewValue
'The change was only committed to the client recordset

On Error Resume Next
'Get rid of the current file to make room for the new one
Kill "c:\hcado.dat"

On Error GoTo Proc_Err
'Save the recordset to disk
rst.Save "c:\hcado.dat", adPersistADTG

rst.Close
Set rst = Nothing

MsgBox "Saved to: c:\hcado.dat", vbInformation

Proc_Exit:
    Exit Sub

Proc_Err:
    MsgBox Err.Description
    Resume Proc_Exit

End Sub

Sub RstPersistence_Open()

'This example will show you how to
'take a recordset, disconnect it from the database,
'store it on disk and then sync it to the db
'The data dump happened in RstPersistence_Save
```

```
'The resync happens here
'From "Microsoft Access 2000 Development Unleashed" (SAMS)
'By: Forte, Howe, Ralston

Dim conn As ADODB.Connection
Dim rst As ADODB.Recordset
Dim strSQL As String
Dim strMsg As String

On Error GoTo Proc_Err

strSQL = "Select * From Customers Where CustomerID='ALFKI'"

'Open a NEW recordset from Disk
Set rst = New ADODB.Recordset
rst.Open "c:\hcado.dat", , adOpenStatic, adLockBatchOptimistic, adCmdFile

'Shows the Original Value vs Saved on Disk
strMsg = "Value in DataSource: " & _
                rst!CompanyName.OriginalValue
strMsg = strMsg & vbNewLine & _
    "Value on Disk          : " & rst!CompanyName

'Display the values
MsgBox strMsg, vbInformation, "Original Value vs Saved on Disk"

'Ok, now update the database with the disk's version
'must reconnect to the database now
Set conn = New ADODB.Connection
With conn
    .Provider = "Microsoft.Jet.OLEDB.4.0"
    .ConnectionString = "data source=c:\sample.mdb"
    .Open
End With

'reconnect the recordset to the
'the database and resync
rst.ActiveConnection = conn
rst.UpdateBatch

MsgBox "Database Re-Synced!", vbInformation

Proc_Exit:
    Exit Sub

Proc_Err:
    MsgBox Err.Description
    Resume Proc_Exit

End Sub
```

Data Definition with ADOx

With ADO, you can easily perform data definition. To create and modify tables, queries, and other data objects like indices, you have to use a special ADO Library called ADOx. To use ADOx, you have to set a reference to Microsoft ADO Ext. 2.1 For DDL and Security from Tools, References in the VBE as shown in Figure 7.8.

FIGURE 7.8

Microsoft ADO Ext. 2.1 For DDL and Security.

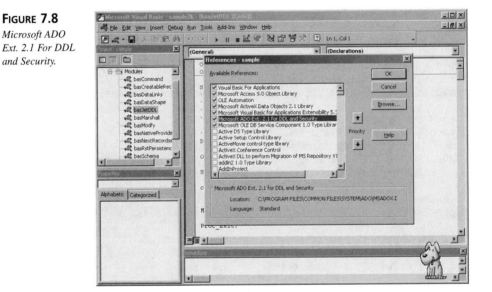

When you have your reference set, you are ready to use ADOx.

The Catalog Object

When using ADOx, everything revolves around a `catalog` object. A `catalog` represents a database. With Access, all you have to do is set the `catalog`'s `ActiveConnection` property to a valid `ADO Command` object to start working.

```
Dim cat As ADOx.Catalog
Set cat = New ADOx.Catalog
'Point the Catalog Object to
'The Current Database
cat.ActiveConnection = CurrentProject.Connection
```

Creating a Database

To create a new blank database with ADOx, you have to use the `Create` method of the catalog object and pass it the path of the new database as shown in Listing 7.10.

LISTING 7.10 CREATING A DATABASE WITH ADOx

```
Sub CreateDataBase()
'This procedure will create a new database
'using ADOx
'From "Microsoft Access 2000 Development Unleashed" (SAMS)
'By: Forte, Howe, Ralston

'The Catalog Object in ADOx
Dim cat As ADOx.Catalog

On Error GoTo Proc_Err

Set cat = New ADOx.Catalog

cat.Create "provider=Microsoft.JET.OLEDB.4.0;" & _
    "data source=C:\newdb.mdb"

MsgBox "Database Created!", vbInformation

Proc_Exit:
    Exit Sub

Proc_Err:
    MsgBox Err.Description
    Resume Proc_Exit

End Sub
```

Creating Tables and Fields

To create a table and its fields, you can create an ADOx `table` object and append columns to it as shown in Listing 7.11.

LISTING 7.11 CREATING TABLES AND FIELDS

```
Sub CreateTable_JOLT40()
'This example creates a table and
'fields in the current database
'From "Microsoft Access 2000 Development Unleashed" (SAMS)
'By: Forte, Howe, Ralston
```

continues

LISTING 7.11   CONTINUED

```
'ADOx Objects
Dim cat As ADOx.Catalog
Dim tbl As ADOx.Table

On Error GoTo Proc_Err

Set cat = New ADOx.Catalog
'Point the Catalog Object to
'The Current Database
cat.ActiveConnection = CurrentProject.Connection

Set tbl = New ADOx.Table
'This creates the actual table
With tbl
    .Name = "Customer_ADO"
    .Columns.Append "CustomerID", adInteger
    .Columns.Append "Name_Prefix", adWChar, 25
    .Columns.Append "Name_First", adWChar, 25
    .Columns.Append "Name_Last", adWChar, 50
End With

cat.Tables.Append tbl

Proc_Exit:
    Exit Sub

Proc_Err:
    MsgBox Err.Description
    Resume Proc_Exit

End Sub
```

Creating a Linked Table

To create a linked table in Access, you have to create a table and then not append any fields to it. Then you have to set two properties:

- `Jet OLEDB:Link Datasource`
- `Jet OLEDB:Remote Table Name`

Set Link Datasource to the path of the back end database you want to link to. Set Remote Table Name to the name of the table in the backend database. Listing 7.12 shows a full example.

LISTING 7.12   CREATING A LINKED TABLE

```
Sub CreateAttachedJetTable()
'Creates a Linked Access table
'From "Microsoft Access 2000 Development Unleashed" (SAMS)
'By: Forte, Howe, Ralston
Dim cat  As ADOx.Catalog
Dim tbl  As ADOx.Table

Set cat = New ADOx.Catalog
' Open the catalog
cat.ActiveConnection = CurrentProject.Connection

Set tbl = New ADOx.Table
' Create the new Table
tbl.Name = "Customers_Linked"
'Shortcut for creating table
Set tbl.ParentCatalog = cat

' Set the properties to create the link
tbl.Properties("Jet OLEDB:Link Datasource") = "F:\backend\datafile.mdb"
tbl.Properties("Jet OLEDB:Remote Table Name") = "Customers"

' Append the table to the tables collection
cat.Tables.Append tbl

Set cat = Nothing

Proc_Exit:
    Exit Sub

Proc_Err:
    MsgBox Err.Description
    Resume Proc_Exit
End Sub
```

Setting a Field's Properties

In ADOx, after you have created a field, you can use the ADOx Column object to set properties specific to your field. You can set a field to be an AutoNumber by setting its AutoIncrement property to True as shown here:

```
Dim col As ADOx.Column
'Point the Column Object to the
'CustomerID Field
Set col = tbl.Columns("CustomerID")
'Set the Column to an AutoIncrement Field
col.Properties("AutoIncrement") = True
```

There are other properties that you can set for a column object. Table 7.4 summarizes them all and maps them to their old DAO equivalent.

TABLE 7.4 THE Field OBJECT'S PROPERTIES

DAO Field		*ADOx Column*	
Property	*Value*	*Property*	*Value*
Attributes	dbAutoIncrField	AutoIncrement	True
Attributes	dbFixedField	ColumnAttributes	adColFixed
Attributes	dbHyperlinkField	Jet OLEDB:Hyperlink	True
Attributes	dbSystemField		
Attributes	dbVariableField	ColumnAttributes	Not adColFixed

Creating an Index

Creating an index in ADOx will have to use the key object. After creating a key object, you have to append a field to it and then specify if it is going to be primary, unique and what sort order to use as shown here:

```
Set idx = New ADOx.Index
'This sets the index to
'be the primary key and sets it
'to descending order
With idx
    .Name = "PrimaryKey"
    .Columns.Append "CustomerID"
    .Columns("CustomerID").SortOrder = adSortDescending
    .IndexNulls = adIndexNullsDisallow
    .PrimaryKey = True
End With
'Appends the index to the table
tbl.Indexes.Append idx
```

By default, the IndexNulls property is adIndexNullsDisallow which indicates that Null values aren't allowed in the index and that no index entry will be added if a field in the index contains Null. Table 7.5 fully describes the acceptable values for the IndexNulls property and also maps them back to their old DAO equivalent.

TABLE 7.5   VALUES FOR THE IndexNulls PROPERTY

DAO	ADOx	Description	
	Required	Ignore Nulls	Index Nulls
True	False	adIndexNullsDisallow	A Null value isn't allowed in the index field; no index entry added.
False	True	adIndexNullsIgnore	A Null value is allowed in the index field; no index entry added.
False	False	adIndexNullsIgnoreAny	A Null value is allowed in the index field; index entry added.

The code in Listing 7.13 brings all the examples together and creates a table, AutoNumber field, and PrimaryKey index on the table.

LISTING 7.13   CREATING A TABLE WITH AN AutoNumber AND PrimaryKey

```
Sub CreateCreateAutoNumberrPK()
'This example creates a table and
'fields in the current database
'From "Microsoft Access 2000 Development Unleashed" (SAMS)
'By: Forte, Howe, Ralston


'ADOx Objects
Dim cat As ADOx.Catalog
Dim tbl As ADOx.Table
Dim idx As ADOx.Index

On Error GoTo Proc_Err

Set cat = New ADOx.Catalog
'Point the Catalog Object to
'The Current Database
cat.ActiveConnection = CurrentProject.Connection

Set tbl = New ADOx.Table
'This creates the actual table
With tbl
    .Name = "Customer_ADO"
    .ParentCatalog = cat
```

continues

7

ADVANCED ADO

LISTING 7.13   CONTINUED

```
    .Columns.Append "CustomerID", adInteger
    'Set the AutoNumber field
    .Columns("CustomerID").Properties("Autoincrement") = True
    .Columns.Append "Name_Prefix", adWChar, 25
    .Columns.Append "Name_First", adWChar, 25
    .Columns.Append "Name_Last", adWChar, 50
End With
'Append the table to the catalog
cat.Tables.Append tbl

'This creates the index object
Set idx = New ADOx.Index
'This sets the index to
'be the primary key and sets it
'to descending order
With idx
    .Name = "PrimaryKey"
    .Columns.Append "CustomerID"
    .Columns("CustomerID").SortOrder = adSortDescending
    .IndexNulls = adIndexNullsDisallow
    .PrimaryKey = True
End With
'Appends the index to the table
tbl.Indexes.Append idx

'Clean up
Set cat = Nothing

Proc_Exit:
    Exit Sub

Proc_Err:
    MsgBox Err.Description
    Resume Proc_Exit

End Sub
```

Creating Relationships in ADOx

To create a relationship in ADOx, you have to create a key object, append its properties, and append the new key to a table object. Use the following syntax:

```
cat.Tables("Products").Keys.Append key
```

The code in Listing 7.14 brings this all together and creates a new relationship.

LISTING 7.14 CREATING A RELATIONSHIP

```
Sub CreateForeignKey()
'Will create a Relationship in
'Northwind from Products to Categories
'From "Microsoft Access 2000 Development Unleashed" (SAMS)
'By: Forte, Howe, Ralston

Dim cat As ADOx.Catalog
Dim key As ADOx.key

On Error GoTo Proc_Err

'Create the ADOx Objects
Set cat = New ADOx.Catalog
Set key = New ADOx.key

' Open the catalog to the current database
cat.ActiveConnection = CurrentProject.Connection

'Set the properties of the new Key object
With key
        'The name of the Key in the
        'database, must be unique
        .Name = "CategoriesProducts"
        'The type of key that it is
        .Type = adKeyForeign
        'Set the "ONE" of the one to many
        .RelatedTable = "Categories"
        'The field name in the "many" table
        .Columns.Append "CategoryID"
        'The "one" field in the "one" table
        .Columns("CategoryID").RelatedColumn = "CategoryID"
        'Specify the cascades
        .UpdateRule = adRICascade
End With

    'Specify the many table here and
    'append the new key object to it
    cat.Tables("Products").Keys.Append key


Proc_Exit:
    Exit Sub

Proc_Err:
    MsgBox Err.Description
    Resume Proc_Exit

End Sub
```

7

ADVANCED ADO

Creating Queries in ADOx

To create a query in ADOx, you have to use an empty ADO command object and set its command text. Then append it to the current catalog object like so:

```
cmd.CommandText = "Select * FROM Categories"
'Append the query to the collection
cat.Views.Append "qryCategories", cmd
```

When you are referring to a query in Access, you have to remember that Microsoft Jet 4.0 handles all your table, query, and field, and index objects for you. Microsoft Jet defines Access queries as one of two types:

- Views
- Procedures

A view is considered a row-returning, non-parameter query while a procedure will contain everything else.

Creating a View

Microsoft Jet will handle the definition of your query for you. So to create a view, just create the query as you would normally via a command object as shown in Listing 7.15.

LISTING 7.15 CREATING A VIEW IN ADOx

```
Sub CreateView()
'Create a new Query (View)
'From "Microsoft Access 2000 Development Unleashed" (SAMS)
'By: Forte, Howe, Ralston

Dim cat As ADOx.Catalog
Dim cmd  As ADODB.Command

Set cat = New ADOx.Catalog
Set cmd = New ADODB.Command

' Open the catalog
cat.ActiveConnection = CurrentProject.Connection
' Create the query
cmd.CommandText = "Select * FROM Categories"
'Append the query to the collection
cat.Views.Append "qryCategories", cmd

Set cat = Nothing

Proc_Exit:
    Exit Sub
```

```
Proc_Err:
    MsgBox Err.Description
    Resume Proc_Exit

End Sub
```

Creating a Procedure

As with a view, creating a procedure is straightforward. Just define your `commandtext` and append it to the catalog as shown in Listing 7.16.

LISTING 7.16   CREATING A PROCEDURE

```
Sub CreateProcedure()
'Create a Query (Procedure)
'From "Microsoft Access 2000 Development Unleashed" (SAMS)
'By: Forte, Howe, Ralston

Dim cat As ADOx.Catalog
Dim cmd As ADODB.Command

Set cat = New ADOx.Catalog
Set cmd = New ADODB.Command

' Open the catalog
cat.ActiveConnection = CurrentProject.Connection

'Create the Command
cmd.CommandText = "Parameters [@Region] Text;" & _
    "Select * from Employees where Region = [@Region]"

'Create the Procedure
cat.Procedures.Append "qryEmployeesRegion", cmd

Set cat = Nothing


Proc_Exit:
    Exit Sub

Proc_Err:
    MsgBox Err.Description
    Resume Proc_Exit
End Sub
```

7

ADVANCED ADO

Modifying a Query's SQL Statement

To modify a current query's SQL statement, you first have to create a command object based on a current query in your database. Then modify its commandtext property and then reset the command as shown in Listing 7.17.

LISTING 7.17   RESETTING A SQL STATEMENT

```
Sub ModifyQuerySQL()
'Change a query's SQL
'From "Microsoft Access 2000 Development Unleashed" (SAMS)
'By: Forte, Howe, Ralston
Dim cat As ADOx.Catalog
Dim cmd As ADODB.Command

On Error GoTo Proc_Err

Set cat = New ADOx.Catalog
Set cmd = New ADODB.Command

' Open the catalog
cat.ActiveConnection = CurrentProject.Connection

' Get the query from the database
Set cmd = cat.Procedures("qryEmployeesRegion").Command

' Update the SQL Statement
cmd.CommandText = "Parameters [forms]![frmOrder]![txtRegion] Text;" & _
    "Select * from Employees " & _
        "Where Region = [forms]![frmOrder]![txtRegion] "

'Save the updated query
Set cat.Procedures("qryEmployeesRegion").Command = cmd

Set cat = Nothing

Proc_Exit:
    Exit Sub

Proc_Err:
    MsgBox Err.Description
    Resume Proc_Exit

End Sub
```

You'll notice that in the ADO code shown in Listing 7.17, setting the `Procedure` object's `Command` property to the modified `Command` object saves the changes. If this last step were not included, the changes would not have been persisted to the database. This difference results from the fact that ADO `Command` objects are designed to be temporary. This is very important because DAO considered `Querydefs` as permanent objects. You may think that the following ADO code examples are equivalent:

```
Set cmd = cat.Procedures("qryEmployeesRegion ").Command
cmd.CommandText = "Parameters [@Region] Text;" & _
    "Select * from Employees where Region = [@Region]"
Set cat.Procedures("qryEmployeesRegion ").Command = cmd
```

and

```
cat.Procedures("qryEmployeesRegion ").CommandText = _
 "Parameters [@Region] Text;" & _
 "Select * from Employees where Region = [@Region] "
```

Although they look like they will do the same thing, the second piece of code will not actually update the query in the database. In the second example, you can use the command object with its new SQL in your VBA code; however, when you are done working with it, the SQL changes will not be saved back to the database. In the first example, because you are explicitly saving the cmd, the changes will be reflected in the database.

Summary

This chapter covered a lot of ground on ADO and ADOx. As you can see, ADO and ADOx are fully featured, flexible, and very powerful. ADO and ADOx are a great new data access technology and as you will see in Chapters 15 and 1. ADO is just as easy to use with SQL Server as it is with Access. I hope you can take these examples and begin to build great Access applications around ADO and ADOx.

7

ADVANCED ADO

User Interfaces Unleashed

PART

III

Advanced Form Design

CHAPTER 8

Forms will make or break your application. This is true not because forms are necessarily the heart of an Access application, but because that is where users spend the most time. To that end, Microsoft has invested a great deal of time and money in making Access forms both simple and very powerful.

This session does not attempt to explain every detail and feature of Access form development (the subject is huge and there are plenty of good books on the subject for beginners and seasoned veterans alike). To give you as much detail as possible within a workable frame, I will focus on some of the form settings and properties that can simplify your development effort and deliver tremendous functionality. I will then look at how to use some of the controls found in Access, and show you how they can help you develop forms that go beyond mere data entry. By the end of this chapter, you will be able to design forms that not only provide more functionality to your users, but also create forms that are easier to work with and more visually appealing.

This session will start by looking at the properties and settings in Access 2000. Next, I'll look at some of the more advanced controls in the Access toolbox, especially the list and combo box controls. I'll look at the option group and how to use it with command buttons, check boxes, or option buttons. Then I will examine how manipulating subforms can increase the power of your forms without the overhead of multiple pages or numerous extra controls.

Finally, I will look at some of the exciting ActiveX controls that ship with the Office 2000 Developer Edition (ODE), and how to work these into your applications for even more functionality.

Form Properties

Access 2000 forms have 81 defined properties on the Properties page for you to choose from (see Figure 8.1). A complete discussion of them would, and has, taken whole sections of how-to books. I've pulled out the few properties that can have a significant impact on your work as a developer. For a detailed look at other properties, see Alison Balter's excellent book *Mastering Access 97 Development*. Look for the updated edition of this book for Access 2000 as well.

Data Properties

Forms in Access 2000 are closely tied to the data behind them. You can easily create a form and start entering data without writing a single line of code. This type of functionality can be achieved through the use of the data properties, which, as the name suggests, describe the way a form should present and work with data.

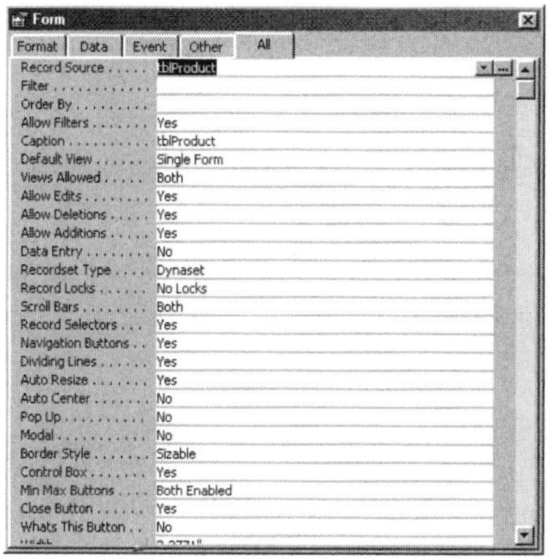

FIGURE 8.1

*The Form
Properties dialog
box.*

Record Source

This is probably the most used property on a form. With it you can bind your forms to
tables, queries, SQL statements, or nothing at all. The property can be set at runtime or at
design time, depending on your needs.

> **NOTE**
>
> If you do not specify a Record Source at design time, you cannot bind individual
> fields on your form to the Record Source.

Allow Edits

When set to True, users can edit data on a form. When False, users cannot. This is a
handy way to quickly make a form read-only.

Allow Deletions

When set to True, users can delete records from the form. Use this property to control
which users can delete records from your database.

Allow Additions

When set to False, users cannot add new records to your database. This is handy when
you are displaying the results of a query in Datasheet mode but don't want your users to
add new records at the end of the result set.

Data Entry

Setting this property to True will restrict your users from seeing existing data, but will enable them to add new records.

Allow Filters, Filter, Order By

These properties enable you to restrict the recordset of a bound form by specifying a WHERE clause in the Filter property or a sort order in the Order By property. The Allow Filters property tells Access whether or not to read these values when the form is opened.

Generally, you might not need to use these properties. By using queries in the Record Source property, you can assign parameters and a sort order in one step versus two when you use the Filter and Order By properties. In addition, by using the Record Source property you can take advantage of optimized queries, which run faster.

Formatting Properties

Forms are what the users see. They might not be the most ingenious part of your application, but the users do not know that. The very important first impression about your application comes from the forms. The way they look, behave, and make their daily tasks easier (or harder) is very important to them and to you, the developer. Setting the formatting properties is a way to control the look and feel of your forms.

Default View

Setting this property tells Access how to open the form. Your choices are

- Single Form: Displays one record at a time.
- Continuous Form: Displays multiple records, each with its own copy of the form in the form's detail section.
- Datasheet: Displays the data in rows and columns like a spreadsheet.

Views Allowed

By setting this property, you can restrict the number of ways users can view your data at runtime. This can be useful if you only want users to see one record at a time, or only want the data presented in Datasheet view. Your choices are

- Form
- Datasheet
- Both

Scrollbars

Setting this property will enable/disable the vertical and horizontal scrollbars on your form.

Record Selectors

This property turns the record selectors on the left-hand side of the form on or off. In single forms, this property is generally turned off; in Datasheet or continuous forms, it's a good idea to turn it on.

Navigation Buttons

If you want Access to handle record navigation, set this property to True. If you want to handle it yourself, set it to False. This will prevent the selector bar from appearing at the bottom of the form.

Border Style

Access forms can be displayed with a variety of borders, each with a specific purpose:

- Sizeable: Allows users to resize the form at runtime. The control box is enabled with the Minimize and the Maximize buttons enabled.
- Dialog: Fixes the size of the form at runtime. The Minimize and the Maximize buttons are disabled. This setting is great for message boxes and pop-up forms.
- Thin: Fixes the size of the forms at runtime. The Minimize and the Maximize buttons are enabled.
- None: No border is present. This setting is best for splash screens.

Control Box

This property determines whether or not the Minimize, Maximize, and Close buttons are displayed.

Min Max Buttons

When set to True, users can minimize or maximize forms on their desktops.

Close Button

When set to True, users can use the control menu to close the form.

8

ADVANCED FORM DESIGN

> **CAUTION**
>
> If you set this property to False, you must provide another way for your users to exit the form. Otherwise they will have to use Crtl+F4 to close the form, or Alt+F4. Besides that, the only other way to close the form is to shut down Access.

Other Properties

Other Properties are as important as the categorized properties described above. They control a few important aspects of the form's behavior and act as an "Advanced" set of properties used to put finishing touches on the form. New in this release of Access is the AllowDesignChanges property described below.

Modal

When this property is set to True, opening the form prevents any other form from receiving the focus until the modal form is closed. This is effective for error messages or critical order of operation functions where the user must do certain actions in certain ways before proceeding.

Pop-up

Pop-up forms are child forms of the Access window. This makes them different from non–pop-up forms, which are children of the form that they are opened in. This means that pop-up forms will sit on top of all other forms and can be placed anywhere on the Access desktop. Custom toolbar forms make good pop-up forms.

Menu Bar, Toolbar

If you have developed custom menus or toolbars you want associated with a particular form, setting this property will cause that menu or toolbar to appear when the form opens.

Shortcut Menu

When set to True, Access will display the menu selected in the Shortcut Menu Bar property whenever the user right-clicks on the form.

Shortcut Menu Bar

If you have developed a custom shortcut menu for the form, selecting it here and setting the Shortcut Menu property to True, will tell Access to display your menu whenever the user right-clicks on the form.

Tag

This property can be used to store any value you want. You can get at it from anywhere in your application and it will be saved with the form.

> **CAUTION**
>
> If you have code behind a form and you set the Has Module property to False, all your code will be deleted. Access warns you of this fact.

Has Module

When set to False, Access will remove all code written behind the form. This "light-weight" form loads very fast.

If a form contains no code behind it, definitely set this property to True. You will elimi-nate an overhead of Access attempting to compile the form on each load. A limited extra functionality can still be achieved without writing code by inserting a hyperlink (described later in this chapter) onto the form in Design view and linking it to an object in a database (see Figure 8.2).

FIGURE 8.2
Edit Hyperlink Properties dialog box.

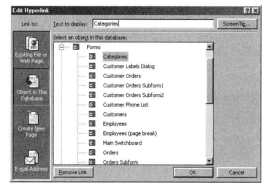

Allow Design Changes

Setting this property to True (All Views) keeps the Form Properties dialog open while the form is running, allowing you to modify changes and see them "live" in your appli-cation. Do not forget to set it back to False (Design View Only) when you are done.

Useful Properties Not on the Property Sheet

As always, things hidden are more interesting to us than those that are evident. The same applies to the hidden form properties. In this case, hidden properties provide extra convenience in developing complex form-driven applications with Access.

OpenArgs

This property is only available at runtime. With it, you can pass a string value from one form and have another form read that value in.

```
'Syntax for sending form:
Docmd.OpenForm "MyForm", "some string value"

'Syntax for receiving form:
Dim x as string
If not isnull(OpenArgs) then
 X = Me.OpenArgs
 'perform special formatting
end if
```

The OpenArgs property is useful when you are using modal forms to gather required information. If you want to format a form in a slightly different way, depending on the logic of your program, you can use OpenArgs to send a "message" to the form and pick it up on the Form_Open event. Inside the event, you can format your form to look differently or even prevent it from scrolling from record to record to concentrate on the one record you must edit. You will not be able to change the form programmatically after you open it as a dialog, so the only way to build logic in a dialog form is through the use of an OpenArgs property.

User-Defined Properties

In the general declarations section of a form, declaring a variable as public or private will create a user-defined property. In order for the property to be accessible from other modules, you must declare your property variable as public. If you need to make this property available to other forms, or would like to add validation when retrieving or setting this value, you can use Property Get and Property Let statements to do the validation.

For example, suppose you are writing a driver's license processing application and one of the requirements is that the driver's age must be at least 16. You could write the following property validation to handle the reading/writing of the property.

In general declarations:

```
' Create intMyAge variable in memory.
Dim intMyAge as Integer
```

```
'Use this code to read in an input value and verify it meets your
'criteria.

Public Property Let MyAge(byval  intAge as Integer)
If intAge < 16 then
      Msgbox "Driver's age may not be less than 16 _ years"
Else
 IntMyAge=intAge
 End if
End Property
```

Use this code to add a `Property Get` statement to make your value available outside your form.

```
Public Property Get MyAge() as Integer
      MyAge = intMyAge
End Property
```

When you want to see the property you created in an IntelliSense drop-down box (as you are coding it), you must declare a form variable as type Form_*name_of_your_form*.

Events

Access has more than 30 events to help you control program flow. It is imperative that you understand in what order events fire. The following indicates the order events fire under different circumstances. Some of the events pass the `Cancel` parameter, which can be set to `True` if you want to stop opening or closing the form. When you set `Cancel` parameter to `True`, Access picks up after the event stopped running, and raises an error 2501. You must handle this error, or risk getting an ugly Access error (see Figure 8.3).

FIGURE 8.3

Access Error 2501 after Cancel *parameter is set to* True.

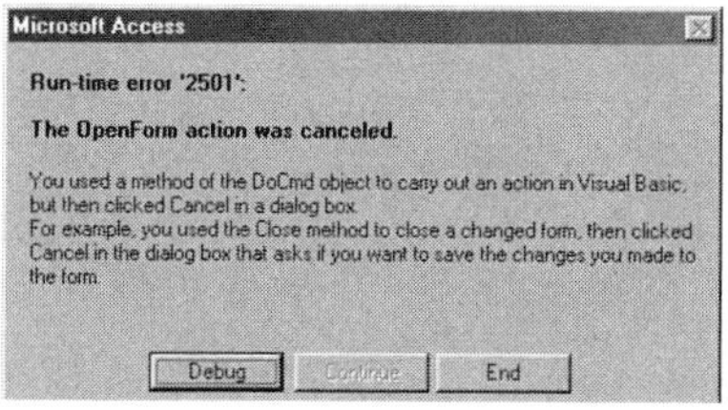

Windows operation system is event based. That means that excluding the timer inside the PC, the only source of any action is the user. The OS responds to the numerous events fired each nanosecond and passes them to the active application. Below is a listing of events that fire when the user works with an Access form.

Form Opens

As the form opens the following events fire in the order described below. Once the `Cancel` parameter is set to `True`, execution of events halts.

1. Open (with cancel option)
2. Load
3. Resize
4. Activate
5. Current
6. First in Tab order Enter
7. First in Tab order Got Focus

> **NOTE**
>
> If there are no controls on the form, the form itself will receive the focus.

If the form has a subform, the following events fire BEFORE the main form's open event.

1. Open (with cancel option)
2. Load
3. Resize
4. Current
5. First Control Enter
6. First Control Got Focus

This allows you to access the fields on the subform, from main form's `Open` event, and cancel if needed.

Form Closes

As the form closes, the following events fire in the order described below. Once the `Cancel` parameter is set to `True`, execution of events halts.

1. Unload (with cancel option)
2. Deactivate
3. Close

Form Sized

As the form is resized, the following events fire in the order described below.

1. Resize
2. Deactivate

Form Maximized

As the form is maximized, the following events fire in the order described below.

1. Resize

Minimized Form Restored

As the form is restored, the following events fire in the order described below.

1. Activate
2. Resize

Access Form Controls

Access 2000 comes with a variety of built-in controls to aid you in development. Some controls, such as the text box, haven't changed much since Access 1.0. Others, such as the list box, have had significant changes. In this session, I'll highlight the capabilities of some of the more interesting controls found in Access.

The `Combo` `Box` Control

Combo boxes create lists of predefined values that your users can pick from to simplify the task of data entry. Most combo boxes are based on queries or SQL statements and typically have one or two columns and a bound field. Although this is usually enough for most developers, there are some interesting capabilities in Access 2000 combo boxes that can add tremendous functionality.

Using the `Not` `In` `List` Event

The `Not In List` event automatically fires whenever a value not found on the list is entered. This gives the developer a chance to examine the value, and then decide how best to handle it.

For example, suppose you provided a combo box of clients, and a user entered a client that was not created yet. Using the following code, you could trap this error and ask the user if he or she wanted to create the client:

```
Dim MyResponse As Variant
Dim Msg As String

'This routine only fires when an item that is not in the list is
'detected.
Msg = "The customer " & NewData & " could not be found, _
do you wish to add the customer?"

'Inform the user that a new value is present.
MyResponse = MsgBox(Msg, vbInformation + vbYesNo, _
"Customer Not Found")

'If yes, add code to handle the new value.
If MyResponse = vbYes Then

MsgBox "Put your add code here", vbInformation _
+ vbOKOnly, "Ready to Add"
Me.cboUser = ""

Else

'If no, enter code to recover or prompt user for _
a valid value.
MsgBox "Please select another customer from the _
list", vbInformation + vbOKOnly, "Select _
Another Customer"

End If

' Notify Access to continue. See the online help file for a
' description of Event Procedure Constants.
Response = acDataErrContinue
```

Making a Combo Box Drop Down Automatically

How many times have you wished you could just tab into a combo box and have the list drop down without having to do a SendKeys command? In Access 97, the following code in the Enter event is all you need:

```
ActiveControl.DropDown
```

That's it!

Creating Your Own Drop-Down Lists

Usually, the values in the drop-down box come from a table or a query. But this is not your only choice. By setting the Row Source Type property to Field List you can choose to view the fields of the underlying table or query. Or you can set the Row Source Type property to the name of the function you create to display a custom list. Even though you might not see the benefit of such an option right away, it comes in handy in situations like adding an extra value to the list like an All value. This option will also help if you need to display a list of right-justified currency values useful for accountants. The latter is implemented by padding the values on the left with spaces, and displaying them in a monospaced font like Courier.

Here's a code sample taken from the Solutions.mdb database, which shows you how to add an extra (All) value to top of the list in the combo box.

```
Function AddAllToList(ctl As Control, lngID As Long, _
        lngRow As Long, lngCol As Long, intCode As Integer) As Variant

'Adds "(All)" to the top of a combo box or list box.
'You can add "(All)" in a different column of the combo
'box or list box by setting the control's Tag property
'to a different column number, or display text other
'than "(All)" by appending a semicolon(;) and the text
'you want to display. For example, setting the Tag
'property to "2;<None>" displays "<None>"

'in the second column of the list.

Static dbs As Database, rst As Recordset
Static lngDisplayID As Long
Static intDisplayCol As Integer
Static strDisplayText As String
Dim intSemiColon As Integer

On Error GoTo Err_AddAllToList
 Select Case intCode
  Case acLBInitialize
 ' See if function is already in use.
  If lngDisplayID <> 0 Then
        MsgBox "AddAllToList is already in use by another control!"
        AddAllToList = False

        Exit Function
  End If

'Parse the display column and display text from Tag property.
        intDisplayCol = 1
        strDisplayText = "(All)"
        If Not IsNull(ctl.Tag) Then
                intSemiColon = InStr(ctl.Tag, ";")
                If intSemiColon = 0 Then
                    intDisplayCol = Val(ctl.Tag)
                Else
                    intDisplayCol = Val(Left(ctl.Tag, intSemiColon - 1))
```

8

ADVANCED FORM
DESIGN

```
                         strDisplayText = Mid(ctl.Tag, intSemiColon + 1)

                    End If
            End If

            ' Open the recordset defined in the RowSource property.
            Set dbs = CurrentDb
            Set rst = dbs.OpenRecordset(ctl.RowSource, dbOpenSnapshot)

            ' Record and return the lngID for this function.
            lngDisplayID = Timer
            AddAllToList = lngDisplayID
    Case acLBOpen
            AddAllToList = lngDisplayID
    Case acLBGetRowCount
    ' Return number of rows in recordset.
            On Error Resume Next
            rst.MoveLast
            AddAllToList = rst.RecordCount + 1

    Case acLBGetColumnCount
    ' Return number of fields (columns) in recordset.
            AddAllToList = rst.Fields.Count

    Case acLBGetColumnWidth
            AddAllToList = -1

    Case acLBGetValue
        If lngRow = 0 Then
                If lngCol = intDisplayCol - 1 Then
                        AddAllToList = strDisplayText
                Else
                        AddAllToList = Null
                End If
            Else
                rst.MoveFirst
                rst.Move lngRow - 1
                AddAllToList = rst(lngCol)
        End If
    Case acLBEnd
            lngDisplayID = 0
            rst.Close
End Select

Bye_AddAllToList:
        Exit Function

Err_AddAllToList:
        MsgBox Err.Description, vbOKOnly + vbCritical, "AddAllToList"
        AddAllToList = False
        Resume Bye_AddAllToList
End Function
```

Retrieving More Than One Value from a Combo or List Box

Using the `Column` property, you can retrieve the value from any column in a combo or list box. The `Column` property is zero-based, so column 1 is read as column 0.

For example, to read the value from the fourth column of a combo box you would type

```
MyVariantvalue = Me!MyCombobox.Column(3)
```

List Boxes

The List Box control is similar to the Combo Box control described above. The differences include the option to view all the choices without having to "Drop Down" the list. And unlike the Combo Box control, List Box allows the selection of multiple values at the same time. This feature is useful when you want to let the user see information about 5 out of 100 entities (invoices, people, CDs, or trucks) in the system you are building. Because most of the features applied to the List Box control have been discussed already, I will concentrate on the differences.

The Multi-Select List Box Control

In Access 2, several tricks were devised to allow users to select several values from a list. Starting with Access 97, picking multiple values is easy with the Multi-Select List Box. However, retrieving the values selected is not quite as intuitive.

Property Settings

To use the Multi-Select List Box you must first set a standard list box to become a Multi-Select List. You do this by changing the `Multi Select` property in the control's property sheet. Your choices are shown in Table 8.1.

TABLE 8.1 MULTI-SELECT PROPERTY CHOICES

Value	Meaning
None	Multiple selection isn't allowed.
Simple	Multiple items are selected or deselected by clicking them with the mouse or pressing the Spacebar.
Extended	Multiple items are selected by holding down Shift and clicking them with the mouse or by holding down Shift and pressing an arrow key to extend the selection from the previously selected item to the current item. You can also select items by dragging with the mouse. Holding down Ctrl and clicking an item selects or deselects that item.

8

ADVANCED FORM DESIGN

To read the values out, you'll need to write a little code. For example, to read the values out of a list of employees, you could write the following code:

```
Dim strMsg As String
Dim strName As String
Dim i As Integer


'Create a string to hold the message.
strMsg = "The following Employees were selected: " _
& vbCr & vbCr

For i = 1 To Me.lstMulti.ListCount

'Test to see if the user selected this row.
    If Me.lstMulti.Selected(i) Then
'If yes, add the first column from the
'selected row to the message string.
        strName = Me.lstMulti.Column(0, i)

' Take the value of item data (the bound
' field) and add it to the string this
' will create the first and last name
' that are displayed.
strName = strName & Chr(32) & _ Me.lstMulti.ItemData(i)

        strMsg = strMsg & strName & vbCr

    End If

Next

MsgBox Msg
```

This code not only reads the value of the list box, but also uses the column property to read the values out of more than just the bound column.

Subforms

Subforms have always provided a great way to show data in one to many relationships. By using the Link Master and Link Child Fields, developers can quickly tie related data together.

Subforms also have another powerful feature. By changing the ControlSource property, developers can insert an unlimited number of subforms into the same main form. By using this technique, developers can create their own container objects, something Visual Basic developers have been able to do for quite a while. Containers let you group controls together and refer to them as a group.

Additionally, subforms are a great way to get around the 22-inch length limit in Access forms. Subforms also let your forms load faster because they will not have to load every potential form, list, or memo field a user might need. Developers can control how data is presented and limit the number of graphics or other resource-intensive forms.

Adding Subforms

There are two methods to add a subform to your forms:

- Select the subform control from the form design toolbox and drag it onto your main form. This creates a blank subform. You must then add a Control Source and set the Link Child and Link Master fields as needed.

- The second way is even simpler. Open your main form in Design view then go out to the database window. With both the Design view of your main form and the database window visible, drag the form you want to use as your subform from the database window to your main form. Access will attempt to link the parent and child fields and set the Record Source for you. Access will also size the subform so that it fits correctly, which can be a real headache for developers who do it manually.

- Use the Subform Wizard that comes with Access.

> **NOTE**
>
> In Access 97 the default state for the Control Wizards was on. In Access 2000 Microsoft has turned them off. To use the wizard, make sure that the Control Wizards button on the ToolBox toolbar is clicked in (see Figure 8.4). When you create a new subform in the forms' Design view, the Subform Wizard will automatically open.

Referencing a Subform

There are several ways to reference a control on a subform. The typical syntax is

```
Forms!MyForm!SubFormControlName.Form!ControlName
```

Access 2000 has improved on this rather lengthy and tedious method because the controls collection is the default collection for the form. Now you can reference the same object this way:

```
Forms!MyForm!SubFormControlName!ControlName
```

or

8

ADVANCED FORM
DESIGN

```
Me!MyForm!SubFormControlName!ControlName
```

Either way you do it, it will work.

Using the expression builder (Ctrl+F2) is a great way to make sure you get the syntax right.

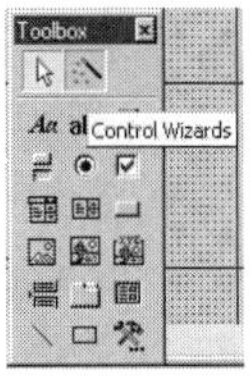

FIGURE 8.4

The ToolBox with the Control Wizards button clicked ON.

Built-In Tab Control

Another way for developers to group controls and preserve resources is by using tab controls. Access 2000 ships with an excellent one built right in. The Developers Edition has a tab strip control that provides similar capabilities, but it is a lot slower to use.

Option Frames

Visual Basic programmers have long enjoyed the ability to create control arrays (that is, the ability to reference a group of controls by the same name, but with a different index). The potential for simplifying property settings or changing values is immense. Unfortunately, Access doesn't provide this capability except in the Option Frame control.

With this control, you can place radio buttons, check boxes, or command buttons (toggle buttons) within the object frame, and then reference each object by its index value. You can turn the visible property of all controls within the frame on or off with one command instead of five or six, and you can use the For Each command to run through the values in the option group instead of testing each one individually.

Pop-up Menus

Windows 95 has made pop-up menus cool. Most users going back to Windows 3x after using 95 for a while curse their inability to right-click on anything. Pop-up menus provide a great way to shortcut to common tasks or provide specialized, on-time features for various controls. Forms, or even individual controls, can have their own pop-up menus, and with a little bit of code you can modify the look of your command bars on-the-fly.

To create a pop-up menu, right-click any toolbar or menu bar and select Customize. Or on the View menu, point to Toolbars, and then click Customize.

1. On the Toolbars tab, click New....

2. In the Toolbar Name box, type the name you want, and then click OK.

3. On the Toolbars tab, click Properties.

4. In the Type list, click Popup.

5. Set the AllowCustomizing property the way you want, and then click Close. *Don't worry—you didn't lose it.*

6. In the Toolbars box on the Toolbars tab, click Shortcut Menus.

7. On the Shortcut Menus toolbar, click the Custom category. That's where you find your new pop-up menu.

8. To complete the menu, do the following.

   Add commands from the Customize dialog box.

   Move or copy commands from other menus.

Hyperlinks

Hyperlinks are great controls that enable users to jump to forms, reports, Excel spreadsheets, Word documents, or even Web pages just by clicking on the hyperlink text. Because there is no code behind them, they are ideal in navigation forms because they can be used on lightweight forms (those with `Has Module` property set to `False`). A hyperlink is an unattached label (a label without a parent control) with `Hyperlink Address` or `Hyperlink SubAddress` property set to anything but `Null`.

Summary

Developers spend enormous amounts of development time on form design. Forms are what your users will identify your application with. Professional, intelligent, and easy-to-use forms will convey the impression of a professional application. A good form provides an intuitive representation of data allowing easy navigation among its controls. Keep in mind that while you might be developing on a large 17-inch or 19-inch screen, the users, your target audience, might still use 15-inch or even 14-inch monitors. You can develop for the lowest common denominator (640×480 resolution) or create a way to resize controls and fonts on your form accordingly. Do not make the form too heavy with code. Remember, Access provides many tools to attach your forms to the data. Making

8

ADVANCED FORM
DESIGN

forms bound is an easy way to let Access handle data access and control. If the requirements of your project suggest a remote database with unbound data forms, consider switching your development package to Visual Basic.

In the Access 2000 world, you can still create some amazing applications. By utilizing the unbound ComboBox, for example, you can filter the records on the form down to the one you want to see and/or edit. By adding the "All" option to some of your Combo Boxes, you can open some powerful search options to your users. Or by checking for existence of data on the form's Open event, you can switch to the Create New Record form in case there is no data to view, edit, or delete.

The forms in the latest version of Access do not offer many new features, but I bet you will like seeing the subforms inside the main form during design process.

Enhancing Forms with ActiveX Controls

IN THIS CHAPTER

ActiveX controls add and extend functionality to Access applications beyond the capabilities provided by Access alone, making it easier to create and maintain applications. The possibilities are limitless.

In this chapter, you will learn about a number of ActiveX controls available today and how to add them to your Access forms. First, I will discuss what ActiveX controls are, where they come from, and other general information.

How to Use ActiveX Controls

You are already familiar with built-in controls such as the text box or command button controls that can be placed on Access forms. ActiveX controls work in much the same way, except the code that supports the functionality of the ActiveX control is stored in a separate file that must be installed before it can be used.

ActiveX controls enable you to easily incorporate additional functionality that is not already available in Access into your applications. For example, you might want to add a calendar or a grid control to your form. ActiveX controls are generally stored in the Windows/system directory and have a file extension of .OCX or .DLL.

ActiveX controls are not part of Access but can be used in Access applications. They run in the same process as the Access application, which provides excellent performance.

In this chapter, I will use ActiveX controls on Access forms. However, the same ActiveX controls can be used in Visual Basic applications, Office applications, and even Web applications.

> **TIP**
>
> Not all ActiveX controls work in all applications. A control that works well in Visual Basic might not work in Access, or vice versa. To determine if an ActiveX control works in Access, review the documentation for the control, or do your own testing.

Types of ActiveX Controls

There are two types of ActiveX controls: design-time controls and runtime controls.

Design-time controls are placed on Access forms but are never seen by the end user. These controls include code that provides functionality of use to the developer. Design-time controls are visible at design time, not at run time, so they remain invisible to the end user. Examples of design-time controls include the `Image` control and the Windows `Common Dialog` control.

Conversely, a runtime control contains a user interface that will be seen by the end user of the application. Examples of this control that will be discussed during this chapter include the `Toolbar` control, `MonthView` control, `ListView` control, and more. This type of control is visible at both design time and runtime. With runtime controls, users are allowed to manipulate the object directly in some way.

Where Can You Get ActiveX Controls?

There are undoubtedly numerous ActiveX controls already on your computer. You might have no idea where you acquired some of these controls. The following are some possibilities:

- Windows
- Microsoft Office applications
- Visual Basic
- Microsoft Internet Explorer
- Other applications
- Third-party vendors
- Downloads from Web sites
- Microsoft Office Developer Kit
- ActiveX controls you create yourself with C++, Java, or Visual Basic. See Chapter 20, "Using Visual Basic with Access," for information about building your own ActiveX controls.

> **TIP**
>
> You are advised to test the control before using it. Many controls are provided as free downloads from the Internet. Determine whether the ActiveX control meets your needs before purchasing the control.

Are ActiveX Controls Safe?

Not necessarily. ActiveX controls are software components that include code. A malicious developer could easily create an ActiveX control that could cause substantial damage to your computer system. You are advised to use ActiveX controls from only trusted vendors.

Can I Use and Distribute ActiveX Controls in My Application?

Just because an ActiveX control is on your computer does not mean you can use and distribute it with your application. The question to ask yourself is, "Do I have a legal right to use the ActiveX controls?"

It is important to carefully read the licensing agreement for the vendor who sold you the control. For example, you might have received controls when you purchased development tools from Microsoft. Read the licensing agreement to determine whether you can use or distribute the controls "royalty free." Similarly, if you purchase ActiveX controls from third-party vendors, read the licensing agreements to determine your rights to use and distribute the controls.

Other controls you might not have purchased might have been downloaded from the World Wide Web. Presumably, you would have no right to distribute those controls with your application. Often, when you attempt to use an ActiveX control in your application, you may be warned that you do not have the right to use and distribute the control.

Licensing agreements are enforceable by law. Improper use and distribution of an ActiveX control is similar to illegally copying a software product. It might be a crime, or might subject the violator to a lawsuit for financial damages.

Using ActiveX Controls

The steps to using ActiveX controls in Access include

1. Install the ActiveX control on the computer.
2. Register the control.
3. Add the control to a form.
4. Set properties of the control.
5. Add code to execute the methods and respond to events.

Installing an ActiveX Control

The ActiveX control must be installed on the computer, or an error will occur when the application tries to use it. This means that whenever you distribute your application, you must make sure to distribute the ActiveX controls as well. This will be discussed in detail later in the chapter.

> **CAUTION**
>
> If you distribute an application that uses ActiveX controls, you must make sure the controls are installed on each computer that runs your application. For example, sample applications for this chapter will not work on your computer unless you have the ActiveX controls installed.

Registering an ActiveX Control

An ActiveX control must be registered before it can be added to an Access form. To determine whether a control is registered, try to insert it in a form as discussed in the next section. If you succeed, the control is already registered. If not, you need to register the control with Access.

Some ActiveX controls are automatically registered when they are installed on the computer. To do this yourself, choose ActiveX controls under the Tools menu while working in form design. The ActiveX controls dialog box will appear. Choose the control you want to register, and then click on the Register button. The ActiveX Controls dialog box will appear. Choose the corresponding ActiveX control (.OCX) file, and then click OK (see Figure 9.1).

FIGURE 9.1

ActiveX Controls dialog box.

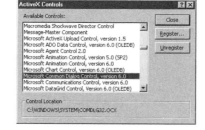

9

ENHANCING
FORMS WITH
ACTIVEX

Adding an ActiveX Control to a Form

If an ActiveX control is registered, you can add it to a form. To do so, switch to Form Design view and choose ActiveX Control under the Insert menu. Instead of the menu, you can also choose the More Controls tool on the bottom right corner of the toolbox (see Figure 9.2).

FIGURE 9.2

The More Controls tool on toolbox.

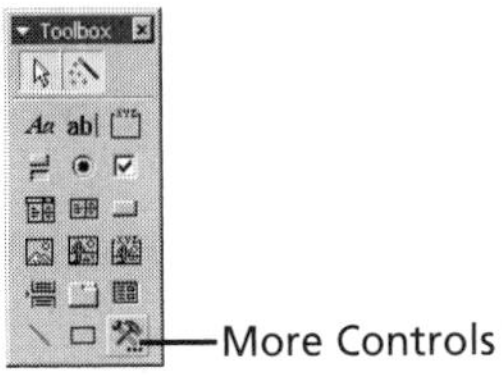

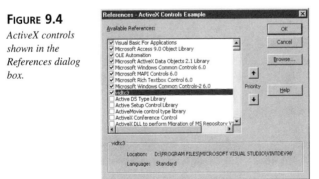

More Controls

The Insert ActiveX Control dialog box will appear. Select the control you want to add to the form, and click the OK button (see Figure 9.3). The dialog box will close. Click the form where you want to place the control.

FIGURE 9.3

Choose an ActiveX control to add to the form.

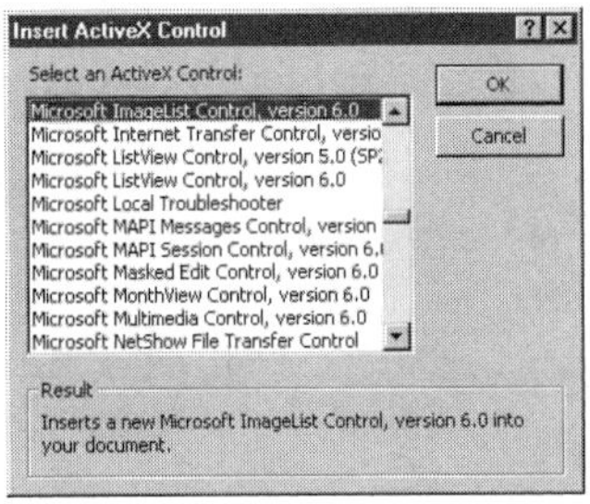

After inserting an ActiveX control in a form, Access maintains a reference to the control's type library. To see all the references of an Access application, choose References under the Tools menu in the Visual Basic Editor (see Figure 9.4).

FIGURE 9.4

ActiveX controls shown in the References dialog box.

Setting the ActiveX Control Properties

ActiveX controls have a property sheet just like any other built-in Access control. In addition, ActiveX controls have a property page that resembles a form, which makes setting properties even easier. To open a property page for the ActiveX control, click on the Build button under Custom Property in the property sheet. In addition, you can right-click on the control itself and choose Properties from the shortcut menu (see Figure 9.5).

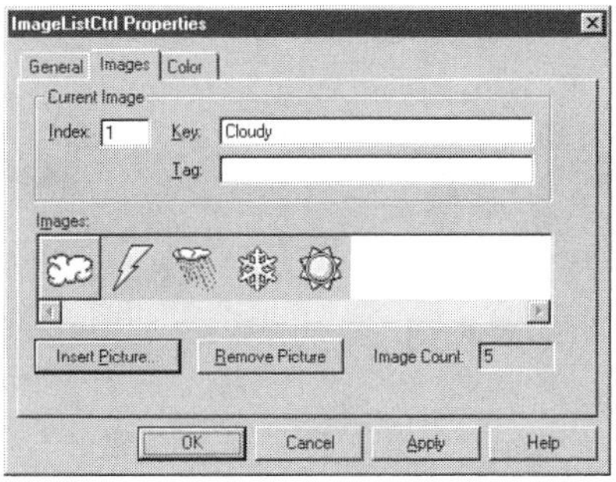

FIGURE 9.5
Property page of ImageList *control.*

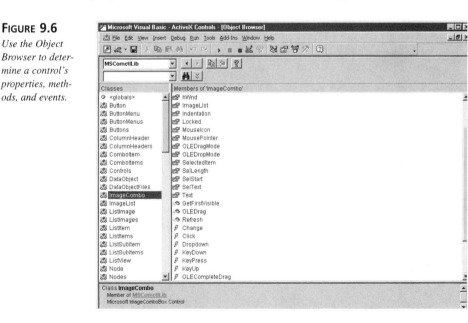

Writing Code to Execute Methods or Respond to Events

Writing code to execute methods or respond to events with ActiveX controls is no different from writing code with built-in Access controls. Use the Object Browser to learn about a control's properties, methods, and events, as shown in Figure 9.6.

FIGURE 9.6
Use the Object Browser to determine a control's properties, methods, and events.

9

ENHANCING
FORMS WITH
ACTIVEX

21 ActiveX Controls

I will now take a whirlwind tour through 21 ActiveX controls. Obviously, volumes can be written about all the ActiveX controls available (there are thousands of them), but these are some of ActiveX controls provided by Microsoft.

> **TIP**
>
> See this chapter's application on the book's CD-ROM for code examples using all 21 of these ActiveX controls.

Table 9.1 provides the name of the control, its file name, and a description.

TABLE 9.1 WHIRLWIND TOUR OF ACTIVEX CONTROLS

ActiveX Control	*File Name*	*Description*
Animation	MSCOMCT2.OCX	Play video (AVI) files on a form
Calendar		Display a calendar on a form
Common Dialog	COMDLG32.OCX	Easily display Open, Save As, Color, Font, Print, and Help dialog boxes
DateTimePicker	MSCOMCT2.OCX	Drop-down calendar for users to input date values
FlatScrollBar	MSCOMCT2.OCX	Scrollbar with a flat look
ImageCombo	MSCOMCTL.OCX	Combo box with images associated with items in the list
ImageList	MSCOMCTL.OCX	Holds bitmaps and images that can be used by other controls
ListView	MSCOMCTL.OCX	Presents a list of data in four different views
MAPIMessages	MSMAPI32.OCX	Send and retrieve messages, display address books, and other mail-related features
MAPISession	MSMAPI32.OCX	Log on and log off MAPI sessions
MonthView	MSCOMCT2.OCX	Calendar interface to view and select date information
ProgressBar	MSCOMCTL.OCX	Displays feedback to the user when a process is occurring

ActiveX Control	File Name	Description
RichText	RICHTX32.OCX	Provides different fonts, colors, sizes, and other formatting to text in textboxes
Slider	MSCOMCTL.OCX	A vertical and horizontal slider control
StatusBar	MSCOMCTL.OCX	Provides a status bar on a form
SysInfo	SYSINFO.OCX	Obtain and respond to system information
TabStrip	MSCOMCTL.OCX	Arranges tabs in multiple rows and display images on tabs
ToolBar	MSCOMCTL.OCX	Provides a toolbar on forms
TreeView	MSCOMCTL.OCX	Displays data in a hierarchical format
UpDown	MSCOMCT2.OCX	Enables users to increment and decrement the value of another control
WebBrowser	SHDOCVW.DLL	Displays a browser on a form

TIP

The chapter code contains working examples that use each of these controls.

Animation Control

Use the Animation control to play video files (.AVI) on Access forms (see Figure 9.7).

FIGURE 9.7

Animation *control example.*

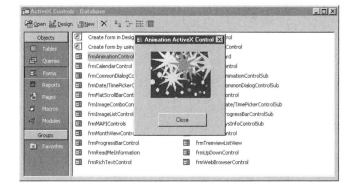

9

ENHANCING
FORMS WITH
ACTIVEX

> **CAUTION**
>
> The Animation control does not support all AVI files. For example, the control will not work if the AVI file contains sound. Also, the AVI file must be uncompressed or compressed with Run-Length Encoding.

The commonly used properties and methods of the Animation control are summarized in Table 9.2.

TABLE 9.2 Animation CONTROL SUMMARY

Item	Description
AutoPlay property	If set to True, AVI file plays in a continuous loop when loaded in the control. If False, AVI file does not play until the Play method is called.
Close method	Closes the currently opened AVI file.
Open method	Opens an AVI file to play.
Play method	Plays an AVI file that is loaded in the control.
Stop method	Stops playing an AVI file that was started with the Play method.

Calendar Control

The Calendar control displays a calendar on an Access form (see Figure 9.8).

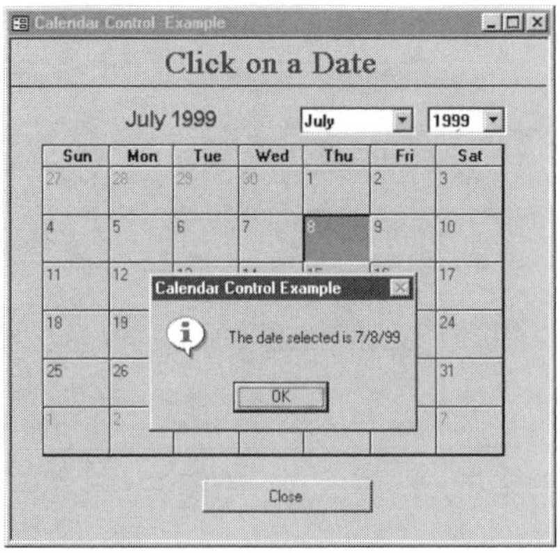

FIGURE 9.8

Calendar *control example.*

The Calendar control is useful for setting and retrieving date values. The appearance of the calendar is very flexible, offering day, month, and year views.

The commonly used properties, methods, and events of the `Calendar` control are summarized in Table 9.3.

TABLE 9.3 `Calendar` CONTROL SUMMARY

Item	Description
Day property	Sets the day of the month (1-31)
Month property	Sets the month to display
ShowDateSelectors property	To display the date selector drop-down list box
Value property	Sets or retrieves the currently selected date
Year property	Sets the year to display
NextDay method	Displays the next day
PreviousDay method	Displays the previous day
Today method	Displays today's date
Click event	Occurs when a user clicks on a date

Common Dialog Control

With the `Common Dialog` control, it is easy to display common Windows dialog boxes such as Open, Save As, Color, Font, Print, and Help dialog boxes (see Figure 9.9).

This control is a design-time control. Simply insert the control in a form and call a method to display the desired dialog box. The following code displays the Color dialog box:

```
Me.ActiveXCommonDialogControl.ShowColor
```

FIGURE 9.9

Common Dialog
control example.

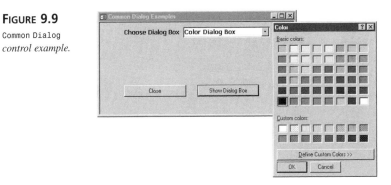

The commonly used properties and methods of the `Common Dialog` control are summarized in Table 9.4.

TABLE 9.4 `Common Dialog` CONTROL SUMMARY

Item	Description
`Color` property	Retrieves selected color in Color and Font dialog boxes
`Copies` property	Number of copies to print from Print dialog box
`Filter` property	Specifies type of file for Open and Save As dialog boxes
`FontName` property	Font selected in Font dialog box
`FontSize` property	Font Size selected in Font dialog box
`Orientation` property	Page orientation (portrait or landscape) from Print dialog box
`ShowColor` method	Displays Color dialog box
`ShowFont` method	Displays Font dialog box
`ShowHelp` method	Displays Help
`ShowOpen` method	Displays Open dialog box
`ShowPrinter` method	Displays Print dialog box
`ShowSave` method	Displays Save As dialog box

`DateTimePicker` Control

The `DateTimePicker` control provides a drop-down month-view calendar so that users can easily enter dates on a form (see Figure 9.10). This is similar to the date control used in Outlook appointment forms.

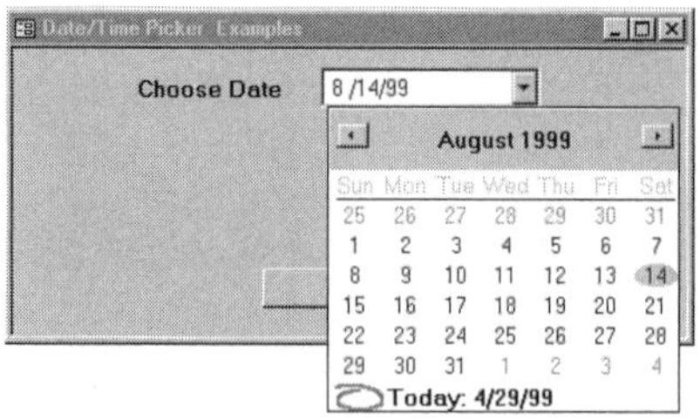

FIGURE 9.10

DateTimePicker control example.

The preceding example shows the drop-down calendar for date selection. A user can also use the up/down arrow keys to modify a date entered in the DateTimePicker. For example, if 7/15/99 is entered in the control, when the month (7), day (15), or year (99) is selected, the up/down arrows can be used to modify the date.

TIP

The appearance of the drop-down calendar can be customized using various color schemes. See the properties in Table 9.5.

The commonly used properties of the DateTimePicker control are summarized in Table 9.5.

TABLE 9.5 DateTimePicker CONTROL SUMMARY

Item	Description
CalendarBackColor property	Sets or retrieves background color in drop-down calendar
CalendarForeColor property	Sets or retrieves foreground color in drop-down calendar
CalendarTitleBackColor property	Sets or retrieves background color of title in drop-down calendar
CalendarTitleForeColor property	Sets or retrieves foreground color of title in drop-down calendar
CalendarTrailingForeColor property	Sets or retrieves foreground color of trailing dates in drop-down calendar
Checkbox property	Places check boxes inside the control
Day, Month, and Year properties	Returns selected value
DayOfWeek property	Returns day of the week
Format property	Displays long dates, short dates, time, and other formats
MinDate and MaxDate properties	Specifies a date range
Second, Minute, and Hour	Returns selected value properties
Value property	Sets or retrieves selected date/time

FlatScrollBar Control

This is a new version of scrollbar that sports a flat look (see Figure 9.11). Using the orientation property, you can position the scrollbar as horizontal or vertical.

FIGURE 9.11

`FlatScrollBar`
control example.

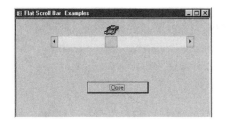

The commonly used properties of the `FlatScrollBar` control are summarized in Table 9.6.

TABLE 9.6   `FlatScrollBar` CONTROL SUMMARY

Item	Description
`Appearance` property	Sets or retrieves appearance of scrollbar. The scrollbar can be set to two- or three-dimensional.
`Orientation` property	Sets or retrieves orientation (horizontal or vertical) of scrollbar.

ImageCombo Control

The `ImageCombo` control is similar to a standard combo box except that images can be associated with each item in the list (see Figure 9.12). This makes combo boxes easier for users to work with.

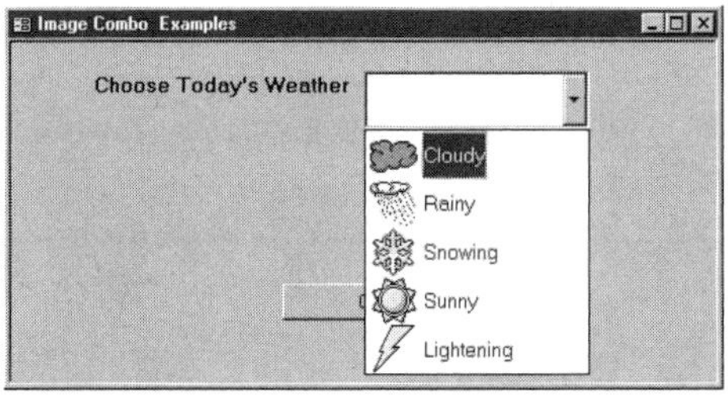

FIGURE 9.12

`ImageCombo` *control example.*

The `ImageList` control is used to obtain images for the `ImageCombo` control. An image can be shown next to the text in the list, as well as in the edit portion of the combo box.

To add items programmatically to the `ImageCombo`, use the `Add` method as follows:

```
With ctlImageCombo.ComboItems
      ' Add Index, ItemName, ListBox Display Name, Image Key Name.
      .Add 1, "Cloudy", "Cloudy", "Cloudy"
      .Add 2, "Rainy", "Rainy", "Rainy"
      .Add 3, "Snowing", "Snowing", "Snowing"
      .Add 4, "Sunny", "Sunny", "Sunny"
      .Add 5, "Lightning", "Lightning", "Lightning"
 End With
```

The commonly used objects, properties, methods, and events of the `ImageCombo` control are summarized in Table 9.7.

TABLE 9.7 `ImageCombo` CONTROL SUMMARY

Item	*Description*
`Collection` object	`ComboItems` collection (1-based)
`Individual` object	`ComboItem` object is an item in the list
`ComboItems` property	Retrieves a reference to `ComboItems` collection
`ImageList` property	Associates an `ImageList` control to `ImageCombo`
`Indentation` property	Sets or retrieves width of indentation (each indent equals 10 pixels)
`SelectedItem` property	Selected item in the list
`Add` method	Programmatically add items to `ImageCombo`
`DropDown` event	Occurs when list portion of control drops down

`ImageList` Control

The `ImageList` control is a design-time control used by developers. The end user will not interact with the control; in fact, it's invisible.

Think of the `ImageList` control as a file cabinet of images. You can store many types of images in the control such as bitmaps (.BMP), icons (.ICO), .GIF files, .DIB files, .CUR files, and .JPG files. Other controls can then use the images stored in the `ImageList` control. Several of the ActiveX controls discussed in this chapter, including the `ImageCombo`, `ListView`, and `Toolbar` controls, use the `ImageList`.

Images are easily added to the `ImageList` with the control's property page (see Figure 9.13). Keep in mind that all images added to the `ImageList` must be the same size. If you want to use different sized images in other controls, use multiple `ImageList` controls.

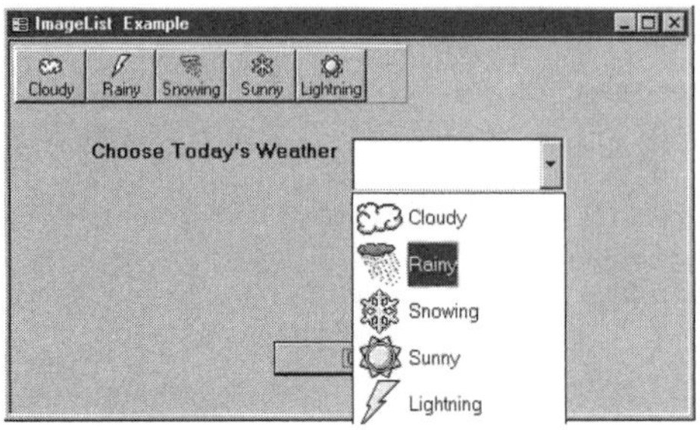

FIGURE 9.13

ImageList *control property page.*

Images added to the `ImageList` are always assigned an index number. Don't rely on it. Instead, always enter a `Key` value for each image.

> **CAUTION**
>
> When items are deleted from the `ImageList` control, the index numbers are renumbered, so do not rely on them. Always use unique `Key` values and refer to images by `Key` value in code.

> **TIP**
>
> Don't be excessive using images in applications. The `ImageList` control consumes a great deal of memory and can slow down your application if a large number of images are used. All images are stored in memory when the form hosting the control is opened.

The commonly used objects, properties, and methods of the `ImageList` control are summarized in Table 9.8.

TABLE 9.8   `ImageList` CONTROL SUMMARY

Item	Description
`Collection` object	`ListImages` collection (1-based)
`Individual` object	`ListImage` object—is an image in the control
`Index` property	A unique index value for each image
`Key` property	A text value (friendly name) to refer to an image
`ImageCount` property	The current number of images in the `ImageList`
`Overlay` method	Draws one image over another
Add images	In code, uses the `Add` method of the `ListImages` collection

For an example of images in a form with the `ImageList` control (see Figure 9.14). The `ListView` control is able to use images because of the `ImageList` control.

> **CAUTION**
>
> After you bind controls to an `ImageList`, you cannot add new images to the `ImageList` control. Make sure to include all images you plan to use when you initially add the control to the form. If you later want to add images to the `ImageList` after another control is bound to it, you must unbind all controls first.

`ListView` Control

The `ListView` control displays a list of items in four different views. An example can be seen in the right pane in Windows Explorer, where users can view files as Large Icons, Small Icons, List, or Details.

In Access forms, lists of data can have this same functionality with the `ListView` control (see Figure 9.14). Items in the list can be arranged with or without column headings. This powerful control is flexible and provides many ways to view data.

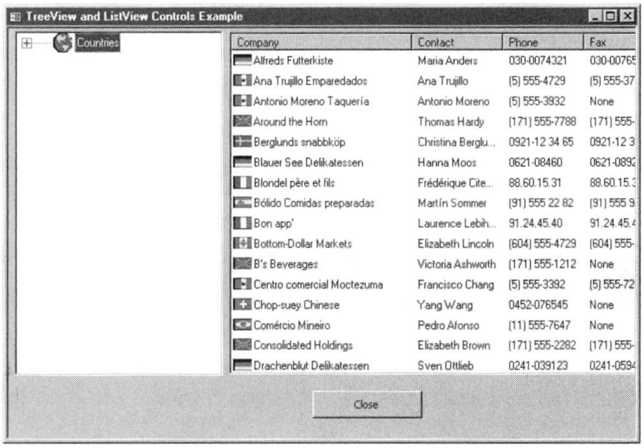

FIGURE 9.14

`ListView` *control example.*

The commonly used objects and properties of the `ListView` control are summarized in Table 9.9.

TABLE 9.9 ListView CONTROL SUMMARY

Item	*Description*
Collection object	ListItems collection (1-based).
Individual object	ListItem object is an item in the list.
Collection object	ColumnHeaders collection (1-based).
Individual object	ColumnHeader object, the heading text for a column header.
AllowColumnReorder property	Reorders columns.
Arrange property	Arranges icons in the control.
ColumnHeaders property	References a collection of ColumnHeader objects.
FullRowSelect property	Selects an entire row.
GridLines property	Displays gridlines in Report view.
HideColumnHeaders property	Hides and unhides column headers in Report view.
LabelEdit property	Enables users to edit labels.
LabelWrap property	Wraps ListItem object labels.
MultiSelect property	Enables users to select multiple objects or items.
SelectedItem property	Determines a selected ListItem.
Sorted property	Determines whether items in collection are sorted.
SortKey property	Determines if items are sorted by ListItem Text property or by a SubItems collection index.
SortOrder property	Sorts by ascending and descending order.
SubItems property	An array of strings displayed in Report view.
View property	Sets appearance of items: Icon (large icon), Small Icon, List, and Report (detail view).

> **TIP**
>
> Using the ListView control in conjunction with the Treeview control provides much of the functionality of the Windows Explorer interface. This is a great way to view data because most users are already familiar with the interface.

MAPISession Control

The MAPI (Messaging Application Programming Interface) controls mail-enabled Access applications. The MAPISession control provides a means to sign on and sign off a MAPI session (see Figure 9.15).

FIGURE 9.15

MAPISession *control example.*

> **CAUTION**
>
> For the MAPI controls to work, MAPI services for a MAPI-compliant email system (such as Microsoft Exchange) must be installed on the computer.

The MAPISession control is a design-time control and has no events. The commonly used properties and methods of the MAPISession control are summarized in Table 9.10.

TABLE 9.10   MAPISession CONTROL SUMMARY

Item	Description
DownloadMail property	Downloads new messages
LogonUI property	Displays a sign-on dialog box
NewSession property	Establishes a new mail session
Password property	Password associated with UserName property
SessionID property	ID of current messaging session
UserName property	Profile used to establish a messaging session
SignOff method	Signs off user and ends messaging session
SignOn method	Logs user into messaging session

MAPIMessages Control

After the user establishes a MAPI session with the MAPISession control, the MAPIMessages control can be used to create new messages, access messages, send messages (with or without attachments), reply to messages, display address books, and more. See Figure 9.15 for an example using this control.

The commonly used properties and methods of the MAPIMessages control are summarized in Table 9.11.

TABLE 9.11 MAPIMessages CONTROL SUMMARY

Item	Description
AttachmentName property	Name of attachment file
MsgCount property	Total number of messages in message set
MsgDateReceived property	Date message received
MsgID property	String identifier of a message
MsgNoteText property	Text body of a message
MsgRead property	Specifies if a message has been read
MsgSent property	Specifies if a message has been sent
MsgSubject property	Subject line of a message
RecipAddress property	Email address of recipient
Compose method	Composes a message
Copy method	Copies a message
Delete method	Deletes a message, recipient, or attachment
Fetch method	Creates a message set from selected inbox messages
Forward Method	Forwards a message
Reply Method	Replies to a message
Save Method	Saves a message
Send Method	Sends a message

MonthView Control

The MonthView control provides a calendar interface to view and select date information and can be customized with color schemes and number of months displayed (see Figure 9.16).

Users can select individual dates on the control or contiguous dates by using the MultiSelect property.

The commonly used properties and events of the MonthView control are summarized in Table 9.12.

FIGURE 9.16

MonthView *control example.*

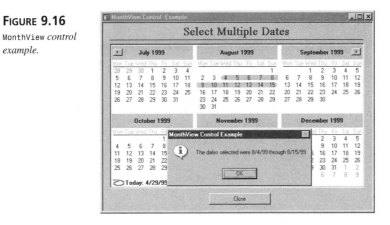

TABLE 9.12   MonthView CONTROL SUMMARY

Item	Description
DayOfWeek property	Specifies day of week
MinDate/MaxDate properties	Range of dates displayed in the MonthView
MaxSelCount property	Maximum number of contiguous days that can be selected at once
MonthBackColor property	Specifies a month's background color
MonthColumns property	Number of monthly columns displayed
MonthRows property	Number of monthly rows displayed
MultiSelect property	Allows multiple selection of dates
SelStart/SelEnd properties	Lower and upper bounds of date range selected
ShowToday property	Enables user to return to today's date
StartOfWeek property	Sets day of week to appear in left-most column
Value property	Date currently selected
DateClick event	Date clicked on the control
DateDblClick event	Date double-clicked on the control
SelChangeEvent	Occurs when a new date or range of dates is selected

ProgressBar Control

It is important to give the users feedback when a process will be lengthy. Otherwise, thinking that the computer has locked up, the user might shut down the application. This could cause program errors, data corruption, and more.

A ProgressBar control provides the user with visual feedback that the computer is busy and approximates how much of the process has been completed (see Figure 9.17). You can customize the appearance of the ProgressBar control, including minimum and maximum values and orientation of the ProgressBar. The ProgressBar can then be incremented as the user waits for the time-intensive process to complete itself.

> **TIP**
>
> Visual feedback provided to users during lengthy processes gives users the perception that the process is speedier than it actually is.

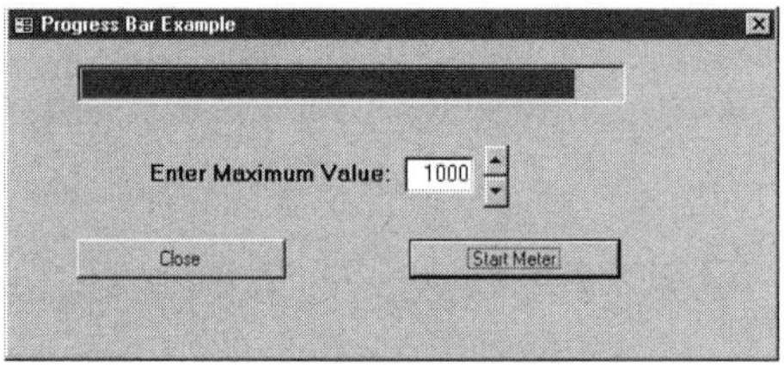

FIGURE 9.17

ProgressBar *control example.*

> **TIP**
>
> With long processes, partially fill the ProgressBar as soon as the process begins. This might be a bit dishonest because it does not accurately reflect the actual work completed. However, if a great deal of time passes before even the first part of the ProgressBar is filled, the user might shut off the computer, thinking it has locked up.

The commonly used properties of the ProgressBar control are summarized in Table 9.13.

TABLE 9.13 ProgressBar CONTROL SUMMARY

Item	Description
Min/Max properties	Minimum and maximum values of the control.
Orientation property	Orientation (horizontal and vertical) of the control.
Scrolling property	Specifies whether progress as displayed in the control is segmented or smooth.
Value property	Value of the control. As value is incremented, progress displayed in the control is increased.

RichText Control

The RichText control provides a text control with extensive formatting capabilities, in contrast to standard textbox controls, which do not provide for mixed fonts and colors (see Figure 9.18). This is not a problem with the RichText control because it features the following:

- Mixed fonts, font styles, font sizes, and font colors
- Superscripts and subscripts
- Paragraph formatting with left, right, and hanging indents
- Capacity for very large text files
- Capability to bind to an Access memo field
- Capability to add bitmaps, icons, and documents

FIGURE 9.18

RichText *control example.*

The commonly used properties, methods, and events of the RichText control are summarized in Table 9.14.

TABLE 9.14 RichText CONTROL SUMMARY

Item	Description
BulletIndent property	Sets or retrieves measurement of indent
FileName property	Filename of the file loaded in the control
MaxLength property	Maximum number of characters the control can hold
MultiLine property	Enables multiple lines of text
RightMargin property	Specifies right margin
ScrollBars property	Displays horizontal or vertical scrollbars
SelAlignment property	Specifies alignment of selected paragraphs
SelBold/SelItalics/ SelStrikeThru/ SelUnderline properties	Formats selected text
SelColor property	Specifies color of selected text
Find method	Searches for text in the control
LoadFile method	Loads a text or .RTF file in the control
SaveFile method	Saves file contained in the control
SelPrint method	Prints selected text
SelChange event	Occurs when selection of text changes or insertion point moves

Slider Control

The Slider control can be used to enter or display a value on a continuous scale (see Figure 9.19). The tick interval, movement properties, and orientation (horizontal and vertical) can be modified.

FIGURE 9.19

Slider *control example.*

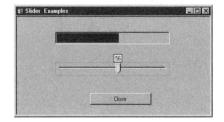

The commonly used properties, methods, and events of the Slider control are summarized in Table 9.15.

TABLE 9.15 Slider CONTROL SUMMARY

Item	*Description*
LargeChange property	Specifies movement of ticks when Page Up or Page Down keys are pressed, or when mouse is pressed on left or right side of slider
SmallChange property	Specifies movement of ticks when left or right arrow keys are pressed
Min/Max properties	Minimum and maximum values of the control
Orientation property	Orientation of the control (horizontal or vertical)
SelectRange property	Specifies a selected range
Value property	Current value of the control
ClearSel method	Clears current selection of the control
GetNumTicks method	Retrieves number of ticks between Min and Max properties
Scroll event	Occurs when there is a movement on the slider

StatusBar Control

StatusBars are used extensively in applications to provide information to the users (see Figure 9.20). Examples include Microsoft Word and Excel.

FIGURE 9.20

StatusBar *control example.*

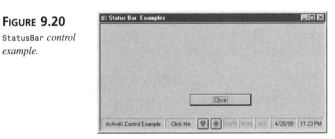

9

ENHANCING
FORMS WITH
ACTIVEX

TIP

The StatusBar control can be positioned on a form with the Align property (top, bottom, left, right, or none). You are urged to place the StatusBar on the bottom of the form to be consistent with other Windows applications.

The `StatusBar` control contains `Panel` objects and a `Panels` collection that can be used to take action programmatically. For example, if a user clicks on a certain panel, a certain action can then be taken.

The commonly used objects, properties, and events of the `StatusBar` control are summarized in Table 9.16.

TABLE 9.16 StatusBar CONTROL SUMMARY

Item	Description
`Collection` object	Panels collection (1-based)
`Individual` object	Panel object is an item in the list
`Align` property	Specifies location of a `StatusBar` on the form (top, bottom, left, right, or none)
`SimpleText` property	Sets or retrieves text in `StatusBar` when `Style` property is set to `Simple`
`Style` property	Sets the style property to display one large panel or all panels
`PanelClick` event	Occurs when a user clicks a panel
`PanelDblClick` event	Occurs when a user double-clicks on a panel

SysInfo Control

The `SysInfo` control is useful to obtain and respond to system information (see Figure 9.21). This powerful control can monitor the following system information:

- The operating system platform, version, and build number
- Events for desktop, monitor size, and resolution changes
- Events for Plug and Play
- Power management properties and events

FIGURE 9.21

SysInfo *control example.*

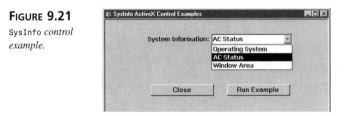

The commonly used objects, properties, and events of the `SysInfo` control are summarized in Table 9.17.

TABLE 9.17 SYSINFO CONTROL SUMMARY

Item	Description
ACStatus property	Detects if using AC power
BatteryFullTime property	When battery is fully charged, indicates number of seconds of battery life
BatteryLifePercent property	Percentage of battery life remaining
BatteryLifeTime property	Returns number of seconds of battery life remaining
BatteryStatus property	Status of battery charge (low, medium, high, charging)
OSBuild property	Operating system build number
OSPlatform property	Operating system (Windows 95, Windows NT)
OSVersion property	Operating system version
ConfigChanged event	Occurs when hardware profile changes
DeviceArrival event	Occurs when new device is added to system
PowerStatusChanged event	Occurs when power status changes
PowerSuspend event	Occurs before system enters suspend mode
TimeChanged event	Occurs when system time changes

TabStrip Control

The `TabStrip` control is useful when a large number of controls need to be placed on a single form (see Figure 9.22). With the `TabStrip` control, multiple controls can be placed on separate tabs. The style and orientation of the tabs on the control can be modified.

FIGURE 9.22

`TabStrip` *control example.*

The commonly used objects, properties, methods, and events of the `TabStrip` control are summarized in Table 9.18.

TABLE 9.18 TabStrip CONTROL SUMMARY

Item	Description
`Collection` object	Tabs collection (1-based)
`Individual` object	Tab object—an individual tab
`ClientHeight`/`ClientWidth`/ `ClientLeft`/`ClientTop` properties	Returns coordinates of display area of the control
`ImageList` property	Associates an `ImageList` control
`MultiSelect` property	Allows multiple selection
`Placement` property	Places tabs on top, bottom, left, or right
`SelectedItem` property	Determines selected tab
`Style` property	Modifies appearance of tabs (tabs, regular buttons, or flat buttons)
`DeselectAll` method	Clears all selected tabs
`Click` event	Occurs when tab is clicked

Toolbar Control

Use the `Toolbar` control to create a toolbar for your Access application. The `Toolbar` control provides users with a graphic interface for commonly used menu items (see Figure 9.23).

The `Toolbar` control includes `Button` objects and a `Buttons` collection. Buttons can be added and removed programmatically from the control. Code can be written to respond to control events, most commonly the `ButtonClick` event.

FIGURE 9.23

Toolbar *control example.*

The commonly used objects, properties, methods, and events of the `Toolbar` control are summarized in Table 9.19.

TABLE 9.19   Toolbar CONTROL SUMMARY

Item	*Description*
`Collection` object	`Buttons` collection (1-based)
`Individual` object	`Button` object—an individual button
`Collection` object	`ButtonMenus` collection (1-based)
`Individual` object	`ButtonMenu` object—drop-down menu from `Button` object
`Align` property	Displays the control on top, bottom, left, or right side of form
`AllowCustomize` property	Enables users to customize the control
`BorderStyle` property	Specifies border style of the control
`ButtonHeight`/`ButtonWidth`	Height and width of toolbar buttons properties
`ImageList` property	Associates an `ImageList` control
`Style` property	Specifies style of the control (standard, transparent, or text to right of image)
`Customize` method	Enables users to customize toolbar
`RestoreToolbar` method	Restores toolbar to original state
`ButtonClick` event	Occurs when a button is clicked
`ButtonMenuClick` event	Occurs when a button menu is clicked

TreeView Control

The `TreeView` control displays a hierarchical list. An example can be seen in the left pane in Windows Explorer. In Explorer, the hierarchical list of folders can be expanded and collapsed for various views. Figure 9.24 shows the use of a `TreeView` control on an Access form.

The `TreeView` control contains `Node` objects. `Node` is an item in the control. Each `Node` can contain text and images. You can programmatically navigate through the hierarchy in the control and expand and collapse nodes.

9

ENHANCING
FORMS WITH
ACTIVEX

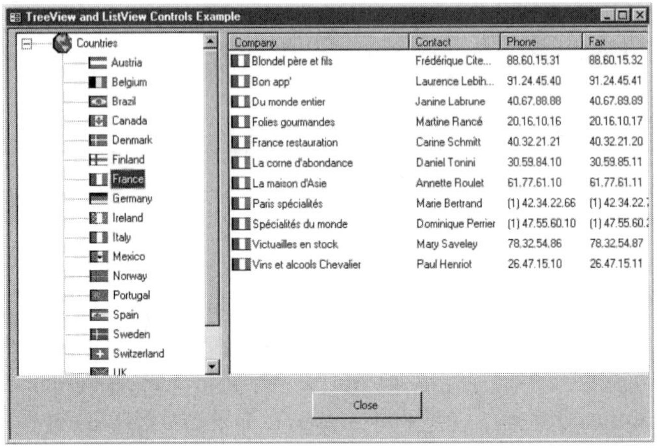

FIGURE 9.24

TreeView *control*
example.

The commonly used objects, properties, and events of the TreeView control are summarized in Table 9.20.

TABLE 9.20   TreeView CONTROL SUMMARY

Item	Description
Collection object	Nodes collection (1-based)
Individual object	Node object—an item in the TreeView control
Checkboxes property	Enables checkboxes in the control
Indentation property	Specifies width of indentation
LabelEdit property	Enables users to edit node labels
LineStyle property	Specifies how style of lines is displayed between nodes
SelectedItem property	Selected node in the control
Sorted property	Specifies how root and child-level nodes are sorted
Style property	Specifies style of each node (text, images, plus/minus, and lines)
AfterLabelEdit event	Occurs after a user edits a node label
Collapse event	Occurs when a node is collapsed
Expand event	Occurs when a node is expanded
NodeClick event	Occurs when a node is clicked

> **TIP**
>
> The Node object also features its own set of useful properties, which include the Child, FirstSibling, LastSibling, Previous, Parent, Next, and Root properties.

UpDown Control

The UpDown control makes it easy for users to change number values with a mouse. The control consists of a pair of arrows that users can click on to increment or decrement values (see Figure 9.25).

The UpDown control can be easily associated with another control, such as a textbox, with the BuddyControl property. There's no need to write specific code. By using the BuddyControl property to associate two controls; you've enabled them to work together. As the user clicks on the up arrow of the UpDown control, the value in the textbox changes automatically.

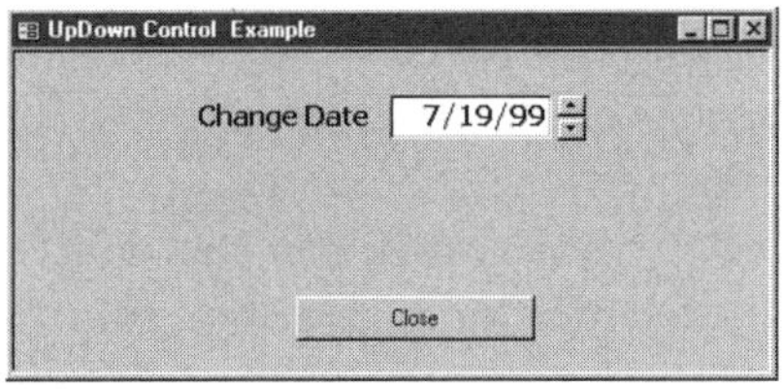

FIGURE 9.25

UpDown *control example.*

The commonly used properties and events of the UpDown control are summarized in Table 9.21.

TABLE 9.21 UpDown CONTROL SUMMARY

Item	*Description*
Alignment property	Aligns UpDown control to left or right of buddy control
AutoBuddy property	Specifies whether BuddyControl property is used to set buddy control
BuddyControl property	Specifies name of control to use as the buddy control
BuddyProperty property	Specifies property used to synchronize UpDown control with its buddy control
Increment property	Specifies amount the value of the control changes
Min/Max properties	Minimum and maximum values of the control

continues

TABLE 9.21 CONTINUED

Item	Description
Orientation property	Specifies orientation of the control (vertical or horizontal)
SyncBuddy property	Specifies whether UpDown control synchronizes its value property with a property of the buddy control
Value property	Current position of scroll value
Change event	Occurs when Value Property changes
DownClick event	Occurs when down or left arrow is clicked
UpClick event	Occurs when up or right arrow is clicked

WebBrowser Control

The WebBrowser control is used to provide a Microsoft Internet Explorer Web browser within an Access form (see Figure 9.26). Because most users already have a Web browser on their computer, why would you ever do this?

- The Web browser is available to users without leaving your Access application.

- Restrict the user's access only to particular Web sites. Some companies have discovered that a great deal of worker productivity is lost due to nonwork-related browsing. With the WebBrowser control, access can be provided only to work-related Web sites. Also, users can be restricted from accessing inappropriate Web sites.

FIGURE 9.26

WebBrowser control example.

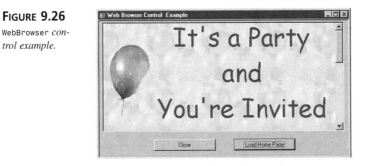

CAUTION

If Microsoft Internet Explorer 3 or greater is installed on your computer, the WebBrowser control is installed. This control cannot be distributed separately with your applications. You must either make sure that users install Internet Explorer, or you must distribute the entire Internet Explorer application to them.

The commonly used properties, methods, and events of the WebBrowser control are summarized in Table 9.22.

TABLE 9.22   WebBrowser CONTROL SUMMARY

Item	*Description*
AddressBar property	Shows address bar
FullScreen property	Maximizes screen
LocationName property	Retrieves friendly name of URL/file
LocationURL property	Retrieves full URL/path
MenuBar property	Shows menu bar
Type property	Retrieves type of document in the control
GoBack method	Navigates to previous item in history list
GoForward method	Navigates to next item in history list
GoHome method	Navigates to Home page
GoSearch method	Navigates to Search page
Navigate method	Navigates to URL or file
Refresh method	Refreshes current page
Stop method	Stops opening a page
DownloadBegin event	Occurs when download of a page begins
DownloadComplete event	Occurs when download of a page is completed
StatusTextChange event	Occurs when status bar text changes
TitleChange event	Occurs when title of document changes

Distributing ActiveX Controls

When you distribute your Access application to others, you will need to include all the ActiveX controls, or your application will not run properly. Each ActiveX control that is used must be correctly installed and registered on the user's machine. The easiest way to deploy an application is to use the VBA Package and Deployment Wizard.

To start the VBA Package and Deployment Wizard, choose Add-In Manager under the Tools menu in the Visual Basic Editor. Select VBA Package and Deployment Wizard. At the bottom of the form, check the load behavior you desire. Click OK. The wizard will then walk you through the steps to create a setup routine of your Access application. The VBA Package and Deployment Wizard does a very good job including all ActiveX controls and other necessary dependent files.

After the end user runs the set-up routine and installs the application and dependent files on his or her computer, the application will run correctly. The VBA Package and Deployment Wizard also makes all the appropriate registry settings on the user's computer.

Summary

Using ActiveX controls will enhance and extend your Access applications. In this chapter, 21 ActiveX controls were explained. See this chapter's application on the book's CD-ROM for examples of all these powerful ActiveX controls.

CHAPTER 10

Reporting Unleashed

After you have done all the work of designing the data structure of your application and have created the forms to assist the users in handling the application's data and processes, it's time to create the reports for the application. The reports are by far the most visible part of your application. People who might never see one of your forms and have no idea how you dealt with security and data layout will see the reports you have created, and they will have requests for more. As a matter of fact, you know you've created a good application when new reports or variations on existing ones are often being requested. This is both rewarding and tedious as reports are probably one of the most challenging objects to work with in Access.

Approaching Reports

This chapter will break the report object down into its constituent parts and explain how each one works. I will also review some tips and tricks for making reports easily do what might seem like complicated tasks. For those tasks that cannot be done simply, I will examine how to manipulate a report with VBA code so it will do almost anything you command. I will also explore bound reports, unbound controls, and subreports.

Reports were designed for creating output for printers. For this reason, there are some unique limitations to the object. Reports do not have an interactive capability like forms, so you cannot dynamically change values or data sources after the report has printed or rendered itself in Print Preview. Also, the appearance of the output is dependent upon the print driver being used because the results are usually viewed on screen or paper. What you see and what you get must conform to the parameters of the printer and paper you are using.

Despite these limitations, Access reports are incredibly flexible tools for presenting data from your application. The key to unleashing their capabilities is to understand the `Report` object and all its parts. The best way to do this is by reviewing it piece by piece.

Understanding the Architecture of Access Reports

Access reports are divided into four major parts or sections: Report Headers/Footers, Page Headers/Footers, Section Headers/Footers, and the Detail section. These sections act as wrappers around your data presentation. The first thing to print on a report is the Report Header/Footer. There is only one Report Header/Footer. The Report Footer prints after all the data, but before the final Page Footer (though it doesn't look that way in the Design view). Each page in a report might have a Page Header/Footer. Though you have access to only one Page section in the Design view of the report, the section prints for each page in the report. You will see how to customize the Page Header/Footer to print differently for different pages. Section Headers/Footers appear for each grouping or banding you place in your report. A report can have as many as ten of these sections, and they can represent themselves in the printout as many times as the data warrants. Section Headers/Footers often cause confusion among report designers when they write expressions in a report. You will see how to manage them so they yield useful information. Finally, the Detail section displays the finest level of information in your report. There is only one Detail section and it is sandwiched between the other section headers and footers in the middle of the Design view. Figure 10.1 shows the sections of a report in Design view.

FIGURE 10.1

Design view of the Categories and Products Report.

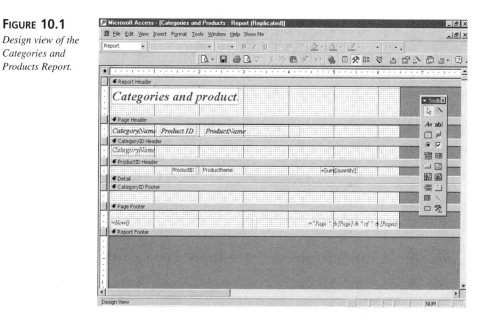

The basic way of presenting data on a report is to place bound controls into the sections and have them present their data when printed. However, it is also possible to place a report into any of these sections so it will make its presentation as a subreport. You will see what's new with subreports in Access 2000 and examine some of the issues involved in using them.

Finally, the Report object, like the other objects in Access 2000, is filled with properties and events that enable you to customize and automate reports. Not much has changed in reports since Access 97, but I will examine how to take advantage of these properties and events to make great reports in Access 2000.

10

REPORTING UNLEASHED

Building a Single Table Report Using the Report Wizard

The Access Report Wizard is probably the most useful wizard in Access, and although it is unlikely to provide you with a report that perfectly suits your needs, chances are that it can do about 90% of the work for you on 90% of your reports. Furthermore, the tasks that it will do for you are some of the most tedious and unexciting chores of report building.

> **NOTE**
>
> The Report Wizard can only create new reports. After you have created a report, you will have to modify it manually.

To create a report using the Report Wizard, simply choose the Report Wizard option from the New Report dialog box. Figure 10.2 shows the selection of the Report Wizard in a New Report dialog box.

FIGURE 10.2

New Report dialog box with Report Wizard and Categories selected.

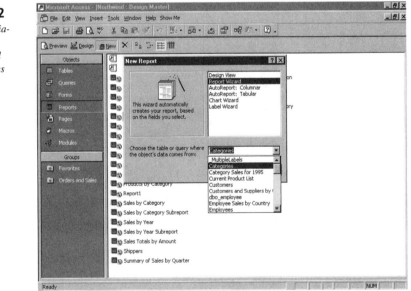

1. Select a data source (in my example I am using the Categories table) and click the OK button.

2. Next, the wizard asks you which fields you want on the report. You can choose them one by one or all at once. The order in which you choose them will affect the sorting and the placement of the controls in the finished report.

3. The next dialog box, shown in Figure 10.3, wants to know how to group the data. Because this is a simple report based on a single table, groupings wouldn't be very useful. You can move to the next dialog box.

   Here you have the ability to determine the sorting of the report. You can sort up to four fields in ascending or descending order. You can choose CategoryID and CategoryName as the fields to sort by.

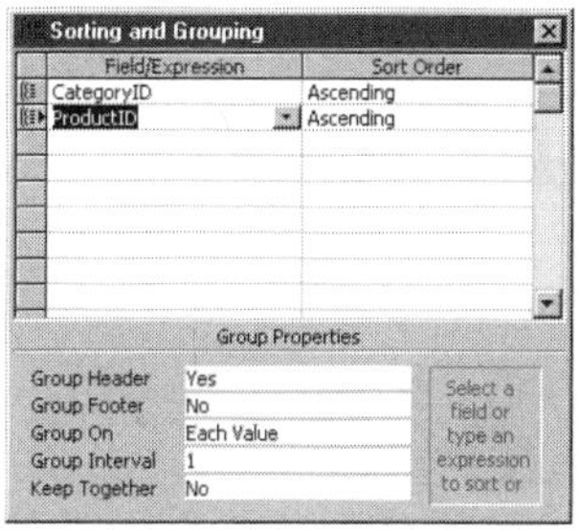

FIGURE 10.3

Sorting and Grouping Property settings.

4. After choosing the sorting order, you can choose a default layout for the report: columnar, tabular, or justified. You can also make the orientation of the printed report either landscape or portrait. Another option is to adjust the fields so they fit on one page. This is not like Microsoft Excel's Fit to Page feature where the contents of the cells are actually rendered in a different font size for printing. This feature only adjusts the width of controls so they will fit on a page. Doing this can make data illegible because it is truncated as the control used to display the data item is not wide enough to show the entire text or number.

   There are several styles to choose from on the next dialog box. These styles treat the headers, labels, and sections of your report differently and can give your report a nice, polished look without a lot of effort on your part.

5. The final dialog box asks you for a name for the report and asks whether you want to view the report or work with it in Design view.

Although the Report Wizard created the report, you can modify it at any time and in any way you like.

The Report Wizard can also create reports based on more than one data source. If you have established a relationship between the tables in your database, the report wizard will act upon them and build a SQL statement for your report.

1. Again, make a new report using the Report Wizard. Go directly to the dialog box where you select the fields and add the Categories table's CategoryName field, as shown in Figure 10.4.

FIGURE 10.4

Selecting fields from the Report Wizard.

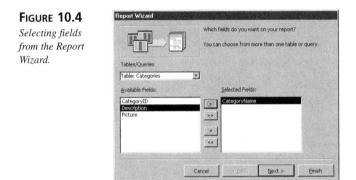

2. Now select the Products Table from the Tables/Queries drop-down list and select ProductName, as shown in Figure 10.5.

FIGURE 10.5

Both fields have been added.

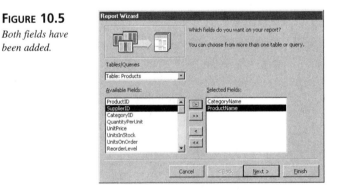

3. Move through the dialog boxes and set the sorting on ProductName.

4. Name the report "Categories and Products" and view the report.

In the Design view of the report, you will notice that the Report Wizard has made a SQL statement for you by using the relationships established during the data design phase of Northwind.

Customizing Reports

It is unusual for a report created with the Report Wizard to exactly meet your needs without some kind of modification. Though you should use the time-saving Report Wizard at every opportunity, there is no substitute for knowing how to customize a report.

With only a few steps and some calculations, you can change the Categories and Products report into a report that shows product orders by category. It will have a multi-table recordsource, groupings, sorting, calculations, headers, and footers. These are the elements that you will use in about 75% of Access reports.

Changing the Recordsource in a Report

The first step to changing a report is to change its recordsource, as shown in Figure 10.6. It would be very difficult to make any meaningful changes to the report without obtaining the correct records and fields.

FIGURE 10.6

Report property window with Recordsource.

From the report's property window, highlight the RecordSource property and click the ellipsis button (...) to start the Query Builder (see Figure 10.7). Add the Order Details table to the query. Also add the Quantity field and the ProductID field from the Products table. Close the Query Builder.

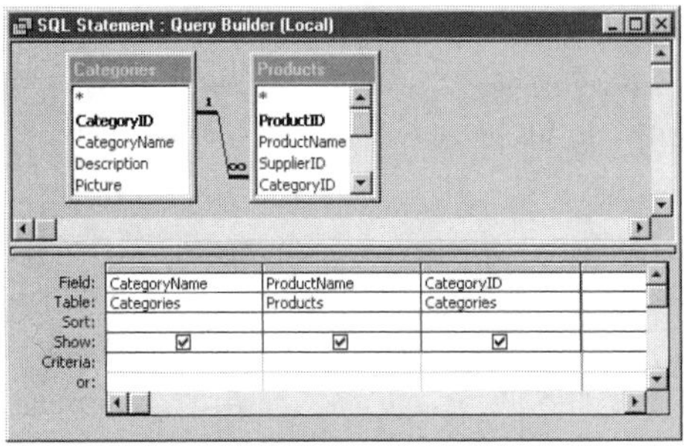

FIGURE 10.7

The Query Builder.

Now that the recordsource has been changed, you can alter the report to present the data in a useful way.

Changing the Grouping Structure in a Report

The most significant modification you need to make is to change the grouping structure of the report. When you assign grouping to a report you are telling the report to gather together the relevant data and present it in a block. These blocks are also called bands and you can create them and alter them through the Sorting and Grouping dialog box. When you create a grouping band, there are several options available.

- Field/Expression   The field or expression which will govern the grouping of the report.

- Sort Order   How the grouping will be presented. Choices are either Ascending or Descending.

- Group Header   When the Group appears on the report, you can choose to have a space in the report precede the presentation of its data. This usually contains the value being grouped and other relevant information.

- Group Footer   The section that follows the group's data. Usually contains totals and other calculations on the group's data.

- Group On   This property determines what will constitute a grouping value. The setting of Each Value will group the data by the entire data item, whereas the

Interval option allows you choose just a part of the grouping data item. The Group On property works in conjunction with the Group Interval property.

• Group Interval   When Group On is set to Interval, this property specifies what the interval will be. Table 10.1 shows the possible values and when they are available.

TABLE 10.1   GROUP INTERVALS AND THEIR LIMITATIONS

Setting	*Value*	*Limitation*
Each Value	0	For Any Data Type
Prefix Characters	1	For Text Fields Only
Year	2	For Date Fields Only
Quarter	3	For Date Fields Only
Month	4	For Date Fields Only
Week	5	For Date Fields Only
Day	6	For Date Fields Only
Hour	7	For Date Fields Only
Minute	8	For Date Fields Only
Interval	9	For Number Fields Only

NOTE

When you decide to group an expression, Access is unable to determine what the result of that expression while the report is in Design view, so Access will present all possible Group On/Group Interval options. Be sure to choose the one that will work with your expression.

KeepTogether   This property affects the printed report and how Access will attempt to keep data on the same page as its group headers/footers. Table 10.2 shows the settings and their effect.

TABLE 10.2 KeepTogether SETTINGS EXPLAINED

Setting	Value	Description
No	0	Page breaks occur without regard to the position of headers, footers, and data.
Whole Group	1	Access tries to keep headers, footers, and data on one page.
With First Detail	2	Access tries to print the group header on the same page as its first detail record.

Implementing Grouping in a Report

For Grouping to be activated, all you have to do is set a header, footer, or both. When you do, a small icon appears next to the field's name in the Sorting and Grouping property window and a new section appears in the report's Design view. Any control placed in this section will create a group based on its values, depending on your optional settings.

For a report to tally the units sold for each product by category, the report needs a grouping by product. It's best to use a unique identifier for this. Though in my example Product Name will probably work just fine, in the real world, products can come in different sizes, weights, and configurations, but share a name. Using the Product ID field will help the report distinguish these differences.

1. From the View menu, choose Sorting and Grouping. Change the `Product Name` sorting property to ProductID and set the `Group Header` property to `Yes`. Also, create a Group footer for Category. You now have all the elements necessary to present a grouped report on category and product.

2. From your field list window, place the ProductID field in ProductID header just to the right of the `CategoryID` control in the Category Header. You can cut and paste the ProductID's caption label control into the Page Header.

3. Next, move the `ProductName` control out of the Detail section and into the ProductID header. You will need to realign it with its caption.

The result is a report that gathers the categories together and then gathers their sales and lists them. As it is, this report only lists products sold in each category, but not how many units have sold. For that, you need an expression.

Using Functions in a Report

To convey complete and accurate information through your reports, you will need to occasionally write functions to perform calculations or other actions for your reports. Calculations in the report can also improve the performance of a report. If you have the choice of writing a function in an underlying query or in the report, you should give careful consideration to choosing to write it in the report. By placing it in the report, you might actually perform the calculation fewer times. This section explains the ins and outs of using functions in a report.

Using Calculation Functions

Calculations on reports are very much the same as calculations anywhere else in Access, except in reports the same expression can give a different result depending upon which section contains the control. The reason for this is simple. When Access cycles through your data to create the groupings you have requested, it is actually looking at different data. So the expression

```
Sum([Quantity])
```

placed in the ProductID header will return a total of the sales for each product. If this expression is placed in the category footer, it will yield a total for all the units sold in the category.

To see this at work, create a text box control in the ProductID header and enter the expression

```
Sum([Quantity])
```

Even though the report does not contain a control named "quantity," a field by this name is in the underlying recordsource and can be used in an expression. Copy the control to the Category footer. View the report in Print Preview mode and you'll see the result shown in Figure 10.8.

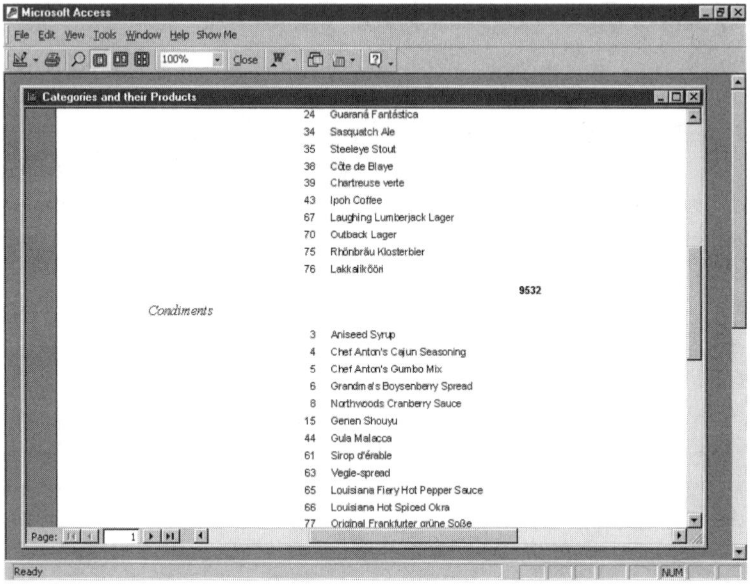

FIGURE **10.8**

The placement of an expression changes the result.

Using an `Immediate IF`

Another useful function to use in reports is the `Immediate IF` function (`IIF()`). This function allows you to create a `IF…Then…Else` test without having to write code. A great use for it is to help summarize or draw attention to important records in the report. It takes three arguments: the condition, what to do when the condition is true, and what to do when the condition is false. A comma separates each argument. To use it, write a test condition that will result in either a true or false resolution (for example, `[sum of quantity]>=500`). The second argument is usually a value to present if the condition is true (for example, "`High`"), and the third argument is a value to present if the condition is false (for example, "`Low`" or "" to display nothing). It is possible to nest `IIF` functions within one another so when a condition is resolved to true, another test is made, and so on. `Immediate IF` statements should be used sparingly as they can be quite slow.

The report could use an `Immediate IF` statement to mark those products which have sales equal to or greater than 500 hundred units. To do this, create a text box control at the right side of the ProductID header and enter the following formula in its control source:

```
=IIF([Sum of Quantity]>=500,"High","")
```

Using User-Defined Functions from the Report's Module

Sometimes, the expression becomes too complex to keep in a single `IIF()` statement. When this happens you can create a function tailored exactly to your needs and then call that function from the report. The example in Listing 10.1 shows how this function could be written in the report's module and called from a control on the report.

While viewing the report in Design view, choose Code from the View menu. This brings you into the reports module where you can create subroutines and functions used in this report.

LISTING 10.1 SHOWS THE FUNCTION

```
How to Replace a Value with a String
Function HiLowTest(dblQuantity As Double) As String
    If dblQuantity >= 500 Then
        HiLowTest = "High"
    Else
        HiLowTest = "Low"
    End If
End Function
```

Now you can replace the `IIF()` function with the following:

```
=HiLowTest([Sum of Quantity])
```

By using this approach you are better able to determine what is going on in the control because you can give the function a meaningful name. Placing the function in the form module also ensures consistency if you are using the same calculation in several places on the report.

Using User-Defined Functions from a Separate Module

There are times when the calculation you are using on a report is also used on a form and by queries. In these cases it might be a good idea to write the function in a separate module object so your application's queries, forms, and reports can always get consistent results. The following example shows a bare-bones function to convert a string to proper case. This is the kind of function that could be called from many places in an application.

This function uses the new `Split()` function in Access's VBA. `Split()` will parse a string into different array elements based on a delimiter you define (spaces are used by default). This new string primitive promises to have many uses in Access 2000. In your database it will take care of the improper capitalization of products such as "Chartreuse verte," "Gravad lax," and "Valkoinen suklaa."

The function is very simple. It takes a string as an argument, parses it into an array (varArray), and then loops through the array, making the first character of each element uppercase with the UCase() function. In order to return words with their first letter capitalized, the function uses the left and right functions to separate the first letter from the left of the word. These groups of letters are then rejoined or concatenated to form the whole word again.

Likewise, the elements of the array are concatenated into one string to recreate the original string, but in proper case. Listing 10.2 shows how this is done.

LISTING 10.2   CAPITALIZING ALL FIRST CHARACTERS AND USING THE NEW SPLIT FUNCTION

```
Function MakeProper(str As String) As String

On Error GoTo MakeProper_Err

    Dim vararray As Variant
    Dim i As Integer
    Dim strTemp As String

    If Len(str) = 0 Then
        Resume MakeProper_Exit
    End If

    ' First, make everything lowercase
    str = LCase(str)

    ' Split() fills an array with the parts of a string
    ' Split() uses a space as a default delimiter
    vararray = Split(str)

    ' Loop through the array and capitalize the first letter of each name
    'and build strTemp

    For i = 0 To UBound(vararray)
        strTemp = strTemp & UCase(Left(vararray(i), 1)) & _
        Right(vararray(i), Len(vararray(i)) - 1) & " "
    Next
```

```
        ' Trim any leading or trailing spaces
        MakeProper = Trim(strTemp)

MakeProper_Exit:
        On Error Resume Next
        Exit Function

MakeProper_Err:
        MakeProper = ""
        Resume MakeProper_Exit

End Function
```

Using Concatenation

Concatenation is extremely common in advanced reports. It enables you to join names and addresses together so they are easier to print and present. When you concatenate two data elements, they can no longer be treated independently. In other words, a form that shows a customer's concatenated last and first name cannot (without a lot of coding) be used to enter new names.

Concatenation is performed with the concatenation operator, the ampersand character [&]. It is also possible to use a [+], but formulas concatenating customer numbers with account numbers can be confusing to a developer or user if the [+] is used. You will see more uses for concatenation in a mailing label example later in this chapter.

Example:

```
="Access" & Space(1) & "2000" & Space(1) & _
 "Development" & Space(1) & "Unleashed"
```

returns

```
"Access 2000 Development Unleashed"
```

You can test this function through the immediate window. From the module's View menu, choose Immediate Window, or press Ctrl+G to gain access to the immediate window.

When in the window, type

```
?MakeProper("access 2000 development unleased") and press enter
```

If everything was entered correctly, you should get "Access 2000 Development Unleashed" as a result.

When concatenating, there are three syntaxes to be aware of:

- Field names must be surrounded by square brackets if there are spaces in the name (for example, [Order ID]), but for clarity, it is a good practice to use brackets as a rule.
- Text strings must be surrounded by quotes ("Attention"). Also consider the use of Chr(34) when dealing with quotes in code.
- Date values must be surrounded by pound signs (#7/27/1997#).

The next step is to employ this function on the report. It will change the product names to proper case. In the Design view of the report, change the control source property of the ProductName control to the following:

```
=MakeProper([ProductName])
```

In some cases, this would be all you have to do. However, in this case, it's not so simple. Because this control has the same name as a field in the report's recordsouce, the function will get confused and return #Error for each record. This is one reason why it's a good idea to follow naming conventions when creating controls on forms and reports. Because you used the Report Wizard to build this report, you did not have much say in how the controls were named. Now is your opportunity to rename this control. Because ProductName is a text box control, you should rename it:

```
txtProductName
```

When you view the report as it appears in Figure 10.9, in Print Preview mode, you can see the few instances where the names were changed to proper case.

So far you have seen how to make a simple report and a more complicated one with the wizard. You have also seen how to modify the report after it was created; you've examined groupings, calculations, concatenation, and the use of custom functions in reports. These topics will carry you through the creation of 90% of the reports you will have to make for an Access database.

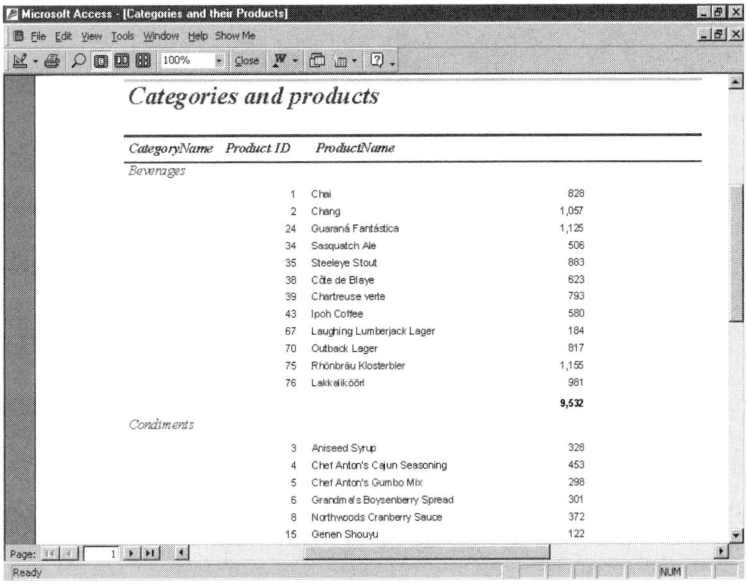

FIGURE 10.9

The products now have names in proper case.

Working with Subreports

Just as forms have a main form/subform capability, reports have a main report/subreport capability as well. Subreports are reports within a report and they are often used to show related records. They can also be used to show subsets of data consistently through different reports. When you use a subreport, you are able to take advantage of the formatting flexibility two reports will give.

When working off a one-to-many relationship between the records in the main report and the records the subreport, the main report is known as the parent and the records in the subreport are its children. Though the effect can often be accomplished with a grouping report configuration, subreports are very useful if you want to print records from several different tables. Figure 10.10 shows a category (Beverages) from Northwind and its subreport of specific products.

10

REPORTING UNLEASHED

FIGURE 10.10

Third page of Northwind's Catalog report shows some of the flexibility offered by subreports.

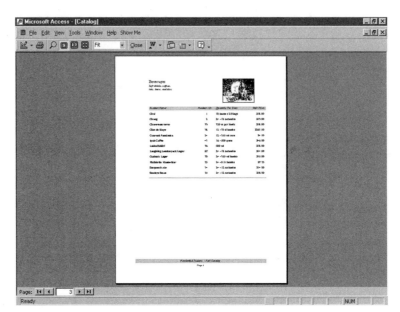

Creating a Simple Subreport

A typical subreport has a one-to-many relationship between the parent records and the child records. Make a note of the related fields between the two tables or queries.

1. Create a report for the parent records. This will be the main report.

2. Create another report for the child records. This will become the subreport.

3. In the Design view of the main report, with the Wizard tool disabled, (disable the wand button on the toolbar) use the Subreport tool to draw a rectangle where the subreport will be placed.

4. Set the subreport's `SourceObject` property to the name of the subreport created in step 3.

5. If the linked fields noted in step one have the same name, Access will automatically fill in the `LinkMasterFields`/`LinkChildFields` properties. If they have different names, the related field name of the main report should be entered in the `ParentLink` property and the `LinkChildFields` property should be set to the related field in the subreport. If the link requires more than one field, separate them with a comma.

NOTE

The LinkChildFields properties require the name of the underlying field, not the name of the report's control displaying the field. The LinkMasterFields will accept the control name. the link requires more than one field, separate them with a comma.

CAUTION

If the main report and the subreport are related, the LinkMasterFields/LinkChildFields properties must be set correctly for the report to work. It is possible to have unrelated main report/subreport construc- tions. Such cases might involve disclaimers or address blocks used in many reports, but displayed as a subreport for consistency and maintainability. It is even possible to have a main report which is based on no records at all.

The display of subreports Access 2000 has been enhanced from the earlier version. In earlier versions, the subreport appeared as a blank empty box in the Design view of the main report. Now it displays more useful information about which fields are being used by the subreport.

Better still, the subreport is editable from the Design view of the main report, as shown in Figure 10.11. You can address the properties and controls of the report as never before. This is sure to save time and aggravation. In earlier versions, the developer had to return to the report container and open the subreport's report object in a separate window to make modifications.

There's another kind of report that doesn't quite fit this form, but is still quite common: mailing labels. The next section will look at this type of report and some of the peculiar aspects of them.

FIGURE 10.11

*Selecting controls
in the subreport
for modification.*

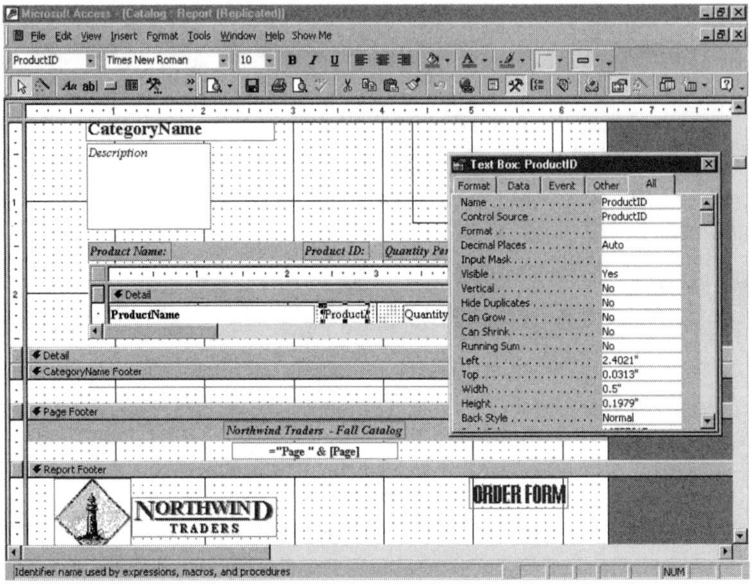

Creating Simple Mailing Labels

Though you might never have a need to create mailing labels per se, the same techniques can be used for a variety of other things, such as name tags for a conference, tabs for your technical documentation, equipment identification tags, and so on. Access provides a Label Wizard that can prepare a report to print labels against hundreds of different formats provided by Avery, Zweckform, and others. These formats can also be altered with the wizard or later.

To create labels, simply create a new report, select Label Wizard from the New Report dialog, and choose Customers as the records source. Click the OK button to start the Label Wizard.

1. Choosing the format for your labels couldn't be easier than selecting the matching manufacturer's product number. The dialog in Figure 10.12 shows the exact measurements of some of the hundreds of common labels known to Access, and it will automatically format your report to accommodate them. You have to choose the unit of measurement, whether the forms are individually sheet fed (most common) or continuous, and whether they are measured in English units (inches) or metric units. Each selection you make for measurement and label type changes the choices of product numbers. You can filter the selection by the label manufacturer. Avery is the default because they are the most widely used and many other manufacturers conform to their measurements and will label their products with a compatible product number.

TIP

If you ever find yourself in a situation where there are no preset label formats that match your needs, you can create your own label format through the Custom dialog.

2. When you have found the label product that matches the labels you are using, move to the next dialog in the Wizard to choose the font and size of the lettering. Because Windows allows you to choose any font and font size you like, it is possible that you might choose a font and a size which is too large for your label. The dialog box shows you what your label might look like with the font and size you have chosen, so you are unlikely to be surprised when they are actually printed.

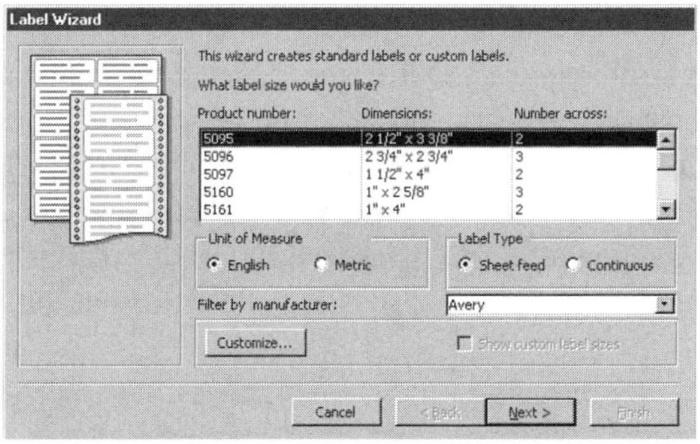

FIGURE 10.12

Choose the label template that matches the labels you are printing on.

3. The Next button will take you to the dialog box, shown in Figure 10.13, where you determine how the label will look. The large blank area on the right contains the merge fields for your prototype. You can move the fields from the data source by double-clicking on them or by using the > button. In order to get a new line, you must place your insertion point at the end of a prototype line and press Enter. After a line is created, you cannot separate its elements into separate lines. To delete something from the prototype, you can select it with your mouse pointer and press Delete. Entering text in the prototype box is the same as entering text anywhere else: Just point, click, and type. Everything you do in the prototype box will affect every label.

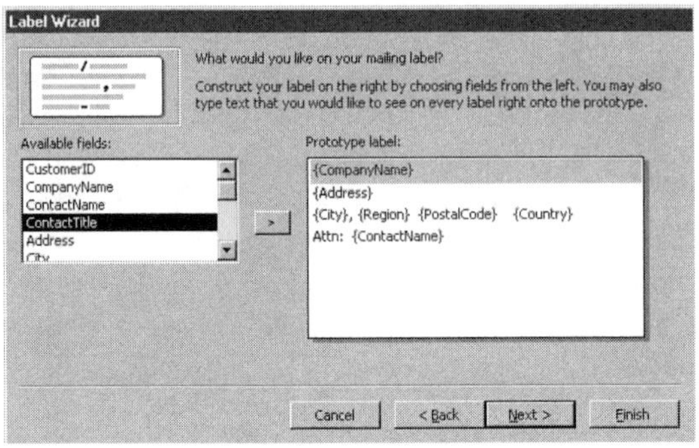

FIGURE 10.13

A completed proto-type label.

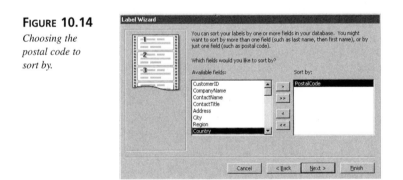

The prototype shown in 10.13 will create a label with the company name at the top, followed by the address and the individual to whose attention the mail will be sent. Notice that a comma and a space follow the {city}. These were typed in and will appear on every label. The same applies to Attn: at the bottom of the label.

4. Moving to the next step in the Label Wizard gives us the option of changing the sort order for the labels. You can choose to sort by more than one field (for example, last name and then first name) or by just one field. The labels will be sorted in the order they are found in the recordsource if no selection is made. When creating mailing labels, you might be able to take advantage of bulk mailing rates if you sort the outgoing mail by ZIP code, so choose PostalCode as the field to sort on (see Figure 10.14).

FIGURE 10.14

Choosing the postal code to sort by.

5. The final dialog box prompts us to name the report. Because these are customer mailing labels, the report could be called "Customer Mailing." You also have the option of opening the report in Design view or in Print Preview mode. Choosing the Modify the Label Design option will let you see that the label report is just a creative use of the properties of the report.

The result of the wizard's efforts is a small report containing a field for each line you defined in the prototype. Notice that the wizard has concatenated separate fields to make a single line out of city, region, and postal code. Notice also that the Wizard has surrounded the fields with the `Trim()` function. Trim makes sure there are no leading or trailing spaces to throw off the alignment of your labels. If you were to create this label report manually, you would have to create the concatenation yourself and you would also have to call the trim function in each control. The report is also perfectly sized for the type of label you chose. The height and width of the report will keep your data printing on the labels column after column and page after page.

The `Grp Keep Together` property is also set to Per Column. This, combined with the other property settings, gives you a report that is two columns wide and four labels deep on each page.

If you have worked with labels before, a couple of questions probably come up right away. What happens if the address is more than one line? How do you move the region and postal codes if the name of the city is really long or really short? The `Can Grow` and `Can Shrink` properties for these controls are set to `Yes`, so they will be able to adjust to these conditions automatically. There is no need to create conditional statements to account for these issues.

Publishing a Report

As great a tool as Access is for managing and presenting data, it is not the be-all-end-all of data managing and reporting. It is not always practical to give everyone an Access client so they can review and print the data in an Access report, and distributing a printed report to more than a few users is a clumsy and cumbersome task. Furthermore, some of your users will want to manipulate the data from a report after they receive it. The report might contain exactly what your users are looking for, but its form and layout might leave it nearly useless to them. Sometimes the data of an Access report needs to be published or distributed in other, more creative and accommodating ways than a simple report.

Exploring the Methods for Publishing Reports

In this section I will examine ways to publish Access reports through Word, Excel, and email. There are several different formats that can help you tailor your reports to fit your users' needs. Data Access Pages are another new way to distribute your reports over the Web, but because they are separate objects entirely, they are covered thoroughly in Chapter 26, "Using Access Data Pages."

The first decision you must make when publishing data is whether the users want a summarized and formatted version of the data or whether they want the raw data itself. If the users want the raw data itself and are not interested in layout, calculations, groupings, and so on, you might serve them better by sending them the data through the export of a query or table rather than by sending them a report. The steps for exporting a query or a table are very similar to exporting a report, but there are some different options to choose from when dealing with recordsets.

The crucial thing to keep in mind when publishing a report is that the published report will not reflect changes made to its recordsource and the users will not be able to drill down through summary information to see more detail. If these are acceptable limitations, the rest of the chapter is relevant to you and your needs.

Using Access's Built-In Methods of Exporting Reports

Access provides seven options, shown in the dialog in Figure 10.15, for exporting or publishing reports. Each of the options is a different file format in which to render the report's information or layout. The following table describes each.

TABLE 10.3 ACCESS REPORT EXPORT OPTIONS

File Format	File Extension	Description
Access	*.mdb, *.adp, *.mdw	Exports the whole report to another Access database.
Excel	*.xls	Turns the report's output into an Excel spreadsheet compatible with versions 5 and 7.
Excel	*.xls	Turns the report's output into an Excel spreadsheet compatible with versions 97 and 2000.
HTML	*.html, *.htm	Generates a hypertext markup language version of the report. Each page of the report is rendered as a separate HTML file and is indexed with its page number (for example, SalesByCategory.html, SalesByCategory2.html...). Hypertext links are automatically created to navigate from one page to another.
Text	*.txt, *.csv, *.tab, *.asc	The most universally accepted file format, it can be read by almost any application. All formatting information is lost.

File Format	File Extension	Description
Rich Text Format	*.rtf	Accommodates most word processors and maintains most standard formatting information in the document.
Snap Shot Format	*.snp	A file format unique to Access that enables you to send the report to people who do not have Access. All they need is Microsoft's SnapShot Viewer.

FIGURE 10.15

The Exporting dialog box.

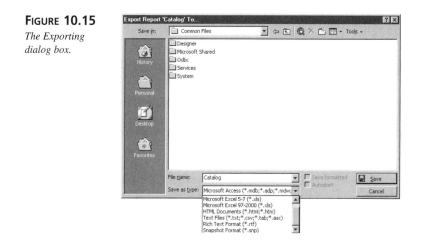

To choose any of these, all you have to do is select the report and choose Export from the File menu. From the resulting dialog box, you can choose the location and the file name and format.

Using Office Links to Publish Reports

Another way to publish is through Office Links. While viewing a report in Print Preview mode, you can select the Office Links toolbar button to send the current report to Word or Excel. From there, you can save the report to a location where others can view it.

Watching for Problems when Publishing

When using Text and Excel as the output format, you might lose some formatting information, so check to see if the report is intelligible in these formats before using them.

Using Email to Publish Reports

Emailing a report can be done from Access through any MAPI compliant email system (for example, Microsoft Exchange). With the report in Print Preview or with it closed and

10

REPORTING UNLEASHED

selected in its container, just choose Send To from the File menu. You can send the report as an email attachment in either HTML, Excel, DOS Text, RTF, or SnapShot format.

Someone wanting to view a report rendered in SnapShot format must have the SnapShot Viewer in order to do so. The SnapShot Viewer allows the user to view the report as if she had Access, and check the report through a Print Preview mode. This is especially useful when emailing reports because it makes for a hassle-free viewing of the attachment.

For more on writing the code for emailing reports and other objects from Access, see Chapter 18, "Using ActiveX Automation."

> ## TIP
>
> When exporting or emailing a report based on a parameter query or with parameters built into its functionality, the report might not work. Consider basing the export version of the report on a static table created from the same parameter settings.

Modifying a Report at Runtime

Because a report is an object like any other object in Access, it is possible to write code to manipulate its properties and respond to its events to suit your purposes. The rest of this chapter will review the Report object and its properties and events so it can be harnessed most effectively.

Because forms and reports are so much alike, this section will only deal with the characteristics that are unique to the reports or have some aspect of their behavior that is peculiar to reports. Events for reports and sections can be divided into design-time and runtime. This distinction is important when trying to solve thorny report problems. Design-time properties can only be set and addressed in Design mode. Once the report is running, it is not possible to alter them. The runtime properties can be accessed by code while the report is opening, formatting, or printing, giving you dynamic control of how the report will look and what it will contain.

In order to modify a report at runtime (or design-time for that matter), it is crucial to possess a thorough understanding of the report's properties, events, and objects. Following is a review of these elements.

Filtering and Sorting

These properties work very much like their counterparts in forms. With the `Filter` property you can limit the contents of the report beyond what the underlying recordsouce has provided. The filtering only takes effect if the `FilterOn` property is set to `Yes`. To see this in action, follow these steps:

1. Open the Catalog report in Design view.
2. Change its `FilterOn` property to `Yes`.
3. Enter the following statement in the `Filter` property:

   `[CategoryName]="Beverages"`
4. View the report in Print Preview mode. Only Beverages should appear in the catalog.
5. Return to Design view and set `FilterOn` to `No`.
6. View the report in Print Preview mode. All categories are now available in the catalog.

To use these properties in code, you could create statements such as these:

`Reports![Catalog].FilterOn=True`

or

`Reports![Catalog].Filter=[CategoryName]="Beverages"`

GroupKeepTogether

When creating multicolumn reports, it might be necessary to keep the groups intact in a column or on a page. There are a couple of options to choose from:

- `WholeGroup` When chosen in conjunction with the `Keep Together` property found in the Sorting/Grouping property window, it will attempt to keep the entire group on the same page or in the same column as the group's header.
- `WithFirstDetail` This is probably a more realistic option. The header will reside in the same column or on the same page as the first record of its detail. Used in conjunction with the `Keep Together` property of the Sorting/Grouping property window.

HasData

When a main report performs calculations against data in a subreport and there is no data in the subreport, the expression might display #Error?. You can use the `HasData` property to determine if there is supporting data for a report or control. The `HasData` property returns three values:

TABLE 10.4 `HasData` PROPERTY VALUES

Value	Description
Unbound report	The report has no recordsource
Bound report, but no records	The report has a recordsource, but the recordsource returns no records
-1—Bound report with records	The report has a recordsource and the recordsource returns at least one record

A simple formula can check to see if the calculation should be performed:

```
="Category has " & if([CategorySubRpt].[Report].[HasData] = -1, _
[CategorySubRpt].[Report]![CatCount],0) & " products."
```

Report Events (Runtime)

The following events are some of the events that fire when the report is run. That is, they are raised when the report is being printed, selected, and so on. These are the events you would use to control behavior that involves interaction with the user or with the report's data.

Open

`Open` is the first event a report fires. It runs before the underlying query is opened. This makes it a good place to program changes to the query or to pass parameters to the query. Code written in the `Open` event will execute before anything else happens in the report. After the `Open` event has completed, the report will take the steps needed to load its data.

Activate/Deactivate

`Activate` and `Deactivate` fire when the report becomes the active window (or in the case of `Deactivate`, is no longer the active window) or the report starts printing.

NoData

In the past, Access would produce an `#Error?` when a report opened on an empty record-set or its filter returned no rows. Thankfully, that problem has been corrected and now controls are simply blank when bound to an empty recordsource. However, the `NoData` property will still fire when there are no records for the report to present. It might be a courtesy to the users simply to let them know that there are no rows to present and cancel the report. If you have a report for orders by customer, the code in Listing 10.3 would cancel the report when there are no orders for a given customer.

Listing 10.3 Canceling a Report When There Is No Data

```
Private Sub Report_NoData(Cancel as Integer)
        ' Alert the user
MsgBox "There are no orders for this customer."
' Cancel the report opening
        Cancel=True
End Sub
```

Error

If a report's underlying table is exclusively opened by another user or simply does not exist, the Jet Engine raises an error and the report's `Error` event fires. The event is hooked into the `AccessError` method of the Access `Application` object, so you cannot use `Err.Description` in your handling of the error.

The best way to handle errors in reports is through the report's class module.

Page

This is the event that enables you to make last-minute changes to a report before it prints or is viewed in Print Preview mode. Some things (for example, drawing borders around pages and maybe calculating some special totals) are easier to do after the report has been formatted, but before it prints.

The report's `Line` method will draw a line around the report before printing:

```
Me.Line (0, 0)-(Me.ScaleWidth, Me.ScaleHeight), , B
```

Close

`Close` occurs when you close the report and just before the `Deactivate` event. You may want to close a parameter-providing form along with a report, or change the Z position of the other windows. These tasks and other mopping-up routines can be programmed into the `Close` event.

Section Properties

An Access report can have as many as 25 sections: Report Header/Footer, Page Header/Footer, Detail section, and up to ten Group Headers/Footers.

The Section property provides an array indexing all the sections in the report. Sections can be referenced by their index number in the array (you can also use an Access constant). Sections are different from other Access property arrays in that they do not return a value of their own; rather, they only return a reference to the section. To make the report header visible, you can employ the following code:

```
Reports![Categories and Products].Section(1).visible=true
```

or

```
Reports![Categories and Products].Section(acHeader).visible=true
```

TABLE 10.5   SECTIONS AND THEIR INDEXES AND CONSTANTS

Section	Index	Name/Constant
Detail	0	acDetail
Header	1	acHeader
Footer	2	acFooter
Page Header	3	acPageHeader
Page Footer	4	acPageFooter
Group Level 1 Header	5	Field name of Group
Group Level 1 Footer	6	Field name of Group
Group Level 2 Header	7	Field name of Group
Group Level 2 Footer	8	Field name of Group
Group Level 3...Header/Footer	9...	Field name of Group

Name

As noted in Table 10.5, sections of a report also expose a Name property that you can use in a reference. At any time, you can name a section for greater clarity and reference that section by the name you have assigned.

Height

This property sets a vertical measurement in inches for the section.

Visible

The Visible property controls whether the section is visible. The values are True or False.

Section Properties (Design-Time)

Sections have a group of properties that can only be read or set at design-time. It's important to distinguish them from other properties that are available at runtime after they are set. Following is a description of the design-time properties.

CanGrow/CanShrink

CanGrow and CanShrink are separate properties that enable you to determine whether a section can vertically resize itself to accommodate the changing size of its controls. If you have placed a control in a section with CanGrow set to True that expands for some data records, setting the CanGrow property of the section will enable that data to be properly displayed.

Controls might not grow and shrink as expected if they touch one another. Because these property settings do not affect horizontal size or position, it is important to make sure that controls are not overlapping at all.

Large controls like OLE objects might inhibit the shrinking of other controls in a section because the growing and shrinking is done line by line. Shrinking would require a blank picture in the OLE control.

Page Headers/Footers cannot grow or shrink, so controls placed within them are confined to the size of the section.

NewRoworCol

When you are creating column reports, the settings of the NewRoworCol give you plenty of control over how your report looks. Experiment with the settings described in Table 10.6.

TABLE 10.6 NewRoworCol PROPERTY SETTINGS

Name	Value	Description
None	0	Settings in the Page Setup dialog control the breaks between columns or rows. This is the default setting.
BeforeSection	1	Every section starts a new column or row. If there is room, a new section can share the column or row.
AfterSection	2	After a section has printed, a new column or row is created.
Before&AfterSection	3	Each section starts a new column or row.

RepeatSection

A common complaint among Access users and developers writing reports occurs when a group spills over to a new page and leaves the group header behind on the preceding page. The `RepeatSection` property, when set to `True`, will print the current group's header on the new page.

Section Properties (`Runtime`)

The following properties are available to the developer at runtime to alter the behavior and appearance of reports in response to data and other conditions.

ForceNewPage

A step up in sophistication from the page break control, the `ForceNewPage` property can be addressed while your report is printing. By setting this property based on data in a recordsource, you can control how pages break in relation to your sections. Table 10.7 describes the settings for the property.

TABLE 10.7   `ForceNewPage` PROPERTY SETTINGS

Name	Value	Description
None	0	Default setting, current section is printed on current page.
BeforeSection	1	Moves the current section to the top of a new page.
AfterSection	2	When a section has completed, the next section will be printed at the top of a new page.
Before&AfterSection	3	The current section prints at the top of a new page and the next section is moved to a new page as well.

KeepTogether

This is a fair-weather property—it only works when all the conditions are right. When set to `True`, Access attempts to print an entire section on one page. If it is unable to do so, it retreats and tries to make a new page. If this new page fails, the group will be spread across more than one page. Unlike the `KeepTogether` property for groups, the `KeepTogether` property for sections only concerns itself with one section at a time.

MoveLayout, NextRecord, and PrintSection

The following properties give the developer the finest level of control over what gets printed and how it gets printed.

- `MoveLayout` A setting of `True` will enable Access to advance to the next print location on the page. A setting of `False` will prevent the report from advancing to the next print location on the page.

- `NextRecord` Could be likened to the `MoveNext` method because when set to `True`, the report will move to the next record in the `RecordSource`. When set to `False`, the report does not advance to the next record.

- `PrintSection` `True` will print the section, `False` will not.

These properties control how the report reads data from its source, how it prepares the page for printing, and whether or not to print the section. When used together, the three properties can repeat data, make blank rows, print different rows on the same line, or select rows to suppress in the data.

Table 10.8 details how to use the properties to get these results.

TABLE 10.8 SETTINGS TO CONTROL WHAT GETS PRINTED

Desired Result	MoveLayout	NextRecord	PrintSection
Print every row, one after another	True	True	True
Leave a blank	True	True	False
Repeat a row	True	False	True
Leave a blank, hang on to same row of data	True	False	False
Print different rows on the same line	False	True	True
Stay on the same line, but skip a row of data	False	True	False

FormatCount

The `FormatCount` property is incremented every time a section is formatted for printing. A section can be formatted more than once. This can happen when a section is supposed to fit on a page, but does not. In this case, Access will format it once on the original page and then format that section again on the new page, setting its `FormatCount` property to 2. This can have important implications if you are performing calculations from your `Format` event because the calculation might occur more than once if they are not controlled by this property.

PrintCount

The PrintCount property is incremented every time a section is printed. A section can be printed more than once. This can happen when a section is supposed to fit on a page but does not. In this case, Access will attempt to print it once on the original page and then again on the new page, setting its PrintCount property to 2. This can have important implications if you are performing calculations from your Print event because the calculation can occur more than once if it is not controlled by this property.

HasContinued/WillContinue

These are two properties of limited usefulness. They are set when a section has run or will run onto a new page. They are of limited usefulness because the Access report writer is unable to distinguish if the overlap is caused by actual data or just white space. Because of this, the WillContinue property is usually set to true for every page in a report. It seems that the only way to defeat this lack of intelligence is to make sure the section height divides evenly into the printable vertical space on a page.

The HasContinued property is set from the Format event. It is True when the section has been continued from the previous page. However, it is very difficult to do anything with the property because its value is set too late to take advantage of the data in the report.

Building Reports Programmatically

Probably the largest challenge facing a developer of reports would be to come up with a report for data that is constantly changing. Consider a periodic report of products sold by region. Consider also that the report must look like a crosstabulation. If the report is based on a crosstab query, the column names used as column heads will probably change every month. This would present a problem for the bound controls on the report. One solution for this is to programmatically build the report each time it is requested. This can be done with a VBA module.

The VBA module presented could, with some alteration, be placed in a report's Open event and simply alter an existing report, but to get the full feel of completely creating a report from nothing but code, it needs to be a separate module.

The example uses DAO for the sake of simplicity. Because ADO does not create crosstab queries, DAO saves us the step of creating a temporary table and will enable most readers to use a familiar data access technique while concentrating on the report issues.

Creating the RecordSource

First, you need to create the data source. A function named `MakeCrosstabQuery`, shown in Listing 10.4, will take two date arguments: `datFrom` and `datTo`. They will define the period for the report. The function will create the querydef if it does not exist, but if it does, it will simply update the SQL property of the querydef. It will be called from the function that will create the report, but it could also be used by itself for other purposes.

LISTING 10.4 How to Make a Crosstab Query Programmatically

```
Function MakeCrosstabQuery(datFrom As Date, datTo As Date) As Boolean

    ' Errors will be handled inline
    On Error Resume Next

    Dim db As Database
    Dim qrydef As querydef
    Dim strSQL As String

    Set db = CurrentDb

    ' Make sure we know all the objects in the container by
    ' using the refresh method
    db.QueryDefs.Refresh

    ' Get the query
    Set qrydef = db.QueryDefs("Quantity Shipped by Region")

    ' If the query does not exist, create the object.
    The Err object will return error code
    ' 3265 if the object doesn't exist.
    If (3265 = Err) Then

        Set qrydef = db.CreateQueryDef("Quantity Shipped by Region")

        ' Since we've made a new object, refresh the container
        db.QueryDefs.Refresh

        ' Reset the error before proceeding
        Err = 0

    End If

    ' For clarity and brevity, assume the dates are correct
    datFrom = CStr(datFrom)
    datTo = CStr(datTo)

    ' Build the SQL statement
```

continues

10

REPORTING UNLEASHED

LISTING 10.4   CONTINUED

```
strSQL = strSQL & "TRANSFORM Sum([Order Details].Quantity) "
strSQL = strSQL & "AS SumOfQuantity "
strSQL = strSQL & "SELECT Products.ProductName "
strSQL = strSQL & "FROM Products INNER JOIN "
strSQL = strSQL & "(Orders INNER JOIN [Order Details]
ON Orders.OrderID = "
strSQL = strSQL & "[Order Details].OrderID) ON Products.ProductID =
[Order Details].ProductID "
strSQL = strSQL & "WHERE (((Orders.OrderDate) Between #" & datFrom &
"# And #" & datTo & "#) AND "
strSQL = strSQL & "((Orders.ShipRegion) Is Not Null)) "
strSQL = strSQL & "GROUP BY Products.ProductName "
strSQL = strSQL & "ORDER BY Orders.ShipRegion "
strSQL = strSQL & "PIVOT Orders.ShipRegion; "

    ' We're pretty sure we've got a query object now, so just change
    ' its SQL statement by setting the SQL property
    qrydef.SQL = strSQL

    If (Err) Then
        ' Pass the error to your error handler here
        Exit Function
    End If

    ' Close the query object
    qrydef.Close
    db.QueryDefs.Refresh

End Function
```

With the query created and ready to go, you can now build the report.

The function, PrepareCrosstabReport() will take two date arguments: datFrom and datTo. They will be passed to MakeCrosstabQuery. It will also use a database icon, a recordset object, the all-important Report object, and a couple of other variables to be used as counters.

Creating the Report Object

PrepareCrosstabReport() will create the new query, open it, and then create a new report object that conforms to the specifics of the new query. With that report object the function in Listing 10.5 will proceed to place controls in the report's sections, position them, and bind them to the data source. Because Access enumerates the controls as they are created, it seems easier to make sure that the data controls are sequential with one another and the labels are sequential with one another and so on. To this end, the function creates the labels and bound controls in separate loops. The report footer is created using the DoCmd object's RunCommand method and is then made visible by setting its visible property to True. A separate loop creates and positions the controls which contain the Sum() function. The Detail section height is set, the recordsource is assigned, and finally the report is opened.

LISTING 10.5   USING CODE TO CREATE THE CROSSTAB REPORT

```
Public Function PrepareCrosstabReport(datFrom As Date, _
datTo As Date) As Boolean
On Error GoTo PrepareCrosstabReport_Err
    Dim db As Database
    Dim DocName As String
    Dim rs As Recordset
    Dim rpt As Report
    Dim i As Integer
    Dim x As Integer

    Set db = CurrentDb()

    'Reset the query to use the new dates and then open it
    MakeCrosstabQuery datFrom, datTo

    Set rs = db.OpenRecordset("Quantity Shipped By Region")

    ' Create the Report Object
    Set rpt = CreateReport("", "")
    rpt.Caption = "Quantity Shipped by Region Between " & _
        datFrom & " and " & datTo

    ' Now we need to create the controls we need
    Dim ctlNew As Control

    ' We've got no more than nine controls to fill, so....
    If rs.Fields.Count - 1 > 9 Then
        x = 9
    Else
        x = rs.Fields.Count - 1
    End If

    ' Create, position, bind and format the controls
    For i = 0 To x
        Set ctlNew = CreateReportControl(rpt.Name, acTextBox, acDetail)
        With ctlNew
            .Height = 270
            .Width = 1080
            .Top = 0
            .Left = (60 + .Width) * i
            rpt("text" & i).ControlSource = rs.Fields(i).Name
```

continues

10

REPORTING
UNLEASHED

Listing 10.5   CONTINUED

```
        End With
    Next

    For i = 0 To x
        Set ctlNew = CreateReportControl(rpt.Name, acLabel, acPageHeader)
        With ctlNew
            .Height = 270
            .Width = 1080
            .Top = 0
            .Left = (60 + .Width) * i
            ' Control Indexes are assigned without regard to your wishes,
            ' so keep track!
            rpt("label" & i + x + 1).Caption = rs.Fields(i).Name
        End With
    Next

    DoCmd.RunCommand acCmdReportHdrFtr
    rpt.Section(acFooter).Visible = True

    For i = 0 To x
        Set ctlNew = CreateReportControl(rpt.Name, acTextBox, acFooter)
        With ctlNew
            .Height = 270
            .Width = 1080
            .Top = 0
            .Left = (60 + .Width) * i
            ' Control Indexes are assigned without regard to your wishes,
            ' so keep track!
            If i = 0 Then
                rpt("text" & i + (2 * x) + 2).ControlSource = "='Total'"
            Else
                rpt("text" & i + (2 * x) + 2).ControlSource = _
                        "=sum([" & rs.Fields(i).Name & "])"
            End If
        End With
    Next

    rpt.Section("detail").Height = 0

    rpt.RecordSource = "Quantity Shipped By Region"

    DoCmd.OpenReport rpt.Name, acViewPreview   'Normally this
    would be printed

    prepareCrosstabReport=True
```

```
PrepareCrosstabReport_Exit:
    Set rpt = Nothing
    rs.Close
    Exit Function

PrepareCrosstabReport_Err:
    prepareCrosstabReport=False
    MsgBox Error$
    Resume PrepareCrosstabReport_Exit

End Function
```

Now there is a report based on a crosstab that is dynamically created each time the report is requested. Because the report uses its intended recordsource, there's never a problem when the column headings change or when there are a different number of regions to report against—within the limits of the report.

Creating Sections

Sections can be created programmatically. However, not all sections can be created the same way. To create group headers and footers, Access provides the `CreateGroupLevel` function. Because the standard five sections (Report Header/Footer, Page Header/Footer, and Detail) are not part of the grouping scheme of reports, there is a different way to create them.

The `CreateGroupLevel` function takes four arguments:

- `StrReport`   A string identifying the report you want to modify.
- `StrExpr`   The group level expression, usually a field name, the parsing of a data item, or date.
- `FHeader/FFooter`   Boolean values to create the complementary group header and group footer sections. `True` creates the section and `False` does not.

  ```
  createGroupLevel "_Categories and products","newGroupSection",1,1
  ```

  or

  ```
  intSection=createGroupLevel ("_Categories and products",
      "newGroupSection",1,1)
  ```

To create the report or page header/footers, use the `RunCommand` method of the `DoCmd` object:

```
DoCmd.RunCommand acCmdReportHdrFtr
```

10

REPORTING
UNLEASHED

Tips and Tricks

Most applications have in them at least one report that poses a particularly vexing problem. To handle some of these problems, this section assembles some tips and tricks that will help add some sparkle to your applications' reports.

Make a Biweekly Grouping

If you are grouping on a date and you want to group your data biweekly (like a payroll), set the `Group On` property to weekly and the `Interval` property to 2.

Hide Repeating Data

In a simple tabular report, information is repeated row after row. To prevent this, set the `HideDuplicates` property of the offending control to `Yes`. This will give you the look of a grouping without using group sections and will enable the data defining the group and its first line of detail to print on the same line.

Group Data Alphabetically

With a report that lists customer by `CustomerName`, you could break the groups into alphabetically distinct groupings with a character designating the group (like a phone book) by following these steps.

1. Set the `GroupOn` property in the Sorting/Grouping property window to Prefix Characters.

2. Set the `GroupInterval` value to 1, as shown in Figure 10.16. This is very important because it tells Access how many prefix characters to use when making a distinction. This value will pay attention to the first character of the customer name.

3. Set the customer name control's control source to

   `=Left([CustomerName],1)`

Make Numbered Lists

Using the `Running Sum` property in conjunction with the control source can enable your report to number the items in list. Figure 10.17 shows an example of a report with numbered items. The sequence can reset for each group or it can run through the entire report.

1. Place a control on a report to hold the number.

2. Set the control's controlsource to =1. This will be the seed for the numbering scheme.

3. Set the control's Running Sum property to Overall or Over Group.

FIGURE **10.16**

Grouping settings.

FIGURE **10.17**

Result of numbering.

CategoryName	Product ID	ProductName
Beverages		
1	1	Chai
2	2	Chang
3	24	Guaraná Fantástica
4	34	Sasquatch Ale
5	35	Steeleye Stout
6	38	Côte de Blaye
7	39	Chartreuse verte
8	43	Ipoh Coffee
9	67	Laughing Lumberjack Lager
10	70	Outback Lager
11	75	Rhönbräu Klosterbier
12	76	Lakkalikööri
Condiments		
1	3	Aniseed Syrup
2	4	Chef Anton's Cajun Seasoning
3	5	Chef Anton's Gumbo Mix

Create Empty Lines Every *n* Spaces

This chapter discussed how the MoveLayout/NextRecord/PrintSection properties could create blank lines. Listing 10.6 is an example of that code. It could be put in most reports. Simply change the intSkipLine constant value to change the spacing.

LISTING 10.6   CREATING EMPTY LINES EVERY *n* SPACES

```
Option Compare Database

Dim intCurrLine As Integer
Const intSkipLine = 3

Private Sub Detail_Format(Cancel As Integer, FormatCount As Integer)

    If intCurrLine Mod (intSkipLine + 1) = 0 Then
        Me.NextRecord = False
        Me.PrintSection = False
    End If

    intCurrLine = intCurrLine + 1

End Sub

Private Sub Report_Open(Cancel As Integer)

    cLines = 0

End Sub
```

Reset Page Number for New Groups

Because the Page property of the group section is read/write at runtime, it is possible to change it every time the group's header is formatted. The Page property should not be confused with the Pages property, which cannot be written at runtime. The following code will reset the page numbers and is most useful when groups span more than one page.

```
Sub GroupHeader_Format
        Page=1
End Sub
```

Draw Vertical Lines

Creating a vertical line on the report can be accomplished with just a few lines of code. Set your positions and call the report's Line method to draw the line during the Format event. You have to measure in twips (1,440 per inch). An example of drawing a line with code is in Listing 10.7.

LISTING 10.7 DRAWING VERTICAL LINES WITH CODE

```
Private Sub Detail_Format(Cancel As Integer, FormatCount As Integer)

    Dim x1 As Single

    'Horizontal position in inches translated into twips
    x1 = 3 * 1440
' Use the Line method of the report, it takes
x1,y1 for starting coordinates and
y1,y2 for ending coordinates
    Me.Line (x1, 1)-(x1, 32000)

End Sub
```

Move Page Numbers for Even-Odd Pages

If your report needs to place even-numbered pages' page numbers to the right and odd-numbered pages to the left, this function will help. You might also want to use this with Creating Gutter for binding. An example of this technique is shown in Listing 10.8.

LISTING 10.8 CHANGING THE POSITION OF EVEN AND ODD PAGE NUMBERS

```
Private Sub Detail_Print(Cancel As Integer, PrintCount As Integer)

    If (Me!txtpagenumber Mod 2 = 0) Then
        txtpagenumber.TextAlign = 3 'Left
    Else
        txtpagenumber.TextAlign = 1 'Right
    End If

End Sub
```

Identify the User Printing the Report

If your Access database is secure, you can identify the user ID of the user printing the report, or use that ID to look up a full name. In an unbound control, enter the following expression as the control source.

```
=currentuser()
```

or

```
=dlookup("UsersTable","[FullName]","[UserID]= " & currentuser() & ")
```

Align Pages for Binding

When pages are bound into a book, the contents of the page must allow room for the page to be bound at the spine of the book. This means that the contents of odd pages must be shifted right and the contents of even pages must be shifted left. The code in Listing 10.9 accomplishes this.

LISTING 10.9   ALIGNING REPORT PAGES FOR BINDING

```
Private Sub PageFooterSection_Format(Cancel As Integer, _
    FormatCount As Integer)
    Dim ctl As Control
    If (Me.Page Mod 2 = 0) Then 'we have an even page
        For Each ctl In Me.Controls
            .Left = .Left + 1440 'shift everything left 1 inch
        Next
    Else 'we have an odd page
        For Each ctl In Me.Controls
            .Left = .Left - 1440 'shift everything right 1 inch
        Next
    End If
End Sub
```

Calculate Page Totals

An Access report will generate an error if you try to place an aggregate function (for example, Sum()) in a control located in the page header/footer. Because the request for a page subtotal on a report often comes up, this is more than inconvenient. With some very simple code, it is possible to calculate the page's subtotal and then display it through an unbound control in the page footer. For the following code example to work, follow these steps:

1. Build a simple report on the Invoices table. Place the CompanyName field and the ExtendedPrice field in the Detail section.

2. Place the ExtendedPrice field in the Detail section a second time and name it RunningSum. Set its Visible property to No and its Running Sum property to Over All.

3. Create an unbound text box control named txtPageSubtot in the page footer.

4. Enter the code shown in Listing 10.10 in the PageFooter's OnPrint event:

LISTING 10.10 CALCULATING A PAGE SUBTOTAL

```
Option Compare Database
Dim x As Double
Private Sub PageFooterSection_Print(Cancel As Integer, PrintCount As
Integer)
    txtpagesubtot = RunningSum - x
    x = RunningSum

End Sub
```

Now the report will give a page subtotal.

Fine Control Manipulation

Rather than selecting controls on a report and running the risk of moving them, try some of the following techniques:

- Click the ruler to select the controls at that measurement.
- Click on the background of the report and drag over controls to select them without moving them.
- Use the Tab key to move from one control to another.
- Control+Arrow will make fine movements of a control easy. It will also move a control from one section to another.
- Shift+Arrow will size controls without moving them.

Summary

This chapter has explored the Report object, its parts, and its peculiarities in detail. You have seen several ways to distribute the reports beyond simple paper-based interoffice mail and you've reviewed some tips and tricks for accomplishing some difficult tasks. With some practice and experimentation, Access reports can do almost anything you want. Though reports have changed very little over the years, VBA for Access has improved quite a bit and can be harnessed to make your reports shine. There are few instances where some hard work and creativity cannot turn a client's request into a finished report.

Because an application (and its developer) can live or die by the quality of its reports, it is critical that developers understand how to get as much out of them as possible. In Access 2000 a new object, Data Access Pages, is now available to display and distribute information on the Web. Though these will probably not supplant reports for some time to come, it is an exciting and valuable new feature. Chapter 26, "Using Data Access Pages," is dedicated to it in this book.

VBA Unleashed

IN THIS PART

Creating Objects with Class Modules

Creating objects is one of the most efficient ways to write and maintain applications. Before discussing the benefits of using objects, let's review some definitions.

Objects are things. People, cars, and buildings are all types of objects. In programming, the word *object* is used to describe one specific thing, such as a form or control. You undoubtedly have had experience with these types of built-in objects.

Microsoft Access has become increasingly object-oriented, empowering us to create custom objects and to add properties and methods to those objects. Examples of custom objects might include a customer object, invoice object, user object, data connection object, and sound object. The code in this chapter includes numerous custom objects for your use. See "Creating Objects with Class Modules.mdb," as shown in Figure 11.1.

Figure 11.1

See custom objects in this book's CD sample code.

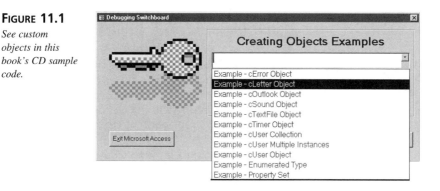

Objects are created using a class module. A class module is a portable, self-contained unit of code designed for a specific purpose. The class specifies the properties and methods that each object in that class will have.

Developers often confuse the terms object and class. A *class* is a description or template of the properties and methods of an object. It does not have a life of its own. When developers want to use the code in the class module, an instance of the class is created. That instance is an *object*.

Therefore, it is inaccurate to state "creating an instance of an object." The object *is* the instance! An individual object is defined as an instance of a class. Multiple objects can be created from the class, each with different property values.

> **TIP**
>
> This chapter deals with creating objects using class modules. Remember, form modules are class modules. You can add properties and methods to forms in the same way that you can add properties and methods to custom objects.

Exploring the Benefits of Using Objects

There are many benefits to creating and using objects, including hiding complex code functionality, using IntelliSense, easier code creation and maintenance, and more.

Hide Complex Functionality

Hiding complex functionality is one of the benefits of using objects. An advanced developer can create complex routines such as Windows API procedures, data access code, string routines, and more. Less experienced developers can enjoy the benefits of the object by calling its properties and methods without having to understand the code that makes the object work.

Use of Microsoft's IntelliSense Technology

The only thing a developer needs to do to use an object is to specify that object and choose its property or method using IntelliSense technology (see Figure 11.2). For example, one of the objects included in this chapter is an error-handler object that can be used in Access applications. Because all the code for the error handler is included in the cError object, a developer simply needs to specify the object and the property or method she wants to use. For example, if the developer would like to have an email sent whenever an error occurs in the application, all he or she needs to do is call the "email" method:

```
cError.email
```

FIGURE 11.2

Objects allow you to use Microsoft IntelliSense technology.

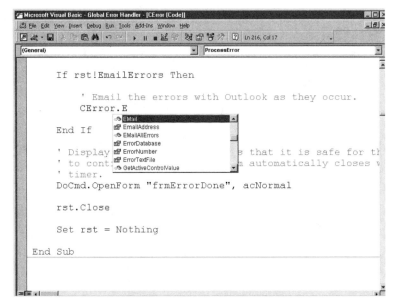

Notice how easy it is to use objects. With Microsoft IntelliSense technology, you simply type the object name (`cError`), type a period, and all properties and methods of the object will appear. This greatly facilitates writing code quickly and accurately.

Organize Code

Creating classes helps organize code so it is easier to read, review, and maintain. All code for a particular functionality is contained within the class. Packaging code into one neat bundle with properties and methods characterizing an object is called *encapsulation*.

Allow Viewing Objects in the Object Browser

Packaging code in classes allows developers to use the Object Browser to review properties, methods, and other information. Later in the chapter, I will examine a custom object in the Object Browser.

Create Multiple Instances of the Object

Imagine you have code that is reused often in an application. In fact, the code can be used an unknown number of times simultaneously. An example is data connection code. Every time a user searches for a new customer, opens a form, or accesses a combo box, data must be retrieved from the server. Rather than duplicate code in each of these procedures, a better approach would be to create a `Data Connection` object that enables code to retrieve data from the server.

Make Code Easy to Update and Maintain

By using classes, you can use a single unit of code multiple times in an application without repeating the code. If, for example, you repeat data access code in numerous procedures, every single place the data access code is located must be found and revised whenever a change must be made. This is very time-consuming and inefficient. On the other hand, if a Data Connection object is used, all updates or changes to the data access code need to be changed in only one place—the class module.

Limit Access to Code

Classes enable you to control who can use the code and under what circumstances. With classes, you can protect properties and methods by controlling when they are exposed outside the class.

Make Code Easily Portable

Because a class module is a self-contained unit of code, it can easily be moved from one Access application to another.

Reviewing Objects, Properties, and Methods

Before discussing how to create objects, let's review the basics. It is essential to understand the terms *object*, *properties*, and *methods*, or the rest of this chapter will make no sense.

An *object* is an item that can be programmed, manipulated, or controlled. In Access, objects include forms, text boxes, command buttons, and more. In this chapter, I will actually create my own custom objects.

A *property* is a characteristic of an object. A property can be thought of as an adjective because it describes or characterizes an object. In Access, properties of a text box include Name, Visible, Forecolor, and more. Most properties of an object can be both set and retrieved. In this chapter, you will learn how to create your own properties and control whether the properties can be set or retrieved.

A *method* is an action that can be taken on an object. A method can be thought of as a verb. For example, one method of an Access form is Close. I will create custom methods for the object in this chapter.

Creating Classes

Class modules are used to create a class. The class defines properties, methods, and events providing a clearly defined and well-documented public interface.

Inserting a Class Module

Creating a class is actually very simple. Adding properties and methods to the object involves a little more work.

To create a class, insert a class module in your access application and name it. The name of the class module is the name of your object.

To insert a class module, choose Class Module under the Insert menu. The Visual Basic Editor will open. In the code window, write any properties, methods, and events for the object. Before going any further, name the class module (see Figure 11.3).

> **TIP**
>
> Take great care in properly naming the class module because it will be the name of your object. This will be how developers access your code through IntelliSense technology. It also might be helpful to precede the name of the object with your company's initials so you can easily see which custom objects were created at your company.

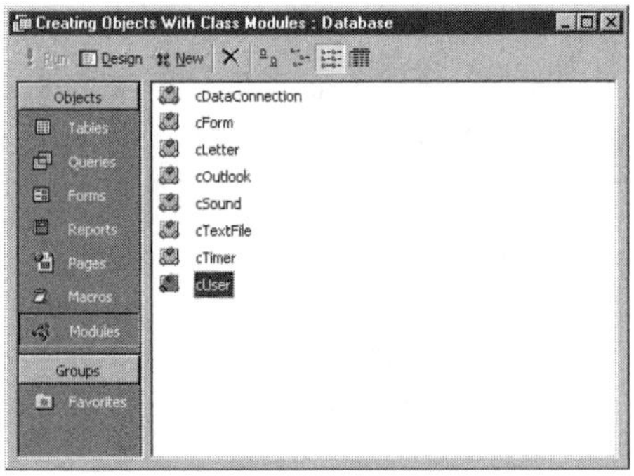

FIGURE 11.3

Properly name the class module.

Creating Properties

There are two ways to create properties of a class: public variables or property procedures.

> **TIP**
>
> The chapter code includes numerous objects. The simplest example, a cUser object, is used for illustration in the next few pages. The cUser object will hold information about the current logged-in user, including his or her name. This object can be used whenever the current user's name is needed in the application, such as during error handling and recording the author of notes or documents. In this example, the cUser object will be used to record the login dates and times, and an event of the object will be used to display a welcome message to the user when he or she logs in.

Using Public Variables

A property can easily be created by simply declaring a public variable in the declaration section of the class module. The following examples create a Name and UserType property of the cUser object:

```
Public Name as String
Public UserType as String
```

After this simple step, users can set and retrieve these property values. To set the property, the code is as follows:

```
cUser.Name = "Steve"
cUser.UserType = "Management"
```

To retrieve the property, the code is as follows (see Figure 11.4):

```
MsgBox cUser.Name
```

Using Property Procedures

Properties can also be added to objects by using a special type of VBA procedure called a *property procedure*. There are three types of property procedures: Property Let for retrieval of a property value, Property Get to set a property value, and Property Set to pass an object as a property.

Property procedures let you restrict who can set and retrieve property values. The key to understanding how property procedures work lies in the fact that the value of the property is hidden in a private module-level variable. Therefore, the first step is to create a private module-level variable and then create the Property Let and Property Get statements.

FIGURE **11.4**

Easily set and retrieve object properties with IntelliSense.

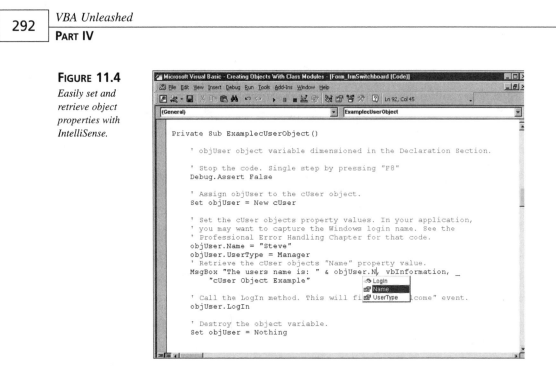

TIP

Property procedures can be set as public or private just like any other procedure. Public property procedures are accessible to all other procedures in all modules; private property procedures are accessible only to procedures in the module in which they are declared.

Private Module Variable Creation

With property procedures, the value of the property is hidden in a private module variable. The creator of the class determines whether a property is exposed to the outside world.

The following is an example of creating a private module-level variable for the Name and Type properties of the cUser object:

```
Option Explicit

' Create Private Variable in Declaration Section
Private mstrName as String
Private mUserType as String
```

Property Let

The `Property Let` procedure is used to set the value of a property. If you do not want others to have the ability to set a property value, do not include a `Property Let`.

The following example creates a `Property Let` procedure for the `Name` property of the `cUser` object:

```
Public Property Let Name (UserName as String)
    ' Take the value passed in (UserName) and save it in private
    ' variable (mstrName
    mstrName = UserName
End Property
```

Let's break down this property procedure. First, because the `Property Let` procedure exists, the `Name` property can be set because it is exposed to the outside world. A developer might set this property as follows:

```
cUser.Name = "James"
```

When `James` is passed into the property procedure, it is received in the variable `UserName`. The `Property Let` procedure takes the value of the variable `UserName` (James) and hides it away in the private module variable, `mstrName`. The preceding procedure passes in one parameter, but actually many parameters can be passed into a property procedure. A property value can only be retrieved if a `Property Get` procedure exists.

Property Get

A `Property Get` procedure enables the retrieval of a property value. If you do not want others to be able to retrieve a property value, do not include a `Property Get` statement. The `Property Get` statement obtains the value of the property, which is hidden away in the private variable, and returns it as the property value. The following example shows a `Property Get` statement for the `Name` property of the `cUser` object:

```
Public Property Get Name () as String
    ' Take the value hidden in the private variable (mstrName) and
    ' put it in the property value.
    Name = mstrName
End Property
```

A user can easily retrieve the value of a property (if a `Property Get` statement exists) by using the following code:

```
MsgBox cUser.Name
```

> **TIP**
>
> The data type of the Property Let must be the same as the Property Get. For example, the Property Let for the Name property accepts a string argument. The Property Get procedure must return a string data type as well.

Property Set

The Property Set statement enables you to create a property procedure that sets a reference to an object. Use the Set keyword within the Property Set procedure when assigning the object.

In this example, the cForm object is used. The cForm object has a Form property that must be passed a Form object. The code in the cForm class module is as follows:

```
Option Compare Database

' Declare private module level variable
Private mobjForm As Form

Public Property Get Form() As Variant

    ' Take the object hidden in the private variable (mobjForm) and
    ' put it in the property value.
    Set Form = mobjForm

End Property

Public Property Set Form(FormObject)

    ' Take the object passed in (FormObject) and save
    ' it in private variable (mobjForm)
    Set mobjForm = FormObject

End Property
```

When frmPropertySet is loaded, the form is passed into the Form property. Because it is an object, the Set keyword is used. The form object's name can then be retrieved for a message box. The following is the code for the frmPropertySet form:

```
' In this example, the "cForm" object is used. The "cForm" object has a
' "Form" property. When this form (frmPropertySet) loads, it is passed
' as an object into the "Form" property. When you click on the
' "Property Set" button, the form name is retrieved.

Private mobjForm As cForm

Private Sub cmdClose_Click()
```

Creating Objects with Class Modules

CHAPTER 11

295

11

CREATING OBJECTS
WITH CLASS
MODULES

```
        DoCmd.Close acForm, "frmPropertySet", acSaveNo

End Sub

Private Sub cmdPropertySet_Click()

    MsgBox "The form object (in the 'Form' property) has a name of: " _
        & mobjForm.Form.Name, vbInformation, "Property Set Example"

End Sub

Private Sub Form_Load()

    Set mobjForm = New cForm

    Set mobjForm.Form = Forms!frmPropertySet

End Sub

Private Sub Form_Unload(Cancel As Integer)

    Set mobjForm = Nothing

End Sub
```

Public Variable or Property Procedures

The easiest way to create properties of a class is to use public variables. However, there
are some disadvantages. Public variables are always exposed to the outside world.
Therefore, you have no control over who sets or retrieves property values. This could
create problems in your application if others change a property value that you are relying
on.

Another advantage of property procedures is that read-only and write-only properties can
be created. For example, if you want to create a Password property, you might want to
allow users to set the password but not retrieve it (write-only). To create a write-only
property, include a Property Let statement, but do not include a Property Get.

With property procedures, you can also perform an action in code when a property is
either set or retrieved.

Creating Enumerated Data Types

An enumerated type is a property value that can be provided to a developer who uses
your object. For example, when setting a form's visible property, you might have noticed
after typing the equal sign that you can choose True or False from a drop-down list (see
Figure 11.5).

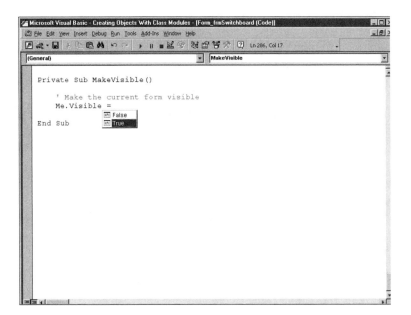

You can provide these property values likewise by creating enumerated types.

In the declaration section of the class module, use the Enum keyword to specify property values. For example, with the cUser object, assume you want to provide for the Type property a drop-down list with the following values: Manager, Staff, or Unknown. The code in the declaration section is as follows:

```
Public Enum UserList
    Manager
    Staff
    Unknown
End Enum
```

The next step would be to use the enumerated data type (UserList) as the data type of the Type property of the cUser class. The following example shows how, with a property created as a public variable:

```
Example 1: Property declared as a string variable
Public UserType as String
Example 1: Property declared as an enumerated data type
Public UserType as UserList
```

Property values can easily be set by using the drop-down list provided by IntelliSense (see Figure 11.6).

Creating Objects with Class Modules

CHAPTER 11

297

11

CREATING OBJECTS
WITH CLASS
MODULES

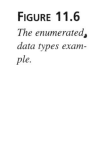

FIGURE 11.6

The enumerated data types example.

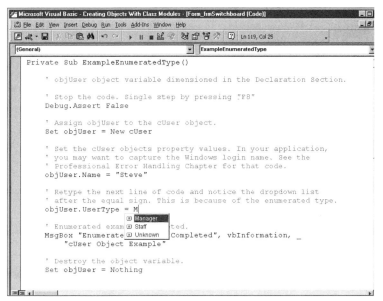

To determine which property value was chosen from the enumerated data types, each data type is numbered beginning with zero and is incremented by one.

TIP

Property values entered are not restricted to the enumerated data types. In the preceding example, the enumerated data type has three members: Manager, Staff and Unknown. VBA does not prevent a developer from ignoring the values in the list and typing a different value (such as FullTime). To restrict choices to the items in the list, use the numeric values of the enumerated items. For example, if there are three items in the list (and numbering starts at zero), do not allow any items less than zero and greater than two.

Creating Methods

A *method* is an action that can be taken on an object. To create a method for a class, simply create a public sub procedure or function. Let's assume that every time a user logs in to the application, you want to keep track of the date and time. The following code creates a Login method that enters in a table the date and time each user logs in.

```
Public Sub Login()

    ' Create an object variable for the recordset
    Dim rst As ADODB.Recordset

    ' Create a string variable
    Dim strSQL As String

    ' SQL statement for tblUsers
    strSQL = "SELECT * FROM tblUsers"

    ' Create an ADO Recordset
    Set rst = New ADODB.Recordset

    ' Open the recordset
    rst.Open strSQL, CurrentProject.Connection, adOpenKeyset, _
        adLockOptimistic

    ' Add a new record
    rst.AddNew

    ' Record the data and time the user logged in.
    With rst
        !Name = Me.Name
        !Date = Date
        !Time = Time
    End With

    ' Save the new record
    rst.Update

    ' Close the recordset
    rst.Close

    ' Destroy the object variable
    Set rst = Nothing
End Sub
```

Using Methods

To use the method when the application opens, the code is simply

```
cUser.login
```

Notice that users of the method do not have to understand the ADO code to update a value in the database. They can simply use any properties or methods available for the object that is conveniently displayed by IntelliSense.

Creating Events

Objects in Access have events. For example, a form object has a Load event, and a command button has a Click event.

You can create events for your custom objects as well. To do so, use the Event keyword in the declaration section and specify the name of the event. For example, let's add a Welcome event that will occur when a user opens the application. In the declaration section of the class module, include the following code to create the event:

```
Event Welcome()
```

To use the event, Raise the event in a method of the object. Let's raise the Welcome event in the Login method of the cUser object.

When the user starts the application, the Login method will be called. This will trigger the Welcome event, which will display a splash screen welcoming the user with a personalized message using his name. The code is as follows:

```
Public Sub LogIn()
    RaiseEvent Welcome
End If
```

Those are the only steps needed to create an event and to raise the event in the class module. The next section will show how to use the event in a form.

Using Events

TTo use the Welcome event from a form module, declare the object variable for cUser in the declaration section of the module and use the WithEvents keyword. The WithEvents keyword is required to expose and use the events of the cUser object. The code is as follows:

```
' Place in declaration section of the module
Private WithEvents objUser As cUser
```

> **TIP**
>
> WithEvents can be used only within class modules (form modules are class modules). WithEvents cannot be used in standard modules.

After declaring the module-level variable using the WithEvents keyword, examine the combo boxes at the top of the module window. In the left column box, choose the object cUser. Then, in the combo box on the right side, you will see the events of the cUser object. Choose the Welcome events, and the procedure will appear in the code window, where you can write code to respond to the event.

The following example shows code responding to the Welcome event (see Figure 11.7).

FIGURE 11.7

The procedure using the Welcome event of the cUser object.

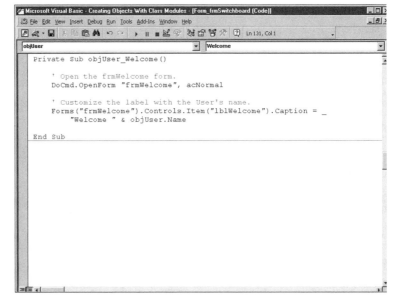

As a result, the user will see a welcome splash screen each time she opens the application (see Figure 11.8).

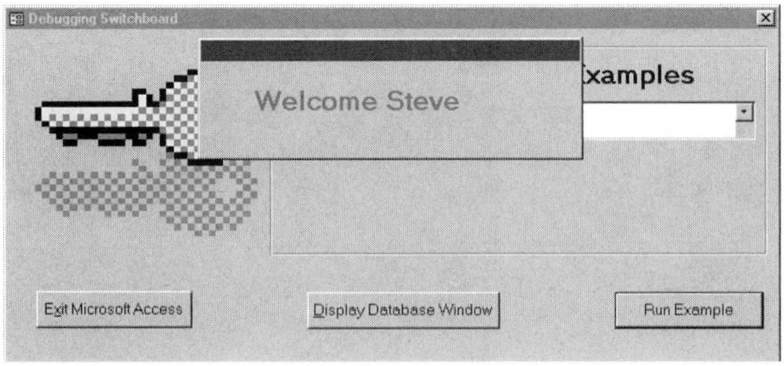

FIGURE 11.8

The welcome splash screen.

Firing the Initialize and Terminate Events

Class modules automatically include initialize and terminate events. To use these events, choose the event from the combo box at the top of the code window.

The initialize event fires whenever an object is created. For example, if you want certain code to run whenever the cUser object is created, put the code in the initialize event.

The terminate event occurs when the object is destroyed. This is a good place to put clean-up code to close database connections, release object variables, and so on.

Using Objects

At this point, the cUser object exists with properties and methods. To use it in the class module, simply type the name of the object and a period. IntelliSense will show a list of properties and methods for the object.

To use the object within the class that creates the object, use the Me keyword. For example, to set the user's name:

```
Me.User = "Steve"
```

Using the object from outside the cUser class module (in forms or standard modules) involves a two-step process. First, declare an object variable to use as a reference to the object. Second, use the Set keyword to create a reference from the object variable to the object.

Creating an Object Variable

A *variable* is a chunk of memory set aside to store or retrieve information. Undoubtedly, you have a great deal of experience with "simple variables," such as strings and integers. The following are examples of declaring and using two simple variables:

```
Dim strName as String
Dim I as integer

StrName = "James"
I = 10
```

In the preceding examples, the variables include a specific type of data, and the information is stored and can be retrieved as needed.

An Object variable is declared with the Dim statement just like simple variables:

```
Dim objUser as cUser
```

Assigning an Object Variable to an Object

The Set keyword is used to assign the reference of the object variable to the object. For example:

```
Set objUser = New cUser
```

> **CAUTION**
>
> Always declare the Dim and Set statements on separate lines. Do not combine the Dim and Set statements on a single line such as Dim objUser = New cUser. If you do so, the code will execute more slowly, and you will not know exactly when the object becomes instantiated (comes into memory).

Using the Object

After creating and setting the object variable, properties and methods of the object can be used with IntelliSense. Using the dot syntax, properties can be set and retrieved, and methods can be executed.

Setting a property value: Object.Property = Value

Retrieving a property value: MsgBox Object.Property

> **TIP**
>
> If you discover, while attempting to use an object, that IntelliSense shows no properties and methods for the object, that is a tip-off that you might not have created or set an object variable. Sometimes, however, IntelliSense does not show items even though your code is correct. Be bold—assume that your code is correct and test it. Microsoft has not provided IntelliSense for all code items.

Releasing the Object

When you are done with the object variable, release it by setting the object equal to Nothing. In this way, valuable resources can be reclaimed. The proper syntax is as follows:

```
' Release the Object Variable
Set objUser = Nothing
```

> **TIP**
>
> When you dimension an object variable, immediately go to the bottom of the procedure and set the object variable equal to `Nothing`. This prevents you from forgetting to release object variables after writing a long procedure.

Creating Multiple Instances of an Object

A class has a defined set of properties and methods. It is like a template or framework. To illustrate, consider opening a new document in Microsoft Word. When you create a new Word document, you can use a template, such as Contemporary Letter. After choosing the template, you can make custom changes to the document. These changes are made to the new document, *not* to the template. The same principle applies to classes.

When the class is instantiated (created), the instance of the object contains the basic set of properties and methods (a template). From that point on, the object becomes unique, with its own set of property values and methods.

One of the benefits of class modules is that multiple instances of the class can be created. Each instance begins with the basic set of properties and methods, but each instance can be customized differently after the object is created. For example, let's say five `cUser` objects are created. All five can have differing property values and methods. For example, one `cUser` object might have a `Name` property value of `James`, and another `Steve`.

To create multiple instances of the object, simply create additional object variables and assign each object variable to a new object. Consider the following code:

```
Public Sub ManyUsers()

    Dim objUser1 as cUser
    Dim objUser2 as cUser

    Set objUser1 = New cUser
    Set objUser2 = New cUser

    ObjUser1.Name = "James"
    ObjUser2.Name = "Steve"

    MsgBox "Current users are: " & objUser1.Name & " and " objUser2.Name

    Set objUser1 = Nothing
    Set objUser2 = Nothing

End Sub
```

Examining More Object Examples

The chapter examples include numerous classes for your use (see "Creating Objects with Class Modules.mdb" on the CD-ROM accompanying this book). Each object will be briefly summarized.

Text File Object

The chapter code includes a `cTextFile` object that can be used to read and write information to a text file (see Figure 11.9).

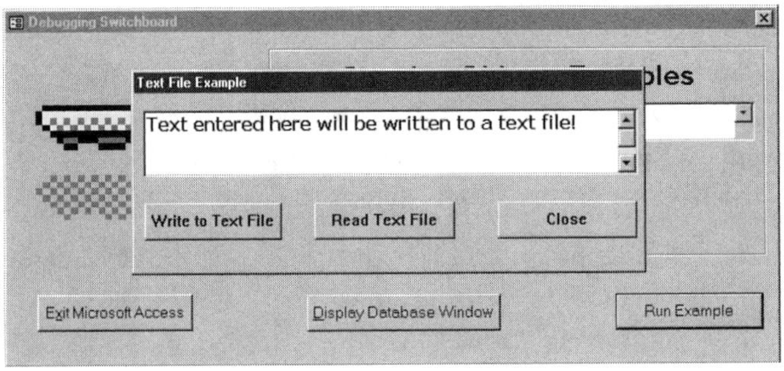

FIGURE 11.9

The TextFile *object example.*

The class module includes the following code:

```
Private pintFreeFile As Integer
Private pvarInfo As Variant

Public Function ReadLineText(strFileName As String) As String

    pintFreeFile = FreeFile
    Open strFileName For Input As pintFreeFile
    Line Input #pintFreeFile, pvarInfo
    ReadLineText = pvarInfo
    Close #pintFreeFile

End Function

Public Function ReadAllText(strFileName As String) As String

    pintFreeFile = FreeFile
    Open strFileName For Input As pintFreeFile
    Do Until VBA.EOF(pintFreeFile)
        Line Input #pintFreeFile, pvarInfo
        ReadAllText = ReadAllText & vbCrLf & pvarInfo
    Loop
    Close #pintFreeFile
```

```
End Function

Public Sub WriteLineText(strFileName As String, strText As String)

    pintFreeFile = FreeFile
    Open strFileName For Append As pintFreeFile
    Write #pintFreeFile, strText
    Close #pintFreeFile

End Sub
```

Timer Object

A cTimer class module is included in the chapter code. This class module is used for two purposes: as a stopwatch to see how many seconds have passed, and to create a "wait state" to hold off code execution for a number of seconds. The code in the cTimer class module is as follows:

```
Option Explicit

Private msngStart As Single

Public Sub Wait(lngSeconds As Long)

    Do Until Timer > msngStart + lngSeconds
        DoEvents
    Loop

End Sub

Public Sub StartTimer()

    msngStart = Timer

End Sub

Public Function ElapsedTime() As Long

    Dim sngTimerStop As Single
    sngTimerStop = Timer

    ElapsedTime = sngTimerStop - msngStart

    msngStart = 0
    sngTimerStop = 0

End Function
```

The frmTimer in "Creating Objects with Class Modules.mdb" demonstrates how to use the timer to determine elapsed time and create a "wait state." See Figure 11.10.

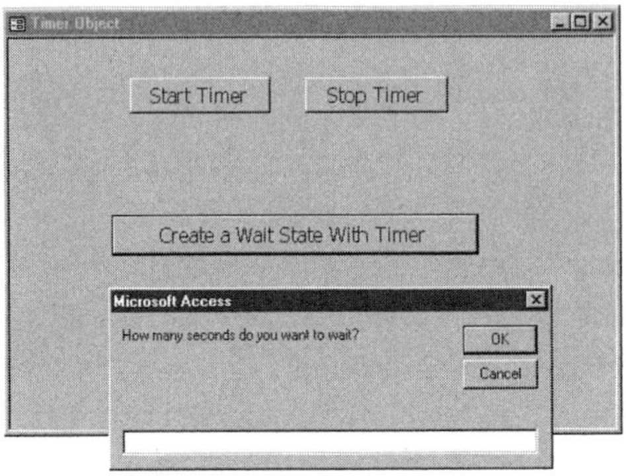

FIGURE 11.10

*Use the timer
object for elapsed
time and a wait
state.*

Sound Object

A cSound class module is included in the chapter code to play sounds in Access applications. The cSound class module contains only one method (PlaySound) that passes the sound file to a Windows API call:

```
' Windows API call.
Private Declare Function sndPlaySound Lib "winmm.dll" Alias _
"sndPlaySoundA" (ByVal lpszSoundName As String, ByVal uFlags _
As Long) As Long

Public Sub PlaySound(SoundFile As String)

    ' Play the Sound File.
    sndPlaySound SoundFile, 1

End Sub
```

The following code instantiates and uses an objSound object (see Figure 11.11):

```
Dim objSound As cSound

Set objSound = New Sound

' If using Windows NT use the path "C:\WINNT"
objSound.PlaySound "C:\Windows\chimes.wav"

Set objSound = Nothing
```

Letter Object

A cLetter class module is included in the chapter code to create letters in Microsoft Word. The letter is created using a mail merge. A Word template is used to produce the letter, and a SQL statement obtains the data for the letter. The ShowWord method (a Boolean) determines whether Word is actually made visible to the user. Sometimes, you might want letters sent directly to the printer without editing.

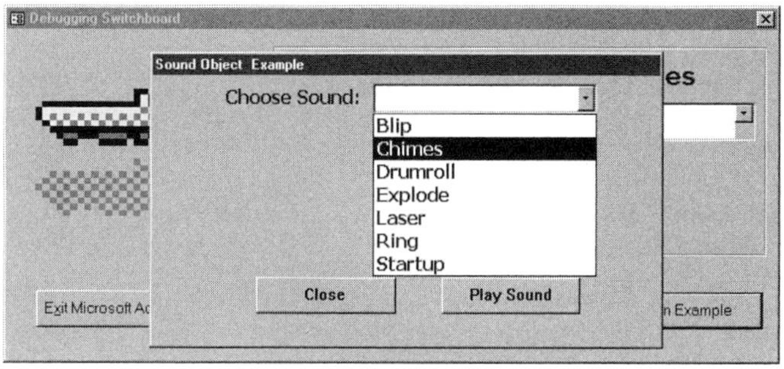

Creating Objects with Class Modules

CHAPTER 11

307

11

CREATING OBJECTS
WITH CLASS
MODULES

FIGURE 11.11

The Sound *object
example.*

The following is the code in the cLetter class module:

```
Option Explicit

Private objWord As Word.Application

'local variable(s) to hold property value(s)
Private mvarTemplate As String 'local copy
Private mvarSQLStatement As String 'local copy

Public Property Let SQLStatement(ByVal vData As String)
    mvarSQLStatement = vData
End Property

Public Property Get SQLStatement() As String
    SQLStatement = mvarSQLStatement
End Property

Public Property Let Template(ByVal vData As String)
    mvarTemplate = vData
End Property

Public Property Get Template() As String
    Template = mvarTemplate
End Property

Public Sub CreateLetter(DatabasePath As String, ShowWord As Boolean)

    ' Write the Customer data to a temporary temp file to use with
    ' the mail merge. This is faster than getting the data directly
    ' from Access.
    DoCmd.OutputTo acOutputQuery, "qryCustomers", _
        acFormatRTF, "C:\Temp.RTF", False

    objWord.Documents.Add (Me.Template)

    ' Run Mail Merge
    With objWord.ActiveDocument.MailMerge
```

```
            .MainDocumentType = wdFormLetters
            .OpenDataSource Name:="C:\Temp.rtf"
            .Destination = wdSendToNewDocument
            .Execute
        End With

        If ShowWord Then
          Me.ShowWord
        End If

End Sub

Friend Sub ShowWord()

    ' Show Word to the user.
    objWord.Visible = True

End Sub

Private Sub Class_Initialize()

    ' Resume to the next line following the error.
    On Error Resume Next

    ' Attempt to reference Word which is already running.
    Set objWord = GetObject(, "Word.Application")

    ' If true, Word is not running.
    If objWord Is Nothing Then
        ' Create a new instance of the Word application.
        Set objWord = New Word.Application
        ' If true, MS Word is not installed.
        If objWord Is Nothing Then
            MsgBox "MS Word is not installed on your computer"
        End If
    End If

End Sub

Private Sub Class_Terminate()

  Set objWord = Nothing

End Sub
```

The following code instantiates an `objLetter` object and uses its properties and methods:

```
' Dimension variables.
Dim objLetter As cLetter
Dim strPath As String
```

```
strPath = CurrentProject.Path

' Assign object variables to cLetter object.
Set objLetter = New cLetter

' Word template to use for the document.
objLetter.Template = strPath & "\Business Services Letter.Dot"

' SQL statement used to get data for the form.
objLetter.SQLStatement = "SELECT * FROM tblCustomers"

' Call the "CreateLetter" method to create the letter.
objLetter.CreateLetter strPath & "\Objects.mdb", True

' Destroy the object variable
Set objLetter = Nothing
```

Outlook Object

A cOutlook class module is included in the chapter code to display an Outlook New Message form (see Figure 11.12). If you want to enable users to enter Outlook messages from within your Access application, simply call the NewEmailMessage method.

FIGURE 11.12

Display the Outlook New Message Form in Access applications.

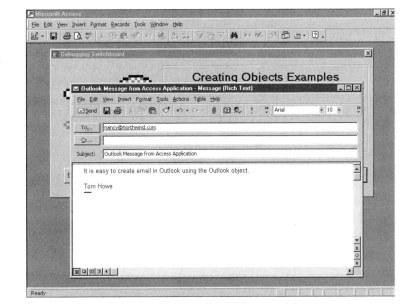

The following is the code in the cSound class module:

```
Option Explicit

Private mobjOutlook As Outlook.Application
Private mMyItem As Object

Public Sub NewEmailMessage(EmailAddress As String)

    ' Create a new Outlook email message
    Set mMyItem = mobjOutlook.CreateItem(olMailItem)

    mMyItem.To = EmailAddress

    mMyItem.Display

End Sub

Private Sub Class_Initialize()

    ' There is no reason to use "GetObject" to automate to Outlook.
    ' Outlook will always open one instance of the application.
    ' Use the "New" keyword.

    ' Set the object variable to the Outlook application.
    Set mobjOutlook = New Outlook.Application

    ' If true, MS Outlook is not installed.
    If mobjOutlook Is Nothing Then

        MsgBox "MS Outlook is not installed on your computer"

    End If

End Sub

Private Sub Class_Terminate()

    ' Release the object variable.
    Set mobjOutlook = Nothing

End Sub
```

The following code instantiates an `objOutlook` object and calls the `NewMailMessage` method:

```
' Dimension object variables.
Dim objOutlook As cOutlook

' Assign object variables to cOutlook object.
Set objOutlook = New cOutlook
```

```
' Call the "NewEMailMessage method.
objOutlook.NewEmailMessage "nancy@northwind.com"

' Destroy the object variable
Set objOutlook = Nothing
```

Implementing an Error Handler Object

See the sample code for Chapter 13, "Professional Error Handling." A class module provides for extensive error handling, including

- Logging errors to an Access table
- Logging errors to a text file
- Handling Email errors
- Handling record errors on an Outlook calendar

See the cError object in the Object Browser, as shown in Figure 11.13.

FIGURE 11.13

The cError *object in the Object Browser.*

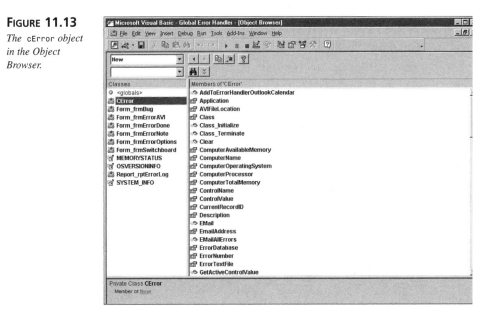

Using Objects with VBA Collections

VBA collections provide a way to treat your custom objects as a group. For example, if five cUser objects exist and you want to perform an action on each object, it is easier and more efficient to treat all five objects as a group rather than individually.

You are probably already familiar with built-in collections such as the "forms" and "controls" collections. VBA also has a collection object. A *collection* is a way of treating a group of objects as a unit. In life, we deal with collections all the time. An orchestra conductor might say, "All wind instruments stand up." It would be less efficient for the conductor to say, "Mary, Jim, John, Joe, Sally, stand up." Similarly, we can treat objects that we create as a unit or collection.

The most important concept here is that a collection is an object with its own properties and methods. A collection object has the following characteristics:

- It is an object with properties and methods.
- Different types of objects can be added to the collection.
- The size is variable, meaning it expands and contracts as items are added and removed from the collection.
- The items in the selection cannot be sorted.
- Items in the collection are index-based one (start counting at the numeral 1).

Creating VBA Collections

Because collections are objects, you create a collection the same way you create objects. First, declare an object variable to use as a reference to the collection. Second, use the Set keyword to create a reference from the object variable to the collection. The following code creates a collection of users:

```
Dim Users as Collection
Set Users = New Collection
```

TIP

You might find it helpful to name a collection the plural name of the objects contained in the collection. The object that will be added to the collection in this example is User. Therefore, the collection is named Users (plural).

VBA Collection's Properties and Methods

The collection object has a very simple structure, with only one property and three methods, as shown in Table 11.1:

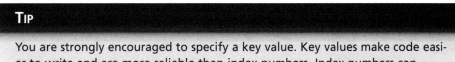
TABLE 11.1 THE COLLECTION OBJECT'S PROPERTIES AND METHODS

Name	Type	Description
Count	Property	Indicates how many items are in the collection.
Add	Method	Used to add items to a collection.
Remove	Method	Used to remove items from a collection.
Item	Method	Used to refer to items in the collection. This is the default method.

Adding Items to a Collection

To add items to the collection, use the Add method of the collection object.

```
Collection.Add Item [, Key][, Before][, After]
```

Then pass the object variable for each object added to the collection. For example, to add two users to the collection, use the object variable for each user: objUser1 and objUser2. The next parameter is the Key value (a friendly name) to use to refer to the object. If a key value is not specified, each item in the collection must be referred to by index number.

> **TIP**
>
> You are strongly encouraged to specify a key value. Key values make code easier to write and are more reliable than index numbers. Index numbers can change if items are removed from the collection or inserted into specific locations of the collection using arguments of the Add method.

In the following example, two users will be added to the Users collection.

```
Dim User1 as cUser
Dim User2 as cUser
Dim Users as Collection

Set User1 = New cUser
Set User2 = New cUser
Set Users = New Collection
```

```
User1.Name = "James"
User2.Name = "Steve"

Users.Add User1, User1.Name
Users.Add User2, User2.Name

Set User1 = Nothing
Set User2 = Nothing
Set Users = Nothing
```

The preceding code adds the object User1 to the collection. The key is specified with the value of the Name property of the object. The User2 object is added in the same manner.

Note that there is a "before" and "after" argument for the Add method of collections to specify the order for an object in a collection.

Referring to a Specific Object

Objects in the collection can be referred to by number or key value. When referring to items in a collection by number, remember that the items are indexed-based one, which means that you begin counting at 1. The easier way to refer to an object in a collection is by its key name. The following code shows how to refer to the specific object User2 using both these methods. Although Item does not need to be specified (it is the default method), it makes the code easier to read and maintain.

```
' Refer to an object in a collection by index number.
MsgBox Users.Item(2).Type

' Refer to an object in a collection by key value.
MsgBox Users.Item("Steve").Type
```

Looping Through Items in a Collection

The easiest and most efficient way to loop through objects in a collection is to use a For Each loop. A For Next loop can be used as well, but it is slower.

To use a For Each loop, specify the object to examine in the collection. The code is as follows:

```
' Must declare object variable.
Dim User as cUser

For Each User in Users
    MsgBox User.Type
Next User
```

> **TIP**
>
> The preceding example will examine each user in the collection. Notice that the individual users had object variables named User1 and User2. To use the For Each loop, specify a generic object variable named User. This object variable need not be assigned to an object variable with the Set keyword. Its only purpose is use with the For Each loop.

Removing Individual Objects

To remove specific objects from the collection, use the object's index number or key value.

```
' Remove object by index number.
Users.Remove 2

' Remove object by key value.
Users.Remove "Steve"
```

Removing All Objects

To remove all objects from a collection, do not loop through all items in the collection and call the remove method. A much faster approach is to reassign the collection object to a new collection.

```
' Remove all objects from a collection.
Set Users = New Collection
```

Releasing the Object Variable

Collections are objects. Just as you would with any other object variable, be sure to remember to release the object variable by setting it to Nothing.

```
' Release the collection object variable.
Set Users = Nothing
```

Summary

Creating objects is an efficient way to write and maintain applications. The benefits include code that is better organized, easier to write and maintain, easier to use with IntelliSense, and more portable. Also, complex functionality can be hidden from developers who use the object, and developers can create multiple instances of the object.

Debugging Access Applications

CHAPTER 12

Using the Debugging Tools in Microsoft Access and the debugging techniques discussed in this chapter can save an enormous amount of development time. Taking the time to study these tools and techniques will result in significant long-term benefits.

Don't assume that you only need these debugging tools to create complex applications. In even the most simple applications, program errors are not readily apparent or easy to find.

It is essential that program errors be discovered and fixed immediately. Although some errors might have little or no consequence, others can corrupt the database or worse.

Eliminating Logic Errors

Logic errors occur when the code does not produce the expected result(s). The logic might be flawed or the program flows incorrectly. When the code executes, but does not produce the desired result, expect a logic error.

Most of the time spent debugging an application involves discovering and fixing logic errors. This chapter will provide you the techniques and tools to resolve these errors.

Examples of logic errors include

- A procedure attempting to use a field in a database that has no data (a null value)
- Incorrect mathematical calculations
- Processing of an operation in code in the wrong order

Working with the Visual Basic Development Environment (IDE)

A radical change occurred in Access 2000's design environment. Access now incorporates the Visual Basic Integrated Development Environment (IDE) just like Visual Basic 5/6, Word 97, and other Office 97/2000 products. This editing environment now provides a standard means to develop applications within the various products. The debugging techniques in this chapter can be utilized in Access as well as Visual Basic and Microsoft Office development. To open the IDE, while in a form design mode, under the View menu choose Code. The IDE includes various windows that can be opened and closed, such as the Project window, Properties window, Immediate window and more. To open a window in the IDE, select the window under the View menu. Close the window by clicking the close button in the upper-right corner of the window. The next time you open the IDE, all the windows will be displayed as they were the last time the IDE was closed.

When a form is opened in Design view, you can work with controls and properties just like in earlier versions of Access. However, you must open the Visual Basic IDE to view code for the form. (See Figure 12.1.) Actually this is a completely separate application from Access.

FIGURE **12.1**

The Visual Basic Integrated Development Environment (IDE).

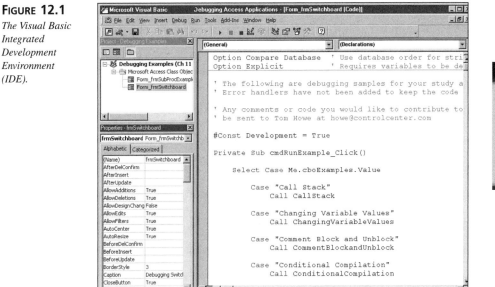

Although the Visual Basic IDE is a separate application, it works in conjunction with Access. If the Visual Basic IDE is open, the Visual Basic IDE will also be closed when you quit Access. To close the Visual Basic IDE, choose Close and Return to Microsoft Access under the File menu.

Let's now examine the windows in the Visual Basic IDE.

The Project Explorer

The Project Explorer displays a list of the forms, reports, and class modules in your Access application. (See Figure 12.2.) Right-click on any of these objects to view the code or go into Design mode for a form. To open the Project Explorer, choose Project Explorer under the View menu or press Ctrl+R.

FIGURE 12.2

The Project Explorer window.

The Code Window

The Code window shows the code for forms, modules, and class modules. (See Figure 12.3.) As a developer, you will most likely spend many hours entering and modifying code in the Code window. To open the Code window, choose Code under the View menu or press F7. There are two drop-down lists at the top of the Code window. The list on the left is used to choose an object such as a form or control on a form. The list on the right side is used to choose the procedure for the selected object.

FIGURE 12.3

The Code window.

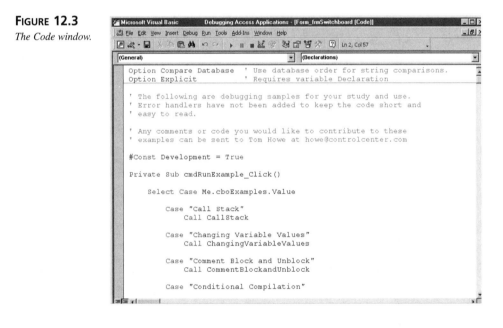

The Properties Window

Use the Properties window to set and view the properties of forms, reports, or controls on forms and reports. (See Figure 12.4.) To open the Properties window, choose Properties under the View menu or press F4.

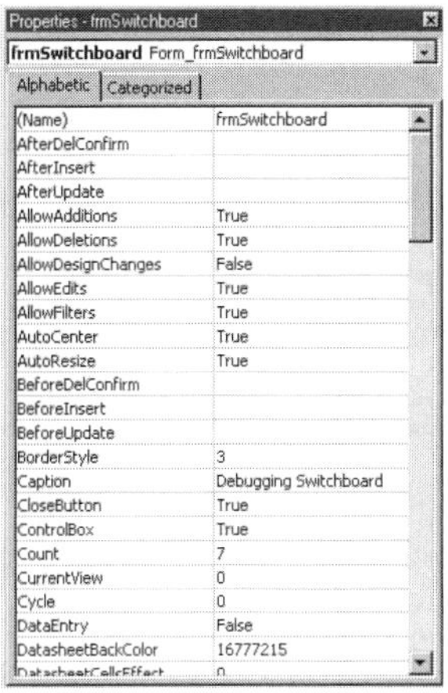

FIGURE 12.4

The Properties window.

The Immediate Window

The Immediate window can be used to evaluate and set variables, run procedures, and output `Debug.Print` statements. To open it, choose Immediate window under the View menu or press Ctrl+G. The Immediate window will be discussed in detail later in this chapter.

The Locals Window

The Locals window shows expressions, values, and types of all variables that are currently in scope. To open the Locals window, choose Locals window under the View menu. Details related to the Locals window will be discussed later in this chapter.

The Watch Window

The Watch window can be used to evaluate expressions while the application runs. To open the Watch window, choose Watch window under the View menu. Details related to the Watch window will be discussed later in this chapter.

The Object Browser

To open the Object Browser, choose Object Browser under the View menu or press F2. Use the Object Browser to examine objects, properties and methods. (See Figure 12.5.)

FIGURE 12.5

*The Object
Browser.*

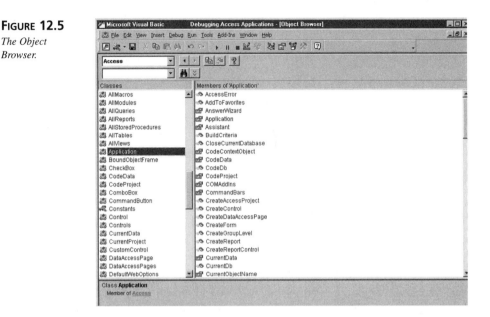

The Call Stack Window

The Call Stack window shows procedures that have been previously called. To open the Call Stack window, choose Call Stack from the View menu or press Ctrl+L. Details related to the Call Stack window will be discussed later in this chapter.

> **TIP**
>
> As shown previously, there are numerous windows that can be shown in the IDE. It is much easier to develop in the IDE with screen resolution set to 1024×768 or higher. Better yet, try the new multi-monitor feature in Windows 98 and Windows 2000.
>
> To easily work with the windows, learn the shortcut keys to quickly open and close the windows. The windows can be resized and moved as needed. But beware that if you undock a window by dragging it to a different location, it is hard to re-dock it. The trick is to double-click on the title bar to dock and undock the window.

Working with the Debug Object

The Debug object has two methods that are helpful in debugging applications:
Debug.Print and Debug.Assert.

Debug.Print

With `Debug.Print`, you can print information to the Immediate window. This method may be used either in the Immediate window itself or in the code.

> **TIP**
>
> To print information to the Immediate window, use the `Debug.Print` statement in code. While testing expressions or running functions in the Immediate window, you do not need to type `Debug.Print`. Instead Type a question mark ?, which will provide the same result.

In the Immediate window, you can test built-in functions, values in a recordset, and more. (See Figure 12.6.) For example, the following tests the built-in function `Len`:

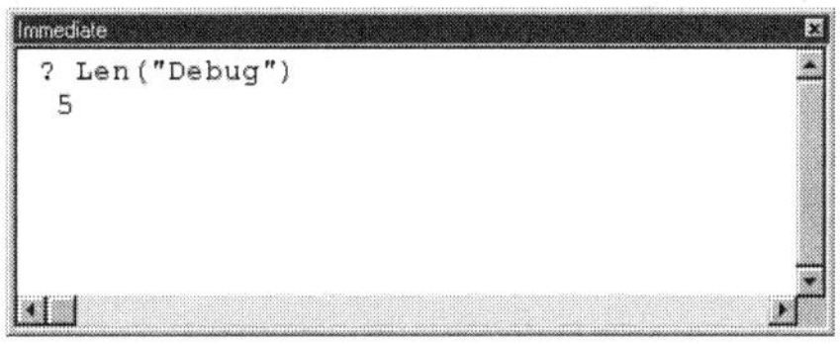

FIGURE 12.6

Use `Debug.Print` *in the Immediate window to test built-in functions.*

```
Immediate
  ? Len("Debug")
      5
```

By placing `Debug.Print` in your code, values and other information can be printed to the Immediate window. When the following code executes, the value of the state will be printed to the Immediate window:

```
Sub Demo ( )
        Debug.Print rst.States
        Select Case rst.States
                Case "Washington"
                        MsgBox "Washington"
                Case "Oregon"
                        MsgBox "Oregon"
                Case "California"
                        MsgBox "California
        End Select
End Sub
```

The Immediate window does not wrap the text, so keep your output brief. It is not necessary to remove `Debug.Print` statements from your code because the end user will never see the Immediate window. However it will have some impact on performance if you use lots of them.

Debug.Assert

`Debug.Assert` will conditionally suspend execution on a particular line of code. For example, if a statement of code reads `Debug.Assert False`, the code will stop execution on that line of code. This will allow you to then step through the code and debug any errors.

> **TIP**
>
> Never use the `Stop` keyword in your code. This will not only stop the execution of your code, but if you forget to remove it, your code will also stop when users run your application. Always use `Debug.Assert False` instead because this statement of code is always removed by the compiler.

Using the Immediate Window

To open the Immediate window, go to the Visual Basic Editor and choose Immediate Window under the View menu or press Ctrl+G. The Immediate window can be used to evaluate and set variables, to run functions and sub procedures and to output `Debug.Print` statements.

Evaluating Variables

To evaluate variables in the Immediate window, enter a question mark followed by the variable name. For example, `? strName`. Remember, you can also determine the value of a variable by hovering the cursor over the variable while in break mode.

Changing the Value of Variables

To change the value of a variable in the Immediate window, enter the variable name followed by an equal sign and the new value. For example, `intI = 10`.

Evaluating Built-in Functions

To evaluate built-in functions in the Immediate window, enter a question mark followed by the built-in function. For example, `? Now`.

Running Custom Functions

To run your own functions in the Immediate window, enter a question mark followed by the name of your function and any parameters. For example, `? MyFunction`.

Running Custom Sub Procedures

To run your own sub procedures in the Immediate window, simply enter the name of your sub procedure and any parameters. For example, type `MySubProcedure`. Do not use a question mark in front of the sub procedure.

> **TIP**
>
> When running a sub procedure or function in the Immediate window, enter the sub procedure or function name (do not use a question mark in front of the procedure name). If the sub procedure or function is in a form module, enter the name of the form name in front of the procedure name (for example, `frmTest.MySubProcedure`).

Tips for Using the Immediate Window

Because you will spend a great deal of time using the Immediate window, the following tips might prove useful.

Running Statements in the Immediate Window

To run a statement of code in the Immediate window, place the cursor anywhere in the statement of code. It is not necessary that the cursor be at the beginning or end of the statement of code.

If there are several statements of code in the Immediate window, you do not need to delete the statements of code after the statement you want to run. Simply put the cursor anywhere in the statement of code you want to execute and press Enter.

Moving Around in the Immediate Window

Use the mouse and arrow keys to move the insertion point. The Home key moves the insertion point to the beginning of the current line of code; the End key moves the insertion point to the end.

The Page Up and Page Down keys move through the code a page at a time.

To move the insertion point to the beginning of the Immediate Window, press Ctrl+Home. Use Ctrl+End to move the insertion point to the end of the Immediate window.

Deleting Code in the Immediate Window

To quickly highlight all the code in the Immediate Window to delete it, press Shift+Ctrl+Home if you are at the end of the code in the Immediate window. This will highlight all the code; then press Delete.

If the insertion point is at the beginning of the code in the Immediate window, press Shift+Ctrl+End to highlight all the code. Then press the Delete key.

Using the Debugger

It is easy to debug applications in Access 2000 by stopping execution of the code in certain places and stepping through the code to observe the program flow.

Setting Breakpoints

A breakpoint stops the execution of code. To set a breakpoint, put the cursor on a statement and choose Toggle Breakpoint under the Run menu of the Visual Basic Editor, or press F9. Remember that you cannot set a breakpoint on a blank line, a comment only line, or a statement of code containing a `Dim` statement. Another way to set the breakpoint is to click on the gray left margin of the code window next to a statement of code. This will put a large red dot in the left border indicating that a breakpoint is present.

When the program is run, execution will stop on the statement where the breakpoint is located. (See Figure 12.7.) The code module will open automatically and the statement of code will be highlighted in yellow. You can then step through the code, view or change the value of variables, and more.

FIGURE 12.7

Code execution stopped at breakpoint.

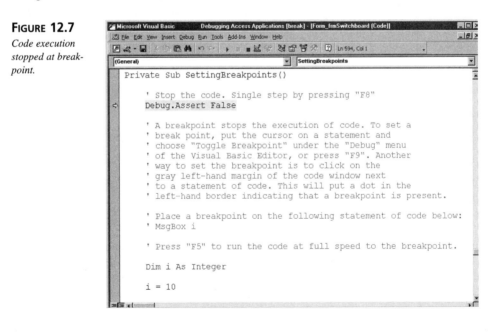

```
Private Sub SettingBreakpoints()

    ' Stop the code. Single step by pressing "F8"
    Debug.Assert False

    ' A breakpoint stops the execution of code. To set a
    ' break point, put the cursor on a statement and
    ' choose "Toggle Breakpoint" under the "Debug" menu
    ' of the Visual Basic Editor, or press "F9". Another
    ' way to set the breakpoint is to click on the
    ' gray left-hand margin of the code window next
    ' to a statement of code. This will put a dot in the
    ' left-hand border indicating that a breakpoint is present.

    ' Place a breakpoint on the following statement of code below:
    ' MsgBox i

    ' Press "F5" to run the code at full speed to the breakpoint.

    Dim i As Integer

    i = 10
```

To eliminate a breakpoint, choose Clear All Breakpoints from the Run menu or press Ctrl+Shift+F9.

Stepping Through Code

When code execution stops due to a breakpoint, the statement of code highlighted in yellow has not executed. You can move forward through your code by using several stepping techniques.

Single-Stepping Through Code

Choose Step Into under the Debug menu in the Visual Basic Editor or press F8 to execute one statement of code at a time. Single-stepping through code is the most effective way to observe program flow and variable values in code.

> **TIP**
>
> Some developers find the Debug toolbar to be a great help. To open the toolbar, go to the View menu, and then choose Toolbars, Debug.

Step Over

At times, you will have one procedure call other procedures. The procedures you are calling might be rock solid (in other words, fully tested and error-free). Use Step Over under the Debug menu or press Shift+F8 to execute the procedure you are calling at full speed so you do not have to step through each statement of code.

After the calling procedure has finished executing, the code will again stop executing. At this point, you can continue to single-step through the code.

Step Out

Let's assume you are stepping through a procedure which calls another procedure. When you are in the called procedure, you can quickly execute the rest of the procedure and return to the original procedure by choosing Step Out from the Debug menu or press Ctrl+Shift+F8. This is useful when you forget to "step over" until you are already into the procedure.

Run to Cursor

When stepping through code, you can execute the code at full speed to the location of your cursor. This is helpful when you step through a statement of code and then want to run at full speed to another section of the code. One example is looping structures. After stepping through a loop several times to verify that it is working correctly, put the cursor at the end of the loop and choose Run to Cursor from the Debug menu, or press Ctrl+F8.

Set Next Statement

When stepping through code, you can set the next statement that you want to execute. To do so, right-click the line of code that you want to execute next. Then click on Set Next Statement from the shortcut menu.

Continuing Code Execution

After stepping through code to verify the code is working correctly, you might want to continue executing the code at full speed. To do so, choose Continue under the Run menu or press F5.

Rerunning Code

After you discover and have fixed the error while stepping through code, you can rerun the code without stopping and restarting the application. The yellow arrow in the left border shows the statement of code which will execute next. You can click on the yellow arrow, drag it up to a previous line of code, and rerun the code that you previously stepped through.

Determining Variable Values

While debugging your application, you can easily discover the value of a variable by hovering the mouse over the variable while in break mode. (See Figure 12.8.)

The Immediate window can also be used to get a variable's value. For example, the following text in the Immediate window will return the value of a variable named strName:
`? strName.`

Using Microsoft IntelliSense While Debugging

When a program error occurs and you have found the offending line of code, check the syntax with the use of IntelliSense. IntelliSense provides for rapid development by suggesting properties and methods of objects as you type code. For example, after typing the name of an object (for example, `Recordset` or `Application`), type a period and see if you have used the correct name and spelling of the property or methods. If you do not see the property or method in the drop-down list, this is a tip-off that the syntax might be incorrect.

FIGURE **12.8**

Determining a variable's value in break mode.

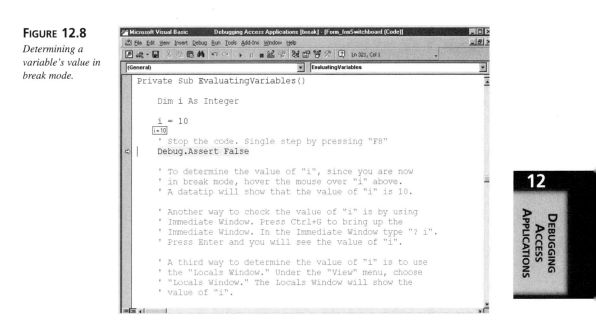

Using the Locals Window

The Locals window will show you expressions, values, and types of all variables that are currently in scope. (See Figure 12.9.) To display the Locals window, choose Locals window under the View menu.

FIGURE **12.9**

The Locals window shows variables in current scope.

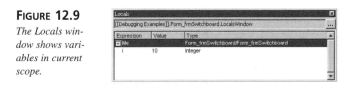

Tip

The Locals window can be used to change the value of variables. Double-click on the variable value and enter the new value.

Using the Watch Window

The Watch window can be used to evaluate expressions while the application runs. For example, if you want to see anywhere in the application where the variable strName is changed, you can use the Watch window.

The first step is to choose Add Watch under the Debug menu. In the Add Watch dialog box, enter the expression you want to watch (for example, `strName = "Smith"`). In the dialog box, also choose whether you want to evaluate the expression in certain procedures, modules, or the entire application. (See Figure 12.10.) Specify the Watch Type in the dialog box:

- Watch Expression—Monitors the expression
- Break When the Value is True—Stops the code in break mode when the expression is True
- Break When Value Changes—Stops the code in break mode when the value of the expression changes

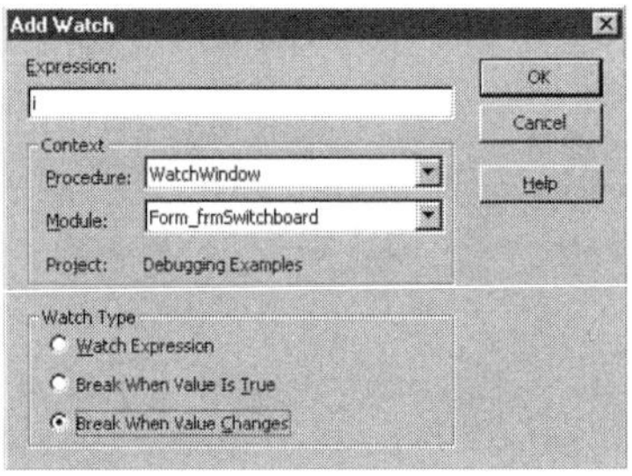

FIGURE 12.10

Use the Add Watch dialog box to create a Watch expression.

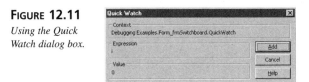

To create a Watch expression quickly, highlight an expression in your code. Then choose Quick Watch from the Debug menu or press Shift+F9. Choose the Add button on the Quick Watch Dialog box. (See Figure 12.11.)

FIGURE 12.11

Using the Quick Watch dialog box.

Viewing the Call Stack

Your application can include procedures that call other procedures that, in turn, can call other procedures, and so on. When debugging your application, it might not be obvious "how you got here" or what list of procedures have been executed. The Call Stack window will show you.

Think about it this way. Stepping through code moves you forward, into the future. The Call Stack is a historical view. It shows what procedures have been previously called.

(See Figure 12.12.) To open the Call Stack window, choose Call Stack from the View menu or press Ctrl+L.

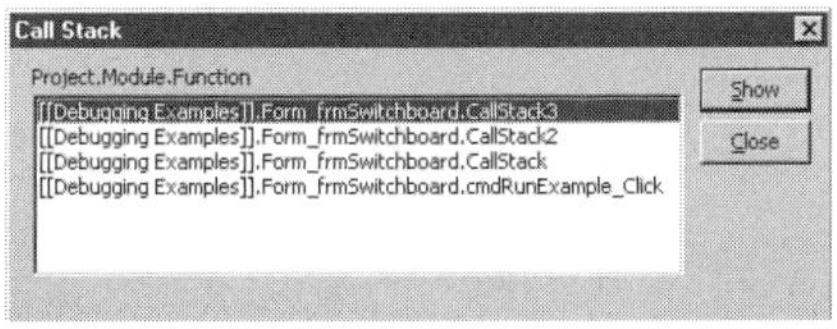

FIGURE 12.12

Use the Call Stack window to show what procedures have been called.

> **TIP**
>
> To jump to a procedure, select it from the Call Stack window and click on the Show button (or simply double-click on the procedure).

Using Conditional Compilation

Maintaining a single version of an application is much easier than creating multiple versions. Let's say you have an application used by many offices. Most of the application is generic and can be used by all the office but a small amount of code needs to be customized for each individual office. If you decide to create multiple versions, updating and maintaining all the versions will be quite a chore. Any new generic code will have to be added to all versions. Also, multiple versions add a great deal of complexity to the maintenance and distribution of the applications.

The better choice would be to create a single version of the application that operates differently under different circumstances. You can choose which part of the code in the application is compiled or run based on the circumstances.

As an example, assume specific code needs to be run for the Los Angeles office that does not apply to any other office. First, decide on a constant for the office, for example, LA. Enter the constant as a conditional compilation argument for the application. In the Visual Basic Editor, under the Tools menu, choose the Application's Properties. The Project Properties dialog box will open. Select the General tab. In Conditional Compilation Arguments enter LA = -1. This sets a constant equal to True.

Now you can enter code that only executes for the LA version of the application. Do so by putting the code in a conditional compilation construct. For example:

```
#If LA Then
        ' This code will run in the LA version of the application.
#End If
```

Conditional compilation can also be a useful debugging tool. Let's say you often want to comment out sections of code. Set a conditional compilation argument `fComment = -1`. This comment flag can then be used with a conditional compilation construct to comment out sections of code:

```
#If fComment Then
        ' This code will run.
#End If
```

Writing Solid Code

There is no way to completely eliminate the need to debug applications. However, if the following guidelines are used, code will more likely run correctly and be error-free.

Declare Variables on Separate Lines of Code

It is much easier to check if a variable is declared by referring to variables that are listed on separate lines rather than in a long text string. In addition, there is no speed penalty for using this technique for compiled applications.

> **TIP**
>
> You might also find that grouping declared variables by data type will also make it easier to refer to variables.

Declare Variables with the Narrowest Scope

Use local variables as much as possible. This will not only prevent scoping issues but can also help performance.

Use Specific Datatypes

Always declare a datatype and use the smallest datatype possible. If you do not declare a datatype, a variant datatype will be used. This is not only inefficient because of the additional resource requirements, but any type of data can be put in a variable with a variant datatype. This can certainly lead to program errors. For example, if a variable should only hold numbers, if a variant datatype is used, an error can occur if data other than numbers or objects are used with the variable.

Destroy Object Variables

Eliminate resource errors by destroying object variables. If an object variable exists named `objWord`, specifically destroy the object variable at the end of the procedure with `Set objWord = Nothing`.

Use TypeOf Keyword

Often you can pass controls to a generic procedure. For example, say you pass list box and combo box controls to a generic procedure that loads values using the AddItem method. If you pass a control that is not a list box or combo box (for example, a command button), an error will occur because the control does not have an AddItem method. In the procedure, use the TypeOf keyword to check what type of control was passed in to eliminate the error.

Use Me Instead of Screen.ActiveForm and Screen.ActiveControl

When debugging an application, the Immediate window has focus. Therefore, Screen.ActiveForm and Screen.ActiveControl will not work. Use the Me keyword instead to refer to the current form.

Use an Error Handler

When an error does occur, the error handler can be a real timesaver to help find the particular statement of code that failed, the information about the type of error, line number, and much more. See Chapter 13, "Professional Error Handling," for additional information.

Use Option Explicit

Force the declaration of all variables by placing Option Explicit at the top of every code module. You can make this the default by checking the Require Variable Declaration option in the program options. By declaring all variables, errors due to misspelled variable names can be eliminated.

0 or 1 Based?

In VBA, some items are 0 based, others are 1 based. This is determined by whether you start counting at 0 or 1. For example, arrays are 0 based while collections are 1 based. If you are not sure if an item is 0 or 1 based, look it up. A wrong guess will certainly produce an error.

Fix Errors Immediately

The temptation is to ignore errors when developing an application. For example, you are creating a new feature in an application and you come across a bug in another part of the application. It is best to stop and fix the bug. This is hard because you are focused on your own development. However, bugs can be hard to find later and reproduce. The best rule of thumb is if you come across a bug, fix it—now.

Use Comments

Let's face it, months, weeks, or even days after writing code, it is hard to remember all the details about a particular procedure. Comment your code heavily to make it easier to maintain. Comments do not slow down the code because they are stripped out by the compiler. To create a comment, put a single quote in front of the statement of code. Commented lines of code are shown in green in the code window.

> **TIP**
>
> To block comment and uncomment code, use the Comment Block and Uncomment Block items on the Edit toolbar in the IDE.

Use the Line Continuation Character

It is difficult to quickly review code if you have to scroll to the right to see code that is not shown on a single screen. Make sure that all the code is visible in the code window by using the underscore (_) as a line continuation character. The underscore will treat all the lines of code as if it were on a single line. A common example is a SQL statement:

```
Dim strSQL as String
StrSQL = "SELECT * FROM tblErrorLog" & _
"ORDER BY tblErrorLog.ErrorLogID;"
```

Use Small Procedures

Lengthy procedures are hard to understand and debug. Break procedures into small logical units. As a rule of thumb, if you cannot print a procedure on a single sheet of paper, you should consider breaking it into smaller procedures.

Use Standard Naming Conventions

Using naming conventions will help you as well as other developers more easily understand and debug your code. A common complaint when a developer takes over an application from another developer is how hard it is to understand the code. Using naming conventions to name objects and variables makes the debugging process significantly easier.

Never Use Stop

Do not use Stop in your code to enter break mode. As mentioned earlier in the chapter, use Debug.Assert instead. The correct syntax is Debug.Assert False.

If you forget to remove Stop in your code before distribution of your application, your application will not run correctly. Debug.Assert is stripped out of the code when the application is compiled.

Don't Debug with Message Boxes

Using message boxes in the past has been a common technique to debug code. The idea is to place message boxes throughout the code to find the offending statement in the code:

```
Sub Demo ( )
MsgBox 1
        Select Case rst.States
MsgBox 2
                Case "Washington"
MsgBox 3
                        MsgBox "Washington"
MsgBox 4
                Case "Oregon"
MsgBox 5
                        MsgBox "Oregon"
MsgBox 6
                Case "California"
MsgBox 7
                        MsgBox "California"
MsgBox 8
            End Select
MsgBox 9

End Sub
```

By watching which message boxes appear before the code fails, you can discover which line of code has the error. A much better approach is to set a breakpoint and walk through the code. Setting a breakpoint is better because

- It is much quicker than entering a bunch of message boxes.
- Message boxes are modal so you cannot switch to the code window to review the code.
- While stepping through the code with the debugger, you can watch the value of variables, change the value of variables, and more.
- When the error is fixed, you do not have to take time to remove the message boxes.
- You do not have to worry about accidentally shipping your applications without removing the message boxes.

Application Testing

Before distributing an Access application, make sure to fully test the application. See Chapter 2, "Planning the Development Process," for additional information.

Practice Debugging Techniques

The sample code for this chapter gives you the opportunity to practice the debugging techniques discussed in this chapter. (See Figure 12.13.)

FIGURE 12.13

Practice debugging techniques with chapter sample code.

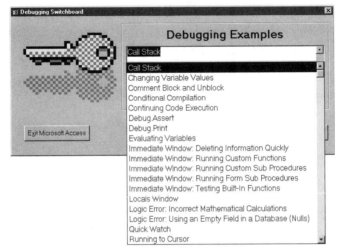

Summary

Access 2000 has powerful debugging tools. Learning how to use these debugging tools is an essential skill for any Access developer. This chapter included tips for using the Integrated Development Environment (IDE), the Immediate window, the Locals window, and the Watches window. The Debugger and debugging techniques were discussed. Also conditional compilation and tips for writing solid code were covered. With the information and techniques discussed in this chapter, creating and maintaining applications should be quicker and easier.

Professional Error Handling

CHAPTER 13

The hallmark of a professional application is error handling. If the application doesn't elegantly handle errors, users will be frustrated no matter how sophisticated an application is or how many features it has.

Without error handling, a program may abruptly shut down, especially if they're using a "runtime" version of your application. This can frustrate users because they have no idea what happened, why it happened, or whether it's safe to continue working.

When an error does occur, users should be provided feedback that allows them to clearly understand how to recover. Cryptic error messages are almost as bad as no feedback at all (see Figure 13.1). How many users understand, or find helpful, error messages such as `Illegal operation`, `Overflow`, or `General Protection Fault`?

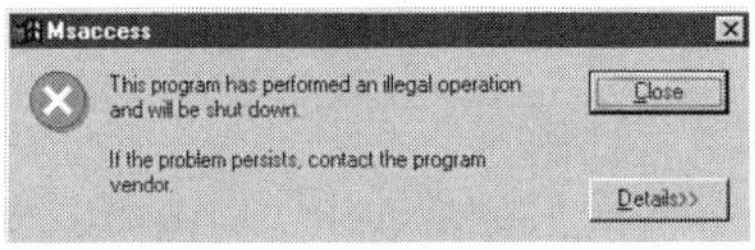

FIGURE 13.1

Example of a cryptic error message.

Without comprehensive error handling, developers also lose valuable feedback about how their application functions under actual use. When support calls are received, it's time-consuming for developers to find and fix errors. Certainly, it's in a developer's best interest to quickly resolve program errors.

Without error handlers, developers must rely on users to explain what they were doing when the program error occurred. A user's typical response might be "I don't know." This leads to the unnecessary and time-consuming work of trying the find and fix the errors. This chapter shows how to develop a powerful error handler that helps the application's users as well as the developer.

There are three types of program errors: syntax errors, logic errors, and runtime errors.

Eliminating Syntax Errors

Let's start with the easiest type of program error to deal with—the syntax error. Syntax errors occur when code is written improperly. An example would be a misspelled variable or keyword or missing code:

```
Dim strName as
```

Obviously, an essential piece of code is missing in the statement. The data type isn't stated. A correct statement would read as follows:

```
Dim strName as String
```

One key to eliminating syntax errors is to insert `Option Explicit` on the first line of every module. This will require you to declare all variables you use in the application.

It's important to declare all variables for several reasons. A misspelled variable name can have drastic consequences. If the variable is to insert a value in the database, inappropriate data can be inserted without any notification of the error. After all, VBA treats a misspelled variable as just another variable. In the following example, the variable `BankBalance` on the second line is misspelled:

```
BankBalance  = 4,576.98
RS!BankBalance = BankBalence
```

VBA doesn't recognize `BankBalence` as a keyword, so it assumes that you want it to create a new variable of `Variant` data type with a default value of `Empty`. As a result, the database is updated with `Empty` instead of the desired value of $4,576.98.

It's also important to declare variables to optimize your application. Because undeclared variables use the `Variant` data type, significant storage space can be lost. For example, the difference in the storage size for a variable that holds the number 5 is as follows:

> `Dim bytNumber as Byte`   (1 Byte)
> Undeclared variable (numeric data only)
> (16 Byte)
> Undeclared variable (character or string data)
> (22 Byte)

In this example, the undeclared variable is assigned as a `Variant` data type. To force variable declaration, go into the Microsoft Visual Basic Editor by opening a code module. From the Tools, Options menu, open the Options dialog box. On the Editor page, turn Require Variable Declaration on (see Figure 13.2). This will insert `Option Explicit` at the top of each new module; however, it won't update old modules. Be sure to insert `Option Explicit` in any modules you've previously created.

Other types of syntax error can occur as well, such as

```
Msggbox "Hi"
```

or

```
EndSeb
```

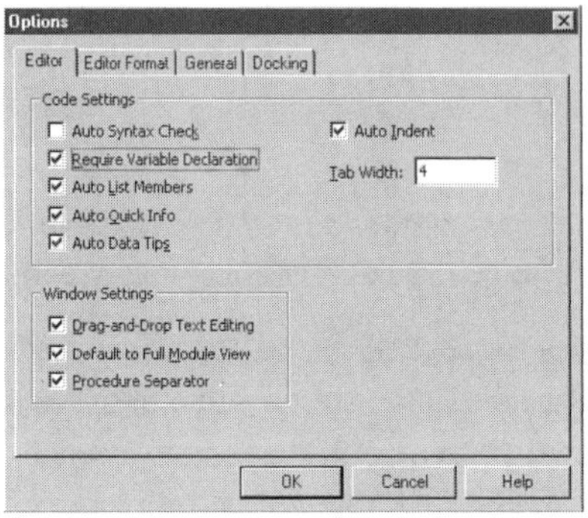

FIGURE 13.2

Select Require Variable Declaration to force variable declaration.

These misspelled reserved words will produce syntax errors. As you type code you are often informed of these errors with highlighted text and a warning message.

> **TIP**
>
> In the Visual Basic Editor, under the Tools, Option menu, on the Editor page, turn Auto Syntax Check off. This won't disable syntax checking, but it will get rid of the annoying dialog box that pops up whenever there's a syntax error. The error will still be shown as the code is highlighted in red.

In the Options dialog box, you can modify some compiler settings. On the General page, the Compile on Demand option enables the application to run faster because modules aren't compiled until they're loaded for execution. On today's faster computers, it's recommended that you turn this option on to eliminate errors.

Also in the General page is a Background Compile option. Turn this option on to enable background compiling while the computer is idle. Background Compile can improve runtime execution speed. To use this feature, Compile on Demand must also be enabled.

It's also important that all modules are compiled and saved before an application is distributed to assure that all syntax errors have been found. From the Debug menu, choose Compile and Save All Modules to compile and save every module in the database, whether or not they are now loaded.

Eliminating Logic Errors

Logic errors occur when the code doesn't produce the expected results. The logic might be flawed, or the program might flow incorrectly. When the code executes but doesn't produce the desired result, expect a logic error.

To resolve logic errors, use Microsoft Access's powerful debugger. See Chapter 12, "Debugging Access Applications," for a complete discussion of these issues.

Eliminating Runtime Errors

There's no way to eliminate all runtime errors, but you can plan for them. This is why an error handler is essential. A professional application includes an error handler in every procedure; nothing is left to chance.

A Simple Error Handler

Before discussing a comprehensive error handler, let's start with a simple example:

```
Sub Demo ( )
    Dim I as Integer
    On Error GoTo ErrorHandler
    ' Program error on this line of code
ExitHere:
    Exit Sub
ErrorHandler:
    MsgBox "An error occurred"
    Resume ExitHere
End Sub
```

This simple error handler follows normal programming conventions, as discussed in the following sections.

On Error GoTo ErrorHandler

This statement by convention is put near the top of the procedure, after all the Dim statements. It's located near the top of the procedure so all code that might produce an error follows it. If an error occurs in the code, this GoTo statement will *branch* (pass program control) to the error handler. The error handler is located at the ErrorHandler label. ErrorHandler isn't a reserved word, but the name of the error handler procedure (you can use your own name).

> **TIP**
>
> You can easily find labels because they are flush left and are followed by a colon.

ExitHere

This label is an exit point for the procedure. It's good practice to have only one exit point in a procedure. If the procedure executes without an error, the `ExitHere` code executes and the procedure will finish. The code in the `ErrorHandler` won't execute because it appears at the very end of the procedure. The code never gets to that point in the procedure because it has already exited the procedure.

The `ExitHere` label is the ideal place to insert any cleanup code. For example, you can release any object variables by setting them to nothing, closing a database, setting the hourglass back to the default, and turning on screen updating.

An `On Error Resume Next` statement should usually be the first statement in your exit routine. This is necessary because some cleanup statements might cause an error themselves. For example, if the error occurred before a database could be opened and the object variable in the database is set to `Nothing` in the exit procedure (`Set db = Nothing`), an error will occur.

> **TIP**
>
> If this is a slow procedure and you're turning the hourglass on at the beginning and off again at the end, you need to be careful that it doesn't get "stuck" on if an error occurs. `Docmd.Hourglass false` is an example of cleanup code you should put in the `ExitHere` code to execute before you exit the procedure, whether or not an error occurred.

> **TIP**
>
> In `ExitHere`, set the hourglass back to the default. You can turn an hourglass on at the beginning of a procedure. If the error occurs before you turn the hourglass off at the end of the procedure, execution of the code will branch to the error handler and the hourglass won't get turned off. If the hourglass is set back to the default in the exit point, it will always be reset.

The following is an example of an exit routine with cleanup code:

```
ExitHere:
    On Error Resume Next
        DoCmd.Hourglass False
        DoCmd.Echo True
        DoCmd.SetWarnings False
    Set rst = Nothing
    Set db = Nothing
    Exit Sub
```

ErrorHandler

This is the location of the error handler that handles runtime errors. It appears, by convention, at the bottom of the procedure. The code in the error handler will execute only if a program error occurs. The error handler should include more than just a message box, as shown in the preceding simple example. It's advisable to include a `Select Case` statement to respond specifically to all possible errors the developer can anticipate (see the later section "Responding to Errors"). The end of the error handler should have a `Resume` statement.

Resume ExitHere

This transfers program execution to the `ExitHere` code.

Program Flow with Error Handling

Notice how the program flow changes when there's an error handler. If the code has no error, program flow looks like this (notice that the error handler never executes):

```
Sub Demo ( )
    On Error GoTo ErrorHandler

    Good code

ExitHere:
    Exit Sub
ErrorHandler:
    MsgBox "An error occurred"
    Resume ExitHere
End Sub
```

If a code statement contains an error, the program flow will be different because the error handler will have been executed:

```
Sub Demo ( )
    On Error GoTo ErrorHandler

    Bad Code
```

```
ExitHere:
    Exit Sub

ErrorHandler:
    MsgBox "An error occurred"
    Resume ExitHere
End Sub
```

The Err Object

VBA provides an `Err` object that provides much of the information you need for the error handler. The `Err` object is global in scope, so you don't need to create an instance of it.

The `Err` object has the following properties:

- `Err.Number`— The error number of the current error. This number can be used to respond to different types of errors that occur.
- `Err.Description`— The description of the error.
- `Err.Source`— The object or application that originally generated the error.
- `Err.HelpFile`— A path to a Windows help file. This property, when used with `HelpContext`, can be used to provide a Help button in an error message dialog box.
- `Err.HelpContext`— Context ID for a topic in a help file.
- `Err.Last DLL Error`— A system error code produced by a call to a dynamic-link library (DLL).

The `Err` object has two methods.

Err.Clear

The `Clear` method clears the properties of the `Err` object. Each of the following will clear the properties of the `Err` object:

- Call `Clear` method of the `Err` object (`Err.Clear`).
- Use any type of `Resume` statement.
- Exit a procedure.
- Use the `On Error` statement.

Err.Raise

The `Raise` method generates a runtime error. Generating a runtime error is useful for testing your application. You can simulate a runtime error by passing the error code to the `Raise` method of the `Err` object. Also, when your application calls an external dynamic-link library (DLL), you can pass the error value back to your application to handle the error.

When raising errors, you can generate user-defined errors. Make sure that your user-defined error number is unique and add your error number to the constant `vbObjectError`. For example, to create error number 50, assign `vbObjectError + 50` to the number argument:

```
Err.Number = vbObjectError + 50
```

The following is an example of using the `Raise` method:

```
Sub Demo(intNumber)
    If intNumber = 110 Then
        ' Raise an error
        Err.Raise vbObjectError + 50, "My Application", _
            "The number cannot be greater than 100", _
            "c:\MyApp\MyApp.Hlp", MyContextID
    End If
End Sub
```

The `Raise` method has five arguments: `Number`, `Source`, `Description`, `HelpFile`, and `HelpContext`. (These arguments are the same as those of the `Err` object.) The syntax would be

```
Err.Raise (Number, Source, Description, HelpFile, HelpContext)
```

By using named parameters, you can pass only the arguments you want, making your code more self-documenting:

```
Err.Raise Number:= vbObjectError + 50, Description:= "My Custom Error"
```

> **TIP**
>
> To learn about the properties and methods of the `Err` object, refer to the object browser. In any code module, press F2, choose the VBA library, and click `Err Object` under classes. You can then review all the properties and methods. After highlighting a property or method, press F1 for help on that topic.

Responding to Errors

A great deal of custom code in a procedure's error-handling section should use a `Select Case` statement. Try to anticipate every possible error that can occur and list the error number in a `Select Case` statement within the error handler. You can then deal with the error as appropriate.

An anticipated error can be dealt with in numerous ways:

- A message box can present users with information about the error.
- A message box can present users with information that helps them resolve the error (for example, There is no disk in the disk drive).
- Ignore the error and continue to execute the code.
- Ignore the error and exit the procedure.
- Take corrective action in code to enable the code to continue executing successfully.
- Branch to another place in the code.

The following code illustrates this point:

```
ErrorHandler:
    Select Case Err.Number
        Case 11
            If MsgBox("You divided a number by zero, enter a " & _
                " different number. Do you want to try again? ", _
                vbQuestion + vbYesNo) = vbYes Then
                Resume
            Else
                Resume ExitHere
            End If
        Case Else
            MsgBox "An unexpected occurred. Error Number: " & _
            Err.Number & " Error Description: " & Err.Description
            Resume ExitHere
    End Select
End Sub
```

You might even want to create generalized procedures that handle errors of a particular type. For example, if you review the table of Access and Jet errors in the Access and Jet Database Errors.mdb , you will find that the errors between the numbers 58 and 76 involve file type errors. These include File already exists, Disk full, Too many files, and more. You could create a general procedure that deals with that group of errors and call the procedure from the Select Case statement in the error handler:

```
ErrorHandler:
    Select Case Err.Number
        Case 58 To 76
        ' General procedure that handles file type errors
        Call FileTypeErrors
        Case Else
            MsgBox "An unexpected occurred. Error Number: " & _
        Err.Number & " Error Description: " & Err.Description
            Resume ExitHere
    End Select
End Sub
```

The Resume Statements

The following Resume statements enable you to branch the program execution to difference statements of code when an error occurs.

Resume

Resume transfers execution of the code to the same line of code that failed. When the error handler provides users with feedback on how to resolve the error, use the Resume statement to return to the statement of code that previously failed. This is used when the reason for program error has been corrected and you want to rerun the code that originally failed.

Resume Next

This transfers execution of the code to the line of code *after* the line that failed. This will allow the remaining code in your procedure to execute.

The following diagram illustrates the program flow for various Resume statements (see Figure 13.3):

FIGURE 13.3

The flow of error handling with Resume.

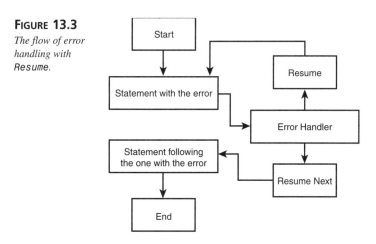

Getting Additional Error Information

The error handler should automatically record all error information developers need. The more information the error handler collects, the easier it is for developers to find and fix the error.

Although the `Err` object provides a great deal of information, it doesn't provide everything. A well-designed error handler should provide the following additional information about the error:

- *Line number*—Identifies the line number where the error occurred. Consider assigning a predefined range of line numbers to each module. Line numbers can be inserted on the left side of a module in front of statements of code. With the global Find available in Access, you can quickly go to the exact line number where the error occurred if line numbers aren't repeated. In a procedure, line numbers don't have to be in order.

TIP

You would expect the `Err` object to provide the line number but it doesn't. To obtain the line number, use the `Erl` function, which you can see in the code examples for this chapter.

- *Name of the form or report*—Provides the name of the form or report where the error occurred. This is a matter of simply passing the form or report name to the error handler.
- *Name of procedure*—Provides the name of the procedure where the error occurred.
- *Name of active control*—Provides the name of the active control when the error occurred.
- *Value of active control*—Provides the current value in the active control when the error occurred. Often an error will occur only if certain values are entered into a control. If, for example, errors occur when a value of greater than 20,000 is entered in a text box, this error type can easily be identified by returning the text box's value in the error handler for logging.

CAUTION

The active control will be passed to the error handler. Some controls have a value; others don't. The error handler should pass the `ActiveControl` to a procedure that evaluates the type of control using the `TypeOf` built-in function. If the control is a text box, obtain the value of the text box for the error handler. However, if, for example, it's a command button, don't obtain a value to prevent an error from occurring.

- *ID of current record*—Provides the ID of the current record on the form when the error occurred. Have you ever noticed that a certain customer record produces most program errors? By returning the current record ID in the error handler, you can compare that customer record with others that don't produce the error. Often, a required field is missing data.

- *Name of program*—Provides the name of the application where the error occurred.

- *Error level*—An arbitrary set of error values you can set—for example, 1–5. With this information, the urgency of the support call can be gauged.

- *User name*—The name of the current logged-on user. Ever notice how certain users have the most errors? Finding out who had the error can be invaluable. Many times, you will discover that the problem isn't program errors, but rather an untrained user. To obtain the current user's name, an application logon screen can be used, or the Windows 95/98/NT logon name can be obtained with a Windows API call.

> **TIP**
>
> The Windows API call to obtain the current logged-on Windows 95/98/NT user is in the error handler in the code examples for this chapter. See the UserName property and the GetUserName function.

- *Date and time*—The date and time the error occurred. This information is helpful to analyze the frequency of errors over time. A simple graph should indicate that program errors occur less frequently over time.

- *Notes about the error*—Users can enter what they were doing or give feedback about the error. This information can be entered in an input box or form. Users can then use a simple form to provide information about what they were doing when the error occurred. Let users know this is optional. Some users will never enter a note about the error, whereas others will appreciate the opportunity to provide feedback.

With the information that can be retrieved with the Err object and with other methods described here, developers should have sufficient information necessary to resolve runtime errors quickly and effectively.

13

PROFESSIONAL ERROR HANDLING

A Comprehensive Error Handler

Now that you've seen how to construct a procedure-level error handler in a procedure and retrieve information about the error, it's time to create a comprehensive error handler.

The first decision should be how to design the error handler and where to put the code. Certainly, the entire error handler could be placed in each procedure. However, this method would create a great deal of redundant code. Also, if the error handler were later modified, changes would have to be made in every procedure.

> **TIP**
>
> See the procedure-level error handler in the code examples for this chapter. Although using the global error handler is more efficient, it will be helpful to review the basics regarding procedure-level error handling if you aren't experienced with error handlers.

The better approach uses a global error handler for the entire Access application. The global error handler is an object, created with a class module.

> **TIP**
>
> To extend the global error handler even further, use Visual Basic to create a component that can be used with any Component Object Model-compliant (COM) application. The error handler could be used to trap errors in Access, Word, Excel, VB, and many other applications. See Chapter 19, "Integration with Office 2000," for more information.

The Error Class Module (Object)

A class module called cError in the chapter code provides the properties and methods needed for an effective error handler. The cError object encapsulates all the code in a class module you can now use. Using this object is easy with the benefit of Microsoft's IntelliSense technology.

> **TIP**
>
> If you are new to class modules, see Chapter 11, "Creating Objects with Class Modules," for details on how to create classes.

cError **Object Properties**

The cError object has properties for the values you want to capture with the error handler. Table 13.1 specifies these properties.

TABLE 13.1 cError PROPERTIES

Property	Description
Application	Name of the program that created the application (for example, MS Access)
AVIFileLocation	Name and full path of AVI (video) file used in initial error notification form or dialog box
Class	Name of the class module
ComputerName	Name of the computer where the error occurred
ComputerTotalMemory	Total memory on the computer
ComputerAvailableMemory	Available memory on the computer
ComputerOperatingSystem	Operating system and version information
ComputerProcessor	Computer processor information
ControlName	Name of the active control
ControlValue	Value of the active control
CurrentRecordID	ID of the current record
Description	Description of the error as returned by the Err object
EmailAddress	Email address used to email error information
ErrorDatabase	Name and full path of the database (such as Access or SQL Server database) containing the error table
ErrorNumber	Error number returned by the Err object
ErrorTextFile	Name and full path of the text file containing the error information
HelpContext	Help file context ID returned by the Err object

13

PROFESSIONAL
ERROR HANDLING

continues

TABLE 13.1 CONTINUED

Property	Description
HelpFile	The name and full path of the Help file returned by the Err object
LastDllError	System error code for the last call to a DLL
Level	Arbitrarily set value to determine error urgency
LineNumber	Line number of statement where error occurred
Note	Note by a user indicating what he was doing when the error occurred
Now	Date and time the error occurred
Procedure	Name of the procedure
SoundFile	The name and full path of the sound file
Source	Name of the object or application that originally generated the error
User	Name of the user who encountered the error
WaitStateFlag	A flag used set a wait state to stop code from continuing to execute
UserEnterNoteFlag	A flag to indicate whether users are asked to enter notes about the error

When an error does occur, most, if not all, of these properties are set. The information can then be retrieved from the cError object and then used in a message box, email, calendar entry, and error table in a database or a text file.

cError **Object Methods**

The methods of the cError object provide useful error information for developers. For example, the error information can be sent by email to the developer or logged in a database. Table 13.2 specifies the methods in the cError object.

TABLE 13.2 cError METHODS

Method	Description
AddToErrorHandlerOutlook Calendar	Add the error information to an Outlook calendar called Error Handler
Clear	Clears the Err object

Method	Description
Email	Sends the developer an email using Outlook whenever an error occurs
EmailAllErrors	Sends the developer an email with an attachment including all the information in the error table
GetActiveControlValue	Retrieves the value of the active control when the error occurred
MessageBox	Presents users with a message box with details about the error
MsgErrorDetails	Summarizes the error information for the message box or email message
OfficeAssistant	Pops up the Office Assistant when an error occurs and asks users if they want to enter a note about the error
PlaySound	Plays a sound when the error occurs to get the user's attention
ProcessError	Controls processing of the error information based on the error options set up by the organization
ShowAVIForm	Pops up a form that includes an AVI file to inform users that an error occurred
UserInputBox	Presents an input box to users so that they can provide feedback about the error
UserName	Retrieves the user's Windows/Windows NT logon name
WaitState	Creates a wait state to stop code from continuing to execute
WriteErrorToTable	Writes the error information to an error table in a database
WriteErrorToTextFile	Writes the error information to a text file

Reviewing the cError Object in the Object Browser

As you can see, the cError object in the chapter code has many properties and methods. To quickly review the objects' properties and methods, open the Object Browser and choose the cError class module (see Figure 13.4).

FIGURE **13.4**

*The cError object
in the Object
Browser.*

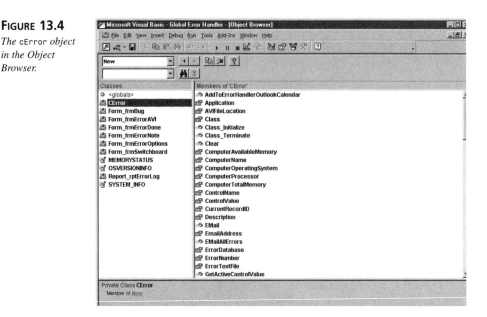

Processing the Error

When a program error occurs, the error handler in the procedure passes the information
to the cError object. The ProcessError method determines how the error is processed.
This method refers to the tblErrorOptions table (discussed later in this chapter) for
information such as whether users can enter a note about the error and whether the error
information is emailed. The code in the ProcessError method follows:

```
Public Sub ProcessError()
    Dim rst As ADODB.Recordset
    Dim strSQL As String
    Dim strVal As String

    strSQL = "SELECT * FROM tblErrorOptions"

    ' Create ADO Recordset
    Set rst = New ADODB.Recordset

    ' Open ADO Recordset
    rst.Open strSQL, CurrentProject.Connection, adOpenKeyset, _
        adLockOptimistic

    Me.ErrorTextFile = rst!ErrorTextFileName

    Me.UserEnterNoteFlag = rst!UserEnterNoteAboutError
```

```
Me.AVIFileLocation = CurrentProject.Path & rst!AVIFileLocation

Me.SoundFile = CurrentProject.Path & rst!SoundFile

Me.OfficeID = rst!OfficeID

Me.OfficeName = rst!OfficeName

Me.OfficePhoneNumber = rst!OfficePhoneNumber

Me.OfficeFaxNumber = rst!OfficeFaxNumber

If rst!PlaySound Then

    ' Play a Sound when the error occurs
    CError.PlaySound

End If

If rst!ShowOfficeAssistant Then

    ' Show the user the office assistant
    CError.OfficeAssistant

End If

If rst!ShowAVIForm Then

    ' Show the user the Error AVI Form
    CError.ShowAVIForm

    ' Wait to continue the code until the form is closed.
    Me.WaitState (True)

    'Close the AVI Form
    DoCmd.Close acForm, "frmErrorAVI", acSaveNo

End If

' Open the Error Note form so the user can enter a note.
If Me.UserEnterNoteFlag Then

    DoCmd.OpenForm "frmErrorNote", acNormal

    ' Wait to continue the code until the form is closed.
    Me.WaitState (True)

    ' Close the Error Note form.
    DoCmd.Close acForm, "frmErrorNote", acSaveNo
```

13

PROFESSIONAL ERROR HANDLING

```
      End If

      If rst!ErrorsToAccessTable Then

            ' Write the error to the Error Log Access Table
            CError.WriteErrorToTable

      End If

      If rst!ErrorsToTextFile Then

            ' Write the error to a text file
            CError.WriteErrorToTextFile

      End If

      If rst!ErrorsToTextFile Then

            ' Write the error to a text file
            CError.WriteErrorToTextFile

      End If

      If rst!AddToErrorHandlerCalendar Then


            CError.AddToErrorHandlerOutlookCalendar

      End If

      If rst!ShowMsgBoxErrors Then

            ' Show the user a message box of the error.
            CError.MessageBox

      End If

      ' Display a form that indicates that it is safe for the user
      ' to continue working. The form automatically closes with a
      ' timer.
      DoCmd.OpenForm "frmErrorDone", acNormal

      rst.Close

      Set rst = Nothing
```

As you can see, this method relies on properties as well as other methods of the cError object. Review the code in the cError class module for additional information.

The End User's Experience

How should errors be handled from the end user's viewpoint? The first priority should be to get the user's attention so she stops working and gets her hands off the keyboard. Remember that the error could be critical, such as causing corrupted data to be inserted in the database.

By calling a few `cError` methods, the Office Assistant will pop up, an AVI form will appear, and a sound will provide user with audio feedback that an error has occurred (see Figure 13.5). The chapter code also includes an AVI form to notify the user of an error (see Figure 13.6). By utilizing the `cError` class module, the code to make this happen is simple:

```
CError.OfficeAssistant
CError.AVIForm
CError.Sound
```

FIGURE 13.5

Using the Office Assistant to indicate that an error has occurred.

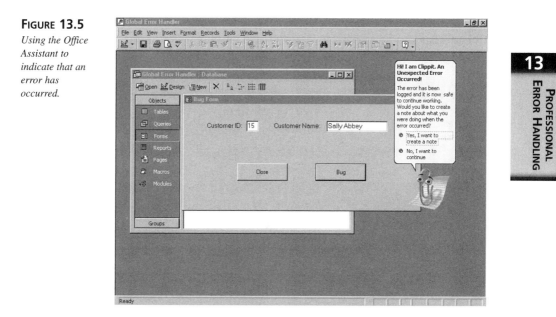

You then can use the `cError` object to present an error note form or an input box, which enables users to indicate what they were doing when the error occurred (see Figure 13.7). Some users will appreciate the opportunity to provide feedback; others will skip this step. The Error Note form indicates that entry of a note is optional.

FIGURE 13.6

Using an AVI form to indicate that an error has occurred.

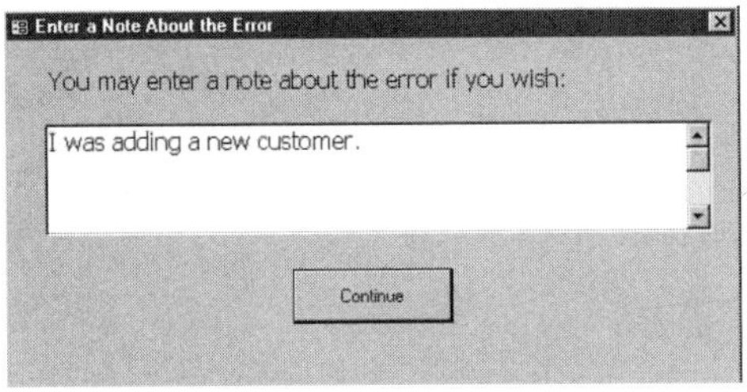

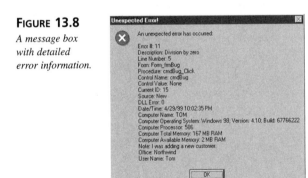

FIGURE 13.7

A form to allow users to enter a note about the error.

FIGURE 13.8

A message box with detailed error information.

The user can also be shown a message box with detailed information about the error (see Figure 13.8).

The last step is to provide a message to inform users that the error has been recorded and they can safely continue their work (see Figure 13.9). This is done with a form that closes automatically in three seconds.

Therefore, when an error occurs, users are assisted every step of the way—they aren't abruptly thrown out of the application. The error handler allows the code to continue safely and will keep the application running. Users are immediately notified of the error and given a chance to provide input and feedback. Finally, users are assured that the error has been forwarded to the developer and that it's now safe to continue working. By handling errors in this manner, your users will be enamored of your professional application—as you should be!

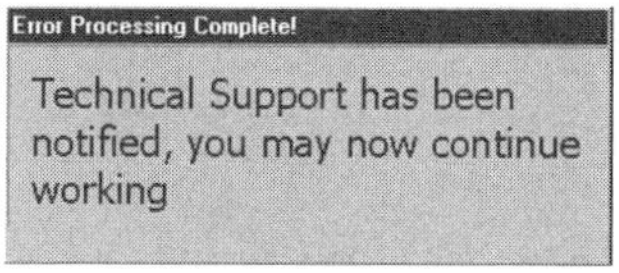

FIGURE **13.9**

Inform the user that it's safe to continue working.

Error Processing Complete!

Technical Support has been notified, you may now continue working

Discovering Computer Problems

Have you ever noticed that certain computers in the office always seem to generate program errors? This issue is perhaps one of the most difficult to troubleshoot. The problem could be hardware related, configuration issues, conflicts with other applications, or something else.

Notice that the error handler has several methods to help deal with this issue. The cError object includes properties (as shown in Table 13.1) to capture the computer name, total and available memory on the computer, operating system, and processor type.

All this information might be useful in determining why one workstation is having problems when all the other computers in the organization work fine. The most frequent problem is that of memory—when an error occurs, check the total and available memory information.

Error Reporting

Now that you are familiar with the end user's experience, how does a comprehensive error handler help you as the developer? With the cError object, you can compile and analyze the program errors in several ways:

- *Error handler Access report*— The error handler report in the Access database contains all the information from the error table for all the errors (see Figure 13.10).
- *Email individual errors*—Every time an error occurs, the details of the error can be emailed to you using the Email method (see Figure 13.11).

13

PROFESSIONAL
ERROR HANDLING

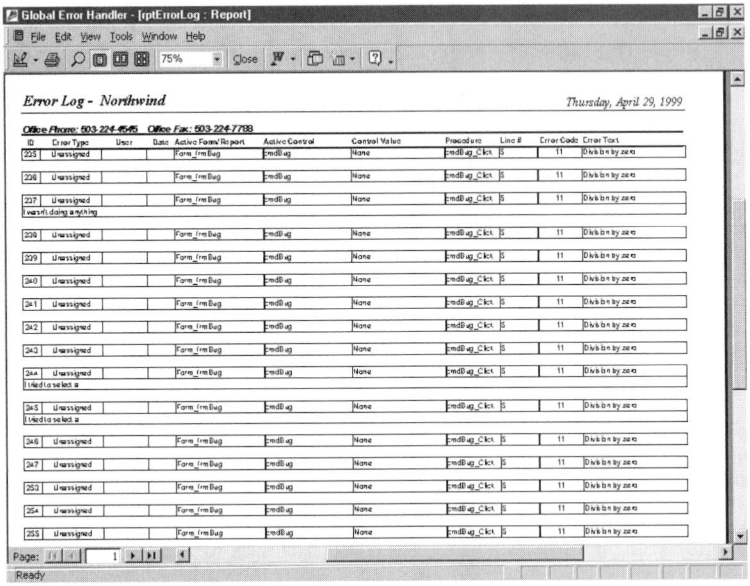

FIGURE 13.10

Access report of all errors.

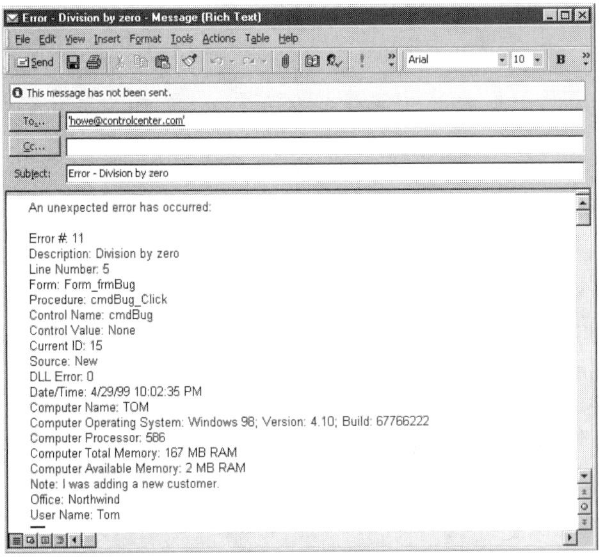

FIGURE 13.11

Email of an individual program error.

- *Email all errors*—All error information in the error table can be emailed to you as an attachment to an Outlook message using the EmailAllErrors method. The error log table is saved as an Excel spreadsheet and attached to the email message.

- *Save error information in an Access database*—By using the `WriteErrorToTable` method whenever an error occurs, the error is added to the error table in the Access database.

- *Save error information in a text file*—By using the `WriteErrorToTextFile` method, all errors can be saved in a designated text file for later review.

- *Save error information on an Outlook calendar*—All errors can be added to an Outlook calendar so the data can be viewed with the many built-in Outlook views as well as custom views. The `AddToErrorHandlerOutlookCalendar` method makes it easy to send all error information to the error handler calendar (see Figure 13.12).

FIGURE 13.12

Outlook error handler calendar.

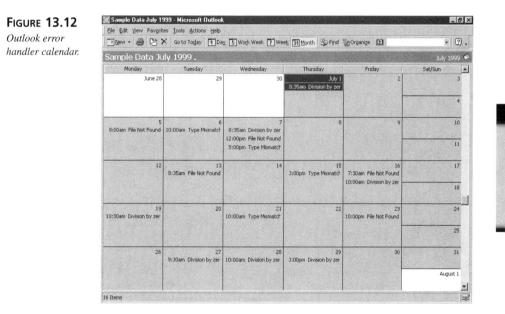

By using one or more of these reporting methods, you receive immediate notification when an error occurs. You will have all the information needed to discover and fix the error, as well as reporting tools for historical analysis.

Error Options

As you can see, a comprehensive error handler has a great number of options and possibilities. Some organizations will want to use all the options contained in the `cError` object; others might not.

The options are all contained in the `tblErrorOptions` table.

13

PROFESSIONAL
ERROR HANDLING

TABLE 13.3 OPTIONS AVAILABLE IN THE ERROR HANDLER

Option	Description	Data Type
AccessErrorTableName	The name of the Access table that includes the error information	Yes/No
AddToErrorHandlerCalendar	Add the error to the error handler Outlook calendar	Yes/No
AVIFileLocation	The full path to the AVI file used in the AVI form	Text
DatabaseName	The name of the database where the error table is located	Text
DatabasePath	The full path to the database	Text
EmailAddress	The email address to use when errors are sent via email	Text
EmailErrors	Email the error information when an error occurs	Yes/No
ErrorsToAccessTable	Save the error information in an Access table	Text
ErrorsToTextFile	Save the error information a text file	Text
PlaySound	Play a sound when the error occurs	Yes/No
ShowAVIForm	Show the user the AVI form when an error occurs	Yes/No
ShowMsgBoxErrors	Show the user a message box with information about the error	Yes/No
ShowOfficeAssistant	Show the user the Office Assistant when an error occurs	Yes/No
SoundFile	The full path to the sound file	Text
UserEnterNoteAboutError	Have the user enter a note about the error	Yes/No

Depending on what options are chosen, the error handler will work differently for each office. A table is used for storing the error options information so the code can be "table-driven." Rather than shuffle through the code to hard-code new option values, the options can simply be entered in the Error Options table. Because the code looks to the Error Options table for information, it's much easier to maintain.

Of course, you wouldn't want users entering data directly into an Access table. The frmErrorOptions form allows offices to easily update and change error options (see Figure 13.13).

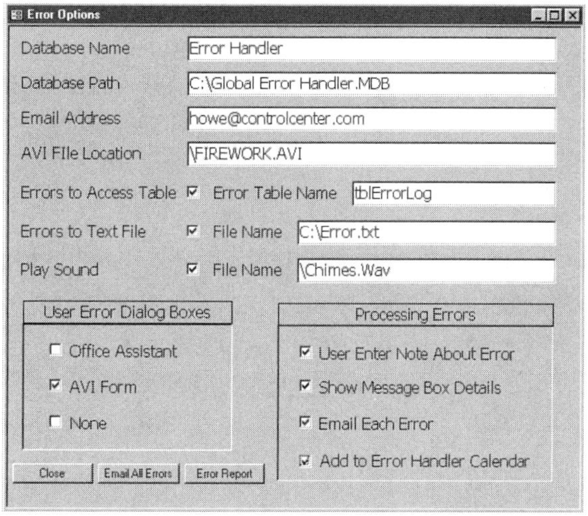

FIGURE 13.13

Error options form to select error-handling options.

At this point, you not only have a powerful error handler but also an error handler that's easy for an office to use and maintain.

Windows API Calls

All the functionality of the comprehensive error handler couldn't be programmed within Microsoft Access; a few Windows API calls were necessary.

The error handler obtains the name of the user who encountered the error. Rather than have a user log on to the application to get this information, the error handler obtains the user logon name from the Windows API. This Windows API call obtains the logged-on user's name under Windows 95/98/NT:

```
' Windows API call to get Windows User's Name.
Private Declare Function GetUserName Lib "advapi32.dll" _
  Alias "GetUserNameA" (ByVal lpBuffer As String, nSize As Long)
```

When the error occurs, a sound can be played to alert users. A Windows API call is also needed for this feature:

```
' Windows API call to play a sound
Private Declare Function sndPlaySound32 Lib "winmm.dll" Alias _
  "sndPlaySoundA" (ByVal lpszSoundName As String, _
  ByVal uFlags As Long) As Long
```

Other Windows API calls can get the computer name, computer memory information, operating system, and computer processor information.

Errors in Various Applications

Access applications today incorporate other applications and components. Accordingly, the errors that can occur can originate from many sources. A typical Access application might have an error occur in Access itself, or in VBA, DAO, ADO, or other applications used with Automation, such as Microsoft Word. Each application has its own error codes you can return in the error handler.

> **TIP**
>
> See the Access and Jet database Errors.mdb in the code samples for this chapter. The Access table in this database includes error numbers and error description of Access and Jet Database errors.

Error Handling With Nested Procedures

Often in your code, you might have one procedure call another procedure that, in turn, calls a third procedure and so on. If an error occurs, how is it handled?

A call list is maintained automatically to keep track of all procedure calls (see Figure 13.14). You can review the call list at any time in the Visual Basic Editor by choosing Call Stack from the Tools menu.

FIGURE 13.14

Call stack window.

When an error occurs, the error handler in the current procedure handles the error. However, if one doesn't exist, the error handler in the calling procedure handles the error. In other words, VBA searches backward through the call list until an error handler is found.

> **CAUTION**
>
> Consider how dangerous the preceding scenario could be: an error handler that you didn't anticipate might handle the error. You might have that error handler resuming to a statement of code in a completely different procedure than the one where the error occurred. It's therefore essential that an error handler be included in *every* procedure.

Advanced Error Topics

Now that you've learned how to handle syntax errors, logic errors, and runtime errors, now look at some more advanced error-handling issues.

Error Event Procedures

Access forms and reports have an OnError event procedure that's useful to display a custom error message when an Access error occurs.

Two arguments are passed to the Error event procedure:

- DataErr is the error number returned by the Err object. By using this argument, you can respond to the particular error type. If, for example, DataErr is 11, a division-by-zero error occurred.

- Response determines whether an error message is displayed. By using this argument, you can control how an error is reported. To ignore the error and supply a custom error message, use the constant acDataErrContinue. To display the default Access error message, use the constant acDataErrDisplay.

A typical code example would look something like this:

```
Private Sub Form_Error(DataErr As Integer, Response As Integer)
    Dim strMessage As String
    If DataErr = 11 Then
        Response = acDataErrContinue
strMessage = "Check the value, you have divided a number by
zero."
        MsgBox strMessage
    End If
End Sub
```

13

PROFESSIONAL
ERROR HANDLING

On Error GoTo 0

This disables error handling within a procedure. The Err object also is reset as though the Clear method of the Err object is called (Err.Clear). The Err.Clear method was discussed earlier in this chapter.

On Error Resume Next

AccessError Method

This method can be used to return a description of a Microsoft Access error. For example, typing ? AccessError(11) in the Immediate window returns Division by zero (see Figure 13.15).

FIGURE 13.15

Using the AccessError *method in the Immediate window.*

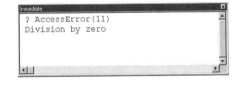

```
? AccessError(11)
Division by zero
```

Useful Error Functions

The following are useful error functions:

- IsError is used to determine whether a variant is an error data type (returns a Boolean).

- CVErr converts a value to an error data type, assigning it to a variant variable.

Setting Error Trapping Options

In the Visual Basic Editor, some option settings regarding how Access handles errors can be found on the General page of the Tools, Option menu (see Figure 13.16):

- *Break on All Errors*—When an error occurs, the code breaks on that line whether or not there's an error handler. This choice is best for debugging your application, but be sure to turn it off before distributing your application.

- *Break in Class Module*—When an error occurs, the code breaks on that line only in class modules, if there's no error hander.

- *Break on Unhandled Errors*—When an error occurs, the code breaks on that line in all procedures that do not contain a error handler.

FIGURE 13.16

Setting error-trapping options.

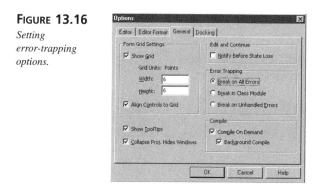

13

PROFESSIONAL
ERROR HANDLING

TIP

You can disable the Break on All Errors setting in a procedure by placing the following code at the top of the procedure:

```
Application.SetOption "Break On All Errors", False
```

Summary

Error handling is critical. A professional application that elegantly handles program errors ensures that a user's experience is pleasant. Error handling also is the best way to save you time in finding and correcting program errors. Hopefully, the comprehensive error handler included in the chapter code will be of great use to you.

Application
Optimization

CHAPTER 14

Application optimization is a topic of endless conversation and debate among developers. We all want to have optimal solutions, but exactly what does "optimal" mean? Some would define optimal as having raw speed, so the fastest technique would always be the optimal one. Others would contend that the optimal solution is the one that provides the most reliability, even if the approach is ponderously slow and overly cautious. Still others consider maintainability and extensibility the optimal goal. Who's right? The answer is, as it is so often in life, they are all right and they are all wrong. Optimization is really a balancing act between all three of these goals.

An optimal solution is certainly one that provides adequate speed to the user. A user usually will not accept a slow application. However, if that solution proves to be just a fast way to scramble and lose data, the developer has made an unwise trade-off. If an application has acceptable speed and has been reliable, the chances are good that the users will want the application revised in the future. However, unconventional design decisions and unorthodox execution of that design can make this otherwise well-regarded application difficult to enhance and extend.

Applications are like cars in some respects. Few of us would want to get behind the wheel of an extremely fast car that handled poorly and had weak brakes. Likewise, we want the car that starts every day and takes us where we need to go with as little fuss as possible. Finally, the repair and maintenance bills should not break the bank. Though this chapter concentrates on optimizing your application for speed, please keep in mind the need for your applications to be reliable, stable, and extensible as well.

This chapter will explore many techniques for optimizing your applications. Almost all of them have some limitations, and some of them are actually counterproductive at times. Even the best ones might not be applicable to your particular problem. Taken as a whole, some techniques will cancel out other efforts. However, judiciously applying this the lessons of this chapter to your development efforts should improve your applications' performance in some way.

The only way to find if these techniques will work for you is to experiment with them. The results will often surprise you. An approach that worked wonders one time might have no discernible effect in another instance. Optimization is complex because the environment in which we work is complex and ever-changing, but also because the goal of true optimization is a truly elusive one.

There are hundreds of things to discuss when writing about optimization. In the interest of order, this chapter will cover the topics from the most removed to the most intimate, from the hardware and operating system to different coding techniques.

Strengthening the Foundation: Hardware and Windows Optimization

Every part of Access 2000 lends itself to many opportunities to tune the application for performance, but none of them will amount to much if the machine you are running the application on is antiquated or has insufficient memory. It will usually be cheaper to purchase hardware in order to improve performance than to pay for software development to accomplish the same result. Hardware is cheaper than software and hardware upgrades benefit all the compatible software running on a machine.

It should come as no surprise that an Access application (or any application for that matter) will run faster on a fast machine. If you have the opportunity to upgrade the machine your application is running on, take it. Microsoft's published minimum requirements for running Access or Microsoft Office 2000 are exactly that: minimum requirements. Developers will quickly find that any serious attempt to run an Access 2000 application on a machine with those minimum requirements will lead to disappointment. The platform for running the applications should really meet a minimum standard of

- 133MHz Pentium processor
- 32MB of RAM (especially when running on NT)
- If you have to choose between upgrading the processor or installing more RAM, choose the RAM. With the worldwide collapse of chip prices, increasing RAM is the cheapest way to boost the performance of a PC. Keep in mind that the requirements for a development machine are much, much higher. A developer should have at least a 200MHz Pentium (Pro or II) with 32–64MB of RAM, among other things.

14

APPLICATION OPTIMIZATION

- Regardless of how much RAM the users' PCs have, it is still possible to run out of memory. Access, like any serious database, needs lots of memory to operate well. Steps should be taken to ensure as much memory is available to your application as possible.

- To this end, remove any screen savers, wallpaper (unless it's just a tiled bitmap), background pictures, and anything else that might be running needlessly. Only applications that are necessary should be taking cycles from the processor when your database is running. The more memory you provide for your Access application, the faster it will run.

- Don't use RAM disks. There is no place in modern, 32-bit operating systems for them.

- Empty the recycling bin and delete your temporary files (especially Internet files and email!) regularly. Databases need lots of disk space to operate, and these files can consume acres of space before you realize it.

- Take advantage of disk defragmentation utilities. Depending on the operating system used, defragmentation might be automatic. Computer files are not stored in one piece. As you create, edit, save, and delete files, your PC spreads them out over any available space. The .MDB file is no different. If your hard drive is fragmented, even simple searches take much longer than necessary because the computer has to move all over the drive to find what you've requested.

- Avoid disk compression (including NTFS compression). Running the database on a compressed drive will have a significant negative effect on the performance of your application.

- Buy more hard drive space. Depending upon what your application does, you might need available free space of as much as 5–10 times the size of your .MDB file. A lack of available space will hinder the performance of large queries, lengthy transactions, compilation, maintenance, imports, and action queries. Hard drive prices have also fallen dramatically in recent years.

- Disable the Journal in Outlook. The Journal feature of Outlook generates a log entry every time you open and close an application. This log can get very large and steal disk space and cycle time from your application.

- Reclaim leaked memory. Applications are very good at claiming memory, but they are not as good at giving it back to you. Over time, many applications, including Access, will reduce the real amount of memory available. Closing Access occasionally will allow Windows to reallocate this memory for you.

- Install Windows and Office locally. Do not run them over the network. It seems strange to write this now, but there are places out there that still do otherwise.

- Adjustments to the swap file (virtual memory) can also help enhance the performance of your application. When Access runs out of RAM, it borrows drive space from the virtual memory allocation and treats this space like additional RAM. If there is not enough virtual memory, Access must continually read and write to the disk in order to perform its operations. Increasing this allocation can boost the performance of your database. However, keep in mind that reading and writing to disk is astronomically slower than working in RAM. Increasing the size of the swap file will only help performance if the disk is defragmented.

> **TIP**
>
> Make sure the swap file is not running on a compressed drive or partition. Dealing with the compression will slow the reading and writing of the temporary files that will need to be written to this area.

Many of the preceding issues might be out of your control, but when developing an Access solution, you should consider and propose them when necessary. As a developer of an Access database, you have more control over whether to use the remaining optimization possibilities.

> **TIP**
>
> Many developers have machines that are much faster than the machines their applications will run on. Be sure to test your application on a machine comparable to your users' machines. If the hardware configurations vary, develop for the lowest common denominator machine.

14

APPLICATION OPTIMIZATION

Installing the Application for Optimal Performance

The way you configure the files your application uses can have an effect on the performance of your application. These guidelines should help your application behave well and make the rest of the chapter useful.

- Separate the data from the application. Creating one .MDB file to contain all the tables, placing it on the network, and installing another .MDB file with the queries, forms, reports, and so on, on the desktop should be standard practice. It will also improve performance, multiuser access, and maintainability. Of all the suggestions in this chapter, you should disregard this one only for a very compelling reason.

- Use a current version of the workgroup file (system.mdw). Although it is possible to use earlier versions of the workgroup file with your application, the current version will provide better performance.

- Compact the database regularly. You should compact the database after large imports, deletes, and updates as well. Compacting the database reclaims the empty space between data pages (slack) and recalculates the database statistics used in query optimization. (More on that later.) Compacting the database also frees disk space for other processes. Access 2000 gives you a new opportunity to compact the database when the database closes. Check Compact on Close in the Tools, Options dialog box on the General tab. Some developers have found that earlier versions of Access needed to be compacted twice in order to really benefit from the process. Try launching your database from a separate MDB file and have this launcher application perform a compact when it starts your database. When combined with the Compact on Close option, you will have a double compact on every use.

- Install an .MDE version of your application whenever possible. There are a couple of advantages to this. An .MDE requires compiled modules; and compiled modules run faster than decompiled modules. An .MDE also needs less RAM and less drive space than an .MBD, thus enhancing performance.

> **TIP**
>
> Before installing an .MDE, make sure your users understand that none of them will be able to modify the application in this form. With the overwhelming popularity of Access, many users insist on having the ability to modify the application later. You should also thoroughly test the application because MDEs kick out error messages that are really difficult to understand.

Optimizing the Configuration of the Jet Database Engine

A well-tuned machine and an optimized installation of your database won't yield all the possible performance improvements if you have not optimized the application itself. The actual database application consists of several things. Most important among them is the Jet database engine itself. Jet is at the heart of almost everything that takes place in an Access database application, and you can optimize it just as you can optimize other features of Access. Your efforts to optimize Jet should come after you have developed most, if not all, of the application, and spent sufficient time evaluating different optimization techniques within the application.

Jet 4.0, which comes with Access 2000, has some advantages over its predecessors. Features such as new data types, text compression, indexing of memo fields, ANSI SQL-92 implementation, SQL Security management, greater flexibility with foreign key indexes, a vastly improved replication scheme, and improved locking abilities promise to improve performance in many ways. This book fully explains these exciting features in other chapters. You should see those chapters for more information on them. Here we will only treat their performance implications.

The Jet engine takes care of most optimization issues without any intervention from the user or developer. Of all the complex things that Jet does, you can only see about 15 of them by way of the Registry. These settings are not very straightforward and you should tinker with them with care. Changing a setting might have the opposite effect you intended. Even if your application seems to run faster, you might have fatally affected other important things like stability or concurrency management. See Table 14.1 for a listing of the Jet Registry settings available to you.

14

APPLICATION OPTIMIZATION

TABLE 14.1 REGISTRY SETTINGS FOR JET 4.0

Key	Description	Default Value	Key Location	Constant for SetOption Method
ExclusiveAsyncDelay	In an exclusive environment, the number of milliseconds Jet must wait before it commits implicit transactions.	2000	\HKEY_LOCAL_MACHINES \SOFTWARE\MICROSOFT\JET 4.0\ENGINES\JET 4.0	dbExclusive AsyncDelay
FlushTransactionTimeout	When a value is entered here, the SharedAsyncDelay and ExclusiveAsyncDelay are disabled. This sets the number of milliseconds before starting asynchronous writes, provided no pages have been added to the cache.	500	\HKEY_LOCAL_MACHINES \SOFTWARE\MICROSOFT\JET \4.0\ENGINES\JET 4.0	dbFlushTransaction Timeout
ImplicitCommitSync	Determines whether the system must wait for implicit transactions to be completed before continuing with processes. If set to No, Jet will process implicit transactions asynchronously.	No	\HKEY_LOCAL_MACHINES \SOFTWARE\MICROSOFT\JET \4.0\ENGINES\JET 4.0	dbImplicit CommitSync
			\HKEY_LOCAL_MACHINES	dbLockDelay

TABLE 14.1 CONTINUED

Key	Description	Default Value	Key Location	Constant for SetOption Method
LockDelay	Number of milliseconds Jet will wait before retrying lock attempts.	100	\SOFTWARE\MICROSOFT\JET\4.0\ENGINES\JET 4.0	
LockRetry	Number of repeated attempts Jet will make to lock a page.	20	\HKEY_LOCAL_MACHINES\SOFTWARE\MICROSOFT\JET\4.0\ENGINES\JET 4.0	dbLockRetry
MaxBufferSize	Jet's cache size in kilobytes.	0	\HKEY_LOCAL_MACHINES\SOFTWARE\MICROSOFT\JET\4.0\ENGINES\JET 4.0	dbMaxBufferSize
MaxLocksPerFile	Maximum number of locks permitted for a single transaction. If the transaction requires more locks, the transaction is then split into multiple transactions, which can be committed individually and partially. This setting can be used to prevent some problems that occur with Novell NetWare 3.1.	9500	\HKEY_LOCAL_MACHINES\SOFTWARE\MICROSOFT\JET\4.0\ENGINES\JET 4.0	dbMaxLocksPerFile

continues

14

APPLICATION OPTIMIZATION

TABLE 14.1   CONTINUED

Key	Description	Default Value	Key Location	Constant for SetOption Method
PagesLockedToTableLock	(New to Access 2000) Provides exclusive access to a table for updates by providing programmatic control over the number of page locks before which Jet will attempt to lock the entire table. A setting of 50 will cause Jet to attempt a table lock at the 51st page lock. If the table lock fails, Jet will try again at the 101st page lock. Zero disables the feature.	0	\HKEY_LOCAL_MACHINES \SOFTWARE\MICROSOFT\JET \4.0\ENGINES\JET 4.0	
PageTimeout	The amount of time that a non–read-locked page is held in the cache before it is refreshed. The amount of time is measured in milliseconds.	5000	\HKEY_LOCAL_MACHINES \SOFTWARE\MICROSOFT\JET \4.0\ENGINES\JET 4.0	dbPageTimeout
RecycleLVs	Determines whether Jet will recycle OLE, memo, and binary pages.	0 (disabled)	\HKEY_LOCAL_MACHINES \SOFTWARE\MICROSOFT\JET \4.0\ENGINES\JET 4.0	dbRecycleLVs

TABLE 14.1   CONTINUED

Key	Description	Default Value	Key Location	Constant for SetOption *Method*
SharedAsyncDelay	In a shared environment, the number of milliseconds Jet must wait before it commits implicit transactions.	50	\HKEY_LOCAL_MACHINES \SOFTWARE\MICROSOFT\JET \4.0\ENGINES\JET 4.0	dbSharedAsyncDelay
Threads	Number of background threads in use by Jet.	3	\HKEY_LOCAL_MACHINES \SOFTWARE\MICROSOFT\JET \4.0\ENGINES\JET 4.0	N/A
UserCommitSync	Determines whether or not the system waits to complete write operations before continuing with processes. If set to No, the Jet engine will process explicit transactions asynchronously.	Yes	\HKEY_LOCAL_MACHINES \SOFTWARE\MICROSOFT\JET \4.0\ENGINES\JET 4.0	dbUserCommitSync
CompactByPKey	Determines the sort order for the primary keys. A setting of 1 makes Jet reorder records by their primary key value. A setting of 0 leaves the records in their order of entry (natural order).	1	\HKEY_LOCAL_MACHINES \SOFTWARE\MICROSOFT\JET \4.0\ENGINES	N/A

continues

14

APPLICATION OPTIMIZATION

TABLE 14.1 CONTINUED

Key	Description	Default Value	Key Location	Constant for SetOption Method
SystemDB	Full path and name of workgroup file.	access_path\system.md	\HKEY_LOCAL_MACHINES \SOFTWARE\MICROSOFT\JET \4.0\ENGINES	N/A
PrevFormatCompact WithUNICODE Compression	(New in Access 2000) Allows or prevents the compression of stored text and memo field data. Compression is permitted by default.	1	\HKEY_LOCAL_MACHINES \SOFTWARE\MICROSOFT\JET \4.0\ENGINES	
JetShowPlan	Not installed by default. When created by the developer and set to 0n (case-sensitive), Jet creates and appends a text file named showplan.out in the current directory. As queries are executed, the execution plans are logged to this file. Disable after development.	Not installed by default.	\HKEY_LOCAL_MACHINES \SOFTWARE\MICROSOFT\JET \4.0\ENGINES\JET 4.0	N/A

Safely Changing the Jet Settings

There are three ways to change the Jet Registry settings:

- Directly edit the default values through RegEdit.exe.
- Create a user profile to override the default settings and call that user profile with the /profile command line option.
- Enable your application to temporarily override the default settings by using the SetOption method of the database object.

The third option is preferred. Not only is it simple to use, but employing this technique enables you to tune each application separately. You can even change the settings at different times within the application to really optimize performance. This technique never changes the default settings, so new projects start from a common baseline.

There is no need to employ API calls to temporarily override these Registry values. The database engine provides a method and it takes two arguments. The syntax is as follows:

```
DBEngine.SetOption ConstantNameofSetting, value
```

For example, the performance of a batch of updates might benefit from having Jet wait longer before committing the implicit transactions. The code to temporarily lengthen the SharedAsyncDelay wait period to 1 second (1000 milliseconds) would be

```
DBEngine.SetOption dbSharedAsyncDelay, 1000
```

This setting remains in effect until your application specifically changes it with another SetOption method, the DBEngine goes out of scope, or the application terminates. SetOption does not write values to the Registry. You cannot override the default settings for SystemDB, CompactByPkey, or threads with the SetOption method.

> **NOTE**
>
> If your application uses an ODBC data source, review the Registry settings under \HKEY_LOCAL_MACHINES\SOFTWARE\MICROSOFT\JET\4.0\ENGINES\ODBC.

Tools to Measure Performance

It is important to know whether the cumulative effect of your efforts have helped or hindered your application. You can employ several tools to monitor and evaluate the relative performance of one technique over another. The first is a timer to measure the amount of time a process takes to execute. The second is an undocumented function to count disk, cache, and lock operations. The third is Access's ability to publish a query execution plan for your review. You can apply the first two tools against almost any techniques discussed in this chapter. Query execution plans are only relevant to optimizing queries.

Although VBA offers a `Timer()` function, it might not be sufficiently accurate for evaluating your optimization efforts. The VBA `Timer` function records the passage of time in seconds since midnight. Because it measures time in a single-precision floating point value, it might not be accurate enough for your needs—especially for elapsed time under 1 second. Many developers have also used the `GetTickCount` function. Although this function appears to return time in milliseconds, because it is tied to the clock timer in the PC, its result is actually measured in increments of 1/18 of a second and not in true milliseconds. The Windows API offers a timer that actually tracks the time in milliseconds. The `timeGetTime()` function measures the passage of time from the moment Windows was started. Because it uses a different hardware timer than `GetTickCount`, it returns time measured with millisecond accuracy.

By using `timeGetTime()`, we can insert a line of code before and after any critical executions and get a very accurate measurement of how long an action has took to complete.

To use this API call, we need two things: a declaration of the function, and a global variable to hold the starting time of our timer. In the declarations section of a module, enter the following three lines:

```
Private Declare Function a2ku_apigettime Lib "winmm.dll" _
Alias "timeGetTime" () As Long
Dim lngstartingtime As Long
```

Now we can create a subroutine to start the clock and a function to stop the clock.

```
Sub a2kuStartClock()
    lngstartingtime = a2ku_apigettime()
End Sub
Function a2kuEndClock()
    a2kuEndClock = a2ku_apigettime() - lngstartingtime
End Function
```

Listing 14.1 illustrates how to use these functions to evaluate the performance of a query.

LISTING 14.1   TIMING THE EXECUTION OF A QUERY

```
Sub QueryTimer(strQueryName As String)

Dim db As Database
Dim qry As QueryDef
Dim rs as Recordset

Set db = CurrentDb()

Set qry = db.QueryDefs(strQueryName)

'Start the clock
a2kuStartClock

Set rs = qry.OpenRecordset()

'Stop the clock and print the result to the debug window
Debug.Print strQueryName & " executed in: " & a2kuEndClock & _
    " milliseconds"

rs.Close

End Sub
```

> **NOTE**
>
> For the most accurate measurement, be sure to place the a2kuStartClock call and the a2kuEndClock call as tightly as possible around the procedure you are reviewing.

Looking Behind the Scenes

Although timing is certainly important, by itself it doesn't say much about performance while you are developing. Chances are that your development effort takes place on a fast machine, and you are probably running against a set of test data smaller than the real application will use. Furthermore, a timer doesn't give any indication of how your application will run on a different machine with less memory or a slower drive. To look behind the scenes of your application, we can use another undocumented function: ISAMStats. ISAMStats is undocumented and unsupported, so use the information it provides as a general guide only. When used, it will provide measurements of six important performance-affecting operations. It keeps a tally of all the disk reads, disk writes, cache reads, read-ahead cache reads, lock placements, and lock releases. The function is readily available in Access 2000 and earlier versions of Access. The syntax is very simple:

```
DBEngine.ISAMStats(option,[reset])
```

There are six options for the *Option* argument:

Argument for *Option*	Description
0	Disk writes
1	Disk reads
2	Cache reads
3	Cache reads (from read-ahead cache)
4	Locks placed
5	Locks released

The optional reset argument enables you to reset the individual counts to zero. In order to use the function to measure performance, you must either subtract one reading from an earlier reading, or reset the meter to zero and then perform your operation. Listing 14.2 provides one way to employ the ISAMStats function to measure performance:

LISTING 14.2   ONE WAY TO USE ISAMStats TO GAUGE PERFORMANCE

```
Sub PrintStats()

Dim i As Integer

Debug.Print
Debug.Print "Disk Reads: " & ISAMStats(0, False)
Debug.Print "Disk Writes: " & ISAMStats(1, False)
Debug.Print "Cache Reads: " & ISAMStats(2, False)
Debug.Print "Read-Ahead Cache Reads: " & ISAMStats(3, False)
Debug.Print "Locks Placed: " & ISAMStats(4, False)
Debug.Print "Locks Released: " & ISAMStats(5, False)

For i = 0 To 6
   ISAMStats i, True
Next

End Sub
```

PrintStats gives you some idea why one technique might be faster than another technique. This information might also help you make an informed choice between two approaches that take the same number of milliseconds to execute. By looking under the hood, you can see how a different hardware configuration or a larger set of data might adversely affect one approach's performance.

The `A2KU_TimeClock` and the `PrintStats` functions are only useful to you if you use them to compare one technique to another. Furthermore, you will only get reliable results if you average their output over many tests in varying conditions. You can easily combine these two functions into one function to conduct and report on such iterative tests.

We will employ these two functions later in the chapter to illustrate how to use them and to show how different the two approaches really are.

Optimizing the Database from the Start

Relational databases, including Access, rest on tables of information. The design of those tables and the relationships between them will have far-reaching effects on the performance of your application. If the tables are not normalized, indexed, and related to one another properly, every query and code routine will be subject to a time-consuming workaround. The greatest thing you can do for the performance of you database is to design the tables correctly.

Designing Data Tables for Performance

Aside from general rule so normalization, the following points should be kept in mind when building tables.

- When working with linked tables, make the links permanent.
- Using simple subdatasheets in tables, where the subdatasheet is another table and the master/child links use indexed fields, has a negligible negative effect on performance; however, a more complex subdatasheet construct might compromise performance. Use subdatasheets in queries instead of tables. This way, you can use them only when you need them, and not every time you open a table.
- Input masks, lookups, and validation rules should also be used only where they are needed: forms. It's best to keep your tables as simple and light as possible.
- Do not create data fields larger than necessary. Access provides room for data by that data item's field size. You can waste a lot of space (and time) by using data types or property settings too large for the data contained in those fields.

Normalizing Data to Enhance Performance

This book has already covered normalization, so we won't cover it here except to make a few points.

- A normalized database saves disk space because it doesn't repeat data needlessly.

- A normalized database uses fewer data pages and fewer index pages, making searches less time-consuming.

- A normalized database makes it more difficult to have conflicting or confusing data because there's little repetition.

- When does breaking normalization make sense? It makes sense to base parts of your application on non-normalized tables if those tables are temporary tables, the creation of which is time-consuming. However, the data should be stored permanently in a normalized structure. Keep in mind that you will have to create the routines to update the normalized structure from actions taken against the non-normal structure—this can compromise performance. Break normalization rules only as a last resort.

- Another aspect of normal form you can usually break without penalty is the data repetition rule because it affects incidental data items. Often there are extraneous bits of information relating to a customer or a product that you should, if strictly following the rules, store in different tables. An example of this would be day and evening telephone numbers, fax numbers, cellular telephone numbers, pagers, email addresses, and so on.

- Break normalization rules when it makes sense. Breaking normalization can, at times, improve performance for parts of your application. But keep in mind that it carries a high cost in terms of reliability, data integrity, and maintainability.

The ideal normalization scheme would have you create a contact table with a customer ID field, a contact type field, and another field to contain the telephone numbers and email addresses. This is probably overkill, and the added integrity and flexibility would not be worth the cost. It's perfectly reasonable to keep this information in the customer table and take advantage of the performance gain. However, the rule is to normalize as much as possible. That's what Jet expects, and it performs best with normalized data.

Creating Indexes to Speed Queries

- Indexes can speed data retrieval performance 1000%.

- Indexes can also slow updates and data entry, so don't create indexes that you don't need.

- Create a primary key that means something to your data and to your users. Allowing Access to create your primary key by inserting an AutoNumber field is nearly useless from a performance standpoint. Unless your users have no other means of identifying their data records, you should use something more meaningful. Try the telephone number, Social Security Number, account number, vendor code, and so on. For an index to really boost your performance, you must actually query against it.

- Index all the fields against which your application will exercise criteria. Creating indexes on multiple fields in your tables will make it easier to optimize queries created later in the development process.

- Index fields on both sides of an expected join. Because the Order Number fields relates to both the Orders Detail and Orders tables, both tables should have an appropriate index. But if you are going to run many reports by order date, these fields might need indexes too.

Establish Relationships Early to Improve Performance

Establish the relationships between tables in the Relationships window. When you create a relationship here, you have the ability to define the properties of that relationship. You'll also alert Jet to its existence. Jet is then able to use all that information to create a more effective optimization plan when you query the data. This improves performance.

Put simply, normalize your data, create indexes where they are necessary, be economical with data types and sizes, and remember to keep tables simple. They exist to store data, not to present it.

Boosting Query Performance

Although your users might never see a query in your application, the queries are doing most of the work. A relational database would be useless without its ability to execute queries against the data. However, queries are not all created equally. Even if you have

taken all the steps necessary to normalize your data and have created all the indexes you need, you could have queries that do not perform as fast as they could. You could even have two queries with identical result sets but different performance measurements.

To understand how to optimize queries, you need to understand how Jet handles them. Each query goes through four steps:

1. Definition—A SQL statement is created using one of several tools.

2. Compilation—The SQL string is broken down or "tokenized" into parts.

3. Optimization—Using a cost-based algorithm, Jet formulates and tests different ways to yield a result set that satisfies the underlying SQL statement.

4. Execution—Using the optimal plan, Jet delivers a result set to the user.

You can define a query through the QBE grid; a SQL string executed in code; a SQL string in the rowsource property of a form, report, or control; or any means that will fundamentally create a SQL string.

Jet places tokenized parts into a hierarchical internal structure. The parts are very similar to the keywords of a SQL statement. The base tables used by the query (From) are at the foundation. The columns of the result (Select) set are next. The criteria or restrictions (Where) the query must satisfy are next. How the base tables relate (Join) follows. Finally comes how the result set should be sorted (Order by). This structure informs the optimization phase.

This is the most complex step. Jet evaluates and calculates a cost for each possible approach. It does this by attacking the query from two angles: accessing the base tables, and exploiting the joins between them. Understand how Jet thinks about queries might help you design faster queries in the future.

There are three ways for Jet to get rows of data from your tables:

- Scan—This is the most expensive approach. In a scan, Jet must read every row of information without using an index. Your query will force Jet to scan a table if

  The query is restricted on a nonindexed field.

  The query's criteria qualify a large percentage of the rows in the table.

- Index—Jet employs the index of the table to read the rows of the table. Although Jet might read a data page more than once, it is still a much faster approach than a scan.

- Rushmore Optimization— This is available only when there are restrictions set against more than one index in the query. Rushmore enables Jet to read far fewer data pages, even none at all in some cases. When Rushmore optimization is used, Jet has to read only index pages, which is extremely efficient.

Obviously, you should avoid scans when possible and try to make the best use of indexes. But how do you make sure that the best choice, Rushmore optimization, is working for your query? There is no way to turn Rushmore on or off, and there's no obvious indicator to check either. It's always on, but only certain kinds of queries can take advantage of it. The following three conditions must exist for your queries to benefit from Rushmore optimization.

Queries must have multiple indexes.

Criteria restrictions must be against these indexed fields.

The criteria statement must use those indexes in one of three ways:

- Index Intersection— A criteria expression with the "AND" operator. Jet could use Rushmore optimization on the following set of restrictions because both fields are indexed.

  ```
  WHERE CompanyName='Ernst Handle' And City='Graz'
  ```

- Index Union— A criteria expression with the "OR" operator. Jet could use Rushmore optimization on the following set of restrictions because both fields are indexed.

  ```
  WHERE CompanyName='Ernst Handle' Or City='Graz'
  ```

- Index Counts— Aggregate queries that return only a count of records. Rushmore will optimize the query even if there are no restrictions set in the Where clause.

  ```
  SELECT Count(*) FROM Customers;
  ```

Be sure you have multiple indexes on all the tables that could benefit from them. Also, try to express your queries in ways that cause intersections or unions of those indexes. Those two design tips will take care of the base table operations of the query execution plan.

Once Jet has figured out how it can access the data in the individual tables, it must figure out how the tables relate to each other. This is the join strategy phase of the optimization. You can also anticipate the execution plan's join strategies by reviewing their types in Table 14.2.

14

APPLICATION OPTIMIZATION

TABLE 14.2   JOIN TYPES: HOW THEY WORK AND HOW TO KNOW THEM

Join Type	How It Works	How to Recognize	Acceptable Use
Index-Merge	Indexes do most of the work.	Indexes used on both sides of the join. At least one of the indexes does not allow nulls (primary key). All tables must be native Jet format.	Whenever possible.
Index	The first table is scanned, and then rows in second table are found by using an index.	Index on the related field(s) of the second table. Nulls allowed in these indexes. Restrictions do not use indexes.	If there are few records in second table, if its records do not appear in result set, or if the first tables criteria is very restrictive.
Merge	Both tables scanned at the same time.	Two tables sorted by their joined fields. Data from both tables appears in result set.	Both tables are large and sorted by their related fields.
Lookup	Second table scanned and sorted before join.	No index on the tables' joined field(s).	When the second table is small and there is no index on the second table's related field.
Nested iteration	Row-by-row iteration through each table in the relationship.	No indexes on either side of join.	Only on very small tables and when there is no alternative.

Jet will choose one of these plans over another depending on several other factors. These factors are

- Number of records in each base table
- Number of data pages used by the base tables
- Location and type of table—local ISAM or ODBC
- The selectivity of the tables' indexes—duplicates or nulls allowed
- Number of index pages

Evaluating the Type of Result Set for Optimum Performance

Jet also considers the result set you have requested. For instance, to present a dynaset, it might employ a plan that will efficiently present the first page of data, even if that plan is slow at presenting the remaining records. To create a dynaset, Jet creates a set of unique key values that point to rows in the underlying base tables. This way, Jet only needs to retrieve the keys up front and can present the rest of the record when the user needs them. In a snapshot, however, Jet gathers all the records and columns for the result set before presenting the result. If the entire snapshot cannot fit in memory, it will overflow to the swap file, negatively affecting performance. You might get better performance from a large dynaset because of its key cursor system than you would from a large snapshot.

First, Jet evaluates and scores the base table access options available to it. Each base table access plan receives a score. Next, Jet evaluates the join options available to it and scores them. Jet will only consider joining a relationship's result to a base table—it will not consider joining the results of one join to the results of another join. This helps limit the amount of time Jet spends optimizing queries. After analyzing each available join strategy with each available base table access strategy and considering the recordset type you requested, it chooses a plan.

For execution against non-ODBC tables, Jet cleans, reduces in size, and submits the plan for execution.

This compiling and optimizing happens the first time you create or edit a query and run it. It is possible for a query to decompile. If you modify a query and save it but do not run it, it will remain decompiled. Also, if you modify table indexes or the schema of your data, your queries might no longer be optimized. Always open the queries in Design view, save them, and then run them before delivering your applications. This will ensure that your queries compile.

Jet performs some complex cost assessments in order to optimize your queries. Among these complex evaluations is a review of the database's statistics. These statistics tell Jet how many data pages, index pages, tables rows, and so on, exist in the database. These statistics can be skewed when the database is abnormally terminated, transactions are rolled back, or if the database is in need of compaction. When optimizing, always compact the database first.

As discussed earlier, Jet creates an execution plan for each query. By creating a Registry entry

14

```
\HKEY_LOCAL_MACHINES\SOFTWARE\MICROSOFT\JET\4.0\ENGINES\DEBUG
```

and setting its string value to ON, Jet will create or append a text file in your current directory with a query execution plan. Many of the topics discussed so far appear in that query optimization plan. You cannot alter the plan, except by altering your data schema, query construction, or query restrictions. The more detailed the plan, the better. Listing 14.3 shows the execution plan for the query, Quarterly Orders in Northwind.

LISTING 14.3   EXECUTION PLAN FOR A QUERY THAT TAKES ADVANTAGE OF RUSHMORE OPTIMIZATION

```
--- Quarterly Orders ---

- Inputs to Query -
Table 'Customers'
    Using index 'PrimaryKey'
    Having Indexes:
    PrimaryKey 91 entries, 1 page, 91 values
      which has 1 column, fixed, unique, primary-key, no-nulls
    PostalCode 91 entries, 1 page, 87 values
      which has 1 column, fixed
    CompanyName 91 entries, 3 pages, 91 values
      which has 1 column, fixed
    City 91 entries, 1 page, 69 values
      which has 1 column, fixed
Table 'Orders'
- End inputs to Query -

01) Restrict rows of table Orders
      using rushmore
      for expression "Orders.OrderDate Between #1/1/98# And #12/31/98#"
02) Outer Join result of '01)' to table 'Customers'
      using index 'Customers!PrimaryKey'
      join expression "Orders.CustomerID=Customers.CustomerID"
03) Sort Distinct result of '02)'
```

You can see the base table section, with the indexes analyzed and the number of entries, databases, index pages, and values being assessed. Notice also that Rushmore can optimize this query because of the index over the Order Date field of the Orders table. The plan recognizes the join between the Orders table and the Customers tables as an outer join. The indexes and Rushmore make this is a well-optimized query. If you're not sure how well-optimized your query is, you can check its execution plan. SHOWPLAN is undocumented and unsupported. Certain queries will not produce plans, and some plans are wrong, but you can still make cautious use of it.

Listing 14.4 shows a poorly optimized query.

LISTING 14.4   A POORLY OPTIMIZED QUERY EXECUTION PLAN THAT DOES NOT BENEFIT FROM JET OPTIMIZATION

```
SELECT Customers.CustomerID, Customers.CompanyName
FROM Customers INNER JOIN Orders ON
Customers.CustomerID = Orders.CustomerID
WHERE ((Not (Orders.ShipCountry)="USA"));

--- Customers with Shipping Address Outside USA ---


- Inputs to Query -
Table 'Orders'
Table 'Customers'
    Using index 'PrimaryKey'
    Having Indexes:
    PrimaryKey 91 entries, 1 page, 91 values
      which has 1 column, fixed, unique, primary-key, no-nulls
    PostalCode 91 entries, 1 page, 87 values
      which has 1 column, fixed
    CompanyName 91 entries, 3 pages, 91 values
      which has 1 column, fixed
    City 91 entries, 1 page, 69 values
      which has 1 column, fixed
- End inputs to Query -

01) Restrict rows of table Orders
      by scanning
      testing expression "Not Orders.ShipCountry="USA""
02) Inner Join result of '01)' to table 'Customers'
      using index 'Customers!PrimaryKey'
      join expression "Orders.CustomerID=Customers.CustomerID"
```

The clue to this query's weakness is in how it handles the restriction. Because the restriction does not use an index, the query must scan the table and test each record to see if the criterion is satisfied. Table scans are costly. An index would have made this query much more efficient.

Increasing the Speed of Queries

The query optimization in Jet is quite sophisticated, but that doesn't mean you can't help it. Following are some tips to help make sure your queries run faster:

- Create indexes for all the fields you intend to use in your criteria clauses.
- Create indexes on both sides of the joins in your queries.

14

APPLICATION OPTIMIZATION

- Use primary keys instead of unique indexes. Because primary keys prohibit null values, your query might be able to take advantage of more join types.

- Don't display any unnecessary columns in the result set. Each column takes time to process and display.

- Refrain from using complex expressions in queries.

- Avoid the `IIF()` (immediate IF) function. `IIF()` must evaluate both the true and the false consequences before it can yield a result. Doing this for each record can seriously impede performance.

- When using nested queries, move all the calculations to the last query in the series.

- Use `Count(*)` instead of `Count([CustomerID])` because Rushmore can process `Count(*)` faster—it doesn't have to check for null values before counting.

- If possible, use the Between operator to reduce the number of rows in the result set instead of greater than and less than operators by themselves.

- Usually, placing a restriction on the "one" side of a relationship is most efficient, but this is not always so. Try moving the restriction to the "many" side of the relationship to see if performance improves. Be sure to check the result set carefully after any change in the criteria.

- Normalized tables can store their data in fewer data pages and fewer index pages. Normalize as a rule and break normalization only when no other alternative presents itself.

- Experiment with subqueries instead of joins or complex OR criteria where appropriate. The optimal choice depends on many discreet factors and only experimentation can help you decide which to use.

- Use outer joins only when necessary, as they will automatically require a table scan of the dominant (preserved) table in the join.

- Use saved, parameterized queries instead of SQL statements in code. Jet has already compiled parameterized queries and created an execution plan for them (though they are not available in SHOWPLAN.OUT). Using compiled and saved queries will eliminate Jet's need to evaluate and optimize your SQL string. Access compiles SQL strings used as record source or row source of forms, reports, or controls, so they can remain as they are.

- Always deliver compiled queries.

- Use queries instead of DAO for data manipulation whenever possible. Queries (SQL) are almost always faster than DAO for these tasks.

- Select your recordset types with care. You need a dynaset if you want to add or edit data. A snapshot or a forward-only snapshot might be suitable if you only want to read data. Snapshots might take longer to open, but they will scroll faster.

- If you are opening a recordset simply to add data, open with the `dbAppendOnly` option. This keeps it from having to retrieve any rows.

- Test pass-through queries when using client/server data. Also, investigate Access 2000's extensive new client/server capabilities. Pass-through queries are not always faster than queries against attached server tables, but they usually result in less network traffic.

- Large action queries might perform better if you set the `UseTransaction` property to `False`. With transactions, Access creates temporary tables. Sometimes these tables are quite large and will hinder the performance of the queries.

- When querying data from a server, use the `CacheStart`, `FillCache`, and `EndCache` methods to handle the data coming from the server.

- When dealing with server data, avoid local processing. Local processing would be things like complex `Group By` where the `Distinct` keyword has been used, employing the LIKE operator on text or memo fields, multiple aggregate functions in a crosstab query, or crosstab queries with `ORDER` clauses. Also, avoid complex outer and inner join combinations. These constructs will cause the server to send massive amounts of data to the local PC for processing, causing very poor performance.

- Compact the database regularly and often to ensure the statistics used by Jet to optimize your queries are accurate.

- If at all possible, fill your application with at least as much test data as it will have when it is installed for your users. This way Jet can optimize the queries with statistics that will accurately reflect the real conditions under which your queries will run.

- Index fields for sorting.

- If your data is mostly static, consider using a make table query of the data you need instead of querying the database repeatedly.

- Avoid using domain aggregate functions (`Dlookup()`) on tables which are not in the query.

Queries are the most complicated aspect of Access. Luckily, Jet goes a long way to making sure they will run well for us. The information contained here will help you help Jet make your query operations as fast as possible. Check your experiments with the SHOWPLAN and the `PrintStats` and `QueryTimer` subroutines to see which combination of solutions will give you the best performance.

Getting Your Forms to Run Faster

Because your users will spend most of their time working with the forms you provide for them, you will have to take care to make sure all your other optimization efforts are not cancelled out by slow forms. The basic watchwords for forms are to keep them light and be frugal.

In the Beginning...

When your application starts, the first thing your users see is the startup form. This might be a splash screen with the name of the application and other information, or it could be a switchboard for navigating your application. Whichever it is, it's a good idea to remove the code from this form. Put the forms' startup code into a standard module and run only those routines that are essential to starting the application. Because the form will load faster, it makes a good first impression on the user. Some of the operations might be able to wait until later to run. After you've removed the module from the form, set its `HasModule` property to `No`. This creates a lightweight form and it should perform better. However, by changing the `HasModule` property of the form, you will erase all the code behind the form and behind the controls. Make sure you place those subroutines and functions in a standard module before changing the property.

The startup form should not have ActiveX controls on it. ActiveX controls take longer to load than all the other controls. If an ActiveX control is required on the startup form, you might want to limit the number of other controls on the form.

Set the Startup Form option instead of using AutoExec macros.

Getting Faster Images

Using images in the interface of your application plays to the graphical strengths of Access. However, just because Northwind moves along quickly showing employee photographs does not mean that you can just put graphics into your application without concern. This section discusses using graphics in your database.

Try using the `Image` control for images. It's much more efficient than the bound or unbound object frames for displaying some graphics.

Access must paint or render every control on a form when you load it. Not surprisingly, it takes longer to render controls that overlap. To make sure your tightly placed controls don't accidentally overlap, use the Format, Vertical Spacing and Format, Horizontal Spacing commands.

Strive for the lowest possible color depth on graphic images; black-and-white is best. The more depth you give the bitmap, the more memory and processing time is required to paint it.

Keep graphics and other large data types (memos and OLE objects) off the primary forms and out of the primary tables and queries. Call them into view with a separate form or query only when requested by the user. This prevents the expenditure of time and resources to present something very large and memory-intensive when it might not be necessary. The memory used by forms containing OLE objects is not released to your application until you close the form, so be sure to close these forms when you are finished with them.

The Basic, Fast Form

The single most common performance drag on a form is the number and type of controls. Every control taxes memory and resources, some more than others. Relatively speaking, a bound object frame weighs about 40 times as much as a line. An ActiveX control can be even heavier, depending on what constitutes the control and what it does.

When choosing which controls to place on a form, keep Table 14.3 in mind. As a rule of thumb, the more functionality a control affords you, the more resources it will take. The following table lists the controls found on the form design toolbar. Counting the properties available for each control and adjusting that number to account for the complexity of the task accomplished by each control derives the relative weight. This is a general guide only. What you do with the form controls will really determine how they use resources.

14

APPLICATION
OPTIMIZATION

TABLE 14.3   RELATIVE WEIGHTS OF FORM CONTROLS

Control Type	Relative Weight
Rectangle	1
Line	1
Page Break	1
Tab Page (not including the controls within)	4
Image (not including the image within)	6
Tab Control	6
SubForm (at least)	6
Label	8
Option Button	8
Command Button	8
Checkbox	8
Option Group (not including the controls within)	8
Toggle Button	9
Text Box	10
List Box (at least)	10
Combo Box (at least)	20
ActiveX Controls	>=20
Object Frame (not including the image within)	30
Bound Object Frame (not including the image within)	40

Some controls are several orders of magnitude heavier than others, so substitution can be a profitable optimization technique. There are many times when a list box can substitute for a combo box or even a subform. Images can often use the image control instead of the object frame, and the native tab control can help divide your form into faster loading pieces by rendering only the controls on the visible page. With users becoming more familiar with hypertext links on the Internet, you might be able to substitute hyperlinks for command buttons. If you have the opportunity to use a lighter control without sacrificing functionality, take it.

There are some other techniques to make your controls perform better:

- Limit the number of fields displayed in list boxes and combo boxes to the barest minimum. Also, index the found field and the displayed fields. Turn off the AutoExpand feature of combo boxes by setting it to No. Making Access watch and act upon every key stroke is a performance drain. Use this feature only when you can't avoid it. If you must use the `AutoExpand`, make sure the column the user is typing is a text type field. Access can only do the `AutoExpand` function on text. If the underlying data is not text, it will have to spend time converting the data and the entries.

- If you are hiding the combo box's bound field, avoid using expressions in that field or in the display fields. The combo box will not display the results as quickly as if you had calculated them ahead of time and read the results from a table.

- Avoid using restricted queries as the basis of a combo box or list box. Try to base them on single table if possible. You might find a performance boost if you can make a table from the query and remake it when necessary.

- When refreshing forms, or any control which displays data that might have changed, use the `Requery` method, it is much faster than the Requery Action of a macro. Be sure to use this method after deletes and updated, especially in a multi-user application.

- Instead of having one large and lengthy combo box, see if the form's functionality would accommodate several combo boxes that limit each other. For instance, one combo box could select states. That selection would limit the contents of a second combo box to cities in the selected state. This would be faster and more efficient than scrolling through one combo box with all the states and cities listed in it.

- Just as you must be frugal with the number and type of controls you place on your forms, you also need to consider the number of fields presented in the form's underlying recordset. Although forms will always load data more quickly from a table than from a query, there is a caveat. When you open a form based on a table, all the fields of the table are loaded, even if the form does not display them. There are times when it is better to open the form from a query instead, so you can exclude unnecessary fields from the recordset.

- Sort the underlying recordset of a form only as a last resort. Forcing the underlying recordset to reorder the records at the same time as the form is configuring itself for presentation can noticeably slow the form's opening.

- When writing code behind the form (CBF), use the `Me` keyword. This constant always refers to the active form and will work faster than other references.

- Index the Link Child field and Link Master fields of a mainform/subform construction. This will greatly improve the lookups that these forms do so often.

- If your users are not going to edit the records of a subform, set the subform's properties accordingly. `AllowEdits`, `AllowAppend`, and `AllowDeletes` affect performance because they provide functionality to the form. You can gain speed by

14

APPLICATION
OPTIMIZATION

getting rid of unused functionality. Likewise, you can gain speed by selecting the correct functionality. If you are opening a form for data entry, set its `DataEntry` property to `Yes` to keep it from retrieving records it doesn't need.

- Be conservative about setting form and control properties at runtime. Set these properties only when necessary and only when it will not hamper performance.

- Do you really need a dynaset? Would a snapshot be faster?

- Just as it is possible to gain speed by hiding controls from view with page breaks and tabs, it is possible to gain speed by hiding forms. A good practice is to invisibly load a few of the most common forms in the application when you get a chance. That opportunity might be at startup or when the form is first requested. To load a form invisibly, open it with the `WindowMode` argument set to `acHidden`:

  ```
  DoCmd.OpenForm "formname",,,,,acHidden
  ```

- When it comes time for the user to see the form, it can appear by issuing the following command:

  ```
  Forms("formname").setfocus
  ```

- If the user will need the form again, hide it instead of closing it. The `Hide` method will remove it from view, while keeping it loaded in memory.

  ```
  Formobject.hide
  ```

- By avoiding the query loading, form loading, and control rendering steps, you can really boost the performance of the interface. The trade-off is that forms will consume memory while hidden and this could adversely affect other parts of your application. Although you can't use this technique for all the forms in your application, you can apply it to the most commonly used forms.

When dealing with very large recordsets, try not to present all the records to the user at once. Most users wouldn't know what to do with tens of thousands of records at one time anyway. But if your users are in a multiuser application, and the form is opening a recordset against large tables or queries, your performance is going to suffer from network bottlenecks, cache limitations, record and page locks, and user overload. It is better to find a logical way to break the data into logical subsets with a restriction. Better still is to present the user with only one record at a time by requesting the record by its primary key or by an indexed field. On smaller applications, this might yield negative performance results, but on larger, multiuser systems, it's really the only way to go. To do this, rewrite the SQL statement in code, programmatically change the form's `Record Source` property, and requery the form.

Get the Reports Printed Faster

What good is a fast database, if it takes all day to print a report?

The single biggest performance-affecting difference between forms and reports is the way they handle their sections. In a form, there is a form header, a detail section, and a form footer. In a report, there is a report header, a report footer, a page header, a page footer, section headers, section footers, and a detail section. When you open a form, the query behind the form runs only once. When you open a report, it has to create a query (based on the one in the record source) for each section in the report. If you have a complex query, that report must run it or parts of it several times.

Here are several things you can do to speed the production of reports:

- Keep the query behind the report as simple as possible.

- Move the calculations onto the report. When you place a calculation in the query, the calculation must resolve for every row in the query. However, if you perform the calculation in the report, it calculates as needed and the user will see a response from the application as soon as Access has calculated one report page of data.

- Try to base the query on as few tables as possible. Because the report will run your query more than once, it might help to create a table of the needed result set. The report can run through a table much more quickly than it can execute the query over again. This will be especially helpful if you have based your reports on queries with subqueries.

- Avoid subqueries in the source of a report. Reports need a lot of memory, and a query with subqueries consumes more memory than might be necessary.

- Do you really need the subreport? Not only do subreports make it more difficult to format your output the way you want, but they also consume memory and hinder your report's performance. Subreports have a place though. If you have lots of domain functions, you might find that a subreport is faster than more than a couple of those function calls.

- Avoid sorting or grouping on expressions. The report will have to calculate each expression more than once to get the sorting and grouping to display correctly. Have these values calculated before they get to the report.

- Index all the fields used for sorting or grouping. Because indexes already sort records by default, it is very easy for a report to order and group the data straight from indexed fields.

- The record source should not contain aggregate domain functions (DLookup). Again, this requires the report to take many trips through the data—these trips will delay the display of the report.

- There is no use in showing your users an empty report with #Error# all over it. If your report has no data, send a message to that effect to the user and close the report. You can determine whether the report has data to present by using the NoData or HasData properties.

Many of the techniques for enhancing form performance apply to reports. This section addressed those that were specific to reports.

Writing Fast Code

When it comes to code, there are a few things you can do to make your functions and subroutines run more quickly. Although the differences between one technique and another might be measured in large fractions of a second, using the fastest technique can afford you more opportunities to enhance features later. Users have only so much patience with their applications. When they come back for modifications, you had better have some slack built into the performance to insert things like audit trails and complex validation routines without trying the users' patience.

If you've taken the time to explore and implement some of the techniques discussed so far, you'll find that your code will be easier to optimize. The greatest impediment code encounters is poor database design. If the database design is poor, almost every function and subroutine must be some type of kluge and workaround. A workaround always takes more time to execute than the standard technique.

However, there are a few simple rules to follow, and several alternative techniques to ensure that your application's functions and subroutines will execute as rapidly as possible. Few if any of these things will have a dramatic effect by itself, but when taken together and executed repeatedly, the cumulative effect can be significant.

How Code Uses Memory

Access calls modules, and all the subroutines and functions contained in them, into memory using a "call-tree loading" method. This means that if function A of module one calls function B of module one, which in turn calls function C of module two, Access will load all of module one and all of module two into memory. Both modules will remain in memory. Therefore, it makes sense to group modules in logical ways. If functions and modules will be calling each other often, put them in the same module to reduce the overhead and module load times. Also, delete any functions and subroutines your application does not need.

VBA also loads a module if you reference its module public variables. Be sure to keep those public variables grouped in modules in a logical way.

Maintaining Your Modules

VBA must compile modules before they run. This doesn't mean they won't run if you don't specifically compile them. It means that VBA will have to temporarily compile a module for you before it can run it. It will have to compile every time you want to run it as well. This can seriously affect performance.

When you compile a module, VBA reduces it to a much smaller, faster executing form. Though the original code is always stored in the .MDB file, Access only loads and executes the compiled VBA code. VBA code also has no white space, no comments, no headers, and takes much less memory than the source code you wrote. If you try to run a decompiled routine, VBA must load the entire source code (white space, comments, and dead code included) into memory and compile it before executing. This compiling behavior also applies to forms and reports with code behind them.

Compiling Code

You can compile your code by choosing the Debug, Compile *projectname* menu command. Be sure to compile your applications before distributing them.

Getting Decompiled

A module decompiles when edited. A report or form decompiles when you make any changes to it, even if you don't touch the code. Creating a new form or report can also decompile your code. During development, you can rely on the Tools, Options, General commands to Compile on Demand. This will cause VBA to compile your applications modules while you work. A feature new to Access 2000 is the Background Compile Option. By compiling your application in the background, VBA relieves you of some of the downtime for compiling.

If you ever take the time to check, you'll see that a compiled application needs more disk space than a decompiled application. This is because the source code and the compiled code are stored in a compiled application. There really isn't a performance hit for this. Because the compiled code is only loaded into memory and runs faster than the source code, you actually get a significant performance gain.

Because Access permanently loads modules, you will want to consider the overhead of many modules in your design. You should make sure there are no unused functions or routines in your application. Remove any code that you have remarked out during the development effort. The compiler must deal with this dead code. This will add delays to your development schedule. During development, you might also want to close the project occasionally to clear memory. Even if you have completely compiled your application, you still want to load as little code as possible.

Make an MDE and Stay Compiled

The surest way to know that your application remains in a compiled state for your user is to create an .MDE file for distribution. An .MDE contains no source code and never decompiles.

Below the module level issues of grouping, memory management, and compiling, there are some specific tips on writing your code that might help you create faster applications.

Use `Option Explicit`

Always use `Option Explicit`. `Option Explicit` requires you to dimension all your variables. If you fail to dimension your variables, you will be force VBA to use the largest and most flexible data type to accommodate your variables. As usual, the largest and most flexible type is also the slowest. Dimming your variables is a good practice for reasons of readability and data integrity too.

Choose Variable Sizes with Care

When dimensioning a variable, use the smallest possible variable size. Don't use a double when an integer will do. Use fixed-length strings instead of variable-length strings when possible.

Save Stack Space with String Variables

String variables one of the most common data types used in code. They can be broken into three different types:

- Local fixed-length (of no more than 64 characters in length)—These use two bytes per character and do not use heap space.
- Local fixed-length (more than 65 characters in length)—These strings also use two bytes per character, but in heap memory. They also require four bytes in the stack to point to the variable in the heap.
- Local variable-length (length doesn't matter)—The amount of heap space depends upon the length of the string. Four bytes of stack memory are used as a pointer to the variable in the heap.

When dealing with strings, the objective should be to reduce the amount of stack memory you are using. Try changing strings to local variable-length strings or make them static fixed-length stings. Following is an example of a variable length string being declared as a static fixed-length string in order to conserve stack memory.

```
Dim strString as string
Static strString as string * 30
```

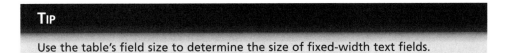

TIP

Use the table's field size to determine the size of fixed-width text fields.

Specific Object Type Declarations

When declaring object types, be specific. If your code is going to cycle through a form's text box controls, declare the object variable as a text box and not simply as a control. This way, VBA will not be required to resolve what kind of control you are addressing. Instead of

```
Sub CycleControls(cntl as control)
```

use

```
Sub CycleControls(cntl as TextBox)
```

to save on execution time.

14

APPLICATION OPTIMIZATION

Use In-Line Code Instead of Calls to Other Functions

A classic battle between maintainability and speed arises when your function or subroutine calls to another function or subroutine. This technique is very maintainable, but it is also less efficient than keeping all the attention inside a single routine. There might be times when you should choose speed or maintainability, but don't do it just to gain a few milliseconds.

Toggle True and False

When flipping a flag from true to false, there is no need to go through the task of checking the value flag in an `If...Then...Else` construct. You can save time and lines of code by reversing the value with a NOT operator. By setting a Boolean variable to what that variable is not, you reverse it.

Instead of

```
If bFlag = False then
  bFlag=True
Else
  BFlag=False
EndIF
```

use this

```
bFlag=Not bFlag
```

It takes much less time to execute one line of code than several with an evaluation.

Len( ) Instead of Empty String

To test a string variable to see if there are any characters, use the `Len()` function instead of comparing it to an empty string (""). The `Len()` function will evaluate faster than the comparison to the zero length string.

```
Sub CheckString(strString as string)
  If Len(strString) then
    MsgBox "Here is the string: " & strString
  EndIf
End Sub
```

True and False Evaluations Instead of Zero

Because `True` and `False` are binary, they are easier to evaluate than the number zero. Use `True` and `False` as follows:

```
Function ShowNumber(dblNumber as Double) as string
  If dblNumber then
    ShowNumber ="The number is " & dblNumber
  EndIf
End Function
```

Fast Object References

Use variables to refer to objects repeatedly. It is much faster to reference an existing variable of a form, control, report, or query than it is to refer back to the object again. Instead of referencing a form again

```
Forms![frmMyForm].Height=500
Forms![frmMyForm].Width=500
```

try declaring a variable and referring to it this way:

```
Dim frm as Form

Set frm=Forms![frmMyForm]

frm.Height=500
frm.Width=500
```

When dealing with more properties of an object, you can reduce the amount of referencing with the `With...End With` construct. This is especially useful when the path of the reference is long.

```
With Forms![frmMainForm]![txtCustomerName]
  .left=200
  .top=300
  .height=200
  .width=100
End With
```

`ME` represents the active form, so you don't have to dimension a variable or refer to an object to use it. Because it only works in CBF, you will not be able to put it into generic standard modules.

```
With ME
  .Height=500
  .Width=500
End With
```

Fast Array Uses

Use arrays. They reside in memory and will run extremely fast. They take an infinitesimally small amount of time to enlarge, but they also use only as much memory as they need at any given moment. If you don't know how many elements you are going to place into the array, make it a dynamic array rather than a large static one with lots of empty space.

If you need to empty the array, but not destroy its structure, you can use the `Erase` keyword. This will enable you to have a clean array of a certain size without rebuilding it.

```
Erase myArray
```

Conversely, if you want to enlarge the array without destroying the data it contains, use the `Redim` with `Preserve`.

```
ReDim Preserve myArray(Ubound(myArray+1))
```

Arrays can often manage the data from a recordset. Instead of having a DAO recordset open with all its overhead, use the `GetRows()` method and close the recordset. This frees memory and can alleviate multiuser issues. `GetRows()` takes one argument: the number of rows to load into the array.

```
Dim db as Database
Dim rowArray as Variant
Dim rs as Recordset

Set db=CurrentDB()
Set rs=db.openrecordset("Quarterly Orders")

RowArray=rs.GetRows(rs.RecordCount)

rs.close
...
```

After the data is loaded into the array, you can manipulate it in any way you like, or you can place it on an unbound form.

Use Constants When Possible

In order for VBA to get the current value of a variable, it must be resolved each time you reference it. Constants don't have to be resolved like this. Constants also improve the readability of your code. Instead of typing 12 to represent the 12 months of the year everywhere, create a constant (maybe called `AllMonths`) and set it to 12. VBA will read the constant much more quickly and other developers will know what you are talking about when they see your constant. The downside of constants is that their value can be set only once and never changed. Constants can only be used to represent values internal to the application or to represent values that don't change in the world. In short, constants can only be used for internal or eternal values.

The Proper Use of Bookmarks

Use bookmarks to navigate back to a previous record. Bookmarks are an extremely fast way to move around records in the interface. Keep in mind that there are two different bookmarks: one for forms and one for recordsets. A form bookmark is an array of variants dynamically assigned to each record in the underlying recordset clone. The DAO bookmark is a byte array that identifies each record in a recordset. Bookmarks are a navigational convenience, destroyed and re-created with the recordsets and clones. Don't rely on them except under controlled or inconsequential situations. They do not represent a record and they have nothing to do with the primary key. They only represent a record's temporary position in a series of rows. Any data manipulation should use techniques that adhere to the design of a relational database and not simply by your position in a recordset or clone. Because you should always use a requery method after updates and deletes, you will destroy and re-create the bookmarks each time. If your interface uses bookmarks under these circumstances, you need to control the deletes and updates closely.

The following code could use a form's bookmark to return to a previous record after performing an update.

```
Private Sub Findit_AfterUpdate()

Dim rsclone As Recordset
Dim recordID As Variant
Dim IDValue As Long

Set rsclone = Me.RecordsetClone

IDValue = Me![Findit]
recordID = "ID = " & IDValue

rsclone.FindFirst recordID

bm = rsclone.Bookmark

Me.Bookmark = bm

End Sub
```

Using the bookmark to return to the previous record is 1300 percent faster than executing a FindFirst to accomplish the same thing.

Close and Destroy

Fast code is clean code. Make sure that you close recordsets when you are finished with them and set objects to nothing when they are no longer needed. Having these objects hanging around consumes memory that other parts of your application could be using.

```
rs.Close
Set db=Nothing
```

Use SQL Instead of DAO

Cycle through recordsets only when there is no alternative. The Jet database is optimized to use SQL to manipulate data and data structures. Use queries instead of DAO at every opportunity. There are few cases where DAO will be faster than a well-built query. Queries have execution plans and can take advantage of indexes where DAO cannot.

If you must address your data through an object model, use ADO instead of DAO. ADO is the new standard for addressing data manipulation and data definition through the object model. DAO is frozen in time and will have no further extensions or enhancements. This book discusses ADO in several other chapters, including Chapters 6, "Introduction to ActiveX Data Objects," and 7, "Advanced ADO."

Use the Index Number of Collections

When dealing with collections, use their index number if possible. These index numbers are the collection's internal identification. They are much faster to use than any other property (such as name) of the collection's object. The following example shows two different ways to reference the current database. The reference to Currentdb() will automatically refresh the database's collections, which takes time. The first reference (dbEngine(0)(0)) does not refresh the collection.

```
Set db=DBEngine(0)(0)
```

is faster than

```
Set db=Currentdb()
```

```
Set cntl=Forms!frmMyForm(0)
```

is faster than

```
Set cntl =Forms![frmMyForm]![myControl]
```

Using the index number of a collection member is especially useful in loops.

Making Faster Loops

When looping through a collection, use `For...Each` instead of `For...Next`. When looping through the controls on a form

```
For Each cntl on frm
...
Next
```

will run faster than a simple `For...Next` loop.

If you need to loop through the collection objects, you will want to avoid refreshing the collection unnecessarily. Even on a small database, refreshing the collection can crush the performance of your application.

When using a `For...Next` loop, you can save time by not reciting the variable on the `Next` line.

```
For i = 1 to 100
......do what you want
Next
```

The benefit of this is especially noticeable in nested loops. Also, don't recalculate the limit on the `For` line. The upper limit should be established before the loop is entered.

```
reccount=rs.recordcount/2
For i=1 to reccount
...
Next
```

If you don't establish the value of the upper limit ahead of time, the loop will recalculate the value for each pass. This is a waste of time.

Ban `IIF()` from Code

Do not use the `IIF()` function in code. This function must evaluate all expressions contained with in it before it yields a result. A standard `If...Then...Else` structure is faster.

Arranging the `Select Case`

When using a `Select Case` construct, arrange the structure with the most frequently encountered cases at the top. Because a pass through the `Selections` will try each case in order, arranging them with the most common occurrence first will enable the execution to exit the structure as soon as possible.

14

APPLICATION
OPTIMIZATION

Use `.Execute`, Not `RunSQL`

Avoid `DoCmd`-based code when ever possible. `DoCmd` is the highest level of VBA code, a holdover from the macros. When there is an alternative, take it.

```
DoCmd RunSQL "..."
```

will be slower than

```
Querydef.Execute
```

Use `A2KU_Timer`

When timing applications, use the `A2KU_Timer` provided in this chapter. It's nearly 1000 percent faster than the alternatives.

Test the Efficiency of Transactions

Transactions don't always save time. At one time, you could count on a transaction enhancing the speed of your queries. This isn't so anymore. Though transactions can still use their caching ability to speed the performance of queries by reducing disk accesses, they can also slow them down by having to create temporary data files on disk in anticipation of a rollback. Transactions are now implicit by default, so you will only know if transactions will improve performance by testing your particular situations against a realistically sized set of test data.

Control Refreshes

Turn off `Application.Echo` or control the repainting of a screen. It takes time to refresh the screen, and this can slow your application.

Reference ActiveX and Use Early Binding

Take advantage of early binding. When using ActiveX controls, make sure you have a reference to the underlying OCX file for that control. Check Tools, References. Early binding can greatly enhance performance.

Upsize to Client/Server

Keep the design of your application open to the possibility that you might upsize to SQL Server or Oracle. If this happens, you can employ passthrough queries and use stored procedures stored on the server. This will greatly improve performance.

Bread and Circuses

If you can't beat 'em, make it look fast. If a process takes enough time to cause the user to get bored, give him some kind of status screen to let him know that something is going on and your application hasn't gone into an infinite loop. Users often think the application is running quickly just because they have feedback.

Summary

This chapter covers techniques for optimizing you application from the computer it runs on to the esoteric For...Next variable use. Applications must perform well, typically with a response time of under one second for most data retrieval operations. The techniques explained in this chapter will help you attain that standard.

The simplest way to get an application to run faster is to upgrade the machine it is running on. You can also alter the Registry settings at will to suit any particular process you are running. Table and query design was covered at length to make sure your application has a foundation that can support high performance. Interface issues were covered to ensure that your application presents itself to the users in a way that doesn't keep them waiting. Finally, the chapter covers coding techniques to squeeze every last millisecond out of the application's performance.

By starting from the ground up, trying these different approaches, and testing them in your particular situation, you should be able to get the best performance from your applications that you possibly can. Taking this chapter as a whole can make dramatic differences in your applications.

14

APPLICATION OPTIMIZATION

Access Client Server

IN THIS PART

- Introducing Access Data Projects and the Visual Tools   *417*

- Developing Access Front-Ends to Microsoft SQL Server   *441*

- Access 2000 Front-Ends to Oracle   *469*

Introducing Access Data Projects and the Visual Tools

CHAPTER 15

With Access 2000, Microsoft has integrated SQL Server with Access using OLE DB as the glue. You can take advantage of this integration when using Access Data Projects or ADPs, a brand new feature of Access 2000. The authors recommend that ADPs are best suited for SQL Server 7.0. If you plan to use something other than SQL Server 7.0 as your back end, look at Chapter 16, "Developing Access Front-Ends to Microsoft SQL Server," and Chapter 17, "Access Front-Ends to Oracle." This chapter will show you how to use ADPs with SQL Server 7.0.

Introducing Access Data Projects

As an Access user, you know that Access uses the Microsoft Jet database engine to store its data and process its queries. Many Access applications use an ODBC Database Server as their data store. These applications might consist of: linked tables, SQL pass-through queries, and ODBCDirect. In applications like these, you are using the Jet engine and ODBC to communicate with your linked tables, and the application is a regular MDB file.

Microsoft has realized that you need more integration with Database Servers. In Access 2000, you have available a brand new database project called Access Data Projects (ADP) to integrate with SQL Server 7.0. Because ADPs are hard wired to the SQL Server OLE DB provider, you can only use them with SQL Server 7.0 or SQL Server 6.5 with Service Pack 5 installed.

> **CAUTION**
>
> If you intend to use ADPs with SQL Server 6.5, SP 5, you should also read the Office 2000 release notes and run a SQL file on your server before ADPs will work with SQL Server 6.5.

The Pros and Cons of ADPs

When you are considering the advantages of ADPs versus MDBs, you have to look at the pros and cons. The advantages of using ADPs are

- Using ADPs, you can edit table structures in Access, but using linked tables on a server, you cannot.
- With ADPs, you have one connection for all your database objects, but in MDBs you do not. For example, in an MDB with linked tables, a form with 10 controls on it has 10 connections to the database. With an ADP, there is only one connection.

- ADPs are easy to use.

- ADPs enable you to use Access as your development tool.

The disadvantages of using ADPs are

- ADPs limit you to using only SQL Server, you cannot use them with Oracle or Sybase.

- ADPs are new technology and with all new technology may not be perfected yet.

- You cannot store any local tables or queries.

After looking at the pros and cons of ADPs and reading through this chapter, you should have all the knowledge that you need to determine if you will want to use ADPs with your applications.

Using ADPs

An ADP application is an Access 2000 application with an ADP extension. It uses SQL Server as the database engine.

> **Note**
>
> Before you can use an ADP, you must either install SQL Server on your machine or have network access to an existing SQL Server. To install SQL Server, desktop edition, on your Windows 95/98 computer, just follow the directions found with the SQL Server 7.0 setup instructions. If you do not have SQL Server 7.0, you can install the Microsoft Data Engine (MSDE), which is SQL Server desktop without a user interface from your Office 2000 Setup CD in the /SQL folder.

Creating an ADP

To create an ADP, open Access and select File, New from the main menu. A dialog box will appear as shown in Figure 15.1. This dialog will ask you what type of Access application you want to create. Your choices are Database, Project (Existing Database), and Project (New Database).

If you select Database, you will create a normal Access MDB file that uses Microsoft Jet as the database engine. If you select Project (Existing Database), you will create an ADP that will communicate to an already existing SQL Server database. If you select Project (New Database), you will create an ADP and a new SQL Server database on your server.

15

ACCESS DATA PROJECTS AND THE VISUAL TOOLS

FIGURE 15.1

*The File, New
dialog box.*

You will now create a sample project based on an existing SQL Server database.
Double-clicking on the icon will then prompt a file location for the ADP as shown in
Figure 15.2.

FIGURE 15.2

*The file location
prompt.*

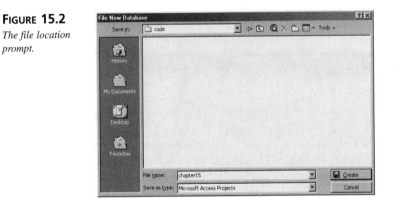

After you have created the ADP file, Access will prompt you for the SQL Server database information as shown in Figure 15.3. Remember that when using Data Links (as
you did in Chapter 7, "Advanced ADO"), you must enter the server name, username,
password, and database name of the database that you want to use. For the current example, you will be using the SQL Server version of Northwind that ships with SQL Server
7.0. After you have connected to the database, Access Project will come up with some
new items in the database container as shown in Figure 15.4.

FIGURE **15.3**

Creating the data link.

NOTE

If you want to follow along with this example on your computer, make sure that you have SQL Server 7.0 installed. You can install the local version of SQL Server with the SQL Server version of Northwind from the Office 2000 CD.

FIGURE **15.4**

The new database container for ADPs.

The New Database Container

The database container for ADPs (refer to Figure 15.4) is different from the one for MDB files. The new database container displays the following:Tables, Views, Stored Procedures, Database Diagrams, Forms, Reports, Pages, Macros, and Modules. Table 15.1 summarizes each item in the database container.

TABLE 15.1   THE DATABASE CONTAINER OBJECTS FOR ADPS

Item	Description
Tables	A listing of all the tables in the SQL Server database. As opposed to linked tables, you have access to add, edit, and delete tables directly on the server.
Views	A listing of all the views in the SQL Server database. You have access to add, edit, and delete views directly on the server.
Database Diagrams	A listing of all the database diagrams on the server. You can create a diagram with the same tools as in Visual InterDev 6.0.
Forms	Access forms in your application. These forms are not on the server but in your ADP file. They can be bound to tables, views, and stored procedures.
Reports	Access reports in your application. These reports are not on the server but in your ADP file. They can be bound to tables, views, and stored procedures.
Pages	Data Access Pages in your application. These reports are not on the server but exist as HTML files on disk. (See Chapter 26, "Using Data Access Pages" for a full discussion of DAPs.) They can be bound to tables, views, and stored procedures.
Macros	All your Access macros. These macros are not on the server but in your ADP file.
Modules	All your Access modules. These modules are not on the server but in your ADP file.

Working with ADPs and Existing SQL Server Databases

As you work with your ADP projects, you may need to add, edit, and delete database objects. This section will show you how to work with SQL Server objects that reside in your ADP.

Working with SQL Server Tables

Because ADPs do not link database tables like traditional Access MDB applications do, you have direct access to a SQL Server table in your Access database container. If you delete or rename your table in Access, you will be deleting or renaming it in SQL Server as well. Although this is very convenient, this can also be dangerous. You will want to make sure that you implement SQL Server security in your application to limit your users' access to the tables.

If you want to edit a table, select it, and press the Design button. This will bring up the SQL Server 7.0 table designer as shown in Figure 15.5.

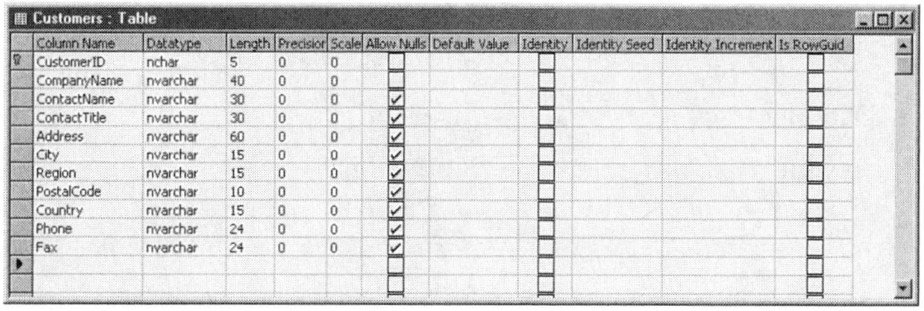

FIGURE 15.5

SQL Server table designer in Access 2000.

The SQL Server table designer shown in Figure 15.5 is very similar to the table designer in Access. Enter the name of the table columns and all the columns' properties in the designer. Table 15.2 summarizes the column properties that you can set.

TABLE 15.2   THE SQL SERVER TABLE DESIGNER PROPERTIES

Property Name	Description
ColumnName	The name of the column. It must be a valid SQL Server column name.
DataType	The data type of the column. Valid SQL Server data types are listed in Table 15.3.
Length	The length of the column.
Precision	The precision of the column. Used with numeric columns.
Scale	The scale of the column. Used with numeric columns.
Allow Nulls	Whether or not the column allows Null values.
Default Vale	The default value for the column.
Identity	Indicates whether the column is an Identity column. Only one column in a table can be an Identity.
Identity Seed	The starting seed of the Identity column.
Identity Increment	The increment value of the Identity column.
Is RowGuid	Determines whether the Identity column is a GUID.

15

ACCESS DATA PROJECTS AND THE VISUAL TOOLS

The SQL Server data types are shown here:

- Binary
- Bit
- Char
- Datatime
- Decmil
- float
- Image
- Int
- Money
- nchar
- ntext
- Numeric
- nvarchar
- Real
- Smalldate
- Smallint
- Smallmoney
- Text
- Timestamp
- Tinyint
- uniqueidentifier
- Varbinary
- Varchar

SQL Server Views

Using the Views section in the database container, you can administer your SQL Server views. One of the greatest advantages of using ADPs is that you can create a view right in Access and save it on the server. To create a view, click on the New button, and the SQL Server view designer will appear as shown in Figure 15.6. Look familiar? It should, because it is modeled after the famous Access QBE designer.

FIGURE 15.6

The SQL Server view designer.

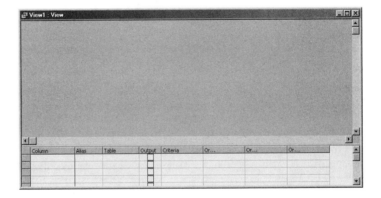

When you are in the designer, you can add tables by selecting Query, Show Table from the main menu. This will bring up the Table/Views list for you to drag into the designer as shown in Figure 15.7. For each table, you can join fields, just as in the QBE. Selecting the SQL button will display the SQL as shown in Figure 15.8. Using the SQL view can be very helpful if you are trying to learn SQL, or if you want to create a SQL statement to copy and paste into your code.

FIGURE 15.7

The SQL Server view designer with tables for use.

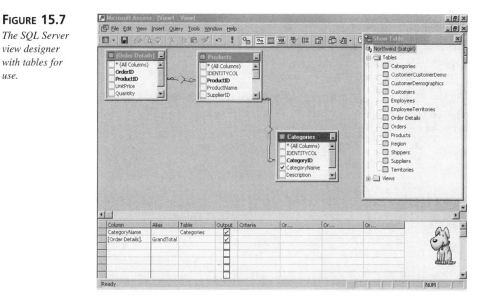

FIGURE 15.8

The SQL Server view designer in SQL view.

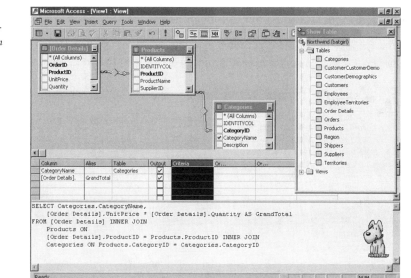

15

ACCESS DATA PROJECTS AND THE VISUAL TOOLS

You can use the criteria section to specify criteria, column aliases, aggregates, and sorting. After you have created your view, you must save it before running it because it is an object in your SQL Server.

Stored Procedures

All the Stored Procedures on your SQL Server can be managed in Access. Enter the stored procedure section of the database container, and you can add, edit, rename, or delete any stored procedure. To add stored procedures select New from the database container options. You will be brought to the Access stored procedure editor shown in Figure 15.9.

FIGURE 15.9

The Access stored procedure editor.

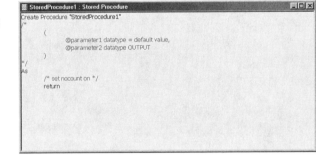

Although the stored procedure editor may look very basic, what you can do with it is very powerful. You can create any valid Transact SQL stored procedure right in Access and save it on the SQL Server. For more information on Transact SQL, see *Sams Teach Yourself TSQL in 21 Days* by Sams Publishing.

You can also run stored procedures by double-clicking on them. If the stored procedure has a parameter in it, Access will prompt you for it as shown in Figure 15.10.

FIGURE 15.10

A stored procedure parameter.

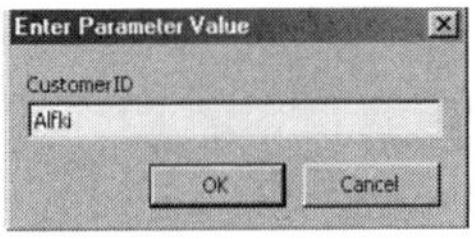

Database Diagrams

Perhaps the coolest features of ADPs are the database diagrams. For those of you who are new to the Microsoft database tools that are now part of ADPs, database diagrams are a visual way to manage and design your database tables. The SQL Server database version of Northwind by default will have a relationships database diagram. This diagram will show you the relationships of your database and give you the capability to edit relationships, edit tables, and add/remove columns right in the window.

To work with the database diagram, double-click on the relationships diagram, and you will be presented with the diagram shown in Figure 15.11.

FIGURE 15.11

The SQL Server database diagram.

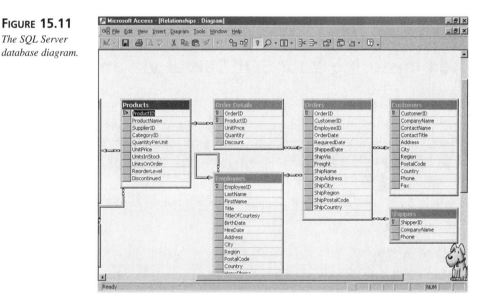

You can move and resize the tables by dragging and dropping with your mouse. You can also zoom and limit your view to certain tables. And the best feature is that you can print this all out as documentation. By right-clicking on a table, you can choose to view the column properties of a particular table, and you will have access to the table designer as shown in Figure 15.12!

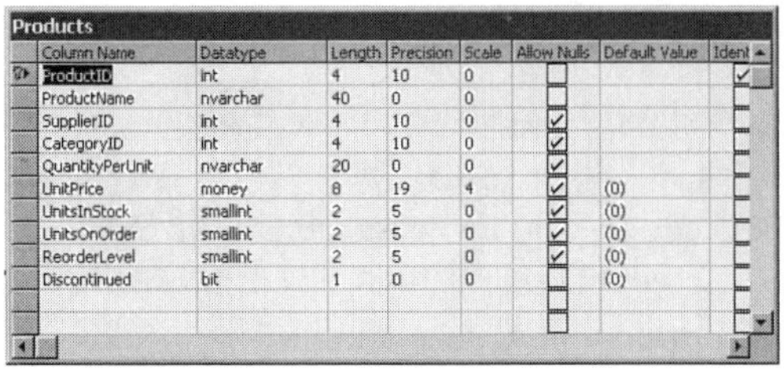

FIGURE 15.12

The SQL Server database diagram with column properties shown.

Forms, Pages, Reports, Macros, and Modules

Using forms, pages, reports, macros, and modules is just like using these objects in Access 2000, with the exception that the current database data objects (tables, views, and stored procedures) are now SQL Server objects and not Access objects.

Administering Your SQL Server via an ADP

Although there is no room in this book for a complete lesson in SQL Server database administration, it is important to show you that you can administer a SQL Server database via your ADP. To administer your SQL Server, the ADP user must have the correct permissions on the SQL Server. You will want to grant the ADP user full admin permissions. In addition, you will want to administer your SQL Server from a different ADP that you use to distribute your applications.

The three areas in which you can administer your SQL Server databases are

- Backup/Restore
- Replication
- Security

Back Up/Restore

To back up your current SQL Server database, you can choose Tools, Database, Utilities, Backup from the main menu. Access will prompt you for a backup location as shown in Figure 15.13. This will save your SQL Server database backup in a format that SQL Server can restore via its normal restore feature. In addition, if you choose Tools, Database, Utilities, Restore from the main menu and select a valid backup file, you can restore your SQL Server database from its backup.

FIGURE 15.13
A SQL Server backup via Access.

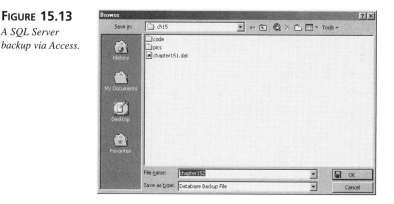

SQL Server Replication

In Access you can create new publications, synchronize replicas, and resolve conflicts. To create a new publication, select Tools, Replication, Create Publication from the main menu. You will be brought to the replication dialog shown in Figure 15.14. Select the database from this diagram and click on the Create Publication dialog. This brings you to the SQL Server 7.0 Create Publication Wizard shown in Figure 15.15.

FIGURE 15.14
A SQL Server replication dialog.

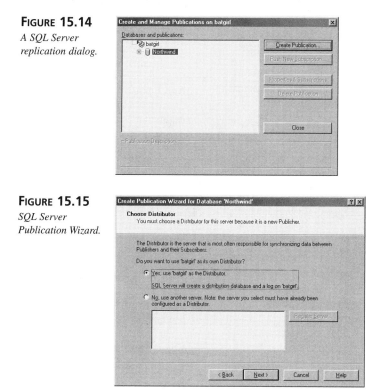

FIGURE 15.15
SQL Server Publication Wizard.

Enter the wizard and follow the directions for creating a publication. It is pretty simple to create a publication, and you even have the option to create a subscriber in an Access Jet MDB file. (For more on replication options, see Chapter 22, "Replication and JRO.") To synchronize a database with a replica, click on the select Tools, Replication, Synchronize options from the main menu. You can also configure SQL Server to automatically synchronize on a schedule via Enterprise Manager.

Security

You can also manage SQL Server database security from Access 2000. With Access 2000, you can manage SQL Server security by selecting Tools, Security, Database Security. This will bring up a security dialog box similar to the one used in Access security as shown in Figure 15.16. You can add, remove, and edit users and their access rights as well as security groups.

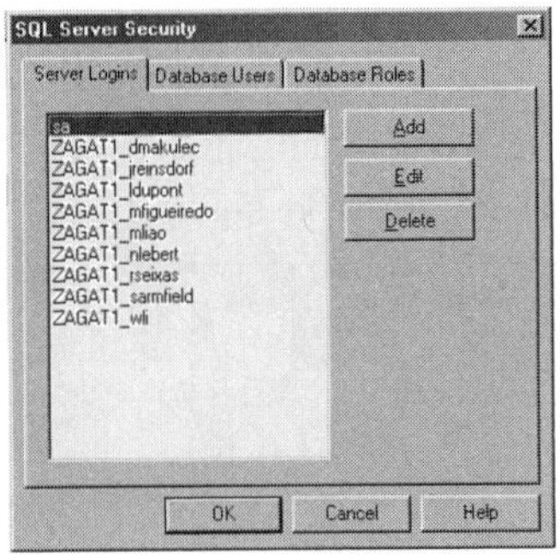

FIGURE 15.16

The Access 2000 ADP security features use the SQL Server 7.0 security model.

You can create Logins for users to actually log in to the database, Users and Roles. A typical user is DBO for Database Owner and Guest for guest. Roles are SQL Server roles that a user can be in, such as "System Administrator." For more information on SQL Server security, see the SQL Server books online.

Reconnecting to the SQL Server Database

What happened when you develop an ADP at your site and then release it to users at another site? You will have to resync the ADP so that it will connect to the correct SQL Server database. If you remember Chapter 7, you used Microsoft Universal Data Links to manage our OLE DB connection string information in ADO. By setting a reference to the Microsoft OLE DB Service Component 1.0 Type Library as shown in Figure 15.17, you can use the UDL's automation interface to resync your ADP with the correct SQL Server database.

FIGURE 15.17

Setting a reference to the OLE DB Service Component.

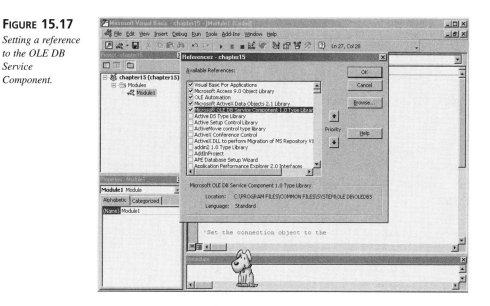

After your reference is set, you can assign a string to the `PromptNew` method of the `DataLink` object. Then assign this string to the `CurrentProject.OpenConnection` method to make the ADP connect to a new SQL Server database. The code in Listing 15.1 shows you how to accomplish this.

LISTING 15.1 UPDATING YOUR ADP'S CONNECTION

```
Sub UpdateConnection()
'Procedure that will use the
'UDL Automation Interface to
'Create a connection object
'And then use that connection
'to resync the ADP
'From "Access 2000 Unleashed" (SAMS)
'By:Forte, Howe, Ralston

Dim strConnect As String
Dim rst As ADODB.Recordset
'The Microsoft UDL Reference
Dim udl As MSDASC.DataLinks

On Error GoTo Proc_Err

'Create the Data Link Object
Set udl = New MSDASC.DataLinks
```

continues

LISTING 15.1 CONTINUED

```
'Set the connection object to the
'Prompt a new Data Link dialog
strConnect = udl.PromptNew

'Take the connection information from
'The UDL and resync the ADP
CurrentProject.OpenConnection strConnect


Proc_Exit:
    Exit Sub

Proc_Err:
    MsgBox Err.Description
    Resume Proc_Exit

End Sub
```

> **NOTE**
>
> The CurrentProject.Connection that an ADP uses the MSDataShape OLE DB Provider in addition to the SQL Server OLE DB Provider. I have discovered that some features of ADO when using the OLE DB Provider for SQL Server in VB (or Access 2000 with a separate connection) without MSDataShape behave slightly differently. Please visit the Microsoft KnowledgeBase for any updates on limitations to using your Access 2000 code in Visual Basic.

Creating a Project Based on a New Database

You can demonstrate how to use the tools in ADPs by creating a SQL Server database from scratch. This example will create a very simple database application, however, it is set up to teach you what potential ADPs have. To begin, open Access 2000 and select File, New from the main menu and then select Project, New Database from the New dialog. Next, Access will bring you to the Create SQL Server Database Wizard as shown in Figure 15.18. This wizard will ask you to provide a server name, user name, password, and database name. When you supply all the information, Access will create the database for you on the server that you specified. Now you are ready to begin creating the database application.

FIGURE 15.18

The SQL Server Database Wizard.

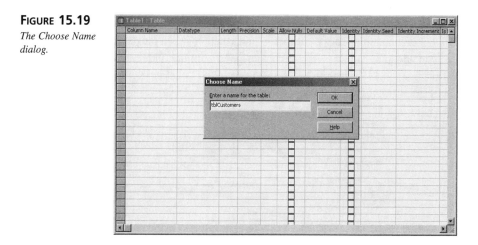

Creating Tables

You are going to create a simple workflow tracking system. To do so, you will have to create a few tables. To create a table, click Create Table in Design View from the Database Container. Notice that you will be asked to name the table before you do anything else, because the object will exist on the server and must follow the rules of the server.

FIGURE 15.19

The Choose Name dialog.

You will need to create two tables in the designer, tblIssue and tlkpTransactionType. The details of tblIssue are in Table 15.3 and the details of tlkpTransactionType are in Table 15.4.

TABLE 15.3   DESIGN FOR TABLE: TBLISSUE

Column Name	Data Type	Notes
IssueID	Int (4)	Identity, Primary Key
TransactionTypeID	Int (4)	Will be a Foreign Key
TransactionComments	Text (16)	
RecDate	Datetime	Default Value:getdate()
CompleteDate	Datetime	AllowNulls=True

TABLE 15.4   DESIGN FOR TABLE: TLKPTRANSACTIONTYPE

Column Name	Data Type	Notes
TransactionTypeID	Int(4)	Identity, Primary Key
TransactionDesc	Varchar(50)	

Setting a Table's Properties and Indexes

To set table properties and indexes, you can select View, Properties from the main menu. This will bring you to the dialog shown in Figure 15.20. You can select an index and set its attributes such as uniqueness, fill factor, and whether it is a clustered index or not. Because you added a Primary Key via the designer, a unique index is created already.

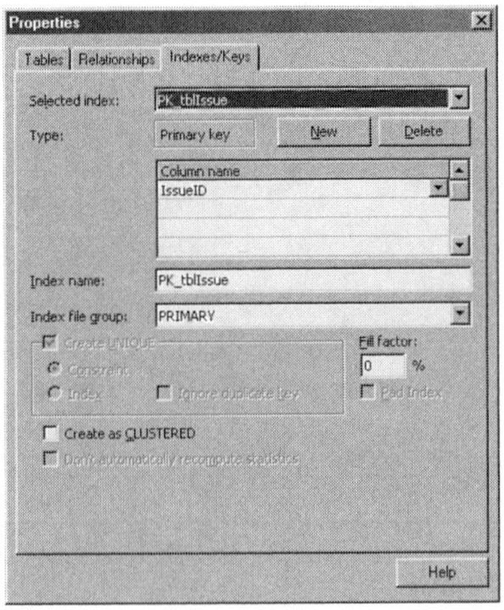

FIGURE 15.20

*The Table
Properties dialog.*

Creating Relationships via a Diagram

Now that you have created two tables (when is an application ever THAT easy?), you need to define a relationship between tlkpTransactionType and tblIssue. Creating relationships are very easy with ADPs. ADPs leverage the skill that you have in Access for creating relationships. To create a relationship visually with a database diagram, select Database Diagrams in the database container and add a new diagram by selecting New. To show the tables to include in the relationships, select View, Show Table from the main menu. Drag the two tables from the Show Table dialog box to the diagram as shown in Figure 15.21. To create the actual relationship, drag the field from tblkTransactionType to tblIssue. Dragging the field will display a Relationships dialog (shown in Figure 15.22). This dialog will enable you to set the fields that are to be used in the relationship. After you create the relationship, save the diagram. Remember that you can now use the diagram as documentation for your database.

FIGURE 15.21

The database diagram in design mode.

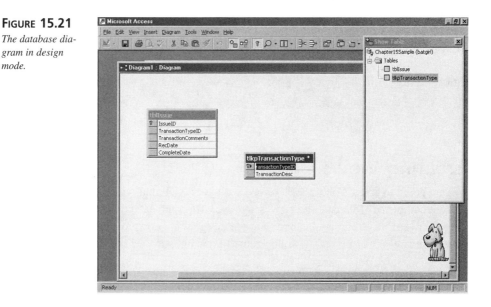

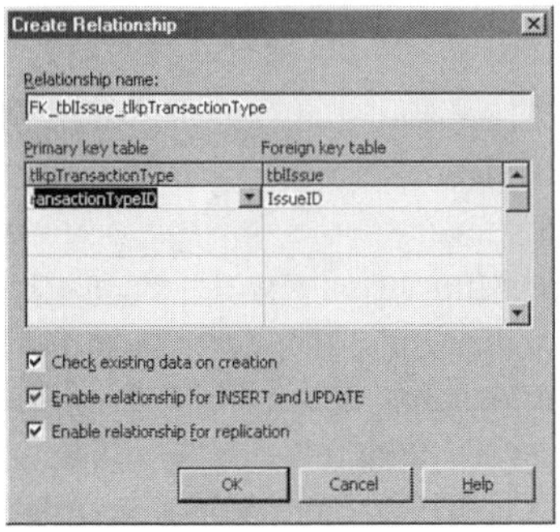

FIGURE 15.22

Relationship properties.

Creating Cascades via Triggers

Because SQL Server 7.0 does not support cascading updates and cascading deletes via its relationships, you would have to specify them via triggers. To create or manage a table's triggers, right-click the table in the database container and select Triggers from the context menu. This will bring up the dialog shown in Figure 15.23. Select a trigger to edit if the trigger already exists, or click New to create a new trigger.

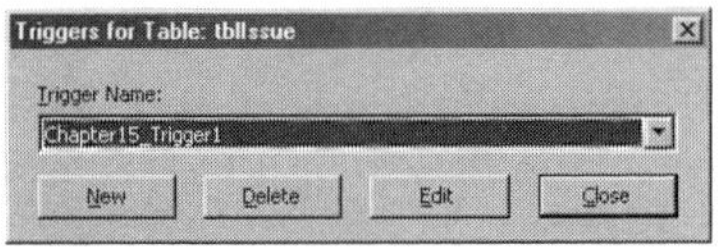

FIGURE 15.23

Managing triggers.

Creating Views

you are going to create a SQL Server View with your ADP that will show all the Issues that are completed. To create the view, select New from the database container and then drag the two tables from the database into the designer as shown in Figure 15.24. You have created a simple view that produced the following SQL in Listing 15.2.

LISTING 15.2   A SIMPLE VIEW

```
SELECT tlkpTransactionType.TransactionDesc, tblIssue.IssueID,
    tblIssue.TransactionComments, tblIssue.RecDate,
    tblIssue.CompleteDate
FROM tblIssue INNER JOIN
    tlkpTransactionType ON
    tblIssue.TransactionTypeID = tlkpTransactionType.TransactionTypeID
WHERE (tblIssue.CompleteDate IS NOT NULL)
```

FIGURE 15.24

The view designer.

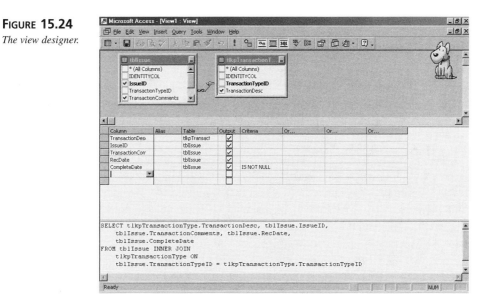

Creating Stored Procedures

To create a stored procedure, open the designer and enter in the TSQL. You are going to create a simple stored procedure that will select one Issue based on the issue number. The TSQL code to do so is shown in Listing 15.3.

LISTING 15.3 A SIMPLE STORED PROCEDURE

```
Create Procedure SelectOneIssue

        @IssueNumber int
As
SELECT tlkpTransactionType.TransactionDesc, tblIssue.IssueID,
    tblIssue.TransactionComments, tblIssue.RecDate,
    tblIssue.CompleteDate
FROM tblIssue INNER JOIN
    tlkpTransactionType ON
    tblIssue.TransactionTypeID = tlkpTransactionType.TransactionTypeID
WHERE   tblIssue.IssueID=@IssueNumber
```

Creating the Access Application

To show you just how easy it is to create an Access application with an ADP, see the simple Form shown in Figure 15.25. It is bound to the table tblIssue, and you can go ahead and enter in data, filter, etc just as you would in a normal MDB file. Creating a report is just as easy in Access 97 against Jet data, just use the wizard to get you started and then create your report.

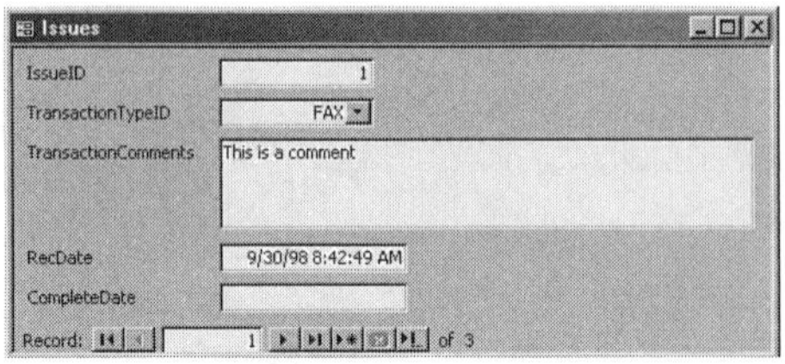

FIGURE 15.25

Our Access form.

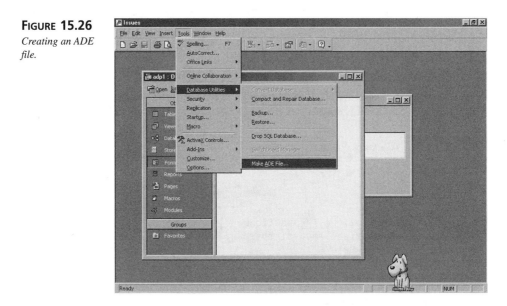

Creating—ADE Files

Access 97 introduced a new concept, an MDE file. An MDE file was a compiled and locked version of your MDB file. Access 2000 enables you to create MDE files for MDB files and ADE files for ADP files. To create an ADE file, select Tools, Database Utilities, Make ADE File from the main menu as shown in Figure 15.26. Then select a file location and Access will make your ADE file for you. Now all forms, reports, pages, and modules will be locked from the user.

FIGURE 15.26

Creating an ADE file.

A Final Note: Upsizing an Access 97 Database to SQL Server and ADPs

In the past, the Access to SQL Server Upsizing Wizard did not do all that much. It would move your Tables to SQL Server for you and that was about it. Your queries remained in Access running against linked tables, not all that efficient of a result. If you run the

Upsizing Wizard from an MDB file in Access 2000, you will get better results. The wizard will convert all your Jet "Views" or select queries to SQL Server views and all your Jet "Procedures" (everything else) to SQL Server Stored Procedures if possible. Then the wizard will create a new ADP project for you based on the new SQL Server database. Although there are still many limitations of the wizard, it is worth taking a look at; it can at least get you started. The wizard is very straightforward to use, so to get started just choose Select Tools, Database Utilities, Upsizing Wizard.

Summary

As you can see, using Access 2000 with a SQL Server database just got a whole lot easier! ADPs are a very powerful tool that enables you to create, edit, and manage remote SQL Server objects while still in Access. SQL Server developers, beware! Access has now entered the Client Server market.

Developing Access Front-Ends to Microsoft SQL Server

Ever since the introduction of Microsoft Access, it has been a great front-end tool for external databases. Although Access 2000 has some incredible new features for working with SQL Server 7.0 in Access Data Projects (ADPs), these features do not work well with SQL Server 6.5, and they do not work at all with any other ODBC database server. This chapter will show you how to develop applications with SQL Server 6.5 or Sybase System 10 as a back-end. Chapter 17, "Access 2000 Front-Ends to Oracle," will show you how to develop applications with an Oracle Enterprise Server as a back-end.

Client/Server Architecture: OLE DB Versus ODBC

A client/server system is defined as having a database server as a back-end data store (like SQL Server or Oracle) and a client application that talks to the back-end database. (A three-tier system, which you hear about all the time, is a similar architecture, except that all the business logic code is located in a separate logical, and usually physical, tier.)

Access MDB front-ends to SQL Server fall into the client category of this architecture, while using ODBC to communicate to the back-end database. Access databases using ODBC load the Jet database engine to broker all communications between the server and your Access client. Access ADP front-ends to SQL Server use the newer OLE DB technology to natively communicate with the server without loading Jet at all. Whereas the OLE DB approach has several significant advantages, ADPs' largest shortcomings are that they do not support any other database servers than SQL Server. Although ODBC and MDBs might not be as slick as the new ADPs, they are very powerful and useful, as you will see in this chapter.

Setting Up Your SQL Server Front-End Connection

In order to start working with a back-end SQL Server database, you will have to establish a communications link with the database. Because you will be using ODBC to communicate to the back-end database, you will have to make sure that you have the proper ODBC drivers installed on the machine that you will be using. A default installation of Access 2000 will install the SQL Server ODBC driver on the machine for you. (If you are using Sybase SQL Server, you will need to install the Sybase SQL Server driver, which is not on the Office CD.) After you install Access 2000 with the ODBC drivers, you are ready to start working with the back-end database. You have two data access methodologies: linked tables or SQL pass-through queries. Most applications use both.

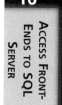

In order to work with either linked tables or SQL pass-through queries, you must set up an ODBC System Data Source.

Setting Up an ODBC Data Source (DSN)

A System DSN is a place for you to store all your ODBC connection information on each machine. Each DSN has a unique name so your application can use it. To create a DSN on your machine, follow these steps:

1. Go to Control Panel and enter "OBDC." This will bring up the DSN dialog box. Select "SQL Server" and click "Finish." This will bring you to the Create DSN Wizard as shown in Figure 16.1.

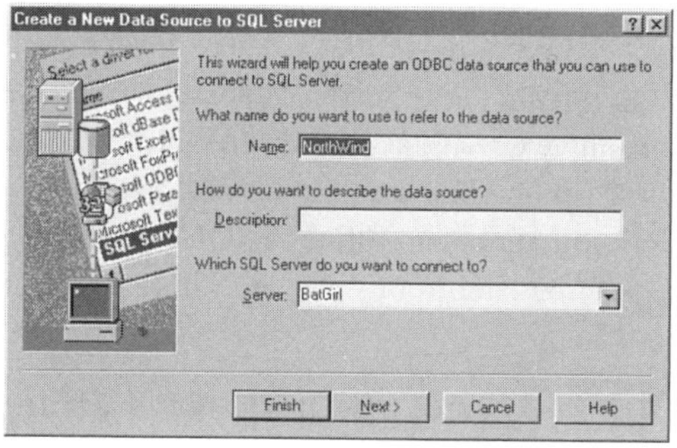

FIGURE 16.1

Creating a new DSN in Control Panel.

2. On the first page of the Wizard shown in Figure 16.1, enter a unique name of the DSN (like "Northwind"), an optional description, and the server name that the SQL Server resides on. Click Next when you are done entering this information.

3. On the second page, enter the SQL Server security information. If you want to use standard SQL Server security (or you are not sure), check the With SQL Server Authentication Using a Login ID and Password Entered by the User checkbox, and then enter the username and password and click Next. (If you use the default SQL Server security, the user will be "SA" with a blank password.)

4. The third page, shown in Figure 16.2, asks you what database on the SQL Server you would like to connect to. Change it to whatever database you are using. For this demo, I will change it to the SQL Server version of Northwind.

5. The fourth page will ask you about ODBC specific items like tracing. Accept the defaults and click Finish.

6. The last page gives you the opportunity to test your ODBC connection. It is wise to check it here and then go back and make any necessary corrections.

Now you are ready to use the SQL Server database in your Access 2000 application.

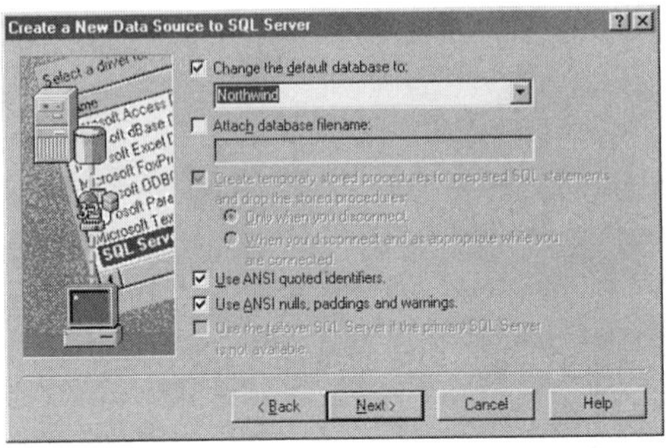

FIGURE 16.2

Specifying a default database when creating a DSN.

Linking Tables

To begin working with the ODBC datasource that you just created, the most commonly used and easiest solution is to link the SQL Server database tables to your .MDB file. This way you can run some simple queries against those tables for combo boxes and list boxes. For really small tables, you might even want to bind a form directly to the table and let users enter data. (For more on bound forms to SQL Server data, see the "Using Forms in Your Application" section later in this chapter.) To link to ODBC database tables, you must follow these steps:

1. Make sure that the ODBC datasource is set up on your machine. (See "Setting Up an ODBC Datasource (DSN).")

2. Open your Access database and choose File, Get External Data, Link from the main menu.

3. A list of all the ODBC datasources will appear. Select the DSN that you want to work with and click OK.

4. Access will display a dialog of all the tables available to link to (see Figure 16.3). As you select your tables, you can specify to save the database password with the tables so your users will not be given an ODBC login screen when they first launch your application.

5. Access will then link the tables to your .MDB file. It will prefix a "dbo_" in front of each table because each SQL Server tables is specified as "Database Owner."

6. If your SQL Server table does not have a unique key in its table, Access will not be able to link it as read/write, so it gives you the opportunity to create a *local* unique index, as shown in Figure 16.4. If you choose to use this technique, the table will be read/write and Jet 4.0 will manage the index for you on the client machine.

FIGURE **16.3**

Selecting the tables from the ODBC database that you want to link to.

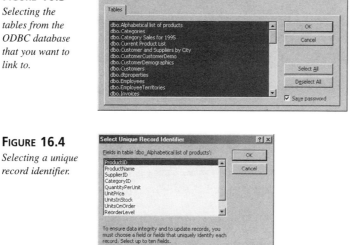

FIGURE **16.4**

Selecting a unique record identifier.

After your table is linked, you can use it as any other linked table in Access. You can create queries, forms, and reports that refer to these linked tables.

Disadvantages of Linked Tables

Linking tables from an ODBC data source to Access can be very inefficient and dangerous. The Jet engine must broker all communication to the SQL Server for your linked table. If Jet cannot use a unique index on the Server, the server might download all the records for Jet to process. Imagine this scenario. You link to a table with 5 million records. You create an Access query asking for about 500 records with query criteria not on any unique index. Depending on your table design, the SQL Server might return all 5 million records for Jet to sort through! If you are running on a low-end machine, this can take hours.

To really harness the power of a back-end SQL Server, you will have to use stored procedures. A stored procedure on a SQL Server is like a saved query in Access. They are compiled SQL statements that execute on the server and can accept parameters. Many developers send SQL statements to the server because it's faster than using a linked table. This method is still slower than using a stored procedure. Because a stored procedure is compiled, it will have an execution plan established on the server for the greatest speed. Using stored procedures represents the largest performance gain that you can get for the least amount of effort.

In addition to increased speed, stored procedures also offer reduced network traffic. You only send the server a small 1KB execute instruction, not a 100KB or larger uncompiled SQL statement. Also, the server will only send you back the data you need.

The Best of Both Worlds: Filling Tables at Startup

Because I tend to use stored procedures as the basis for everything in my Access client/server applications, I usually use linked tables for my lookup data that fills combo and list boxes on forms (and reports too!). To achieve the best performance, you can create exact replicas of the server tables that you are interested in using and fill them at the startup of your application. Doing this will require fewer network connections to the database server in your application. Of course, you can only use this technique with relatively static tables (tables that change only infrequently).

> **NOTE**
>
> This technique, although extremely useful, is not available in ADPs that were discussed in Chapter 15, "Introducing Access Data Projects and the Visual Tools." This is because these local tables live in a Jet database, and ADPs do not load the Jet engine.

Stored Procedures and SQL Pass-Through Queries

It makes sense to base an Access report or reports on stored procedures because they are so fast and powerful. The problem is that you cannot link to a stored procedure the way you can link to a table on the SQL Server. You can use a SQL pass-through, however, to obtain the same functionality though. A SQL pass-through query is a SQL statement sent directly to the SQL Server for processing. The Jet engine does not process the query (the back-end database does), and Access will display only the results. SQL pass-through queries take advantage of the processing power of the database server.

Creating advanced stored procedures is beyond the scope of this book; however, if you can create a view in an ADP (see Chapter 15 for more information), you can copy and paste the outputted SQL into a stored procedure. Listing 16.1 shows an example of a stored procedure from the SQL Server Northwind database that will provide Order Information between a parameterized date range. Listing 16.1 creates a stored procedure called sp_OrdersByDate that accepts two date parameters, @StartDate and @EndDate.

Developing Access Front-Ends to Microsoft SQL Server

CHAPTER 16

447

16

ACCESS FRONT-
ENDS TO SQL
SERVER

LISTING 16.1 A SIMPLE STORED PROCEDURE

```
CREATE PROCEDURE dbo.sp_OrdersByDate
@StartDate datetime,@EndDate datetime AS

SELECT Customers.CustomerID, Customers.CompanyName,
Orders.OrderDate, [Order Details].Quantity,
[Order Details].UnitPrice, Quantity*UnitPrice As TotalAmount

FROM Customers INNER JOIN Orders ON
Customers.CustomerID = Orders.CustomerID  INNER JOIN
[Order Details] ON Orders.OrderID = [Order Details].OrderID

Where OrderDate Between @StartDate and @EndDate
```

Running a stored procedure is easy. Log into the SQL Server and type in an EXECUTE command in the SQL window. If your stored procedure accepts any parameters, you will have to provide them here. To run the sp_OrdersByDate stored procedure you created in Listing 16.1 from the SQL Server T/SQL tool, you will have to call it like this:

```
Execute sp_OrdersByDate @StartDate='07/01/94', @EndDate='09/30/94'
```

The results of the sp_OrdersByDate stored procedure are shown in Figure 16.5. This stored procedure returns Customer's Orders sorted by dates with the total amount of each order.

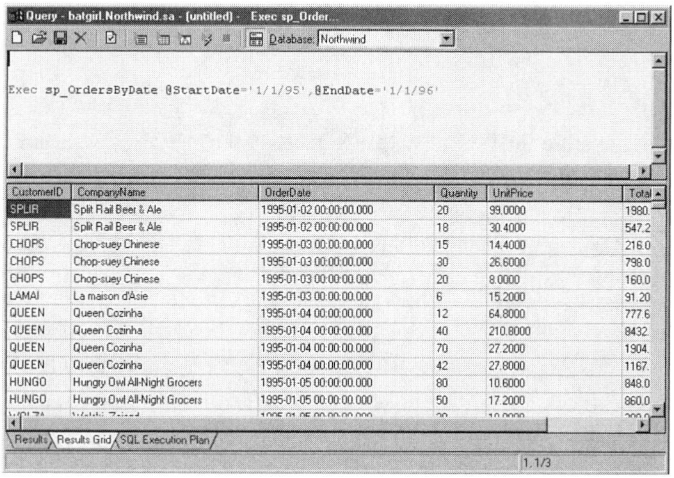

FIGURE 16.5

The results of the executed stored procedure.

Basing Access Reports on Stored Procedures via Pass-Through Queries

To execute a stored procedure in a SQL pass-through query, all you have to do is use the Execute syntax discussed earlier. You can set up a SQL pass-through query in Access by selecting Query, SQL Specific, Pass-through from the main menu when in Query Design view as shown in Figure 16.6.

FIGURE 16.6

Setting up a SQL pass-through query in Access.

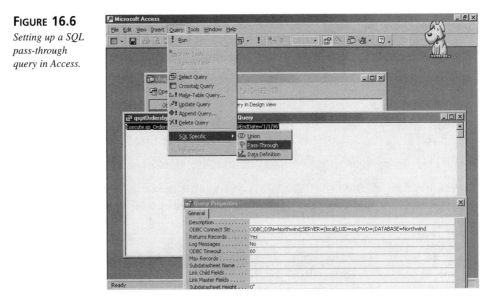

You cannot use the QBE Grid with a SQL pass-through; you will have to type in the SQL directly into the SQL window. You have to use SQL syntax that is compliant to your target server. (This chapter uses Microsoft SQL Server 6.5. You will have to change the syntax for another database server. Chapter 17, "Using Access 2000 Front-Ends to Oracle," focuses on Oracle syntax.)

After you type in your SQL string, you must set the ODBC connection string. The connect string tells Access what ODBC database to send the SQL to for processing. You must choose Tools, Properties to set the ODBC connect string property. Access provides a nice builder for you if you click on the ellipses next to the property. You can either type in a valid ODBC string or use the builder provided at the end of the property sheet. Use the builder and you will have to choose a valid ODBC datasource from those installed on your system as shown in Figure 16.7.

Save the pass-through query as qsptOrdersbyDate. Notice that when you save a pass-through query, it has a different icon than a normal query (see Figure 16.8).

FIGURE 16.7
*Valid DSNs on
your system.*

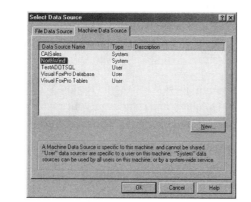

FIGURE 16.8
A saved pass-through query.

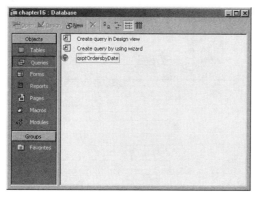

Reporting Against SQL Server in Access 2000

If you ask experienced developers what they like most about Microsoft Access, many will say that it has one of the best reports engines around. Access makes it easy to create great reports very quickly, even when that data does not come from an Access database. The capability to easily report ODBC data makes Access an excellent choice for all enterprise reporting.

There are many ways to report ODBC data. The simplest way is to link to ODBC tables and then create an Access query to base your report on. Although this is the fastest way to create reports, it is not advisable for the same reasons described earlier in the chapter.

Traditionally, SQL Server database servers have much more processing power and RAM than an average desktop. I am going to look at ways to increase the performance of your Access client/server reports by taking full advantage of the powerful server your database resides on.

For the examples, I will continue to use the database on my SQL Server called "Northwind."

To run a report on a SQL pass-through query, just run the Report Wizard on the qsptOrdersbyDate SQL pass-through query and customize your report as needed. It's that easy. A report in the sample database available on this book's companion CD is shown in Figure 16.9. Save the pass-through query as qsptOrdersbyDate.

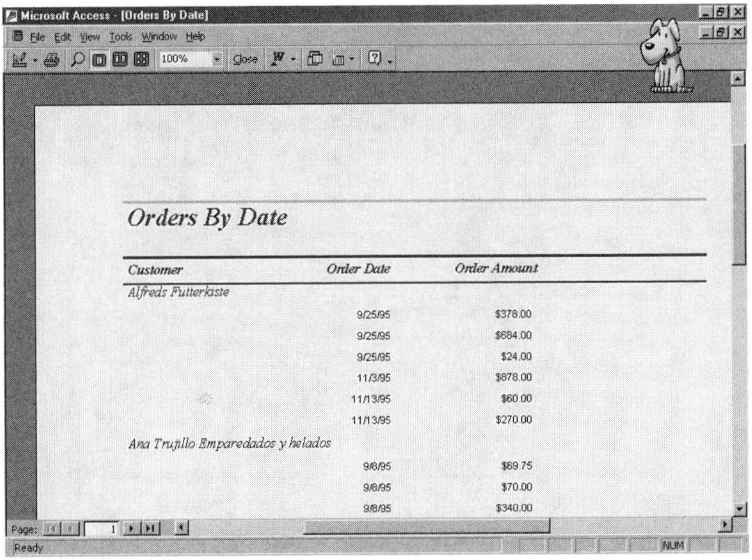

FIGURE 16.9

A report based on a stored procedure.

Advanced Features: Providing Parameters for the Stored Procedure at Runtime

You might be accustomed to using parameter queries in Access for your reports that require a user to enter dates or other criteria information at runtime. In Access, if you reference the form field in your query criteria, you can dynamically ask the user for parameters, as shown in Figure 16.10. Using the stored procedure approach, you will have to re-create the Execute statement with the new parameters inside your qsptOrdersbyDate pass-through query every time you run the report. In your parameter collection form

shown in Figure 16.10, there is code on the Click event to rewrite the SQL in the pass-
through. This code will then execute the stored procedure with the new date range
parameters. The code to do this is shown in Listing 16.2; please note that you need a reference to DAO 3.6 in your project to run this code. To set a reference to DAO 3.6 in your
application, open a module and then from the main menu in the VBE Editor choose
Tools, References. In this dialog, place a check next to DAO 3.6 Object Library.

FIGURE 16.10

*The Collect
Parameters form
used to run
reports.*

LISTING 16.2   CODE TO REWRITE THE SQL STATEMENT AND RUN THE REPORT

```
Private Sub cmdPrint_Click()
'''''''''''''''''''''''''''''''''''''''''''
'Purpose: Reset the SQL Code to call
'the Stored Procedure with new parameters
'From "Microsoft Access 2000 Development Unleashed" (SAMS)
'By: Forte, Howe, Ralston
'''''''''''''''''''''''''''''''''''''''''''
Dim db As DAO.Database
Dim strSQL As String

On Error GoTo Click_Err

strSQL = "Execute sp_OrdersByDate @StartDate=" & _
    Chr(39) & Me.txtStartDate & Chr(39) & _
        ",@EndDate=" & Chr(39) & Me.txtEndDate & Chr(39)

Set db = CurrentDb
db.QueryDefs("qsptOrdersbyDate").SQL = strSQL

DoCmd.OpenReport "rptOrdersBydate",acViewPreview

Click_Exit:
    Exit Sub

Click_Err:
    MsgBox Err.Description
    Resume Click_Exit

End Sub
```

Additional Filtering of a Report at Runtime

Sometimes the Where clause in a stored procedure does not fully limit the information that you need. You might return 500 orders and want to filter out more orders based on an amount at runtime. Access provides two methods to filter reports via the DoCmd.OpenReport method: You can supply a filter name as a saved query at runtime, or you can pass it a Where clause to filter the report by. Figure 16.9 shows the parameter collection form altered to accept a filter for a report with an Order Amount greater than a dollar amount. If the user decides to use the filter in addition to the date parameters, there is code to call the BuildCriteria method of the Application object. A valid filter should be something like OrderAmount>500. The BuildCriteria method will construct a valid filter for you. After you construct the filter, you use it with the DoCmd.OpenReport method. Listing 16.3 shows the code to both change the SQL pass-through and create and apply the filter.

LISTING 16.3   USING THE BuildCritera METHOD TO PROVIDE A REPORT FILTER

```
Function BuildWhere(curAmt As Currency) As String

'Build Where Clause with Access' BuildCriteria Method
BuildWhere = _
    BuildCriteria("TotalAMount", dbCurrency, ">=" & curAmt)

End Function


Private Sub cmdPrint_Click()
''''''''''''''''''''''''''''''''''''''
'Purpose: Reset the SQL Code to call
'the Stored Procedure with new parameters
'Also Add a Filtering Capability
'The Filter is set via
'Access' Where Clause Property
'of the DoCmd.OpenReport Method
'From "Microsoft Access 2000 Development Unleashed" (SAMS)
'By: Forte, Howe, Ralston
''''''''''''''''''''''''''''''''''''''
Dim db As DAO.Database
Dim strSQL As String

On Error GoTo Click_Err

strSQL = "Execute sp_OrdersByDate @StartDate=" & _
    Chr(39) & Me.txtStartDate & Chr(39) & _
        ",@EndDate=" & Chr(39) & Me.txtEndDate & Chr(39)

Set db = CurrentDb
```

Developing Access Front-Ends to Microsoft SQL Server

CHAPTER 16

453

16

**ACCESS FRONT-
ENDS TO SQL
SERVER**

```
db.QueryDefs("qsptOrdersbyDate").SQL = strSQL

'Here we determine if a Filter is Required
'A filter is required if the Checkbox is clicked
If Me.chkFilter Then
    'Apply the Filter
    DoCmd.OpenReport _
        "rptOrdersBydate", acViewPreview, , BuildWhere(Me.txtFilter)
Else
    'No Filter Selected
    DoCmd.OpenReport "rptOrdersBydate", acViewPreview
End If

Click_Exit:
    Exit Sub

Click_Err:
    MsgBox Err.Description
    Resume Click_Exit

End Sub
```

Lastly, it is a good idea to display a label control dynamically to alert the user to the filter and its amount. In addition, you should also alert the user to an empty report with the NoData report event. The code to do this follows in Listing 16.4:

LISTING 16.4   REPORT CODE TO HANDLE THE FILTER AND NoData

```
Private Sub Report_NoData(Cancel As Integer)

'No Data!
'From "Microsoft Access 2000 Development Unleashed" (SAMS)
'By: Forte, Howe, Ralston
On Error Resume Next

'Alert User to Empty Report
MsgBox "This Report Contains No Data" & _
    vbNewLine & "Please Try a different Selection Criteria", _
        vbCritical, Me.Name

'Prevent the Report From Opening
Cancel = True
End Sub

Private Sub Report_Open(Cancel As Integer)
On Error Resume Next
```

continues

LISTING 16.4   CONTINUED

```
'Check to see if the Filter was applied
If Forms!frmPrintReport!chkFilter Then
'Fill the caption with the Filter Criteria
    Me.lblFilter.Caption = _
        "Report Filtered for Orders > $ " & _
            Forms!frmPrintReport!txtFilter
    Me.lblFilter.Visible = True

End If

End Sub
```

Using Forms in Your Application

Forms are usually at the center of your Access applications. It is no different when you have an Access front-end to SQL Server. You can use forms in two types of modes—bound and unbound. The following sections will show you how to work with forms in both bound and unbound mode.

Bound Forms

It makes sense to base your Access forms on stored procedures as well; however, stored procedures are read-only. If your users are accustomed to bound forms and you want to use them instead of linked tables, there is nothing to do except write a query to limit the number of records that will be displayed on the form. Using a bound form based on a stored procedure/SQL pass-through query will change the parameters at runtime (as shown in Listing 16.2) and open the form. If you have a large amount of data or need to update data, you will have to use ADO code and unbound forms as shown in following sections to optimize performance.

Unbound Forms

When you use a bound form, there is a level of overhead involved, especially with linked tables. With a linked table, Jet has to manage the ODBC communication for you and there is an ODBC connection to the server for each bound control on the form. This can add up to a lot of connections and a lot of memory. A great alternative to using bound forms is to use a technique called unbound forms. With unbound forms, you can ask the user to enter in the PrimaryKey or other search value, and then use that value to open an ADO recordset and fill in the text boxes with those values, as shown in Figure 16.11.

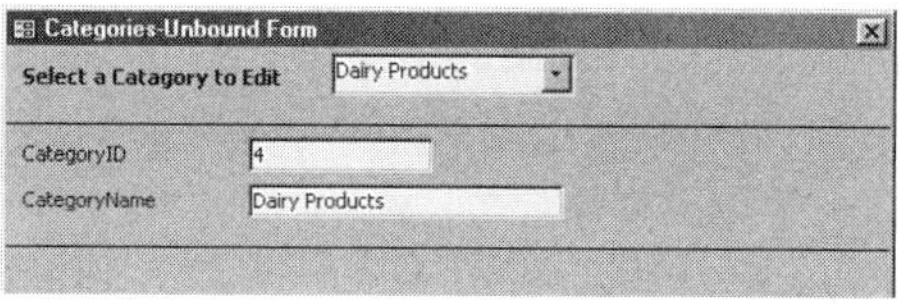

FIGURE 16.11

*An unbound
Access form.*

You can fill the combo box with a SQL pass-through query based on a stored procedure and then use the code in Listing 16.5 on the After Update event.

LISTING 16.5   FILLING A FORM WITH VALUES FROM AN ADO RECORDSET

```
Private Sub cboFind_AfterUpdate()
'This code will fetch the records
'based on the primary key
'and fill in the values in an unbound form
'From "Microsoft Access 2000 Development Unleashed" (SAMS)
'By: Forte, Howe, Ralston

Dim conn As ADODB.Connection
Dim rst As ADODB.Recordset
Dim strSQL As String

On Error GoTo Proc_Err

DoCmd.Hourglass False

Set rst = New ADODB.Recordset
Set conn = New ADODB.Connection

'Create SQL String based on what the user chose in
'the combo box
strSQL = "Select * From Categories Where CategoryID=" & Me.cboFind

'Set up an ADO connection to the SQL Server
With conn
    .Provider = "SQLOLEDB"
    .ConnectionString = "data source=batgirl;" & _
            "user id=sa;initial catalog=Northwind"
    'read only mode
    .Mode = adModeRead
    .Open
End With

'Open the recordset
rst.Open strSQL, conn

'Fill the values
Me.CategoryID = rst!CategoryID
Me.CategoryName = rst!CategoryName
```

continues

LISTING 16.5   CONTINUED

```
'clean up
rst.Close
conn.Close

Set conn = Nothing
Set rst = Nothing

Proc_Exit:
    DoCmd.Hourglass False
    Exit Sub

Proc_Err:
    MsgBox Err.Description
    Resume Proc_Exit
End Sub
```

After you start building unbound forms, you will want to update, delete, edit, and perform other operations in ADO. The next section will describe how to use ADO and the OLE DB Provider for SQL Server.

Advanced Features of the SQL Server OLE DB Provider

In order to use the OLE DB Provider for SQL Server, you first need to be sure it is installed on your computer. Luckily, if you install Access 2000, the OLE DB Provider for SQL Server will be installed by default. After you have the Provider installed, you will need to use a connection object. To set up a connection object, use the following syntax shown in Listing 16.6.

LISTING 16.6   CONNECTING TO SQL SERVER VIA OLE DB

```
Sub SQLServer()
'This procedure will connect to SQL Server
'From "Microsoft Access 2000 Development Unleashed" (SAMS)
'By: Forte, Howe, Ralston

Dim conn As ADODB.Connection
Set conn = New ADODB.Connection

With conn
    .Provider = "SQLOLEDB"
    .ConnectionString = "data source=BATGIRL;" & _
        "user id=sa;initial catalog=Northwind"
```

```
        .Mode = adModeRead
        .Open
End With

MsgBox "Connected to " & conn.Provider, vbInformation

End Sub
```

Next Recordset

One feature of SQL Server that you will not be allowed to do with Jet is to execute two select statements as one. Using this feature, you can then execute a SQL statement with multiple return recordsets using one recordset object. Listing 16.7 shows you how to use two recordsets with one recordset object. To do this you have to use the NextRecordset method of the recordset object.

LISTING 16.7   USING NextRecordset

```
Sub NextRst(strCustomerID As String)
'Use ALFKI or ANTON for an example
'This procedure will use 2 recordsets in one
'From "Microsoft Access 2000 Development Unleashed" (SAMS)
'By: Forte, Howe, Ralston

'This example opens a recordset
'based on a SQL Statement that will
'return two recordsets

Dim cmd As ADODB.Command
Dim conn As ADODB.Connection
Dim rst As ADODB.Recordset
Dim strSQL As String

Set conn = New ADODB.Connection

'Connect to the SQL Server
With conn
    .Provider = "SQLOLEDB"
    .ConnectionString = "data source=batgirl;" & _
        "user id=sa;initial catalog=Northwind"
    .Open
End With

'A SQL Statement that will produce two recordsets
'You can only do this against a provider/data engine that
'supports multiple resultsets
```

continues

LISTING 16.7 CONTINUED

```
strSQL = "select * From Customers Where CustomerID=" & _
    Chr(39) & strCustomerID & Chr(39)
strSQL = strSQL & vbNewLine
strSQL = strSQL & "Select * From Orders Where CustomerID=" & _
    Chr(39) & strCustomerID & Chr(39)

Set cmd = New ADODB.Command

With cmd
    .CommandText = strSQL
    .ActiveConnection = conn
    .CommandType = adCmdText
End With

Set rst = cmd.Execute

'This will open the first recordset
Do Until rst.EOF
    Debug.Print rst!CompanyName
    rst.MoveNext
Loop

'Grab the next recordset
Set rst = rst.NextRecordset

Do Until rst.EOF
    Debug.Print rst!OrderDate
    rst.MoveNext
Loop

rst.Close
conn.Close

Set rst = Nothing
Set cmd = Nothing
Set conn = Nothing
End Sub
```

Executing Commands with Parameters

Earlier in the chapter I emphasized the importance of using stored procedures in your application whenever possible to take advantage of the speed and reduction of network traffic they offer. When it comes to writing ADO code, using stored procedures provides the same benefits. In ADO, when you use a command object with the SQL Server

Developing Access Front-Ends to Microsoft SQL Server

CHAPTER 16

459

16

ACCESS FRONT-
ENDS TO SQL
SERVER

OLEDB provider, you can map that command object to a stored procedure on the server and use all its parameters, input, and output with parameter objects. As with most things in ADO, there are many ways to accomplish this task. In the following sections, I will explore some of the most common ways that you can use stored procedures and command objects; however, it is up to you to figure out which one will be best suit your coding style. Along the way, I will throw in my personal experiences and comments to help you decide which methodology to use.

The Long Way

Perhaps the most code intensive way to execute a stored procedure is the best place to start. Although no one in their right mind will want to code command objects in this way, learning this way first will accomplish a few things. First you will definitely appreciate the other ways to execute commands; and second, you will fully understand the relationship between the connection, command, and parameter objects that you will be using in all of your future code. To execute a command with parameters, you will have to create a command object and a parameter object, and then append the parameter object to the command, as shown in Listing 16.8.

LISTING 16.8 EXECUTING A COMMAND WITH PARAMETERS

```
Sub ExecuteCommandwithParms()
'This procedure will execute a stored procedure w/ parameters
'From "Microsoft Access 2000 Development Unleashed" (SAMS)
'By: Forte, Howe, Ralston

Dim conn As ADODB.Connection
Dim cmd As ADODB.Command
Dim prm As ADODB.Parameter

Set conn = New ADODB.Connection

'Establish a connection to the database
With conn
    .Provider = "SQLOLEDB"
    .ConnectionString = "data source=Batman;" & _
        "user id=sa;initial catalog=pubs"
    .Open
End With

'Set up a command object
Set cmd = New ADODB.Command
```

continues

LISTING 16.8   CONTINUED

```
With cmd
    .ActiveConnection = conn
    .CommandText = "byroyalty"
    .CommandType = adCmdStoredProc
End With

'Set up the parameter
Set prm = New ADODB.Parameter
With prm
    .Name = "@percentage"
    .Direction = adParamInput
    .Type = adInteger
    .Value = 50
End With
cmd.Parameters.Append prm

'Open a recordset based on the executed command
Dim rst As ADODB.Recordset
Set rst = cmd.Execute

'Loop through the results
Do Until rst.EOF
    Debug.Print rst!au_id
    rst.MoveNext
Loop

'Clean up
rst.Close
conn.Close
Set rst = Nothing
Set conn = Nothing
Set cmd = Nothing
Set prm = Nothing

End Sub
```

Using `Create Parameters`

An easy way to deal with stored procedure parameters without writing a ton of code is with the `CreateParameter` method of the command object. This method does not force you to create an actual parameter object of each parameter in your stored procedure, saving you perhaps more than a hundred lines of code if you have a lot of parameters. I have found that this is the least code-intensive and most reliable way to execute a command against both SQL Server 6.5 and 7.0. As shown in Listing 16.9, using `CreateParameter` creates a parameter object for you under the covers, without all that extra code.

LISTING 16.9   EXECUTING A COMMAND WITHOUT A PARAMETER OBJECT

```
Sub ExecuteCommandwithCreateParms()
'Execute a Parameter Query w/o
'Having to create Parameter Objects
'Here we use the CreateParameter method
'From "Microsoft Access 2000 Development Unleashed" (SAMS)
'By: Forte, Howe, Ralston

Dim conn As ADODB.Connection
Dim cmd As ADODB.Command

Set conn = New ADODB.Connection

'Establish a connection to the database
With conn
    .Provider = "SQLOLEDB"
    .ConnectionString = "data source=batgirl;" & _
        "user id=sa;initial catalog=pubs"
    .Open
End With

'Set up a command object
Set cmd = New ADODB.Command
With cmd
    .ActiveConnection = conn
    .CommandText = "byroyalty"
    .CommandType = adCmdStoredProc

    'Set up the parameter info
    'Here we use the Create Parameter Method
    'Of the Command Object to simplify your code
    .Parameters.Append .CreateParameter("@Percentage", _
        adInteger, adParamInput, , 50)

End With

'Open a recordset based on the executed command
Dim rst As ADODB.Recordset
Set rst = cmd.Execute

'Loop through the results
Do Until rst.EOF
    Debug.Print rst!au_id
    rst.MoveNext
Loop

'Clean up
rst.Close
conn.Close
```

continues

LISTING 16.9   CONTINUED

```
Set rst = Nothing
Set conn = Nothing
Set cmd = Nothing

End Sub
```

Using Refresh

Using the `Refresh` method of the command object's parameter collection is very similar to the `CreateParameter` method, except you do not have to create any parameter objects. Instead, you connect to the database, set your command object equal to the stored procedure that you will be using, and then refresh the parameter collection. This will give the collection the parameters you need, and it is up to you to fill them in. As shown in Listing 16.10, this option gives you the advantage of great flexibility in your code (you can create generic command classes); however, this method works 100 percent of the time with SQL Server 7.0 only. Using SQL Server 6.5, I had some issues that led me to wait until a future ADO release to use `Refresh`. (You can never be too safe with your data!) Even with this limitation, you might want to learn the syntax and usage of the `Refresh` method for your future programming, or when using SQL Server 7.0. One important thing to note is that you are making an extra roundtrip when you use the 'refresh' method to go to the database and fetch the parameter information. Although it's the easiest to use, you want to check on the performance before you make it your standard.

LISTING 16.10   USING Refresh WITH A COMMAND

```
Sub ExecuteCommandwithParmRefresh()
'Execute a Parameter Query w/o
'Having to use Parameter Objects
'Helpful with Stored Procedures that have
'A whole lot of Parameters
'This procedure will execute a stored procedure w/ parameters
'From "Microsoft Access 2000 Development Unleashed" (SAMS)
'By: Forte, Howe, Ralston

Dim conn As ADODB.Connection
Dim cmd As ADODB.Command

Set conn = New ADODB.Connection

'Establish a connection to the database
With conn
```

```
    .Provider = "SQLOLEDB"
    .ConnectionString = "data source=batgirl;" & _
        "user id=sa;initial catalog=pubs"
    .Mode = adModeRead
    .Open
End With

'Set up a command object
Set cmd = New ADODB.Command
With cmd
    .ActiveConnection = conn
    .CommandText = "byroyalty"
    .CommandType = adCmdStoredProc

    'This example uses the Parameter's Refresh
    'Method to get the parameters from the server
    'And then fill their values before execute
    'Avoids the need to Create/Append Parameters
    .Parameters.Refresh
    .Parameters("@Percentage").Value = 50
End With

'Open a recordset based on the executed command
Dim rst As ADODB.Recordset
Set rst = cmd.Execute

'Loop through the results
Do Until rst.EOF
    Debug.Print rst!au_id
    rst.MoveNext
Loop

'Clean up
rst.Close
conn.Close
Set rst = Nothing
Set conn = Nothing
Set cmd = Nothing

End Sub
```

Handling Return Values

Sometimes the stored procedures will return a value indicating success or failure of the
procedure, or it may return the newly added CustomerID value. In either case, you will
want to know the return value of that parameter. ADO enables us to query the parameter
collection after you execute the command to retrieve any return parameters.

Listing 16.11 runs a command object against a very simple stored procedure that returns the value of 55. The procedure is shown here:

```
CREATE  PROCEDURE sp_CmdWithPram  AS
/*Return Value*/
Return 55
```

After you execute the command object, you will have to query its parameters collection after using a Refresh (see the preceding section) via its ordinal position as shown here:

```
cmd.Parameters(0).Value
```

LISTING 16.11   QUERYING THE RETURN VALUES

```
Sub CommandReturnValues()
'This procedure will execute a stored procedure
'and query its return values
'A copy of the Stored Procedure:
'CREATE  PROCEDURE sp_CmdWithPram  AS
'
'/*Return Value*/
'Return 55

'From "Microsoft Access 2000 Development Unleashed" (SAMS)
'By: Forte, Howe, Ralston

Dim conn As ADODB.Connection
Dim cmd As ADODB.Command

Set conn = New ADODB.Connection
Set cmd = New ADODB.Command

'Establish a connection to the database
With conn
    .Provider = "SQLOLEDB"
    .ConnectionString = "data source=batgirl;" & _
        "user id=sa;initial catalog=northwind"
    .Open
End With

'Set up the command object to
'point to the Stored Procedure
With cmd
    .CommandText = "sp_CmdWithPram"
    .CommandType = adCmdStoredProc
    .ActiveConnection = conn
    .Parameters.Refresh
End With

cmd.Execute
```

```
MsgBox "return value: " & cmd.Parameters(0).Value

conn.Close
Set conn = Nothing

End Sub
```

Not Using a `Command` Object

For a row returning parameterized stored procedure, you can open one without using a `Command` object at all. To do this, you have to construct a SQL statement and use the open method of a recordset object as shown here:

```
rst.open 'exec sp_SimpleProc @OrderID=1', conn
```

Using a Connection Class

As you begin to rely more on code in your applications, you should get in the habit of trying to write generic, reusable code as often as possible. Although I try to show you as much class module programming as possible in this book, creating a `connection` class is one of the most important examples that I can show you. It is a real world-class module that you can make use of immediately, not only in Access programming, but in any VBA host, including the other Office 2000 applications and Visual Basic 5 and 6.

When you program with ADO, you should get into the habit of using a connection class. A connection class is a generic object that will create and return an ADO `Connection` object for you. If all of your data access code in your application relies on this particular class module to create connections to the database for it, you will only have to maintain this small piece of code when the database connection information changes. (That never happens, right?)

In this chapter, you will create a simple class module called DBConnection that will have one public method, `Connect`. `Connect` is just a simple VBA function that returns an ADO `Connection` object. The function, show in Listing 16.12, creates an ADO `Connection` object and then sets the function equal to that `connection` object. (The `connection` class is very simple. You can enhance the class module to use a Microsoft UDL file as described in Chapter 7, "Advanced ADO," for the most reusability.)

LISTING 16.12   A GENERIC Connection CLASS

```
Function Connect() As ADODB.Connection
'Reusable Component to Connection to a database
'Can use this component to centralize where the
'the data connection exists, so you only have to
'change the database connection info in one place
'From "Microsoft Access 2000 Development Unleashed" (SAMS)
'By: Forte, Howe, Ralston

Dim conn As ADODB.Connection
Set conn = New ADODB.Connection

'SQL Server Connection Information
With conn
    .Provider = "SQLOLEDB"
    .ConnectionString = "data source=batgirl;" & _
        "user id=sa;initial catalog=airline"
    .Open
End With

Set Connect = conn

End Function
```

Using the `Connection` Class in Your Applications

Using the connection class in your applications is simple. Wherever you have ADO code to connect to the back-end database, you create a `DBConnection` object to create the ADO `Connection` object for you, as shown in Listing 16.13. This will enable you to hide all the connection-specific code in one generic reusable class module or COM object for reuse later.

LISTING 16.13   USING THE Connection CLASS

```
Sub UseConnect()
'Uses the Reusable Component to Connection to a database
'From "Microsoft Access 2000 Development Unleashed" (SAMS)
'By: Forte, Howe, Ralston

Dim conn as ADODB.Connection
Dim oConnect as DBConnection

Set oConnect= New DBConnection
Set rst=oConnect.Connect

End Sub
```

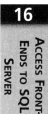

Summary

This chapter showed you the basics of using Access 2000 as a front-end to SQL Server. In this chapter we discussed how to create an Access application using the SQL Server OLE DB Provider. You can use ADO in your unbound forms to display and manipulate SQL Server data efficiently. Once again, if you are planning to use a version of SQL Server earlier than 7.0, you will want to use the techniques in this chapter. If you will be using 7.0 or higher, check out ADPs in Chapter 15, "Introducing Access Data Projects and the Visual Tools."

CHAPTER 17

Access 2000 Front-Ends to Oracle

IN THIS CHAPTER

Despite the prevalence of Oracle in the work of Access developers, there is very little written on the subject of using Access with it. This chapter will attempt to fill that gap.

Although new, the Access Data Project (ADP) is available to you for sophisticated client/server development, but there are plenty of times when you will need to retain the rich development environment of a regular Access application. Some of these situations include when you are prototyping an application or when you need to take advantage of the heterogeneous data management capabilities of Access.

Oracle is an extremely powerful and sophisticated database, and this chapter will in no way reveal all of its workings and complexity. However, by following some simple techniques and guidelines, you can harness much of that power without too much trouble.

Essentially, good Access/Oracle development requires that you approach Oracle on its own terms and let it do the data management for you because that is what it does so well. Though this sounds obvious, it can be a challenge in practice. Although many Access developers are called upon to use Oracle as part of their design, they often are not invested with as much control over Oracle's data schema as they are with Access's. Very often they find that they must negotiate a less-than-optimal data arrangement or data warehouse. Additionally, many Access developers find themselves presented with the task of developing against Oracle with little more than an ODBC driver and a user account. This chapter will explore ways of overcoming these challenges as well as ways to use some of the more basic Oracle tools, which, with a little prodding, should be made available to you.

Accessing Oracle Data with Access

There are several ways to use Oracle data with Access. This chapter will focus on two ways: basic ODBC techniques, though not ODBC programming; and ADO programming. During development, these two approaches can be used together, but your final product may benefit from using just one.

These two basic approaches manifest themselves in three ways:

- Table linking (ODBC)
- SQL pass-through queries (SPT) (ODBC)
- Direct connections through ADO

Table Linking

Because it is so easy for Access to link tables from many data sources, most Oracle data comes to Access through these linked tables. The linked tables use ODBC despite the fact that ADO is the default data management model for Access 2000. This means that you must have the ODBC drivers as well as the latest version of ADO installed to appreciate this section.

To create a link to a table in Oracle you must have the following:

- A compatible ODBC driver for Oracle.
- A network connection to the Oracle database using either SQLNet or Net8 (for Oracle 8). Oracle provides and controls its own network connection. Without one of these tools, you will not be able to connect to Oracle over the network.
- The ODBC driver included with Access.

Through ODBC, you establish a connection to the database; manage the tables, views, and procedures; and submit your SQL statements for parsing and execution.

Creating an ODBC Connection String

The ODBC manager on the client machine communicates between your process and the ODBC driver you are using for your data source. In order to make a connection to Oracle, you must first construct an ODBC connection string. This string is composed of the following optional pieces listed in Table 17.1:

TABLE 17.1 ODBC CONNECTION STRING ARGUMENTS

Section	Description
DSN	Data Source Name
UID	User ID
PWD	Password
Database	If the DSN does not name the database, it can be specified here
APP	The application using the connection

An ODBC connection string might look something like this:

```
ODBC;DSN=MSOracleDriver;UID=Scott;SERVER=empexample;;TABLE=SCOTT.DEPT
```

Every part of the connection string is optional, so if your string is missing necessary information, the user will be prompted for it.

Creating a Database Server Name

To prepare to use ODBC with Access, you should create a Database Server Name through ODBC. This is a very simple process. The following steps will create a DSN for Oracle.

1. Start the ODBC Data Sources from the control panel.

2. In the ODBC Data Source Administrator, click the Add button to create a new data source for Oracle.

3. Select either the Oracle ODBC Driver, Microsoft ODBC Driver for Oracle, or another ODBC Driver for Oracle. Click Finish. At this point, you will be prompted for information similar to the following dialog box. The exact dialog box you receive will vary depending upon the driver and its version (see Figure 17.1).

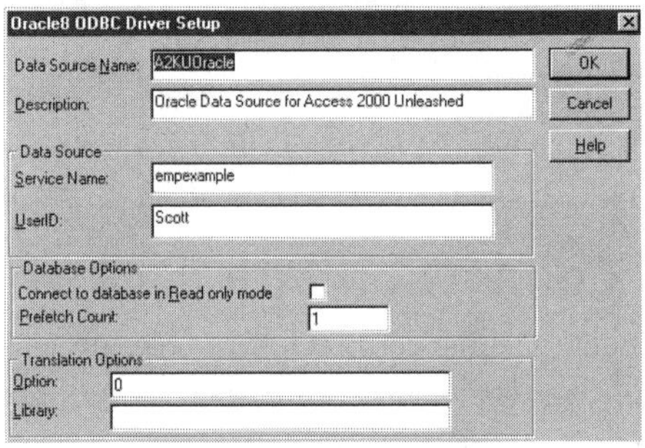

FIGURE 17.1

Filling out the DSN information.

Once you've created the DSN, you can call upon it to link your Oracle data to your database.

Understanding the Cost of an Oracle Connection

Creating the connection to an Oracle database is much more expensive in time and resources than creating a connection to a Jet database. When programming through ODBC, RDO, DAO, ODBC Direct, or ADO, you would try to maintain the connection and refer to it repeatedly within your application. Access does this work for you when you link a table from Oracle. It keeps the connection open and you can refer to it by referring to the Table object. Figure 17.2 shows how the linked tables can be used to build a query.

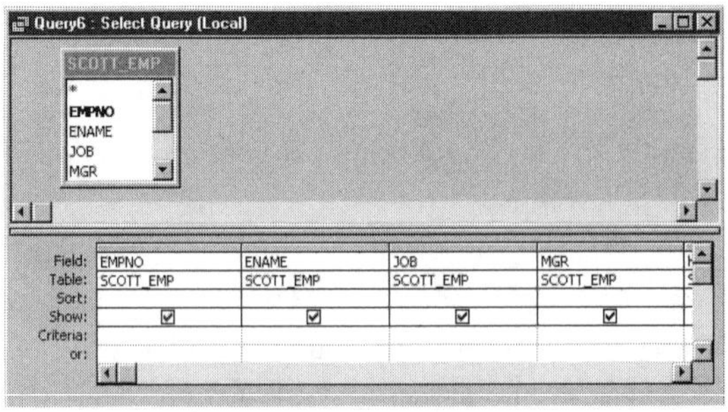

FIGURE 17.2

Use linked tables to build queries as if they were local tables.

```
SELECT SCOTT_EMP.ENAME, SCOTT_DEPT.DNAME
FROM SCOTT_DEPT INNER JOIN SCOTT_EMP ON SCOTT_DEPT.DEPTNO =
SCOTT_EMP.DEPTNO
WITH OWNERACCESS OPTION;
```

But that convenience is expensive. When you query the linked tables, your SQL statement is written in Access, so Oracle does not know what it is. The ODBC driver and Jet have to work together to resolve the statement. The ODBC driver parses the query and may be able to send a rudimentary fragment of your SQL statement to Oracle, usually referring to one table at a time, for processing. However, this usually results in Oracle sending massive amounts of data over the network to the desktop to be processed by Jet. Because Jet is the only data engine that understands the full SQL statement, all the processing will happen at the desktop. This may be unavoidable at times, but it should not be confused with real client/server design.

If you need to browse data or examine the schema of the tables and you have no Oracle tools, linking is an appropriate technique. Linking is also acceptable if you are querying the Oracle data with data that must remain local or comes from more than one source (heterogeneous query). However, if you need to homogeneously query Oracle data, you should consider other approaches.

SQL Pass-Through Queries (ODBC)

One such approach is a SQL pass-through query (SPT).

By using the same ODBC connection you used for linking, you gain access to the Oracle database and shift the burden of processing your query to the server—where it belongs. Of course in an SPT, all the data sources you reference in the SQL statement must reside on the Oracle database and the SQL statement must conform to Oracle's dialect, but these are small concerns when weighed against the increased response time and the reduced network traffic. In SPT queries, the only thing you send to the server is the SQL statement, and the only thing it sends back is the result.

To create a SPT, follow these steps:

1. Create a new query.
2. From the Query menu, choose SQL Specific.
3. Select SQL pass-through.
4. From the SQL editor view of the new query (the only design view available), select View and then Properties.
5. Enter the ODBC Connection string into the ODBC Connect Str property setting.

17

ACCESS 2000
FRONT-ENDS TO
ORACLE

The ODBC connection string could look like this:

```
ODBC;DSN=EmpExample;UID=SCOTT;PWD=tiger;DBQ=empexample;
```

TIP

To save time, you can copy the ODBC connection string from a linked table.

6. Type the Oracle SQL statement.

An example of the SQL statement could look like this:

```
Select * from emp
```

Upon execution, Access passes this SQL statement directly to Oracle through the ODBC connection. Jet is not involved at all in its execution. Oracle will receive the statement, respond to it, and send the result, if any, back to the sender.

Some situations where SPTs could be used with Oracle data are

- To issue SQL statements to alter the schema of an Oracle database
- To retrieve selected fields and particular rows from Oracle
- To check the number of rows affected by an update SQL statement
- To serve as the recordsource of a simple bound form showing a small number of records
- To create, replace, and execute views and stored procedures in Oracle.

You should always test the option of using SPT queries to see if they will benefit your application.

Understanding SPT Property Requirements

When you create a pass-through query, you must specify whether or not the query will return records. Queries that insert, update, delete, or alter do not return records, while queries that select usually do. If you do not set this query property correctly an error will result.

Understanding SPT Syntax Requirements

You must also write the SQL statement in Oracle's SQL syntax, which differs in important ways from the Access syntax generated by the QBE grid. Access 2000 supports a SQL dialect that more closely conforms to ANSI-92 standard SQL, but if you have been writing Access SQL since version 1.1, a review of the differences will help you use Oracle effectively.

Oracle does not require you to end the SQL statement with a semicolon [;] when creating SPT queries, even though it requires them when you run SQL statements from SQL PLUS. A semicolon at the end of a SPT statement will cause an error.

Square brackets are not required to identify table or field names in Oracle. Using them will cause an error.

Although Access changes the period [.] of SCOTT.EMP to the underscore [_] in SCOTT_EMP when you link the table, you must use Oracle's native delimiter when making an SPT statement. Oracle's will only work with the period [.].

Understanding Case Sensitivity

Oracle SQL statements are not case sensitive, with the exception of the values you are comparing in the Where clause. The following two statements are identical:

```
Select eName, job FroM eMP
SELECT ENAME, JOB FROM EMP
```

However, only the first of the following two statements will return the correct result

```
Select ename, job form EMP where JOB='MANAGER'
Select ename, job form EMP where JOB='manager'
```

Understanding the Select Statement

The Select keyword works exactly as it does in Access. Select tells Oracle which fields (or columns) to return in the result. Column names listed after the Select keyword must exist in the tables mentioned in the following From clause.

```
SELECT ename, job, hiredate....
```

The tables or views used by the query are listed in the From clause, just as in Access. As in Access, the order of the table name or views does not affect the outcome of the query.

```
Select ename, job, hiredate FROM Emp
```

Understanding the Where Clause

The Where clause will give most Access developers problems when they first develop queries against Oracle data because it encompasses the most differences between Access SQL and Oracle SQL. In Oracle, the Where clause not only limits the records returned from the server as it does in Access; it also explains the relationships between the tables and views used in the query.

In its implementation familiar to most Access developers, the Where clause restricts records in the result and looks like some of the following examples:

17

ACCESS 2000
FRONT-ENDS TO
ORACLE

```
Select * from Emp WHERE MNG=7698
Select * from  EMP WHERE HIREDATE between '1/1/1990' and '1/1/1995'
Select * from EMP WHERE Ename like 'M%'
```

Understanding Relationships

When more than one table is involved in the query, the `Where` clause in Oracle states the relationship

```
SELECT emp.ename,dept.dname
FROM emp,dept
WHERE (emp.deptno=dept.deptno) AND (emp.ename like 'M%')
```

The SQL statement shown above returns records that are equal on each side of the relationship through their related fields as specified in the `Where` clause (emp.deptno=dept.deptno). To return records that are not represented on both sides of the relationship, you must construct an outer join. In Oracle, an outer join is created by placing a (+) on the side of the relationship that will display the null value when no match exists. A good way to remember it is to put the (+) sign on the side that will show the extra, though blank, entries. The SQL statement below represents a left outer join that will show all employees whether or not they have a matching department code.

```
SELECT emp.ename,dept.dname
FROM emp,dept
WHERE emp.deptno(+)=dept.deptno
```

Relationships in Oracle can also be written as expressions. This is not possible in Access. Although using expressions in a relationship is not common, it can be a powerful tool when dealing with less than optimal data arrangements and the peculiar things you can encounter when dealing with legacy systems and data warehouses. The SQL statement below shows how you can use an expression to represent a relationship.

```
Select emp.ename, dept.dname
From emp, dept
Where (emp.deptno=dept.deptno+10)
```

Using Wildcards/Position Markers

Access takes either the * or the ? as wildcards. The * will stand in for any number of text characters when used in the `Where` clause and the ? will hold just one place. In Oracle, you have the same capabilities, but the % substitutes for the * and _ holds a single space. These wildcards can be used as follows:

```
Select * from emp where ename like 'M%'
Select * from emp where ename like 'J___S'
```

Using Null/Not Null

Oracle handles null evaluations the same way that Access does.

```
SELECT * FROM emp WHERE comm IS NULL
SELECT * FROM emp WHERE comm IS NOT NULL
```

Constructing Insert Statements

An Access query that inserts new values into an existing table would generate a SQL statement that looks something like this:

```
INSERT INTO SCOTT_EMP ( EMPNO, ENAME, JOB, MGR, HIREDATE, SAL, DEPTNO )
SELECT '9999' AS Expr1, 'JP' AS Expr2, 'SALESMAN' AS Expr3,_
7698 AS Expr4,
#7/27/1997# AS Expr5, 2380 AS Expr6, 10 AS Expr7;
```

However, Access will also accept a "Values" clause like the one shown below for Oracle, but you would have to type it yourself.

In Oracle you can simplify that SQL statement as follows:

```
INSERT INTO EMP ( EMPNO, ENAME, JOB, MGR, HIREDATE, SAL, COMM, DEPTNO)
VALUES( 9998, 'JP', 'SALESMAN', 7698, _
TO_DATE('7/27/1997','MM/DD/YYYY'), 2380,0,10)
```

Notice how Oracle uses the To_Date() to verify that the value entering a date type field is really a date. There is more on this and other Oracle functions later in the chapter.

Constructing Update Statements

Issuing an Update SQL in Oracle is not very different from doing so in Access. Following is the Access QBE generated SQL against an attached table followed by the SPT SQL to do the same thing:

```
UPDATE SCOTT_EMP
SET SCOTT_EMP.SAL = [7000]
WHERE ((([SCOTT_EMP].[EMPNO])=9999));
```

Oracle's version is simpler than that of Access with fewer parenthetical clauses and no square brackets. Also, because the ODBC connection string directs the SQL statement directly to the Scott table space, there is no need to preface the table name situations.

```
UPDATE emp
SET sal=7000
WHERE empno = 9999
```

Using `Group By/Having`

Access's QBE grid takes care of the syntax when you create a grouping query. In Oracle, you have to take care of these issues yourself. As in Access, Group By distills your data down to a representation of each value in the designated columns. Any other columns of data displayed in the result must be viewed through an aggregate function (for example, Sum(), Avg(), and so on).

In the following SQL statement:

```
SELECT deptno, count(*)
FROM emp
WHERE deptno <>10
GROUP BY deptno
HAVING count(*) <6
```

Oracle will get all the records with a deptno other than 10 and then group these qualifying records together as part of the Group By operation. Finally, Oracle will search the results returned by the record count (count(*)) and suppress any rows whose count is fewer than 6. The only real differences between this SQL statement and an Access SQL statement are the parentheses and square brackets.

However, the functions you are able to employ with this or any other query differ quite a bit.

Functions in Oracle Versus Access

In Access, SQL statements are checked for references to functions, either VBA functions or functions you have created. The Jet Expression Service allows any function you put into a SQL statement to operate. You cannot use VBA or your own functions in a SPT query. The reason for this is very simple. SPTs do not use Jet at all. Oracle receives the SQL as a string and it must be understandable to Oracle. Though it is possible to create similar custom functionality in Oracle, those skills are beyond the scope of this chapter.

The next section will review some of the more commonly used Oracle functions you can use with an SPT query.

Many of the functions offered by Oracle are very similar to the string functions in Access. This section explains those functions, which either do not exist in Access or are slightly different from similar functions in Access. Consult your Oracle documentation for a complete listing of Oracle functions.

Strings

Most of the data types you will deal with will probably be strings or they will be other data types that are converted into strings at some point. Typically, you are going to want to search strings, replace parts of strings, concatenate strings, parse them, change their case, or in some way alter them to fit your forms and your report. This section discusses some of the most common aspects of string manipulation that you will encounter when working with Oracle.

Concatenation

Oracle concatenates using two vertical bars (¦¦) where Access would use an ampersand (&) or a plus sign (+). The following SQL statement illustrates concatenation:

```
SELECT ename¦¦deptno
FROM emp
```

Initcap, Lower, Upper

Initcap(string) takes a string argument and capitalizes the initial character of each word in the string.

Similarly, Upper and Lower capitalize all members of a string or change them to lower-case respectively

```
SELECT INITCAP(ename)
FROM emp
```

Returns the following result:

```
INITCAP(ENAME)
----------
Jp
Allen
Ward
Jones
Martin
Blake
Clark
Scott
King
Turner
Adams
James
Ford
Miller


SELECT UPPER(ENAME)
FROM emp
```

Returns the following result:

```
UPPER(ENAME)----------

JP
ALLEN
```

```
WARD
JONES
MARTIN
BLAKE
CLARK
SCOTT
KING
TURNER
ADAMS
JAMES
FORD
MILLER

SELECT LOWER(ename)
FROM emp
```

Returns the following result:

```
LOWER(ENAM
----------
jp
allen
ward
jones
martin
blake
clark
scott
king
turner
adams
james
ford
miller
```

Instr

Instr returns the position of a character you are searching for and can be very useful for parsing stings at their spaces or at a comma. If the character you are searching for is not found, a 0 value is returned. The Instr function is case sensitive, unlike in Access.

Instr takes four arguments:

- String—required. The literal string or a reference to the string you want to search through.
- Set—required. The character or characters you want to find.
- Start—optional. At what position should the search begin. The default is 1, or the first character.

• Occurrence—optional. If you are only concerned about the second or third encounter of the Set, you can enter a 2 or a 3 here.

Compare this SQL statement with neither the occurrence nor the start arguments specified:

```
Select ename, instr(ename,'A') from emp
```

returns

```
ENAME        INSTR(ENAME,'A')
----------   ----------------
JP                         0
ALLEN                      1
WARD                       2
JONES                      0
MARTIN                     2
BLAKE                      3
CLARK                      3
SCOTT                      0
KING                       0
TURNER                     0
ADAMS                      1
JAMES                      2
FORD                       0
MILLER                     0
```

When a SQL statement uses the occurrence argument (2), it will search for the second appearance of the requested character.

```
Select ename, instr(ename,'A',1,2) from emp
```

```
ENAME        INSTR(ENAME,'A',1,2)
----------   --------------------
JP                           0
ALLEN                        0
WARD                         0
JONES                        0
MARTIN                       0
BLAKE                        0
CLARK                        0
SCOTT                        0
KING                         0
TURNER                       0
ADAMS                        3
JAMES                        0
FORD                         0
MILLER                       0
```

LTrim/RTrim

Access has three functions for trimming characters from a string: LTrim() for removing from the left, RTrim for removing from the right, and Trim for removing from both sides at the same time. Oracle has only LTrim and RTrim. Access's trimming functions and Oracle's trimming functions differ in another important way.

In Access, the trimming functions only remove spaces, but in Oracle, they will remove any set of characters you want.

The trim functions take two arguments:

- String—required. The literal string or a reference to the string you want to affect.
- Set—optional. The characters you want to find within the string argument.

You could use the LTrim/RTrim functions to remove the word 'THE' from the beginning of titles by executing the following statement

```
Select LTrim(Title,'"THE ') from Books
```

It's critical to note that the LTrim/RTrim functions are case sensitive and they ignore character order. This means that book titles will be altered as they are in Table 17.2.

TABLE 17.2 BEFORE AND AFTER LTrim

Before	*After Trimming*
The Great Access Book	Great Access Book
How to Develop in Access	ow to Develop in Access
THE ETHICAL DEVELOPER	ical Developer
Access 2000 Development Unleashed	Access 2000 Development Unleashed

The LTrim/RTrim functions do not care if the order of the string is different or if it repeats itself several times (as in THE ETH... of The Ethical Developer). You will probably need to combine these functions with Instr, Substr, and Decode to get the result you really want.

Soundex

Since 1888, the Census Bureau has been using an algorithm to classify names that are similarly spelled. This algorithm is called Soundex. It works by taking the first letter of a word, and then assigning a number for every following consonant. Different consonants are assigned the same number (for example, [T] and [D] both translate into 3) based on the interpretation of their sound. The algorithm goes through the word until it has a four-character code. Words that have too few consonants to generate four characters are filled in with 0s. A vowel is eliminated unless it is the first character in the word. Soundex codes would look like this:

```
Select ename, soundex(ename) from emp
ENAME      SOUN
---------- ----
JP         J100
ALLEN      A450
WARD       W630
JONES      J520
MARTIN     M635
BLAKE      B420
CLARK      C462
SCOTT      S300
KING       K520
TURNER     T656
ADAMS      A352
JAMES      J520
FORD       F630
MILLER     M460
```

Soundex can be very useful for a fuzzy search in lists of names and titles. An SQL statement such as the following:

```
Select ename from emp where soundex(ename) like soundex('muller')
```

Would yield matches to names such as:

```
Mailer
Miller
Molar
Moller
Muler
Mulronsky
```

The Soundex function does not interpret the context of the characters, so some results may not be intuitive at first glance and words of varying length can match one another. Despite these caveats, it can be very useful when searching mailing lists and company directories.

Substr

Substr could be compared to the Mid function in Access. Oracle has no direct equivalent of the Right() and Left() functions found in Access. Like Access's Mid() function, the Substr() function takes three arguments:

- String—the literal string or reference to manipulate.
- Start—an explicit or derived value to begin the manipulation.
- End—an explicit or derived value to represent the number of characters affected to the right of the Start position.

In a situation where a customer's name is

MacIntyre, Alastair

you can use the `Substr()` function along with the `Instr()` function to parse the name into separate fields.

```
SUBSTR(CustomerName,INSTR(CustomerName,', ')+2) = Alastair
SUBSTR(CustomerName,1,INSTR(CustomerName,', ')-1)=MacIntyre
```

In the first case, the `Substr` takes all the characters in the string from 2 spaces after it finds the "," to the end of the string. By leaving the third argument empty, the function assumes the length of the string. In the second case, the function takes all the characters from the start of the string to the comma, less one position.

Decode

For better or worse, many Access developers have come to rely on the immediate `If` (`IIf()`) function in queries. Oracle does not provide a comparably named function. The Oracle function you would use in its place is `Decode`.

`Decode` is a series of `If`/`Then` tests ending with an `Else`. In this respect, it is more like a `Case Select` construct than an `IIf()`.

```
DECODE(value, if1,then1,if2,then2,...,else)
```

The number of `If`/`Then` conditions you can use is nearly endless.

The following SQL statement is a simple use of the `Decode` function to translate cities to regions:

```
Select loc,
DECODE(LOC,'NEW YORK','MID-ATLANTIC','DALLAS','SOUTH','BOSTON','NEW
ENGLAND','CHICAGO','MIDWEST','UNKNOWN') REGION
FROM dept
```

The result of this query shows how the regions have been substituted and the unknown city has been handled by the `Else` part of the function.

```
Select loc, DECODE(LOC,'NEW YORK','MID-ATLANTIC',
'DALLAS','SOUTH','BOSTON','NEW ENGLAND','CHICAGO',
'MIDWEST','UNKNOWN') REGION from dept


LOC             REGION
-------------   -----------
NEW YORK        MID-ATLANTIC
DALLAS          SOUTH
CHICAGO         MIDWEST
BOSTON          NEW ENGLAND
SUMMIT          UNKNOWN
```

Mathematical Calculations in Oracle

Since good database design proscribes persisting most calculation results, you won't be able to create meaningful interfaces or reports without an understanding of Oracle's functions. Oracle's functions are very similar to the functions you would find in VBA or Access. This section highlights some of the differences between Oracle functions and Access's functions.

Ceil()

Ceil() has no real counterpart in Access. Ceil takes one argument, value, and returns the smallest integer that is larger or equal to the value argument.

```
CEIL(34.2)=35
CEIL(-2.4)=-2
```

Floor()

Floor(), the opposite of Ceil(), does not have a counterpart in Access. It takes one argument, value, and returns the largest integer that is smaller than or equal to the value.

```
FLOOR(34.2)=34
FLOOR(-2.4)=-3
```

Nvl()

The Null Value Substitute function (Nvl()) is similar to NZ() in VBA. It enables you to substitute a value when the given argument is null. This can help prevent math errors caused by math on a null value.

It takes two arguments:

- Value—required. A literal or a reference to a value.

- Substitute—required. What the function will return if value is null.

```
NVL(value, substitute)
NVL(238,15)=238
NVL(null,15)=15
```

Round()

Round() has been missing from Access for a long time. In Access 2000, users finally get it. The function takes two arguments:

- Value—required. A literal value or a reference to be assessed.

- Precision—optional. The number of decimal places to which to round. Zero places is the default.

Sign()

`Sign()` works exactly like `Sgn()` in Access. It returns 1 for a positive number and –1 for a negative number.

Trunc()

Rather than rounding the number up or down, `Trunc()` simply chops the number off without regard to the value beyond its truncating position. `Trunc()` takes two arguments:

- `Value`—required. A literal value or a reference to be assessed.
- `Precision`—required. The number of decimal places to retain. Zero places is the default.

Greatest/Least

`Greatest` and `Least` are used to make a choice between two or more arguments. It can be used with numbers, characters, and dates. When used with dates, as in the example following, literal dates must be handled with the `To_Date()` function; otherwise, they will be interpreted as literal strings and the results will probably not be what you expect.

This example uses the `Least` function to see which comes first, the date in the Hiredate field or the date of January 1, 1985.

The `Least` function chooses the earliest or smallest value among the choices, whereas `Greater` chooses the largest value among the choices.

```
SELECT ENAME, LEAST(HIREDATE,TO_DATE('1-JAN-85')) FROM EMP;
```

```
ENAME        LEAST(HIREDATE)
----------   ---------
JP           01-JAN-85
ALLEN        20-FEB-81
WARD         22-FEB-81
JONES        02-APR-81
MARTIN       28-SEP-81
BLAKE        01-MAY-81
CLARK        09-JUN-81
SCOTT        01-JAN-85
KING         17-NOV-81
TURNER       08-SEP-81
ADAMS        01-JAN-85
JAMES        03-DEC-81
FORD         03-DEC-81
MILLER       23-JAN-82
```

Date Calculations in Oracle

There is probably no data type more troublesome than dates. This section will explain some of the functions that deal with and render dates in Oracle.

Arithmetic

Date is a data type in Oracle, just as it is in Access. Also as in Access, dates store more than what you see. In Oracle, a date column stores the year, month, date, hour, minute, and second. This means you can perform arithmetic operations on dates. However, unlike numbers, when you add a number to a date, you get a new date. When you subtract one date from another, you get a number representing the elapsed time between the dates. Depending on the formatting you choose, this elapsed time could appear as anything from years to seconds. It's even possible to arrive at a number that is not an integer—just like Access.

SYSDATE

The Sysdate() function reaches into the operating system and returns the date and time it finds there.

```
Select SYSDATE FROM sys.Dual
```

This SQL statement will return the system's date from Oracle's small function testing table.

Add_Months

If an employee's first review should occur after 6 months of employment, you can use Add_Months to schedule the review.

Add_Months takes two arguments:

- Date—required. A literal or a reference to a valid date.
- Count—required. The number of months to add to the Date.

The following SQL will determine when the first review should occur.

```
SELECT ename, hiredate, add_months(hiredate,6)
FROM emp
ENAME       HIREDATE   ADD_MONTH
----------  ---------  ---------
JP          27-JUL-97  27-JAN-98
ALLEN       20-FEB-81  20-AUG-81
WARD        22-FEB-81  22-AUG-81
JONES       02-APR-81  02-OCT-81
MARTIN      28-SEP-81  28-MAR-82
BLAKE       01-MAY-81  01-NOV-81
CLARK       09-JUN-81  09-DEC-81
```

```
SCOTT       19-APR-87 19-OCT-87
KING        17-NOV-81 17-MAY-82
TURNER      08-SEP-81 08-MAR-82
ADAMS       23-MAY-87 23-NOV-87
JAMES       03-DEC-81 03-JUN-82
FORD        03-DEC-81 03-JUN-82
MILLER      23-JAN-82 23-JUL-82
```

Often when scheduling events, a specific amount of lead time is needed to make preparations. This calls for subtracting dates from one another. You can do this by entering a negative number for the Count argument of Add_Months().

Months_Between

In order to calculate elapsed time, you could subtract one date or time from another, but because months have different numbers of days, it could get complicated. Months_Between() returns the difference between two dates in months, taking into account which months fall between the dates.

The following SQL statement converts the months to years by dividing by 12. The SQL also uses the round function to get a more manageable result.

```
SELECT ename, hiredate, ROUND(MONTHS_BETWEEN(SYSDATE,hiredate)/12,2)
"YEARS SERVICE"
FROM emp
```

```
ENAME       HIREDATE  YEARS SERVICE
----------  --------- -------------
JP          27-JUL-97          1.56
ALLEN       20-FEB-81         17.99
WARD        22-FEB-81         17.99
JONES       02-APR-81         17.88
MARTIN      28-SEP-81         17.39
BLAKE       01-MAY-81          17.8
CLARK       09-JUN-81         17.69
SCOTT       19-APR-87         11.83
KING        17-NOV-81         17.25
TURNER      08-SEP-81         17.44
ADAMS       23-MAY-87         11.74
JAMES       03-DEC-81         17.21
FORD        03-DEC-81         17.21
MILLER      23-JAN-82         17.07
```

Next_Day()

When events occur on a given day of the week before or after a certain day (like most secular holidays, some religious holidays, and paydays) it can be tricky to look forward and know what dates these events will fall on. The Next_Day() function helps determine what these dates will be.

Next_Day() takes two arguments:

- Date—a literal or a reference to a valid date
- Day—the textual expression of the day of week ('Sunday', 'Monday', and so on)

The following SQL statement shows each employee's first payday, assuming everyone gets paid every Friday.

```
SELECT ename, hiredate, next_day(hiredate,'Friday') "PAYDAY!"
FROM emp
```

```
ENAME       HIREDATE  PAYDAY!
----------  --------- ---------
JP          27-JUL-97 01-AUG-97
ALLEN       20-FEB-81 27-FEB-81
WARD        22-FEB-81 27-FEB-81
JONES       02-APR-81 03-APR-81
MARTIN      28-SEP-81 02-OCT-81
BLAKE       01-MAY-81 08-MAY-81
CLARK       09-JUN-81 12-JUN-81
SCOTT       19-APR-87 24-APR-87
KING        17-NOV-81 20-NOV-81
TURNER      08-SEP-81 11-SEP-81
ADAMS       23-MAY-87 29-MAY-87
JAMES       03-DEC-81 04-DEC-81
FORD        03-DEC-81 04-DEC-81
MILLER      23-JAN-82 29-JAN-82
```

To_Date()

The purpose of To_Date is to convert literals into recognizable Oracle dates. You will use it often in Update and Insert SQL statements. Without it, you may not be able to perform date calculations on your data.

To_Date() takes two arguments:

- String—required, a string representing a date (for example, "July 27, 1997"). "DD-MON-YYYY" is the default format.
- Format—optional,

```
SELECT TO_DATE('27-jul-97','dd-mon-yyyy') "Formatted Date"
FROM sys.dual
```

```
Formatted Date
---------
27-JUL-1997
```

Year 2000 Concerns

Oracle does not automatically window dates like Access does.

The two SQL statements which follow illustrates how Oracle assigns all dates to the current century (the century of `Sysdate()`) unless instructed otherwise.

```
SQL> SELECT MONTHS_BETWEEN('27-JUL-2001','27-JUL-1997') FROM SYS.DUAL
MONTHS_BETWEEN('27-JUL-2001','27-JUL-1997')
-------------------------------------------
                                        48


SQL> SELECT MONTHS_BETWEEN('27-JUL-01','27-JUL-97') FROM SYS.DUAL
MONTHS_BETWEEN('27-JUL-01','27-JUL-97')
---------------------------------------
                                  -1152
```

It is vital that you address this issue in your development efforts.

When dealing with dates, you can use the format mask RR to window the century according the following scheme. If the year is 0–49, Oracle will assign the date to the 21st century. If the year is between 50 and 99, it will place the date in the 20th century.

```
SQL> SELECT TO_CHAR(TO_DATE('000727','RRMMDD'),'DD-MON-YYYY') RRMMDD,
TO_CHAR(TO_DATE('000727','YYMMDD'),'DD-MON-YYYY') YYMMDD
FROM SYS.DUAL
RRMMDD        YYMMDD
----------- -----------
27-JUL-2000 27-JUL-1900     CONVERSION
```

Understanding Views and Stored Procedures

Passing a SQL statement to Oracle for processing is a great way to improve performance and reduce network traffic, but keeping the SQL statements is not the very best solution possible. To really tap the power of Oracle, benefit from work already done on the database, reduce your maintenance chores, and secure your work and preserve the integrity of your data, you will want to use Oracle views and stored procedures.

A view in Oracle is simply a query saved in Oracle. Like a `Select` query saved in Access, it is compiled and has an execution plan. This means it will run faster than the ad hoc query you send through the SPT.

The benefits of using views are many. You can call it by its name, which is usually much shorter than the average SQL statement, thereby further reducing network traffic. Because the view resides in Oracle, it will have an added level of security, especially beneficial in those applications which remain open or only lightly secured. Because your application is probably not the only one using the Oracle data, you can take advantage of views that have already been built, thereby saving time and assuring consistent results across different applications.

You can create a view right from Access or with other Oracle development tools. In order to make a view, or make any schema change for that matter, your Oracle account must have a Resource permission. Check with your database administrator to have this level of permission granted to your account.

Because this chapter is taking advantage of Oracle from Access, everything I do will use only Access as its tool. If you have the option of using SQL Plus or other Oracle administrative tools, you should consult the Oracle documentation on how to use them.

Creating a View

A view is merely a SQL statement that returns records. Because a view is part of the database schema, it can be created, altered, used, and dropped with SQL.

Consider the following simple SQL statement in Oracle's SQL dialect:

```
Select * from emp where SAL>3000
```

You could create this in Access and execute it as a pass-through query, or you could create a view in Oracle and simply call that view.

Creating a view from Access requires that you create a SQL pass-through to the server and issue a data definition SQL statement from it. These statements begin with the keywords `Create`, `Alter`, `Drop`, and so on. To create a view, your statement should follow this syntax:

```
Create [or Replace]
View
[ViewName]
AS
[record returning SQL Statement]
```

To create a view of the preceding SQL statement, the following data definition SQL could be issued from a SPT:

```
Create or Replace View MyView As Select * from emp where SAL>3000
```

The keywords "or Replace" would allow you to avert an error should MyView already exist on the server. You may not want to include "or Replace" all the time, so use it with care.

Executing the query now will create an Oracle view that returns all the columns from the emp table with salaries greater than 3000.

You can verify the view's creation by attempting to link it as if it were a table. You can use it as a linked table, or in any valid SQL statement in an SPT.

```
Select * from MyView
```

or

```
Select MyView.ename, dept.deptno from MyView, Dept
Where MyView.deptno=Dept.deptno
```

Connections to Oracle Through ADO

Creating SPTs is a great way to interact with Oracle because it allows the server to do the work instead of Jet. As a matter of fact, Jet's not involved at all. You can get all the benefits of the SPTs, and much more, by making a connection to Oracle through ADO. This approach will enable you to effectively validate data, dynamically construct SQL statements, and execute stored procedures after manipulating and validating variables to use in those procedures. Also, your code can respond to your users in ways that your queries cannot.

Creating a connection to Oracle used to involve a lot of complex ODBC API calls or RDO, which was a DAO-like wrapper around ODBC. Now, we have ADO and OLEDB to present a fast, uniform, and flexible interface to a wide variety of different datasources and types, including Oracle.

For a detailed explanation of ADO and OLEDB see Chapter 6, "Introduction to ActiveX Data Objects," and Chapter 7, "Advanced ADO."

This section will look at ways of using ADO/OLEDB to connect to Oracle, issue SQL statements for data manipulation, and define data.

When using SPTs, Oracle does the work of resolving the SQL statement and rendering a result set, but the query is ad hoc. Oracle has no plan for it, so performance might be less than optimal. Furthermore, if several applications need the same query or procedure performed, it would have to be developed over and over again and distributed to all the different applications. A better approach may be to create a view or a stored procedure on the server that can be shared by a variety of applications, ensuring consistent results. Because the query or stored procedure has an execution plan, it may perform better than an ad hoc submission.

We've already seen how to create a view or a stored procedure by using an SPT. The SQL statement is the same, but using ADO code to make the connection and create the view or stored procedure is quite a bit different.

The examples in this chapter use the Oracle Native OLEDB Provider from Microsoft. This provider interfaces with Oracle's Call Interface (OCI). However, at this time, not everything that can be done through the OCI can be done through the OLEDB provider, or any other object interface for that matter. By far, most of the things that will need to do with Oracle can be performed through the existing functionality.

The code in Listing 17.1 will create a view in Oracle, and then open it and display the results in the debug window.

LISTING 17.1 CREATING A VIEW IN ORACLE FROM ACCESS

```
Function CreateOracleView() As Boolean

    Dim conn As New ADODB.Connection
    Dim cmd As New ADODB.Command

On Error GoTo CreateOracleView_Err

    With conn
        .Provider = "MSDAORA"
        .ConnectionString = "Data Source=empexample; _
          User ID=Scott;password=Tiger"
        .Open
    End With

    cmd.ActiveConnection = conn
    cmd.CommandType = adCmdText

    ' The Create or Replace SQL statement saves us some error handling
    cmd.CommandText = "Create or Replace View MyView As _
        Select * from emp where SAL>2000"
    cmd.Execute

CreateOracleView_Exit:
    conn.Close
    Set conn = Nothing
    Set cmd = Nothing
    Exit Function

CreateOracleView_Err:
    ' Failure
    CreateOracleView = False

    ' Find out what errors occured by looping through the Errors
    With conn
        For i = 0 To .Errors.Count - 1
            errDesc = errDesc & .Errors(i).Description & Chr(13)
```

continues

LISTING 17.1   CONTINUED

```
      Next
   End With

   ' Notify the user
   MsgBox "The following error(s) occured:  " & errDesc

   Resume CreateOracleView_Exit

End Function
```

Parameters

In Access, a developer can create parameter queries so that the same basic execution plan is used with different criteria values. Unfortunately, Oracle does not expose its views' parameters through OLEDB providers. An alternative is to replace existing views, as seen previously, or to use the OLEDB provider's command object to append and feed parameters for SQL statements that are then passed to Oracle.

The code in Listing 17.2 demonstrates how this is done.

LISTING 17.2   USING ORACLE PARAMETERS FROM ACCESS VBA

```
Function OracleParams(SalAmnt As Long) As Boolean

   Dim conn As New ADODB.Connection
   Dim rs As New ADODB.Recordset
   Dim rsfield as New Field
   Dim cmd As New ADODB.Command

   ' Make the connection
   With conn
       .Provider = "MSDAORA"
       .ConnectionString = "Data Source=empexample;_
          User ID=Scott;password=Tiger"
       .Open
   End With

   ' Use server side cursors in this case
   With rs
       .CursorLocation = adUseServer
   End With

   ' Build the command object
   With cmd
       cmd.ActiveConnection = conn
       ' Set the CommandType to accept a SQL statement
       cmd.CommandType = adCmdText
```

```
' Set the CommandText
cmd.CommandText = "Select * from emp where sal > ?"
' Create the parameter and Append it to the cmd object's
' Parameter collection
cmd.Parameters.Append _
    cmd.CreateParameter("SAL", adNumeric, adParamInput)
' Assign the SalAmnt's value to the command object's first
' parameter
cmd(0) = SalAmnt
End With

' Execute the command and assign the result set
' to the ADO recordset object
Set rs = cmd.Execute

If conn.Errors.Count = 0 Then
    OraclParams = True
End If

rs.MoveFirst

While Not rs.EOF
    strfield = ""
    For Each rsfield In rs.Fields
        strfield = strfield & "   " & rsfield
    Next
    Debug.Print strfield & Chr(9)
    rs.MoveNext
Wend

End Function
```

Creating Stored Procedures

A stored procedure in Oracle is similar to a code module in Access. It executes a set of steps on the server.

The main benefits of stored procedures are their speed, reliability, and security. They can be used to enforce business rules, validation, and transactions. The main drawbacks of Oracle's stored procedures is in the making and debugging of them. Oracle does not provide a development environment that would be familiar to an Access/VB developer. This makes building, maintaining, and replacing stored procedures difficult. Though Oracle8 provides a schema interface that validates procedures when you create them, it is still tough going. Additionally, stored procedures are specific to the server you are using, so if you have to migrate to another server, you'll have to rewrite the stored procedures.

N-tier architectures were developed partly in response to these drawbacks. There is no compelling reason to place all complex business logic on the server (just as there is no compelling reason to place it all on the client), so stored procedures themselves are becoming much simpler as other objects are handling business rules and other tasks.

This section will create and call a simple stored procedure from Access.

To create procedures in your own schema you must have the Create Procedure system privilege that is part of the Resource role. To create procedures in someone else's schema, you must have Create Any Procedure privileges. Consult your Oracle Database Administrator if you are not sure of your permissions.

Procedures break down into the following pieces:

- Declaration of arguments
- Beginning of processes
- Commitment of processes
- Exception handling
- Rollback of commitment
- Error handling

A simple stored procedure that adds a record to a simple To table with two fields would look like Listing 17.3:

LISTING 17.3 AN ORACLE PROCEDURE TO ADD A NEW RECORD

```
(Ename CHAR, EJob CHAR) IS
BEGIN
INSERT INTO SCOTT.TESTTABLE
VALUES(Ename, EJob);
COMMIT;
EXCEPTION
WHEN OTHERS THEN
ROLLBACK;
RAISE;
END;
```

In this case the stored procedure takes two arguments, a name and a job title, and supplies them to the SQL statement.

Access can create this procedure by way of an SPT as follows:

```
CREATE OR REPLACE PROCEDURE MyStoredProcedure
(Ename CHAR, EJob CHAR) IS
BEGIN
INSERT INTO SCOTT.TESTTABLE
```

```
VALUES(Ename, EJob);
COMMIT;
EXCEPTION
WHEN OTHERS THEN
ROLLBACK;
RAISE;
END;
```

Once this procedure is created, it can be executed through an SPT or through VBA.

Calling a Stored Procedure

Calling it from an SPT is a bit different than calling a view:

```
{call MyStoredProcedure }
```

The curly brackets mimic the syntax Oracle expects when addressed through its *call* interface, which is the interface used by OLEDB provider.

However, running the stored procedures from VBA through OLEDB provider for Oracle looks a bit different. The following function in Listing 17.4 takes advantage of the fact that stored procedures expose their parameters in a way that can be used in VBA. By supplying a stored procedure name, the name of the table into which you are going to insert a new record, and filling out the required arguments in the paramArray of the function, most stored procedures could be executed with the function in Listing 17.4, or a variation of it.

17

ACCESS 2000
FRONT-ENDS TO
ORACLE

LISTING 17.4 EXECUTING A STORED PROCEDURE WITH PARAMETERS FROM ACCESS VBA

```
Function RunOracleStoredProcedures(ProcName As String,
    DestTable as String, _
    ParamArray ParamArgs() As Variant) As Boolean

    Dim conn As New ADODB.Connection
    Dim rs As New ADODB.Recordset
    Dim i As Integer
    Dim cmd As New ADODB.Command
    Dim rsfield As Field
    Dim strfield As String

    With conn
        .Provider = "MSDAORA"
        .ConnectionString = "Data Source=empexample;_
            User ID=Scott;password=Tiger"
        .Open
    End With
```

continues

LISTING 17.4 CONTINUED

```
cmd.ActiveConnection = conn
cmd.CommandType = adCmdStoredProc
cmd.CommandText = ProcName

For i = 0 To UBound(ParamArgs())
    With cmd.Parameters(i)
        .Type = adChar
        .Direction = adParamInput
        .Value = ParamArgs(i)
    End With
Next

cmd.Execute

' Now we'll review the result in the debug window
' You would not need this code in reality    rs.Open
"Select * from " & destTable, conn, _
    adOpenForwardOnly, adLockReadOnly

rs.MoveFirst

While Not rs.EOF
    strfield = ""
    For Each rsfield In rs.Fields
        strfield = strfield & "    " & rsfield
    Next
    Debug.Print strfield & Chr(9)
    rs.MoveNext
Wend

Set rs = Nothing
conn.Close

RunOracleStoredProcedures = True

End Function
```

Calling many simple stored procedures from code gives you the ability to create complex procedural logic from within the familiar surroundings of VBA while taking advantage of the rich debugging and error-handling capabilities.

Creating an Unbound Interface to Oracle

Given the performance limitations and heavy network load of linked tables, Access applications using Oracle should consider using an unbound user interface when ever possible.

Creating an unbound interface frees you to employ n-tier architecture in your application, increasing your application's scalability and maintainability. It also allows you to mix your tools more freely. You can use ADO, ADOX, DAO, RDO, and so on where you think one may offer an advantage over another, or where it may simply be more familiar to you. An unbound interface makes future migrations to another development platform, like VB, easier than it would be from a bound interface. And by ensuring that the data processing work is performed on the server, you may gain some performance benefits as well.

The following exercise will create a simple, unbound interface to Oracle that looks and feels like a bound form. In order to show ADO's flexibility, there are SQL statements as well as recordset methods being employed.

The form will display records from the EMP table. You will be able to insert and delete records from the Oracle database. You will also be able to edit the records without having to consciously save each changed record.

Building an Unbound Interface

To start, build a form like the one in Figure 17.3.

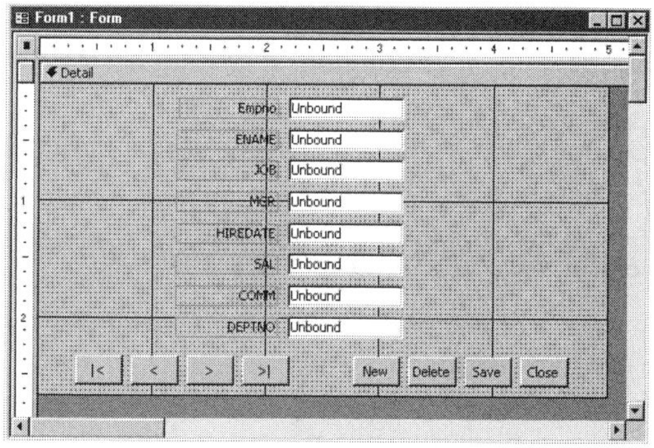

FIGURE 17.3

Data form in Design view.

For simplicity, the control names will correspond to the field names of the EMP table:

- Empno
- Ename
- Job
- Mgr
- Hiredate

- Sal
- Comm
- Deptno

The navigation and manipulation buttons will be named as follows:

- BtnGotoFirst
- BtnGotoPrevious
- BtnGotoNext
- BtnGotoLast
- BtnEdit
- BtnNew
- BtnDelete
- BtnSave
- BtnClose

Creating Global Variables

The basic tasks of this form can be handled in many ways. For simplicity and focus, the connection to the database, the recordset used by the form, and a flag to indicate if the data is being edited will be handled by three global variables declared in standard module:

```
Global conn As ADODB.Connection
Global rs As ADODB.Recordset
Global EditRec As Boolean
```

Loading Data and Initializing the Form

The code listed in Listing 17.5 will trigger the data loading and initialization of the application from the OnOpen event of the form.

LISTING 17.5 CREATE AN OPEN CONNECTION TO ORACLE AND FILL THE FORM

```
Private Sub Form_Open(Cancel As Integer)

    Set conn = New ADODB.Connection
    Set rs = New ADODB.Recordset

    With conn
        .Provider = "MSDAORA"
        .ConnectionString = "Data Source=empexample;_
```

```
            User ID=Scott;password=Tiger"
        .Open
    End With

    rs.CursorLocation = adUseClient
    rs.Open "Select * from emp", conn, adOpenStatic, _
        adLockOptimistic, adAsyncFetch

    FillForm

    EditRec = True

End Sub
```

Oracle does not return recordsets, but the OLEDB provider you are using allows you to capture the results of a SQL statement as a recordset. The OLEDB provider masks Oracle's call interface so it appears to you and behaves like any other data handled by OLEDB. By using a global recordset, you can quickly and easily fill the form's controls with the first record of data. It then sets the EditRec flag to true to indicate that the form's data is now ready to be edited. The OnOpen event calls the FillForm function listed in Listing 17.6.

LISTING 17.6 FILLING THE FORM WITH DATA

```
Function FillForm() As Boolean

On Error GoTo FillForm_Err

    [Empno] = rs(0)
    [ENAME] = rs(1)
    [Job] = rs(2)
    [MGR] = rs(3)
    [HIREDATE] = rs(4)
    [SAL] = rs(5)
    [COMM] = rs(6)
    [DEPTNO] = rs(7)

    FillForm = True

FillForm_Exit:
    Exit Function

FillForm_Err:
    FillForm = False
    Exit Function

End Function
```

Programming the Navigation Buttons

In order to move through the recordset, you need to program the navigation buttons as shown in Listings 17.7 through 17.10.

LISTING 17.7   GO TO FIRST RECORD

```
Private Sub btnGotoFirst_Click()

    On Error Resume Next

    rs.MoveFirst

    If Not rs.BOF Then
        FillForm
    End If

    CurrentContext Me

End Sub
```

LISTING 17.8   GO TO PREVIOUS RECORD

```
Private Sub btnGotoPrevious_Click()

    On Error Resume Next

    rs.MovePrevious

    If Not rs.BOF Then
        FillForm
    End If

    CurrentContext Me

End Sub
```

LISTING 17.9   GO TO NEXT RECORD

```
Private Sub btnGotoNext_Click()
    On Error Resume Next

    rs.MoveNext

    If Not rs.BOF Then
        FillForm
    End If
```

```
    CurrentContext Me

End Sub
```

LISTING 17.10   GO TO LAST RECORD

```
Private Sub btnGotoLast_Click()

    On Error Resume Next

    rs.MoveLast

    If Not rs.BOF Then
        FillForm
    End If

    On Error GoTo 0

    CurrentContext Me

End Sub
```

The current state of the navigation buttons depends on your position within the record set. The CurrentContext function, which takes the form as an argument, controls when to activate or deactivate the different navigation buttons, as shown in Listing 17.11.

LISTING 17.11   ACTIVATING AND DEACTIVATING THE NAVIGATION BUTTONS

```
Sub CurrentContext(frm As Form)

    Dim bFirstRec As Boolean
    Dim bLastRec As Boolean

    bFirstRec = (rs.AbsolutePosition = 1)
    bLastRec = (rs.AbsolutePosition = rs.RecordCount)

    With frm

        If Not bFirstRec And Not bLastRec Then
            !btnGotoFirst.Enabled = True
            !btnGotoPrevious.Enabled = True
            !btnGotoLast.Enabled = True
            !btnGotoNext.Enabled = True
            GoTo CurrentContext_Exit
        End If
```

continues

LISTING 17.11 CONTINUED

```
    If bFirstRec And bLastRec Then
        !btnEdit.SetFocus
        !btnGotoFirst.Enabled = False
        !btnGotoPrevious.Enabled = False
        !btnGotoLast.Enabled = False
        !btnGotoNext.Enabled = False
        GoTo CurrentContext_Exit
    End If

    If bFirstRec Then
        !btnGotoLast.Enabled = bFirstRec
        !btnGotoNext.Enabled = bFirstRec
        !btnGotoLast.SetFocus
        !btnGotoFirst.Enabled = Not bFirstRec
        !btnGotoPrevious.Enabled = Not bFirstRec
        GoTo CurrentContext_Exit
    End If

    If bLastRec Then
        !btnGotoFirst.Enabled = bLastRec
        !btnGotoPrevious.Enabled = bLastRec
        !btnGotoFirst.SetFocus
        !btnGotoLast.Enabled = Not bLastRec
        !btnGotoNext.Enabled = Not bLastRec
        GoTo CurrentContext_Exit
    End If

End With

End Sub
```

Updating Oracle Data Using the Form

So far, you can view data only, but none of the changes you make will be saved. The function in Listing 17.12 will use the Update method of the ADODB recordset to pass your changes along to Oracle as soon as you make them. This gives your interface behavior similar to a hyperactive bound form, when in fact it is not bound at all. This function, shown in Listing 17.12, must be called out of the AfterUpdate event of each text box.

LISTING 17.12 THE UpdateField FUNCTION

```
Function UpdateField(FieldName As Variant, NewValue As Variant) As Boolean

    If EditRec = False Or IsEmpty(EditRec) Then Exit Function
```

```
    Dim rsOrigSource As String
    Dim errDesc As String
    Dim i As Integer

    On Error GoTo UpdateField_Err

    ' Keep the original recordset's source around in the event of a
    ' failure
    rsOrigSource = rs.Source

    ' Attempt to update the field using the update method of the recordset
    rs.Update FieldName, NewValue

    ' Success
    UpdateField = True

UpdateField_Exit:
    Exit Function

UpdateField_Err:
    ' Failure
    UpdateField = False

    ' Find out what errors occured by looping through the Errors
    With conn
        For i = 0 To .Errors.Count - 1
            errDesc = errDesc & .Errors(i).Description & Chr(13)
        Next
    End With

    ' Notify the user
    MsgBox "The following error(s) occured:  " & errDesc

    ' Must counter the Update method with the CancelUpdate method
    ' otherwise you won't be able to manipulate the recordset object
    rs.CancelUpdate

    ' Close the existing recordset
    rs.Close

    ' Open the recordset with the old source, thereby setting
    ' the form back to its original condition
    rs.Open rsOrigSource, conn, adOpenStatic, adLockOptimistic,
adAsyncFetch

    ' Call FillForm
    Forms![form1].FillForm

    Resume UpdateField_Exit

End Function
```

The `UpdateField` function can be called from each `AfterUpdate` event by selecting all the text box controls at the same time and pasting in the expression in Listing 17.13. An alternative to saving changes immediately would be to buffer the changes and then save them when you move to a new record. You could also take advantage of ADO's ability to call a stored procedure in Oracle and pass the new values to its parameters.

LISTING 17.13 EXPRESSION TO SAVE CHANGES TO FIELDS AFTER UPDATE

```
=UpdateField(screen.activecontrol.[Name],screen.activecontrol)
```

Now when you cycle through the records and change a data item for an employee, the change is saved to Oracle as soon as you move to another field.

Adding Oracle Data Using the Form

To add a new record, you need to clear all the controls on the form and set the `EditRec` flag to false. The code in Listing 17.14 could be written into the `btnNew OnClick` event.

LISTING 17.14 PREPARING THE FORM FOR A NEW RECORD

```
Private Sub btnNew_Click()

    ClearForm
    EditRec = False

End Sub
```

A Utility function needs to be written to clear the form for edits and inserts. For our purposes, this can be located in a standard module behind the form. The function is exceedingly simple and is shown in Listing 17.15.

LISTING 17.15 CLEAR THE FORM

```
Sub ClearForm()

        Me![Empno]  = ""
        Me![ENAME]  = ""
        Me![Job]  = ""
        Me![MGR]  = ""
        Me![HIREDATE]  = ""
        Me![SAL]  = ""
        Me![COMM]  = ""
        Me![DEPTNO]  = ""

End Sub
```

Saving Oracle Data Using the Form

When it comes time to save the record, you can execute the following code from the btnSave Onclick event. It checks to see that you are entering a new record by checking the EditRec flag and then fills out a SQL statement and executes it in a command object. This technique is shown in Listing 17.16 as a way to address Oracle as it is customarily.

LISTING 17.16   ADDRESSING ORACLE THROUGH SQL AND ADO

```
Private Sub btnSave_Click()

    Dim cmd As New ADODB.Command
    Dim strCmdtxt as string

    ' If we are not editing a record then..+.
    If EditRec = False Then

        ' make sure the command object is properly configured and then
        ' construct and execute the Insert SQL statement
        With cmd
            .ActiveConnection = conn
            .CommandType = adCmdText
                with Me
                        strCmdtxt = strCmdtxt & "insert into emp values ("
                        strCmdtxt = strCmdtxt & "'![Empno] ',"
                        strCmdtxt = strCmdtxt & "'![ENAME] ',"
                        strCmdtxt = strCmdtxt & "'![Job] ',"
                        strCmdtxt = strCmdtxt & "'![MGR] ',"
                        strCmdtxt = strCmdtxt & "' to_date('" &![HIREDATE] &
                        "','MM/DD/YY') ',"
                        strCmdtxt = strCmdtxt & "'![SAL] ',"
                        strCmdtxt = strCmdtxt & "'![COMM] ',"
                end with

            .Execute
        End With
    End If

    ' Close, configure and reopen the recordset
    With rs
        .Close
        .CursorLocation = adUseClient
        .Open "Select * from emp", conn, adOpenStatic, adLockOptimistic,
        adAsyncFetch
    End With

    ' Fill the form, you may want to handle this differently.
    FillForm
```

continues

LISTING 17.16   CONTINUED

```
    ' Put the application back in edit mode
    EditRec = True

End Sub
```

Deleting Oracle Data Using the Form

The same basic approach is taken to delete a record. The code in Listing 17.17 will delete the current record from Oracle when executed from the OnClick event of btnDelete.

LISTING 17.17   DELETE THE CURRENT RECORD

```
Private Sub btnDelete_Click()

    Dim cmd As New ADODB.Command

    ' If we are not editing a record then...
    If EditRec = True Then

        ' make sure the command object is properly configured and then
        ' construct and execute the Delete SQL statement
        With cmd
            .ActiveConnection = conn
            .CommandType = adCmdText
            .CommandText = "Delete from emp where empno= " & Me![Empno]
            .Execute
        End With
    End If

    ' Close, configure and reopen the recordset
    With rs
        .Close
        .CursorLocation = adUseClient
        .Open "Select * from emp", conn, adOpenStatic, adLockOptimistic,
        adAsyncFetch
    End With

    ' Fill the form, you may want to handle this differently.
    FillForm

End Sub
```

To make the navigation buttons reflect the context of your form's navigation through the available records, the code in Listing 17.18 can be written into the form's OnCurrent event.

LISTING 17.18   POPULATE FIELDS WITH DATA, THEN CHECK CURRENT CONTEXT OF THE
FORM

```
Private Sub Form_Current()

On Error Resume Next

    Dim bFirstRec As Boolean
    Dim bLastRec As Boolean

    If Not rs.BOF Then
        With Me
            ![Empno] = rs(0)
            ![ENAME] = rs(1)
            ![Job] = rs(2)
            ![MGR] = rs(3)
            ![HIREDATE] = rs(4)
            ![SAL] = rs(5)
            ![COMM] = rs(6)
            ![DEPTNO] = rs(7)
        End With
    End If

    CurrentContext Me

End Sub
```

Closing the Connection to Oracle

When closing the form, close the connection to Oracle and set the connection and
recordset objects to nothing. In other applications, you may want to keep the objects
around. The function in Listing 17.19 will handle these housekeeping chores.

LISTING 17.19   CLEANING UP ON Close

```
Private Sub btnClose_Click()
On Error GoTo Err_btnClose_Click_Err

    DoCmd.Close

Exit_btnClose_Click_Exit:
    conn.Close
    Set conn = Nothing
    Set rs = Nothing
    Exit Sub

Err_btnClose_Click_Err:
    MsgBox err.Description
    Resume Exit_btnClose_Click_Exit

End Sub
```

By managing other recordset objects, persistent recordset objects, and by using the OLEDB provider's simplification of the Oracle call interface, you can create an entire unbound interface to Oracle, thereby taking full advantage of the speed, scalability, and robustness of Oracle in your Access application.

Summary

In this chapter I explored some of the different ways to use Oracle in your Access solution. You saw the convenience of Linked tables, but you also learned of their drawbacks. SQL pass-through queries overcome the problems caused by local processing of linked tables. You saw how to create and use them, with a review of the SQL and function differences you must negotiate with Oracle to get the results you want.

Giving Oracle ad hoc instructions in a SPT is not a good way to use Oracle to the fullest in most cases. To learn to use Oracle fully, you created, modified, and ran views and stored procedures using only Access tools. This makes Oracle put its query executing plans to work, while at the same time drastically cutting network traffic when compared to using linked tables. This is Oracle development more than Access development.

Finally, to demystify the use of Oracle, you created a simple unbound interface was created that almost anyone could build—even if they do not have permissions to create and modify views and procedures. By using the OLEDB provider for Oracle, the techniques used to build that interface look almost identical to any other unbound interface using OLEDB provider.

This chapter was intended as a primer for using Oracle, but no single chapter can cover everything you will possibly need to develop your next great Oracle application. Microsoft's Web site and Oracle Press have some excellent material available for further study.

Interoperability

IN THIS PART

Using ActiveX Automation

CHAPTER 18

Today, more than ever, developers are asked to build more sophisticated applications faster and integrate them with other software.

Fortunately, with ActiveX Automation (formerly called OLE Automation), applications can work together to provide a comprehensive software solution. This can substantially speed up development time because instead of creating a feature, developers can integrate and use other software that has the feature.

This chapter will cover the principles and techniques for ActiveX Automation. Chapter 19, "Integration with Office 2000," will specifically explain how to use ActiveX Automation to integrate Access with the rest of Microsoft Office.

What Is ActiveX Automation?

ActiveX technology is based on Microsoft's Component Object Model (COM). ActiveX Automation enables programs to interact with each other. Automation specifically enables one program to access and manipulate another program's objects from outside that application. An example of Automation is printing letters or reports in Microsoft Word from Microsoft Access.

Why Use Automation?

Using Automation is an effective way to build and extend applications. Automation can substantially speed up development time because rather than developing and testing a feature from scratch, you can "borrow" the functionality from another application.

There is no reason today to build your own word processor or spreadsheet functionality within your Access application. It is much easier to use Automation and some of the techniques discussed in this chapter to automate Word or Excel for that functionality. This enables a developer to focus on features not provided by other programs that can be of benefit to users.

Distinguishing Automation Server Versus Automation Client

When two applications are interacting with one another, it is important to distinguish which application is exposing its objects and which application is using those objects. The Automation Server is the application that exposes the Automation objects. The Automation Client (or sometimes referred to as Automation Controller) is the application that decides which objects to use and when to use them.

For example, if a command button on an Access form is clicked and prints a letter in Word, the Automation Server is Word and the Automation Client is Access.

Determining Automation Resource Requirements

Because Automation involves one application controlling another, at a minimum, two programs are open. Whenever multiple applications are running, additional processing power and memory is required. What requirements are necessary to automate from Access to Word, for example, is a subjective decision. What one user might find satisfactory, another might find unacceptable. The minimum acceptable performance would be a Pentium II processor with 24MB of RAM. Certainly, a Pentium processor would substantially improve performance; however, RAM is more beneficial than processing power. If Automation performance is not acceptable, you should increase the amount of RAM first and upgrade the processor second.

Understanding the Big Picture

There are three steps to Automation:

1. Get the Automation object. Either create a new one or reference an existing one.

2. Use the Automation object as needed in your application.

3. Release the Automation object.

As an example, if you would like to print letters or reports in Word from Access, the first step would be to create or get a reference to the Word application. Next, use Word's objects, properties, and methods (such as open, modify, or print a document). Finally, release the Word application.

Creating and Setting a Reference to Another Application

To automate to another application, it is necessary to set a reference to the other application by creating an object variable and assigning it to an instance of the application.

Setting a Reference to Another Application

With Automation, you are interacting or using an application outside of Microsoft Access. Whenever an application or component is used outside of Access, you must set a reference to that application. To do so, go to the Visual Basic Editor and choose Tools, References. A Reference dialog box will display a list of type libraries, programs, DLLs, and ActiveX controls (see Figure 18.1). Set a reference to the application you would like to automate. For example, to set a reference to Word 2000, check the box next to Microsoft Word 9.0 Object Library.

FIGURE 18.1
The References dialog box.

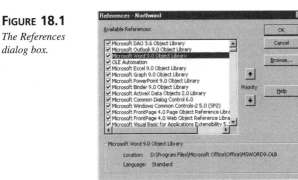

TIP

If you cannot find the item that you would like to set a reference to in the References dialog box, click the Browse button to locate the application in the file system.

After you have set a reference to another application, you can review and use its objects, properties, and methods.

Reviewing Objects, Properties, and Methods

Before discussing how to use another application's objects, let's review some basics. It is essential to understand the terms object, properties, and methods, or the rest of the Automation chapter will make no sense.

An *object* is an item that can be programmed, manipulated, or controlled. In Access, objects include forms, text boxes, command buttons, and more. With Automation, other applications and their objects can be programmed and manipulated from Access. Microsoft Office has more than 500 objects that can be programmed, manipulated, or controlled. For example, Word has a Document object and Excel has a Workbook object.

A *property* is a characteristic of an object. A property can be thought of as an adjective because it describes or characterizes an object. In Access, properties of a text box include Name, Visible, Forecolor, and more. Likewise, when using objects in other applications, those objects have properties that can be manipulated via Automation. For example, similar to an Access form, Word and Excel applications can be set to visible or invisible. Most properties of an object can be both set and retrieved.

A *method* is an action that can be taken on an object. A method can be thought of as a verb. For example, a method of an Access form is Close. An example of a method in Excel is Quit which closes the Excel application.

Understanding Object Models

When automating to another application, it is helpful to review its Object Model to understand what objects are available to work with. The *Object Model* is a representation (in outline form) of an application's objects. This is a quick and easy way to determine what objects in the application are available to program, manipulate, or control. Object Models for various applications can be found in the Help files. Object Models for the Microsoft Office programs are shown in Chapter 19.

Using the Object Browser

Another way to quickly determine the objects available in an application is to use the Object Browser. The advantages of the Object Browser are that it includes properties, methods, and events, and it has links to online help. The Object Browser is a helpful tool to quickly search, find, and learn about the various objects of an application.

To use the Object Browser in the Visual Basic Editor, under the View menu, choose Object Browser or press F2. See Figure 18.2.

18

USING ACTIVEX
AUTOMATION

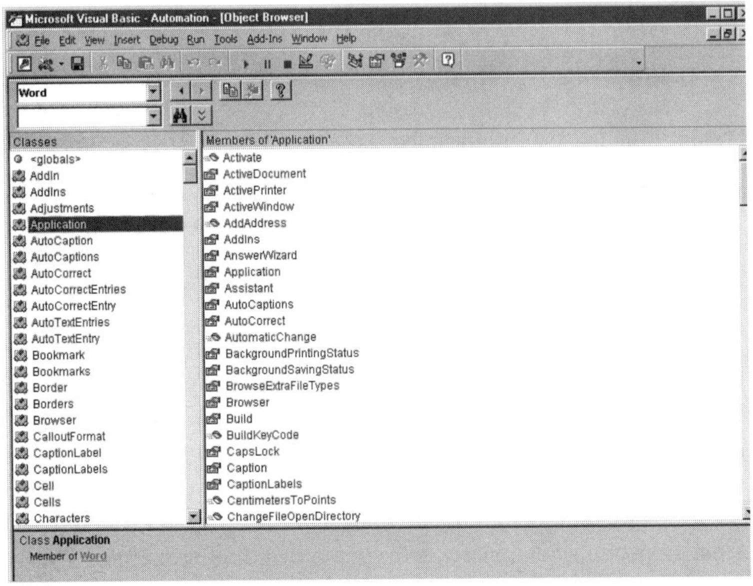

FIGURE 18.2

*Object Browser
showing Microsoft
Word objects.*

When first opening the Object Browser, the combo box in the top left corner will be set to All Libraries. With this setting, the Object Browser is showing all objects for all referenced libraries. The first step might be to select the application in the combo box for the objects that you want to review. For example, if Word is selected, only Word objects will be shown.

The other combo box can be used to search for a particular item. For example, if you want to search for a message box in all libraries, set the top combo box to All Libraries, and in the combo box beneath it type MsgBox and click on the binoculars icon (see Figure 18.3).

The lower left pane of the Object Browser is entitled Classes. The classes list shows the available types of objects in the selected type library. When an item is selected in the classes list, the properties, methods, and events are shown in the Members Of list.

The lower-right pane, entitled Members, shows the items related to the particular class chosen on the left side. For example, if the application object is selected, the right pane Members will show all the application's objects properties, methods, and events. The Members Of list displays the properties, methods, events, and constants that are associated with the selected object in the classes list.

Where does the Object Browser get information about the objects, properties, and methods? Most applications that ship today contain a type library file which has information about the application's objects, properties, methods, and constants. The Object Browser shows information from the type library. Type library files usually have a .TLB or .OLB file extension.

FIGURE 18.3

Search for MsgBox in the Object Browser.

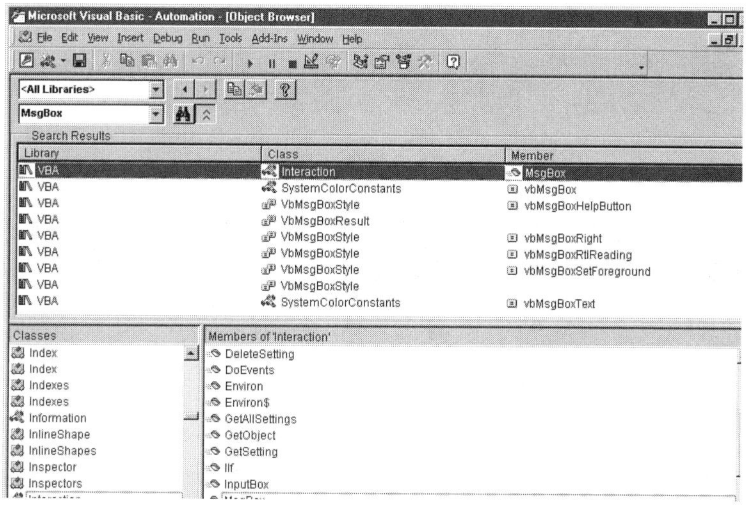

> **TIP**
>
> By default, the items listed in the Classes and Members panes are in alphabetical order. It is useful to right-click on the panes in the shortcut menu and choose Group Members. This will re-sort the items in the list by putting together all the properties, methods, and events. The items within each property, method, and event are sorted in alphabetical order.

At the very bottom of the Object Browser, the syntax is shown for the item selected. For example, with the Access `Application` object selected and by choosing the `Dlookup`, the correct syntax is shown at the very bottom of the Object Browser. For further information, after an item is selected, press F1 to review the online help for the item.

Creating an Object Variable

A *variable* is a chunk of memory set aside to store or retrieve information. Undoubtedly, you have had a great deal of experience with simple variables, such as strings and integers. The following are examples of declaring and using two simple variables:

```
Dim strName as String
Dim I as integer

StrName = "Bob"
I = 10
```

In the preceding examples, the variables include a specific type of data and the information is stored and can be retrieved as needed.

`Object` variables are declared with the `Dim` statement just like simple variables:

```
Dim objWord as Word.application
Dim objExcel as Excel.application
```

> **TIP**
>
> Fully qualify all objects used in Automation. Instead of
>
> ```
> Dim objWord as Application
> ```
>
> use
>
> ```
> Dim objWord as Word.Application
> ```
>
> Several referenced programs might have an application object. Fully qualifying the object variable assures that the code will run properly.

Referencing an Application That Is Already Running

After creating an object variable, the next step is to actually reference the application you want to automate. However, remember, you have no idea whether the application you want to automate is already open on the user's computer. If you want to automate Word, the user might already have Word open. If this is the case, you might want to use the current instance of Word for your Automation session. Otherwise, you will be opening a separate instance of Word and rapidly consuming additional resources on the computer.

To determine whether an instance of the application is running, use the `GetObject` function. The `GetObject` function will reference an application that is already running.

```
' Declare objWord as an Object Variable.
Dim objWord As Word.Application

' Use "GetObject" function to use an application that is already running.
Set objWord = GetObject(, "Word.Application")
```

Assigning an Object Variable to an Application

The Set keyword is used to assign the reference of the object variable to the object. For example:

```
Set objExcel = Excel.Application
```

Object variables hold a pointer to an object. When an object variable is assigned to the Excel application, the object variable contains a pointer to the Excel application; it does not hold the entire Excel application within the variable. When objects are passed from one procedure to another, they are always passed by "reference," never by "value."

Creating an Instance of the Application

If the application is not open or you want to create a new instance of the application, use the New keyword. The following example would create a new instance of Microsoft Word:

```
' Declare objWord as an Object Variable.
Dim objWord As Word.Application

' Create a new instance of Microsoft Word.
Set objWord = New Word.Application
```

18

USING ACTIVEX
AUTOMATION

CAUTION

Always declare the Dim statement and Set statement on separate lines. Do not combine the Dim and Set statements on a single line such as

```
Dim objWord = New Word.application.
```

If you combine the Dim and Set statement on one line, the code will execute more slowly and you will not know exactly when the object is instantiated (comes into memory).

Using `GetObject` and the `New` Keyword Together

If an application is already open, use it; do not open another version of the application. If the application is not running, create a new instance of the application. To accomplish this, use the `GetObject` function to see if the application is running, and the `New` keyword to start a new instance of the application (if necessary).

```
' If Word is running, use it. If Word is not running, create an instance
' of Word._

' Declare objWord as an Object Variable.
Dim objWord As Word.Application

' An error will occur with GetObject if Word is not running. Ignore the
' error.
On Error Resume Next

' Attempt to reference Word which is already running.
Set objWord = GetObject(, "Word.Application")

' If objWord is Nothing (an uninstantiated Object Variable), Word is
' not running.
If objWord Is Nothing Then

        ' Create a new instance of the Word application.
        Set objWord = New Word.Application

        ' If objWord is still "Nothing" assume MS Word 9.0 is not
        ' installed on the computer.
        If objWord Is Nothing Then

                MsgBox "MS Word 2000 is not installed on your computer"

        End If

End If

' On Error GoTo ErrorHandler (Put Error Handler Code Here!)
```

> **NOTE**
>
> The New keyword can only be used if you can create a reference to the application's type library.

Using Early Versus Late Binding

Notice that the object variable in the Dim and Set statements specifically references the Word.Application. This is referred to as early binding. At compile time, the object variable is bound to the Word application's type library. This will result in the code executing much faster because much of the work is done at compile time rather than at runtime.

On the other hand, if objWord were declared as an object, the binding to the Word application's type library would not occur until runtime. This would slow the execution of the code substantially.

The following example summarizes the point:

```
' Use early binding, it's faster.
Dim objWord as Word.Application

' Late binding, this code is slower.
Dim objWord as Object
```

> **TIP**
>
> In the Automation.mdb included in Chapter 19 there are speed test examples that show that early binding is substantially faster than late binding.

Using the CreateObject Function

The most efficient Automation code will declare object variables with a specific class (early binding), use the GetObject function to determine if the application is already running, and use the New keyword to create an instance of the application if it is not running.

Unfortunately, in some cases, it is not possible to use Early Binding or the New keyword. The CreateObject function is useful in these circumstances.

When Other Applications Cannot Be Referenced

When using Automation from some applications (fortunately not Access), you cannot create a reference to another application (there is no references dialog box). Examples include Outlook 97/98 and Internet development. In these cases, you are forced to use late binding and the `CreateObject` function. The following is an example of Automation code you can write within Outlook to automate to Word.

> **NOTE**
>
> You can still use the `GetObject` function to determine whether or not Word is currently running. The `CreateObject` function creates a new instance of the application.

```
' Declare objWord as an Object Variable.
Dim objWord As Word.Application

' An error will occur with GetObject if Word is not running. Ignore the
' error.
On Error Resume Next

' Attempt to reference Word which is already running.
Set objWord = GetObject(, "Word.Application")

' Error 429 occurs if Word is NOT running.
If Err.Number = 429 Then

        Err.Number = 0

        ' Create a new instance of the Word application.
        Set objWord = CreateObject("Word.Application")

        ' If error 429 occurs again, assume MS Word 9.0 is not installed
        ' on the computer.

        If Err.Number = 429 Then

                MsgBox "MS Word 2000 is not installed on your computer"

        End If

End If


' On Error GoTo ErrorHandler (Put Error Handler Code Here!)
```

When Users Have Different Versions of the Application

In some companies, different users can be running different versions of an application. Some users might be using Word 95, others Word 97, whereas still others are using Word 2000. A few users might even have multiple versions of Word on the same computer!

With the CreateObject function, you can pass as a parameter which particular version of Word to use. The following example uses CreateObject to open Word 97:

```
' Declare objWord as an Object Variable.
Dim objWord As Word.Application

' Create a new instance of a Word 97 application.
Set objWord = CreateObject("Word.Application.8")
```

> **NOTE**
>
> The version number for Office 95 programs is 7.0; Office 97 is 8.0; and Office 2000 is 9.0. You can also pass a parameter with the version number when using the New keyword.

Using the Automation Object's Properties and Methods

After you have an instance of the object, you can program, manipulate, and control the object's properties and methods.

Setting an Object's Properties

This is where Automation really pays off. You can now work with other applications to use their features and functionality. In the same way that you work with an object's properties in Access, you can work with the Automation object's properties. The following examples use properties in Word and Excel:

```
' Setting an Automation Object's Properties
objWord.Visible = True
objExcel.Cells(1,1).Value = "Yearly Sales"
```

Setting an Object's Methods

With Automation, you can execute an object's method. The following are a few examples:

```
' Executing an Object's "Add" Method
objWord.Documents.Add
objExcel.Workbooks.Add
```

> **TIP**
>
> Chapter 19 includes numerous examples of automating to Microsoft Office applications. In that chapter, objects, properties, and methods of various applications will be discussed in detail.

Releasing the Automation Object

When you are done with the object variable, release it by setting the object equal to `Nothing`. In this way, valuable resources can be reclaimed. The proper syntax is as follows:

```
' Release the Object Variable
Set objWord = Nothing
```

> **TIP**
>
> When you dimension an object variable, immediately go to the bottom of the procedure and `Set` the object variable equal to `Nothing`. This prevents you from forgetting to release object variables after writing a long procedure.

Putting It All Together

I have now reviewed all the steps to make Automation work. Let's now look at a code sample that puts it all together. This example will print a Word document with Automation. All the steps previously discussed are included in the code: creating or getting a reference to Word; using Word's objects (specifically the `PrintOut` method); and releasing the `Automation` object.

```
' Declare objWord as an Object Variable.
Dim objWord As Word.Application

' An error will occur with GetObject if Word is not running. Ignore the
' error.
On Error Resume Next

' Attempt to reference Word which is already running.
Set objWord = GetObject(, "Word.Application")

' If objWord is Nothing (an object variable that does not refer to an
' object), Word is not running.
If objWord Is Nothing Then

        ' Create a new instance of the Word application.
        Set objWord = New Word.Application

        ' If objWord is still "Nothing" assume MS Word 9.0 is not
        ' installed on the computer.
        If objWord Is Nothing Then

                MsgBox "MS Word 2000 is not installed on your computer"

        End If

End If

' On Error GoTo ErrorHandler (Put Error Handler Code Here!)

' Open a Word document.
objWord.Documents.Open ("C:\Automation\Northwind Magazine Ad.doc")

' Print the Word document
objWord.PrintOut Background:=False

' Close Word
objWord.Quit

' Release the object variable.
Set objWord = Nothing
```

18

**USING ACTIVEX
AUTOMATION**

TIP

Admittedly, this is a very simple example. Chapter 19 covers more complex
Automation code and the Automation.MDB file for that chapter has thousands
of lines of Automation code for your use.

Closing the Automation Server Application

During the course of an Automation session, you can use a current instance of the application that is running, or open a new instance of the application. It is important that you close the Automation Server application under the appropriate circumstances.

If the application is already running when you start the Automation session, and you use that instance of the application, do not close the application at the end of the Automation session. Users will become exceedingly frustrated if applications they use are closed by your code.

If, on the other hand, you create a new instance of the application, you should close the application at the end of the Automation session. If not, the application will remain open unused by the user, but taking up valuable computer resources.

To close an application, use the appropriate method for the application. For example, with Excel, call the `Quit` method as follows:

```
' Close the Excel application by calling the "Quit" method.
objExcel.Quit
```

Using the `UserControl` Property to Determine How an Application Was Opened

The `UserControl` property enables you to determine whether an application or document was created or opened by the user or programmatically. If the `UserControl` property (a Boolean) is true, the application or document was opened by the user; if false, the application or document was opened programmatically.

The following example opens Word programmatically and then tests how Word was opened using the `UserControl` property.

```
' Declare objWord as an Object Variable.
Dim objWord As Word.Application

' Open Word programmatically.
Set objWord = New Word.Application

' Check the UserControl property to see if Word was opened
' by the user or opened programmatically.
If objWord.Application.UserControl Then

        MsgBox "The Word application was opened by the user".

Else

        MsgBox "The Word application was opened programmatically".

End If

Set objWord = Nothing
```

Using `WithEvents` to Expose Events of the Automation Server

Using Automation as discussed so far in this chapter is analogous to a one-way telephone call. Access, for example, has controlled and directed Word to do certain things. Using the `WithEvents` keyword, you can actually create a two-way communication between Access and Word. Access can direct Word to print a letter or report and Word can respond back to Access when certain events occur.

First, it is important to determine what events can be reported back by the calling application. The easiest way to determine this is to use the Object Browser. Click on the application object and see if there are any events listed. Word 97 had only two events exposed by the `Application` object (`DocumentChange` and `Quit`). Word 2000 now has 12 events exposed by the `Application` object. See Figure 18.4, which shows the Object Browser. When referring to an object, different icons indicate properties (a finger pointing to a sheet of paper), methods (green flying erasers), and Events (lightning bolts).

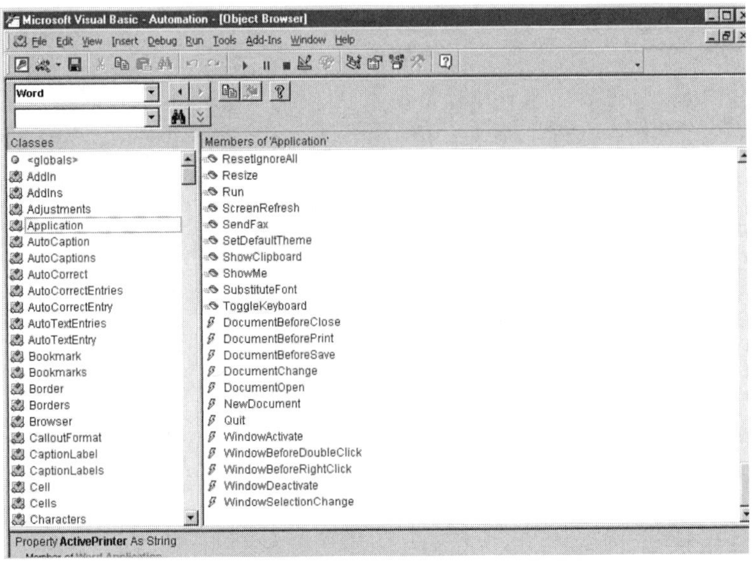

FIGURE **18.4**

*The Object
Browser shows
Microsoft Word
2000 exposed
events.*

Microsoft Excel exposes even more events than Word. Excel 2000's application object
exposes 21 events (see Figure 18.5).

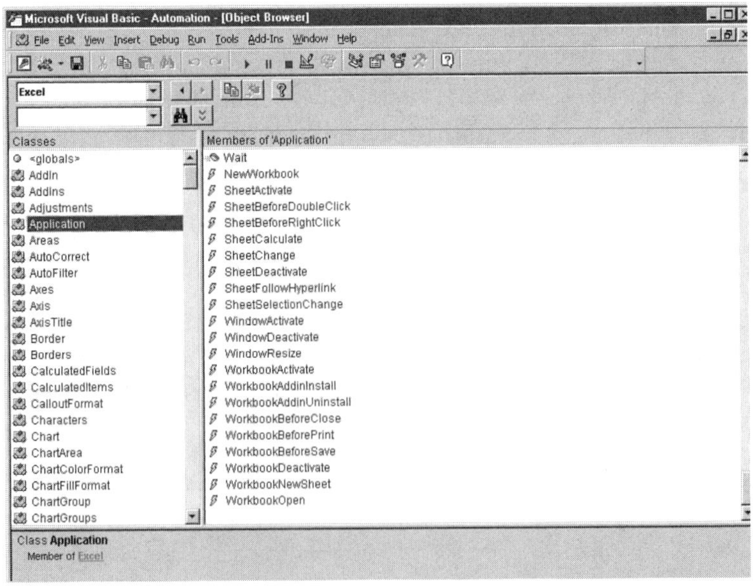

FIGURE **18.5**

*The Object
Browser shows
Microsoft Excel
2000 exposed
events.*

Making `WithEvents` Work

Normally, when using Automation within a procedure, you dimension the object variable in a procedure as follows:

```
Dim objWord as Word.application
```

To use `WithEvents`, move the `Dim` statement out of the procedure and create a module-level variable instead. Because a module-level variable will be used, the `Dim` keyword should be changed to `Private` or `Public`. You can also use the `WithEvents` keyword to expose the events of the application.

```
' Declare module level variable using "WithEvents" keyword.
Private objWord WithEvents as Word.application
```

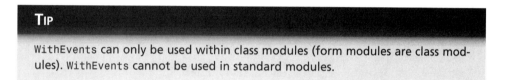

TIP

`WithEvents` can only be used within class modules (form modules are class modules). `WithEvents` cannot be used in standard modules.

See Figure 18.6, which shows how to declare a module-level variable using the `WithEvents` keyword.

18

USING ACTIVEX
AUTOMATION

FIGURE 18.6

Declare module-level variable using the `WithEvents` *keyword.*

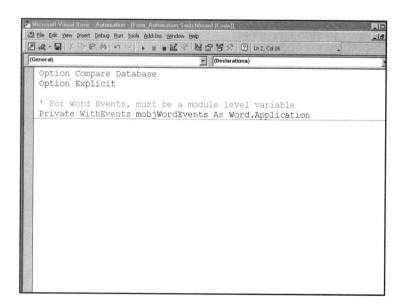

After declaring the module-level variable using the `WithEvents` keyword, examine the combo boxes at the top of the module window. In the left column box, choose the application that is the Automation Server. Now, in the combo box on the right side, you will see the events that are exposed by the application. Choose any of these events and the procedure will appear in the code window where you can write code to respond to the event.

Figure 18.7 shows procedures using the exposed Word events `Document Change` and `Quit`.

FIGURE 18.7

Procedures using exposed events of Microsoft Word.

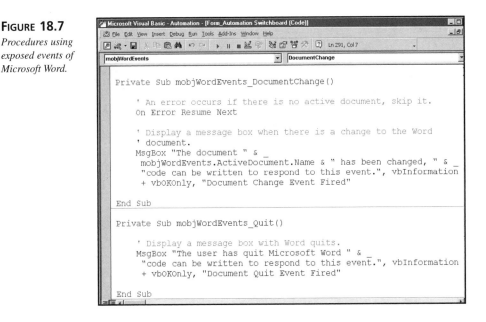

Using the Automation Tips and Techniques

Traditionally, `Automation` has received a lot of bad press because of poor performance. In reality, with reasonable hardware and proper coding techniques, `Automation` runs efficiently today. Please keep in mind the following concepts when using `Automation`.

Set References, Use Early Binding, and the New Keyword

To start an Automation session, set a reference to the application with the references dialog box. Use a specific class when dimensioning the object variable and use the New keyword to instantiate a new instance of the object. All these issues have been discussed previously in this chapter.

Use an Existing Application If It Is Already Open

Do not open a new instance of an application in every Automation session. If an application is already open on the user's machine, use the existing instance of the application for the Automation session.

Turn ScreenUpdating Off

During a typical Automation session with Word or Excel, a tremendous amount of screen updating and paints are occurring. As far as performance is concerned, if ScreenUpdating is turned off, the performance improves because processing will be less intensive. The best technique is to turn ScreenUpdating off, complete all the Automation work, and then turn ScreenUpdating back on at the end. The user then sees the completed document at one time when it is completed. The following code illustrates this:

```
' Turn Off Screen Updating.
Application.ScreenUpdating = False

' Automation Code Runs Here!

' Turn On Screen Updating.
Application.ScreenUpdating = True
```

TIP

I once mistakenly distributed an application with ScreenUpdating left on, which slowed down the application's performance. In the next version, ScreenUpdating was turned off to improve performance. I received so many complaints from users that I had to revise and redistribute the application with ScreenUpdating turned back on. The users explained that while the screen was being refreshed, they had an opportunity to read the document, to start reviewing it, or to make sure it was the correct document to print. By forcing the user to wait until all the automation work was complete before making the document visible, they lost three to five seconds of review time. They also thought it was somewhat cool to watch the documents being "magically" constructed piece by piece on the screen. Therefore, the lesson was to consider the "processing time" of human beings in reviewing the documents, not just the processing of the computer.

Give the Users Feedback

If an Automation session will take some time, definitely give the users feedback to indicate that progress is being made. This might mean showing a progress meter, an hourglass cursor, or some other visual cue. If not, the user might turn off the computer thinking it is locked up. Remember, with Automation, more than one application is open. If the computer is abruptly shut off, devastating consequences can result.

You know as a developer that providing visual feedback, such as a progress meter, can in fact slow down the time it takes to complete the process. Nevertheless, what is important is not the real time it takes to complete a process, but the "perceived" time. Users report that a process seems to take less time when visual cues are provided even though, in fact, the process actually took longer.

> **TIP**
>
> I created an application for an aerospace company that involved very sophisticated Excel Automation code. While the process was occurring, a small icon of an airplane flew across the screen. The users were more excited about the little airplane flying across the screen than the complex Automation code doing the work.

Have the Automation Server Run the Code

It is always faster to let the Automation Server run its own code. For example, if an Access application automates to Word, first create the instance of the Word document object. Then, place all the VBA code, which controls and manipulates Word (such as changing fonts or styles of the text, or printing the document), in Word.

In other words, have an application run its own code. If Word's objects, properties, or methods are being used, put the VBA code in Word. Otherwise, cross-process communication is occurring between Access and Word for each statement of code. By following this technique, you will substantially improve performance.

> **TIP**
>
> VBA code in applications such as Word and Excel are placed in templates. To make it easier to distribute templates, place the templates in a shared folder on the network server. Under the Tools menu in Word, for example, under File Locations, workgroup templates can be set to that network drive location. When changes need to be made to the code or new templates added, they can simply be copied to the network drive where the workgroup templates are stored.

Use the `With/End With` Construct

There are two good reasons to use the `With/End With` construct. First, the code runs more efficiently because the object is referenced once instead of with each statement of code. The second reason is readability. Think of every dot as a speed bump on a race-track. The fewer dots the better! Consider the following examples:

Example 1: The object is referenced on each line of code, which will cause it to more slowly. It is also harder to read.

```
objExcel.Range("F6").Select
objExcel.ActiveCell.FormulaR1C1 = "Yearly Sales"
objExcel.Range("G6").Select
objExcel.ActiveCell.FormulaR1C1 = "Sales Summary"
objExcel.Range("F7").Select
```

Example 2: The object is referenced only once, which will cause it to run more quickly. The code is also easier to read.

```
With objExcel

        .Range("F6").Select
        .ActiveCell.FormulaR1C1 = "Northwind Traders"
        .Range("G6").Select
        .ActiveCell.FormulaR1C1 = "Sales Summary"
        .Range("F7").Select

End With
```

Release Object Variables

As discussed earlier, always release the object variable at the end of the Automation session by setting it equal to Nothing to reclaim valuable resources.

Do Not Display Dialog Boxes and Message Boxes

Generally, avoid actions that cause the Automation session to stop, such as dialog boxes and message boxes. If a stoppage does occur, it might not be seen by the user because another application might have focus at the time.

Use Error Handling

Automation adds a great deal of complexity to an application. The benefit of using features from other applications has the downside that more can go wrong. It is essential that an Error Handler be in place to handle any errors that might occur during an Automation session. With Microsoft Office applications, the server application can return error information. See Chapter 13, "Professional Error Handling," for additional information about Error Handling.

Summary

In this chapter, the principles and techniques of Automation were discussed. Automation enables applications to work together affording the developer an opportunity to create complete software solutions. It is certainly easier to learn these principles than to create a word processor, spreadsheet, or other feature that is already included in another application. Creating an instance of another application, using the application, and closing the automation session were discussed. Many automation tips were covered to improve the performance of Automation. Chapter 19, "Integration with Office 2000," will discuss integrating Access applications with other Microsoft Office 2000 applications.

CHAPTER 19

Integration with Office 2000

In the preceding chapter, the principles and techniques of Automation are discussed. Now, let's apply that knowledge using all the applications in Microsoft Office 2000.

In this chapter, you will learn how to automate from Access to other Microsoft applications such as Word, Excel, PowerPoint, Outlook, Graph, MapPoint, FrontPage, and the Binder.

> **TIP**
>
> See the chapter code examples. There are thousands of lines of automation code for Access, Word, Excel, PowerPoint, Outlook, Graph, FrontPage, and MapPoint (see Figure 19.1).

FIGURE 19.1

The Automation.MDB file.

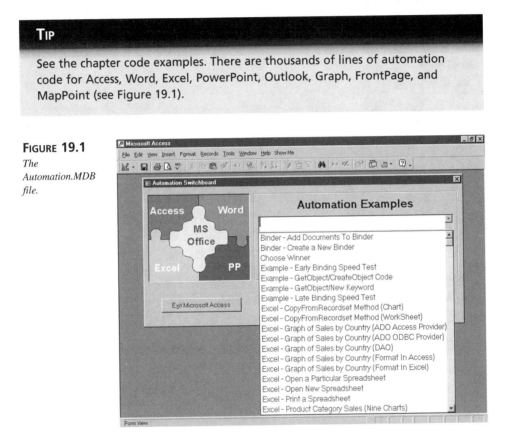

Why Integrate with Office 2000?

Office 2000 is an entire suite of products to help meet the needs and demands of customers. These products offer a tremendous number of features that have been developed and fully tested by Microsoft. Office 2000 exposes hundreds of objects that developers can manipulate programmatically using VBA. No other office suite today provides the power and integration that Office 2000 offers.

To create a full-featured application, you can utilize the many features of Office 2000 applications as described following.

Using Word

Word is an excellent choice to create invoices, letters, interoffice memos, and business reports. Word is a terrific report writer!

As a developer, you can create fancy documents in Access or Excel, but why go through the effort? Word has all the styles and formatting capability you will ever need.

Using Excel

When you need to crunch numbers, Excel is a great choice. Create impressive graphs and charts for office meetings, customer proposals, Board of Director meetings, and more.

Using PowerPoint

When it's show time, choose PowerPoint. Impressive, high-quality presentations can be produced with relative ease. Create effective demonstrations for product sales, staff meetings, Board of Director meetings, investor presentations, and more.

Using Outlook

Outlook provides numerous features that you can plug into your application. Use Outlook's email for company email, Internet email, automatic mailing of orders to the shipping department, automatic ordering of products as needed, billing of customers, and more.

Rather than build a calendar in your application, automate to Outlook for these features. Employees can maintain their own personal calendars as well as an office calendar.

Outlook provides task management, which can be used for employees' personal to-do lists, office to-do lists, special projects, and more.

Outlook contacts can be used to maintain separate personal and office Rolodex files. Certainly, a contact management database can be created in Access, but why go through the effort when Outlook is ready to use today?

Using Graph

Microsoft Graph is a useful tool to graph data in Access and other Office applications.

19

INTEGRATION WITH
OFFICE 2000

Using MapPoint

MapPoint is a useful tool to search for and display map information. With Automation, an address can be read from a database. A map can then be displayed showing the exact location of the address.

Using FrontPage

The Web is essential in today's business world. Use FrontPage to create and modify Web pages and for other Web development.

Using Binder

The Office Binder provides a way to integrate office documents within a unified container. With Automation, Word, Excel, and PowerPoint, documents can be integrated within the Binder so that users can work with all these documents together.

All the documents can then be saved in this Binder format so that whenever the user wants to work on them again, he or she opens the Binder, where all the office documents are conveniently accessible.

Using the Right Tool

The first, and perhaps most important, decision a developer makes is in answer to the question, "What tool should I use for this feature?"

Resist the urge to develop all features within Access just because you are familiar with that application. VBA now extends to *all* Office products. It is much easier now than in the past to switch to Word or Excel and become comfortable with programming very quickly.

Think of Automation as a set of services that your application can plug into via Automation:

- Access—database services
- Word—word processing and desktop publishing services
- Excel—calculation and financial services
- PowerPoint—presentation services
- Outlook—email, calendar, contacts, tasks, and other services
- Graph—graphing and chart services
- MapPoint—mapping services
- FrontPage—Web development services
- Binder—document container services

VBA Everywhere

Visual Basic for Applications (VBA) is a powerful development language that exists throughout the Office products. This unifying programming language allows developers to easily integrate Office applications with unified software solutions.

Using the Macro Recorder to Write Code

The Macro Recorder is a terrific code writer and can be used for rapid development in Word, Excel, and PowerPoint. To access Macro Recorder in these applications, choose Macro under the Tools menu, and then select Record New Macro (see Figure 19.2).

FIGURE 19.2

The Record Macro dialog box.

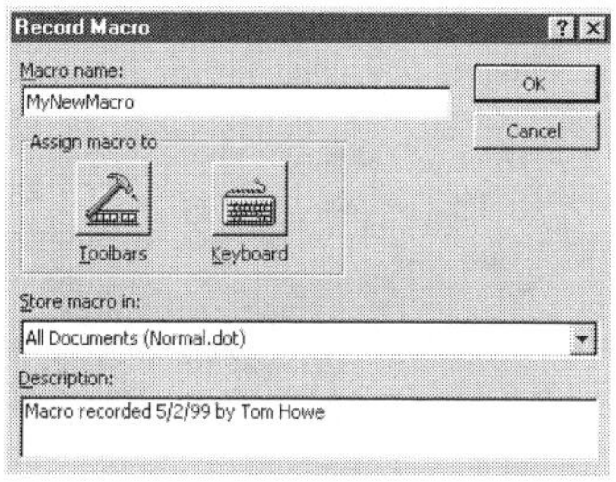

In the Record Macro dialog box, name the macro and choose OK to start the Macro Recorder. On the document, you will see a small toolbar with two buttons. By moving the mouse to hover over each button, you can see there is a Stop Recording and Pause Recording button. In addition, the mouse features a small cassette tape icon to indicate that the Macro Recorder is running (see Figure 19.3).

While the Macro Recorder is running, any action you take within the application will be converted to VBA code. You can type text in the document, format the text, and even save and print the document. When you finish the tasks you want to record, click the Stop Recording button. To review the VBA code that was written by the Macro Recorder, choose Macro under the Tools menu, and then select Macros on the cascading menu. Select the macro that you recorded and click on the Edit button. The Visual Basic Editor will open and show the VBA code written for that macro (see Figure 19.4).

19

INTEGRATION WITH OFFICE 2000

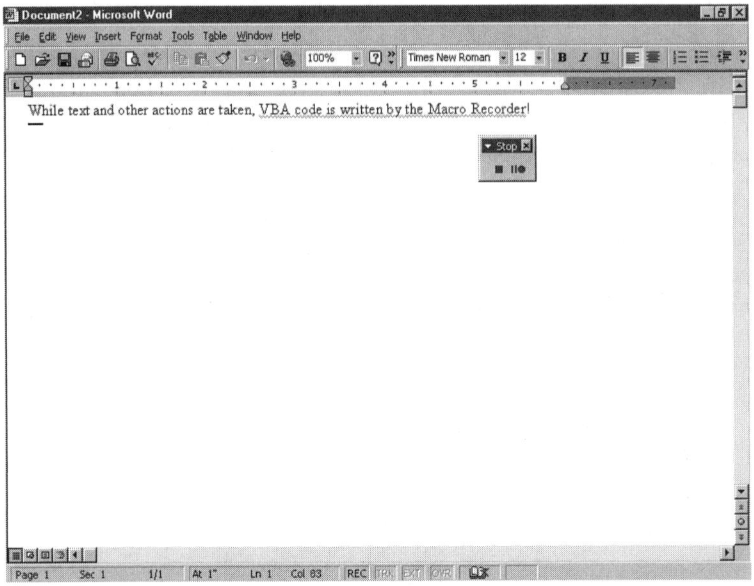

FIGURE 19.3

A Word document with the Macro Recorder running.

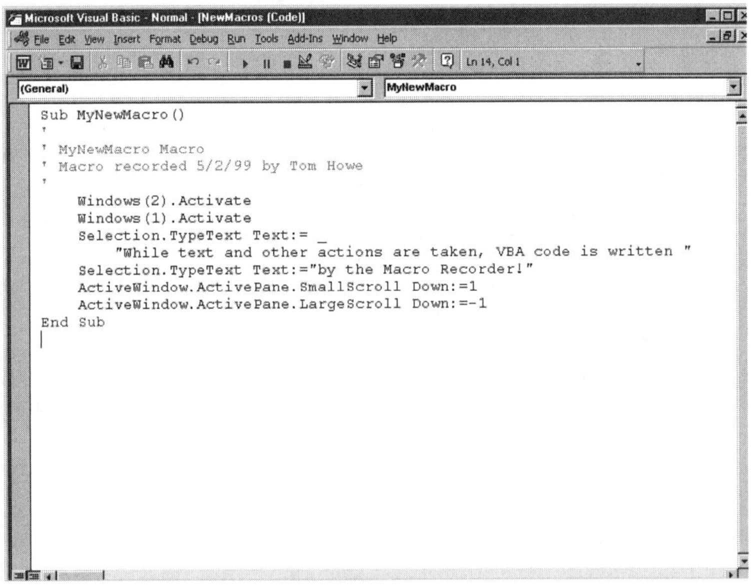

FIGURE 19.4

VBA code written by the Macro Recorder, as shown in the Visual Basic Editor.

TIP

The Macro Recorder does not always write the most optimized code, so you might want to review the code before using it in your application. Reformatting the code using the `With`/`End With` construct is a good idea.

Using Auto Macros

Word, Excel, and PowerPoint include Auto Macros that can be used to run code under various circumstances, as illustrated by the following examples of Auto Macros in Word:

- AutoExecute—runs when you start Word
- AutoNew—runs when you create a new file
- AutoOpen—runs when you open a file
- AutoClose—runs when you close a file
- AutoExit—runs when you close Word

To use an Auto Macro in the Visual Basic Editor, create within the module a function with the name of the Auto Macro. For example, to create an Auto Open Macro, you would follow this procedure:

```
Private/Public Sub AutoOpen ()
    ' Code to run when the document opens.
End Sub
```

Microsoft Forms

Office products, including Word, Excel, and PowerPoint, feature a separate forms package called Microsoft Forms. At times, such as when using other applications, these forms might come in handy.

Developers experienced with Access forms will have no difficulty with Microsoft Forms. To create a Microsoft Form, follow these steps: Under the Insert menu in the Visual Basic Editor, choose User Form or press Shift+F7. Use the control toolbox to add controls to a form. VBA code can be written to respond to control and form events, and ActiveX controls can be added to forms.

19

INTEGRATION WITH
OFFICE 2000

> **TIP**
>
> Microsoft Forms are distinct from forms within Access, Visual Basic, and Outlook. These are all separate forms packages. You cannot, for example, convert an Access form to a Microsoft Form, or vice versa.

Object Browser

As you work with the various applications covered in this chapter, don't forget to use the Object Browser. The previous chapter discusses in detail how to use the Object Browser.

To use the Object Browser in the Visual Basic Editor, choose Object Browser under the View menu, or press F2 (see Figure 19.5).

FIGURE 19.5

The Object Browser showing Microsoft Word objects.

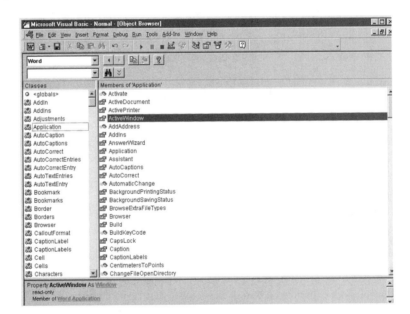

Class Arguments for Office Applications

To automate with other applications, you need to know the class arguments:

Application	Class Argument
Access	`Access.Application`
Binder	`Office.Binder`
Excel	`Excel.Application`
	`Excel.Sheet`
	`Excel.Chart`
FrontPage	`FrontPage.Application`
Graph	`Graph.Application`
MapPoint	`MapPoint.Application`
Outlook	`Outlook.Application`
PowerPoint	`PowerPoint.Application`
Word	`Word.Application`
	`Word.Document`

Automation Example

The basics of Automation (such as automating Word, creating or getting a reference to Word, using Word's objects, and releasing the automation object) are covered in the previous chapter.

The following example of printing Access information in a Word report demonstrates all those steps. Don't forget to set a reference to Microsoft Word.

```
Private Sub AccessApplicationReport()

Dim objWord As Word.Application

DoCmd.Hourglass True

' Resume to the next line following the error.
On Error Resume Next

' Attempt to reference Word which is already running.
Set objWord = GetObject(, "Word.Application")

' If true, Word is not running.
If objWord Is Nothing Then

' Create a new instance of the Word application.
Set objWord = New Word.Application
```

19

INTEGRATION WITH OFFICE 2000

```
' If true, MS Word 8.0 is not installed.
If objWord Is Nothing Then

MsgBox "MS Word 8.0 is not installed on your computer"

End If

End If

' On Error GoTo ErrorHandler (Put Error Handler Code Here!)

' Open a new word document based on the "Normal.dot" template.
objWord.Documents.Add

' Activates Word
objWord.Activate

' Show Word to the user.
objWord.Visible = True

' Create a heading for the report.
With objWord.Selection
.TypeText vbTab & vbTab & "Access Application Report"
.StartOf Unit:=wdStory, Extend:=wdExtend
.Font.Bold = True
.Font.Size = 20
.EndKey Unit:=wdLine
.TypeParagraph
.TypeParagraph
.Font.Bold = False
.Font.Size = 16
End With


' Put information about this Access Application in the Word document.
With objWord.Selection
.TypeText "Application Item" & vbTab & "Value" & vbCrLf
.TypeText "Database Name and Path" & vbTab & _
        Application.CurrentDb.Name & vbCrLf
.TypeText "Current Form Name" & vbTab & Forms.Item(0).Name & vbCrLf
.TypeText "Current Active Object" & vbTab & _
        Application.CurrentObjectName & vbCrLf
.TypeText "Current User Name" & vbTab & Application.CurrentUser & vbCrLf
.TypeText "Current Jet Version" & vbTab & _
        Application.DBEngine.Version & vbCrLf
.TypeText "Application Compiled" & vbTab & Application.IsCompiled & vbCrLf
.TypeText "Number of References" & vbTab & _
        Application.References.Count & vbCrLf
.TypeText "Current Mouse Pointer" & vbTab & _
        Application.Screen.MousePointer & vbCrLf
.TypeText "User Control" & vbTab & Application.UserControl & vbCrLf
.TypeText "Application Visible" & vbTab & Application.Visible & vbCrLf
```

```
.StartOf Unit:=wdStory
.MoveDown Unit:=wdLine, Count:=2
.StartOf Unit:=wdLine
.EndOf Unit:=wdStory, Extend:=wdExtend
.ConvertToTable Separator:=wdSeparateByTabs, NumColumns:=2, _
NumRows:=11, Format:=wdTableFormatColorful2, _
        ApplyBorders:=True, ApplyShading _
:=True, ApplyFont:=True, ApplyColor:=True, ApplyHeadingRows:=True, _
ApplyLastRow:=False, ApplyFirstColumn:=False, ApplyLastColumn:=False, _
AutoFit:=True, AutoFitBehavior:=wdAutoFitFixed
.EndOf Unit:=wdStory

End With

' Turn paragraph markers off.
objWord.ActiveWindow.ActivePane.View.ShowAll = False

DoCmd.Hourglass False

' Release the object variable.
Set objWord = Nothing

End Sub
```

Automating Word

This section covers specific issues and examples for automating Microsoft Word.

The Word Object Model

The previous example shows code that includes all the steps to make automation work. Now, I will focus on the objects, properties, and methods available in Word. The object model is very informative in this regard.

An *object model* is a representation (in outline form) of an application's objects. This is a quick and easy way to determine which objects in an application are available to program, manipulate, or control.

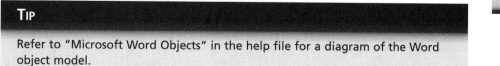

TIP

Refer to "Microsoft Word Objects" in the help file for a diagram of the Word object model.

The Word object model is quite comprehensive. There are more than 180 Word objects that can be manipulated with VBA. Frequently used Word objects are summarized in Table 19.1. The objects that also have collections end with (s):

TABLE 19.1 WORD OBJECTS

Word Object	Description
Application	The entire Word application. You do not usually need to reference the application object from within Word. If using Word from another application, you will use this object.
AutoCaption(s)	A caption that can be added automatically.
AutoCorrect	AutoCorrect feature in Word.
Character	Characters within an opened document.
CommandBar(s)	A particular command bar referred to by index number or name.
DefaultWebOptions	Default settings for publishing or saving as a Web page.
Dialog(s)	A built-in dialog box.
Dictionary(s)	A dictionary in Word.
Document(s)	An opened document referred to by index number or name.
Email	An email message for a document.
EmailSignature	Email signature information.
Find	An object used to find a word, selection, range, and more.
Paragraphs	A collection of paragraphs.
Range	A defined starting and ending point in a document. A document might have more than one range.
Replacement	An object specifying a replacement criteria.
Selection	The current selection in Word. There can only be one selection in Word at a time.
Table(s)	A single table in a document.
Template(s)	A document template.
WebOptions	Settings to override DefaultWebOptions.
Window(s)	A particular window referred to by index number or name.
Words	A collection of words.

Using Word Templates

As discussed in the last chapter, automation code runs fastest in the automation server. In other words, when automating Word's objects, properties, and methods, the VBA code should be placed in Word templates, rather than copied into Access.

To create a Word template, open a new Word document. After all code has been added, choose Save As under the File menu to save the document as a document template (.DOT extension).

To add code to the template, use the Macro Recorder as discussed earlier in this chapter. Simply turn on the Macro Recorder, perform the actions you want to automate, and the Macro Recorder will write the VBA code.

So how do you call the VBA code in Word from Access? Actually, it is very easy. Use the Run method. The code is as follows:

```
' Run Macro in Word that formats the document.
objWord.Run "FormatDocument"
```

Again, running the code in Word will be much faster because cross-process communication need not occur for each automation instruction. With the code in Word, the VBA code runs in a single process.

> **TIP**
>
> There are examples in the chapter code showing the same automation code in Access versus in a Word template. A timer demonstrates the speed difference. Placing the automation code in Word is substantially faster.

Although code runs faster when put in a Word template, doesn't it create a distribution headache? Not if managed correctly. Templates can be saved either on each workstation or as workgroup templates on the server. The advantage of saving the templates as workgroup templates is that if you make a change to a template, or if you add a new template, you only need to copy the changes into the shared directory on the server. However, when the templates are used, network traffic will occur. Some developers write simple applications that copy the templates from the server to each workstation when the application starts up.

To provide users access to the workgroup templates (on the server), choose Options under the Tools menu. In the File Locations tab, set the path to the workgroup templates (see Figure 19.6).

19

INTEGRATION WITH
OFFICE 2000

FIGURE **19.6**

File locations in Word Options.

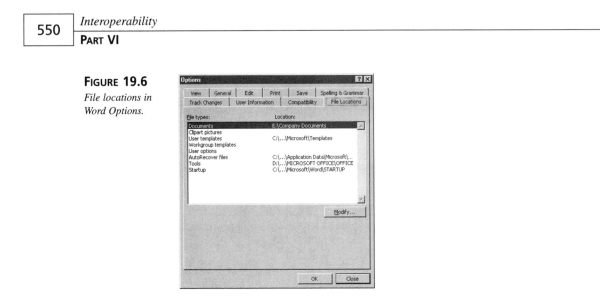

Inserting Data in Word Documents

Word is a terrific report writer. Corporate data can be presented in Word documents that can be easily modified by end-users. The following is an example of a magazine ad created with corporate data (see Figure 19.7).

FIGURE **19.7**

Creating reports in Word.

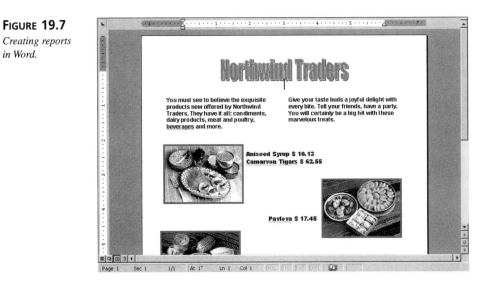

There are three features that can be used to send data from Access or SQL Server databases to a Word document: Mail Merge, Bookmarks, and Find and Replace. The sample code in this chapter demonstrates all these techniques.

Mail Merge

End users often use Word Mail Merge to assemble documents. This can also be done with automation.

Of the three methods of Word automation discussed in this section, Mail Merge is the preferred method of data integration.

To create the Mail Merge automation code, turn on the Macro Recorder and complete the steps for a Mail Merge just as an end user would. Under the Tools menu, choose Mail Merge and complete each step in the Mail Merge Helper dialog box.

When choosing a data source for the merge document, you can select an Access table or query as the data source. You will find that if you output the data to an RTF file first and use the RTF file as your data source, the automation code will run significantly faster. Several examples of this are included in the chapter code.

A key advantage of the Mail Merge technique is that end users themselves can insert fields of data into the document. In the mail merge document, users can insert fields from the Mail Merge toolbar. This empowers users to create their own documents and relieves developers from the necessity of creating reports. When properly designed by developers, templates can provide data fields that users might need to create Word reports of their own (see Figure 19.8).

FIGURE 19.8

Users can create Word reports.

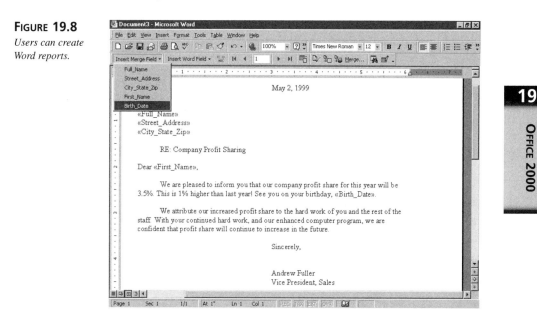

19

INTEGRATION WITH OFFICE 2000

The code in the template to run the mail merge in the Automation.MDB chapter code sample is

```
Private Sub RunMailMerge()

With ActiveDocument.MailMerge
.MainDocumentType = wdFormLetters
ActiveDocument.MailMerge.OpenDataSource Name:= _
"C:\Automation\Automation.MDB", ConfirmConversions:=False, _
ReadOnly:=False, LinkToSource:=True, AddToRecentFiles:=False, _
PasswordDocument:="", PasswordTemplate:="", WritePasswordDocument:="", _
WritePasswordTemplate:="", Revert:=False, Format:=wdOpenFormatAuto, _
Connection:="QUERY qryEmployeeLetters", SQLStatement:= _
"SELECT * FROM [qryEmployeeLetters]", SQLStatement1:=""
.Destination = wdSendToNewDocument
.Execute
End With

End Sub
```

Bookmarks

Another way to insert data in Word documents is to use Bookmarks. A Bookmark in a document is a placeholder where data can be inserted later. When the code runs, each Bookmark is searched, for and the applicable data is inserted at the appropriate place.

One disadvantage of Bookmarks is that developers themselves must insert the bookmarks in the template and write the code (or use the macro recorder to create it) to search for the bookmarks and insert the data. End users cannot create their own documents with data, as with the Mail Merge technique.

Another disadvantage of the Bookmark method is that Bookmarks are not readily apparent when Word templates are open, making it difficult to find and identify them.

To use this method, create a Word template with all the standard document text. Insert bookmarks where you want to insert data by choosing Bookmark under the Insert menu. Give the Bookmark a name and choose the Add button.

Use the Macro Recorder to write the VBA code as you go to bookmarks and insert text. Code in this chapter includes an example of automation using Bookmarks. The VBA code is as follows:

```
Selection.GoTo..... What:=wdGoToBookmark, Name:="MyBookmark"
Selection.TypeText "New Text"
```

Find and Replace

With this technique, text is inserted in the document as a placeholder where data is to be inserted (for example {First Name}). The code searches for the placeholder text with a

Find and replaces it with the appropriate data. In other words, {*First Name*} could be found and replaced with "Steve."

One of the advantages of using this method instead of Bookmarks is that placeholder text can be seen more easily and is more descriptive than bookmarks. Again, as with Bookmarks, use the macro recorder while doing a search and replace in order to create the VBA code. An example of the Find and Replace code is

```
With Selection.Find
.ClearFormatting
.Text = "{Find Text}"
.Replacement.Text = "New Text"
.Forward = True
.Wrap = wdFindContinue
.Format = False
.MatchCase = False
.MatchWholeWord = False
.MatchWildcards = False
.MatchSoundsLike = False
.MatchAllWordForms = False
.Execute Replace:=wdReplaceAll
End With
```

Word Automation Code Examples

The following examples demonstrate code to automate specific properties and methods of Word objects.

Formatting Word Documents

Word has extensive formatting capabilities. To automate document creation, VBA code can be used to format a Word document:

```
' Formatting Text
With Selection.Font
        .Size = 14
        .Bold = True
End With

' Formatting Paragraphs
With Selection.ParagraphFormat
        .LeftIndent = InchesToPoints(0)
        .RightIndent = InchesToPoints(0)
        .SpaceBefore = 0
        .SpaceAfter = 0
        .LineSpacingRule = wdLineSpaceSingle
        .Alignment = wdAlignParagraphLeft
        .KeepWithNext = False
        .KeepTogether = False
```

19

INTEGRATION WITH
OFFICE 2000

```
         .PageBreakBefore = False
         .NoLineNumber = False
         .Hyphenation = True
         .FirstLineIndent = InchesToPoints(0)
         .OutlineLevel = wdOutlineLevelBodyText
End With

' Setting Line Spacing to Double Space
Selection.ParagraphFormat.LineSpacingRule = wdLineSpaceDouble

' Adding a Page Break
Selection.InsertBreak Type:=wdPageBreak

' Adding a Section Break
Selection.InsertBreak Type:=wdSectionBreakNextPage
```

Using Document Styles

A *style* is a group of formatting instructions that can be named and assigned to text.
Styles enable formatting of several blocks of text or paragraphs with a single command.
In addition, styles help provide consistent formatting throughout the document.

```
' Applying the Heading Style to Text
Selection.Style = ActiveDocument.Styles("Heading 1")

' Creating a New Style
ActiveDocument.Styles.Add Name:="MyNewStyle", Type:=wdStyleTypeParagraph
With ActiveDocument.Styles("MyNewStyle")
        .AutomaticallyUpdate = False
        .BaseStyle = "Heading 5"
 End With
 With ActiveDocument.Styles("MyNewStyle").Font
        .Name = "Times New Roman"
        .Size = 12
        .Bold = False
        .Italic = False
        .Underline = wdUnderlineSingle
        .StrikeThrough = False
        .DoubleStrikeThrough = False
        .Outline = False
        .Emboss = False
        .Shadow = False
        .Hidden = False
        .SmallCaps = False
        .AllCaps = False
        .ColorIndex = wdAuto
        .Engrave = False
        .Superscript = False
        .Subscript = False
        .Scaling = 100
```

```
        .Kerning = 0
        .Animation = wdAnimationNone
    End With
```

AutoCorrect

AutoCorrect fixes easily misspelled words (for example, "teh" can be changed to "the"). You can also use AutoCorrect to save typing (for example, convert "MS" to "Microsoft").

AutoText

AutoText is a database that stores frequently used text and graphic objects that can be inserted easily into documents. The chapter code has examples of inserting text and photographs to documents.

```
' Create an AutoText Entry.
NormalTemplate.AutoTextEntries.Add Name:="Microsoft", _
     Range:=Selection.Range

' Insert an AutoText Entry.
NormalTemplate.AutoTextEntries("Microsoft").Insert _
     Where:= Selection.Range
```

AutoSummarize

AutoSummarize analyzes each sentence of a document to create a summary. The summary can be displayed several ways: as highlighted text within the document, as an abstract in the beginning of the document, in a new document, or by itself with no other document showing. AutoSummarize can even be used to create a summary of Web pages.

```
' AutoSummarize a Document (summary put in a new document).
ActiveDocument.AutoSummarize Length:=25, Mode:=wdSummaryModeCreateNew, _
     UpdateProperties:=True
```

Document Views

After creating a document for the user, present the document in the appropriate view: Normal, Online Layout, Page Layout, Outline, or Master Document.

```
' Normal View
ActiveWindow.View.Type = wdNormalView

' Online Layout
ActiveWindow.View.Type = wdOnlineView

' Page Layout
ActiveWindow.View.Type = wdPageView
```

19

INTEGRATION WITH
OFFICE 2000

```
' Outline View
ActiveWindow.ActivePane.View.Type =wdOutlineView

' Master Document
ActiveWindow.ActivePane.View.Type = wdMasterView
```

Table of Contents

In the past, creating a table of contents was a laborious task. Now, with Word, this is largely an automated process. The trick is to use styles in your document. When you set up styles to format Heading 1, Heading 2, and so on, Word can rely on this information to create an accurate table of contents automatically.

```
' Create a Table of Contents.
With ActiveDocument
        .TablesOfContents.Add Range:=Selection.Range, _
            RightAlignPageNumbers:= _
          True, UseHeadingStyles:=True, UpperHeadingLevel:=1, _
          LowerHeadingLevel:=3, IncludePageNumbers:=True, _
            AddedStyles:=""
        .TablesOfContents(1).TabLeader = wdTabLeaderDots
 End With
```

Footnotes

Footnotes help the reader locate and evaluate information that supports a point made in the document.

```
' Create a Footnote.
ActiveDocument.Footnotes.Add Range:=Selection.Range, _
Reference:=Selection, Text:="My New Footnote"
```

Headers

Headers appear at the top of each page of a document.

```
' Create a Header.
ActiveWindow.ActivePane.View.SeekView = wdSeekCurrentPageHeader
    Selection.TypeText Text:="My Header"
```

Footers

Footers appear at the bottom of each page of a document.

```
' Create a Footer.
ActiveWindow.ActivePane.View.SeekView = wdSeekCurrentPageHeader
    If Selection.HeaderFooter.IsHeader = True Then
        ActiveWindow.ActivePane.View.SeekView = wdSeekCurrentPageFooter
    Else
        ActiveWindow.ActivePane.View.SeekView = wdSeekCurrentPageHeader
    End If
    Selection.TypeText Text:="My Footer"
```

Hyperlinks

Hyperlinks enable users to jump easily to other parts of a document, to open an entirely different document, and even to jump to electronic documents on the Internet.

```
' Create a Hyperlink to a Bookmark in the Existing Document.
ActiveDocument.Hyperlinks.Add Anchor:=Selection.Range, Address:="", _
        SubAddress:="MyBookmark"

' Create a Hyperlink to Another Document.
ActiveDocument.Hyperlinks.Add Anchor:=Selection.Range, Address:= _
        "C:\MyDoc.doc", SubAddress:=""

' Create a Hyperlink to a Web Site.
ActiveDocument.Hyperlinks.Add Anchor:=Selection.Range, Address:= _
        "http://www.microsoft.com/office/", SubAddress:=""
```

Creating Tables

A table contains information by rows and columns. Word makes it easy to create tables with a wide range of flexibility.

```
' Create a Table.
ActiveDocument.Tables.Add Range:=Selection.Range, NumRows:=3,
NumColumns:=_3,
        Selection.Tables(1).AutoFormat, Format:=wdTableFormatClassic3, _
        ApplyBorders:=True, ApplyShading:=True, ApplyFont:=True, _
        ApplyColor:=True, ApplyHeadingRows:=True, _
        ApplyLastRow:=False, ApplyFirstColumn:=True, _
        ApplyLastColumn:=False, AutoFit:=False

' Inserting Rows in a Table
Selection.InsertRows 1

' Inserting Columns in a Table
Selection.InsertColumns
```

Page Setup

The Page Setup dialog box controls margins, paper size, orientation, paper source, and layout. All these settings can be adjusted with code:

```
' Setting Margins
With ActiveDocument.PageSetup
        .TopMargin = InchesToPoints(0.5)
        .BottomMargin = InchesToPoints(0.5)
        .LeftMargin = InchesToPoints(0.5)
        .RightMargin = InchesToPoints(0.5)
End With

' Set Page Layout to Landscape.
ActiveDocument.PageSetup.Orientation = wdOrientLandscape
```

Print Preview

To present a Print Preview of a document, use the following code:

```
' Print Preview
ActiveDocument.PrintPreview
```

Printing Documents, Envelopes, and Labels

The following examples show how to print documents, envelopes, and labels with code:

```
' Printing Entire Document
Application.PrintOut FileName:="", Range:=wdPrintAllDocument, _
        Item:= wdPrintDocumentContent, Copies:=1, Pages:="", _
        PageType:=wdPrintAllPages, Collate:=True, Background:=True,
        PrintToFile:=False
' Printing Envelopes
ActiveDocument.Envelope.PrintOut ExtractAddress:=False, _
        OmitReturnAddress :=False, PrintBarCode:=False, _
        PrintFIMA:=False, Height:=InchesToPoints(4.13), _
        Width:=InchesToPoints(9.5), Address:="Tom Howe", _
        AutoText:= "ToolsCreateLabels1", ReturnAddress:=_
        "1001 SW Fifth Avenue, Suite 1100",ReturnAutoText:= _
        "ToolsCreateLabels2", AddressFromLeft:=wdAutoPosition,_
        AddressFromTop:=wdAutoPosition, ReturnAddressFromLeft:=_
        wdAutoPosition, ReturnAddressFromTop:=wdAutoPosition


' Printing Labels
Application.MailingLabel.DefaultPrintBarCode = False
    Application.MailingLabel.PrintOut Name:="2160 Mini", _
        Address:="Tom Howe"
```

> **TIP**
>
> When printing voluminous documents or reports printed on a daily basis, consider using a timer routine to print the reports in the middle of the night when printers are available and network traffic is minimal.

Word Fields

A *Word field* is a special code that is used to insert particular information, such as page numbers, dates, and more. To insert a field in a document, choose Field under the Insert menu.

When working with documents, you can toggle between the text and field code in the document by using the shortcut key Alt+F9.

The fields can be updated manually with the shortcut key F9 or automatically when the document is printed.

Some commonly used Word fields are listed in Table 19.2.

TABLE 19.2   WORD FIELDS

Word Field	Description
Ask	Prompts user for text to attach to bookmark
CreateDate	Date document was created
Fill-in	Prompts user for text to insert in the document
Hyperlink	Opens and jumps to specified file
If	Evaluates arguments conditionally
MergeField	Inserts a Mail Merge field
Next	Goes to next record in the Mail Merge
SectionPages	Inserts total number of pages in a section

The following shortcuts will help when working with field codes:

Shortcut Key	Description
Alt+F9	Switches between field codes and data in the field
Ctrl+F9	Creates field characters
Ctrl+Shift+F9	Unlinks the field codes
Delete	Deletes a field code
F9	Manually updates the field codes

19

INTEGRATION WITH
OFFICE 2000

Document Summary Information

When a new document is created and saved, information must be saved for later searches and retrieval. Information to identify a document is contained in the Word Properties dialog box (see Figure 19.9).

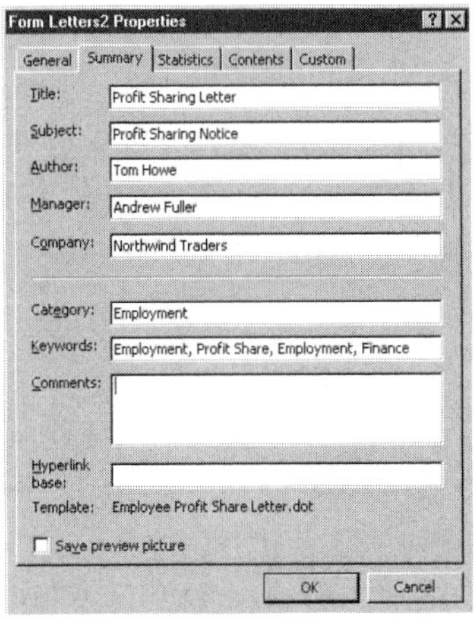

FIGURE 19.9

Word document summary information.

The following information can be associated with a document:

- Document name
- Document size
- Date and time of creation
- Last modified date and time
- Template document based on
- Keywords to identify document
- Document location
- Author name
- Manager name
- Company
- Category
- Comments
- Document statistics
- Contents information

It is even possible to create custom properties to meet the specific needs of an organization. See the Custom tab in the Properties dialog box.

Other Word Features

Word contains many advanced desktop publishing features, such as

- Multicolumn layouts
- The capability to import graphics from other applications
- Embedded TrueType fonts
- Borders and shading
- Backgrounds and textures
- Word Art
- Extensive drawing tools

Automating Excel

This section covers specific issues and examples for automating Microsoft Excel.

Excel Object Model

There are more than 140 Excel objects that can be manipulated with VBA.

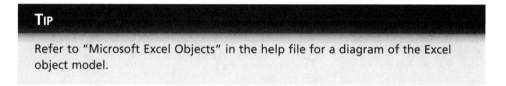

TIP

Refer to "Microsoft Excel Objects" in the help file for a diagram of the Excel object model.

Table 19.3 summarizes commonly used Excel objects. The objects that also have collections end with (s):

TABLE 19.3   EXCEL OBJECTS

Excel Object	Description
Application	The entire Excel application
Characters	Characters in an object that contains text
Chart(s)	A chart in a workbook
CubeField(s)	A hierarchy or measure field from an OLAP cube
DefaultWebOptions	Default settings for publishing or saving as a Web page
Dialog(s)	A built-in dialog box
DocumentProperty(s)	Built-in or custom document properties
Name(s)	A defined name for a range of cells

continues

TABLE 19.3 CONTINUED

Excel Object	Description
PivotCache(s)	A memory cache for a PivotTable report
PivotTable(s)	A PivotTable report on a worksheet
PublishObject(s)	An item in a workbook that has been saved to a Web page
Range	A cell, row, column, or selection of cells containing contiguous blocks of cells, or a 3D range
Shape(s)	An object, such as a picture, in the drawing layer
ShapeRange	A subset of shapes on a document
Style(s)	A style description for a range
WebOptions	Settings to override DefaultWebOptions
Workbook(s)	An opened workbook referred to by index number or name
Worksheet(s)	An opened worksheet referred to by index number or name

Excel Automation Code Examples

The following examples demonstrate code to automate specific properties and methods of Excel objects.

Formatting Excel Documents

Excel has extensive formatting capabilities. The following examples demonstrate how to format column headings and column data and how to call the AutoFit method:

```
' Format column headings.
With objWorkSheet
    'Bold column headings.
    .Cells(1, 1).Font.Bold = True
    .Cells(1, 2).Font.Bold = True
End With

' Format the data in the worksheet.
With objWorkSheet.Columns
```

```
      With .Item(2)
          .NumberFormat = "0.00"
          .AutoFit
      End With

      ' Use the "AutoFit" method to format the data.
      .Item(1).AutoFit

End With
```

Creating Charts

Use the Macro Recorder to create automation code quickly. Use the Chart Wizard to select the chart desired. The following automation code creates various types of charts:

```
' Create a Pie chart.
      objChart.ChartWizard Source:=objSheet.Cells(1, 1).CurrentRegion, _
            Gallery:=xlPie, Format:=4, PlotBy:=xlColumns, _
            CategoryLabels:=1, SeriesLabels:=1, HasLegend:=2, _
            Title:="Product Sales (Pie Chart)"

' Create a Column chart.
      With ObjChart.ActiveChart
.ChartType = xlColumnClustered
            .SetSourceData Source:=_
            Sheets("Top 5 Product Sales").Range("A1:B6"), _
            PlotBy:=xlColumns

    End With

' Create a Doughnut chart.
      With ObjChart.ActiveChart
.ChartType = xlDoughnut
            .SetSourceData Source:=_
            Sheets("Top 5 Product Sales").Range("A1:B6"), _
            PlotBy:=xlColumns
            .Location Where:=xlLocationAsNewSheet, Name:="Doughnut Graph"
                .HasLegend = True
            .ChartTitle.Characters.Text = "Product Sales (Doughnut Chart)"
    End With
```

The automation code creates charts in Excel (see Figure 19.10).

19

INTEGRATION WITH
OFFICE 2000

FIGURE 19.10

Creating charts in Excel.

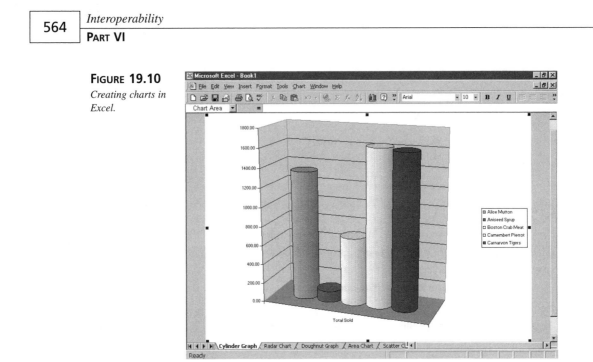

Using the Parent Property

Excel includes an application object and workbook object. You can access all other objects by using the properties of these top-level objects. Generally, automation code starts with top-level objects and works down the hierarchy. In Excel, code may start with the application object, move to the workbook object, and then travel down the hierarchy to the worksheet and cell levels.

When you open an object in the application's object hierarchy, you can traverse the hierarchy in both directions. Use the `Parent` property to travel up the hierarchy. For example, if you are working with a particular worksheet, you can access the workbook that contains the worksheet by using the parent property. The code is as follows:

```
Private Sub ParentPropertyDemo()

    Dim objExcel As Excel.Application
    Dim objWorkBook as Excel.WorkBook

    ' Create a new instance of the Excel application.
    Set objExcel = New Excel.Application

    ' Open a new Excel workbook.
    ' Make sure the spreadsheet from the chapter code
    ' is in the following path.
    objExcel.Workbooks.Open _
        ("C:\Automation\Sales by Country Data.xls")
```

```
   ' Set objWorkBook to Active WorkBook
   Set objWorkBook = objExcel.ActiveWorkBook

   ' Get the name of objWorkBook ("Sales by Country")
   MsgBox objWorkBook.Name

   ' Get the name of the application object using the
   ' parent property ("Microsoft Excel").
   MsgBox objWorkBook.Parent.Name

      ' Maximize window.
      objExcel.WindowState = xlMaximized

      ' Show Excel to the user.
      objExcel.Visible = True

      ' Use the Quit method to terminate Excel.
      'objExcel.Quit

      ' Release the object variable.
      Set objExcel = Nothing

End Sub
```

In this example, a workbook is opened. By using the Parent property of the workbook object, it is referring upward in the object hierarchy to the Excel application object.

Automating PowerPoint

This section covers specific issues and examples for automating Microsoft PowerPoint.

The PowerPoint Object Model

There are more than 85 PowerPoint objects that can be manipulated with VBA.

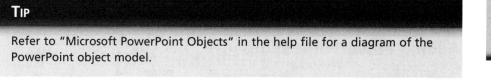

TIP

Refer to "Microsoft PowerPoint Objects" in the help file for a diagram of the PowerPoint object model.

Table 19.4 summarizes commonly used PowerPoint objects. The objects that also have collections end with (s):

TABLE 19.4   POWERPOINT OBJECTS

PowerPoint Object	*Description*
ActionSetting(s)	Setting that defines how a shape or text range reacts to mouse actions during a slide show
AnimationSetting(s)	Animation setting for a shape during a slide show
Application	The entire PowerPoint application
Cell	A cell in a table
CellRange	A collection of cells in a table column or row
ColorScheme(s)	The color scheme for a slide, handout, and more
Column(s)	A column in a table
DefaultWebOptions	Default settings for publishing or saving as a Web page
DocumentWindow(s)	A document window
Pane(s)	A portion of a document window
Presentation(s)	An opened presentation referred to by index number or name
Row(s)	A row in a table
Selection	A selection in a document
ShapeRange	A set of shapes on a document
SlideRange	A set of slides
SlideShowWindow(s)	The window in which a slide show runs
Table	A table on a slide
TextRange	Text attached to a shape
WebOptions	Settings to override DefaultWebOptions

PowerPoint Automation Code Examples

The following examples demonstrate code to automate specific properties and methods of PowerPoint objects (see Figure 19.11).

Adding PowerPoint Slides

The Add method is used to add PowerPoint slides to a presentation:

```
' Add a slide.
Set ppPres = objPP.Presentations.Add
```

FIGURE 19.11

*A PowerPoint pre-
sentation created
with automation.*

Adding Transition Effects

The following code adds a transition effect to a slide:

```
' Add a transition effect to a slide.
objPresentation.Slides(5).SlideShowTransition.EntryEffect = _
   ppEffectFade
```

Adding Data and Formatting Slides

The following code adds data and formats a slide:

```
With objPresentation.Slides(5).Shapes(1)
.TextFrame.TextRange.Text = "Sales Totals"
        .Shapes(1).TextFrame.TextRange.Characters.Font.Size = 80
    End With

    With objPresentation.Shapes(2).TextFrame.TextRange
        .Text = Chr$(CharCode:=13) + "Board Of Director Meeting" _
            + Chr$(CharCode:=13) + "Sales Summary Information"
        .Characters.Font.Color.RGB = RGB(0, 0, 255)
        .Characters.Font.Shadow = True
    End With
```

19

**INTEGRATION WITH
OFFICE 2000**

```
With objPresentation.Shapes("Rectangle 3").TextFrame.TextRange._
    Characters(1, 53).Font
    .Size = 36
    .Color.SchemeColor = ppFill
End With

End With
```

Adding a Photo to a Shape on a Slide

The following code adds a photo and formats a slide:

```
Dim strFileName as String
strFileName = ADOrs!Photos

objPresentation.Shapes.AddPicture(FileName:=strFileName, _
 LinkToFile:=msoFalse, SaveWithDocument:=msoTrue, _
Left:=110, Top:=260, Width:=250, Height:=250).Select
```

Running a PowerPoint Presentation

The following code starts a PowerPoint presentation:

```
ObjPresentation.SlideShowSettings.Run
```

Automating Outlook

This section covers specific issues and examples for automating Microsoft Outlook.

The Outlook Object Model

There are more than 55 Outlook objects that can be manipulated with VBA.

> **TIP**
>
> Refer to "Microsoft Outlook Objects" in the help file for a diagram of the Outlook object model.

Table 19.5 summarizes commonly used Outlook objects. The objects that also have collections end with (s):

TABLE 19.5 OUTLOOK OBJECTS

Outlook Object	Description
Action(s)	A specialized action of an item
AddressEntries(s)	Address information for delivery of a message
Application	The entire Outlook application
AppointmentItem	An appointment in the Calendar folder
Attachment(s)	An attached document to an Outlook item
ContactItem	A contact in the Contact folder
DistListItem	Distribution list in a Contact folder
DocumentItem	A document in an Outlook folder
Explorer(s)	The window that displays the contents of a folder
Folders	A collection of MAPIFolder objects
Inspector(s)	The window that displays an Outlook item
Items	A collection of Outlook items in a MAPIFolder
JournalItem	An entry in a Journal folder
NameSpace	The root object to access data
NoteItem	A note in the Notes folder
Pages	A collection of pages of an Inspector
PostItem	A post in a Public folder
PropertyPage(s)	A custom property page
Recipient(s)	A user or resource in Outlook
SyncObject(s)	A synchronization profile for a user
TaskItem	A task in the Tasks folder

19

INTEGRATION WITH
OFFICE 2000

Outlook Automation Code Examples

The following examples demonstrate code to automate specific properties and methods of Outlook objects.

Adding and Displaying Outlook Folders

The following code adds a subfolder and displays a Public folder in Outlook:

```
' Add a subfolder to the default calendar folder.
Set objSubFolder = objOutlook.GetNamespace("MAPI").GetDefaultFolder_
    (olFolderCalendar).Folders.Add("New Calendar")
```

Adding a New Task and Displaying Task Items

The following code adds a new task and displays task items:

```
Dim objOutlook As Outlook.Application
Dim objTaskFolder As Object
Dim objTaskItem As Object

Set objTaskItem = objOutlook.CreateItem(olTaskItem)

With objTaskItem
    .Subject = "This is the subject of a task"
    .Body = "This is the body of a task"
    ' You can also add a reminder, time, and date.
    .Save
End With

' Go to tasks folder.
Set objTaskFolder = objOutlook.GetNamespace("MAPI")._
    GetDefaultFolder(13)

' Show the items in the Task folder.
objTaskFolder.Display
```

Creating an Email Message with an Attachment

It is easy to send email from Access applications using Outlook with automation (see Figure 19.12).

FIGURE 19.12

Send Outlook email with an attachment from Access.

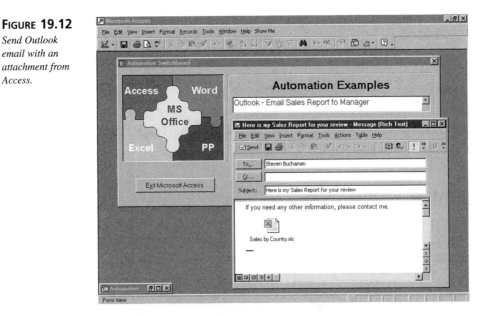

The following code creates a new email message and attaches an Excel spreadsheet:

```
Dim objOutlook As Outlook.Application
Dim objRecipient As Recipient
Dim objAttachment As Attachment
Dim objMailItem As MailItem

' Create a Mail Item.
Set objMailItem = objOutlook.CreateItem(olMailItem)

With objMailItem
' Create a recipient for the email message.
   Set objRecipient = .Recipients.Add("Steven Johnson")
   objRecipient.Type = olTo

   ' Set the Subject, Body, and Importance of the mail item.
   .Subject = "Here is my Sales Report for your review"
   .Body = "If you need any other information, _
         please contact me." & vbCrLf & vbCrLf
   .Importance = olImportanceHigh

   ' Attach an Excel spreadsheet and graph called "Sales by Country."
   Set objAttachment = .Attachments.Add_
         ("C:\Automation\Sales by Country.xls")

   ' Resolve each recipient's name.
   For Each objRecipient In .Recipients
       objRecipient.Resolve
   Next

   ' Display the email message.
   .Display

   ' Send the email message.
   .Send

End With
```

Creating Outlook Items

The following code creates various Outlook items:

Outlook Item	Code to Create the Item
Appointment	`Set objItem = objOutlook.CreateItem(olAppointmentItem)`
Contact	`Set objItem = objOutlook.CreateItem(olContactItem)`
Journal	`Set objItem = objOutlook.CreateItem(olJournalItem)`
Mail Message	`Set objItem = objOutlook.CreateItem(olMailItem)`
Note	`Set objItem = objOutlook.CreateItem(olNoteItem)`

19

INTEGRATION WITH
OFFICE 2000

Displaying Default Outlook Folders

Table 19.6 shows the constant to use with the `GetDefaultFolder` method to display a default Outlook folder:

TABLE 19.6 OUTLOOK FOLDER CONSTANTS

Outlook Folder	*Constant for* `GetDefaultFolder` *Method*
Calendar	`GetDefaultFolder(olFolderCalendar)`
Contacts	`GetDefaultFolder(olFolderContacts)`
Inbox	`GetDefaultFolder(olFolderInbox)`
Journal	`GetDefaultFolder(olFolderJournal)`
Notes	`GetDefaultFolder(olFolderNotes)`
Tasks	`GetDefaultFolder(olFolderTasks)`

Display an Outlook Public Folder

The following code displays an Outlook Public folder:

```
Dim objOutlook As Outlook.Application
    Dim objNameSpace As Outlook.NameSpace
    Dim objPublicFolders As Outlook.Folders
    Dim objAllPublicFolders As Object
    Dim objOfficeContacts As Object

    Set objNameSpace = objOutlook.GetNamespace("MAPI")
    Set objPublicFolders = objNameSpace.Folders("Public Folders")
    Set objAllPublicFolders = objPublicFolders.Folders("Favorites")
    Set objOfficeContacts = objAllPublicFolders.Folders("Office Contacts")

    ' Display the public folder "Office Contacts."
    objOfficeContacts.DisplayThe
```

Finding an Outlook Item

The following code demonstrates how to find a contact in Outlook:

```
Set objItem = objContactItems.Find("[File As] = 'Zelko, John'")
objItem.Display
```

Filtering Outlook Items

The `Resolve` method is used to filter Outlook items. The following code returns only the contact items with the First Name of "Steve":

```
Set objFilter = objContactItems.Restrict("[First Name] = 'Steve'")
```

> **TIP**
>
> The code for this chapter contains an entire Internet email application. Email can be sent from Outlook to groups of individuals in an Access database.
>
> The chapter code also includes examples of letters created in Word that can be automatically sent to contacts in Outlook.

Automating Graph

This section covers specific issues and an example for automating Microsoft Graph.

Graph Object Model

There are more than 10 Graph objects that can be manipulated with VBA. Table 19.7 summarizes commonly used Graph objects. The objects that also have collections end with (s):

TABLE 19.7   GRAPH OBJECTS

Graph Object	Description
Application	The entire Microsoft Graph application
AutoCorrect	Graph AutoCorrect feature
Axis(s)	A single axis in a chart
Chart	A Graph chart
ChartArea	The area of a specified chart
ChartGroup(s)	One or more series of points plotted in a chart
DataSheet	A Graph datasheet
DataTable	A data table in a specified chart
Legend	A legend in a specified chart
PlotArea	The plot area of a specified chart
Series(s)	A series in a specified chart

Creating Graphs

Sophisticated documents often include graphs and charts. Word and other Office products share Microsoft Graph, which can be used to create and format graphs.

In Access it is very easy to create graphs on forms using a wizard. Often, however, you might want to show different types of graphs of specific data. Rather than create six forms with different graphs, you can manipulate the graph on one form with automation code to give the user various graphic views of the data (see Figure 19.13).

FIGURE 19.13

A single form can show many types of graphs.

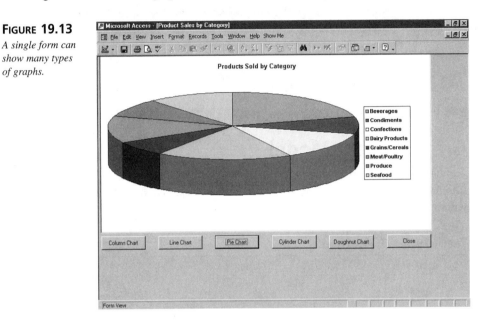

Graph Automation Code Examples

After the form is created with a graph, use the Chart object and change the ChartType property to show various graphs. For example, to change the column chart to a pie chart, the code in the Access form is as follows:

```
Dim objChart As Graph.Chart

    ' Assign object variable to chart on form.
    Set objChart = Me.objProductsSold.Object

    ' Change the chart type to a Pie Chart.
    objChart.ChartType = xl3DPie

    ' Show legend on chart.
    objChart.HasLegend = True

    ' Destroy the object variable.
    Set objChart = Nothing
```

By simply using the properties and methods of Microsoft Graph, you can format and change the chart as needed to add data pointers, legends, labels, background patterns, and more.

> **TIP**
>
> When automating to an application for charting capabilities, you can use Microsoft Excel or Microsoft Graph. Generally, you should use Excel because of its more extensive object model.

Automating MapPoint

This section covers specific issues and an example for automating Microsoft MapPoint.

The MapPoint Object Model

MapPoint objects can be manipulated with VBA.

> **TIP**
>
> Refer to "Microsoft MapPoint Objects" in the help file for a diagram of the MapPoint object model.

Table 19.8 summarizes commonly used MapPoint objects.

TABLE 19.8 MAPPOINT OBJECTS

MapPoint Object	Description
Application	The entire Microsoft MapPoint application
Location	A MapPoint location
Map	A MapPoint map
PushPin	A MapPoint push pin

MapPoint Automation Code Examples

The following example automates to MapPoint to display a particular map (see Figure 19.14). This could be used to open a map showing the location of customers.

```
' Set a reference to MapPoint 1.0.

Dim objMapPoint As MapPoint.Application
Dim objMap As MapPoint.Map

Set objMapPoint = New MapPoint.Application

' Open a Map of Portland, Oregon
Set objMap = objMapPoint.OpenMap("C:\Maps\Portland, OR.ptm")

' Release the object variable.
Set objMap = Nothing
Set objMapPoint = Nothing
```

FIGURE 19.14

Present maps in Access applications using MapPoint.

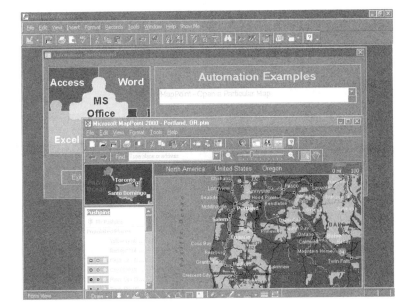

Automating FrontPage

This section covers specific issues and an example for automating Microsoft FrontPage.

FrontPage Object Model

FrontPage objects can be manipulated with VBA.

19

INTEGRATION WITH
OFFICE 2000

> **TIP**
>
> Refer to "Microsoft FrontPage Objects" in the help file for a diagram of the FrontPage object model.

Table 19.9 summarizes commonly used FrontPage objects. The objects that also have collections end with (s):

TABLE 19.9 FRONTPAGE OBJECTS

FrontPage Object	Description
Application	The entire FrontPage application
HomeNavigationNode	Navigation node for the home page
Theme(s)	A FrontPage theme
Web(s)	A FrontPage Web
WebFile(s)	A file in a Microsoft FrontPage-based Web
WebFolder(s)	A folder in a Microsoft FrontPage-based Web
WebWindow(s)	A window opened on a Microsoft FrontPage-based Web

FrontPage Automation Code Examples

With automation you can, among other things:

- Create a new Web, or open an existing one
- Create or open Web folders
- Create, open, or modify Web files
- Apply themes

The following example automates to FrontPage to create a new Web or add a new Web page, inserts Access data into the page, and applies a theme:

```
' Set references to ADO 2.1 and FrontPage 4.0 Web Objects.

Dim objFrontPage As FrontPage.WebWindow
Dim objWeb As Web
Dim objWebFile As WebFile
Dim objWebWindow As WebWindow
Dim strSQL As String
Dim ADOrs As ADODB.Recordset
Dim Conn As ADODB.Connection
```

```
Set objFrontPage = New FrontPage.WebWindow
Set objWeb = Webs.Open("C:\Automation\Web")

Set objWebFile = ActiveWeb.RootFolder.Files.Add_
    ("Category Sales Summary.htm")

' Create ADO Connection Object
Set Conn = New ADODB.Connection

' Create ADO Recordset
Set ADOrs = New ADODB.Recordset

With Conn
    .Provider = "Microsoft.JET.OLEDB.3.51"
    .Open "C:\Automation\Automation.mdb"
End With

strSQL = "SELECT Categories.CategoryName AS Category, _
    Sum([Order Details].UnitPrice) AS Price FROM _
    (Categories INNER JOIN Products ON Categories.CategoryID = _
    Products.CategoryID) INNER JOIN [Order Details] _
    ON Products.ProductID = [Order Details].ProductID _
    GROUP BY Categories.CategoryName _
    HAVING (((Sum([Order Details].UnitPrice))>0));"

' Open ADO Recordset
ADOrs.Open strSQL, Conn

Set objWebWindow = Webs(0).WebWindows(0)

objWebWindow.Visible = True

' Activate the Web window.
objWebWindow.Activate

' Open the Web file.
objWebFile.Open

' Insert the heading.
objFrontPage.ActiveDocument.Body.insertAdjacentText "BeforeEnd", _
    "Category Sales Summary"

' Insert the data from the database.
Do Until ADOrs.EOF

    objFrontPage.ActiveDocument.Body.insertAdjacentText _
    "BeforeEnd", ADOrs!Category.Value & vbTab & vbTab & ADOrs!Price.Value

    ADOrs.MoveNext
```

```
Loop

' Change the theme of the Web page to "artsy"
objWebWindow.ActivePageWindow.ApplyTheme "artsy", fpThemePropertiesAll

' Save the Web page.
objWebWindow.ActivePageWindow.Save

' Close the recordset.
ADOrs.Close

' Turn hourglass off.
Screen.MousePointer = 0

' Release object variables.
Set ADOrs = Nothing
Set objWeb = Nothing
Set objWebFile = Nothing
Set objWebWindow = Nothing
Set objFrontPage = Nothing
```

Automating Binder

This section covers specific issues and an example for automating Microsoft Binder.

Binder Object Model

Binder objects can be manipulated with VBA.

> **TIP**
>
> Refer to the Office Binder help file for a diagram of the Binder object model.

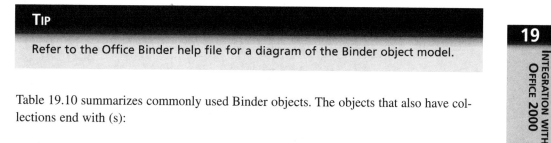

Table 19.10 summarizes commonly used Binder objects. The objects that also have collections end with (s):

TABLE 19.10 OFFICE BINDER OBJECTS

Binder Object	*Description*
Binder	A Microsoft Office Binder
DocumentProperty(s)	A built-in or custom property of a binder document
PageSetup	Page setup attributes
Section(s)	A section in a binder

A Binder Automation Code Example

The following code creates a new Binder and adds Office documents to the Binder:

```
Dim objBinder As Binder

Set objBinder = New Binder

With objBinder
    ' Add a Word Document to the Binder.
    .Sections.Add FileName:="C:\Automation\Northwind Magazine Ad.doc"
    .Sections(1).Name = "Northwind Magazine Ad"
    ' Add an Excel Spreadsheet to the Binder
    .Sections.Add FileName:="C:\Automation\Sales by Country Data.xls"
    .Sections(1).Name = "Automation Spreadsheet"
    ' Add a PowerPoint Demonstration to the Binder
    .Sections.Add FileName:="C:\Automation\Board Of Director _
            Meeting.ppt"
    .Sections(1).Name = "Board Of Director Meeting Presentation"
End With

objBinder.Visible = True

' Save Binder.
' objBinder.SaveAs "Automation.odb"

Set objBinder = Nothing
```

The automation code creates an Office Binder with various Office documents (see Figure 19.15).

FIGURE 19.15

Automating the Microsoft Binder.

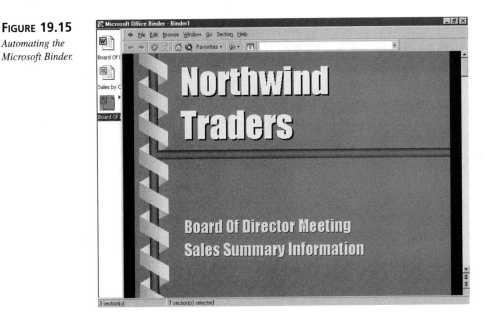

Securing Documents, Templates, and Code

Documents, forms, templates, and code modules can be password-protected. To do so, go to the Project Explorer Window in the Visual Basic Editor. To password-protect the entire project, right-click the Project and choose Properties. Click the Protection tab and enter a password. In the same manner, individual forms, templates, documents, and code modules can be password protected.

Summary

Automating to other Microsoft WebWindows is a great way to extend Access WebWindows. Office 2000 includes an entire suite of feature-rich products that expose hundreds of objects that can be manipulated programmatically using VBA.

This chapter includes numberous examples to automate to Word, Excel, PowerPoint, Outlook, Graph, MapPoint, FrontPage, and the Binder.

19

INTEGRATION WITH
OFFICE 2000

Using Visual Basic with Access

CHAPTER

20

Access is a powerful development tool, but it does not do everything. Visual Basic (VB) is a terrific adjunct to Access. VB can be used to create standalone ActiveX code components and ActiveX controls.

This chapter assumes that you have no experience developing with Visual Basic. Using step-by-step instructions, you will learn how to create ActiveX controls that you can use in your Access applications. Also, step-by-step instructions are provided to create code components in Visual Basic that can be used in Access, Visual Basic, and Office applications.

> **Tip**
>
> To work through the examples in this book you can use any version of Visual Basic 6. If you do not have Visual Basic 6, the Learning Edition is the least expensive version.

You might ask, "What is the difference between Visual Basic and Visual Basic for Applications (VBA)?" VBA is a programming language used in Visual Basic, Access and other Office applications. The VBA used in Office 2000 and Visual Basic 6 is bit by bit identical. Visual Basic 6 is the development environment you will use in this chapter to create components and ActiveX controls.

Creating ActiveX Code Components

With Visual Basic, you can create ActiveX code components and use them in Access applications. As an example in this chapter, you will create an ActiveX code component to play a sound file in Access applications.

> **Tip**
>
> The ActiveX components and ActiveX controls discussed in this chapter are included on the book CD-ROM. These components must be registered before you can use them. To register the components, open the project file and compile it. Later in this chapter, you will find additional information about registering components.

What Is an ActiveX Code Component?

An *ActiveX code component* is code in the class module that is compiled into an executable (EXE) or dynamic link libraries (DLL). An advantage of creating ActiveX code components is that you can use the components in any COM-compliant application. Therefore, rather than be restricted to a particular Access application only, the code can be used in numerous Access applications, Visual Basic applications, Office applications, and more.

In Chapter 11, "Creating Objects with Class Modules," you created a sound object using the cSound class module. In the class module, a sound file is passed to a Windows API call to play the sound on the computer. The code in the class module appears in Listing 20.1.

LISTING 20.1 cSOUND CLASS MODULE

```
Option Explicit

' Windows API call.
Private Declare Function sndPlaySound Lib "winmm.dll" Alias _
        "sndPlaySoundA" (ByVal lpszSoundName As String, _
        ByVal uFlags As Long) As Long

Public Sub PlaySound(SoundFile As String)

    ' Play the Sound File.
    sndPlaySound SoundFile, 1

End Sub
```

The problem with this class module is that it can be used only in the Access application in which the module exists. If another Access application is created, the class module must be imported into the new application. However, if you decide to make a change to the class module in the future, you will have to go to every class module in every Access application and make the change to each one individually.

By creating an ActiveX code component for the sound object, all Access applications (as well as other applications) can use the ActiveX code component. If a change must be made, it must be made in only one place.

What Is the Difference Between an ActiveX EXE and an ActiveX DLL?

When you create an ActiveX code component in Visual Basic, you can create either an ActiveX EXE or an ActiveX DLL. What's the difference?

An ActiveX EXE is an *out-of-process* component. This means that it runs in its own process space, separate from the calling application. If an ActiveX sound component is compiled as an EXE, it will run in a separate process space than the Access application will run. The calls from the Access application are communicated cross-process to the sound component. This is slower than if the ActiveX component ran in-process. However, one advantage of an ActiveX EXE is that, if it crashes, the calling application (your Access application) will not crash as well.

An ActiveX DLL runs in the same process space as the calling application. Because no cross-process calls are made, the speed is substantially faster. However, if the DLL crashes, the calling application will likely crash as well. Most of the time, you will likely use ActiveX DLLs.

> **TIP**
>
> An ActiveX DLL runs in the same process as the Access application that calls it. Therefore, an ActiveX DLL is substantially faster than an ActiveX EXE.

Creating an ActiveX Code Component

To create an ActiveX code component to play sounds, open Visual Basic. In the New Project dialog box, shown in Figure 20.1, choose ActiveX DLL. You will use an ActiveX DLL project because the component will run in the same process, as will the Access application that calls it.

When the project opens in the IDE, you will notice one class module named Class1. In the Project Properties window, rename this class module cSound.

In Access, open the Chapter 11 Access application Creating Objects with Class Modules.mdb. Open the cSound class module in Design view, and copy the contents of the module into the Clipboard. Return to the Visual Basic project, and paste all the contents into the code window for the cSound class module, as shown in Figure 20.2.

FIGURE 20.1

Choose ActiveX DLL from the New Project dialog box.

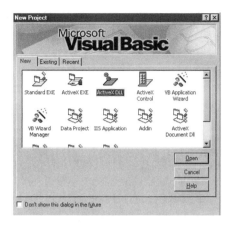

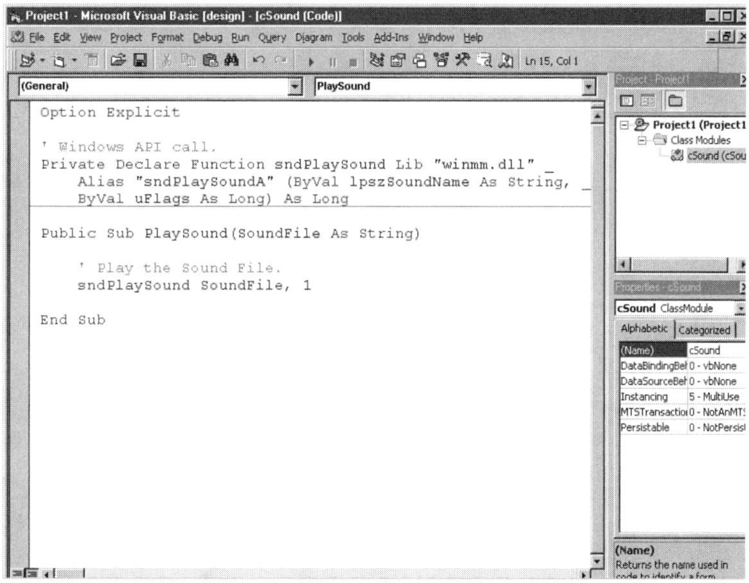

FIGURE 20.2

Copy the cSound code into the class module.

In the Project Properties window, there is an `Instancing` property. The default is set to `Multiuse`. Because ActiveX components contain class modules, you can create multiple instances of the class. This is useful because one unit of code can be used many times. With the `Instancing` property set to `MultiUse`, your Access application can create the sound object from this component. However, if numerous instances of the class are requested, only one is created. This reduces memory requirements, but when a second request for the object is made, it cannot run until the first request is completed. Most of the time, you will use the `Multiuse` default settings.

> **TIP**
>
> There are six settings for the `Instancing` property. Because this chapter is an overview of Visual Basic for Access developers, these property settings are not discussed in detail. See the Visual Basic Help for additional information.

The next step is to modify the project properties. Choose Project1 Properties under the Project menu.

Under the General tab in the Project Properties dialog box, shown in Figure 20.3, enter the project name `cSoundObject` (the project name cannot include spaces). In Project Description, enter `cSound Object`. The project description can include spaces, and this is the name that will be used when referencing the object in the References dialog box.

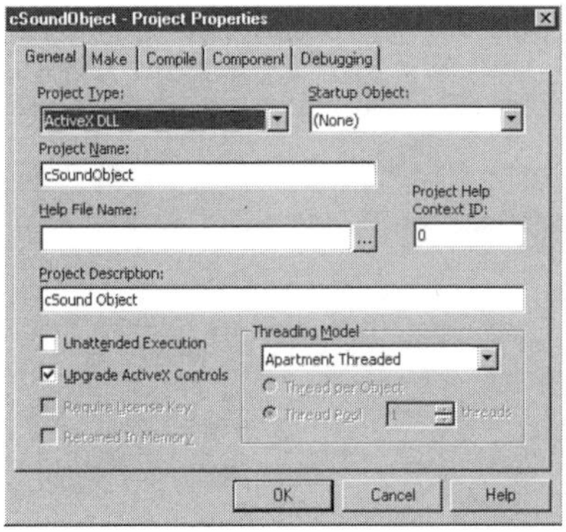

FIGURE 20.3

The Project Properties General tab.

Under the Make tab in Project Properties, shown in Figure 20.4, you can specify a version number. It is a good idea to check the Auto Increment check box so that each time you compile the component, a new version number is provided. In the Version Information section, you can enter a company name, copyright, product name, and other information. The rest of the settings do not have to be changed for this example.

Under the Compile tab, shown in Figure 20.5, the default is Compile to Native Code. Most of the time, you will not want to change this setting. If you choose Compile to P-Code, the code will run slower, but the component will be smaller in size. For information about other settings under the Compile tab, see the Visual Basic Help file.

FIGURE 20.4

The Project Properties Make tab.

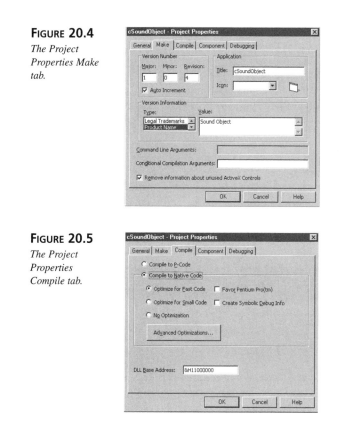

FIGURE 20.5

The Project Properties Compile tab.

Under the Component tab, shown in Figure 20.6, the default is set to Project Compatibility. This is the setting you should use as a developer when creating the component on your computer. The other options, No Compatibility and Binary Compatibility, are discussed later in the section, "Distributing ActiveX Components."

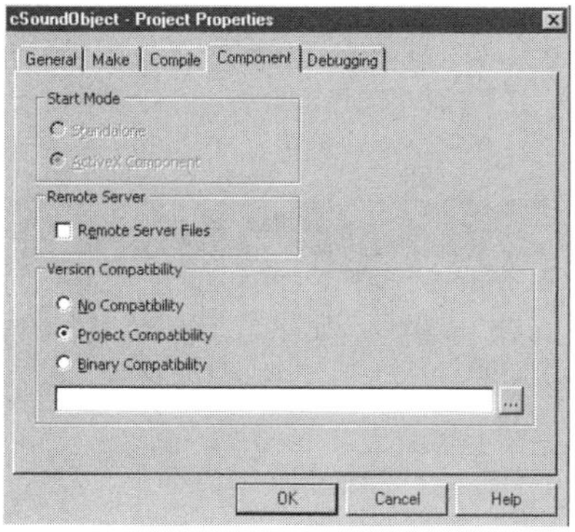

FIGURE 20.6

The Project Properties Component tab.

For this example, do not make any changes under the Debugging tab. Click OK to close the Project Properties dialog box.

Save the project and all the cSound class module by choosing Save Project under the File menu. It is best to save the project (.vbp file) and class module (.cls file) in the same directory (for example, Sound Object).

Compiling the DLL

Now that the project has been created and saved, the DLL can be compiled so that the object can be created and used. This is very easy to do. Choose Make cSound Object DLL from the File menu. You will likely be prompted to save this DLL in your Visual Basic directory. Instead, save the cSound object DLL in the same directory as your project file.

> **TIP**
>
> Saving the compiled DLL in the same directory as your project file makes it easy to locate.

The DLL has now been created and registered on your computer. In Visual Basic, whenever you have compiled a DLL, you can immediately begin to use it on the developer machine. Additional steps, covered in a later section, describe how to distribute the DLL to users on other computers.

> **NOTE**
>
> If you look at the directory in which you saved the project files (see Figure 20.7), you will see numerous files. Visual Basic saves forms, modules, and other objects as separate files on the disk. In contrast, Microsoft Access includes objects within one MDB file.

> **TIP**
>
> This example shows how to create an ActiveX DLL. The process to create an ActiveX EXE is very similar. To begin, open Visual Basic and start with an ActiveX EXE in the New Project dialog box.

FIGURE 20.7

Visual Basic saves the objects as separate files.

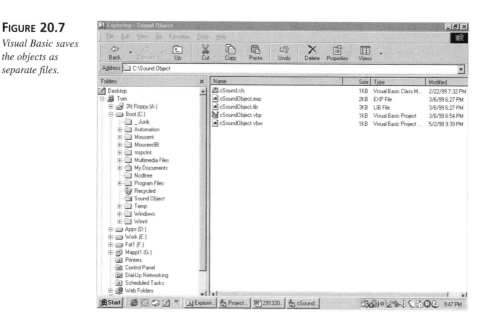

Using the cSound ActiveX Component

Now that the component has been created, you can use it from an Access application. The Access application must set a reference to the DLL and instantiate and use a Sound object.

Here's how to use the component: First, open a blank Access database. Give it a name (for example, Sound) and save it. Next, create a blank form in design mode, and add a command button to test the component. Open the event procedure for the Click event for the command button. In the code module window, set a reference to the cSound ActiveX component, and then choose References under the Tools menu. In the References dialog box, click the check box next to the cSound object. The cSound object name is the name specified in the Project Description in Project Properties. Click the OK command button to close the References dialog box.

It is necessary to set a reference to the cSound object, because this is a component external to the Access application. Notice that you will use the cSound object without any class module in your Access application.

In the command button Click event, enter the following code:

```
Private Sub cmdSound_Click()

    Dim objSound As cSound
```

```
Set objSound = New cSound

' If using Windows NT, use the path "C:\WINNT"
objSound.PlaySound "C:\Windows\chimes.wav"

Set objSound = Nothing
```

```
End Sub
```

Did you notice as you typed the code that IntelliSense appeared for the object?
(See Figure 20.8.) This is a terrific benefit for writing code faster and better.

FIGURE 20.8

IntelliSense
appears for the
cSound *object.*

With only a few lines of code, you can see how easy it is to create a sound object from
the ActiveX code component and use its properties, methods, and events. Also, you can
now use this cSound component from other Access applications. Changes will also be
simplified because all Access and other applications are using the same component. If
you decide to add or modify any of the properties, methods, or events of the component,
you have to make changes in only one place, in the component itself.

Using the Component in Other Applications

In addition to Access, you can use the cSound component in other COM-compliant
applications. You might want to use the component in VB, Office, Outlook, and Web
development.

Distributing ActiveX Components

When distributing components to end users, several issues arise:

- Installing the component
- Component Registry settings
- Component compatibility

Installing the Component

The easiest way to install components on the end user's computer is to use the Package and Deployment Wizard that comes with Visual Basic. This wizard creates a setup program that will install the component and make all the Registry settings on the computer. However, there are third-party installation programs as well.

Creating Setup Files with the Package and Deployment Wizard

Start the Package and Deployment Wizard, and on the first screen, click the Browse button to locate your project file (for example, cSoundObject.vbp and Figure 20.9).

FIGURE 20.9

The Package and Deployment Wizard initial screen.

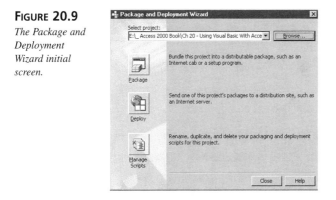

On the next screen, specify a Packaging Script (see Figure 20.10). For this example, choose "None."

On the next screen, specify the Package Type (see Figure 20.11). There are three Package Types:

- Standard Setup Package: Creates a standard Windows setup.
- Internet Setup: Creates an Internet setup.
- Dependency File: Setup includes only dependency files.

20

USING VISUAL
BASIC WITH
ACCESS

Figure 20.10

Specify a Packaging Script.

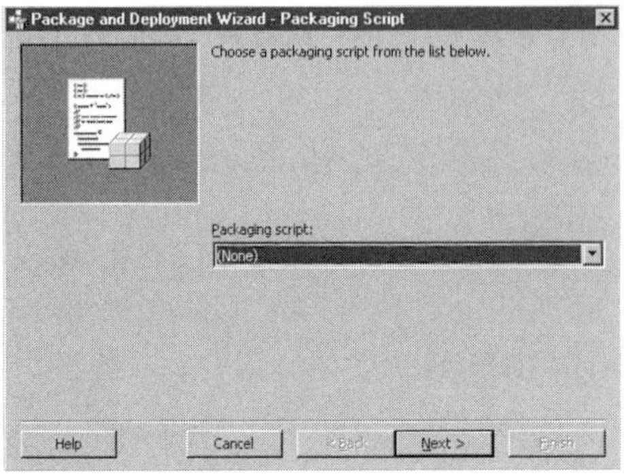

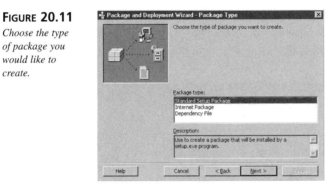

For this example, you will use the Standard Setup Package.

Figure 20.11

Choose the type of package you would like to create.

On the next screen, specify where you want your setup files located (see Figure 20.12). A folder will automatically be created if one does not exist.

Figure 20.12

Specify the package folder.

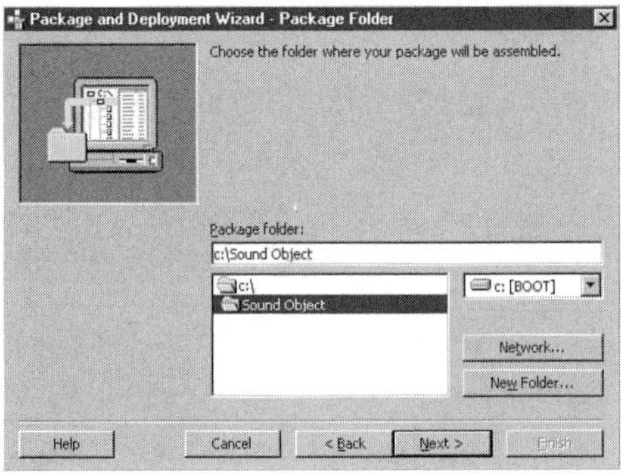

The next screen will show the files to be included in the setup (see Figure 20.13). The Package and Deployment Wizard does a good job of automatically including necessary files in the list. Notice that the component appears in the list, as well as the VB runtime file and other files. If you want to add other files to the setup, click the Add button.

> **TIP**
>
> The VB runtime file must be installed on the end user's computer for the component to work. After initially installing the VB runtime file, you might want to uncheck the VB runtime file's boxes to keep the setup file small.

FIGURE 20.13

Specify included files.

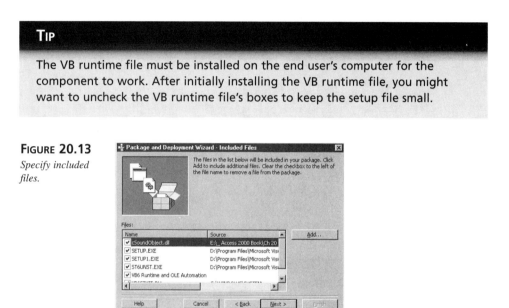

On the next screen, specify cab options (see Figure 20.14). A single cab (compressed) file can be created for a network or CD setup, or multiple cab files can be created for a floppy disk setup.

FIGURE 20.14

Specify cab options.

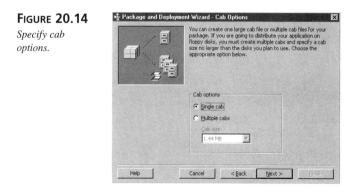

20

USING VISUAL
BASIC WITH
ACCESS

On the next screen, indicate the installation title (see Figure 20.15). Specify a friendly name because this is what end users will see if they run the setup program.

On the next screen, indicate the Start menu items (see Figure 20.16). You can create a program group that the end user can use to start an application with the Start button. Because this is a component, you would not specify a program group.

On the next screen, specify where the component will be installed (see Figure 20.17). You might want to install the component in your application directory for easy maintenance, rather than in the Windows/System directory.

On the next screen, specify whether the component will be installed as a shared file (see Figure 20.18). Shared files can be used by more than one application.

FIGURE 20.17
*Specify install
locations.*

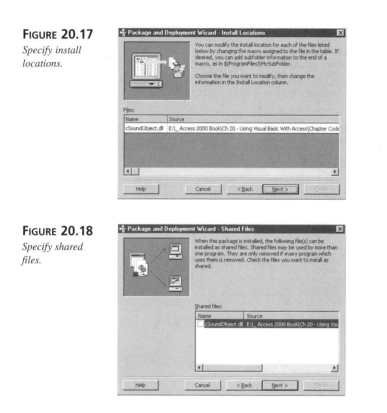

FIGURE 20.18
*Specify shared
files.*

On the last screen, a script name can be specified to save a setup script so that all the
options need not be selected the next time setup files are created (see Figure 20.19).
Click the Finish button to create the package.

FIGURE 20.19
*Specify a script
name and create
the package.*

The cab file(s) will then be created, and a Packaging Report will open with additional information. You can save the report if you like.

All the setup files are now located in the package folder you specified (see Figure 20.20). These files can be distributed to the user so that the component can be installed.

FIGURE 20.20

Setup files created.

The user can simply double-click the setup icon (or use Add/Remove Programs in the Control Panel) to install the component and other necessary files (see Figure 20.21).

Deploying Files with the Package and Deployment Wizard

After the setup files are created using the Package and Deployment Wizard, you must distribute the setup files to the end user. The Deploy part of the Package and Deployment Wizard includes a wizard to simplify this process.

Start the Package and Deployment Wizard, and on the first screen, click the Browse button to locate your project file (for example, cSoundObject.vbp and Figure 20.22). Then, click Deploy.

FIGURE 20.21
The setup created for the user.

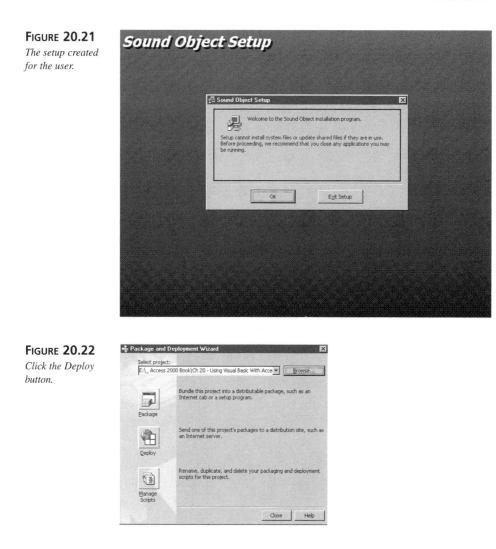

FIGURE 20.22
Click the Deploy button.

On the next screen, specify a Deployment Script (see Figure 20.23).

FIGURE 20.23

Specify a Deployment Script.

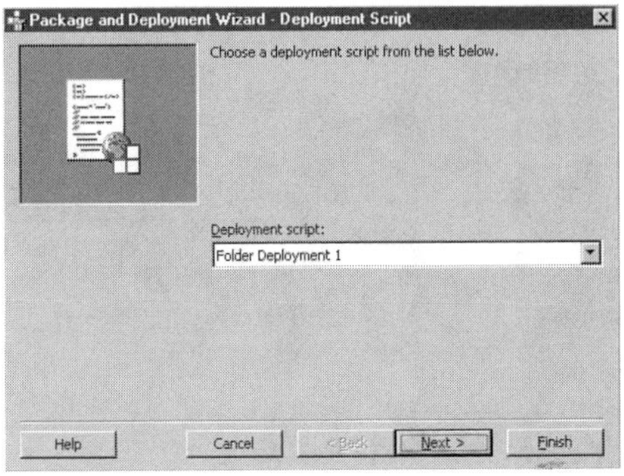

On the next screen, specify the package you want to deploy (see Figure 20.24).

FIGURE 20.24

Specify the package to deploy.

On the next screen, specify the deployment method. You can deploy to a local or network folder or to a Web server (see Figure 20.25). In this example, a folder will be used.

FIGURE 20.25

Specify the deployment method.

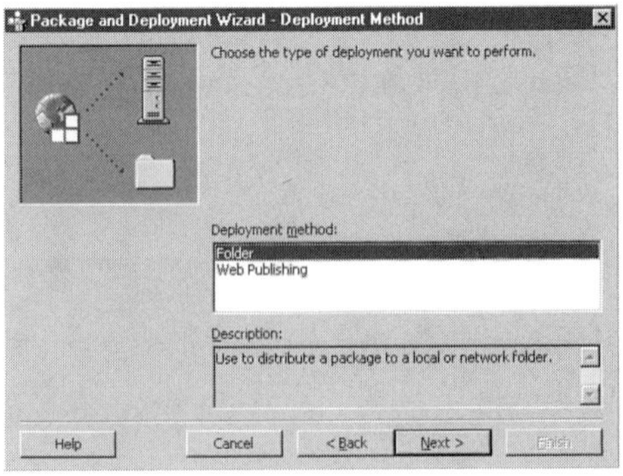

On the next screen, specify the folder to which you want to deploy a package (see Figure 20.26). This may be a folder on your network server.

FIGURE 20.26

Specify the deployment folder.

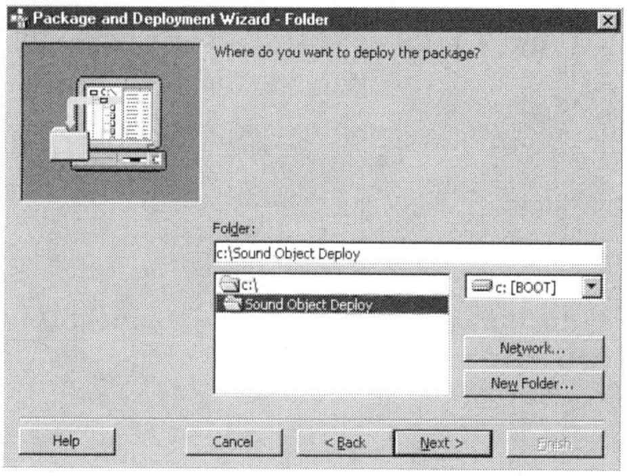

On the last screen, a script name can be specified to save a deploy script so that all the options need not be selected the next time the Deploy wizard is run (see Figure 20.27). Click the Finish button to deploy the package.

FIGURE 20.27

Specify a script name and deploy the package.

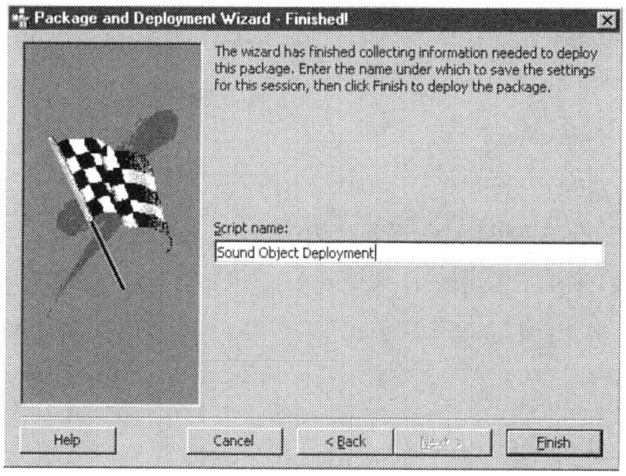

A Deployment Report is then created, which can be saved.

Component Registry Settings

For components to work, information must be stored in the Windows Registry. Specifically, a globally unique identifier (GUID) is assigned to the component. This is a randomly generated unique identifier.

When an application is installed using a setup created by the Package and Deployment Wizard, all the Registry settings are created automatically.

20

USING VISUAL BASIC WITH ACCESS

If the Package and Deployment Wizard is not used, components can be registered manually.

If the component is an ActiveX EXE, the component is registered when it is run from the DOS command line. Also, an ActiveX EXE can be registered by double-clicking on it in Windows Explorer.

If the component is an ActiveX DLL, use REGSVR32.EXE to register the component. REGSVR32.EXE is located on your computer in the Windows/System32 directory (or Winnt/System32 in Windows NT).

Enter the following in the Run command to register the component (see Figure 20.28):

```
REGSVR32.EXE "C:\Components\SoundObject.Dll"
```

FIGURE 20.28

Manually register an ActiveX DLL with REGSVR32.

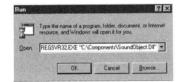

You can also manually unregister components. For ActiveX EXEs, run the executable from the command line, and append /UNREGSERVER as a parameter. For ActiveX DLLs, run REGSVR32, and append the /U parameter.

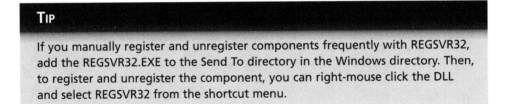

TIP

If you manually register and unregister components frequently with REGSVR32, add the REGSVR32.EXE to the Send To directory in the Windows directory. Then, to register and unregister the component, you can right-mouse click the DLL and select REGSVR32 from the shortcut menu.

Component Compatibility

As mentioned before, a component must be properly registered to work. The component will be assigned a GUID in the Windows Registry. But what happens if a component is installed and changes are made to the component later? When the modified GUID is installed, does it have to be reregistered and/or assigned a new GUID?

To answer these questions, you must go back to the Component tab in Project Properties. On the tab, there are three options under Version Compatibility: No Compatibility, Project Compatibility, and Binary Compatibility.

When developing the component, choose Project Compatibility. This will manage the Registry settings as you compile and recompile the component on the development computer.

When the component is initially shipped, choose Binary Compatibility (see Figure 20.29). In the textbox under that option, a DLL must be referenced to maintain compatibility. Navigate to the DLL using the ellipsis button. Whenever a new DLL is compiled, it will be compatible with the prior version of the component because it will refer to the DLL you specified.

CAUTION

Even with Binary Compatibility, if you change the interface of the component, the calling application will fail when the component is used. For example, if the method called PlaySound is changed to PlayMusic in the cSound component, the component will no longer be compatible. In that case, choose the No Compatibility option and redistribute the component with your Access application.

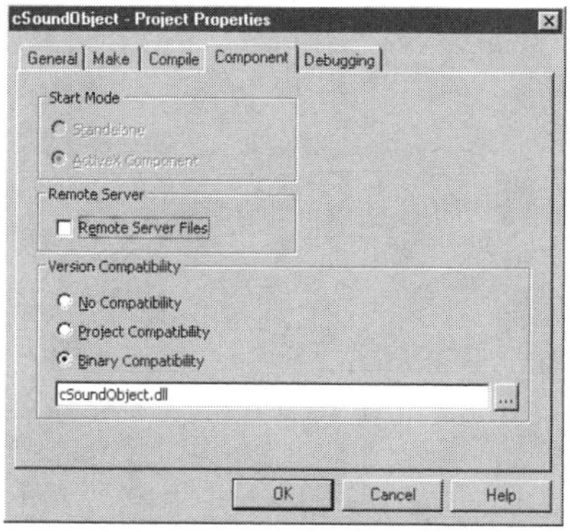

FIGURE 20.29

Choose Binary Compatibility and reference a DLL.

> **TIP**
>
> Take care not to delete the DLL referenced for Binary Compatibility. Create a DLL with a special name, and save it in a secure location. A naming example is Binary–cSoundObject.dll to alert you that this DLL is used for binary compatibility.

When do you use No Compatibility? Let's assume that you distribute the cSound component and later decide to eliminate the PlaySound method, replacing it with another method. All applications using the component will fail because they rely on the PlaySound method. In such a case, choose No Compatibility so that a new GUID is assigned. It is best in this situation to re-create the setup and distribute it as if it were the first time. In other words, this is a "do over."

> **TIP**
>
> Before reinstalling a component, it is best to uninstall the old version.

The Error Handling Component

In Chapter 13, "Professional Error Handling," an Error Handling class module is provided for extensive error handling, including

- Logging errors to an Access table
- Logging errors to a text file
- Email errors
- Record errors on an Outlook calendar

The code for this chapter includes a more comprehensive error handler using a cError component (cErrorObject.dll). The entire ActiveX DLL project is included so that you can utilize a "global error handler." With the DLL, you can use the error handler for program errors in all Access, VB, Office, and other applications.

> **TIP**
>
> In the chapter code are an Access application and VB application that use the cError component to log all errors to the global error handler.

Global Error Handling Data

The data for the `cError` global error handler is contained in an Access database named Global Error Handler Data.mdb. The database contains two tables. All error information is saved in the tblErrorLog table. The other table, tblErrorOptions, has settings to how the global error handler runs. A form in the database, frmErrorOptions, provides an easy interface to modify the error options (see Figure 20.30).

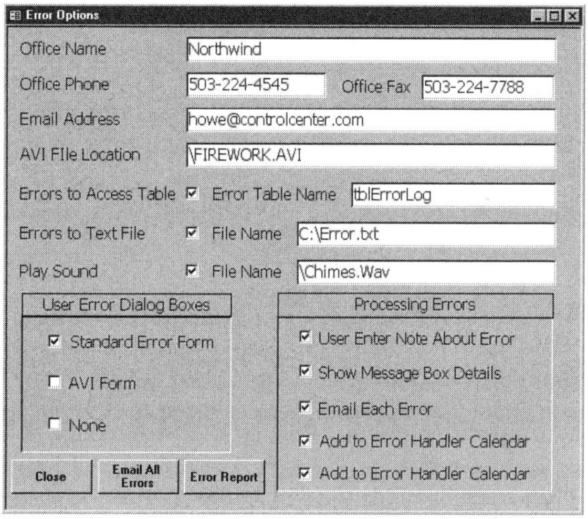

FIGURE 20.30

The Error Options form in the global error handler.

Also, the Global Error Handler Data.mdb includes an error report.

The `cError` Component

The bulk of the work is done by the error handling component. The component contains six class modules:

- `cComputerName`—Gets the name of the computer.
- `cDBConnection`—Creates an ADO connection.
- `cError`—Processes the error information.
- `cSound`—Plays a sound file.
- `cSystemInformation`—Gets computer information such as operating system, processor, and total and available memory.
- `cUserName`—Gets the Windows login username.

20

USING VISUAL
BASIC WITH
ACCESS

Creating ActiveX Controls

Visual Basic is exciting because it allows you to create your own ActiveX controls, giving you enormous power to extend your applications.

Types of ActiveX Controls

In Chapter 9, "Enhancing Forms with ActiveX Controls," 23 Microsoft ActiveX controls are discussed, and the chapter code includes examples of each control.

ActiveX controls are of two types: runtime controls and design-time controls. The runtime controls you looked at in Chapter 9, such as the TreeView and ListView controls, have an interface for user interaction. Design-time controls, on the other hand, are used by developers only; users do not interact with these controls. Examples include the ImageList and CommonDialog controls.

ActiveX Control Attributes

ActiveX controls cannot exist independently. They must be instantiated in a host application, typically a form.

A compiled ActiveX control is saved in a file, typically with an OCX extension. A single OCX file may contain several ActiveX controls. For example, MSCOMCTL.OCX shipped by Microsoft contains the following ActiveX controls: ImageCombo, ImageList, ListView, ProgressBar, Slider, StatusBar, TabStrip, ToolBar, and TreeView.

ActiveX controls are in-process Automation servers. Therefore, an ActiveX control you create and use on an Access form runs in the same process that Access runs in, which results in excellent performance.

Creating a Design-Time ActiveX Control

In Access, when a timer is necessary, developers generally use the On Timer property and Timer event of a form. One problem with this approach is that only one timer can be used. What if you need multiple timers, each working independently.

Visual Basic includes a built-in Timer control not available in Access. The VB Timer control is a design-time control that can execute code at certain intervals. To use the VB Timer control, place it on the form, and set the Interval property in milliseconds (1,000 milliseconds equal one second) (see Figure 20.31). Code in the Timer event executes whenever the interval occurs. Multiple VB timers can be placed on a form, each operating independently.

FIGURE **20.31**

Set the Interval *property of the* Timer *control.*

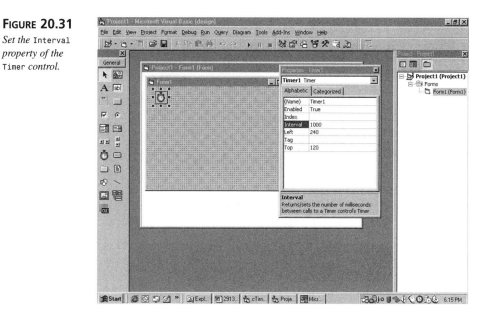

In this section, you will create your own Timer ActiveX control that can be used in Access and other applications.

> ### TIP
>
>
>
> The VB ActiveX Control project and Access database that use the Timer control are both available on the CD-ROM accompanying this book. Remember, the ActiveX control must be registered (compiled) on your computer in order to use it.

Starting an ActiveX Control Project

To create your ActiveX control, open Visual Basic. In the New Project dialog box, choose ActiveX Control (see Figure 20.32).

Creating the Interface

When the project opens, you will see what appears to be a form. Actually, it is not a form, but is called a UserControl object. The UserControl is used to create the interface for the ActiveX control. In the Properties window for the UserControl, change the name from UserControl1 to ctlTimer.

FIGURE 20.32

*Choose ActiveX
Control from the
New Project
dialog box.*

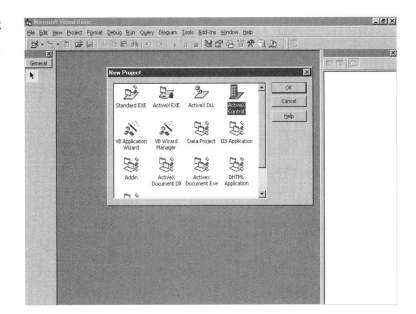

ActiveX controls may include other controls. In your `Timer` control, you will insert a
`PictureBox` control from the toolbox (see Figure 20.33). Name the `PictureBox` control
`picClock` and choose for its `Picture` property the CirClock.bmp from the
Bitmaps\Gauge directory where you installed Visual Basic. This picture of a clock is
what the developer will see when using the design-time control.

Next, insert a VB `Timer` control from the toolbox, and name it `ctlVBTimer` (see Figure
20.34). Notice in the Properties window of the control that there is an `Interval` property.
You will be using this property in your ActiveX control.

Now, you will resize the `UserControl` object. First, move the VB `Timer` control, and
place it directly on top of the `PictureBox` control. Then, choose Send to Back under the
Format menu. This will hide the control. Next, resize the `UserControl` so that it fits
around the `PictureBox` control, as shown in Figure 20.35.

Because this is a design-time control, the end user will never see it. In the `UserControl`
Properties window, set the `InvisibleAtRuntime` property to `True`.

FIGURE 20.33

Insert a
`PictureBox`
control on the
`UserControl`.

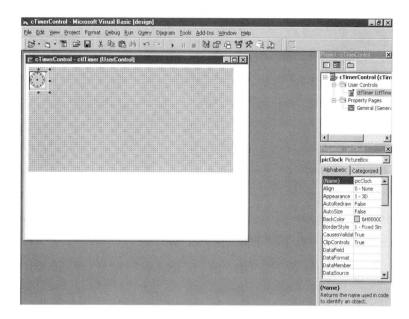

FIGURE 20.34

Insert a VB `Timer`
control on the
`UserControl`.

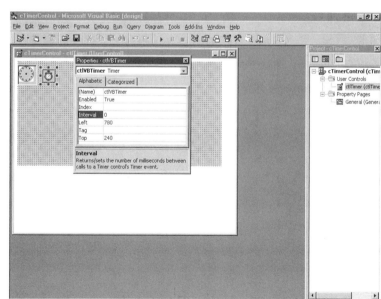

FIGURE 20.35

Resize the
UserControl.

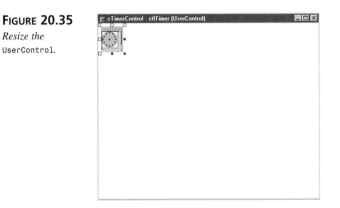

Setting Project Properties

Open Project1 Properties under the Project menu. In the Project Properties dialog box, enter the project name (`cTimerControl`) and project description (`cTimer Control`) as shown in Figure 20.36. Click OK to close the Project Properties dialog box.

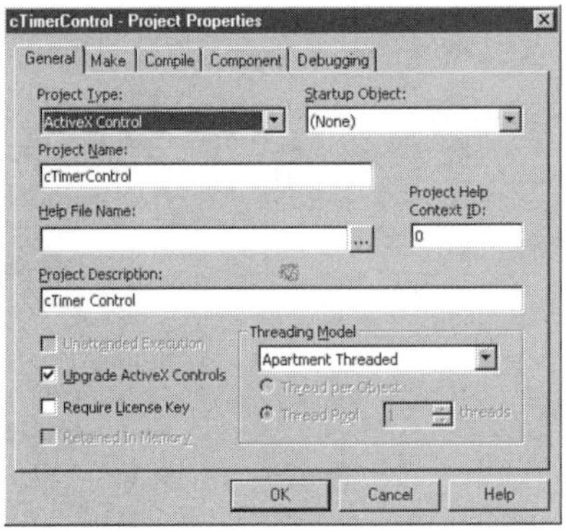

FIGURE 20.36

Specify the project
name and
description in
Project Properties.

Saving the Project

Save the project and `UserControl` by choosing Save Project under the File menu. It is best to save the project (.vbp file) and `UserControl` (.ctl file) in the same directory (for example, `Timer` Control).

Adding a Method and Event

Click the `UserControl` (not the `PictureBox`), and review the list of properties in the Properties window. Notice that there is no `Interval` property. You will have to add this property. Also, a `Timer` event must be added to enter code to execute when the `Timer`

interval occurs. To add properties, methods, and events to an ActiveX control, use the
ActiveX Control Interface Wizard.

Using the ActiveX Control Interface Wizard

Open the ActiveX Control Interface Wizard by choosing ActiveX Control Interface
Wizard under the Add-Ins menu. If you do not see the item under the Add-Ins menu,
choose Add-In Manager, select VB 6 ActiveX Control Interface Wizard, click the Load
on Startup check box, and then click the OK button to close the dialog box.

The first screen of the wizard is the Introduction screen (see Figure 20.37). Click the
Next button.

FIGURE 20.37

*The ActiveX
Control Interface
Wizard:
Introduction
screen.*

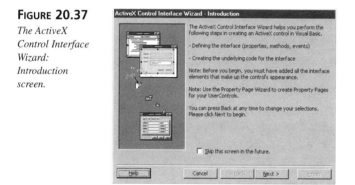

On the right side of the Selected Interface Members screen is a list of standard
properties, methods, and events (see Figure 20.38). Remove all the items on the
rightmost side. On the left side, choose the `Interval` property and `Timer` event, and
move them to the right side so that they are included in the control. Click Next.

FIGURE 20.38

*The Selected
Interface
Members screen.*

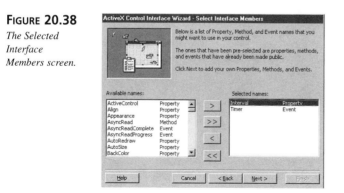

20

USING VISUAL
BASIC WITH
ACCESS

On the Create Custom Interface Members screen, click Next because you have already added the property and event you wanted (see Figure 20.39).

FIGURE 20.39

The Create Custom Interface Members screen.

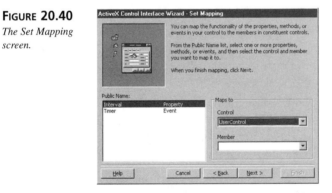

On the Set Mapping screen, select the Interval property and the Timer event, and map them to the UserControl (see Figure 20.40). Then, click Next.

FIGURE 20.40

The Set Mapping screen.

On the Set Attributes screen, choose the Interval property, and make sure that the data type is set to Long (see Figure 20.41). Then, click Next.

On the Finished screen, click the Finished button (see Figure 20.42). The wizard will write code for you to add the Interval property and the Timer event to the ActiveX control. Also, a Summary Report is created that can be saved to disk.

FIGURE 20.41

The Set Attributes screen.

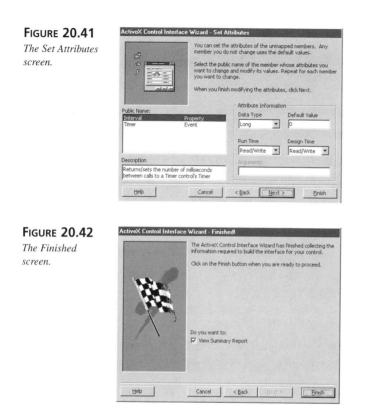

FIGURE 20.42

The Finished screen.

Open the code window for the UserControl, and examine the code (see Figure 20.43). The wizard created a Property Get and Property Let for the Interval property. Also, code was written to add the Timer event.

Adding Code to the ActiveX Control

The ActiveX Control Interface Wizard did a great deal of work for you, but you have to add a little code to complete your Timer control.

Raising an Event

In your ActiveX control, there is a VB Timer control with a Timer event. Your ActiveX control also has a Timer event, which was added with the ActiveX Control Interface Wizard. You have to synchronize these Timer events so that when the VB Timer event fires, it triggers your ActiveX control's Timer event.

20

USING VISUAL
BASIC WITH
ACCESS

FIGURE 20.43

Code created by the ActiveX Control Interface Wizard.

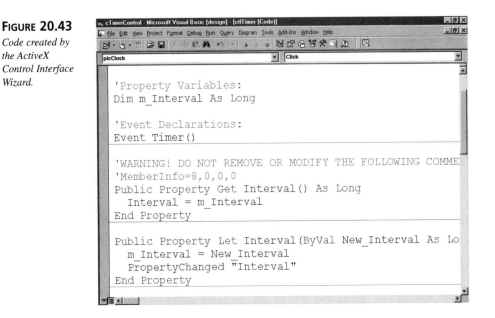

```
'Property Variables:
Dim m_Interval As Long

'Event Declarations:
Event Timer()

'WARNING! DO NOT REMOVE OR MODIFY THE FOLLOWING COMME
'MemberInfo=8,0,0,0
Public Property Get Interval() As Long
    Interval = m_Interval
End Property

Public Property Let Interval(ByVal New_Interval As Lo
    m_Interval = New_Interval
    PropertyChanged "Interval"
End Property
```

To do this, you will "raise" an event in your UserControl. In the code window, choose ctlVBTimer from the object list on the top-left drop-down list. Then, choose Timer from the event list on the top-right drop-down list. A Timer event procedure will then be created (see Figure 20.44). Enter the code shown in Figure 20.40 to "raise" the Timer event:

FIGURE 20.44

The RaiseEvent Timer.

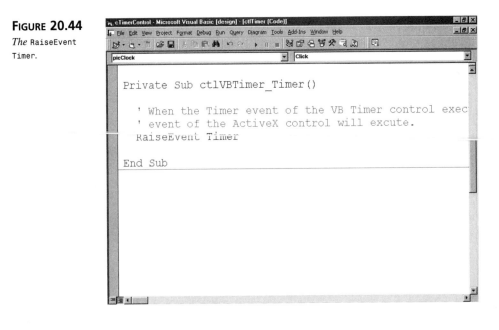

```
Private Sub ctlVBTimer_Timer()

    ' When the Timer event of the VB Timer control exec
    ' event of the ActiveX control will excute.
    RaiseEvent Timer

End Sub
```

What is the effect of this? When the VB `Timer` executes, its `Timer` event fires, which then triggers the `Timer` event of the ActiveX control. This will run the code you create for the `Timer` control.

Using the `ReadProperties` Event

When a developer inserts your `Timer` control on a form, the `Interval` property will be set to determine when the `Timer` event fires. The VB `Timer` control will take care of the time keeping. Therefore, the value in the `Interval` property of your `Timer` control must be synchronized with the `Interval` property of the VB `Timer` control.

ActiveX controls are created and destroyed often, as they are added to forms by developers and when forms that contain the control are opened. To synchronize the `Interval` properties, the `ReadProperties` event is a good choice because it will execute when the form hosting the control opens. The following code will set the value of the `Interval` property in the VB `Timer` control to be the same as your `Timer` control:

```
' When the interval on your control is changed on the form.
' change the interval on the VBTimer control in your control.
UserControl.ctlVBTimer.Interval = Me.Interval
```

Make sure that you save the project.

Testing the ActiveX Control in Visual Basic

Before using your `Timer` control in Access and other applications, let's test it in Visual Basic.

With the ActiveX Control project open, you can add a standard EXE project and test your control on a VB form. To add a project, choose Add Project under the File Menu. In the New Project dialog box, select Standard EXE. Notice that two projects are now displayed in the Project Explorer window (see Figure 20.45).

FIGURE 20.45

Add a project to test the ActiveX control.

Because there are now two projects, set the Startup Project to the Standard EXE (Project1). In the Project Explorer window, right-mouse click Project1. On the menu, choose Set as Startup. Now, when you run the project, the Project1 will start.

Next, close all the ActiveX Control project windows. Under the Windows menu, select any open windows (except Form1), and close each window.

While in the Design view of Form1, open the toolbox. Notice that on the toolbox is a new control named `ctlTimer`. Insert the control on the VB form (see Figure 20.46).

FIGURE 20.46

Insert the `Timer` *control on a VB test form.*

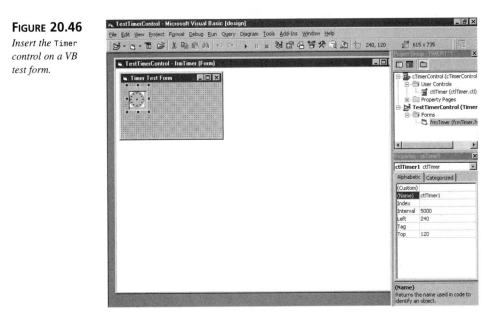

Your `Timer` control on the form can be used just like any other control (for example, `TextBox`). Its properties can be set in the Properties window, and code can be written to respond to events.

In the Properties window, set the `Interval` property to `5000`. Because the control uses milliseconds, the `Timer` event will execute every five seconds.

Next, choose Code under the View menu to open the code window. Choose `ctlTimer1` from the object list and `Timer` from the event list. In the `Timer` event procedure, enter a simple message box as shown in Figure 20.47.

Run the project by choosing Start under the Run menu (or press F5). Every five seconds, the message box will appear (see Figure 20.48). Notice that the control cannot be seen at runtime. Any type code can now be written utilizing your `Timer` control.

FIGURE 20.47

The Timer *event procedure.*

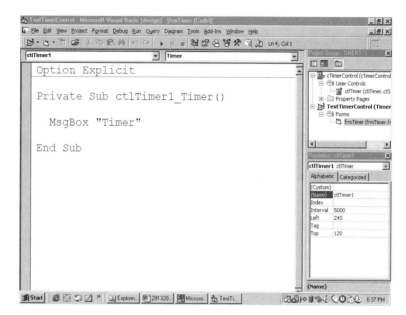

FIGURE 20.48

The message box opens every five seconds.

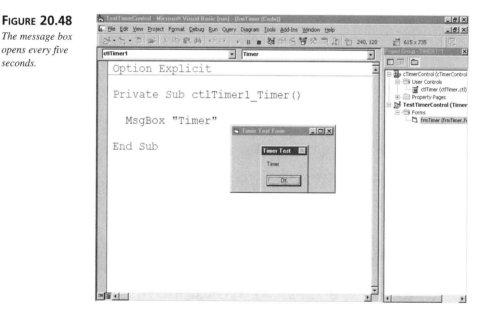

Now that you have tested your `Timer` control in Visual Basic, let's use it in an Access form.

Using the `Timer` Control in an Access Form

Testing your control was very easy in Visual Basic. To use the control in Access, you must compile the control.

Open the ActiveX Control project, and choose Make cTimerControl.ocx from the File menu. Save the OCX file in the same directory as your ActiveX Control project.

The ActiveX control is now compiled, and Registry settings have been made on your computer.

Open a form in design view in an Access database. Choose ActiveX Control from the Insert menu. Choose your `Timer` control (`cTimerControl`) from the list, and then click OK to close the dialog box (see Figure 20.49).

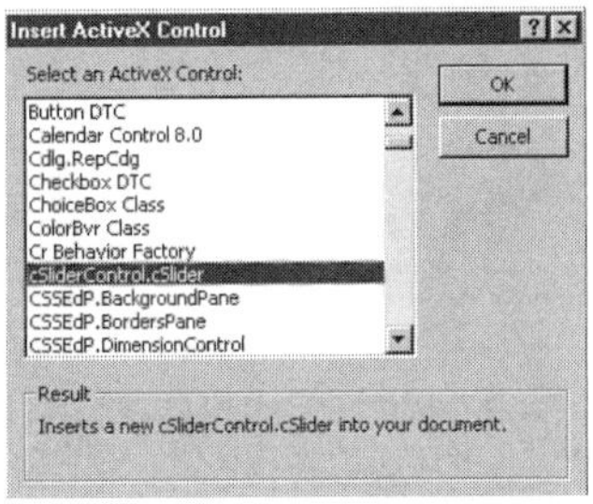

FIGURE 20.49

Choose cTimerControl *from the Insert ActiveX Control dialog box.*

As you did in the VB test form, set the `Interval` property of the control to `5000`, and create a message box in the `Timer` event.

The `cTimerControl` will now work on an Access form.

Using Multiple `Timer` Controls

The beginning of this section mentions that the `OnTimer` event of Access forms is often used as a timer. However, that is only one timer that can be used. You can place several `Timer` controls on a form, and they will all work independently (see Figure 20.50).

Distributing the `Timer` ActiveX Control

Distributing an ActiveX control is essentially the same as distributing ActiveX components. See the section earlier in the chapter titled "Distributing ActiveX Components."

FIGURE 20.50

Multiple `Timer` *controls working independently.*

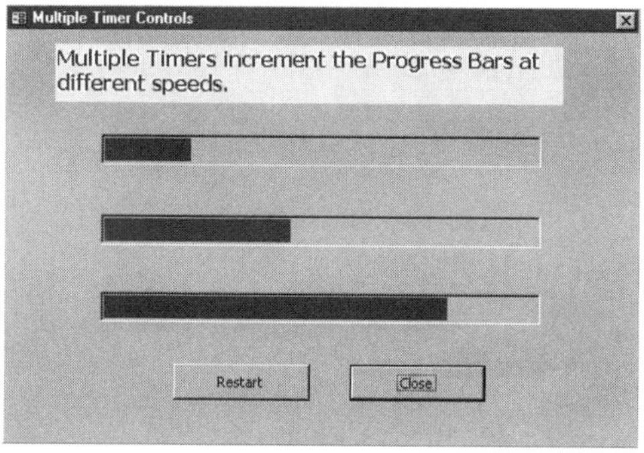

Creating a Property Page

Chapter 9 explains how to use property pages to easily enter property values for ActiveX controls. Figure 20.51 shows the property page for the ImageList control.

FIGURE 20.51

The `ImageList` *control property page.*

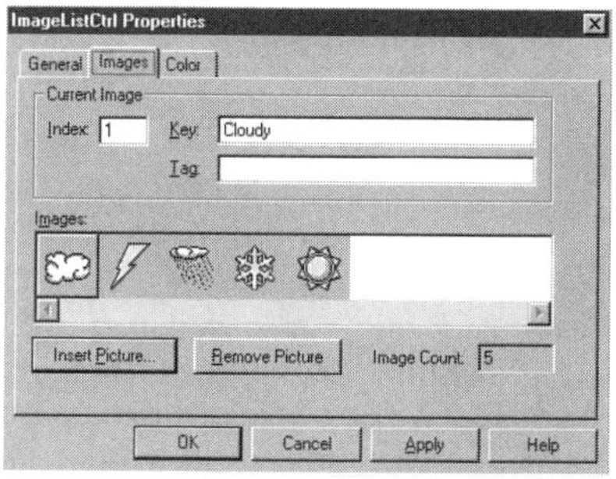

You can create a property page for your `Timer` control as well! In the ActiveX Control project, choose Add Property Page under the Project menu. In the Add Property Page dialog box, choose the VB Property Page Wizard. Click Open to start the wizard.

On the Introduction screen, click Next.

On the Select the Property Pages screen, click Add and add a General page (see Figure 20.52). Use the up arrow on the right side of the screen to list the General page first. Click Next.

On the Add Properties screen, click the General tab. Move the `Interval` property from the left list box to the right list box (see Figure 20.53). Click Next.

FIGURE 20.52

*The VB Property
Page Wizard:
Select the
Property Pages
screen.*

FIGURE 20.53

*The VB Property
Page Wizard: Add
Properties screen.*

On the Finished screen, click Finished. The wizard will create the property page and a
summary report that can be saved to disk. Notice that the property page now exists in the
Project Explorer window (see Figure 20.54).

FIGURE 20.54

*The property page
in the Project
Explorer window.*

Using the Property Page

To use the property page, save and recompile the ActiveX control. In design view of an Access form, insert the `Timer` control, and right-mouse click the control. On the menu, choose `cTimerControl` properties. The property page can be used to enter the `Interval` property (see Figure 20.55).

FIGURE 20.55

Using the property page.

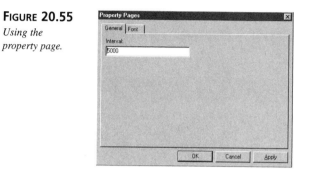

Using the `Timer` Control in Other Applications

Your `Timer` control is not restricted to just VB and Access applications. This same control can be used on a form in Word, Excel, Outlook, and other applications.

Creating a Runtime ActiveX Control

Most ActiveX controls have an interface with which users interact. In this section, you will create a runtime ActiveX control. The sample control will be named `cSlider` and will include a `Slider` control and `UpDown` control. As users increment and decrement the `UpDown` control, the `Slider` control will move.

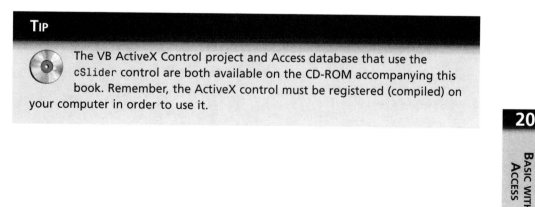

TIP

The VB ActiveX Control project and Access database that use the `cSlider` control are both available on the CD-ROM accompanying this book. Remember, the ActiveX control must be registered (compiled) on your computer in order to use it.

Creating the Interface

As with the design-time control, open an ActiveX Control project. On the UserControl, add a Slider control and UpDown control as shown in Figure 20.56. Notice that ActiveX controls you build can include many other controls.

FIGURE 20.56

Add a Slider *and* UpDown *control to the* UserControl.

Name the objects as follows:

```
UserControl: cSlider

Slider control: ctlSlider

UpDown control: ctlUpDown
```

Then, resize the UserControl.

Right-mouse click ctlUpDown, and choose Properties from the menu to open the property page. On the property page, you will associate the UpDown control with the Slider control using the Buddy property. The controls will then work together without writing any code.

Click the Buddy tab on the property page. In the Buddy Control text field, enter ctlSlider. This will associate the ctlSlider control with the ctlUpDown control. Choose Value from the Buddy Property list so that when the value of ctlUpDown changes, the value of ctlSlider will change. Enable the check box for Auto Buddy, and click OK to close the property page (see Figure 20.57).

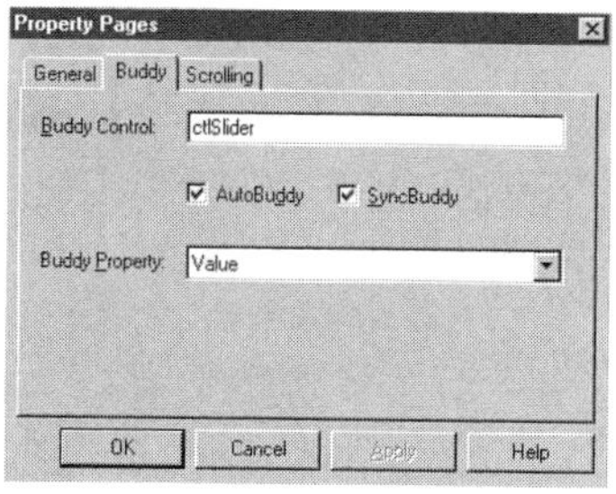

FIGURE 20.57

Set the Buddy properties in the property page.

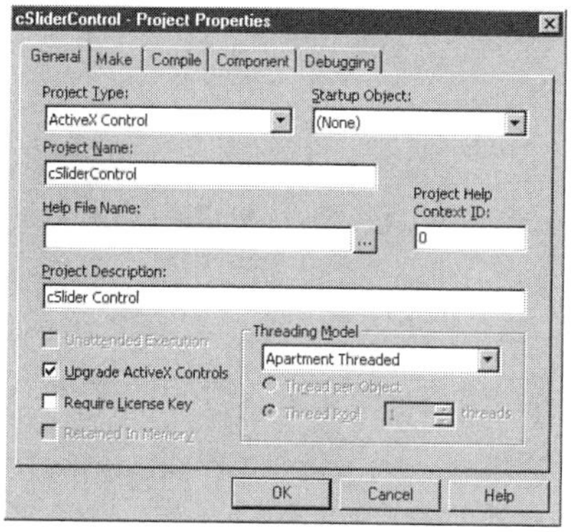

FIGURE 20.58

Specify the project name and description in Project Properties.

Setting Project Properties

Open the Project1 Properties under the Project menu. In the Project Properties dialog box, enter the project name (cSliderControl) and project description (cSlider Control). Click OK to close the Project Properties dialog box (see Figure 20.58).

Saving the Project

Save the project and UserControl by choosing Save Project under the File menu. It is best to save the project (.vbp file) and UserControl (.ctl file) in the same folder (for example, cSlider Control).

Testing the Control on a Visual Basic Form

You test the cSlider control on a Visual Basic form by following the same steps used to test the design-time control discussed earlier.

20

USING VISUAL
BASIC WITH
ACCESS

Using the `cSlider` Control in an Access Form

Open the ActiveX Control project, and choose Make cSliderControl.ocx from the File menu. Save the OCX file in the same directory as your ActiveX Control project. The ActiveX control is now compiled, and Registry settings have been made on your computer.

Open a form in design view in an Access database. Choose ActiveX Control from the Insert menu. Then, choose `cSliderControl` from the list, and click OK to close the dialog box.

The `cSlider` control now works on the Access form (see Figure 20.59). As the `UpDown` control changes, the slider changes as well.

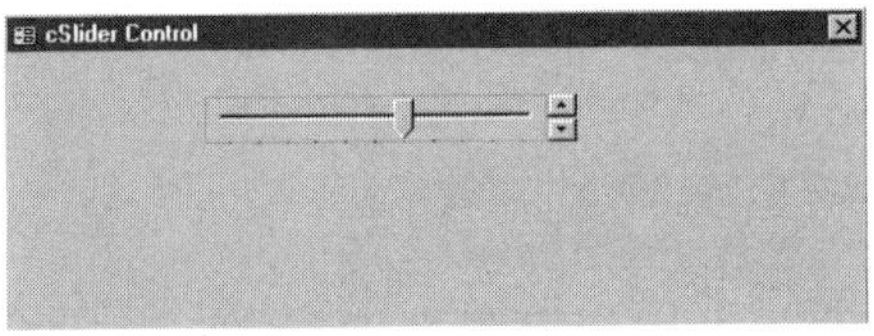

FIGURE 20.59

The ActiveX control on an Access form.

Distributing the `cSlider` ActiveX Control

Distributing an ActiveX control is essentially the same as distributing ActiveX components. See the section earlier in the chapter, titled "Distributing ActiveX Components."

Using the `cSlider` Control in Other Applications

Your `cSlider` control is not restricted to just VB and Access applications. This same control can be used on a form in Word, Excel, Outlook, and other applications.

Creating an Internet Package (Setup)

Use the Internet Package in the Package and Deployment Wizard to use the `cSlider` ActiveX controls on Web pages.

Start the Package and Deployment Wizard, and choose the `cSlider` project file (.vbp file). Click the Package button to go to the next screen (see Figure 20.60). Choose Internet Package, and click Next.

FIGURE 20.60

Choose Internet Package.

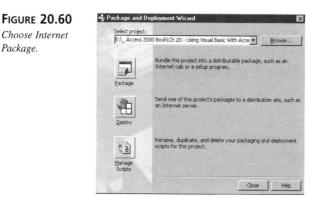

Choose a packaging script (see Figure 20.61). Because this is the first time this Internet Package is completed, choose None and click Next.

FIGURE 20.61

Specify the packaging script.

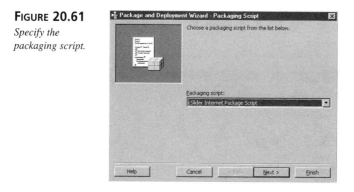

Choose the Internet Package type and click Next (see Figure 20.62).

FIGURE 20.62

Specify the package type.

20

USING VISUAL
BASIC WITH
ACCESS

Specify a folder for the package files, and click Next (see Figure 20.63). The default creates a package folder as a subfolder in your project directory.

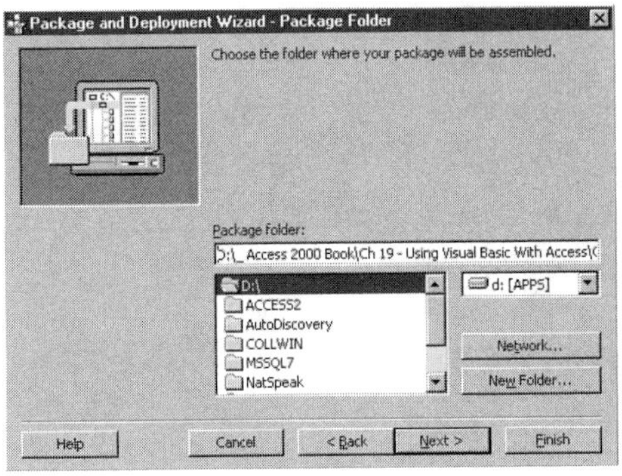

FIGURE 20.63

Specify the package folder.

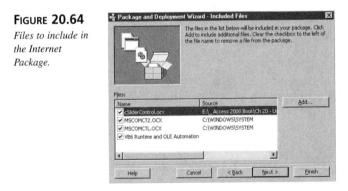

The Included Files screen will show all files necessary to use the ActiveX control. This includes the VB runtime file and any other necessary files (see Figure 20.64). Click Next.

FIGURE 20.64

Files to include in the Internet Package.

On the File Source screen, specify the location of the files to install (see Figure 20.65). The control you create (OCX file) will generally be included in the cab (compressed) file. The default setting for the VB runtime files and other Microsoft files is the Microsoft Web Site. You might want to leave this default setting as is because users will then be able to download these files as needed from Microsoft's Web servers. Click Next to continue.

FIGURE 20.65

Specify the file source.

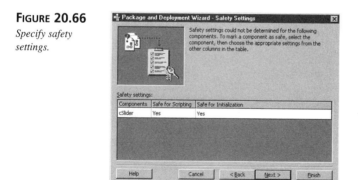

On the Safety Setting screen, the cSlider control is listed. Choose Yes for Safe for Scripting and Safe for Initialization (see Figure 20.66). This is your declaration that the control is safe. Click Next to continue.

FIGURE 20.66

Specify safety settings.

On the last screen, you can specify a script name to save a deploy script so that all the options need not be selected the next time the Deploy wizard is run (see Figure 20.67). Click Finish to deploy the package.

20

USING VISUAL
BASIC WITH
ACCESS

FIGURE 20.67

*Specify a script
name and deploy
the package.*

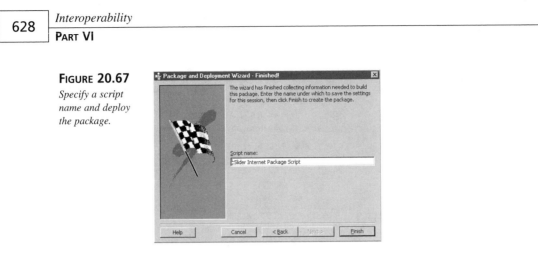

A Deployment Report is then created and can be saved for later use.

Using the `cSlider` Control on Web Pages

Open the folder where the Internet Package was saved. Notice that a
cSliderControl.HTM file was created (see Figure 20.68).

FIGURE 20.68

*Files in the
Internet Package
folder.*

Double-click the cSliderControl.HTM file, and it will open in the browser. The cSlider
control works just in the browser as it did in VB and Access forms (see Figure 20.69).

FIGURE 20.69

The cSlider
*control on a Web
page.*

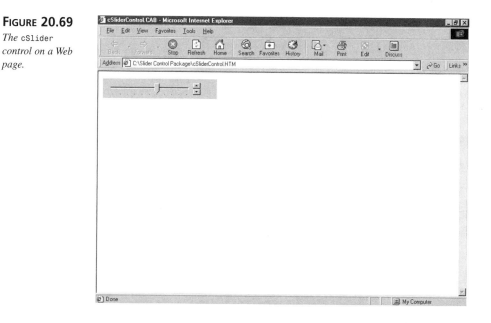

To view the HTML for a Web page, open Microsoft Internet Explorer, and choose
Source under the View menu. Notice in the HTML that the cSlider ActiveX control and
its class ID are shown as follows (see Figure 20.70):

```
<OBJECT CLASSID="clsid:5220cb21-c88d-11cf-b347-00aa00a28331">
    <PARAM NAME="LPKPath" VALUE="LPKfilename.LPK">
</OBJECT>
-->

<OBJECT ID="cSlider"
CLASSID="CLSID:A3251E4A-CCCF-11D2-A8AC-0010A4F61FE6"
CODEBASE="cSliderControl.CAB#version=1,0,0,0">
</OBJECT>
```

20

**USING VISUAL
BASIC WITH
ACCESS**

FIGURE 20.70

ActiveX control object code in HTML.

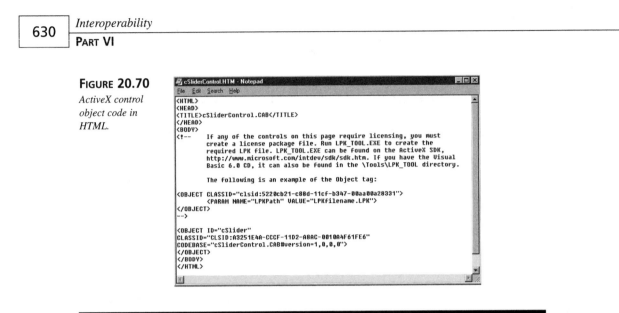

> **TIP**
>
> If you want to use the `cSlider` ActiveX control on another Web page, copy the HTML object code from one Web page to another.

Summary

Using Visual Basic to create ActiveX code components and ActiveX controls can enhance and extend Access applications. With ActiveX code components, the same code can be used in Access and many other applications. This makes maintaining the code much easier because changes to the code have to be made in only one place—the code component.

Visual Basic allows you to create ActiveX controls to use in Access, in other applications, and even in Web pages. You can create runtime controls with an interface users interact with, as well as design-time controls exclusively for developer use.

Multiuser Issues

Multiuser Issues/File Server/Locking

CHAPTER 21

As soon as an Access database leaves its development environment and ventures out into the world to be used by the people for whom it was built, it will suffer from multiuser issues. The most vexing multiuser problem faced by Access developers is record contention caused by the concurrent use of the Access database.

Contention

The important thing to remember is that every multiuser database is subject to the problems caused by locking and contention. Suppressing the error messages, dismissing the issue, or hoping for the best will not make the problem go away. Though multiuser issues sound complex, a thorough understanding of how Jet locks data and handles multiple users is not hard to obtain. Not dealing with multiuser issues will typically create far more complex problems involving users, clients, and reputations. Failure to effectively deal with multiuser concerns will result in the following application problems:

- New records will not be saved—There can be nothing worse than a user entering data into your application and finding that the data has disappeared. The fact that they probably cannot duplicate the error for you does not mean that the problem does not exist; it just means that they are correct in saying the application is unreliable.

- Changes to existing records may not be saved—A client might not even realize that changes were not saved. However, at some point in the future, the balance sheet will be off or there will be too many items in inventory, or an important client's order will be sent to the wrong address. These are insidious problems and they are likely to go undetected for a time. It is usually an innocent bystander who suffers the initial consequences.

- Users will get cryptic messages that the system cannot meet their request for data—Though less dramatic than the other two problems, there's nothing that will disappoint a user like an application throwing in the towel under a light workout.

In Access, multiuser issues are not just about locking records and releasing those locks. Because an Access application exists as a single file and because it can have at least some of its forms directly bound to data, any discussion of multiuser issues must include file level issues, configuration, interface design techniques, and the properties of queries and forms. A typical Access application will require a combination of multiuser tactics because it will encounter multiuser issues in several different ways in the various parts of the application.

Multiuser Issues/File Server/Locking

CHAPTER 21

635

21

MULTIUSER
ISSUES/FILE
SERVER/LOCKING

Configuration

At the file level, an Access application can be configured in several ways to accommodate multiple users. Each has its advantages and disadvantages. Some of these benefits and drawbacks are described here.

- Network deployment—In this configuration, a single MDB file is placed on a network server and users access the database from that server. The data and the executables might be one MDB, or they might be split into more than one file, though all reside on the file server. The advantage of this configuration is ease of maintenance because there is only one executable to update. However, because all the forms, reports, modules, queries, the Access EXE, all DLLs, and so on, must be passed over the network to the desktop, network traffic is needlessly high and performance can be abysmal. A configuration such as this will probably use bound forms as a rule and as you will see later, binding forms to data can exacerbate contention problems.

- Split database with data on network—This configuration has traditionally been called a remote database configuration (note that the use of the word "remote" is undergoing some change in the ever-changing Internet age and might soon be archaic in this context) because the data is separated from the executable or code, yet the data engine remains local. Unlike a client/server configuration, the Access data engine on the user's desktop manages, retrieves, locks, and releases the data in the MDB file on the network server. The multiuser capability of this configuration is dependent upon the various users' data engines working in concert with one another and with the file server's capability to accommodate the traffic. By far the preferred way to deploy most Access database applications, the main advantage to this method is performance and, when done correctly, control. With the data on the network, only data must travel over the wire, so network traffic is greatly reduced. The main disadvantages of this configuration are that every desktop must have Access installed and an MDE (a compiled version of the application's forms, queries, reports, and modules) or MDB version of the client executable thereby increasing the maintenance burden, but there are ways to manage that.

- Replication—In a replication scheme, users share data, but the data is not common as in the network deployment or split database arrangement. In a replication scheme, each user or a small group of users has a private copy of the data, which, through Jet Replication, is kept in sync with another database or databases. One advantage of giving each user his own copy of the data is that the potential for locking issues can be completely eliminated, but they can be traded for replication issues, which can be nearly as tricky as contention issues. Another big advantage of replication implementation is that it allows disconnected users to share data asynchronously. Another drawback to this scheme is that even if only a small group of users shares a common data source, the application may have to deal with contention issues and replication issues together. Finally, replicable databases tend to be much larger than databases that do not employ replication in their design.

- Client/Server Configuration—Access 2000 now enables developers to create client/server setups with Access's new Access Data Project capability. In a client/server configuration, the data is remote and so is the database engine. When SQL Server, Oracle, or some other database server controls your data from a central location, it will also control the locking and manage the multiuser issues. This does not mean that you don't have to worry about them; it means you have to deal with a different set of habits, capabilities, messages, and rules. The major advantages to this configuration are performance, stability, and the capability to handle a large number of users and lots of activity. The greatest disadvantage is cost and increased complexity.

This chapter will explore the issues common to the network configuration: the split database configuration and a client/server implementation. The issues unique to replication are discussed in Chapter 22, "Replication and JRO."

When using Access, there are settings at the database level, in the forms, queries, recordsets, and the level of code execution that need to be set and coordinated in order to make sure the application will reliably handle multiple users. Almost all the topics discussed in this chapter have a place in various parts of an application, and the technique or combination of techniques that you choose will vary from one application to another and from one part of an application to another. The key to multiuser management is planning, prediction, and testing.

Access and Jet Locking

Jet has a locking scheme that can be used to handle multiple users effectively. When Jet is used with Access, as opposed to being used with VB or some other development tool, there are some default behaviors that need to be considered. This section will deal with these development issues.

Locking Overview

Before a multiuser database application can be deployed, it must be positioned at a location where more than one user can access it, and it must be told to open for shared use. There are several ways to do this.

In the Options dialog box (Tools, Options, Advanced) there is the Default open mode option. Here you can tell the database if it should open for exclusive use (only one user at a time) or if it should open for shared use.

When Exclusive is chosen, only one user will be able to open the database. When opened in this way, Access changes the file header of the LDB file, or Access's locking file (for more on this file, see "The LDB File" later in this section), to prohibit any other users from accessing the data. Obviously, this setting must not be selected in a multiuser application. However, maintenance tasks such as compact and repair must be performed on a database that is opened exclusively.

The Shared option allows several users to open the database at once. When this is done, Access will write information about the users in the LDB file when they open the database and will negotiate the locking and releasing of pages and rows.

These and other options are accessible from the command line when starting an Access application. Table 21.1 explains some of these switches.

TABLE 21.1   COMMAND-LINE OPTIONS FOR OPENING ACCESS

Switch	Description
/Excl	Opens the database exclusively. Can be used even when the database's option is set to Shared.
/Ro	Read Only. Though available to multiple users, no changes can be made and no locks are used.
None	Default interpretation. The lack of either the /Excl or /Ro switch will open a database in shared mode or according to its option setting.

> **TIP**
>
> It is critical to prevent users from opening a database in Exclusive mode when it should be shared. This can be prevented by removing the OpenExclusive permission from the users' groups when you configure the security on the application. See Chapter 23, "Security," for more on Access security options.

When in the database, the developer has the option of choosing the default record locking mode. The two choices are row-level locking or page-level locking.

Page-Level Locking Versus Row-Level Locking

In the past, Access was particularly vulnerable to contention problems because of the way it stored records and locked them. Because Access maintains a variable length record it could not implement row-level locking easily. In exchange for the advantages of this record structure, Access had to store records in a static 2KB page (in Access 2000's Jet 4.0 data engine, the data page is now 4KB) structure. When a record was locked, intentionally or incidentally, the entire page was locked. Locking the page also locks the other records in the page along with the one being edited. Though very efficient, this compounded the contention issues and limited the number of concurrent users for Access applications and has been a widely criticized limitation of the development efforts using Access.

In Access 2000, Jet 4.0 offers developers the choice of using row-level locking or page locking as the default record locking approach. Now a user can lock only the record he is editing and not the other records on the page. Because a single record might be locked for only an instant (as would be the case when executing a Delete, Update, or Insert SQL statement), the chance that two users will conflict while editing that record is lower than it would be if several records were locked at the same time under a page-level locking scheme. Previously, the chance for conflict was multiplied by the number of records on the page, and that was difficult to determine. The number of records on a data page depended on the size of the record and when they were entered, so it was difficult to predict the conflict potential.

Row-level locking is the default setting, but that does not mean it is always the best choice. In situations where performance is extremely important, yet record conflicts are infrequent or manageable, the slight overhead of row-level locking might prove to be too much of a compromise. Consider a system like a bank's foreign exchange trading system where records are entered far more often than they are edited. Because such a system would be found in a fast-paced environment and performance is important, the argument could reasonably be made that a performance hit should come only when a conflict occurs, but all other database activities should run as fast as possible. In such a case, a page-locking scheme might be in order.

On the other hand, if concurrence is high and it is unacceptable to have more than one record edited by a user at a time, row-level locking is available to meet that requirement. This would be especially true if a database is very actively edited. Going back to the hypothetical bank example, a database that records deposits and withdrawals from customer accounts must have a high level of availability. It would have to lock some records

exclusively while they are being edited; otherwise, a user runs the risk of having his changes overwritten by a concurrent user. Moreover, when one account record is being edited, that edit cannot prevent anyone else from editing a neighboring record. Row-record locking might also be appropriate in situations where a record needs to be kept open for a period of time while preventing others from editing it. An example of this might be reviewing a customer's information for regulatory compliance or credit qualifications. You would not want that record to change until you have finished the review and rendered a judgment. If a user will typically keep a record open for several minutes, it would be counter-productive to lock several other records for the duration of that single edit. As a matter of good practice, you should avoid locking even a single record for any long period of time unless it is absolutely necessary.

So now developers have the capability to control multiuser behavior at the data page and row levels. This combination affords a great deal of flexibility.

The LDB File

The lock file is a special temporary file created when Access opens a database. It contains information about the locks being managed in the database and the users using the database. When the database is closed, the file is deleted. The file has the same name as the database it serves, except with an LDB extension. It always resides in the same directory as the database.

Optimistic Versus Pessimistic Versus Row-Level Locking

In a multiuser application, the only safe assumption a developer can make is that users will eventually be in contention for the same record. The only reasonable thing to do when faced with this fact is to plan to handle those situations by choosing suitable locking options. There are essentially two options to choose from: optimistic locking and pessimistic locking.

Optimistic Locking

As the default in Access, optimistic locking is the easiest to implement and is usually the right choice. When a record is locked optimistically, the user is working under the belief that contention is unlikely and no lock is placed on the record until the instant it is actually updated. This allows for a high degree of availability for the data because no one is making long-lasting or exclusive claims on the data. Accordingly, when a user opens a record for editing, other users are still able to open that record for editing and the first user to save his changes has the advantage. Though optimistic locking is easy to implement and usually causes few problems for users getting their data, optimistic locks raise one of the oldest multiuser issues known to databases—whose changes should get saved.

If Charles opens a record to edit it and places an optimistic lock on that record, there is nothing to prevent Karen from opening the same record to make a change. If Karen saves her changes before Charles does, Charles will get a message that reads:

```
"The Microsoft Jet database engine stopped the process because you and
another user are attempting to change the same data at the same time."
```

Earlier versions of Access presented a confounding dialog box prompting the user to choose between overwriting the other user's changes, not saving his own changes, or copying the information to the clipboard. This write conflict dialog box simply did not present enough information to make a reasonable choice between its options. The new write conflict dialog box, though harsh in that it offers you no options, is unambiguous. Later I'll examine the write conflict and explore some ways of handling the error better.

Pessimistic Locking

Pessimistic locks are the opposite of optimistic locks. When a record or a page is locked pessimistically, it is no longer available to other users from the moment the user begins editing the record to the time it is saved. Many other databases use this type of locking, so it should be familiar to most developers and the consequences of it will be familiar to users. Although pessimistic locking can eliminate the write conflicts seen with optimistic locking, it is not without problems.

When pessimistic locking is employed, the availability or concurrence of the data can be decreased. If page locking is being used, the problem is amplified because records on the page will also be locked and unavailable for a period of time. If the typical editing process is a time-consuming one and there are many concurrent users, pessimistic locking should be evaluated carefully. Some applications, such as sales and inventory processing, will probably benefit more from the pessimistic lock because control over a record is so important, whereas a time tracking system will probably find pessimistic locking a hindrance to performance. Most of the cautions and reservations that have been presented for pessimistic locking were made in the context of Access's page-locking approach. Now that Access can lock at the row level, pessimistic locking should see wider acceptance and usage.

Row-Level Locking

The principal benefit of row-level locking is the increase in concurrence. By locking only the edited record, more users will be able to gain access to more data without encountering locking conflicts or write conflicts. Using the row-level locking also allows developers to employ pessimistic locking in more applications. By doing so, users will see behavior that is both more familiar to them and more intuitive. Users expect to simply open a record, edit that record, and have their changes saved. In earlier

versions of Access, the page locking approach made the pessimistic lock too expensive in terms of concurrence to use widely. So users had to confront the prospect that someone else could block their changes and developers had to devise schemes to get the behavior their users expected (expanding records, temporary tables, and so on). Row-level locking is a major advance for Jet 4.0 and should make for even more popular and robust applications.

RecordLocks Property and the Bound Interface

When a bound form or a recordset is opened in Access, it is possible to set the locks on the underlying recordset. Of course, these options apply only to a Jet implementation, when using a client/server configuration, Access always assumes "No Locks."

The developer has three choices:

- No Locks—This would be the equivalent of optimistic locking.
- Edited Records—This would be the equivalent of pessimistic locking.
- All Records—This locks all the records in the recordset. This should be used with caution in a multiuser application.

> **TIP**
>
> Although binding the user interface to the data is an easy way to give users access to the data, you give up control when doing so. On a form bound to a pessimistically locked record, the user will receive a slashed-O in the record selector bar; however, he won't know who has the record locked. If the record selector bar is not visible, the user will only hear a beep.

Locking Methods of Jet

Locking is a normal and necessary occurrence in your database, but in order to make sure that the locks are of the correct type and duration, you need to be able to get information about them as they are occurring. This section will help dissect the locking behavior of your application to make sure it conforms to the intended design.

Determining the Status of a Lock

As discussed previously, the actual locking of a record or page of records occurs at different times when locking is done optimistically or pessimistically. Also, different parts of an application (or different applications) can use different locking approaches against the same data at the same time. Because of this, different types of errors will occur at different times. The error received depends upon the status of the lock.

ADO provides a LockType property of the recordset that indicates the type of lock placed on records during editing. The property is read/write before the recordset is opened and it is read-only while it is open. Table 21.2 describes the LockType constants for Microsoft.Jet.OLEDB.4.0. Other providers might provide different options. To determine what options are supported by a provider, use the .Supports method with adUpdate or adUpdateBatch.

TABLE 21.2   JET 4.0's LOCKTYPE CONSTANTS AS SEEN THROUGH MICROSOFT.JET.OLEDB.4.0 PROVIDER

Constant	Description
AdLockReadOnly	Default setting. Recordset cannot be altered, is opened read-only, and no locks are placed on data.
AdLockPessimistic	Pessimistic locking upon editing.
AdLockOptimistic	Optimistic locking upon calling the Update event.
AdLockBatchOptimistic	Optimistic locking for batch update mode.

NOTE

adLockPessimistic is not supported if the CursorLocation property is adUseClient; however, no error will occur. Jet will substitute another similar LockType. This is because by using the adUseClient, the server is not keeping track of your current record, so pessimistically locking it is not possible.

NOTE

The ADOR (ADOR is a subset of the ADO object model that provides only the Recordset and Field objects and can be created ad hoc or passed from server to client) subset (client-side recordset) object only supports adLockOptimisticBatch LockType.

Knowing the status of a record lock is important when developing, testing and supporting an application. Every process that handles data should be reviewed to see that it conforms to the intended design. Doing so is very straightforward. Stop the execution of code and review the LockType property of the recordset as shown in Figure 21.1.

FIGURE 21.1

The recordset's LockType *property will reveal the lock status of the recordset.*

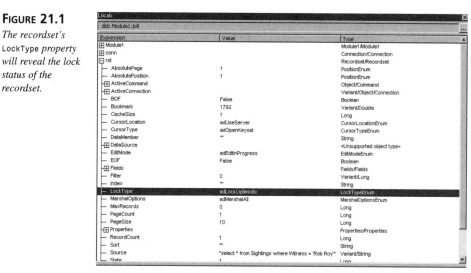

Another property will reveal if the recordset is being edited. The EditMode property will change from adEditNone before the editing occurs, to adEditInProgress while the record is being edited, to adEditNone again when the record has been successfully updated. Other values for the EditMode property are described in Table 21.3.

TABLE 21.3   VALUES FOR THE EditMode PROPERTY OF AN ADO RECORDSET

Constant	Description
AdEditNone	No editing is in progress.
AdEditInProgress	Data in the current record has been modified, but has not been saved.
AdEditAdd	Appears when the AddNew method has been called. Indicates the copy buffer contains a new record that has not been saved to the data.
AdEditDelete	The current record has been deleted.

The value of the EditMode property represents the status of the buffer used for editing and creating records. You can use this value to test if you need to invoke the Update or CancelUpdate methods when operations have been interrupted.

Testing Locks

The way to test the locks you have placed on records is to review the LockType and EditMode properties, but usually the greatest concern to a developer is to the lock placed by another user on the desired data. The only way to test locks is to actually cause a contention error.

Jet's OLEDB provider gives some information about the other user's lock when an error occurs. Upon a conflict, check the

```
Connection.Errors(index).SQLState
```

property to find exactly what kind of error occurred. Table 21.4 describes some of the contention error codes returned by .SQLState.

TABLE 21.4 LOCKING ERROR CODES PROVIDED BY JET 4.0 OLEDB PROVIDER

Code	Message
3006	Database <name> is exclusively locked.
3008	The table <name> is already opened by another user, or it's already open through the user interface and can't be manipulated programmatically.
3009	You tried to lock table <tablename> while opening it, but the table can't be locked because it's currently in use. Wait a moment, and then try the operation again.
3027	Can't update; database or object is read-only.
3046	Couldn't save; currently locked by another user.
3158	Couldn't save record; currently locked by another user.
3164	The field can't be updated because another user or process has locked the corresponding record or table.
3186	Couldn't save; currently locked by user <name> on machine <name>.
3187	Couldn't read; currently locked by user <name> on machine <name>.
3188	Couldn't update; currently locked by another session on this machine.
3189	Table <name> is exclusively locked by user <name> on machine <name>.
3197	The Microsoft Jet database engine stopped the process because you and another user are attempting to change the same data at the same time.
3202	Couldn't save; currently locked by another user.
3211	The database engine couldn't lock table <name> because it's already in use by another person or process.
3212	Couldn't update; currently locked.

Code	Message
3218	Couldn't update; currently locked by user <name> on machine <name>.
3260	Table <name> is exclusively locked by user <name> on machine <name>.
3261	Couldn't lock table <name>; currently in use by user <name> on machine <name>.

The error array also contains other potentially useful information regarding the error lock: information on the other user's lock. The `NativeError` property and the `Number` property tell you about the lock blocking your operation. These combinations and their meanings are shown in Table 21.5.

TABLE 21.5   HOW `NativeError` AND `Number` PROPERTIES OF THE `Connection.Errors` COMBINE TO REVEAL THE `LockType`

User	Property	Value	LockType
You	`Connection.Errors(0).` `NativeError`	–533791822	Pessimistic
You	`Connection.Errors(0).` `Number`	–105514571	Optimistic
Other	`Connection.Errors(0).` `NativeEr`	–2147467259	Pessimistic
Other	`Connection.Errors(0).` `Number`	–2147217887	Optimistic

At this time there is very little you can do with these values, except maybe use them for the timing of another update attempt. However, circumstances where that would make a difference are hard to determine. Consider them properties that might have some usefulness in the future.

Using Page Locking

Access has for years been unable to lock records on its own (there have been cludgy workarounds) and instead locked entire pages as described earlier in this chapter. To take advantage of the performance benefits of page-level locking, turn off the row-level default option. To do this, choose Tools, Options, Advanced and clear the Open databases with row-level locking check box.

Multiuser Locking Error Handling

Every multiuser system will have to anticipate locking errors. Different systems handle these errors in different ways and for different reasons. Different systems also provide different information to the developers and users when locking errors occur. This section will explore some of the lock settings and locking errors that you are likely to encounter while developing with Access 2000. It will also explain some techniques for handling these errors and avoiding them altogether.

Access's Locking Settings

The best way to handle multiuser errors is to avoid them. Access provides several properties that you can set to reduce the frequency of contention issues. These options can be found on the Advanced tab of the Options dialog box. However, they will not, by themselves, handle all such errors.

- Number of Update Retries—Controls the number of times Access will repeat its attempt to save or update a record against a lock. Valid settings are 0–10.
- ODBC Refresh Interval—Refresh interval, in seconds, when using ODBC database. Valid settings are 1–3,600.
- Refresh Interval—Refresh interval, in seconds, for refreshing records in Datasheet or Form view. Valid settings are 1–32,766.
- Update Retry Interval—Time in milliseconds before again trying to save a changed record against a lock. Valid settings are 1–32,766.

Write Conflict

The Write Conflict error (error number 3197 in Table 21.4) has been one of the most confusing errors in Access multiuser environments. User1 opens a record under optimistic locking and while he edits the record, User2 opens the same record, edits it, and saves it. When User1 finishes working with the record and attempts to save it, he will receive an error. In past versions of Access, the user was presented with a confusing dialog box asking him to overwrite the other user's changes (though it didn't say what they were), drop the changes he just attempted to make (never very popular), or copy the data to the Clipboard (then what?).

This error's internal handling has changed. In Access 2000, a Write Conflict will cause Jet to simply ignore User1's changes. Though this sounds harsh, it is better when you consider that most multiuser Access applications are created quickly and by people who might not have a clear understanding of multiuser issues. If nothing else, the treatment of the Write Conflict is at least decisive and final, and users do not have to answer a question they never thought they should have been asked in the first place. If an application needs to handle the write conflict differently, a custom error handler will have to be written.

Locked Record

When, in the normal course of using the application, User1 tries to change a record that User2 is editing, User1 will receive a Locked Record error (error number 3260 in Table 21.4). Typically, an error-handling routine will make a set number of attempts to save User1's record before giving up and telling User1 to try again or give up. If User2's lock is pessimistic, it will be released as soon as the record has been updated to the database. This is typically a very short period of time.

Transactions

A transaction takes separate or atomic processes and executes them as one. The set of processes either succeeds completely (committed) or fails completely (rollback). When a transaction fails, the database is restored (rolled back) to the state it was in before the transaction process began. This ensures that when an item is recorded on a bill of sale, it is also removed from inventory. When one account is credited, another is debited, and when a record is changed, an appropriate entry is made in an audit trail table. In the highly dynamic environment of a multiuser application, a user executing these kinds of updates and appends would very likely encounter locked-record errors on one part of the whole process, leaving accounts out of balance, inventories artificially inflated, or changes made but not completely recorded. In short, transactions help you maintain data integrity against the challenges of frequent and multiple record locks. Transactional processing should be used wherever possible in a multiuser application.

However, transactions are not an unqualified good thing. One thing a transaction does to ensure that all its changes are made is to accumulate locks. Transactions set all the locks, just as your application instructs, but do not release them until the entire process has finished and no errors have occurred. Because many locks could be set and they last longer than they would if they were set as part of a single process, the concurrency of the application is actually reduced. However, a database with high concurrency and low integrity is not worth very much, so this seems like a reasonable trade-off.

Transactions are methods of the `Connection` object in ADO. Table 21.6 describes the three methods.

TABLE 21.6 DEFINING A TRANSACTION

Method	Description
BeginTrans	From this invocation forward, all processes will be as one.
CommitTrans	Ends the series of processes and commits them to the database, provided there are no errors.
RollbackTrans	In the event of an error, cancel the process and set the database back to the state before BeginTrans.

The basic form of a transactional process looks like Listing 21.1.

LISTING 21.1 USING A TRANSACTION IN VBA

```
Function TestTrans() As Boolean
    Dim conn As ADODB.Connection
    Dim rst As ADODB.Recordset
    On error resume Err_TestTrans
    Set conn = New ADODB.Connection
    Conn.BeginTrans
    'execute processes such as SQL statements or .Edit .Update
    ➥.AddNew Methods
    'If everything worked, then commit the transaction.
    Conn.CommitTrans
    Exit Function

Err_TestTrans:
'Something went wrong, cancel the transaction and put everything
➥'back to the way it was.
Conn.RollbackTrans
......
End Function
```

Transactions can be nested, so that the committing of one transaction is dependent upon the committing of another. When nesting transactions, they must be resolved from the innermost or lowest level to the outermost or highest level.

Oracle/SQL Server Locking

When you work with Oracle, SQL Server, Informix, or any other data server engine, Access no longer controls the locking. However, the basic concept is the same—control access to the records in the database so that many users can use the database at the same time.

Data servers do this task extremely well. Because the data is located with the database engine, the record locking and concurrence management can be handled quickly, transparently, and reliably. Each of these applications keep locking information in a memory resident table and can decide on the most effective lock to employ, place the lock, execute the operation, and release the lock in a matter of microseconds.

In the case of Microsoft SQL Server there are three types of locks that it chooses form:

- Shared locks—Used in read-only operations. Shared locks enable other users to read a record or a page that is subject to a shared lock. A record or page can have multiple shared locks imposed on it at one time. Shared locks are released as soon as the data is not needed.

- Exclusive locks— When UPDATE, DELETE, or INSERT SQL statements are executed against the data, an exclusive lock is set. When an exclusive lock is imposed, no other operation can acquire a lock on the affected data until SQL Server releases the lock when the transaction has committed.

- Live locks— A live lock is a request for an exclusive lock which occurs after four repeated denials to make an exclusive lock on data. Live locks occur when there are too many overlapping shared locks. When the situation occurs, SQL Server will apply no more shared locks. Live locks prevent shared locks (from read operations) from monopolizing a table or page and preventing write operations (UPDATE, DELETE, INSERT). Live locks prevent a condition known as "lock starvation."

There are other strategies employed by SQL Server to handle concurrency issues. Among them are dynamic row-level locking (SQL Server 7.0); deadlock avoidance, detection and correction; optimistic concurrency control; and scalable lock escalation.

Dynamic row-level locking the lock manager in SQL Server dynamically adjusts the locks server configuration based on the size and usage of the database. This greatly reduces the need to assess, set, and maintain the lock server manually.

In deadlock avoidance and detection and correction, SQL Server recognizes when two transactions run into conflict. In this situation, SQL Server finds that one transaction has exclusively locked data needed by a second transaction and the second transaction has exclusively locked records needed by the first transaction. The first transaction will not release its locks and the second transaction will not release its locks either. Without intervention by the engine, they would remain in deadlock. SQL Server detects this condition, rolls back one transaction, completes the other, and runs the first one again to break the deadlock.

SQL Server actively avoids deadlocks by greatly reducing the number of table locks.

SQL Server employs an optimistic concurrency control approach to managing its multi-user environment. With an optimistic approach, users can use a server-side cursor to browse the data forward and backward without locking any data. Instead, SQL Server detects if rows have been modified since they were retrieved and then acts accordingly (usually rejecting the change unless accompanied with an explicit locking instruction). This approach makes a large amount of data available without extensive lock management and the overhead that entails.

Summary

This chapter has explored multiuser issues ranging from file configuration, to database settings, to recordset options, to data pages and data records. It has gone into detailed discussions of different locking strategies such as optimistic versus pessimistic locking and the advantages of Jet's new row-level locking capabilities. It has also explained how to determine what type of locks are being used in your database application and how to figure out the cryptic error messages from the OLEDB provider. Taken together, this chapter should help develop effective locking strategies and tactics for your next application, but it can also help you debug a troublesome existing database.

This is really just a survey—nothing will substitute for experience when it comes to developing for a multiuser environment. Contention is a serious issue and requires a developer's attention in every multiuser application. Contention issues will occur, on this there can be no doubt, but Access provides sophisticated tools for avoiding conflicts and handling them when they do occur.

CHAPTER 22

Replication and JRO

As corporations have become even more dependent on their data, their users have become more dispersed and the demands placed on their networks have increased dramatically. In response, software configurations are decentralizing into distributed systems in order to keep everyone informed and to spread the load. This trend brings with it new challenges. How does a corporation know that its users will always have access to their data when they need it? How will users know they are making decisions with the most up-to-date information? Can the data be trusted? Replication is one technique to meet these challenges and answer these questions.

This chapter will cover the creation and management of replicas. It will also introduce you to the new Jet Replication Object (JRO) for coding replication functionality and harnessing its flexibility. Jet has made remarkable improvements in replication. Among them, bidirectional data synchronization with SQL Server, better conflict resolution, the capability to designate priorities in the scheme, column-level resolution, and visibility to give you greater control in defining your replication topology.

When to Use Replication

There are several factors that should be considered when evaluating a replication solution. Not surprisingly, each potential benefit of replication has a drawback. However, there are some situations where replication is a wise choice.

If your application's performance is suffering from excessive lock contention because of heavy traffic or frequent report writing, you may find that dividing the database into two or more replicas and dividing the users between them will cut down on the lock contentions. The two data sources will replicate their changes between each other.

Similarly, if each user requires only a subset of the data in the data source, a partial replication scheme may be a good way to boost performance, cut contention, and secure sensitive data. (An example of this is a human resources application that distributes employee evaluations to department managers, allowing each manager to see only data for his own employees.) For increased speed, a time-tracking system can provide each replica with only that user's time history. Further, a time-tracking system for software developers, for example, might disconnect from the network in order to record that developer's frequent weekend, evening, and client-site work. A synchronization scheme would solve a number of problems in this application.

When you restrict the data a user can see, you are implementing partitioning in your replica scheme and it can be an effective way to keep your data from being updated by users who shouldn't be able to see it. There are three types of partitioning: vertical, horizontal, and vertical and horizontal combined.

When implementing a vertical partition, you are allowing only certain columns to be replicated to another database. You can do this by replicating through a query or view of the data that restricts the number of columns being presented. When replicating through a vertical partition, you must include the primary key in the presentation query.

When horizontally partitioning, you restrict the replication process by limiting the records that are replicated. This can be done with a replication filter or with a query. When replicating through a horizontal partition, you are replicating the entire record.

Horiztonal and vertical partitioning can be combined to restrict the records and the fields replicated simultaneously.

When an application must run every day and around the clock, backing up the data can cause an unacceptable interruption in the service the application provides. Replication could provide the data to a read-only replica at regular intervals, and then the replica could be backed up at regular intervals.

Replication is also a suitable solution when the data users have a high tolerance for data latency. This means that users can tolerate having their data out of date for some period of time greater than instantly. When reports are only run from the system once every hour or more, once a day or more, or if the reports are based on data up to a point in time that has passed (for example, as of the last day of the month, fiscal year end, or as of noon today), replication may be acceptable.

Though replication is usually used to distribute data, it can also be used to distribute other Access objects. I once used replication to update an application in Argentina with development changes made in New York. So, in certain situations, replication can alleviate some support headaches.

When Not to Use Replication

Like anything else, replication is not a panacea. There are definitely times it should not be used.

Replication causes your MDB file to become much larger because the replication process requires that Jet add objects, fields, and data in order to run and control the replications. If the systems you are developing for are short on resources, replication may not be a good idea.

Busy systems that have a high number of transactions may also cause problems for replication. A high frequency of transactions and the locks these transactions place on data usually lead to a high number of conflicts in the synchronization of the data.

Resolving these conflicts can greatly reduce performance. Without robust conflict resolution, replication in your design may prove more bane than benefit.

When the timeliness of the data is of the utmost importance, replication may not be acceptable because replication schemes require that users trade up-to-the-second data for concurrency, performance, and mobility.

Making a Database Replicable

There are several ways to make a database replicable. This chapter will cover the briefcase, the Access UI, and Jet Replication Object (JRO).

Replication Using the Briefcase

The simplest way to replicate data is to use the Briefcase. Though this technique is only suitable for synchronizing your desktop with your laptop and not much else, it is a good solution to a common problem. Also, it will work with files other than Access databases.

Typically, you would use Briefcase replication for yourself or for other users who are going to share data and files between a desktop PC and a laptop.

Before you can use Briefcase replication (or any form of replication for that matter), make sure the database does not have a database password. Then follow these simple steps:

1. Open Explorer.
2. Open Briefcase.
3. Copy your Access database into the Briefcase window and follow the instructions in the resulting dialog boxes starting with the one illustrated in Figure 22.1.
4. Respond to the first dialog by clicking Yes. Your database must increase in size in order to be replicable.
5. Allow the Briefcase to back up your database, if you have the disk space.
6. If you are only going to change the data in the database, tell the next dialog box that the original copy should not accept design changes. If you expect to make changes in the schema of the database, choose Briefcase Copy.
7. When you open either of these databases you will notice that the title bar now designates it as Design Master or Replica.
8. Copy the Briefcase to a removable medium and take it with you. However, if the machines are connected, drag the briefcase to the other machine.

FIGURE 22.1

Designate your database as a replica in the briefcase.

> Briefcase
>
> Briefcase has made an additional replica in the Briefcase folder.   `OK`
>
> You can make changes to the data in either the Design Master or a   `Help`
> replica of your database. However, you can make design changes
> (for example, add fields or change queries) only at the Design
> Master. Which member of the replica set should allow changes to the
> design of the database?
>
> ⦿ Original Copy
> ○ Briefcase Copy

9. When you have finished working off-site, put the updated file back on the original computer and open the Briefcase. Choose Briefcase, Update Selection.

Briefcase will figure out which updates must be made in each direction. When using the Briefcase alone, it is unlikely that you will encounter conflicts in the data. Later in this chapter, you will examine more complex, elaborate, and powerful ways to do replication.

You cannot reverse the conversion of a database into a replica; however, you can restore the database to a nonreplicable version of itself. To do so, follow these steps:

1. From the database you want to convert into a nonreplicable version, choose Tools, Options and go to the View tab. Turn off the System Objects.

2. Create a new database and open it.

3. Import all the objects from the replica into the new database.

4. On the View tab of the Options dialog box, make sure the System Objects option is selected.

5. Delete the s_GUID, s_Lineage, s_Generation, and s_colLineage columns from each table.

6. Save the new database.

Using the Access User Interface

The Access User Interface gives you more flexibility than the Briefcase, but with a little more complexity. With this approach, you can employ replication between different users on a network to share data and other Access objects. When using the Access UI, you are also able to distinguish between objects that will be replicated and objects that will not be replicated. The user interface approach also enables you to control when and with whom you replicate.

1. Exclusively open a database, making sure there is no database password.

2. From the Tools menu, choose Replication, Create Replica as shown in Figure 22.2.

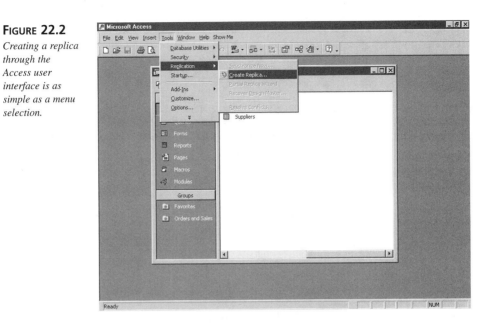

3. Access will close your database and reopen it before continuing. The next step asks you to allow the replica creation process to back up your database. The backup will have the original file name, but with a BAK extension. You should follow this advice.

The conversion process can take a few moments, depending upon the complexity of your database and the number of objects in it. In the process of converting your database to a replica, Access is doing several things.

- It creates a new MDB file and imports all your objects into it.
- It creates a replicable property for each object and sets that property to T so that it will replicate.
- It adds four fields of the types listed in Table 22.1 to each table in your database.

TABLE 22.1 FIELDS ADDED TO A TABLE WHEN IT IS MADE REPLICABLE

Field Name	Field Type	Description
s_ColLineage	OLE Object	Tracks changes to the column or field
s_Generation	Number	Tracks record changes

Field Name	Field Type	Description
s_Lineage	OLE Object	Tracks other changes
s_GUID	AutoNumber	A Global Unique ID to identify the record

These fields help Jet keep track of all the changes being made to your database and then decide what to do when there is a conflict between two database. You are not able to change the data, types, or design of these fields, and they are not visible in your tables unless you make them so. They can also add quite a bit of space to your database. You may find that, depending upon how much data you have and how many objects you have, your database may increase in size from 10 to 100 percent.

If a field has an AutoNumber data type, replication cannot be expected to work properly. It is reasonable to say that all tables could have a record with an AutoNumber of 1, 2, 3.... The only way to resolve these certain conflicts is to change the type of data kept in this field. If the field contains an AutoNumber type with an Increment setting for New Values, Jet changes the Increment to Random to make a conflict less likely. If this proves to be insufficient, it is possible to change this to Replication ID so that every record gets a GUID, thereby creating a unique record identifier. Creating random numbers is slower than Increment, and Replication ID is slower still, but sometimes it is necessary and unavoidable.

Jet also adds more than a dozen tables to the database. These tables are designated as Msys tables and, as such, are subject to change in any future release by Microsoft. You should hesitate before writing any code or creating any process that uses these tables in your application. Jet uses them, and it should be left at that. Table 22.2 gives a brief explanation of the function of each of these tables.

TABLE 22.2 TABLES ADDED TO THE DATABASE WHEN IT IS MADE REPLICABLE

TableName	Purpose
MSysConflicts	Tracks unresolved conflicts. Empty when conflicts are resolved
MSysExchangeLog	Logs various activity details on each synchronization

continues

22

REPLICATION AND JRO

TABLE 22.2 CONTINUED

TableName	Purpose
MSysGenHistory	Prevents attempts to send unchanged records during synchronizations
MSysOthersHistory	Logs various activity details from other replicas
MSysRepInfo	Information about the replica set and design master, including GUIDs
MSysReplicas	GUIDs for each replica in the set
MSysRepLock	Records failed attempts to lock a record during a synchronization
MSysSchChange	Schema changes to the design master are stored here while they are relevant
MSysSchedule	Schedule information when used with Replication Manager
MSysSideTables	Table names and GUIDs for conflicts
MSysTableGuids	Replicated table names and GUIDs
MSysTombStone	Table and row GUIDs for deleted records
MsysTranspAddress	Identifies the replica(s) with which your replica synchronizes

These tables are read-only and some of the data in them is stored as OLE objects, so they cannot be viewed.

Access also adds several properties to the database to control the replication process. These properties are `Replicable`, `ReplicableID`, and `DesignMasterID`.

- `Replicable` tells Jet that the database can be replicated.
- `ReplicableID` uniquely identifies the database and distinguishes it from all other replicas.
- `DesignMasterID` describes the database as the one that governs the changes made to the replicas.

Only the design master will accept design changes. There should be only one database designated as the design master in a replica scheme or replica set. Having more than one can cause data corruption and data loss.

Some objects are needed only by your local application, so you will notice that templates, most system tables, and wizards are not made replicable. However, system tables involved in tracking aspects of the replication process are made replicable and the MsysAccessObjects and MsysCmdbars are made replicable so that schema and menus can be part of your replication scheme.

> **CAUTION**
>
> Replication also reduces the number of nested transaction your database can perform. A replica can only support six nested transactions.

Distinguishing Between Local and Replicable Objects

When you depart from using the Briefcase for replication and start tapping Access's capabilities, one of the first things you will want to consider is whether an object in the database should be local or replicable; what kind of topology you should employ, whether or not the replication process should be managed or unmanaged, direct or indirect.

By default, Access marks all objects for replication. It is likely that your application will have objects that do not need to be replicated. These might be tables that contain local settings, temporary tables, or simple queries that just are not going to change that often (for instance, `Select * from Customers Order by Company Name`). You can control which objects are updated during synchronization by setting the replicable property. When an object is replicable, the property has a check box in the object's property dialog box (actually, it's a value of `T`); when it is local, the box is blank, and the object does not get synchronized. To make an object local follow these steps:

1. Select the object.
2. Click the right-mouse button and choose Properties from the shortcut menu.
3. Turn off the `Replicable` property and click OK.

The design master you are currently working with is a very special database. It is the only one you can make changes to, and it dictates all the changes to the other replicas. Typically, you don't want the design master to be in contact with its replicas because users may get updates of partially developed solutions. It's a good idea to isolate the design master from the replica set until you are certain you want to propagate the changes you have made to the database.

To flesh out the replication topology, you should create more replicas from the replica you just created. Do not continue to create more replicas from the original database because that will just give you a bunch of design masters and that will make your life miserable.

All the replicas you create from this replica—or from a replica of this replica—will be a member of the same replica set. They will share a set of GUID numbers that permit them to exchange data and schema information. The order in which you create these replicas has little bearing on the path or flow your replication takes. Each replica is able to synchronize with any member(s) of the replica set, and you are able to control the flow of the replication.

Upon synchronization, you choose the replica or replicas with which you will exchange information. As shown in Figure 22.2, in the Access Interface, this is done under Tools, Replication, Synchronize Now. The default setting is to choose one replica with which to synchronize; but other options are available too. You have the capability to choose to replicate in the background with all other replicas to which you have a valid path or with a single other replica.

Planning a Replication Topology

Deciding to use replication and creating replicas is only a part of what you have to do to really get the benefits of Access's replication capabilities. You also must decide who will replicate with whom, when they will replicate, how you will ensure that replication will be available when needed, and how you will handle complexities like remote users and slow connections.

These issues are addressed when designing a replication topology, or a map of the replicas. This map is determined by where replicas are located, how the replicas are related, how the replicas are made, and when they replicate. The topology of your scheme is crucial to its performance and reliability. You should take care to evaluate the different available topologies and choose the one that is appropriate for your needs. Don't let your topology happen by accident.

The combination of possible topologies is almost endless when you consider that you can use synchronization in one direction or two. You can force one replica to contain the cumulative changes in another replica, although not delivering its data to any other database. This may be useful to efficiently deliver end-of-day results to a manager's desktop when that manager only reports and analyzes the data, but never updates it. Replication can also follow a more traditional model where two databases synchronize their data so that they both reflect all the changes made in each database.

Figure 22.3 shows just a few possible replication topologies. Take note of the dependencies and the flow.

FIGURE 22.3
Basic replication topologies.

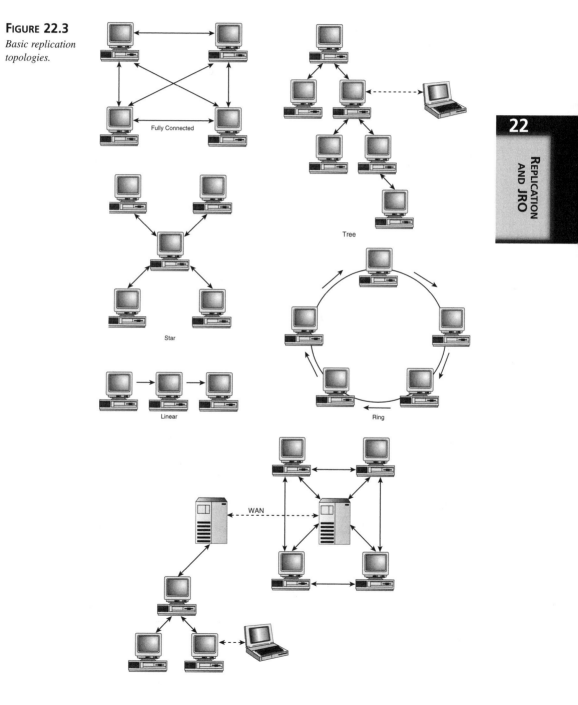

On a local area network (LAN), the users are able to maintain, for the most part, persistent connections to one another. In this case, hub and spoke, ring, multiple connection, linear, and tree and branch topologies can work well. Each of these has its strengths and weaknesses. The topology you choose could be a combination or a hybrid of these basic types. Table 22.3 explains some of the strengths and weaknesses of these basic types.

TABLE 22.3 BENEFITS AND DRAWBACKS OF DIFFERENT TOPOLOGIES

Topology	*Strengths*	*Weaknesses*	*Appropriate Use*
Multiple Connection	Provides the most up-to-date	Network traffic can be heavy. data for users with an even load distribution.	When quick updates are important and users are few.
Star	Low network traffic.	Hub is central point of failure and load is unevenly distributed and may require multiple synchronizations to propagate changes to all users.	Few users on a slow network.
Tree	Low network, strict control over dependencies' traffic.	Uncertain latency, uneven loads, some node failures are more severe than others.	When only some users make updates, the tree can be very efficient.
Ring	Even load distribution, low network traffic.	Fair latency, vulnerable to failure if replication cannot reverse direction.	Use in load-sensitive situations.
Linear	Worst latency, even load distribution, low network traffic	Very vulnerable to failure.	Simple implementation, good only for single-user replica to master configuration.

In a wide area network, where persistent connections might not exist or are simply too slow to keep them persistent, these topologies can be joined by assigning one replica to be the remote synch replica for another topology on the remote LAN. Jet also provides for synchronization over the Internet/intranet.

Whether you are using the Access UI to implement replication or you are using JRO or DAO, these topologies should be considered, before implementing your solution, based on their relative strengths and weaknesses and your application's needs.

Regardless of the approach you use to implement replication, you are the only one who can cause the replication to take place, and you must make those decisions and implement them. In a simple scheme, you can use the Tools, Replication, Synchronize Now dialog box or by triggering synchronization from an event in the application. That event could be at startup or at regular intervals (use a timer on an invisible form) after a certain number of changes have been made.

When synchronizing, you must decide between a managed and unmanaged scheme. If you choose to use a managed scheme, you will also have to choose if the replication will be direct or indirect. Your solution can use different options in different places and at different times, but it is crucial to know what the options are.

Choosing a Managed Scheme

Essentially, a managed scheme employs the Replication Manager and its sister application, Synchronization Manager. The Replication Manager enables you to schedule and control the replication events and resolve their resulting conflicts. The background execution, recordkeeping, and the capability to perform synchronizations as frequently as every 15 minutes make them worth using. Though it is possible to duplicate these functionalities in your own JRO or DAO code, there is usually no reason to do so.

Understanding Direct Synchronization

Direct synchronization occurs when both databases are opened and updated at the same time. To use direct synchronization reliably, you should have a dependable and persistent connection between the replicas.

Understanding Indirect Synchronization

You can use an indirect synchronization approach over a WAN or a slow connection. In an indirect synchronization, one database is opened, and a packet of changes is sent to the Synchronization Manager. When all the change packets have been received, the first database is closed and the second one is opened and updated. This makes the synchronization less vulnerable to a failure in the connection.

Choosing an Unmanaged Scheme

An unmanaged scheme does not rely on the Synchronization Manager. If you have a compelling reason, such as more frequent synchronizations than the manager can accommodate, or some type of event sensitive synchronization (such as when an item's inventory goes below a certain level), you can control the synchronizations through code that you create.

With all that explained, choose Tools, Replication, Synchronize Now and click OK to initiate a synchronization through the Access user interface.

Jet and Replication Objects Model

For the most control over the replication process and the resolution of conflicts resulting from replication, you can use the Jet Replication Object model (JRO). Taking this route enables you to remove the users from the replication process almost completely. With careful planning, JRO can make the benefits of shared data completely painless and invisible for the users of your application.

When programming your replication functionality, you can choose between two object models, which have different capabilities and interfaces. You can use Data Access Objects (DAO) or you can use the new Jet Replication Object. DAO's replication functionality is built into its object model along with its data manipulation capabilities, its security powers, and its data definition features. If you are using ADO to manipulate your data (and that is the default in Access 2000), why load a bulky object like DAO (DAO360.dll is 541KB), thereby duplicating functionality, when you do not need all of it? Instead, reference the specialized and extended capabilities of JRO (MSJRO.dll is 79KB). This chapter will explain handling replication with JRO.

The Jet Replication Object is an interface for replication and basic maintenance in the Jet database engine. This chapter will examine replication between Jet databases only, though you can use JRO to replicate between SQL 7.0 and Jet 4.0. Like Active Data Objects (ADO), Active Data Object Recordset (ADOR), and Active Data Object Extension for DDL and Security (ADOX), JRO follows the current trend toward flatness in the object model. The object model has only a few layers to it, and the methods and properties are easily accessible from the object level. Figure 22.4 illustrates the JRO model.

FIGURE 22.4

The JRO model.

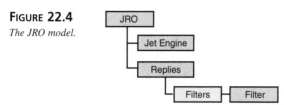

Exploring JRO

JRO exposes a set of methods and properties that enable you harness Access's replication capabilities. This section will examine the object model and explain its parts. Tables 22.4 and 22.5 show the properties and methods of the Replica object.

TABLE 22.4 JRO.Replica PROPERTIES

Name	Member of	Type	Notes
ActiveConnection	JRO.Replica	Object	
ConflictFunction	JRO.Replica	String	
ConflictTables	JRO.Replica	Recordset	Read Only
DesignMasterID	JRO.Replica	Variant	
Priority	JRO.Replica	Long	Read Only
ReplicaID	JRO.Replica	Variant	Read Only
ReplicaType	JRO.Replica	ReplicaTypeEnum	Read Only
RetentionPeriod	JRO.Replica	Long	
Visibility	JRO.Replica	VisibilityEnum	Read Only

TABLE 22.5 JRO.Replica METHODS

Method	Syntax
CreateReplica	Replica.CreateReplica(ReplicaName, Description [,ReplicaType] [, Visibility] [, Priority] [, Updatability])
GetObjectReplicability	Set ReturnValue = Replica.GetObjectReplicability (ObjectName, ObjectType)
MakeReplicable	Replica.MakeReplicable([ConnectString] [, ColumnTracking])

continues

TABLE 22.5 CONTINUED

Method	Syntax
PopulatePartial	Replica.PopulatePartial(FullReplica)
SetObjectReplicability	Replica.SetObjectReplicability (ObjectName, ObjectType, Replicability)
Synchronize	Replica.Synchronize(Target [, SyncType] [, SyncMode])

Tables 22.6 and 22.7 discuss JRO.Filters collections' properties and methods. Table 22.8 covers JRO.Filter properties.

TABLE 22.6 JRO.Filters COLLECTIONS' PROPERTIES

Name	Member of	Type	Notes
Count	JRO.Filters	Long	Read Only
Item	JRO.Filters	Filter	Read Only Default Property

TABLE 22.7 JRO.Filters COLLECTIONS' METHODS

Method	Syntax
Append	Filters.Append(TableName [, FilterType], FilterCriteria)
Delete	Filters.Delete(Index)
Refresh	Filters.Refresh

TABLE 22.8 JRO.Filter PROPERTIES

Name	Member of	Type	Notes
FilterCriteria	JRO.Filter	String	Read Only
FilterType	FilterType	Enum	Read Only
TableName	JRO.Filter	String	Read Only

JRO Properties and Methods Explained

The Jet Replication Object has several properties and methods of its own. The properties are used by JRO to identify the database, assign it a place within your replication topology, and determine how conflicts will be handled. The methods govern the creation of replicas, the synchronization between them, and the extent to which information is transferred between replicas. The Jet Replication Object's Replica object also contains a collection of filters that restrict, through criteria, the data passed between replicas.

`ActiveConnection` Property

`ActiveConnection` is the Connection object to which the Replica belongs. This property can also be a valid connection string if a `Connection` object is unavailable.

As with anything else in ADO, if the `ActiveConnection` property is set to nothing, any related objects will be disconnected from the data source.

`ConflictFunction` Property

You can set the `ConflictFunction` property to the name of the custom conflict resolution function you have created to use when resolving synchronization conflicts. You can create your own conflict resolution functions when the defaults are not

acceptable to you.

In earlier versions of Jet, there were replication errors (duplicate key errors, referential integrity violations, validity problems, and so on), and there were replication conflicts (two users made conflicting changes), and each was handled separately. With Jet 4.0, what were once considered replication errors are now treated together with replication conflicts. This makes resolving replication issues much simpler.

When developing a replication scheme, you should expect to encounter the following types of conflicts:

> Simultaneous Update—Two users have attempted to update the same record at the same time. One of the users will lose the conflict, thus relegating his record to the conflict table.
>
> Unique Key Violation—Upon synchronization, two records have the same value in a field restricted to unique key values.

Table-Level Validation Violations—When a database tries to synchronize and a record violates a validation rule set in the table's design (zero-length strings, values out of range, and so on) a table-level validation conflict occurs and the offending record is rejected.

Referential Integrity Violations—When deleting a record in a replica where that record is the one side of a one-to-many relationship, any record based on a foreign key will be rejected upon synchronization. When updating the primary key of a record in a replica, the change to the primary key will cause its previously related records in other replicas to be rejected. Replica records with foreign keys based on invalid primary keys will be rejected.

With each of these cases, the Conflict Resolver Wizard will present the rejected record to the user. The user can then decide whether to resubmit his changes, abandon his changes, or otherwise modify the data to avoid the conflict.

Microsoft Access uses the built-in Conflict Resolver to resolve these conflicts. The Conflict Resolver Wizard presents each conflict to the user, who must then manually decide which record contains the correct data.

To avoid this process, you can use the `ConflictFunction` property. This enables you to use custom conflict resolution code for resolving data conflicts that occur between replicas upon synchronization, or it can designate one replica in the set to always win the conflict. Set the `ConflictFunction` property to a text string that is the name of the function you want to call. Note that the setting must be the name of a Function procedure; it can't be the name of a Sub procedure. If this property has not been set, Microsoft Access calls the built-in Conflict Resolver.

Your custom conflict resolution function is called after the synchronization is complete. When you create a custom resolution function, you will use the conflict tables in your replica to evaluate the conflicts and update your records or the hub's records using standard data management techniques (DAO, ADO, RDO, or SQL).

When you write custom procedures to resolve conflicts, you override the built-in resolution algorithms. You should carefully consider the situations in which this is necessary. One possible scenario where you may benefit from writing custom conflict resolution functions is when you want to refer to a user's group membership to determine if his changes take precedence over the changes of another user. This approach would enable users to work from different replicas without being subject to that replica's priority in the replication topology.

By default, Jet 4.0 resolves conflicts using two priority-based algorithms, and it avoids conflicts by finding conflicts only at the column level.

In Jet 4.0, a replica is assigned a priority number. This number determines its pecking order in the topology. If two replicas conflict, Jet resolves the conflict based on their priority relationship. The highest priority replica always wins. In the event of a tie, the replica with the lowest ReplicaID (the one created earliest in the topology) wins. This algorithm is similar to the one used by SQL Server 7.0.

A priority is a value from 0 to 100, inclusive. When a replica is created, it receives a default priority of 90 percent of its parent.

Fewer conflicts should occur in Jet 4.0 than in earlier versions. In earlier versions, a conflict occurred if two users edited the same record, even if they made changes to different fields. In Jet 4.0, two users can change different fields of the same record, and no conflict will occur. Column-level tracking of changes will greatly reduce the frequency of conflicts, and it will make it easier for users to resolve those conflicts that do occur.

Column-level change tracking is the default setting in Jet 4.0. If your application needs row-level change tracking, it must be set before the tables are made replicable. To choose between column-level or row-level change tracking, use the replica.MakeReplicable method's columntracking argument. Setting the argument to True will enable column-level change tracking, whereas a False value will set the replica to row-level change tracking. The following method call would make the database replicable with row-level change tracking:

```
Replica.MakeReplicable CurrentProject.Connection, False
```

ConflictTables Property

This property specifies a recordset containing a list of tables and associated conflict tables.

Calling the ConflictTables property returns a recordset of two columns: TableName and its related ConflictTableName, in the replica database, for each table that had conflicts during the synchronization of two replicas. ConflictTables is read-only.

By opening the table named under the ConflictTableNames field of the ConflictTables recordset, you can view the entire record that lost the synchronization conflict and view its replication specific fields.

Listing 22.1 shows a sample of what a simple custom conflict resolution may look like. It uses ADO, ADOX, and JRO to work through all the conflicts by using the ConflictTables property.

LISTING 22.1 SIMPLE CUSTOM CONFLICT RESOLUTION

```
Function CustomDataConflictResolver()

    Dim jro As New jro.Replica
    Dim cat As New ADOX.Catalog
    Dim conflrs As New Recordset
    Dim rs As New Recordset

    On Error Goto CustomDataConflictResolver_Error

    Set jro.ActiveConnection = CurrentProject.Connection
    Set cat.ActiveConnection = CurrentProject.Connection

    ' jro.ConflictTables returns a recordset with all the relevant
    ' conflict table names
    Set conflrs = jro.ConflictTables

    ' For each relevant conflict table, examine the conflicts
    ' and resolve them
    While Not conflrs.EOF

        ' Open the actual conflict table data to analyze the losing records
        rs.Open "Select * From " & conflrs.Fields(1), jro.ActiveConnection

        While Not rs.EOF
            ' evaluate the conflicting records here and
            ' use SQL or ADO to overwrite changes if appropriate
            ' be sure to preserve records, which don't get resolved.
            rs.MoveNext
        Wend

        ' Close the recordset of the losing records
        rs.Close

        ' Get the next conflict table name
        conflrs.MoveNext

    Wend

    ' When you create a custom resolution function,
    ' you have to delete the conflict tables
    While Not conflrs.EOF
        cat.Tables.Delete (conflrs.Fields(1))
        conflrs.MoveNext
    Wend

    CustomDataConflictResolver = True
```

```
CustomDataConflictResolver _Exit:
  Set conflrs = Nothing
  Set rs = Nothing
  Set jro = Nothing
  Exit Function

CustomDataConflictResolver _Error:
  ' Handle the error
  CustomDataConflictResolver = False
  Resume CustomDataConflictResolver _Exit

End Function
```

The way you resolve these conflicts is completely up to you. You can always take the last record, always take records from certain users or groups, accept records based on highest or lowest values, or use some combination of all these approaches.

`DesignMasterID` Property

The `DesignMasterID` is a GUID that uniquely identifies the design master in a replica set. This property is set when the design master is created.

You can set a replica to act as a new design master, and you can make a replica change itself into the design master in the event the original is lost or corrupted; but a replica cannot change a different replica into the design master.

CAUTION

Setting this property at a replica when there is already another design master in the set could break your replica set into two irreconcilable sets of replicas. If this happens, you will not be able to execute synchronizations with all the previous users. Because a design master's GUID will be globally unique, only convert a replica into a design master in the unusual circumstance where a design master is lost or corrupted, and no other design master exits.

Replica Objects

Each database spawned from the design master or from another replica is a `Replica` object when addressed through JRO. The following properties and methods work to distinguish the Replica and control its behavior and interactions with other replicas.

22

REPLICATION AND JRO

ReplicaID Property

This property uniquely identifies a database replica and returns a Variant GUID that uniquely identifies a database replica. This GUID is created with the replica, and it is read-only in the replica.

ReplicaType Property

This property indicates the type of replica. It returns one of the following constants listed in Table 22.9:

TABLE 22.9 REPLICA TYPE Enums

Constant	Value	Description
jrRepTypeNotReplicable	0	Default. The database is not replicable.
jrRepTypeDesignMaster	1	The replica is a design master.
jrRepTypeFull	2	The replica is a full replica.
jrRepTypePartial	3	The replica is a partial replica.

The read-only ReplicaType property determines whether a database is replicable, and if so, in what way is it replicable. If ReplicaType is jrRepTypeNotReplicable. the database has not yet been made replicable. You can use the *ReplicaType* parameter of the CreateReplica method to create full or partial replicas.

RetentionPeriod Property

This property indicates how many days (from 5 to 32,000) to save replication histories. The histories include details of deleted records, schema changes, and other system-specific information. If the database was made replicable with ADO, RDO, or the Replication Manger, the default is 60 days. If the database was made replicable with the Access user interface, the default is 1,000 days.

This property must be set on a design master.

Visibility Property

This property indicates whether the replica is global, local, or anonymous. Visibility governs the interaction between replicas and is determined by one of the following constants listed in Table 22.10.

TABLE 22.10 Visibility Enums PROPERTY

Constant	Value	Description
jRepVisibilityGlobal	1	Default. The replica is global.
jRepVisibilityLocal	2	The replica is local.
jRepVisibilityAnon	4	The replica is anonymous.

You can create any type of replica from a global replica. Changes by a global replica are fully tracked and can be exchanged with any other global replica in the set. The global replica can also exchange changes with any local or anonymous replicas for which it becomes the hub.

Local and anonymous replicas require a global replica at the hub of their topology. They cannot synchronize with other replicas in the replica set. All local and anonymous replicas have a priority of 0; therefore, they will always lose any conflict with the hub. The hub will always assume authorship of any successful change.

Only the hub replica is aware of local replicas, and only it can schedule an exchange to a local replica.

Anonymous replicas should be used in an Internet topology when there is mass distribution of data because system-tracking information is not retained, and the size of the replica reduced. No replicas, not even the hub replica, can actively engage anonymous replicas. The hub replica cannot schedule an exchange to an anonymous replica.

Visibility is permanent and cannot be changed after the replica is created with the CreateReplica method. It is read-only.

CreateReplica Method

This method creates a new replica of the current replicable database.

```
Replica.CreateReplica(RepName, Desc [, ReplicaType] [, Visibility]
  [, Priority] [, Updatability])
```

ReplicaName—A String that specifies the fully qualified path of the full or partial replica to be created.

Description—A String describing the replica to be created.

ReplicaType—Optional. An Enum value indicating the type of replica to be created. The default value is jRepTypeFull. When a replica is a full replica, all data is exchanged during synchronization. In a partial replica, only data matching a filter you created will be exchanged. The constants listed in Table 22.11 are valid for `ReplicaType`.

TABLE 22.11 Enums FOR ReplicaType

Constant	Value	Description
jrRepTypeNotReplicable	0	Default value. Not replicable.
jrRepTypeDesignMaster	1	Replica is design master.
jrRepTypeFull	2	The replica is a full replica.
jrRepTypePartial	3	The replica is a partial replica.

`Visibility`—Optional. An `Enum` value indicating the replica's visibility. The default value is `jrRepVisibilityGlobal`. The constants listed in Table 22.12 are valid for `Visibility`.

TABLE 22.12 Visibility Enums

Constant	Value	Description
jrRepVisibilityGlobal	1	The replica is global.
jrRepVisibilityLocal	2	The replica is local.
jrRepVisibilityAnon	4	The replica is anonymous.

`Priority`—Optional. A `Long` value indicating how one replica will overrule another replica in the event of a conflict. The default value is `-1`, which means that the database should determine the default value. When you create global replicas, their default priority will be set to 90 percent of the parent replica's priority. If you are the database administrator, the entire range (0 to 100) is available to you. Local and anonymous replicas will always have a priority of `0` and cannot be changed. This value is forced with the creation of the replica, and any other value you attempt to assign will be ignored.

`Updatability`—Optional. An `Enum` value indicating the type of updates allowed. The default value is `jrRepUpdFull`. The constant `jrRepUpdReadOnly` prevents users from modifying replicable tables and their records; however, when you synchronize the new replica with another member of its replica set, design and data changes will be propagated to the new replica. The constants listed in Table 22.13 are valid for `Updatability`.

TABLE 22.13 Updatability Enums

Constant	Value	Description
jrRepUpdFull	0	The replica can be updated.
jrRepUpdReadOnly	2	The replica is read-only.

A replica either inherits the exact same characteristics or is more restrictive than the replica that created it. For example, a read-only global replica can only create either a local or anonymous read-only replica, although a local replica can only create another local replica with the same characteristics.

GetObjectReplicability Method

This method indicates whether an object within the database is local or replicated. The syntax of a proper GetObjectReplicability call is shown here.

```
Set ReturnValue = Replica.GetObjectReplicability(ObjectName, ObjectType)
```

This is a Boolean value indicating whether the object is capable of being replicated. In databases that have not been made replicable, this method returns True for all objects by default because they are capable of being replicated even though no replication scheme is in place. If the database is made replicable, these objects will return True on this method. In replicable databases, this method returns False for all new objects by default because new objects are not necessarily part of your replication scheme when they are created. GetObjectReplicability's parameters are defined below.

ObjectName—A String value specifying the name of the object for which to retrieve the replication state.

ObjectType—A String value specifying the type of object specified by *ObjectName*.

The GetObjectReplicability method indicates whether the object is or will be replicated.

The *ObjectName* and *ObjectType* parameters are strings that indicate the name of the object (for example, Customers) and the object's container (for example, Tables). An error will occur if an object of that name and type does not exist in the database or if either of these strings is longer than 64 characters.

See the SetObjectReplicability method for information on how to change an object's replicability.

An error will occur if the object specified by the *ObjectName* and *ObjectType* parameters does not exist.

MakeReplicable Method

This method makes a database replicable and is used as shown here.

```
Replica.MakeReplicable([ConnectString] [, ColumnTracking])
```

ConnectString—Optional. A String value specifying the name and fully qualified path of the database to make replicable. The *ConnectString* overrides the ActiveConnection property.

ColumnTracking—Optional. A Boolean value that determines whether to track database changes by column or by row. The default value is True. Column-level conflict resolution lets you merge two records and only report a conflict if different users have changed the same field. If you frequently have overlapping updates in the same row, setting this option might increase performance.

An error will occur if the *ConnectString* parameter is omitted and the ActiveConnection property has not already been exclusively set. The ActiveConnection property will be set if this method is successful.

PopulatePartial Method

This method populates a partial replica.

```
Replica.PopulatePartial(FullReplica)
```

FullReplica—A String value representing the path and filename of the replica to populate with data.

When you synchronize a partial replica with a full replica, it is possible to find yourself left with "orphaned" records in the partial replica. For example, you have a filter for the Customers table with a FilterCriteria of Region = 'NJ'. If a user changes a customer's state from NJ to OR in the partial replica and then employs the Synchronize method, the change is propagated to the full replica. But the record containing OR in the partial replica is orphaned because it no longer meets the replica filter criteria.

To avoid orphaning records when updating records, use the PopulatePartial method. PopulatePartial clears all records in the partial replica and repopulates it based on the current filters. The PopulatePartial method is similar to the Synchronize method, but it synchronizes any changes in the partial replica with the full replica, removes all records in the partial replica, and then repopulates the partial replica based on the current replica filters. This assures you that changes made to data will not be orphaned because of a filter conflict.

Always use the PopulatePartial method when you create a partial replica and whenever you change your replica filters. If your application changes replica filters, you should follow these steps:

1. Synchronize the full replica with the partial replica in which the filters are being changed.
2. Use the Filter object to make the desired changes to the replica filter.
3. Call the PopulatePartial method to remove all records from the partial replica and transfer all records from the full replica that meet the new replica filter criteria.

If a replica filter has changed, and the Synchronize method is called without first calling PopulatePartial, a trappable error occurs.

The PopulatePartial method can only be invoked on a partial replica that has been opened exclusively. Furthermore, you cannot call the PopulatePartial method from code running within the partial replica itself. Instead, open the partial replica exclusively from the full replica or another database, and then call PopulatePartial.

> **NOTE**
>
> Although PopulatePartial performs a one-way synchronization before clearing and repopulating the partial replica, it is still a good idea to call Synchronize before calling PopulatePartial. When using the direct or Internet synchronization modes, if the call to Synchronize fails, a trappable error occurs. You can use this error to decide whether or not to proceed with the PopulatePartial method (which removes all records in the partial replica). For indirect synchronization, a trappable error does not occur; see the Synchronize method for more information. If PopulatePartial is called by itself, and an error occurs while records are being synchronized, records in the partial replica will still be cleared. This might not be the desired result.

SetObjectReplicability Method

This method sets whether a database object is local or replicated. Setting replicability is accomplished through a method call as shown below.

```
Replica.SetObjectReplicability(ObjectName, ObjectType, Replicability)
```

ObjectName—A String value specifying the name of the object for which to retrieve the replication state.

ObjectType—A String value specifying the type of object specified by *ObjectName*.

Replicability—A Boolean value specifying whether the object is or will be replicated.

The SetObjectReplicability method makes an object local or replicated. If the database has not been made replicable, setting the *Replicability* parameter to False will indicate that the object should be kept local when the database is made replicable. Objects in nonreplicable databases are replicable by default. However, new objects created in a replicable database are not replicable by default. To make a new object in a replicable database replicable, set the *Replicability* parameter to True.

The *ObjectName* and *ObjectType* parameters are strings that indicate the name of the object (for example, Customers) and the object's container (for example, Tables). An error will occur if an object of that name and type does not exist in the database. An error will also occur if either of these strings is longer than 64 characters.

SetObjectReplicability is ignored on objects in the following Microsoft Access collections: Forms, Reports, DataAccessPages, Macros, and Modules. An Access system table, MSysAccessObjects, controls the replicability of these objects and can only be set prior to making the database replicable. The default is True.

See the GetObjectReplicability method for information about how to determine an object's replicability.

Synchronize **Method**

This method makes two replicas synchronize with one another according to their replication properties and the parameters of the method call.

```
Replica.Synchronize(Target [, SyncType] [, SyncMode])
```

Target—A String value specifying the path and filename of the replica with which to synchronize, the name of the synchronizer that manages the target replica, or the name of the Internet server that contains the target replica.

SyncType—Optional. An Enum value specifying the type of synchronization to perform. The default value for the *SyncType* parameter is jrSyncTypeImpExp. The values listed in Table 22.14 are valid for *SyncType*.

TABLE 22.14 SyncType Enums

Constant	Values	Description
jrSyncTypeExport	1	Sends changes from the current replica to the target replica.
jrSyncTypeImport	2	Sends changes from the target replica to the current replica.
jrSyncTypeImpExp	3	This is the default. Sends changes from the current replica to the target replica and vice versa.

SyncMode—Optional. An Enum value specifying the method of synchronization, jrSyncModeIndirect is the default value for the *SyncMode* parameter. The values listed in Table 22.15 are valid for *SyncMode*.

TABLE 22.15 SyncMode Enums

Constant	Value	Description
jrSyncModeIndirect	1	This is the default. Indirect synchronization.
jrSyncModeDirect	2	Direct synchronization.
jrSyncModeInternet	3	Indirect synchronization over the Internet.

The replica identified in the *Target* parameter must be part of the same replica set. If both replicas have the same ReplicaID property setting or are design masters for two different replica sets, the synchronization fails. This is enforced by the provider.

When the *SyncMode* is indirect, the value of the *Target* parameter must be a Synchronizer name. Jet replication leaves the changes in a drop box. The Synchronizer that manages that target replica picks up the changes and applies them. For indirect synchronization to work correctly, a Synchronizer must be running on both the local computer and the target computer.

When the *SyncMode* is Internet, the value of the *Target* parameter must be a Uniform Resource Locator (URL) address instead of a local area network path. An error will occur if a URL is specified in the *Target* parameter and the *SyncMode* parameter is not jrSyncModeInternet.

22

REPLICATION AND JRO

When the *SyncMode* is direct, both replicas are opened simultaneously and synchronized. Over a WAN or remote dialup network, reliability and performance are improved by using indirect synchronization. You can also synchronize with an SQL Server replica in a replica set containing both SQL Server and Jet databases by setting the *Target* parameter to ServerName.Database.Publication and performing a direct (jrSyncModeDirect) synchronization. An error will occur if the *Target* parameter is ServerName.Database.Publication and *SyncMode* is other than direct.

This method can only be used if the database is replicable. An error will occur if the ReplicaType is jrRepTypeNotReplicable and the user attempts to use this method.

Replication Manager is required for installation and configuration of the Synchronizer and Replman should be used to monitor the status for indirect and Internet synchronizations. It is only available in the Microsoft Office 2000, Developer Edition. For more information about Replication Manager, see Replication Manager in Microsoft Access help.

Filters Collection

This collection contains all the Filter objects for the replica. Each filter object enables you to limit the records affected during a synchronization.

The properties and methods of a Filters collection are listed in Table 22.16.

TABLE 22.16 PROPERTIES AND METHODS OF THE Filters COLLECTION

Property	Description
Count property	Return the number of filters contained in the collection
Item method	Access a column in the collection
Append method	Add a new filter to the collection
Delete method	Remove a filter from the collection
Refresh method	Update the objects in the collection to reflect the current database's revised schema

Count Property

This property indicates the number of objects in a collection.

Use the Count property to determine how many objects are in a given collection.

Because numbering for members of a collection begins with zero, you should always code loops starting with the zero member and ending with the value of the `Count` property -1. If you are using Microsoft Visual Basic and want to loop through the members of a collection without checking the `Count` property, use the `For Each...Next` command.

If the `Count` property is 0, there are no objects in the collection.

`Item` Method

This method returns a specific member of a collection by name or ordinal number. A call to the method is shown here.

```
Set object = collection.Item ( Index )
```

It returns an object reference.

Index—A `Variant` that evaluates either to the name or to the ordinal number of an object in a collection.

Use the `Item` property to return a specific object in a collection. If the method cannot find an object in the collection corresponding to the *Index* argument, an error occurs. Also, some collections don't support named objects; for these collections, you must use ordinal number references.

The `Item` property is the default property for all collections; therefore, the following syntax forms are interchangeable:

```
collection.Item (Index)
```

```
collection (Index)
```

Append Method

This method adds a new `Filter` object to the `Filters` collection of a partial Replica. The syntax for the `Append` method is shown below.

```
Filters.Append(TableName [, FilterType], FilterCriteria)
```

TableName—A `String` value specifying the name of the table to which the filter is applied with the `TableName` property.

FilterType—An `Enum` value indicating the `FilterType` property to determine whether the filter is based on a table or a relationship.

FilterCriteria—A `String` value specifying the criteria that a record must satisfy in order to be replicated from the full replica with the `FilterCriteria` property.

An error will occur if the replica is not a partial replica, as defined by the `ReplicaType` property. An error will occur if a filter with the same name and type already exists.

An error will occur if you attempt to add a second `FilterType` `jrFltrTypeTable` with the same *TableName*.

Delete Method

This method removes the `Filter` object from the `Filters` collection of a replica. The following is an example of a call to the filter's delete method:

```
Filters.Delete(Index)
```

Index—A `Variant` value specifying the name or ordinal of the Filter object you want to delete.

If two filters have the same name, the first filter will be removed. Use the ordinal value to explicitly delete a filter when more than one filter has the same name.

An error will occur if a filter with the name or ordinal specified does not exist in the collection.

Refresh Method

This method updates the objects in a collection to reflect objects available from and specific to the provider. Calling the `Refresh` method is straightforward.

```
collection.Refresh
```

Filter Object

This property specifies the criteria that a record must satisfy in order to be replicated from the full replica.

FilterCriteria Property

It sets or returns a `String` value. For filters based on a table, the string should represent a `SQL` `WHERE` clause without the keyword `WHERE`. For filters based on relationships, the string contains the name of the relationship. `FilterCriteria` is read-only after it has been set, and it can only be set using the `Append` method.

The default value is an empty string (`""`).

FilterType Property

This property indicates the type of filter.

It sets or returns an Enum value. The following constants are valid values for the read-only FilterType. You can only set the FilterType with the Append method. Table 22.17 lists the constants for FilterType.

TABLE 22.17 FilterType Enums

Constant	Description
JrFltrTypeTable	Default. The filter is based on a table.
JrFltrTypeRelationship	The filter is based on a relationship.

TableName Property

This property indicates the name of the table to which the filter is applied.

It sets or returns a String value specifying a table name. For filters based on a relationship, this is the table on the *many* side of the relationship. TableName is read-only after it has been set, and it can only be set using the Append method.

Summary

This chapter explored and attempted to explain replication in Access. The capability to replicate data and Access objects can be a great tool for sharing data, spreading the load, propagating application changes, and increasing the number of potential users. To these ends, you examined the relative benefits of the briefcase, replicating through the Access user's interface and the new Jet Replication Object. Important related topics such as topologies and conflict resolution were also covered here and compared.

This chapter should serve as a basis for experimenting and testing replication in your Access 2000 applications to see if Access 2000 is an appropriate part of your solution.

Security

CHAPTER 23

Applications, especially multiuser applications, are not really finished until they have been secured. Without properly implemented security, an application is vulnerable to the worst intentions of malicious hackers and the innocent curiosity of inexperienced users. Yet despite Jet's formidable security capabilities, security is usually neglected or implemented improperly in Access databases. Part of this is undoubtedly because figuring out what the security structure of the database should be is often a daunting task. The instructions for implementing security are confusing, and the way Jet handles security is different from many other database management systems, past and present.

Elements of Security

This chapter will explore the workgroup security model of Jet in detail and will look at many of the practical matters you must consider when securing a database. It will also demonstrate ActiveX Data Object Extensions for Database Definition Language and Security (ADOX) techniques for handling security functionality. ADOX succeeds DAO as the programming interface for data definition and security management. With a simpler object model and, when used with an OLEDB provider, an interface free from native syntactical differences, ADOX will free you from many of the burdens of securing a database, especially those with nontraditional or heterogeneous sources. Because ADOX only handles data source and data-bearing or data-handling objects such as tables, queries, views, and procedures, I will also review DAO and user interface techniques. These will enable you to apply security to the forms, reports, and macros of an Access database client.

There are two options for securing an Access 2000 database application:

- Set a database password
- Implement Workgroup-Based Security

Database Password Security

Setting a database password is a quick and easy way to secure the MDB file. When employed (by choosing Tools, Security, Set Database Password in an exclusively opened database), all users are assigned the same password. When starting the MDB file, each user is prompted for this database password. Everyone has the same password and anyone who knows that password has access to the database. It is easy to see how the database can be compromised when everyone has the same password and privileges and is indistinguishable from everyone else. Additionally, if the password is forgotten, there is no way to recover it. Finally, use of a database password precludes the use of replication. The database password alone is not the best way to secure a serious, multiuser application, but it can be used in conjunction with workgroup security.

Workgroup security is much more complicated than the database password. This chapter will focus on this method.

Workgroup-Based Security

If the database password is database-based (that is, each database is secured as a file or as a set of files, without regard to the identity of the user), Access/Jet is secured based upon how you are identified within a particular workgroup. It is that identity that determines what you are allowed to do. In this sophisticated and flexible system, the identity of the user within a workgroup is central to the functioning of the security in the workgroup security scheme. In this user-based security structure, users are uniquely identified and can be uniquely assigned permissions to databases and to the objects within them. It could be said that the coming discussion of workgroup files, workspaces, and groups is really about enhancing, organizing, and easing the basic tasks of creating and assigning permissions to users.

This user-based system is not administered by Access or Jet. It is administered by the workgroup file (system.mdw). The workgroup file contains the security information on users and groups of users and is consulted by Access/Jet on security matters. In Access, security is always on, it's just not always visible. The workgroup file is always in use, whether you can see it working or not. Because of this, it is very important to know which workgroup you are connected to before setting up a security scheme.

Setting up security this way (with separate administration) means that groups of users can have several database applications secured and administered through one centralized security file. The MDW file used for a database defines the workgroup. The workgroup is a collection of users, their groups, and the databases they can use. As illustrated in Figure 23.1, the database engine relies on its workspace (the workgroup as determined by the MDW file) to supply information on the users for the database in question.

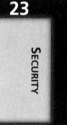

FIGURE 23.1

Notice that there are no database objects in this schematic.

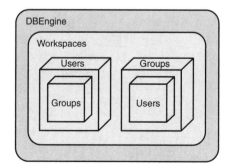

Although the user is the center of the security system, it is impossible to create a user or have a meaningful discussion about him without putting him into the context of a group. A workgroup must exist for security to function. It can have many users or only one, but a workgroup file must be established.

The workgroup file is a special encrypted database that contains the following information:

- User names
- User passwords
- User personal identifiers (PIDs)
- User preferences (toolbar settings and some defaults)
- User's last four opened databases (for the file menu)
- Group names
- Group (PIDs)
- Group members (users belonging to that group)

Workgroup Creation

Out of the box, Access is joined to a default workgroup defined by System.mdw. System.mdw has been created for convenience only. When it was created during the installation, information critical to its security capability was left out, so it is permanently and inherently unsecured. Anyone willing to check Access help files can defeat the security plan of the default system.mdw. You should leave this workgroup file alone and create new ones as needed.

For this task, Microsoft provides a utility called wrkgadm.exe (usually located in …\Microsoft Office\Office\wrkgadm.exe).

This utility enables you to create new workgroups and join existing ones. When creating a workgroup, the resulting MDW file should be placed in a network location common to all expected users. At the time you create the workgroup file, you do not have to have a detailed plan for the security structure of your users; however, it is a good idea to create the workgroup file as early in the development process as possible to avoid any confusion later.

Upon running wrkgadm.exe, you must choose to either join an existing workgroup or create a new one.

After choosing to create a new workgroup file, you must define the workgroup ownership information. There are three fields to fill out as seen in Figure 23.2. The Workgroup

Sketch express

leonardo
07/27/04

Sketch express

leonardo
07/27/04

Administrator has already completed two of these fields for you by borrowing information from the installation of Office 2000 or Access 2000 (see Figure 23.3). You can change these two fields here or leave them as they are; however, you must provide a Workgroup ID.

FIGURE 23.2

Before you finish creating the workgroup, make a note of this critical information.

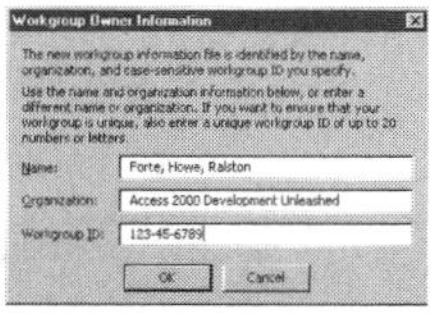

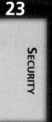

FIGURE 23.3

Access automates some of the new user information with the Workgroup Administrator, but you can still change it.

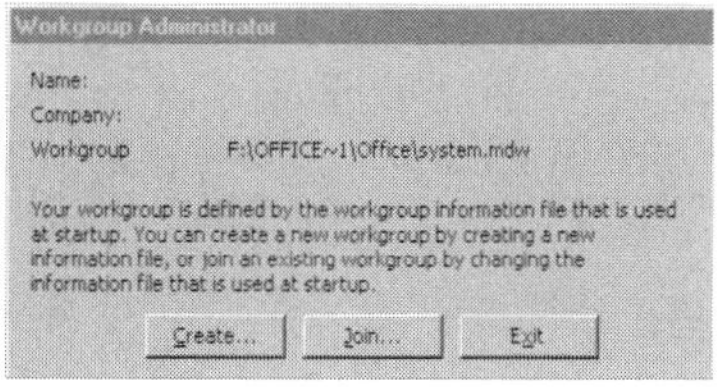

The Workgroup ID provides a seed for the encryption of the workgroup file. This is the piece of information missing from the default installation. Wrkgadm will allow you leave it blank after warning you, but that defeats the whole purpose of creating a workgroup. A Workgroup ID consists of up to 20 alphanumeric characters and is case-sensitive. The string you enter here will ensure that this workgroup is unique by generating a binary ID called the Workgroup Security ID (SID). With the workgroup ID properly secured and hidden, your workgroup cannot be subverted by an imposter. The security system is so particular about this that you will have only one more opportunity to see or change its value ever again. Write this string down, keep it secret, and store it in a separate location from the group of users.

> **CAUTION**
>
> Write down the workgroup ID value and store it in a safe and separate location. You might need it again to re-create the workgroup; however, Jet will never provide it for you—ever.

23

SECURITY

The next step is to find a location for the workgroup file. The workgroup file should be placed in a location where all the intended users have read/write directory access. Although, if your users are very static, it is possible to place a copy of the MDW file on their local machines and replace that copy each time there are changes, the performance gains might not outweigh the administrative overhead. Placing the file on a network drive also improves your chances that the MDW file will be backed up at regular intervals, making disaster recovery much easier.

> **CAUTION**
>
> Resist the temptation to name the MDW file with the same name as the application or data source if they are located in the same directory. The MDW file will create an LDB file to track its own locking activity, just as the data source or executable will. If the MDB and the MDW share a name, they will not conflict with each other, but their LDB files will. A good suggestion is to preface the file name with "SYS" or "SYS_".

Your last chance to change or view the information is presented in the Confirm Workgroup Information dialog box. Make sure you have accurately recorded all this information, especially the workgroup ID, because you might need it later to re-create the MDW file.

If you confirm the information, the workgroup administrator will confirm that your new workgroup has been created and you will be returned to the first dialog box. Notice that you are now joined to the new workgroup. You can now create databases, create users, create groups, assign users to groups, and grant and revoke permissions for that workgroup. If you choose to join a different workgroup, you will be able to work in that group to the extent that your security settings permitted.

In the interest of not wrecking any existing databases, you will use a brand new database created in this workgroup to explore the rest of the security features.

If Access is open, close it and restart it. This will start Access in the workgroup you just created because it is the current default workgroup, though there is no way to tell unless you run the workgroup administrator. Before creating security, it is imperative that you make certain you are joined to the appropriate workgroup.

You can set workgroup membership to a database through the command line of a shortcut, as seen here.

```
Path to Access.exe and MDB /WRKGRP path to workgroup file
[/USER username /PWD password]
```

23

SECURITY

> **NOTE**
>
> The /WRKGRP, /USER, and /PWD command line switches only work for Access databases and not Access projects.

Users and Groups

Users are the basis of the security system. Jet recognizes users and knows what they are allowed to do. What they are allowed to do, or the permissions they have, depends upon the permissions the users have been assigned directly, and what they have inherited through the groups they belong to. A user's permission set is the sum of their group permissions (implicit permissions) and any individual permissions (explicit permissions) he might have. A user always belongs to at least one group, the Users group.

When you log on to a Jet database, you always log on as a user. You cannot log on as a group. The security system will know which groups you belong to and observe the permissions you have been assigned.

Though users are the basic element of the security system, it is difficult to discuss them without also discussing groups because users always belong to at least one group, and groups exist to organize and manage users.

Take the case of a hypothetical Clerk group. Although the group might have no rights to create or modify objects, there might be one person who is designated to revise and create reports. He could be given the explicit rights to create and modify report objects, although no one else in the Clerk group has those rights. Although this works, it creates an administrative headache because the security administrator must now track an individual as well as a group. Chances are, if the security administrator will make one exception, he will make others. A better alternative solution for a report writing clerk would be to join him to a group that has permissions to create and modify reports. This way, the security administrator can track individuals by their functional capabilities rather than by unique security profiles. Groups cannot belong to groups.

> **TIP**
>
> Because reports can be created with the wizards, and the query builder helps users to precisely define recordsources without adding query objects to the query container, it is possible to give extensive permissions for report building—even if the database is secured. This can save you a lot of tedious development efforts.

> **CAUTION**
>
> Because the Users group has all permissions by default, and every user is always a member of it, you must remove all permissions from the Users group in order to successfully secure a database. Otherwise, every user of the database will inherit administrative rights.

Understanding Default User and Group Settings

Before you do anything with security, it is important to know what the default settings are. Jet starts with two groups and one default user. The two groups are Admins and Users. The default user is Admin. Admin is a member of both groups and both groups have all permissions in the database.

When creating other users and groups, the names of groups and the names of users must not conflict. Access uses a naming convention in which groups are plural and users are singular. This seems to be a good rule of thumb to follow.

The most important group is the Admins group because it has special permissions that cannot be granted to groups you create. In order to create, change, or delete a user; create or delete a group; change a group's membership; or clear the passwords of other users; you must be a member of the Admins group. A user who is not a member of the Admins group can view the accounts of other users and can see who belongs to any group, but cannot change any of these things, even for himself. He is only able to modify his own password. For obvious reasons, every database must have at least one member of the Admins group.

Groups are not merely collections of users. Although you are not able to log on as a group and groups cannot possess a password or own a database, they can own Jet/Access objects and have distinct permissions. These capabilities make administration of the database and its users much easier. As a general rule, you should only assign permissions to groups and then make users members of the group. This makes administering security much simpler.

Creating Users

Although users should have few details attached to them that distinguish them from other members of the same groups, they are still necessary to a proper security structure of your database.

To create a user, follow these steps:

1. From the Tools menu, choose Security, and then select User and Group Accounts.

2. Select the User tab and click New.

3. Enter the User Name and a PID (Personal Identifier), as shown in Figure 23.4. The PID must be between 4 and 20 characters in length. It is case-sensitive and serves as the seed for the creation of the SID or security Identifier. You must make a record of the PID because you will never be able to see it again.

FIGURE 23.4

Creating a new user and assigning the personal ID to him.

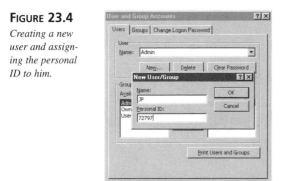

Setting/Changing User Passwords

After a user has been created, you have the option of assigning a password for that user. You are not prompted to do this, but it should be standard practice.

Click on the Change Logon Password tab to set or change a password. The password is case-sensitive, between 1 and 14 characters, and optional. However, because the password is designed to verify if a user is who she says she is when she logs on to the database, everyone should have a password. There is no way to see a password after it has been assigned, so write it down and keep it safe. In a worst case, an administrator can always clear another user's password if the user should forget it. Figure 23.5 shows how the dialog box conceals the passwords from view as you change them.

CAUTION

Professional responsibility precludes me from revealing the techniques available to breach Access security should you forget a password. Remember to use a password that you won't forget, but no one else can know. Once you've decided on a password, commit it to memory or write it down and store it in a separate and secure location.

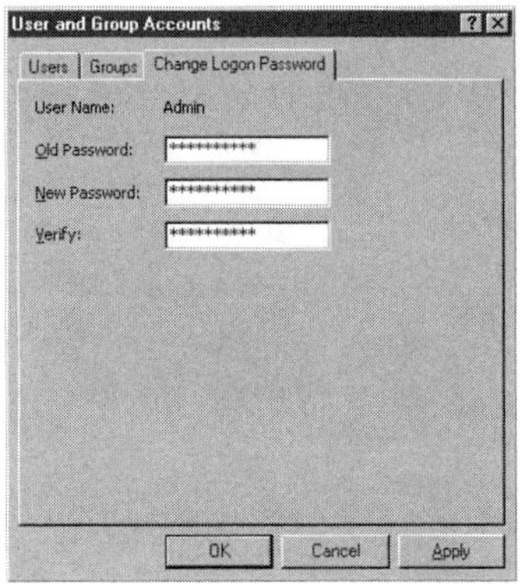

FIGURE 23.5

Changing a user's password through Access's user interface.

Creating Groups

The linchpins of your security scheme should be your groups. As discussed earlier, groups ease your administrative burden by passing on their security profiles to all their members.

To create a group, follow these steps:

1. From the Tools menu, choose Security, and then select User and Group Accounts.

2. Select the Groups tab and click New.

3. Enter the Group Name and a PID (Personal Identifier). The PID must be between 4 and 20 characters in length, case-sensitive and serve as the seed for the creation of the SID or Security Identifier. You must make a record of the PID, because you will never be able to see it again. See Figure 23.6.

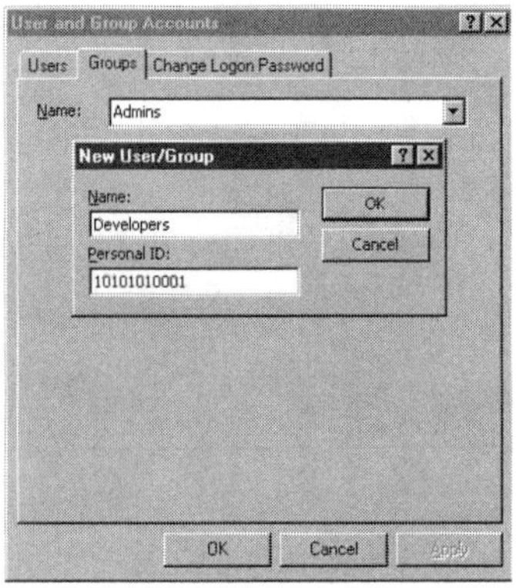

FIGURE 23.6

Creating a group by assigning a name and PID through the user interface.

> **CAUTION**
>
> The PID of a group is the seed that will be used to uniquely identify the group; if you ever need to re-create the group, you will need that PID, so write down and store it in a secure location.

Assigning Users to Groups

Users and groups are so tightly entwined, their creation and assignments are done in the same place. Use the same tab of the User and Group Accounts dialog box where you create users and groups to join them together.

Follow these steps to assign a user to a group:

1. Choose the user you are interested in from the top dialog box.

2. At the bottom of the dialog box, choose the group to which you want to assign this user from the Available Groups list.

3. Double-click on this group or click the Add button to join this user to this group. You can also remove groups from a user by double-clicking on a group name in the Member Of list or by using the Remove button. You can never revoke the membership in the Users group.

To see all the assignment made in the database, use the Print Users and Groups button.

Because security is user-based, you can control group membership from the Users tab only, not from the Groups tab.

Distinguishing Between Default and Special Users and Groups

Access's security structure is not devoid of users and groups when you create a new database. In fact it has a set of default users and groups. These default groups and users must be present in order for security to function. Since Access has to know who's logged in, everyone is identified as the default Admin user, a member of the default Admins and Users groups, when logging in without security being implemented. These groups should not have any role in your final security setup. These default groups are described in this section.

Admins— Unlike the default accounts, the Admins group is unique to any given workgroup because the SID of the Admins group is generated from the SID of the workgroup. The Admins group must always have at least one member and Jet will enforce this rule. Though membership in the Admins group can be revoked, the group imparts certain special and irrevocable privileges. A member of the Admins group can grant permissions to any object in the workgroup. With DAO and ADOX, it is possible to deny these privileges to Admins's members over a database object so that only the object owner has special privileges, but neither DAO nor ADOX can revoke Admins's privileges over groups and user account administration.

Admin— The only default user in Jet. Though invested with no special privileges, it inherits rights from the Admins group. You are logged on to a database as Admin if you do not specifically log on as some other user. As long as the Admins group has another member, you can remove the Admin user from the Admins group. This is a necessary step for properly securing a database and is discussed in the section "Securing a Database Step by Step."

Users— An empty group at creation whose members have full rights by default. Removing all permissions from the Users group is a necessary step for properly securing a database and is discussed in the section "Securing a Database Step by Step."

Owner— The owner is the creator of the object or the user to whom ownership has been transferred. The owner of an object is the most powerful user and has extensive, irrevocable rights. The database object must be owned by a user, but other objects can be owned by groups.

Understanding Permissions

Just as it is difficult to discuss users without groups, it is difficult to cover permissions without talking about objects.

After the users and the groups have been created, it is possible to implement your security plan. The permissions determine what a user or group can or cannot do with an object. The objects range from the database to tables, queries, forms, reports, and macros (modules are no longer subject to security in the user interface) in the database. The types of permissions available vary from object to object and some permissions are dependent on other permissions. For instance, if you have the permission to alter the design of an object, you must have the ability to open it (maybe even exclusively), read it, and write to it. There is no need to memorize the independent and dependent permissions sets. The Access interface will take care of that for you—you just need to know what they all mean. Table 23.1 details the objects, their permissions, and their implications. Permissions for objects are not stored in the MDW file (the MDW file does not know anything about them). They are kept in the database and the user is verified with the MDW file.

TABLE 23.1 PERMISSIONS AND WHAT THEY CAN DO FOR YOU

Permission	Grants	Object
Open Exclusive	Open while barring others from opening.	Database
Open/Run	View in runtime mode.	Database
Read Design	View in design-time mode.	All except Modules
Modify Design	View, change, or delete objects' structure and properties.	All
Administer (Database)	Set database password, create replication master, modify startup options. No security administration.	Database
Administer (Other)	Full rights and privileges including security administration.	All except Database object
Read Data	View data only.	Tables and Queries
Update Data	View and change data, no append or delete.	Tables and Queries
Insert Data	View and append, no change or delete.	Tables and Queries
Delete Data	View and delete, no change or append.	Tables and Queries

If you want to compact or repair a database, you must have the database opened exclusively. You must also open the database exclusively if you want to make changes to a multiuser application that has already been deployed.

One source of confusion often arises regarding queries. You might develop a query for your users, but you do not want them to have access to the underlying tables. There is a way you can enable users to open or run queries without giving them access to the supporting tables. Creatively employing Run Permissions gives you row-level and column-level security on the database because you can restrict users to records by criteria statements (for example, department codes, employee number, current dates, field values, and so on), and they can be prohibited from changing the queries you provided.

Run Permissions is found in the Tools, Options, Tables/Queries tab. Selecting Owner's (as shown in Figure 23.7) gives all users the permissions for running or opening the query possessed by the owner of the query; however, only the owner can modify the query and only the owner can transfer ownership of the query. Selecting Owner's overrides existing permissions for users. This option can also be exercised from the query's property sheet and by using the With OwnerAccess option in a SQL statement. (See the section "Implications When Using SQL" for more on this.)

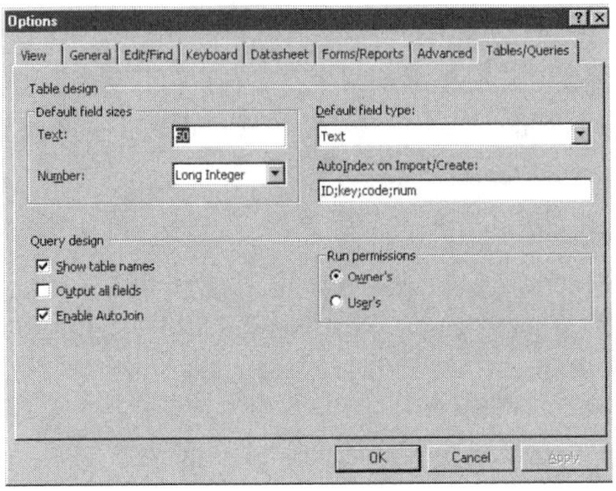

FIGURE 23.7

*Setting the Run
Permissions prop-
erty for a query
through the user
interface.*

In all my years of developing database applications, I haven't met many that could really be called "finished." If the database is being used and its users like it, it is bound to be extended. To accommodate the eventuality that new objects will be created in the future, Access provides a way to handle the security settings for objects that do not yet exist when you implement your security plan. But the name of this feature, <New objectname>, is misleading regarding what it will do for your security scheme.

Choosing the <New objectname> in the Users and Group Permissions dialog does not prevent users from creating database objects, it only determines what permissions the object will have when it is created. Even if you remove all the permissions for <New objectname>, users will still be able to create them. Because these users are the owners of these objects, they are free to assign whatever permissions they want to them. The only way to prevent users from creating objects is by intervening in the security assignments with DAO or ADOX.

The owner of an object is the most powerful user of the object and can do anything with it. He cannot have his rights of ownership revoked or removed. The security user interface might make it appear that permissions for an owner have been revoked, but they really have not. The only way to disfranchise an owner of an object is to transfer ownership.

The user who created the database is the database's permanent owner. His rights to create objects in the database are irrevocable, regardless of what the security user interface says about his privileges. Other users can create objects within the database. They become the owners of those objects. Objects' ownership can be transferred to groups to ease administrative burdens—this way, any member of a group can administer an object or set of objects.

Ownership of objects can be transferred by the database owner or by the object owner. To change the ownership of a database, a user must have Read Design and Read Data privileges to the original database, create a new database in the workgroup of the original, import all the objects into the new database, delete the original database, and rename the new database to the exact same name as the deleted original. (The Access Security Wizard does the exact same set of steps for you.)

Security Implementation Using Startup Options

Beyond a rigorous, properly implemented security scheme, there are a few other things you can do with startup options to augment your Access security. These should never be mistaken for, or used to substitute for, a real security plan, but they can add a little panache to your applications and might even plug an unanticipated hole. By themselves, they might serve to lock down an application just enough for a temporary solution.

Under the startup menu there are a number of options to examine. They are

23

SECURITY

Display Database Window—The place where users can do the most harm is in the database window. By hiding it at startup, less experienced (and usually the most curious) users might not realize it is there to begin with.

Menu Options— Again, giving users access to native functionality can allow a small security hole to appear much larger. Be careful about letting a user close a form in a way other than the one you prescribe, or letting a user save a record without verifying his identity and rights to do so. Disallowing full menus, default shortcut menus, built-in toolbars, and prohibiting toolbar and menu customization can prevent such a breach. Carefully select which, if any, of these features remain active.

Allow Viewing Code After Error— Without proper security (and good errorhandling) users will either see a disturbing and cryptic error message or the code itself, which is an extremely bad and embarrassing thing. Turn this feature off.

AllowSpecialKeys—F11, Control-Break, and Control-G could ruin an application. Disable these features when your application is distributed.

Application Icon— Depending on the environment your application will run in, it might serve to substitute the Access icon with something else. If nothing else, this may throw troublesome users off the scent that they are dealing with an Access application. Substitute it with a BMP or ICO file.

Security Concerns with Replication

Using replication in the database application poses no insurmountable problems to security. The replicas can be secured using user-level security. Any changes made to the Design Master's objects' security bits will propagate to the replicas during synchronization because those permissions reside in the objects themselves. Unfortunately, the workgroup file does not replicate. If the users of the replicated database cannot share a single workgroup file (this is the case in most replication arrangements), the workgroup file must be distributed when new objects are created, or when changes in the security scheme require it.

Another consideration when distributing replicas and MDW files is Admins membership. Because members of this group can add and delete users as well as reset or clear passwords, it is important to carefully select the administrators and have as few of them as possible when they are far afield.

When replication is used, the Database Password feature is unavailable.

Security for Split Databases

Access databases should always be split. That is, their data should reside in one MDB file and the executable parts such as its forms, reports, and modules, should reside in another. How do you secure such an arrangement?

When using linked tables, you must deal with two sets of permissions: one for the source database, and one for the client. At the source, or back-end, there are tables. In the client, there are links to those tables. It is possible to set restrictive permissions on the links, but that does not really make much sense when you think about it. The link is really not much more than a set of properties, a string if you will.

```
Database=C:\Program Files\Microsoft Office\Office\Samples\Northwind.mdb
```

With the understanding that there is no data from the linked table residing in the client database, provide full permissions to the linked table. Doing so will also enable the client's user to re-create the tabledef if needed. With the links unrestricted, you can secure the back-end database's tables in the normal way. This way, unrecognized users will not be able to access the data with other methods.

When it comes time to refresh the links to the source tables, there are three options:

- RefreshLink—Read data permissions on the back-end data table
- RefreshLink—Read design permissions on the back-end data table
- Connect property—None or no permissions on back-end data

If all the permissions have been removed from the back-end data, the third option is the natural choice. These options must be run from DAO or ADOX. The user interface does not permit you to manage the link's security unless you have read data permissions on the back-end data source. The following code shows how this might look.

```
Set tbldef=db.CreateTableDef(strTableName)
With tbldef
  .SourceTableName=strTableName
  .Connect = ";Database=" & strTableName
  .Append tdf 'attach single table - better yet, loop through some -
End With
```

Another way to deal with the link issue is to drop the link entirely and access the back-end tables through a remote database object and SQL statements. You can also take advantage of Access 2000's capability to bind a form to a detached recordset object. See Listing 23.1 for an example of this.

Listing 23.1 Binding a Form to a Detached Recordset Object

```
Dim wrk As Workspace
Dim db As Database
Dim rdb As Database
Dim rs As Recordset
Dim Connstr as String

Set wrk = DBEngine.Workspaces(0)
Set db = CurrentDb()

Connstr = "C:\program files\microsoft office\"
Connstr = Connstr & "office\samples\northwind.mdb"

Set rdb = wrk.OpenDatabase(Connstr, , , "admin")

Set rs = rdb.OpenRecordset("Select * from Customers") ...
```

ADOX is not affected by the linking of a table for one important reason: It does not concern itself with objects located in the current database (`currentdb()`), so the security status of the link is unknowable to it. With ADOX, data would be opened directly in the back-end database. The code in Listing 23.2 opens an ADO connection to the datasource and then assigns permissions to the user named "JP".

23

SECURITY

LISTING 23.2   OPENING A DATABASE AND ASSIGNING PERMISSIONS TO IT THROUGH ADOX

```
Dim cnn As New ADODB.Connection
Dim cat As New ADOX.Catalog

With cnn
    .Provider = "Microsoft.Jet.OLEDB.4.0"
    .ConnectionString = "data source=F:\NorthWind_Traders\& _
        NorthWind.mdb;jet oledb:system database="  & _
        "F:\NorthWind_Traders\sysnwind.mdw; "  & _
        "user id=Chuck;Password=opensesame"
    .Open
End With

Set cat.ActiveConnection = cnn
cat.Users("JP").SetPermissions objName, adPermObjTable, _
    adAccessGrant, adRightFull
....
```

With OwnerAccess Option

Another possibility is to remove all permissions from the tables on the back-end. You can then run queries against the links using `With Owneraccess` option at the end of the SQL statement or as the property setting of the query. This way the query will be able to run or return rows, but users from other applications will not be able to alter data or table structure. A code fragment showing such a SQL statement is listed here.

```
SELECT Customers.*
FROM Customers
WITH OWNERACCESS OPTION;
```

To create a query that runs `With OwnerAccess` option, follow these steps:

1. Remove all permissions from the table(s) in question for the group that will use that query.

2. Using an account that has Read Data and Update Data permission on those tables, make a query and include the column and set the criteria that will give you the desired result.

3. Change the query's permissions options to "Owner's." This will enable the query to run as if it were being run by the owner, but only the owner can make changes to it.

Having a query that can be changed only by its owner can hinder development of a complex database application where there is more than one developer. It is best to assign ownership to a group so that there is more than one person who can change or maintain the query when needed. You will need to reset the query's ownership back to User before transferring it to a group.

Security for Client/Server

When working with data from a server such as SQL Server, Oracle, or Sybase, these servers secure their data themselves—you usually have very little control over that security.

If your application is attached to tables on a server and you want to restrict the write and insert permissions to these tables, you can do so through the Access permissions, either through ADOX (use CurrentProject.Connection) or through the user's interface.

Managing Users

Jet security is user-centric, but that does not mean you should dwell on the user and get involved in lots of details about him. Basically, all he needs to exist is a name, a password, and a PID. To make him useful he needs permissions, and to make him manageable he needs to belong to at least one group. Beyond that, there is little you should do with him. If you get into the habit of customizing users' security profiles, you will create a maintenance nightmare for yourself. After you have created a name, a PID, and a password, you should modify only those settings. Avoid granting object permissions to users. Instead, grant object permissions to groups and then have your users joining the appropriate group.

Listing 23.3 is a simple function that shows how to check for the existence of a user, create a user, delete a user, assign group membership, or check a user's membership in a group.

To create or revamp the user, the subroutine takes a username argument, a PID, a password, and, in a parameter array argument, a list of the groups the user should belong to.

The subroutine checks to see if the user's name is in the .Users collection. If it is, the subroutine deletes the user and re-creates him with the new PID. The function then loops through the parameter array passed in and joins the user to each group. So that the subroutine is consistent with the user interface, it checks to make sure he at least belongs to the default and permission-less Users group. If that function was not passed in, the sub assigns him to that group.

LISTING 23.3   CODE EXAMPLE TO CHECK THE EXISTENCE OF USERS, DELETE THEM, AND ADD THEM

```
Sub ADOXManageUser(strUserName, strPID, strPWD, _
    ParamArray JoinGroups() As Variant)

    Dim cnn As New ADODB.Connection
    Dim cat As New ADOX.Catalog
    Dim Group As Variant

    With cnn
        .Provider = "Microsoft.Jet.OLEDB.4.0"
        .ConnectionString = "data source=C:\Program Files\ & _
            Microsoft Office\Office\Samples\Northwind.mdb; & _
            jet oledb:system database=C:\Program Files\ & _
            Microsoft Office\Office\Samples\sysnwind.mdw; & _
            user id=NWindAdmin;Password=opensesame"
        .Open
    End With

    Set cat.ActiveConnection = cnn

    With cat

        ' We don't anticipate any errors, so
        On Error Resume Next

        ' Check to see if the name already exists
        ' If so, delete him so his groups can be redefined
        ' Deleting the user also removes any group references
        If strUserName = .Users(strUserName).Name Then
            .Users.Delete strUserName
        End If

        ' Create the new user
        .Users.Append strUserName, strPWD

        ' Even if the user exists, we can add him to
        ' a new group if appropriate
        For Each Group In JoinGroups()
            .Groups(Group).Users.Append strUserName
        Next

    ' Before finishing, so we are consistent with the UI,
    ' check to see that he at least belongs to the Users Group
    ' There's no need to loop through the group's members
    ' to determine this, just check the name against the group's
    ' users collection.
    If Not strUserName = .Groups("Users").Users(strUserName).Name Then
        .Groups("Users").Users.Append strUserName
```

```
    End If

    End With

End Sub
```

Enumerating Groups and Users and List Membership

It would be nearly impossible to administer your database if you couldn't programmatically find out who could use the database and in what capacity they could use it. Access VBA provides a way, through ADOX, to list all the users in your database, as well as their group memberships and other information. An example of this code is shown in Listing 23.4.

LISTING 23.4 USING ADOX TO LIST USER INFORMATION

```
Public Sub ADOXGroupsandUsers()

    Dim cnn As New ADODB.Connection
    Dim cat As New ADOX.Catalog
    Dim i As Integer, k As Integer

    With cnn
        .Provider = "Microsoft.Jet.OLEDB.4.0"
        .ConnectionString = "data source=h:\books and articles\ & _
          unleashed\securityexample.mdb; & _
          jet oledb:system database=h:\books and articles\ & _
          unleashed\sysnwind.mdw;user id=Admin;Password=letmein"
        .Open
    End With

    Set cat.ActiveConnection = cnn

    With cat

        Debug.Print

        'Enumerate and list the Groups
        Debug.Print "GROUPS count = " & .Groups.Count
        For i = 0 To .Groups.Count - 1
            Debug.Print "    " & .Groups(i).name
        Next

        Debug.Print
```

continues

LISTING 23.4   CONTINUED

```
'Enumerate and list the Users
Debug.Print "USERS = " & .Users.Count
For i = 0 To .Users.Count - 1
    'Suppress the 'Engine' and 'Creator' Users
    If .Users(i).Groups.Count > 0 Then
        Debug.Print "    " & .Users(i).name
    End If
 Next

Debug.Print

'List the Groups collection of the catalog and their members
Debug.Print "GROUP MEMBERSHIP"
For i = 0 To .Groups.Count - 1
    Debug.Print "    " & .Groups(i).name
        For k = 0 To .Groups(i).Users.Count - 1
            Debug.Print "      " & .Groups(i).Users(k).name
        Next
 Next

Debug.Print

' List the Users collection of the catalog
' and their group memberships
Debug.Print "USER MEMBERSHIP"
For i = 0 To .Users.Count - 1
    'Suppress the 'Engine' and 'Creator' Users
    If .Users(i).Groups.Count > 0 Then
        Debug.Print "    " & .Users(i).name
            For k = 0 To .Users(i).Groups.Count - 1
                Debug.Print "      " & .Users(i).Groups(k).name
            Next
    End If
 Next

End With

End Sub
```

Identifying Current Users with ADOX

The question "Who's logged in right now?" usually comes up, and there was never an elegant way to find out. Now with ADOX, you can use the roster to find out who is using the database at any particular moment. See Listing 23.5 for an example of this.

LISTING 23.5   ADOX Can Let You See Who Is Currently Using a Database

```
Sub UserRoster()
'Procedure that will use the
'User Roster feature or Jet 4.0
'to connect to a database and check
'to see who is in the database
'From "Microsoft Access 2000 Development Unleashed" (SAMS)
'By: Forte, Howe, Ralston

Dim conn As ADODB.Connection
Dim rst As ADODB.Recordset

On Error GoTo Proc_Err

Set conn = New ADODB.Connection

'Open the back-end database
With conn
    .Provider = "Microsoft.Jet.OLEDB.4.0"
    .ConnectionString = "data source=h:\books and articles\ & _
        unleashed\securityexample.mdb; & _
        jet oledb:system database=h:\books and articles\ & _
        unleashed\sysnwind.mdw;user id=Admin;Password=letmein"
    .Open
End With

'Create the recordset based on the
'Number of users in the database
Set rst = conn.OpenSchema(adSchemaProviderSpecific, , _
"{947bb102-5d43-11d1-bdbf-00c04fb92675}")

'For each user print out the computer name
'and other information
Do Until rst.EOF
    Debug.Print rst!COMPUTER_NAME
    Debug.Print rst!LOGIN_NAME
    Debug.Print rst!CONNECTED
    Debug.Print rst!SUSPECTED_STATE

    rst.MoveNext
Loop

Proc_Exit:
    Exit Sub

Proc_Err:
    MsgBox Err.Description
    Resume Proc_Exit

End Sub
```

23

SECURITY

Identifying Users Who Have Blank Passwords

One of the biggest holes any secured database can have is a user with a blank password. Jet security does not require a password, so the password must either be forced, in a custom security interface, or someone has to search the users to see if anyone can open the database with a user name and no password. The function in Listing 23.6 shows how that can be done with ADOX.

LISTING 23.6 AVOIDING THE BLANK PASSWORD SECURITY PROBLEM

```
Public Sub ADOXPasswordCheck()

    Dim strcnn1 As String
    Dim strcnn2 As String
    Dim cnn As New ADODB.Connection
    Dim pwrdtestcnn As New ADODB.Connection
    Dim cat As New ADOX.Catalog
    Dim pwdCat As New ADOX.Catalog
    Dim i As Integer, k As Integer

    strcnn1 = "data source=C:\Program Files\Microsoft Office\Office\"
    strcnn1 = strcnn1 & "Samples\NorthWind.mdb;"
    strcnn1 = strcnn1 & "jet oledb:system database="
    strcnn1 = strcnn1 & "C:\Program Files\Microsoft Office\Office\"
    strcnn1 = strcnn1 & "Samples\sysnwind.mdw; "
    strcnn1 = strcnn1 & "user id=NWindAdmin;Password=OpenSaysaMe"
    With cnn
        .Provider = "Microsoft.Jet.OLEDB.4.0"
        .ConnectionString = strcnn1
        .Open
    End With

    Set cat.ActiveConnection = cnn

    With cat
        For i = 0 To .Users.Count - 1

            'Suppress the 'Engine' and 'Creator' Users
            If .Users(i).Groups.Count > 0 Then

                ' Try to open another connection with a username
                ' and a blank password
                With pwrdtestcnn
                    .Provider = cnn.Provider
                    strcnn2="data source=C:\Program Files\"
                    strcnn2= strcnn2 & "Microsoft Office\Office\Samples\"
                    strcnn2= strcnn2 & "NorthWind.mdb; "
                    strcnn2= strcnn2 & "jet oledb:system database="
                    strcnn2= strcnn2 & "C:\Program Files\"
```

```
            strcnn2= strcnn2 & "Microsoft Office\Office\"
            strcnn2= strcnn2 & "Samples\sysnwind.mdw; "
            strcnn2= strcnn2 & "user id=NWindAdmin;Password='''"
            .ConnectionString = strcnn2

            ' Since we'll usually get an error,
            ' we don't want that to stop us.
            On Error Resume Next
            .Open

            ' No error means the database opened with no password
            If Err = 0 Then

                ' Use the catalog from the current connection
                Set cat.ActiveConnection = pwrdtestcnn
                Debug.Print cat.Users(i).name & _
                  " has a blank password"

                ' Close the new connection
                pwrdtestcnn.Close
            End If
          End With
        End If
      Next
    End With

End Sub
```

Setting/Clearing Passwords

Setting and clearing a password can be done from the interface or from ADOX. The following line of code will change a password.

```
cat.Users("admin").changepassword "oldpassword","newpassword"
```

Setting both arguments of the .changepassword method to zero length string will clear a password. Though a member of the Admins group cannot see another user's password, he can reset any password.

Managing Groups

In order to manage the users more easily, you can assign permissions and object ownership to groups instead of to individuals. This gives you far fewer permission profiles to track.

Managing Group Object Ownership

Since you have the most flexibility available to you when you own an object, you should know how to assess and modify object ownership through code. Listing 23.7 demonstrates how to find out what group an object belongs to and then to change that ownership. The function assigns the object's ownership to a group so that it will be easier to administer.

LISTING 23.7   ASSIGNING OBJECT OWNERSHIP

```
Public Sub ADOXGroupOwnership(strObjectName As String, strGroupName As
String)

    Dim cat As New ADOX.Catalog
    Dim n As String


    ' Here we are working with the client, but if you wanted to
    ' work with another MDB file, just create and open a connection to it
    Set cat.ActiveConnection = CurrentProject.Connection
    With cat
        Debug.Print .GetObjectOwner(strObjectName, adPermObjTable)
        .SetObjectOwner strObjectName, adPermObjTable, strGroupName
        .Tables.Refresh
        Debug.Print .GetObjectOwner(strObjectName, adPermObjTable)
        cat.Tables.Refresh
    End With

End Sub
```

Managing Multiple Apps

With ADOX, your project does not need to load DDL or security functionality if it does not require it, and when it does require it, ADOX comes in a lightweight package with a clear and (if the best intentions are not mislaid) universal programming interface you can reference through msadox.dll.

Though ADOX still has some shortcomings at the time of this writing, it also has great promise. If it lives up to the promise it holds—and, judging from ADO, it probably will—ADOX soon will be the DDL and security programming interface of choice. With it, you can administer and coordinate all visible workgroups from one location. In and of itself, that is not new, but when you consider the possibility of coordinating Oracle or SQL Server security and data definition with your local workgroup—with one common interface—it is really impressive. Currently, you can only perform DDL functionality against Oracle when using the MSDAORA provider and ADOX.

When facing the security and data definition tasks of multiple applications, evaluate ADOX and see if it can serve your needs.

Common ownership of objects is another tactic you should employ for handling multiple applications. Just as ADOX gives you one-stop-shopping for DDL and Security, you should try to unify the ownership of objects as much as possible. The fact that only one entity can own an object in the database at one time should give any serious developer pause. What should happen if the owner of the object leaves and changes must be made to it, but you have found it impossible? Rather than find yourself in that situation, when you have one central point of massive failure, let groups own objects. That way, several individuals will have the rights to change and reassign the object as needed.

Separate applications can share a workgroup, as you saw in Figure 23.1. Take advantage of this as much as possible. Chances are that you will be able to overlap many groups from one application to another, thereby reducing your administrative overhead.

If at all possible, strive for a common file location on the network rather than adopting a replications scheme. Though replication is a fine tool for sharing data and has opened up a world of possibilities for Access applications, its use can come at a high administrative cost.

The key to managing multiple applications is to share objects, users, groups, workgroups, and locations as much as possible. Reducing the number of variables in the maintenance of these applications will make them more reliable and robust.

Implications When Using SQL

Access 2000 provides another new way to handle basic security functionality in a database, including the client. New keywords have been added to the SQL dialect that enable you to create users and groups, add users to groups, drop users or groups, grant permissions on objects to users and groups, or revoke those privileges.

These SQL statements are executed like any other SQL statement, but instead of returning recordsets or altering the data definition of the database, they affect the security settings of the objects they are aimed at.

Create

Create User or Group does exactly what it implies. The user and group collections in the system file of the database are appended with the new user and group entities. One difference between this technique and ADOX is the absence of a PID. PIDs cannot be included with the SQL statements. The following code shows how you would create users and groups through SQL statements.

```
CREATE USER user password[, user password,...]
CREATE GROUP group password[, group password,...]
```

After the user and/or group is created, it can be added to an existing group with the Add User statement. Users are always added to groups in SQL, never the other way around.

Add User

Add User also affects the group collection in the workgroup file. Wherever the workgroup file is affected, it is always the current workgroup. You cannot, using SQL, affect any workgroup file other than the one you are logged in to.

```
ADD USER user[, user,...] TO group
```

Grant/Revoke

After users have been created and added to groups, they can be granted permissions. The Grant keyword enables you to give object permissions to users and groups.

```
GRANT {privilege[, privilege...}] ON
    {TABLE table ¦
    INDEX index ¦
    QUERY query ¦
    CONTAINER}
TO    {user/group[, usergroup,...]}
```

The permissions that can be granted are more limited than you will find in ADOX. They are described in the following list:

Select	Selectsecurity	Create
Delete	Updatesecurity	Selectschema
Insert	Dbpassword	Schema
Update	Updateidentity	Updateowner
Drop		

With SQL, you can grant permissions on tables, indexes, queries, and containers.

After granting privileges, you can revoke them with Grant's opposite, Revoke. The syntax and options are the same as they are in a Grant statement, but the result is exactly opposite.

Drop

After the permissions are removed, you can Drop the user or group. The syntax and options are exactly like Create, except that Drop is the keyword and the result of the query is the removal of an user or group from the workgroup file.

Securing a Database Step by Step

With the almost bewildering number of options and new features in Access security, it is good to know that the basic steps to securing a database have not changed.

By following these steps closely while you implement your security plan, you will have full advantage of Access's security capabilities. Failing to follow these steps could compromise the strength of your security.

1. Create a new workgroup—Be sure to use the wrkgadm.exe discussed earlier in this chapter. Select the option to create a new workgroup file.

2. Open Access using the workgroup file created especially for your new application.

3. Open or create the database you intend to secure.

4. Create a new user and add him to the Admins group.

5. Change the Admin user's password from its default blank to something you will remember, but that few, if any, other people know.

6. Remove all permissions from all objects for the Users group in the database.

7. Close the database.

8. Reopen Access and log in as the new administrator.

9. Open the database you are securing.

10. Run the Security Wizard on the new database. This will save you a great deal of tedious work changing object ownership.

11. Remove the Admin user from the Admins group.

12. Create the users and groups your application needs.

13. Join your users to their respective groups.

14. Assign the appropriate permissions to the groups.

15. Add or remove group permissions as needed.

Common Security Errors

One common problem occurs when users logged in to one workgroup are able to get into another database with their admin accounts.

Most likely this has happened because you created your security in the default system.mdw. The default system MDW is not secure and can never be made secure because it was not seeded with a PID when it was created. Because the admin account is universal, others will be able to enter this vulnerable system. It is also possible that the

Admin user was not removed from the Admin group on your system. Because the Admin user is not unique across workgroups, every workgroup will see Admin as its own Admin. If your workgroup still has Admin as a member of the Admins group, people from other workgroups will be able to log on to your workgroup as administrators.

To solve this problem, you will have to secure the database against a new workgroup file.

Sometimes a database seems to be secured, everyone logs in, but the permissions are not working.

A common problem with secured databases is the failure to strip the users group of all permissions. At birth, all workgroups grant users full rights to everything in the database. All users are, by default, members of the Users group. Even if you grant no explicit administrative rights, all users in the Users group will inherit them by virtue of being in that group. Make sure to remove all permissions from the Users Group.

There is nothing stopping you from creating as many groups as you could ever want. Because the Users group is worthless as a permission-less group, and the Admin groups is super-powerful, you really have no choice but to create a security plan and create groups to satisfy it.

Summary

As vital as security is—even to the simplest databases—it is often neglected or improperly configured. This chapter has explored the ever-growing number of ways to secure a Jet database to protect it from inadvertent misuse and malevolent harm. Planning security from the start of the application and studying these topics to find an implementation that suits your needs will enhance the experience users have with your application, and will mean fewer maintenance headaches for you.

Web Publishing with Access 2000

PART

VIII

Configuring a Web Site for Web Publishing

CHAPTER 24

Most Access developers get extremely intimidated when their boss or client starts talking to them about Web publishing with Access 2000 because most of them are experts in database management and VBA, but do not know much about setting up and maintaining a Web site. This chapter will explain to you how to set up a machine for Web site development, Web site deployment, and how to work with Microsoft Web server technology. By no means will you be a Web server administrator after this chapter, but you will be able to set up a Web site when you are through.

Development Versus Production Environment

Let's clarify some terminology that we will use in this section of the book. There are two different environments with which you will probably be dealing during the life cycle of your development project: the development environment and the production environment. Your development environment is exactly what it sounds like—the place you develop your application. The production environment is the place your application will ultimately reside when it is finished and ready to be viewed by your users or clients. If you create your pages on a Windows 95 machine but place them on a Windows NT Server machine for testing and debugging, the Windows 95 machine is the development machine and the Windows NT Server machine is your development environment.

Ideally, your development and production environments would have identical hardware and software configurations, but would be physically located on two different machines. In the real world, this is not always feasible. Many people (including some of the authors of this book) use Windows 95/98 or Windows NT Workstation as their development environment, and then place the files on a Windows NT Server machine for their final resting place (production environment).

The great thing about Microsoft Web technology is that you can develop and test your Access 2000 Web applications on a Windows 95/98 machine and deploy it to a Windows 2000/NT 4.0 machine without changing any code. Microsoft has provided one Web server technology that works on any of these operating systems. The way to harness this technology is by installing a Web server on your development and deployment machines.

Choosing Your Platform

Microsoft has released three different Web server applications—one for each level of their Windows platforms. One, called Personal Web Server 4.0 (PWS4), runs on Windows 95/98 and provides the most basic Web server functionality. Another, called Peer Web Services 4 (again PWS4), is also a limited functionality Web server, almost identical to the Windows 95/98 version, but with modifications made so it will run properly under Windows NT Workstation. The other, called Internet Information Server 4.0 (IIS4), can only be run on Windows NT Server 4.0. Since the versions that run under Windows 95/98 and Windows NT Workstation are so similar in capabilities and functions, I will refer to them together through the rest of this chapter as PWS, noting differences where applicable.

Some of the features that both products provide are

- The ability to serve basic HTML Web pages
- The ability to implement Active Server Pages applications
- The ability to implement transactional Web applications through the use of Microsoft Transaction Server
- ODBC connection pooling
- The ability to utilize Microsoft's Data Access Components (MDAC)
- Microsoft Message Queue (MSMQ)

> **NOTE**
>
> Version 1.5 of the Microsoft Data Access Components is installed with a standard installation of the Option Pack, but it is recommended you acquire and install the newest version. At the time of this writing, the newest version is MDAC 2.1, shipped with Access 2000.
>
> It should also be noted that there is a difference in the version of the MSMQ that is installed with the Option Pack depending on which operating system you are installing to. The version of the MSMQ installed on Windows NT Server is a fully functional message queue service, whereas the NT Workstation and Windows 95/98 versions are merely clients that can utilize the MSMQ service on a remote server.

Although there are many similarities, there are also some differences, mostly related to performance and scalability, that you should be aware of before choosing which platform to run.

Personal Web Server and Peer Web Services

Personal Web Server and Peer Web Services are great tools for developing applications locally on your workstation without the requirement of running NT Server. They enable you to develop and test your applications prior to moving them to the production Web

24

CONFIGURING A
WEB SITE FOR
WEB PUBLISHING

server. If an application runs properly on PWS, you are assured that it will also run properly when deployed to IIS4.

Because PWS was not designed to host high-volume sites, some of the features that are included with IIS4 are missing, such as Index Server, SMTP Server, and Certificate Server. You are also limited to the number of concurrent client connections with this platform—only one on Windows 95/98 and a maximum of just ten on Windows NT Workstation.

Internet Information Server

Internet Information Server 4.0 is a much more robust Web server application than the Personal Web Server is. It is the recommended platform for all production Web servers, because it will hold up better under high volume. You will also notice performance gains with IIS4 over PWS4. IIS4 has no limitation on the number of concurrent users. Depending on the design of your application, it can potentially handle thousands of concurrent users.

The installation of both is very simple and also quite similar. It is recommended to install only the services that you plan to take advantage of. Loading unused components will create unnecessary load on the workstation/server.

Now you know some basics about each of your choices for Microsoft Web servers—which one do you use? Well, you should definitely use IIS4 and Windows NT 4 Server for your production environment. You would also be better served to develop on an environment as close as possible to the production environment, so I also recommend IIS4 on NT Server 4 as a development environment. Almost every Active Server Pages application that you write will run on either Web platform IIS4 or PWS4—ASP is ASP.

> **NOTE**
>
> There is a difference between the ASP that can run on IIS3 and IIS4. IIS3 uses VBScript 2 but IIS4 uses VBScript 3. All versions of the VBScript engine are backward-compatible, but each version has added functionality. You need to be careful not to require the newer features unless you are sure that your Web server supports them.
>
> If you have installed Internet Explorer 5 on your server, you are running VBScript 5, which contains all the previously included functionality, plus some additional benefits. If you do not have Internet Explorer 5 installed on your

system but would still like to take advantage of the newest scripting engine, you can download the most recent release from www.microsoft.com/scripting/. Two new functions introduced in version 5 are the Eval and Execute functions, which provide the ability to evaluate code at runtime. There have also been changes made that have resulted in performance gains for any application that uses VBScript (including Active Server Pages).

The way to install a Microsoft Web server is by installing the NT 4.0 Option Pack.

What Is the Option Pack?

Only Windows 2000's standard installation includes the files necessary to develop Web applications, but the Web services for NT 4.0 and Windows 95/98 are a free add-on. The installation package that can be used to provide Web development and Web deployment capabilities is the Windows NT Option Pack. Even though it is named the "Windows NT" Option Pack, the same installation package can be used to install Personal Web Server 4 and other Web enhancements on Windows 95/98.

During the installation of Windows NT Server 4.0, you are given the option to install Internet Information Server (version 2), but that does not provide the needed functionality to implement Active Server Pages, Microsoft's key Web development technology and the topic of Chapter 27, "Web Publishing with Access 2000 and Active Server Pages."

NOTE

Now that we are on the topic, we recommend either not installing IIS during a Windows NT Server installation or uninstalling it before we move forward. It is always better to start with a fresh install rather than an upgrade.

Microsoft's most recent release of Web server software is included as part of the Option Pack, which can be obtained from a variety of sources. It will automatically be sent if you are an MSDN subscriber. You can also buy the CD or download it from Microsoft's Web site at

http://www.microsoft.com/ntserver/nts/downloads/recommended/NT4OptPk/
default.asp.

24

CONFIGURING A
WEB SITE FOR
WEB PUBLISHING

The option pack can be installed and run on Windows 95/98, Windows NT Workstation, and Windows NT Server 4.0. Prior to installing the Option Pack on a platform, you are required to install Microsoft's Internet Explorer 4.0 or higher. We recommend downloading and installing the newest release of the browser to have all the most recent patches and bug fixes. (At the time of this writing, it is Internet Explorer 5.0 included with the Office 2000 disks.) Additionally, if you are installing the Option Pack on Windows NT 4.0, you will be required to install Microsoft's Windows NT Service Pack 3.

> **NOTE**
>
> Service Pack 4 is the most recent Windows NT service pack released from Microsoft, but should be installed AFTER installing the Option Pack.

> **NOTE**
>
> If you need to reinstall Service Pack 3 for any reason after you have installed the Option Pack, be sure not to overwrite any of the newer files that Option Pack installed.

Before installing the Microsoft Option Pack, you should be sure that your computer meets the minimum system requirements noted in Table 24.1.

TABLE 24.1   MINIMUM HARDWARE REQUIREMENTS FOR THE INSTALLATION OF THE WINDOWS NT OPTION PACK

Hardware Component	Required	Recommended
Processor	66 MHz 486	90 MHz Pentium
RAM	32 MB	64 MB
Free hard disk space	30 MB	100 MB
Monitor	VGA	Super VGA
CD-ROM drive (optional)	3x	6x

Setting Up Your Web Server

Web servers can be either simple or complicated to install and configure, depending on your application requirements. The reason for the complexity is the extreme amount of control you can maintain with Microsoft's Web servers.

Installation

There are some basic requirements that need to be met before installing the NT Option Pack, such as the installation of Internet Explorer 4.01 and Service Pack 3 (NT only), mentioned earlier.

When you begin installation of the NT Option Pack, there are some further requirements that need to be met for successful application development with Office 2000. There are also a lot of components that can and may be installed unnecessarily if you accept the defaults. In this next section, I will tell you what the different options are, which are required, and which should only be installed if you are planning to use them.

NT Option Pack for Windows 95/98

The components available to you during the installation of the NT Option Pack differ depending on the platform for which you are installing.

Installable Components

Below is a list of the components available to you during installation if you were to choose a "Custom Installation" during setup of the NT Option Pack. Not all these components are each system. The ones that require a certain operating system have been noted. Also noted are the ones that are required to develop Office 2000 Web applications using Active Server Pages or COM objects.

- Certificate Server (Windows NT Server only)— Enables you to create and send digital certificates. This ability allows for an additional layer of security in your Web application. You can create a personalized security certificate for a client that they can download and install to their client software (Web browser). In the future, you are assured that the client is who you think it is.

  This is not required for Office 2000 Web development.

- Option Pack Common Program Files—Contains files common to most of the other components.

  This is required for Office 2000 Web development.

- FrontPage 98 Server Extensions— Enables you to author sites and perform basic administration through Microsoft FrontPage and Microsoft Visual InterDev.

  This is not required for basic development of Office 2000 Web applications unless you decide to use FrontPage or Visual InterDev as your development tool.

NOTE

You can perform some level of development in these tools without having the FrontPage server extensions installed, but you will not be able to take advantage of the built-in wizards, Web-bots, or publishing features. Because the extensions add some overhead to a server (and FrontPage has a habit of occasionally rewriting ASP code), many developers only use these tools to create "shell" code that they later modify in another tool and then transfer to the server using standard FTP software.

- Internet Connection Services for RAS— Manages multiple dial-up connections and phone books.

  This is not required for Office 2000 Web development.

- Microsoft Data Access Components 1.5— This installs ActiveX Data Components (ADO) 1.5 and Remote Data Services components (RDS). It also places necessary drivers and providers on your system that will enable you to connect to databases.

  This is a required component for Office 2000 Web development. After installing this component, you will also need to acquire the latest version of the MDAC components (version 2.1). Since the Option Pack was released, there have been several enhanced revisions that contain bug fixes and additional functionality required for successful Office 2000 development (Web or otherwise).

- Microsoft Message Queue (MSMQ)— Allows applications to pass transaction information to other components without having to wait for a reply. This is a feature that should be investigated if you are developing transactional applications, but the interfaces that you are dealing with are sometimes unreliable. For example, if you are using the MSMQ and there is a momentary disturbance in network connectivity, the MSMQ will continue to attempt completion of the transaction. When the network comes back online, the transaction can be committed.

  This is not required unless you have specific requirements for it and plan to incorporate its services into your application.

- Personal Web Server (Windows 95/98 and Windows NT Workstation only)— This component contains the core Web services.

  It is required if you plan to develop, test, or deploy applications on your workstation.

- Internet Information Server (Windows NT Server only)

  Includes:

  > File Transfer Protocol (FTP) services

  > NNTP services (for publishing newsgroups)

  > Internet Service Manager (ISM)(a snap-in for the MMC): This is a required component that enables you to administer and configure your Web services through the Microsoft Management Console.

  > Simple Mail Transfer Protocol (SMTP) service:This enables you to generate email messages from your application and send it to the destination of your choice.

NOTE

This component enables you to send and receive email, but it does not have any method for securing or controlling access to mail. After mail is received, it is placed in a shared folder and could potentially be accessed by anyone. This component is best used for outgoing mail only (like feedback forms). If you need to send and receive email, you should install email server software (such as Microsoft Exchange Server) that supports both the SMTP and POP protocols and is better able to handle the security involved with multiple users.

  > World Wide Web Server (HTTP Web services): This is required if you plan to develop, test, or deploy Web applications on your server.

  > Sample Web site: If you are new to Web programming, you might want to install this sample Web site and look at the coding conventions and techniques used.

  > HTML version of the ISM (Internet Service Manager): This enables you to manage your Web server remotely via an HTML interface.

- Microsoft Transaction Server (MTS) 2.0—This installs the COM and DCOM manager.

  It is required for Office 2000 Web development.

- Microsoft Index Server (Windows NT Server only)— Enables you to perform full-text search and retrieval of documents residing on your Web server. This is an excellent search tool with many advanced capabilities. If you install it, be sure you use it—having it sit on your system and index all your Web pages can be extremely resource-intensive and a waste if not used.

  This is not required for Office 2000 development.

- Microsoft Script Debugger (Windows NT Server only) allows you to perform real-time ASP script debugging. It can be used to enhance development and testing cycles by automatically opening the active ASP script once an error is detected. Because of security and performance considerations, this should not be installed on a production Web server.

  This is not required for Office 2000 development.

- Windows Scripting Host— Provides the ability to write and run local script files to perform certain functions like certain system maintenance features.

  This is not required for Office 2000 development.

- Microsoft Management Console (Windows NT only)— The main GUI interface in Windows NT to allow you to manage and configure each of the services installed in the NT Option Pack.

  This is a required component if you are installing Windows NT Server. It is not required on NT Workstation (you could use the Personal Web Manager), but it is highly recommended.

- Visual InterDev RAD Support— This enables Visual InterDev applications to be deployed remotely to your server.

  This is not required for Office 2000 Web development.

> **NOTE**
>
> Installing the Visual InterDev RAD Support poses a potential security risk on your system that you should be aware of. This component allows for remote deployment of applications, possibly without your knowledge. As with any development platform, it is possible that the component(s) deployed without your knowledge could have adverse effects on your system.

As you can see, there is quite a lot included with the NT Option Pack. Each of these components adds enhanced functionality, but they are not required for basic Office 2000 Web development and can add unnecessary overhead to your system if installed without reason.

To make it easier to install the NT Option Pack, Microsoft has included three preconfigured install options with the setup package. The components installed with them are noted below.

Minimum, Typical, Custom Installation Options

If you choose the Custom installation, you will be presented with the list of components above and be able to pick-and-choose the ones you want installed. This is not usually necessary or desired, so Microsoft has made two other options available to you.

A minimum installation includes everything necessary to develop basic Office 2000 Web applications. The components installed during a Minimum install are

- Microsoft Data Access Components 1.5
- Personal Web Server (Windows 95/98 and Windows NT Workstation only)
- Internet Information Server (Windows NT Server only)
- Transaction Server
- SMTP Service (Windows NT Server only)

A Typical installation includes all the components named above (Minimal installation) plus the components listed below:

- FrontPage Server Extensions
- Personal Web Server documentation (Windows 95/98 and Windows NT Workstation)
- Internet Information Server documentation (Windows NT Server only)
- Additional documentation: Active Server Pages, SMTP services, ADO, and Index Server (Windows NT Server only)
- Microsoft Index Server (Windows NT Server only)
- Microsoft Management Console (Windows NT Server only)
- Index Server (Windows NT Server only)
- Microsoft Script Debugger
- Windows Scripting Host

> **NOTE**
>
> To get a full install of the Active Server Pages documentation for Personal Web Server, you will be required to perform a Custom install and specifically include that option. For some reason Microsoft decided not to include them with either of these two preconfigured installation options.

If you want any of the advanced components that are not installed automatically, you should perform a custom installation.

One of the components discussed previously, Microsoft Transaction Server, is such a major advancement and integral part of Microsoft's Web strategy that we have dedicated the next section to explaining it in more detail.

Microsoft Transaction Server 2.0

Microsoft Transaction Server (MTS) is a major component of the Option Pack and required for many of the other services to work, including IIS/PWS. MTS is an object request broker and transaction broker. In past years, critical applications had to run on big beefy systems with special software installed in order to perform this functionality.

> **NOTE**
>
> MTS is so crucial to the operation of IIS that in Windows 2000, Microsoft has integrated it into the operating system itself and renamed it COM+.
>
> MTS is required to install Microsoft's Web services because, even if you do not develop towards it, MTS controls all Active Server Pages applications. Every ASP page that is processed is run through MTS (controlling the ASP.DLL)—this is one reason IIS4 has seen such great performance gains over IIS3.

What Is a Transaction Broker?

Good question. A transaction broker manages transactions, but this still doesn't tell us much. Most current database systems, like Microsoft's SQL Server, provide transaction management. A database server is told that a transaction is starting, and then one or more SQL statements are performed on one or more tables in the database. The database server does not commit (make permanent) these changes until it is sent a command to tell it that everything worked correctly. This helps maintain referential integrity through the database and consistency within the application. This ensures that SQL1 will not execute unless SQL2 and SQL3 execute also. If the transaction is not told to commit, it is rolled-back, meaning all the SQL statements are cancelled and the database is restored to the state it was in before starting the transaction.

MTS does for COM objects what database servers do for multiple SQL statements. With good development practice, you will break the application into the smallest possible chunks, then isolate that code so that it can be reused. For a truly scalable application, this code can be migrated to COM and then registered with MTS. Once properly registered, MTS knows which COM objects are a required part of a transaction and tracks the success or failure of each object.

> **NOTE**
>
> Access 2000 (and all previous versions) is limited in its ability to be supported by Microsoft Transaction Server. Although you can still develop towards MTS to gain speed, scalability, and connection pooling, you will have to use an advanced database platform, such as Microsoft's SQL Server, to gain the full level of transactional support available.

In addition to brokering transactions, MTS controls object creation and destruction. This enables COM objects to be created only when needed, speeding application execution and preventing unnecessary overhead on the server.

MTS also handles connection pooling into databases. This enables users to share connections instead of each one having a unique connection. Without connection pooling, 500 users would require 500 connections to a database. MTS allows us to use about 1/10 of those connections. If a connection is not in use, it is borrowed and used for another user, and then released back to the "pool" of available connections. The number of connections is only increased when all available connections are in use. This is a great advancement and has incredible performance gains for applications.

There are a number of good books on the market that give more detail on the operation, configuration, and development considerations for Microsoft Transaction Server. Digging deep into this topic is beyond the scope of this book, but if you will be developing transaction-based applications or applications that need inherent scalability, you should definitely investigate MTS.

Now that you know what to install, how to install it, and what basic functions are provided, let's discuss configuration of your Web services.

Managing and Configuring Your Web Server

There are two different administration interfaces used to configure the Web services depending on whether you are running Windows 95/98 or Windows NT (Workstation or Server). You will need to be comfortable with the interface that relates to the environment and platform you are working with.

Personal Web Manager

The interface that runs on Windows 95/98 is called the Personal Web Manager and has a very simple (if limited) interface to control your Web site. There are five main options from within the interface—Main, Publish, Web Site, Tour, and Advanced. You can get to any of these areas by choosing either the item from the left-hand navigation bar or from the View item on the menu bar.

- The Main screen, shown in Figure 24.1, is where you go to start and stop your local Web services and to view some basic information about your site.

FIGURE 24.1

The Main page of the Personal Web Manager is mostly used to start and stop your Web services.

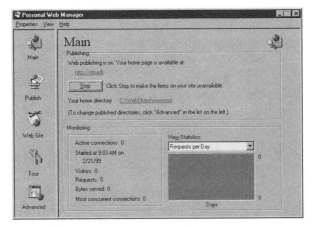

NOTE

You can also start and stop the Web services by right-clicking on the PWS icon in your system tray (bottom-right corner next to your clock) and choosing the desired action.

In addition to starting and stopping the Web service, you can view the physical location of your Web root (your home directory), the Web location of your Web root (just above the start/stop button), and some basic traffic statistics about your site (Monitoring).

- The next page is an interface to the Web Publishing Wizard. Microsoft's documentation states that this wizard will "automatically place a copy of the file in the Webpub directory and add a descriptive link to your home page." However, the wizard is temperamental, so it is usually better to modify the files yourself.

    Choosing Web Site gives you the option of creating a default home page or editing it if you have already created one. This is a very basic tool and probably best left alone if you are a serious Web developer.

- The Tour provides some VERY basic information—probably nothing you do not already know. If you are curious, you can step through the ten informational screens that are available.

- Most of the options that are required to perform your function as a Web developer are located in the Advanced area, as shown in Figure 24.2. From here, you will create your virtual directories, set default documents, and control folder properties.

FIGURE 24.2

You will need to create and manage your virtual directories and Web settings on the Advanced page of the Personal Web Manager.

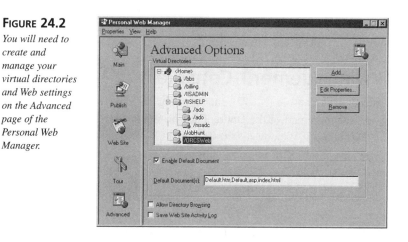

NOTE

The term *virtual directory* has caused confusion for some Web developers. This term is clarified in the section "What Is the Difference Between a Site and a Virtual Directory?" later in this chapter.

Virtual directories will be covered later in the chapter, but it should be noted that there are three access levels allowed when you create a virtual directory: Read, Execute, and Scripts (see Figure 24.3). Always place a check next to Read; if you don't, no one will be able to view your site. If you intend to view Active Server Pages within the virtual directory you are setting up, you need to check the box that allows scripts to run (ASP is server-side VBScript). Take care when enabling the Execute option. With this option enabled for a virtual directory, any executable file placed within can be executed, including script engines (such as Perl) or Windows binary files (such as .exe and .dll files).

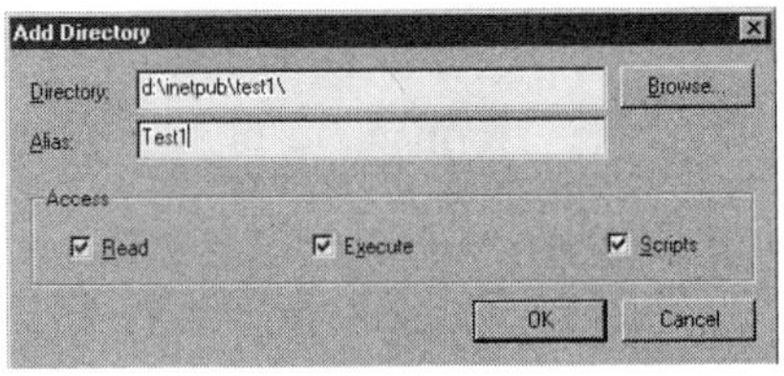

FIGURE 24.3

Access permissions for a new virtual directory within the Personal Web Manager.

The interface used to manage the Web services on a Windows NT/ Windows 2000 system is called the Microsoft Management Console and is quite a bit more involved. If you develop on Windows 95/98 but have someone else who will manage the Windows NT production server(s), you can skip the next section.

Microsoft Management Console

The Microsoft Management Console (MMC), shown in Figure 24.4, is the main tool for controlling all services that are part of the Option Pack on Windows NT and will be a very large and important part of Windows 2000 (Microsoft NT's successor) when it is released. It is a good idea to get comfortable with it now if you plan to use future versions of Microsoft Windows NT.

When you open the MMC, you will notice that the left pane has two options and expanding branches under each. The right pane is the detail pane that will show specifics of the item chosen on the left. The very first item in the list on the left is Console Root—basically the MMC itself. Each item under that is called a snap-in and enables you to perform specific tasks—usually isolated to one service. Windows 2000 will have many snap-ins available in the MMC, so get used to them now.

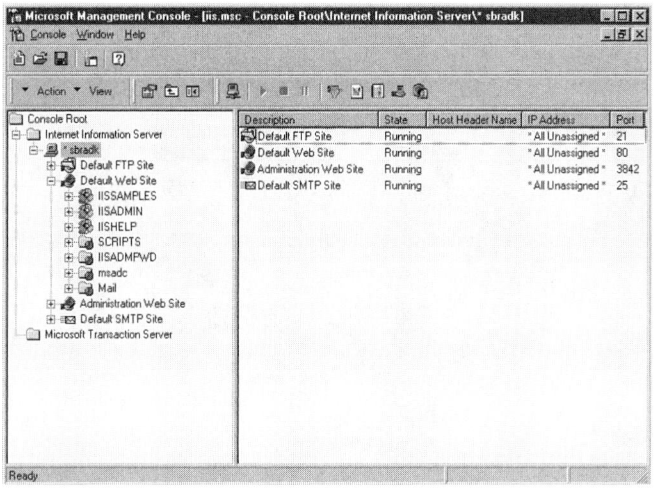

FIGURE 24.4

The Microsoft Management Console (MMC) is the main interface for managing Windows NT's Web services.

Internet Information Server Configuration

The first snap-in you will see (and the only one we will discuss in this book) is the Internet Information Server control. If you expand this branch one level, you will see the netbios name of your local computer listed below. Expanding this one level further will reveal different options depending on the services you have installed.

Usually you will see

- Default FTP Site
- Default Web Site
- Administration Web Site
- Default SMTP Site

Covering each of these is beyond the scope of this book, but we will dig a bit into the Web site configurations because they will affect the operation and performance of your Web application.

Okay, let's step through the different options and screens now. We will make some changes as we go to explain and demonstrate the effect.

First, choose the name of your local server and right-click. As with many Windows application, choosing an item and right-clicking will display a quick-menu of frequently accessed options (see Figure 24.5). Then choose Properties from the option list. This presents the default settings for the entire server. You could get these same options by choosing properties of an individual site, but then you would have to make these changes for each site.

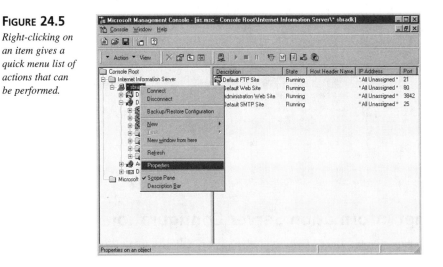

The first thing we want to change if the location of the log files. Option Pack defaults to placing these files at C:\winnt\system32\logfiles\. Looks okay at first, but let's think about this…the log files can grow very large on an active site. Do you really want the potential of choking required disk space from your operating system? I didn't think so.

At the bottom of the Web Site tab, choose the logging properties. Then on the general tab, change the default location of the Web log files. This can be a folder that already exists on your system. We like d:\logfiles—it's off the system partition and easy to find. If you choose the Extended Properties tab, you can change exactly what information is stored in the log files when a client requests a page.

> **NOTE**
>
> DO NOT simply choose everything. Each item you record causes additional disk activity and system overhead. For best performance, choose only the items you really want and need.

Click OK a few times to get back to the main WWW Properties box.

Now let's take a look at the Documents tab. This is where you can specify one or more default documents (see Figure 24.6). This is the information that IIS uses to tell which file to load first. If someone types www.YourSiteName.com without specifying a file, IIS starts at the top of this list and looks for each file until one is found or the end of the list is reached. If the file is not present on the site, or you have not specified at least one default document, the user will receive an error. Because my company, ORCS Web, Inc hosts many clients, we always add index.html to each Web server—that was the UNIX standard and many people are familiar with it.

FIGURE 24.6

Sometimes you will want to change the name of the default document or add more default documents to the list for a particular site.

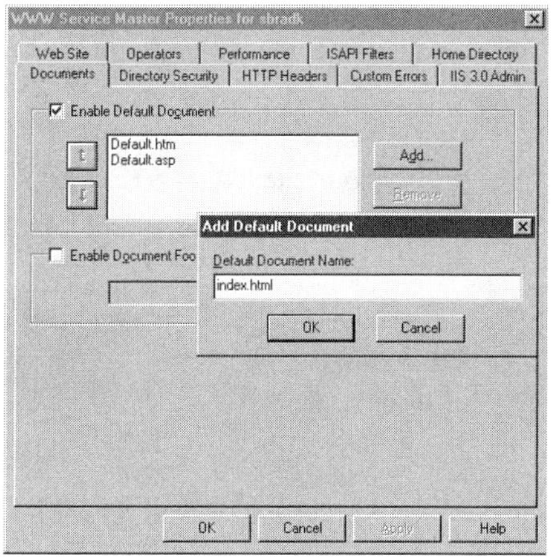

Click your way back to the WWW Properties again and choose the Directory Security tab. The Microsoft Management Console allows you to manage additional security settings that work in conjunction with Windows NT File System (see Figure 24.7). There are three sections to the directory security that IIS controls.

- Anonymous Access and Authentication Control
- Secure Communications
- IP Address and Domain Name Restriction

First choose Anonymous Access and Authentication Control. Here again you have three choices.

- Allow Anonymous Access
- Basic Authentication (Password is sent in clear text)
- Windows NT Challenge/Response

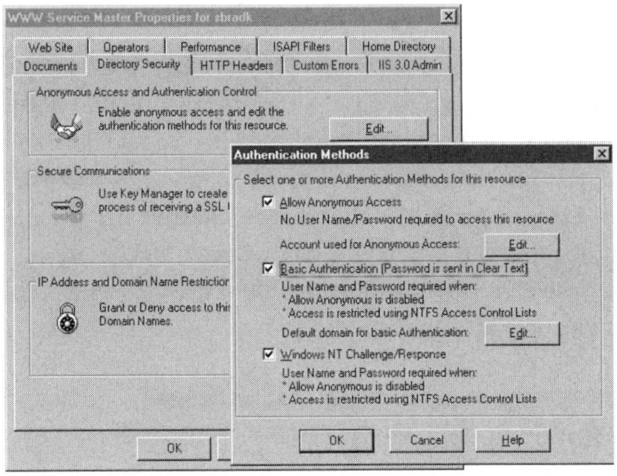

FIGURE 24.7

*Security is almost
always a concern
on any system that
is connected to
the Internet.*

If you want to allow anonymous access to your site, be sure that the first box (Allow Anonymous Access) is checked. This option tells IIS to first check permissions on that file and determine if the IUSER account (explained later in the section titled "What Is IUSER?") has access whenever someone requests a page or file. If so, assume the client is IUSER and process the request. If this option is not checked or the IUSER account does not have access to the file in question, a process is initiated based on the other two settings on this page.

If Challenge and Response is enabled and the client is using Internet Explorer, the username/password combination that was used to log on to the client will be passed to the Web server and authentication will be attempted again. Using Challenge and Response, the transmission of the username/password combination is encrypted and totally secure. If that username/password combination can be matched to an account on the server (either local or domain accounts will work), the user is allowed or denied based on that user's access. If the account cannot be matched, access is denied. If the client is not using Internet Explorer as the browser, authentication can only be done through clear text authentication.

To validate a user on the Web server when the client is not using Internet Explorer, IIS must be set to allow clear text authentication. This method is NOT secure, but is necessary if you must protect areas on your site and cannot know for sure what browser the client will be running.

Usually, enabling both of these options is the best choice. First, IIS will try to authenticate as IUSER (if enabled), and then it will try Challenge and Response. If still unsuccessful, it will attempt basic authentication.

Choosing the Secure Communications option on this screen will open the Key Manager if you have not already installed a secure key. When and if you decide that you want to implement Secure Socket Layer (SSL), this is the place to start. From here, you generate the necessary key request to be sent to a Certificate Authority such as VeriSign. After it processes the request, you will need to enter the certificate into the Key Manager to complete the process.

After you have installed your SSL key, this button changes from Key Manager to Edit. Choosing Edit will enable you to require SSL to access this resource. URLs will need to be formatted `https://` instead of `http://` to view pages at this location (site, folder, virtual directory, and so on).

> **NOTE**
>
> E-commerce is becoming more and more popular. To safely transmit sensitive data (such as credit card numbers) over the Internet, you must implement SSL.

You also have the ability to limit access to your site based on the client's IP address. This is not very convenient unless your server is going to be used for intranet use only. Most client IP addresses on the Internet change every time they log on because of dynamic allocation from their ISPs.

If you decide to restrict based on IP address, you can specify that all clients are granted access except a specified list, or just the opposite—all clients are denied access except the ones specified.

Click your way back to the main Web Site Properties page and let's move to the Home Directory tab shown in Figure 24.8. This is where you specify your application settings.

The "local path" is the physical location of the Web site that we are viewing properties for.

Access Permissions enable you to specify whether this site allows read, write, both, or no access. I have not run into a situation yet where write access was required, so we will leave Read checked.

Content Control has four options:

- Log Access—If this is checked and you also enabled logging on the Web Site tab, all HTTP requests will generate an entry in the Web server log files.

- Directory Browsing Allowed—If this is checked and no default home page is present (or specified on the Documents tab), a list of the files in that folder will be displayed.

- Index This Directory—Tell Index Server to monitor and index the files at this location for possible search.

- FrontPage Web—Exactly as it sounds. Specifies that this location is a FrontPage (or Visual InterDev) Web site and that the FrontPage Server Extensions are supported.

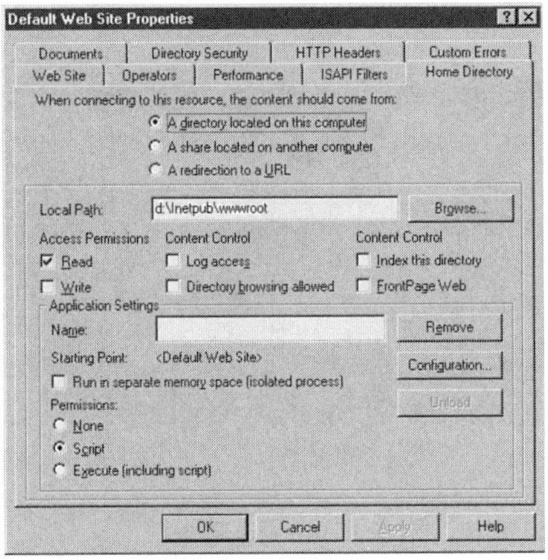

FIGURE 24.8

The Home Directory tab enables you to manage the lowest level of settings for the Web site— such as the physical path on the server.

The bottom third of this dialog box deals with Application Settings. By application, Microsoft means an independent set of Active Server Pages that work together to perform some function. (That's my definition—not Microsoft's.)

On this part of the screen, be sure that the script permissions are selected. This enables Active Server Pages to execute on the server and send their results back to the browser. I have seen quite a few people select execute permissions (because that was the old setting in IIS3), but this is a no-no. Allowing execute is necessary on folders that contain CGI or Perl, but should not be selected otherwise. Placing a executable in a folder marked as execute will potentially enable that program to run on the server and cause undesirable effects.

Choose the configuration tab and let's look at some of the details that are specific to the performance and functionality of your ASP pages.

Under configuration there are three tabs: App Mappings, App Options, and App Debugging. App Mappings is where the file types are specified (by extension) and the executable that should be used to process that is listed. At a minimum, you should leave .asa and .asp specified in this list and related to the ASP.DLL. You will also notice quite a few other mappings listed—if you are sure that you are not using any files of this type, you can remove these mappings and improve the performance of your server.

You can specify whether you want to allow your application to maintain session state and how long each session should last on the App Options tab shown in Figure 24.9. Be careful when modifying any of the settings located on this tab because they can have drastic effects on the operation and performance on the Web site. Most developers take advantage of session state—it's one of the great things about ASP. However, if you can work around it, you will see great improvements in performance by turning off session state.

FIGURE 24.9

Application settings will become very important to your site as you get deeper and deeper into Microsoft Web development.

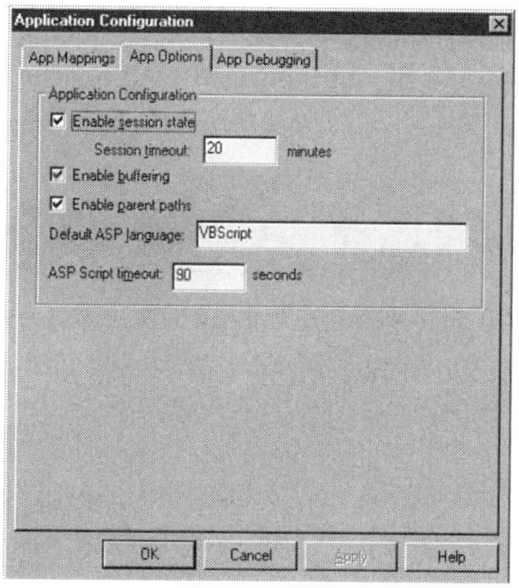

On this page you can also specify whether to enable buffering (yes, this also improves performance), enable parent paths (allows ASP to reference relative paths to the parent directory), and specify your default language (usually VBScript, but can be JScript if you desire). You can also specify the script timeout. Increasing this enables longer scripts to run without error, but this can also tie up your server resources unnecessarily. It is preferable to leave this at 60 seconds and specify a longer script timeout in the individual ASP page if required (`<% Server.ScriptTimeout=180 %>`).

The final tab, App Debugging, is where you specify whether or not you want to allow debugging on either the server side, client side, both, or neither. You can also specify a generic error message to send to clients if your ASP page runs afoul. This is a nice feature because it looks cleaner to the client if you do encounter an error. However, don't do this while debugging, or you won't know what went wrong.

Securing Your Web Applications

One of the problems that users face after installation of IIS or PWS is security—especially if you are developing an e-commerce application or an application that contains sensitive data.

There are some basic steps that can be taken, such as the ones noted later in the "ASP/HTML—Placement and Permissions" and the "Databases—Placement and Permissions" sections. These security settings are required just to allow the basic functionality required by a Web application, but there are some additional measures that can be taken to protect sensitive data and prevent unauthorized people from viewing information on your site.

> **NOTE**
>
> Many companies will implement a firewall between their servers and the rest of the Internet. A firewall allows the company to place certain restrictions on who can access the server and how it can be accessed. Quite often firewalls are told to exclude external access to the server from any port other than port 80 (the default HTTP port). This allows HTTP requests to come through and view the Web application, but it restricts a user from gaining access on any unauthorized ports.

The options that we just discussed and the changes they create were all site-wide. In addition to changing options for an entire site, you can also set specific configurations on a virtual directory.

What Is the Difference Between a Site and a Virtual Directory?

A *site* is a distinct entity on a Web server signified by a unique domain name. Internet Information Server on Windows NT Server is very good at handling multiple sites on a single server. Only hardware resources limit the number of sites you can run on a single NT Server.

A *virtual directory* is always contained within a site and is restricted to that site and that site only. A virtual directory can have its own Web settings that are different from the main Web sites, allowing a great level of control over the content on your site. For example, if you are planning on running CGI on your site (not recommended for performance reasons, but certainly possible), you will want to place all your CGI files into a single virtual directory and mark that directory as allowing execute permissions.

> **NOTE**
>
> Microsoft FrontPage and Visual InterDev are very particular about the way their virtual directories are configured. If you are using either of these tools in your development, it is best to allow that product to create the virtual directories for you. Also, after the program has created the virtual directory, do not manually change any of the settings. Many developers have "broken" their sites by modifying either Web settings or file permissions on a FrontPage or Visual InterDev Web site.

Probably the most exciting thing about a virtual directory is that it can be physically located anywhere on the server. It can even be located on a share drive mapped to another server (this requires special security configurations that are beyond the scope of this book). So if your site is www.YourSite.com, and you map a virtual directory called "user1" to d:\user1\, this will be accessible as http://www.yoursite.com/user1/, even though the folder is in a physically isolated area on the server.

> **NOTE**
>
> Although a virtual directory can be placed anywhere, it can also be located under the physical path for the Web root. The directory structures for your Web application should be thought out in advance. Having many virtual folders that are mapped to obscure areas of the server can cause a maintenance nightmare.

24

CONFIGURING A
WEB SITE FOR
WEB PUBLISHING

One of the most useful benefits of using virtual directories is control access to Web content. Let's say you have your Web root located at d:\wwwroot\, in which you control the content. You also have two coworkers who want their own Web areas where only they control the content. Regardless of whether they map a shared folder or use FTP, it is very hard to keep them from accessing the Web root's files if you simply create folders at d:\wwwroot\user1\ and d:\wwwroot\user2\.

One way of tightening security and restricting users' access to their own content only is to create folders at d:\users\user1\ and d:\users\user2\, and then map virtual directories to these areas.

The second most exciting thing about virtual directories is only available on Windows NT: the ability to specify an "application" starting point. This allows isolation of session/application variables and total isolation between Web applications—even if they exist on the same server.

Although you can create Web applications on Windows 95/98, there is no real way to create multiple applications and take advantage of the application isolation such as you can on Windows NT. On a Windows 95/98 Web server, all the content running under PWS is considered to be the same Web application. Session-level variables created in a virtual directory on Windows 95/98 are available from all other virtual directories on that site. If you plan to host multiple Web applications on the same server, this is yet another reason to use Windows NT.

When viewing the properties of a virtual folder on Windows NT, you can set specific settings different from those of the main site. All the options that were mentioned earlier in the chapter for site-level control are also available for virtual directory-level control. This provides more flexibility and control over individual Web applications, and allows you to make specific settings that might be needed on one application but not on another.

On the Home Directory tab, there is an option to create an application out of the virtual directory whose properties you are viewing. After you specify this folder as an application, it will operate independently of the rest of the Web site. When I say independently, I mean that this newly created application can have its own global.asa file and unique configurations. Also, any session or application-level variables that are defined are available only from within that application. Trying to access these variables from outside the current application—even from a folder on the same server—will be unsuccessful. This allows for isolation and an increased level of security.

> **NOTE**
>
> Global.asa files should always reside at an application's starting point. If you have declared a virtual directory to be an application, the global.asa file should be at the same physical path that you defined as that virtual directory's starting folder.

If you want even further isolation, you can specify that the application should run in its own memory space. Setting this feature requires context switching by the Web server and might have a negative impact on server performance. The benefit is that all processes of this specific application are isolated, and a fault or failure of this one application will not affect other applications running on the same server.

Now that we have our Web service installed and we know how to configure it, are we done? Not quite yet. There are a few other items that you should be aware of and take into consideration for Web application development and deployment. Although you set some basic options when you set up your application, you also need to consider the environment outside of the Web settings. One of the more important considerations is security and how to properly set up your application to allow access to your files and data sources.

What Is IUSER?

During the installation of IIS/PWS on Windows NT, a new user account is created and named IUSER_<machine_name> where <machine_name> is the netbios name associated with the server (in network properties).

When someone accesses a Web page on an IIS server and the server is set to allow anonymous access, IIS first checks the NTFS permissions of the file to see if the IUSER account has access. If IUSER has the appropriate rights to view the page, it is returned to the browser. If the IUSER account does not have rights assigned to this file, or if IIS is set to NOT allow anonymous access, IIS will try to authenticate the user based on the settings within the MMC.

File System Type

Although IIS has some options buried within it to allow for a small level of security for a site, it is insufficient for most needs without the complement of NT Security. I strongly recommend using Windows NT File System (NTFS) on the partition where your Web files and database will reside. This allows you to implement security at a file and folder level and is really the only safe way to configure a production Web server.

24

CONFIGURING A
WEB SITE FOR
WEB PUBLISHING

> **NOTE**
>
> NTFS is only available on Windows NT systems. If you are developing on a Windows 95/98 workstation, you will not be able to maintain as tight a security model as you would on Windows NT. This is one more good reason to deploy your application to Windows NT in production.

Directory Structures and Required Permissions

A fairly standard configuration for a Web server is to have two disk partitions—one small partition (perhaps 1GB) for the operating system and another for all Web-related files and log files. What file system type is used for the OS partition is a matter of preference, but almost always the Web partition is converted to NTFS for security reasons.

During installation of IIS, the path to the Web root was specified. Assuming the root was placed on the second partition, the default path would be D:\Inetpub\wwwroot\. This is the area that IIS will route all Web requests, unless the configuration is modified to send them elsewhere. If you were to look at the properties of this folder within the MMC, you would notice that the IP allocation is set to "all unassigned," so even if you have multiple IP addresses on the server, all requests will be directed to this area. For sake of simplicity, we will assume there is only one site on our server and that the Web path is D:\Inetpub\wwwroot.

ASP/HTML—Placement and Permissions

I'll assume you have a general knowledge of NT permissions for this section and quickly run through the requirements for IIS.

To view an HTML document, the IUSER account (or related NT account if using security) must have at least READ permissions to the file. In order to view an Active Server Pages document, the user must have at least EXECUTE permissions to the file. If you assigned a user general READ permissions (see Figure 24.10), the related NT permissions assigned are READ/EXECUTE (RX). When I say READ and EXECUTE, I am referring to the lowest level of NT permissions—found under "special file permissions" (or "special folder permissions") as shown in Figure 24.11. Although this will allow access to both HTML and ASP pages, it is not totally necessary or the most secure solution (if security is a concern).

Databases—Placement and Permissions

If you are using Active Server Pages to connect to an Access database, the database does not need to be under the Web root. Because the path is specified in the connection string, you can place it anywhere. For security reasons, it is recommended you place the database in a directory structure that is totally isolated from the Web files. D:\databases\ would work just fine. This prevents a mischievous client from typing http://www/your-site.com/database/database.mdb and being able to download the database file.

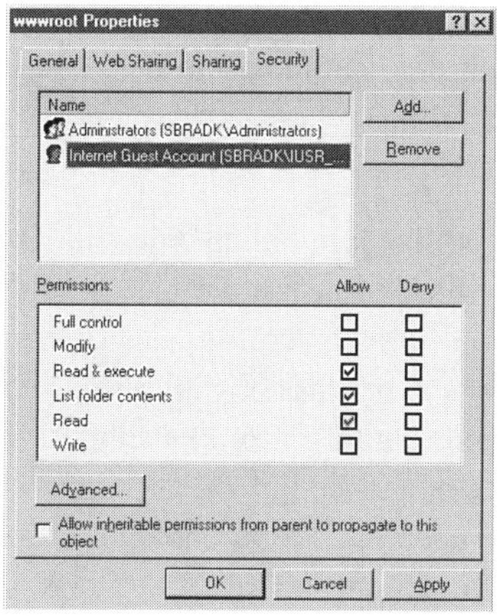

FIGURE 24.10

NTFS on Windows NT has some default permission settings that can satisfy the security needs in most situations.

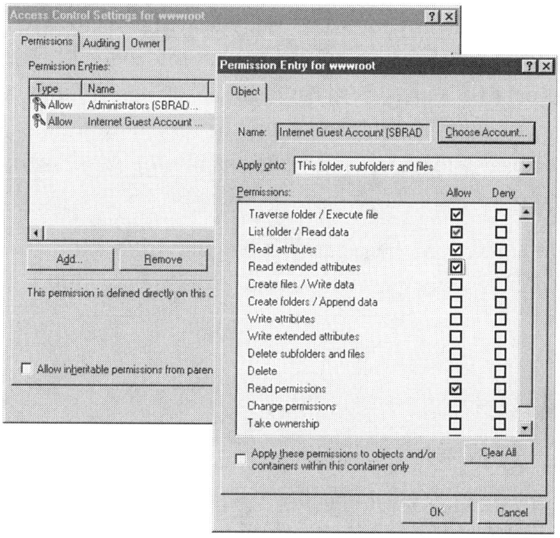

FIGURE 24.11

If you need even greater control over file security permissions, you can get very specific with the special file permissions.

Security on an Access database can be tricky without knowing some of the "quirks." There are two ways to implement security on an Access database—either through Access's built-in security measures, or through the use of NTFS file permissions.

If you have a read-only application that will never insert information into your database, things are straightforward. Simply assign the IUSER account READ access to the database file. If you currently have nothing but read-only data in your application, you probably won't for long. Sure, one of the great benefits of Web applications is to display dynamic information to your users, but that's only half of the game. There is a lot of value added when you start storing information in the database. You can collect user feedback, mailing-list information, and online orders—anything you want. This allows the user to interact more with the site, and helps you provide better service to the client.

Let's say you have a database you will use to store online orders in. Okay, you assign READ/WRITE permissions to the database file and give it a try—it won't work. When an Access database is in use by a user who has write permissions, it creates a lock file. Because the IUSER account has READ/WRITE permissions, Access attempts to create this file but gets an access-denied error. To prevent this error, the entire folder where the database is stored must have CHANGE access for the IUSER account. CHANGE access is necessary because the lock file must be updated as SQL commands are being executed. Just ADD and READ permissions will not suffice.

This really gets ugly if you didn't take my earlier advice and move your database to its own folder. With the database in your Web root, you will need to give the IUSER account the ability to READ/WRITE/DELETE files in that folder—BAD IDEA! In the early stages of our experimenting with Access databases, Web applications, and security requirements, one of the other authors and I did just this. It didn't take long for a hacker to realize that the site was wide open and make changes to our files for us—lesson learned.

If you are using SQL Server, all the security is handled from within the database server itself so you can avoid the potential nightmare of working out your file-level security requirements.

Summary

Developing applications for the Web is very exciting. Many developers and their clients alike are just now realizing the great benefits that can be reaped by Web-enabling their applications. With the information just presented to you, you should be able to install, configure, and perform some basic maintenance on a Microsoft Web server.

Combining this knowledge with the other information provided in this book, you should be well on your way to either developing Office 2000 Web applications or converting existing Office 2000 application to a Web format.

CHAPTER 25

Web Enabling Access 2000 with Office Web Components

As you know, there is no ignoring the Internet. With Office 2000, Microsoft wanted to find a simple way to move as much core Office functionality to the Internet as possible. The result was the Microsoft Office 2000 Web components and Data Access Pages (see Chapter 26, "Using Data Access Pages"). This chapter will introduce you to the Office Web components.

What Are the Office 2000 Web Components?

The Office Web components are a group of COM-based ActiveX controls that provide some of the same basic spreadsheet, chart, and pivot table functionality as you would find in Office proper to an ActiveX-based Web browser. The Office 2000 Web components are composed of

- Office Spreadsheet Control
- Office Chart Control
- Office PivotTable Control

These three graphical controls (Spreadsheet, Chart, and PivotTable) and the DataSource control are based on COM, so they can be controlled from VBScript, JScript, VB, C++, Java, and of course, VBA. Just because these controls are named Web components, do not think that they are only available on Web pages. They will also play a great role in your Access applications. Figure 25.1 shows a simple Spreadsheet control on an Access form.

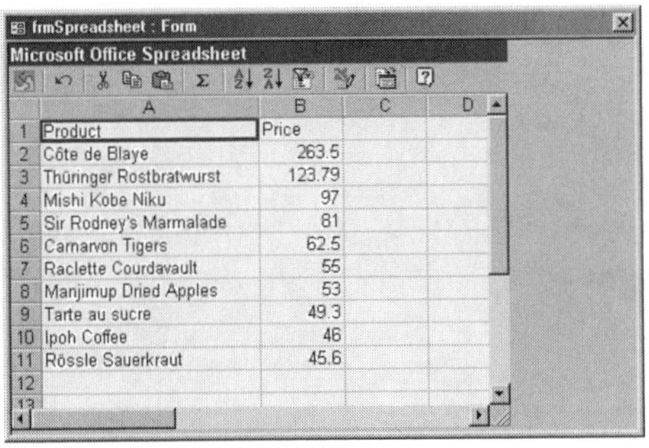

FIGURE 25.1

An Office Web component inside an Access form.

What Do the Office Web Components Do?

Each Web component has a distinct functionality that you will want to incorporate into your applications. The Spreadsheet control is like a mini-Excel in a Web browser or form. Most basic Excel functionality is provided, like recalculation, filtering, and sorting. You can also use the Spreadsheet control as an invisible calculation engine in your Access, VB, or Web applications. The Chart control provides 2D charting and has the capability to be bound to other HTML elements like a Spreadsheet control or record-sets. Chart can also export GIFs for Web browsers that do not support ActiveX controls. The PivotTable control provides the pivot table functionality found in Excel via an ActiveX control. PivotTable can also export GIFs like the Chart control. Lastly, there is the nongraphical DataSource control. DataSource works like the Data control in Visual Basic by connecting to a database and enabling another control to bind to it. Each of these controls is discussed more in depth in the next chapter.

What Are the License Requirements for Using Web Components?

Unlike most ActiveX controls, Web components require the purchase of an Office 2000 user license for the destination machine in order to use them. Your users do not need to have Office 2000 installed, but they do need to have a license for it. This way, if you are in a large organization and want to deploy some of the Web components (and Data Access Pages shown in the next chapter), you can get a site license and begin deployment of the Web components before you deploy Office 2000. That being said, it is obvious that Microsoft intends Web components to be used as intranet tools.

Using the Office Spreadsheet Control

Using the Spreadsheet control is a lot like using Microsoft Excel. There are two ways to use the Spreadsheet control, in either bound or unbound form. Bound involves using the DataSource control, which you will learn about in the next chapter. Let's take a look at the control in an unbound state here.

Getting Started

What makes the Spreadsheet control so easy to use is that you can transfer your Excel spreadsheets to a Web page automatically. In Excel 2000, create a simple spreadsheet. Then click File, Save As Web Page from the main menu. A dialog will be presented to you, as shown in Figure 25.2. This dialog lets you select a particular range or an entire sheet to export. When you want to save data to an interactive Web page, you must define your data as a range in Microsoft Excel. To export a selected range to an Excel Spreadsheet control on your Web Page, choose the Add Interactivity check box as shown in Figure 25.2.

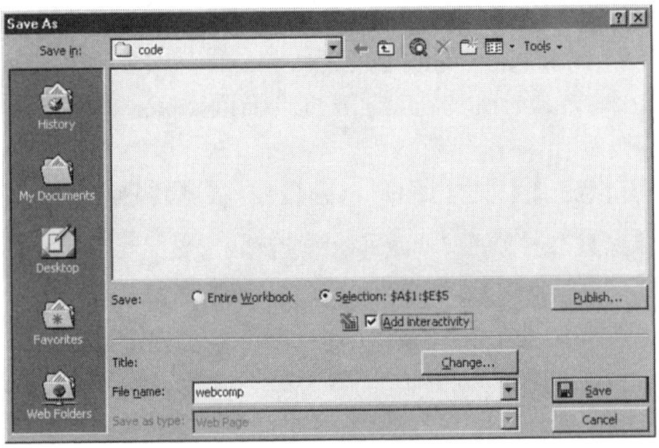

FIGURE 25.2

The Save As Web Page dialog.

After you save your spreadsheet as a Web page via Excel, you can open the Web page in Internet Explorer, as show in Figure 25.3.

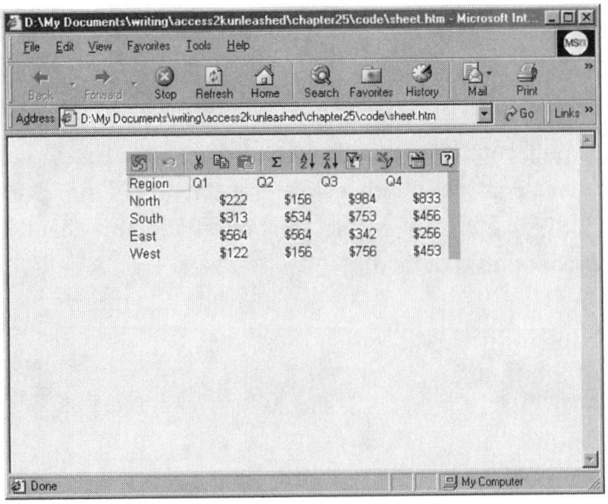

FIGURE 25.3

The result of saving the Excel 2000 spreadsheet as a Web page.

Region	Q1	Q2	Q3	Q4
North	$222	$156	$984	$833
South	$313	$534	$753	$456
East	$564	$564	$342	$256
West	$122	$156	$756	$453

When you have the Web page open, you can right-click on the control and then bring up the Spreadsheet Property Toolbox dialog box, as shown in Figure 25.4. This dialog, created with Dynamic HTML, will allow you to format and control the layout of your control. (For more information on using the control on the Web, see the information on Data Access Pages later in the next chapter.)

FIGURE 25.4

The Spreadsheet Property Toolbox dialog.

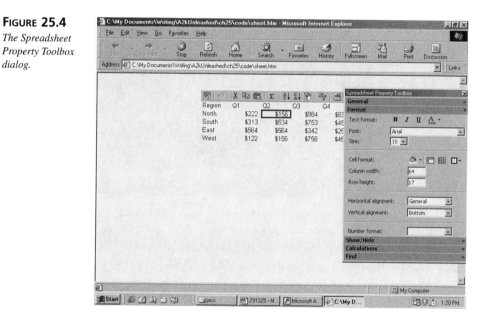

Using the Control in Access

To use the Spreadsheet Web component on an Access form, choose Insert, ActiveX Control from the main menu. This will bring up the Insert ActiveX Control dialog box as shown in Figure 25.5. Scroll down to Microsoft Office Spreadsheet 9.0 and click OK. This will insert the ActiveX Control onto your form in Design mode, as shown in Figure 25.6. Once inserted, rename the control to SpreadSheet1 in the Property dialog.

FIGURE 25.5

The Insert ActiveX Control dialog box.

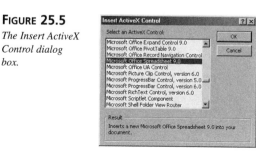

FIGURE 25.6

The Spreadsheet
*control at design
time in an Access
2000 form.*

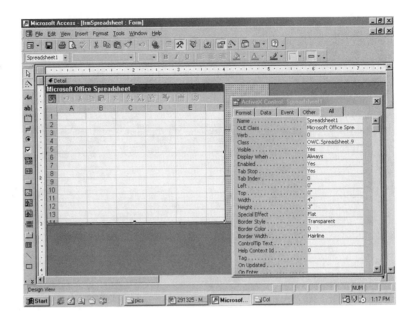

Now that the control is on your form, write some code to get data inside the
Spreadsheet control when the form loads. Listing 26.1 works on a form's load event and
opens an ADO recordset based on the "Ten Most Expensive Products" query in the
Northwind database. Now iterate through the recordset. At each row in the recordset, we
use the ActiveCell's default property to insert the values of the data in the recordset into
the cell of the Spreadsheet control. As we move through the recordset, we must increment the ActiveCell property of the spreadsheet to move the data to the next line of the
spreadsheet. As you can see, this is much like programming Microsoft Excel.

LISTING 25.1   LOADING DATA INTO THE Spreadsheet CONTROL AT RUNTIME

```
Private Sub Form_Load()
'Loads the Spreadsheet ActiveX Control
'With the data from a query in Access
'From "Microsoft Access 2000 Development Unleashed" (SAMS)
'By: Forte, Howe, Ralston

Dim rst As ADODB.Recordset
Dim intCount As Integer

On Error GoTo Proc_Err

Set rst = New ADODB.Recordset
rst.Open "[Ten Most Expensive Products]", CurrentProject.Connection
```

```
'Hardcode the captions
Spreadsheet1.ActiveCell(1, 1) = "Product"
Spreadsheet1.ActiveCell(1, 2) = "Price"

'Start the counter for the loop
intCount = 2

Do Until rst.EOF
    'Fill in the current cell with the
    'the current record from the recordset
    Spreadsheet1.ActiveCell(intCount, 1) = "" & _
        rst!TenMostExpensiveProducts
    Spreadsheet1.ActiveCell(intCount, 2) = "" & _
        rst!UnitPrice

    'Move to the next record and increase the counter
    rst.MoveNext
    intCount = intCount + 1
Loop

rst.Close
Set rst = Nothing

Proc_Exit:
    Exit Sub

Proc_Err:
    MsgBox Err.Description
    Resume Proc_Exit
End Sub
```

Using the Office Chart Control

You might think you've wasted too much time playing with Microsoft Graph in the past are not willing to use another Graph control from Microsoft. Chart is easy to use and very powerful. Like the other controls, it can be used in both bound and unbound mode. I will look at using the control in unbound mode here and in bound mode in the next chapter. In addition, in Chapter 27, "Web Publishing with Access 2000 and Active Server Pages," I will look at how you can use the component to export GIFs for use in Active Server Pages.

Getting Started

As with the other controls, start by creating a simple chart in Microsoft Excel 2000, as shown in Figure 25.7. Choose File, Save As Web Page, and then click the "Selection: Chart" option. Check the Add Interactivity box. The result is show in Figure 25.8. You can now manipulate the chart via client-side scripting code such as VBScript or JScript. In order to use the control in your scripts, you will have to know the properties and methods that it exposes, which you will learn about in the next section.

FIGURE 25.7

A chart in Microsoft Excel 2000.

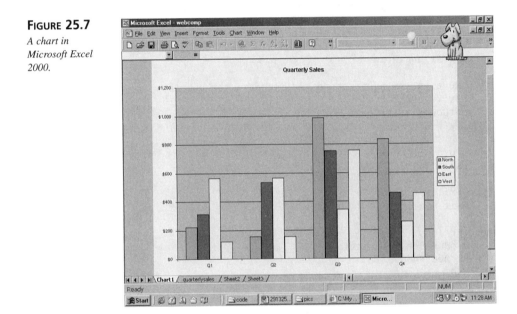

Using the Control in Access

Insert the control via the Insert, ActiveX Control method on an Access form. You must choose "Microsoft Office Chart 9.0" from the list of ActiveX controls. After you have created the control, rename it Chart1 inside the property box. When using the Chart control in unbound mode, there are two important things to remember. First, the Chart control can contain many objects, so each chart that you create will be part of a Charts collection. Second is that you can fill arrays of values for the chart series and an array of values for the chart's series' data.

To demonstrate this, I created a simple crosstab query in the Access 2000 version of Northwind with the following SQL:

```
TRANSFORM Sum(CCur([Order Details].[UnitPrice]*
   [Quantity]*(1-[Discount])/100)*100) AS ProductAmount
SELECT Year([OrderDate]) AS OrderYear
```

```
FROM Products INNER JOIN (Orders INNER JOIN
   [Order Details] ON Orders.OrderID = [Order Details].OrderID)
   ON Products.ProductID = [Order Details].ProductID
WHERE (((Orders.OrderDate)
  Between #1/1/1997# And #12/31/1997#))
GROUP BY Year([OrderDate])
PIVOT "Qtr " & DatePart("q",[OrderDate],1,0)
  In ("Qtr 1","Qtr 2","Qtr 3","Qtr 4");
```

FIGURE 25.8

A Chart *control exported as a Web page.*

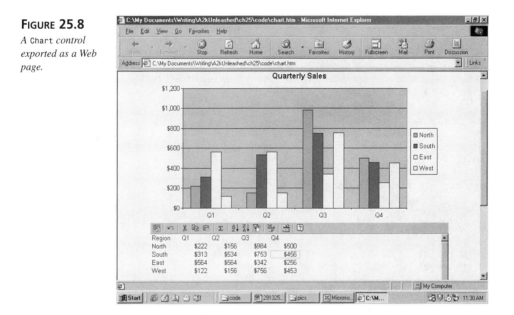

The SQL in the previous example will break out the total sales by quarter and produce an output as shown in Figure 25.9.

FIGURE 25.9

A simple crosstab query in Access 2000.

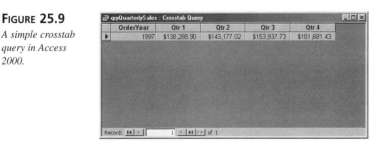

You will now use the simple crosstab query created previously to create an unbound chart on your form's Open event. I previously created two array aHeaders in which I fill in the values of my series headers (in this case the four quarters of a fiscal year). Then you will open up an ADO recordset based on the saved crosstab query called qryQuarterlySales, and then fill the aValues array with the values of the fields of the recordset. The full code listing is shown in Listing 25.2.

LISTING 25.2   CREATING AN UNBOUND CHART

```
Private Sub Form_Open(Cancel As Integer)
'Loads the Chart ActiveX Control
'With the data from a query in Access
'From "Microsoft Access 2000 Development Unleashed" (SAMS)
'By: Forte, Howe, Ralston

Dim ChartSpace1, aHeaders(3), aValues(3)
Dim rst As ADODB.Recordset

On Error GoTo Proc_Err

Set rst = New ADODB.Recordset

'Create an array of items for the chart
aHeaders(0) = "Q1"
aHeaders(1) = "Q2"
aHeaders(2) = "Q3"
aHeaders(3) = "Q4"

'Open a recordset based on a XTAB query
'and fill in the values for the chart bars
rst.Open "qryQuarterlySales", CurrentProject.Connection

aValues(0) = rst![Qtr 1]
aValues(1) = rst![Qtr 2]
aValues(2) = rst![Qtr 3]
aValues(3) = rst![Qtr 4]

Set ChartSpace1 = Me.Chart1

With ChartSpace1

    .Border.Color = chColorAutomatic
    'Can have more than one chart in a
    'chartspace, so you have to refer to
    'the collection
    .Charts.Add
    With .Charts(0)
        .Type = chChartTypeColumnClustered
        .SeriesCollection.Add
```

```
        .SeriesCollection(0).Caption = "1999 Sales"
        'This sets the data to the arrays we
        'created above
        .SeriesCollection(0).SetData _
           chDimCategories, chDataLiteral, aHeaders
        .SeriesCollection(0).SetData _
           chDimValues, chDataLiteral, aValues
        .HasLegend = True
    End With

End With

rst.Close
Set rst = Nothing

Proc_Exit:
    Exit Sub

Proc_Err:
    MsgBox Err.Description
    Resume Proc_Exit

End Sub
```

Using the Office `PivotTable` Control

As with the other two controls that I have explored in this chapter, the `PivotTable` control is available in both bound and unbound modes. The next two sections will explore how to use the controls in unbound mode, whereas in the next chapter you will see how to bind the control to data in a Data Access Page.

Getting Started

Pivot tables are one of the most popular features of Microsoft Excel; they give you the ability to run ad hoc reports while in Excel. Many end users are big fans of pivot tables after they are trained to use them. The ability to create pivot tables and incorporate them as either a part of a Web site or Access form is pretty cool. To start, create a pivot table in Microsoft Excel 2000 as shown in Figure 25.10.

Figure 25.10

A simple Excel 2000 pivot table.

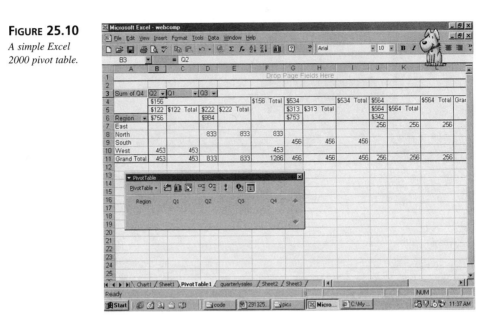

After your pivot table is created, select File, Save As Web Page from the main menu; however, do not click Save on the dialog box, click Publish. This brings up the advanced Save As Web Page dialog as shown in Figure 25.11.

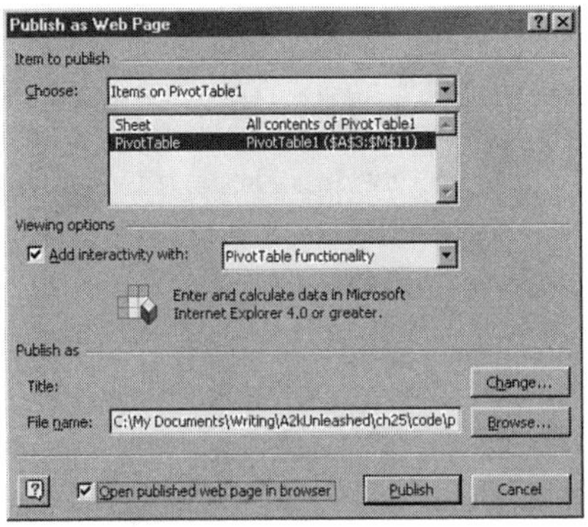

Figure 25.11

The Publish as Web page dialog.

This dialog shown in Figure 25.11 will give you the opportunity to select the items of the pivot table to export and set the viewing options. By setting the viewing options, you can select the Pivot Table option for the output, as shown in Figure 25.11. Excel will produce a Web page, as shown in Figure 25.12.

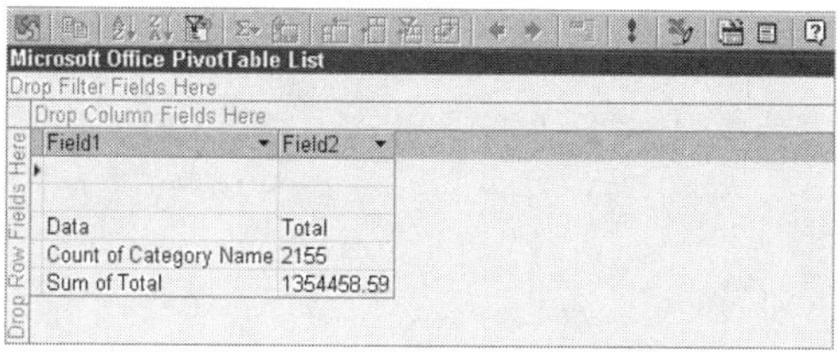

FIGURE 25.12

Excel pivot table exported to Internet Explorer.

Summary

The Office 2000 Web components might represent the future of Office computing. As users hear more and more about computers selling for less than $1000 in the future and the infamous NetPC, Office Web components offer a nice neat package for Office functionality in a Web browser. As business moves to cheaper alternatives to PCs, the Office Web components may play a major role in the evolution of Office and business computing in general. With the ability to use native functions of a spreadsheet PivotTable and charting in an ActiveX control both in Access 2000 and on a Web page, this chapter gave you a great introduction to the Web components.

Using Data Access Pages

As you know, there is no ignoring the Internet. With Office 2000, Microsoft wanted to find a simple way to move as much core Office functionality to the Internet as possible. The result was Data Access Pages and the Microsoft Office 2000 Web components. This chapter will introduce you to Data Access Pages and get you started using them.

Chances are that you have explored with the Internet or your corporate intranet already. Now that you have shown your users some basic Web pages, they ask you if they can have drill-downs, charts and graphs, and more dynamic pages. You reply that you are a database programmer, not a Web programmer, and that is too difficult to do quickly. Microsoft realized your users would want more power and online reporting and created something called Data Access Pages in Access 2000.

What Is a Data Access Page?

You might have noticed the new database container tab called Pages. This tab is for the new database object called Data Access Pages (DAPs), as shown in Figure 26.1. DAPs are subsets of Access forms and reports designed for availability on the Web, but more appropriately, the intranet. These pages are Dynamic HTML pages that can be viewed in Internet Explorer 5.0. They connect to a live database that provides the user with the ability to do form data entry or drill down into a report.

FIGURE 26.1

The new database container tab for Data Access Pages.

Data Access Pages Architecture and Requirements

Data Access Pages use ActiveX controls, Dynamic HTML, ADO, and client-side scripting. With client-side scripting, you need ADO and the OLEDB providers for Access and SQL Server installed on your machine. Only Internet Explorer 4.0 or 5.0 supports ActiveX controls, so you are limited to Microsoft's browser. In addition, Microsoft has made an Office 2000 license required for use of Data Access Pages.

An Office 2000 installation is the only way to guarantee that the Web components, ADO 2.1, and the proper drivers and OLE DB Providers are installed on your users' hard drive.

Creating Your First Data Access Page

Let's get started creating our first Data Access Page. Click on New while in the database container for DAPs. Click Design view. You will be brought to a blank DAP in Design view, as shown in Figure 26.2.

FIGURE 26.2

A blank Data Access Page in Design view.

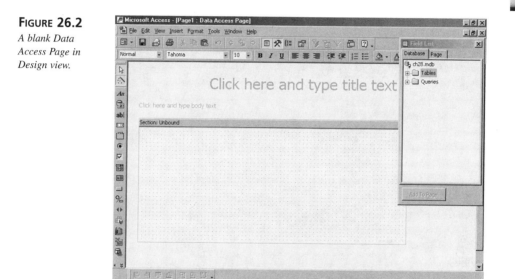

Give your page a title by clicking the top part of the page and typing "Categories." Bring up the field list by selecting View, Field List from the main menu. The field list shown in Figure 26.3 has a listing of all the tables and queries in your current database. This works much like the field list in a typical Access form and report.

FIGURE 26.3

The Data Access Page field list.

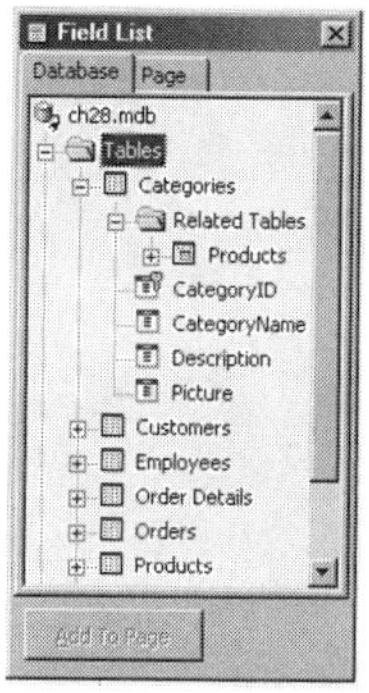

After you have brought up the field list, drill down to the category table and then drag the CategoryName and Description fields to the page.

Now that you have added the two fields to the page, click the Save button on the toolbar or choose File, Save from the main menu. Notice that the Save as Data Access Page dialog comes up, as shown in Figure 26.4. A Data Access Page is NOT stored in the MDB file like all other objects such as tables, queries, forms, reports, macros, and modules. You can quickly find out the path of the DAP by hovering your mouse pointer over a DAP in the database container and viewing the ToolTip, as shown in Figure 26.5.

FIGURE 26.4

Save as Data Access Page.

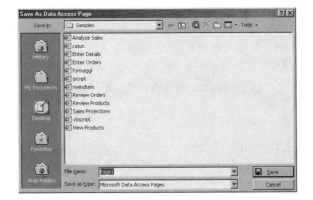

FIGURE 26.5

A ToolTip showing the path of the Data Access Page.

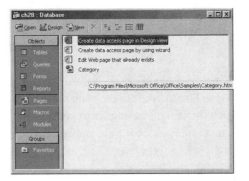

Before I preview the Data Access Page, I'll take a look at the Sorting and Grouping options. Choose View, Sorting and Grouping from the main menu. This will bring up the Grouping and Sorting dialog box as shown in Figure 26.6.

FIGURE 26.6

The Grouping and Sorting dialog for Data Access Pages.

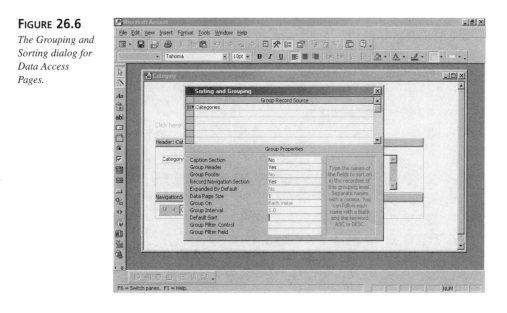

Most of these options are identical to those in reports; however, there are two new ones that you need to look at. The first is Data Page Size, which will control how many records will be displayed at a time. We will set this to 1 so we can view one record at a time. You can experiment with this property to view more records at a time, as we will later on in this chapter. The next property you will want to look at is the Record Navigation Section property, which will give your section a record navigation section.

After you have set these properties, we will want to apply some formatting to our page before we choose to view it. To apply some formatting to your Data Access Page, select Format, Theme to bring up the Theme dialog, as shown in Figure 26.7.

FIGURE 26.7

The Theme dialog.

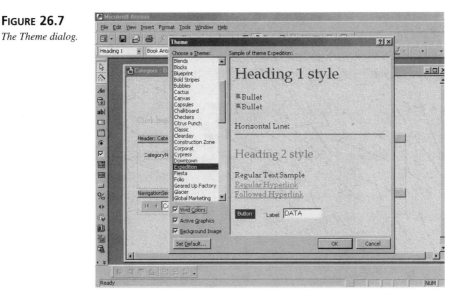

Viewing a Data Access Page

You have two ways to view and use a Data Access Page: as part of your Access application, or via a capable Web browser. To view a Data Access Page from Access, either click on the Page View icon or select View, Page View from the main menu while in Design view. If you want to navigate to a DAP as part of your application, you can use the `OpenDataAccessPage` method of the `DoCmd` object as shown here:

```
DoCmd.OpenDataAccessPage "Category", acDataAccessPageBrowse
```

Figure 26.8 shows the Data Access Page in Microsoft Access. Notice that you can incorporate DAPs into your applications seamlessly as if it were a form or report.

FIGURE 26.8

A Data Access Page shown in Access.

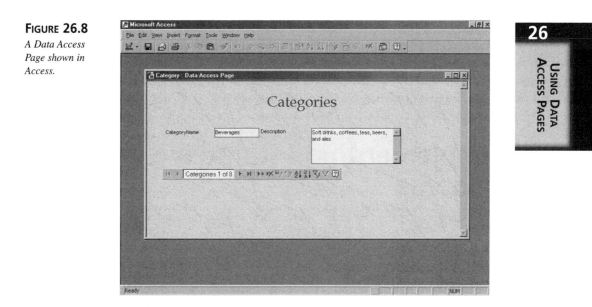

You can also view that Data Access Page in a capable Web browser. All you have to do is open the HTML file directly, either on disk or by uploading the page to a Web server. Figure 26.9 shows the Data Access Page in the Web browser.

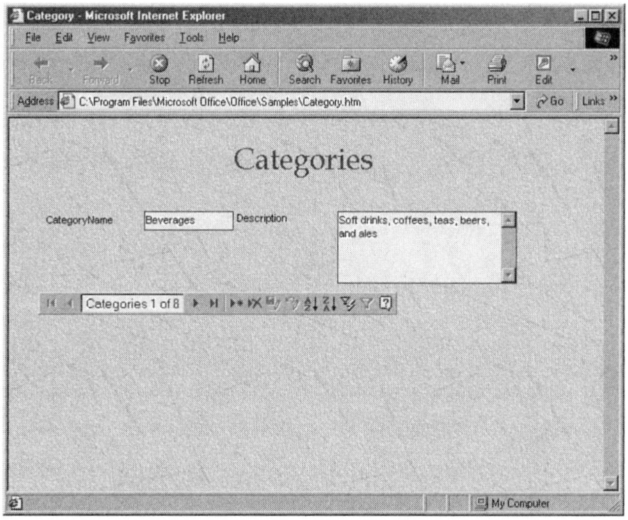

FIGURE 26.9

A Data Access Page shown in Internet Explorer.

Notice that the Data Access Page looks exactly the same in the browser as it does in Access. Also, there is no loss of functionality when you move from Access to a Web page. Inside the Web page, try editing the data and moving to the next record. You will see that the data is bound live to the database--any changes you make in the page will be reflected in the database. If you develop your application around DAPs instead of forms and reports, you can easily transport your application to the Web.

Implementing Interactive Drill-Downs

The great power of Data Access Pages is their ability to create drill-downs based on one-to-many relationships in your database. Let's create a one-to-many drill-down from Categories to Products on our Category Data Access Page. Open our Category page and then bring up the Field List as we did before by selecting View, Field List from the main menu. Drill down to the Products table and drag the ProductName, UnitPrice, and Discontinued fields to the bottom of the detail section. Access will create a new detailed child section that will be a child drill-down section, as shown in Figure 26.10.

> **NOTE**
>
> Even though Microsoft holds you to the Windows-compatible standards to earn the use of its logo in your applications, Microsoft does not hold itself to this standard. Data Access Pages do not contain an Undo feature at all.

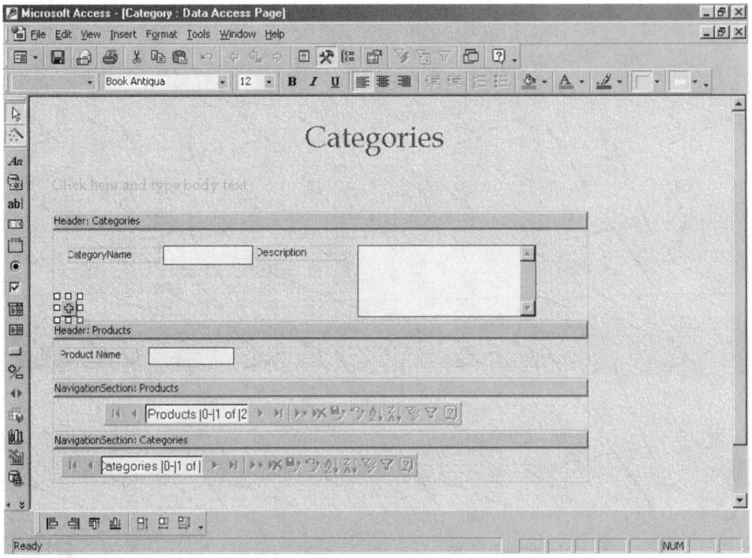

FIGURE 26.10

The child drill-down section for Products in Design view.

In Design view, you will notice a plus (+) sign button. This is for the drill-down capability. You might want to move it to a better location, like the bottom of the detail section. Let's go back to the Grouping and Sorting section. Set the Category section's Data Page Size to 1, the Products section Data Page Size to All, and the Products Record Navigation Section to No. This will give us a drill-down section that shows all the related Products to each Category on your page, as shown in Figure 26.11.

FIGURE 26.11

The child drill-down section for Products in Page view.

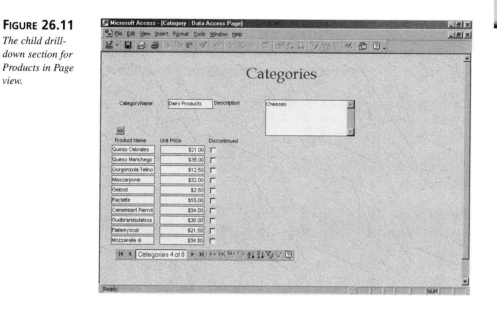

Incorporating the Office Web Components with DAPs

The great power of Data Access Pages is their ability to contain Office Web components that are bound to live data. As you can see in Figure 26.12, you can create some great-looking Data Access Pages using the Office Web components.

To get started, let's create a simple crosstab query in Access's Northwind database. We will create a crosstab with all the product's categories and their quarterly sales figures for 1997. The SQL code to do this is

```
TRANSFORM
  Sum(CCur([Order Details].[UnitPrice]*[Quantity]*
  (1-[Discount])/100)*100) AS ProductAmount
SELECT Categories.CategoryName
FROM (Categories INNER JOIN Products
```

```
ON Categories.CategoryID = Products.CategoryID)
INNER JOIN (Orders INNER JOIN [Order Details]
ON Orders.OrderID = [Order Details].OrderID)
ON Products.ProductID = [Order Details].ProductID
WHERE (((Orders.OrderDate) Between #1/1/97# And #12/31/97#))
GROUP BY Categories.CategoryName
PIVOT "Qtr " & DatePart("q",[OrderDate],1,0)
 In ("Qtr 1","Qtr 2","Qtr 3","Qtr 4");
```

Save this query as QuarterlyProducts and create a new Data Access Page based off this query.

FIGURE 26.12

A Data Access Page with bound Office Web components.

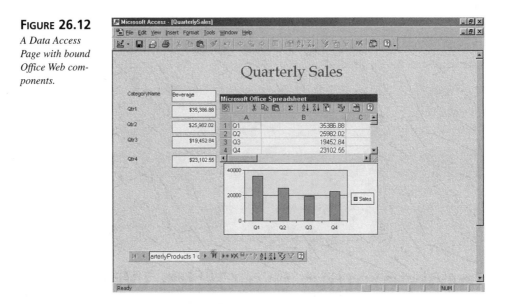

Adding an Excel Spreadsheet Web Component

To add a Microsoft Office Web component to your Data Access Page, select the icon that looks like Excel's from the toolbox, as shown in Figure 26.13, and draw your control on your Data Access Page. After you have sized your control on the page, you will want to bind spreadsheet cells to fields in your page so your spreadsheet will dynamically change when the users scroll through the records. You have to use the DHTML object model, where everything is exposed through the document object. To access a field named txtQ1, enter this in the cell:

```
=document.txtQ1.value
```

Add a cell for each quarter. In the next cell, bind the cell to the control on your page that has the data.

TABLE 26.1 THE VALUES OF YOUR SPREADSHEET CELLS

Q1	=document.txtQ1.value
Q2	=document.txtQ2.value
Q3	=document.txtQ3.value
Q4	=document.txtQ4.value

FIGURE 26.13

The Data Access Page toolbar.

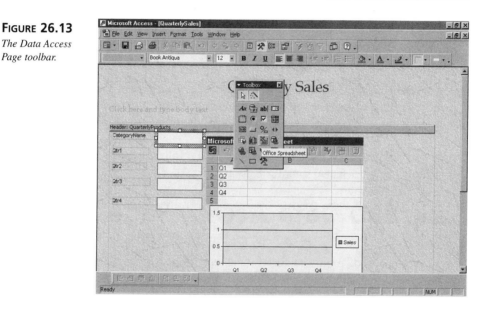

Adding a Chart Web Component

Now that you have added a Spreadsheet control, let's add a Chart control and bind it to the data contained in the Spreadsheet control. As we scroll through the records, not only will the spreadsheet change its values dynamically, but the Chart control will also change based on the data. Let's add a Chart control to our page by clicking on the chart icon and drawing a Chart control on your page. The Chart Wizard will then come up. The first page of the Wizard asks you what type of chart you want to use. The charts that are available to you are like the 2D charts from Excel. Select a chart type that you like and click next. On page two, shown in Figure 26.14, the Wizard asks you whether to bind the chart to a table or query in your database or to a Spreadsheet control already on your page. Choose the Spreadsheet control and click Next. The last page asks you what series on your spreadsheet contains your labels and data. Enter =A1:A4 as your labels and =B1:B4 as your data series.

FIGURE 26.14

*The Data Access
Page Chart
Wizard.*

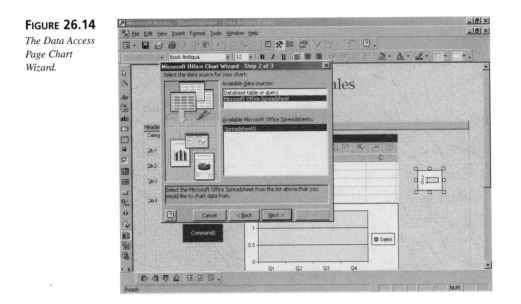

Now, when you look at your chart in Page view and scroll through the records, your chart will update as each new record is presented.

Scripting Data Access Pages

Writing code to control a Data Access Page is not as simple as writing code to control an Access form or report. When you are working with the code behind Data Access Pages, you have to use script to control your page's behavior. When you create a command button or any other object that exposes events, you have to write VBScript (or JavaScript). There is no VBA Editor with Data Access Pages. You have to use something called the Microsoft Script Editor (MSE), as shown in Figure 26.15.

Let's replace the navigation bar supplied by Access with one of our own. Create four command buttons and give them the following captions: Move Previous, Next, First, and Last. Then right-click your page and then select Microsoft Script Editor from the context menu.

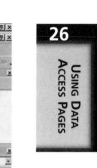

FIGURE 26.15

*The Microsoft
Script Editor
(MSE).*

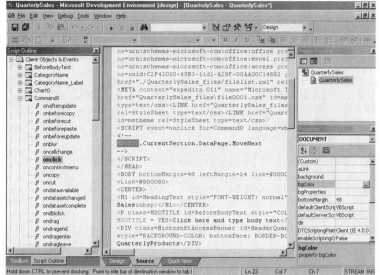

When in the MSE, you can use the Script Outline shown in 26.14 to drill down on the
client objects and events. This section of the MSE enables you to view each object on
your page and look at each event. You can double-click each event and then write some
code. So drill down to each command button and double-click the onClick event. Inside
the MSE's HTML code you will get HTML code like this:

```
<SCRIPT LANGUAGE=vbscript FOR=cmdFirst EVENT=onclick>
<!--
-->
</SCRIPT>
```

There are a few ways to write code for an object; however, the For statement pointing to
the object you need to use is the default method. Inside the script block, enter the following code:

```
MSODSC.CurrentSection.DataPage.MoveFirst
```

Each Data Access Page has a Microsoft Datasource object called "MSODSC" that has
methods of the DataPage object. We will use the MoveFirst, MoveLast, MoveNext, and
MovePrevious methods. After you write the code behind all your command buttons, your
code should look like that in Listing 26.3.

LISTING 26.3 CREATING CUSTOM DATA PAGE NAVIGATION BUTTONS

```
<SCRIPT LANGUAGE=vbscript FOR=cmdFirst EVENT=onclick>
<!--
MSODSC.CurrentSection.DataPage.MoveFirst
-->
</SCRIPT>
<SCRIPT LANGUAGE=vbscript FOR=cmdlast EVENT=onclick>
<!--
MSODSC.CurrentSection.DataPage.MoveLast
-->
</SCRIPT>
<SCRIPT LANGUAGE=vbscript FOR=cmdNext EVENT=onclick>
<!--
MSODSC.CurrentSection.DataPage.MoveNext
-->
</SCRIPT>
<SCRIPT LANGUAGE=vbscript FOR=cmdPrev EVENT=onclick>
<!--
MSODSC.CurrentSection.DataPage.MovePrevious
-->
</SCRIPT>
```

Changing the DAP's DataSource at Runtime

Since your DAPs do not exist inside the MDB file, distribution can become an issue. The most common distribution problem that you may face is that the DAP may not be pointing to the correct database. When you place a DAP onto the Web server or mail the HTML file to someone else, the DAP may be pointing to the wrong MDB file—or worse, the user may not have the same file mappings as you or the other users.

Although this is a problem, DAP data connections are managed by the invisible Microsoft Office Web component called the DataSource control, and the connections are fully scriptable. The DataSource control contains a ConnectionString property that you can change programmatically. To change the string, all you have to do is modify the ConnectionString property of the DataSource control as shown here:

```
MSODSC.ConnectionString = strConnect
```

We are assuming the the name of the DataSource control is MSODSC (MSODSC is the default) and strConnect is a valid OLE DB connection string. It is up to your code to provide a valid connection string.

You might want to ask your users to specify a path to a database each time the DAP loads. To do this, all you have to do is use an InputBox or a common dialog control inside your client-side code. Listing 26.4 shows you how to accomplish this with a very simple InputBox method. Listing 26.4 asks the user to supply the path to an Access database shown in Figure 26.16, and then rebuilds a connection string to assign to the DataSource control. You may want to combine this technique with using a UDL file on the client side to avoid the InputBox.

LISTING 26.4 RECONNECTING YOUR DAP'S CONNECTION STRING AT RUNTIME

```vbscript
<SCRIPT language=vbscript>
<!- -
'This example will refresh the
'link of a DAP in realtime to
'whatever Access database the user wants
'From "Microsoft Access 2000 Development Unleashed" (SAMS)
'By: Forte, Howe, Ralston
Dim strConnect
Dim strPath

'Ask the user for the path to the database
'By Using an Inputbox
strPath=inputbox("Enter in the Path to Northwind","Reconnect", _
    "C:\Program Files\Microsoft Office\Office\Samples")

'For SQL Server, would have to change this to:
strConnect="Provider=SQLOLEDB.1"
strConnect="Provider=Microsoft.JET.OLEDB.4.0"
'Add the provider info with the path
strConnect=strConnect & ";Data Source=" & strPath

'Reset the property of the DataSource control here
'note that by default the control is named MSODSC
'if you have renamed the control manually, you
'must indicate that here
MSODSC.ConnectionString = strConnect

'alert the user that you changed the connection
Msgbox "Connection changed to " & strPath,64

- ->
</SCRIPT>
```

FIGURE 26.16

Asking the user for the connection.

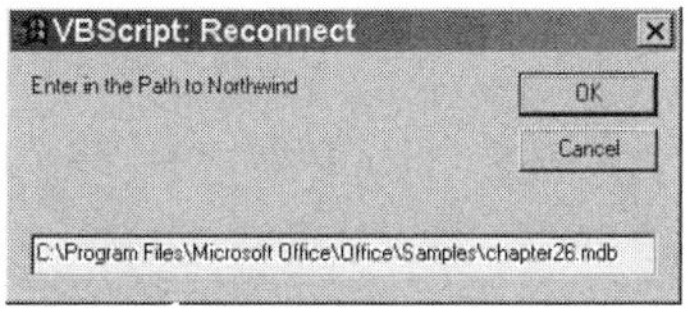

Summary

As you can see, Access 2000 embraces the Internet in a big way. We have had the capability to publish Access datasheets over the Web since Access 95, but now with Data Access Pages and the Office Web components, you start developing normal Access applications for distribution over the Web.

27

Web Publishing with Access 2000 and Active Server Pages

IN THIS CHAPTER

If you want to move past static Web pages, publish your data on-the-fly, and create an interactive Web site, you will want to learn about Active Server Pages (ASP).

Static Web pages are a thing of the past. In order to make your users happy, you need to give them access to the most up-to-date information. Using the Active Server Pages, you can always guarantee that your Web site provides the user with the latest information. ASP also eliminates a lot of maintenance in your Web site. For example, if you were Webmaster for a site that has a User Listing page, you would want to maintain the page with an interactive database. In the old days, you had to manually update the user's information on the HTML page itself every time the information changed. With the ASP you can have members make changes over the Web and the User Listing page will automatically update itself when the next visitor hits your Web site because the data is stored in your Access 2000 database.

Using Active Server Pages

Active Server Pages (ASP) is the latest technology available from Microsoft for publishing your data dynamically on the Web. ASP is a component of Internet Information Server 3.0 and higher, which is available to Personal/Peer Web Server as well. With ASP you can develop the next generation of Web Pages that go beyond the limited functionality of older technology like Common Gateway Interface (CGI) and the Internet Database Connector (IDC). Interactive sites that include personalized customer service, order entry, "shopping cart" applications, and many more interactive features can be built easily with Active Server Pages. Web pages can be customized by the user and be re-created the next time the user visits your site, providing them with a much more personal experience.

With ASP, you can create interactive sites that store global variables set by a user for use during all her visits. Traditionally, client/server systems could keep state between screens with global variables and classes. Maintaining state on a Web page has never been done before, and with ASP it is a very easy process. Prior to Active Server Pages, you needed very complex CGI scripts to remember who was at your site as they navigated through the pages of your site. With ASP, this functionality is built-in, requiring not a single line of code.

Like its predecessor IDC/HTX, Active Server Pages is browser independent and easy to implement and customize. What ASP provides is extreme flexibility in publishing your Web site using Access 2000. This chapter will explain what Active Server pages are and show you how to create Active Server pages, both with the Access User Interface and on your own.

Understanding Active Server Pages

Have you ever gone to a Web site and saw that the URL was something like `http://www.microsoft.com/default.asp`? A file with the .ASP extension is an Active Server Page; Active Server Pages are accessed just like any HTML page through the HTTP protocol. The big difference between HTML and ASP is how the Web server treats the page. Active Server Pages contain standard HTML and instructions for the Web server. These instructions are server-side scripts that will conditionally output HTML based on conditions you set up or records in a database. The Web server will process the Active Server Pages' instructions. The Web server then sends your browser plain HTML.

An Active Server Page is a file that contains HTML or HTML and server-side scripting. When the server processes the ASP file, it will carry out the script on the server and send the browser plain HTML. Because all script is processed on the server, ASP files are browser-independent. If there is no server-side script in the ASP file, the Web server will just output the HTML directly. You can, for example, take a normal HTML page and change its extension to .ASP. You now have an Active Server Page. When you request the ASP file, you will be sent plain HTML because the Server will write the HTML out from the ASP file. If you add some script into the page, for example, to change the background color based on the day of the week, this script will be run on the server and you will only receive HTML with the correct `<Backcolor="XXX">` tag.

VBScript is the default script language of Active Server Pages and will be the focus of the second part of this chapter. VBScript is a subset of Visual Basic and Visual Basic for Applications. If you are already familiar with VB and VBA, you should be at home with VBScript. If you are already familiar with JavaScript, ASP supports JavaScript as well. If you currently use another scripting language like Perl, you can use these languages with ASP, but you will need to obtain a plug-in from the vendor of the script language.

Because your script executes on the server and only the resulting HTML is generated for the Web browser, complex code and business rules contained in your script are protected. If a user chooses to view the source of the document, all they will see is the HTML sent to the browser. The code that ran will not be visible to the browser.

Active Server Pages Versus CGI

Active Server Pages are an integrated part of the operating system and are compile-free. CGI applications are compiled on the target Web Server and run out of process. For each visitor to your Web site, you will have a separate instance of the CGI application running, not all that efficient. A CGI program must be compiled every time a change is made, whereas when you change an ASP file and save it, the script is automatically compiled the next time it is requested. This means that when developing an ASP Web application, you can save the page and immediately preview it in a browser.

The structure of a CGI program was described in the previous section and when compared to an in-process Active Server Page, performance is vastly improved. Because an ASP is in-process, only one instance of the ASP engine will be running for every user of your application and will manage memory with multi-threading. ASP will maintain state automatically for each user who hits your Web site. ASP can easily integrate to legacy data, as well as your Access 2000 database. Whereas it is quite an effort to access ODBC data with CGI, ODBC access is built into Active Server Pages with a powerful ADO. In addition, ADO uses OLE DB providers for Jet, SQL Server, and Oracle as shown in previous chapters, so they are available to you to use in your code as well.

Obtaining Active Server Pages

Before converting all of your application's objects, you need to make sure that you have Active Server Pages installed and working, an ODBC data source or OLE DB Provider set up for your database, and a virtual directory with execute permissions set up for your application. Please refer to Chapter 24, "Configuring a Web Site for Web Publishing," for reference on setting up your Web Server, for reference on setting up your Web Server.

Getting Started with Active Server Pages

With Microsoft Access 2000, you can export any database object as an Active Server Page. When you convert an Access database object to an Active Server Page, the ASP will display an HTML table of the data in your object. Users will not have the ability to update or delete existing records, nor add new records by using a Web browser unless you write this code by hand. The export as ASP functionality is NOT an Access to ASP conversion.

To convert a database object to Active Server Pages using the Access User Interface, start the Wizard by choosing File, Export from the main menu. Choose Active Server Pages as the file type and you see the dialog box shown in Figure 27.1.

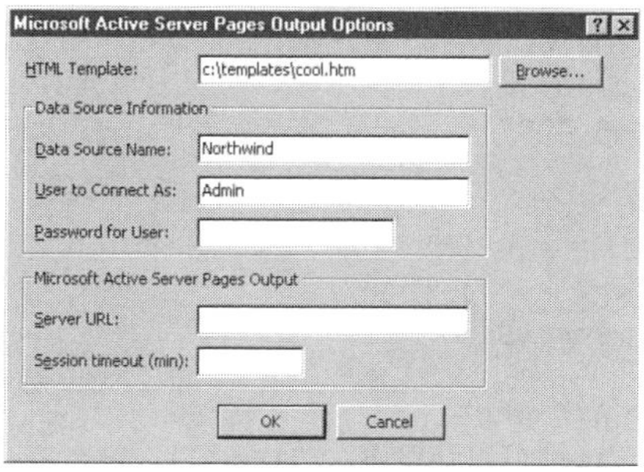

FIGURE 27.1

The Export to ASP dialog box.

The dialog shown in Figure 27.1 asks you for the ODBC data source name, password of your database, and the URL and session timeout. Enter in the any value for the ODBC data source, user name and password because you are going to change the output of the file. For URL, put the URL of the Web server where the ASP file will reside (for example, `www.myserver.com`). A session timeout is how long the ASP will wait until there is no activity at the page to close the connection. The ASP will then destroy the session state information for your user and release this memory back to the server. For session timeout, ASP files use a default of 20 minutes, so enter that amount.

After you are done, your ASP file will be saved to disk. You will want to save the Active Server Page to a virtual directory with execute permissions on your Web server as discussed in Chapter 24. Now that Access has saved the ASP file, you have to know what Access does. Access uses ODBC as its default OLE DB provider for exporting an Active Server Page from the user interface. To overcome this limitation, open the Active Server Page using Notepad. The code generated by the Export Wizard is shown in Listing 27.1.

LISTING 27.1 THE RESULTS OF EXPORTING THE NORTHWIND CUSTOMERS TABLE TO ASP

```
<HTML>
<HEAD>
<META HTTP-EQUIV="Content-Type" CONTENT="text/html;charset=windows-1252">
<TITLE>Customers</TITLE>
</HEAD>
<BODY>
```

continues

LISTING 27.1 CONTINUED

```
<%
If IsObject(Session("NYC_conn")) Then
    Set conn = Session("NYC_conn")
Else
    Set conn = Server.CreateObject("ADODB.Connection")
    conn.open "NYC","Admin",""
    Set Session("NYC_conn") = conn
End If
%>
<%
If IsObject(Session("Customers_rs")) Then
    Set rs = Session("Customers_rs")
Else
    sql = "SELECT * FROM [Customers]"
    Set rs = Server.CreateObject("ADODB.Recordset")
    rs.Open sql, conn, 3, 3
    If rs.eof Then
        rs.AddNew
    End If
    Set Session("Customers_rs") = rs
End If
%>
<TABLE BORDER=1 BGCOLOR=#ffffff CELLSPACING=0><FONT FACE="Arial"
COLOR=#000000><CAPTION><B>Customers</B></CAPTION></FONT>

<THEAD>
<TR>
<TH BGCOLOR=#c0c0c0 BORDERCOLOR=#000000 >
<FONT SIZE=2 FACE="Arial" COLOR=#000000>Customer ID</FONT></TH>
<TH BGCOLOR=#c0c0c0 BORDERCOLOR=#000000 >
<FONT SIZE=2 FACE="Arial" COLOR=#000000>Company Name</FONT></TH>
<TH BGCOLOR=#c0c0c0 BORDERCOLOR=#000000 >
<FONT SIZE=2 FACE="Arial" COLOR=#000000>Contact Name</FONT></TH>
<TH BGCOLOR=#c0c0c0 BORDERCOLOR=#000000 >
<FONT SIZE=2 FACE="Arial" COLOR=#000000>Contact Title</FONT></TH>
<TH BGCOLOR=#c0c0c0 BORDERCOLOR=#000000 >
<FONT SIZE=2 FACE="Arial" COLOR=#000000>Address</FONT></TH>
<TH BGCOLOR=#c0c0c0 BORDERCOLOR=#000000 >
<FONT SIZE=2 FACE="Arial" COLOR=#000000>City</FONT></TH>
<TH BGCOLOR=#c0c0c0 BORDERCOLOR=#000000 >
<FONT SIZE=2 FACE="Arial" COLOR=#000000>Region</FONT></TH>
<TH BGCOLOR=#c0c0c0 BORDERCOLOR=#000000 >
<FONT SIZE=2 FACE="Arial" COLOR=#000000>Postal Code</FONT></TH>
<TH BGCOLOR=#c0c0c0 BORDERCOLOR=#000000 >
<FONT SIZE=2 FACE="Arial" COLOR=#000000>Country</FONT></TH>
<TH BGCOLOR=#c0c0c0 BORDERCOLOR=#000000 >
<FONT SIZE=2 FACE="Arial" COLOR=#000000>Phone</FONT></TH>
<TH BGCOLOR=#c0c0c0 BORDERCOLOR=#000000 >
```

```
<FONT SIZE=2 FACE="Arial" COLOR=#000000>Fax</FONT></TH>

</TR>
</THEAD>
<TBODY>
<%
On Error Resume Next
rs.MoveFirst
do while Not rs.eof
 %>
<TR VALIGN=TOP>
<TD BORDERCOLOR=#c0c0c0 ><FONT SIZE=2 FACE="Arial" COLOR=#000000>
<%=Server.HTMLEncode(rs.Fields("CustomerID").Value)%><BR></FONT></TD>
<TD BORDERCOLOR=#c0c0c0 ><FONT SIZE=2 FACE="Arial" COLOR=#000000>
<%=Server.HTMLEncode(rs.Fields("CompanyName").Value)%><BR></FONT></TD>
<TD BORDERCOLOR=#c0c0c0 ><FONT SIZE=2 FACE="Arial" COLOR=#000000>
<%=Server.HTMLEncode(rs.Fields("ContactName").Value)%><BR></FONT></TD>
<TD BORDERCOLOR=#c0c0c0 ><FONT SIZE=2 FACE="Arial" COLOR=#000000>
<%=Server.HTMLEncode(rs.Fields("ContactTitle").Value)%><BR></FONT></TD>
<TD BORDERCOLOR=#c0c0c0 ><FONT SIZE=2 FACE="Arial" COLOR=#000000>
<%=Server.HTMLEncode(rs.Fields("Address").Value)%><BR></FONT></TD>
<TD BORDERCOLOR=#c0c0c0 ><FONT SIZE=2 FACE="Arial" COLOR=#000000>
<%=Server.HTMLEncode(rs.Fields("City").Value)%><BR></FONT></TD>
<TD BORDERCOLOR=#c0c0c0 ><FONT SIZE=2 FACE="Arial" COLOR=#000000>
<%=Server.HTMLEncode(rs.Fields("Region").Value)%><BR></FONT></TD>
<TD BORDERCOLOR=#c0c0c0 ><FONT SIZE=2 FACE="Arial" COLOR=#000000>
<%=Server.HTMLEncode(rs.Fields("PostalCode").Value)%><BR></FONT></TD>
<TD BORDERCOLOR=#c0c0c0 ><FONT SIZE=2 FACE="Arial" COLOR=#000000>
<%=Server.HTMLEncode(rs.Fields("Country").Value)%><BR></FONT></TD>
<TD BORDERCOLOR=#c0c0c0 ><FONT SIZE=2 FACE="Arial" COLOR=#000000>
<%=Server.HTMLEncode(rs.Fields("Phone").Value)%><BR></FONT></TD>
<TD BORDERCOLOR=#c0c0c0 ><FONT SIZE=2 FACE="Arial" COLOR=#000000>
<%=Server.HTMLEncode(rs.Fields("Fax").Value)%><BR></FONT></TD>

</TR>
<%
rs.MoveNext
loop%>
</TBODY>
<TFOOT></TFOOT>
</TABLE>
</BODY>
</HTML>
```

27

WEB PUBLISHING
WITH ACCESS
2000 AND ASP

What you want to do is change the ADO connection information in the Active Server Page to use OLE DB. To do this you have to change only one line of code—the one that deals with the connection string. The wizard will try to open an ADO connection to the

DSN name that we provided. Because we give a phony DSN name, we will have to change the connection to use the OLE DB Provider for Jet (Access) and point to the MDB file on the server. You must change it to the valid syntax shown in Chapter 6, "Introduction to ActiveX Data Objects." You will change it from this

```
conn.open "NYC","Admin",""
```

to

```
conn.Open "Provider=Microsoft.Jet.OLEDB.4.0;data source="c:\northwind.mdb"
```

Save the file in Notepad and then open up a Web browser via its URL. Figure 27.2 shows the final result of your Active Server Page conversion. You have to open your ASP in your browser using its correct URL. For example you can get to an ASP file on your computer by using HTTP like so: `http://localhost/yourvirtualdirectoryname/filename.asp`.

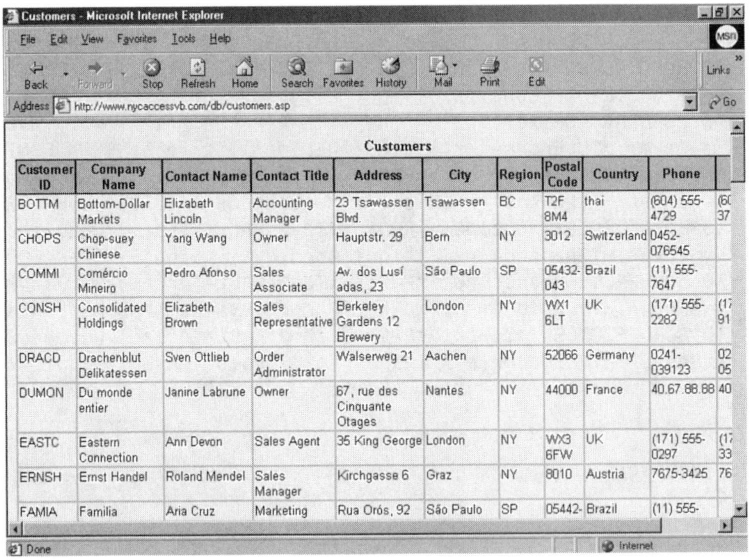

Customers

Customer ID	Company Name	Contact Name	Contact Title	Address	City	Region	Postal Code	Country	Phone	
BOTTM	Bottom-Dollar Markets	Elizabeth Lincoln	Accounting Manager	23 Tsawassen Blvd.	Tsawassen	BC	T2F 8M4	thai	(604) 555-4729	(6C 37
CHOPS	Chop-suey Chinese	Yang Wang	Owner	Hauptstr. 29	Bern	NY	3012	Switzerland	0452-076545	
COMMI	Comércio Mineiro	Pedro Afonso	Sales Associate	Av. dos Lusí adas, 23	São Paulo	SP	05432-043	Brazil	(11) 555-7647	
CONSH	Consolidated Holdings	Elizabeth Brown	Sales Representative	Berkeley Gardens 12 Brewery	London	NY	WX1 6LT	UK	(171) 555-2282	(1 91
DRACD	Drachenblut Delikatessen	Sven Ottlieb	Order Administrator	Walserweg 21	Aachen	NY	52066	Germany	0241-039123	02 05
DUMON	Du monde entier	Janine Labrune	Owner	67, rue des Cinquante Otages	Nantes	NY	44000	France	40.67.88.88	40
EASTC	Eastern Connection	Ann Devon	Sales Agent	35 King George	London	NY	WX3 6FW	UK	(171) 555-0297	(1 33
ERNSH	Ernst Handel	Roland Mendel	Sales Manager	Kirchgasse 6	Graz	NY	8010	Austria	7675-3425	76
FAMIA	Familia	Aria Cruz	Marketing	Rua Orós, 92	São Paulo	SP	05442-	Brazil	(11) 555-	

FIGURE 27.2
Table converted to Active Server Page.

Understanding the ASP Code

As you can see, the code that the Export wizard produces and you change is very simple. All you are doing is opening an ADO connection object and then opening an ADO recordset off that connection object. As you move through the recordset, you are outputting the data to the HTML table. I will cover this further later in the chapter.

Understanding the Limitations of Exporting ASP Pages

Although the Access export does a great job converting your data to Active Server Pages and getting you started, it is not as flexible as you would probably like it to be, nor can it create an entire custom Web application for you. The export does not provide any interactivity to your Web page, allow any updates or deletes, and the ASPs use the slower and less efficient ODBC to connect to the Access database.

You can use the export method to create some quick and dirty Active Server Pages, but if you want more robust Active Server Pages that provide additional functionality or use OLE DB, you will have to learn the basics of Active Server Pages. The next section in the chapter will discuss the basics of ASP.

Active Server Pages 101

In order to be able to create your own Active Server Page applications with Access 2000 as your database backend, you need to learn the basics of Active Server Pages. Although the topic of Active Server Pages can fill a whole book, this section will give you the basics to get you started. Enough material is presented here for you to build a very powerful Web-based application. I will cover

- The ASP engine
- Server-side VBScript
- Application and session objects
- Response and request objects
- The Global.asa file

The Active Server Page Engine

Active Server Pages is a single Internet Server Application Programming Interface (ISAPI) that has been added to Internet Information Server (IIS) 3.0 and higher. When a browser requests a file off the Web server, the ISAPI filter looks to see if the request is for an Active Server Page. If the Web browser requested an Active Server Page, the Active Server engine takes over. The ASP engine then parses out the entire ASP file and from top to bottom, runs the server-side script, and returns HTML back to the Web browser. The next section describes the server-side script.

Server-Side Scripting

Your ASP file contains server-side script and HTML. The server-side script is written in VBScript by default, and that is what I will focus on in this chapter. Visual Basic Scripting Edition, better known as VBScript, is a very powerful server- and client-side scripting language.

VBScript is a subset of Visual Basic. VBScript shares the same syntax and language features as VBA. If you have been using Visual Basic for Applications you can learn VBScript very quickly. VBScript leaves out some important features of VBA, so it will be safe and small to run over the Internet. For example File I/O, DLL calling, and the ability to call OLE Automation has been left out. All data types (Long, String, and so on) have been left out and all data variables use the data type of variant. Table 27.1 from the VBScript documentation lists all the features of VBA that were left out of VBScript.

TABLE 27.1 ALL FEATURES OF VBA NOT SUPPORTED BY VBSCRIPT

Category	*Omitted Feature/Keyword*
Array Handling	Option Base
	Declaring arrays with lower bound <> 0
Collection	Add, Count, Item, Remove
	Access to collections using ! character (for example,
	MyCollection!Foo)
Conditional Compilation	#Const
	#If...Then...#Else
Control Flow	DoEvents
	GoSub...Return, GoTo
	On Error GoTo
	On...GoSub, On...GoTo
	Line numbers, Line labels
	With...End With
Conversion	CVar, CVDate, Str, Val
Data Types	All intrinsic data types except Variant
	Type...End Type
Date/Time	Date statement, Time statement
	Timer
DDE	LinkExecute, LinkPoke, LinkRequest, LinkSend
Debugging	Debug.PrintEnd, Stop

Category	*Omitted Feature/Keyword*
Declaration	`Declare` (for declaring DLLs)
	`New`
	`Optional`
	`ParamArray`
	`Property Get, Property Let,`
	`Property Set`
	`Static`
Error Handling	`Erl`
	`Error`
	`On Error...Resume`
	`Resume, Resume Next`
File Input/Output	All traditional Basic file I/O
Financial	All financial functions
Object Manipulation	`TypeOf`
Objects	`Clipboard`
	`Collection`
Operators	`Like`
Options	`Def`*type*
	`Option Base`
	`Option Compare`
	`Option Private Module`
Strings	Fixed-length strings
	`LSet, RSet`
	Mid statement
	`StrConv`
Using Objects	Collection access using !

VBScript is kept small to ensure that the VBScript compiler will be very quick and efficient. Another reason VBScript has limited functionality is because VBScript can run on the browser as well as the server. If you are running a script in the browser on the client's machine, you do not want to give that script access to the underlying file system to allow unscrupulous VBScript developers to develop a script to reformat your hard drive.

Although some features were left out of VBScript, Table 27.2 from the VBScript documentation lists all the features included in VBScript.

TABLE 27.2 ALL THE FEATURES INCLUDED IN VBSCRIPT

Category	Keywords
Array handling	Array, Dim, Private, Public, ReDim, IsArray, Erase, LBound, UBound
Assignments	Set
Comments	Comments using ' or Rem
Constants/Literals	Empty, Nothing, Null, True, False
Control flow	Do...Loop, For...Next, For Each...Next, If...Then...Else, Select Case, While...Wend
Conversions	Abs, Asc, AscB, AscW, Chr, ChrB, ChrW, Cbool, Cbyte, Ccur, Cdate, CDbl, Cint, CLng, CSng, CStr, DateSerial, DateValue, Hex, Oct, Fix, Int, Sgn, TimeSerial, TimeValue, Dates/Times, Date, Time, DateAdd, DateDiff, DatePart, DateSerial, DateDiff, DatePart, DateSerial, DateValue, Day, Month, Weekday, Year, Hour, Minute, Second, Now, TimeSerial, TimeValue
Declarations	Const, Dim, Private, Public, ReDim, Function, Sub
Formatting Strings	FormatCurrency, FormatdateTime, FormatNumber, FormatPercent
Error Handling	On Error, Err
Input/Output	InputBox, LoadPicture, MsgBox
Literals	Empty, False, Nothing, Null, True
Math	Atn, Cos, Sin, Tan, Exp, Log, Sgr, Randomize, Rnd
Objects	CreateObject, Dictionary, Err, FileSystemObject, GetObject, TextStream
Operators	Addition(+), Subtraction(-) Exponentiation(^) Modulus arithmetic(Mod) Multiplication(*), Division(/), Integer Division(\) Negation(-), String concatenation(&) Equality(=), Inequality(<>)

Category	Keywords
	Less Than(<), Less Than or Equal To(<=), Greater Than(>), Greater Than or Equal To(>=), Is, And, Or, XorEqv, Imp
Options	Option Explicit
Procedures	`Call, Function, Sub`
Rounding	`Abs, Int, Fix, Round, Sgn`
Script Engine ID	`ScriptEngine, ScriptEngineBuildVersion, ScriptEngineMajorVersion, ScriptEngineMinorVersion`
Strings	`Asc, AscB, AscW, Chr, ChrB, ChrW, Filter, Instr, InStrB, InstrRev, Join, Len, LenB, Lcase, Ucase, Left, LeftB, Mid, MidB, Right, RightB, Replace, Space, Split, StrComp, String, StrReverse, LTrim, RTrim, Trim`
Variants	`IsArray, IsDate, IsEmpty, IsNullIsNumeric, IsObject, TypeName, VarType`

27

WEB PUBLISHING WITH ACCESS 2000 AND ASP

Learning VBScript can be done through trial and error by just experimenting with some VBA code and seeing if it will work in VBScript. In addition, Microsoft made available VBScript's documentation to help you use and learn VBScript. Downloadable from www.microsoft.com/vbasic the documentation is available for free. When you download and install the documentation, a full language reference and tutorial is installed on your machine as shown in Figure 27.3.

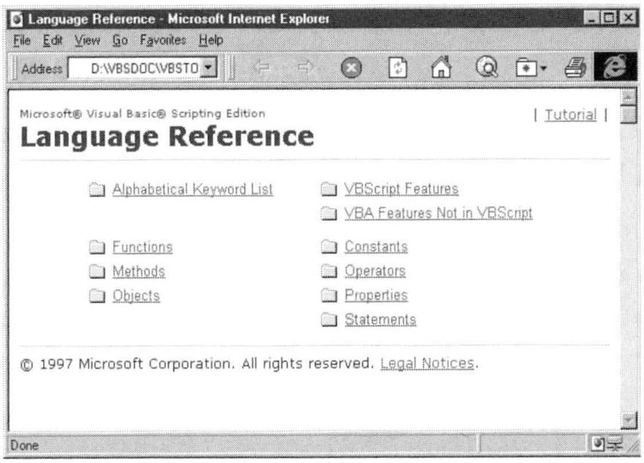

FIGURE 27.3

VBScript's documentation.

Using VBScript with Active Server Pages

Although you can create great looking sites that incorporate VBScript on the client-side (when VBScript actually runs in the Web browser on the local machine), this chapter only deals with the server-side script because that is how the ASP engine will generate HTML for you. Here are a few things you can do with VBScript on the server:

- Create a variable and assign a value to it, make decisions to it, or include it in the HTML output.

- Perform operations on variables using the If…Then, Select Case, and many other operators.

- Create procedures that only run on the server to do logins, data validation, and formatting.

- Dynamically create client-side VBScript to execute on the client in the outputted HTML.

All VBScript that runs on the server is written between <%> tags. You can incorporate pieces of script mixed with HTML. For example, Listing 27.2 is an ASP file that assigns my name to the variable strName and then combines it with HTML to produce a Web page.

LISTING 27.2 A SAMPLE ASP FILE USING A VARIABLE

```
<HTML>
<HEAD><TITLE>Variables</TITLE></HEAD>
<BODY BGCOLOR=#FFFFFF>
<% strName="Stephen Forte" %>
Hello <%=strName%>
</BODY>
</HTML>
```

When a user requests an ASP file with the code in Listing 27.2, the Web server will run the script between the <%> delimiters and produce a Web page in HTML, as shown in Figure 27.4. The HTML of the page produced is shown in Listing 27.3.

Listing 27.3 shows the source of the Web page in Figure 27.4.

LISTING 27.3 THE HTML SOURCE OF THE WEB PAGE IN FIGURE 27.4

```
<HTML>
<HEAD><TITLE>Variables</TITLE></HEAD>
<BODY BGCOLOR=#FFFFFF>
Hello Stephen Forte
```

```
<BR>
</BODY>
</HTML>
```

FIGURE 27.4

The Web page produced by the ASP file in Listing 27.5.

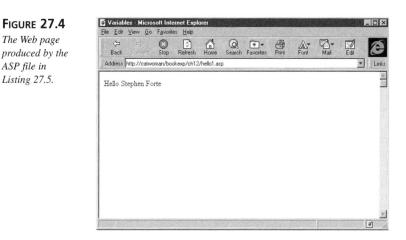

Compare the ASP file in Listing 27.2 and the HTML the ASP file generated in Listing 27.3. Notice that the VBScript code inside the <%> code is not in the HTML because that VBScript produced the HTML final result. The code <%=strName%> was replaced in the HTML output with the value of the variable. This is because anything inside the <%> tags are processed and run on the server and the results of the code are sent to the browser as straight HTML.

In addition to working with strings, the ASP file in Listing 27.4 will use a loop to increase the value of the variable produce HTML.

LISTING 27.4 ASP FILE USING SERVER-SIDE SCRIPTING

```
<HTML>
<HEAD>
<TITLE>Creating Hello World with Incremental Text Size Increase</TITLE>
</HEAD>
<BODY BGCOLOR=#FFFFFF>
<% for i = 3 to 7 %>
        <FONT SIZE=<% = i %>>Hello World</FONT><BR>
<% next %>
<BR>
<BR>
</BODY>
</HTML>
```

When a user requests the ASP file in Listing 27.4, the VBScript will loop five times and increase the font size by one on each loop, producing the Web page in Figure 27.5. The HTML source code is shown in Listing 27.5.

FIGURE 27.5

The Web page produced by the ASP file in Listing 27.4.

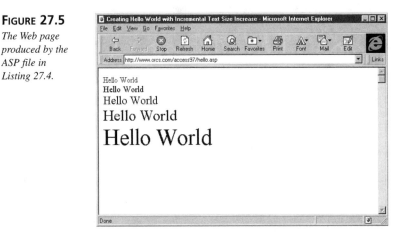

LISTING 27.5 HTML Source from the Web Page Generated by the ASP in Listing 27.4

```
<HTML>
<HEAD>
<TITLE>Creating Hello World with Incremental Text Size Increase</TITLE>
</HEAD>
<BODY BGCOLOR=#FFFFFF>
        <FONT SIZE=3>Hello World</FONT><BR>

        <FONT SIZE=4>Hello World</FONT><BR>

        <FONT SIZE=5>Hello World</FONT><BR>

        <FONT SIZE=6>Hello World</FONT><BR>

        <FONT SIZE=7>Hello World</FONT><BR>
<BR>
<BR>
</BODY>
</HTML>
```

As you can see in the prior two examples, Active Server Pages uses VBScript on the server and produces standard HTML based on your script. To really increase the power of your ASP Web pages, you will want to take advantage of some of the built-in ASP objects, which are discussed next.

The `Application` and `Session` Objects

When using Active Server Pages, ASP has some built in objects available for you to use in your application. The following section will explain to you how to use each of these objects in your ASP applications. This is only an introduction, so you can use the objects in your applications. For a more in-depth discussion on these objects, see *Active Server Pages Unleashed* (ISBN: 1-57521-351-6).

Using the `Application` Object

When developing Active Server Pages, each virtual directory on your Web server is considered an application. ASP will refer to each application as an object. The `Application` object can be used to maintain application-wide information that can be accessed by all users within an application. The `Application` object comes to life when the first user comes to your directory for the first time since your Web Server was last started. The `Application` object will be available to all users who visit your site and lives on until all user sessions time out or the Web server is restarted.

Properties can be added to the `Application` object dynamically that are considered to be global variables available to each page in your application and each user in your application. Using a property of the `Application` object is easy, the syntax in ASP is

```
<%Application("propertyname")=value %>
```

For example, let's say that you want to determine how many users have logged in at the same time. You can set up a property called VisitorNum like this:

```
<%Application("VisitorNum")=0 %>
```

Then as each user logs into your system either through a prompt or by going to your default page, you can increase this global variable by one and display the total number of current users. With this technique you will also want to decrease the variable by one when a user leaves to keep the number accurate. You would increase the property by one when a new user logs in:

```
<%Application("VisitorNum")=Application("VisitorNum")+1%>
```

When a user logs off, you would use

```
<%Application("VisitorNum")=Application("VisitorNum")-1%>
```

To display the current concurrent users of your application at any given point is very easy with ASP. Just do the following in your ASP file:

```
We have <%=Application("VisitorNum")%> Concurrent users!%>
```

In summary, the `Application` object is used to store global variables for use with each page in your application and can be accessed by every user. To maintain state with *individual* users, or use global variables for each individual user, you must use the `Session` object discussed in the following section.

Using the `Session` Object

Perhaps the most important object you can learn in Active Server Pages development is the `Session` object. ASP will maintain state for you and the `Session` object automatically will keep its scope for the current user. If you have 200 users at your page at a time, you will have 200 `Session` objects running. The `Session` object enables you to create custom properties that will be globally scoped for the specific user that comes to your Web site. `Session` objects are what enable you to provide a unique and personalized experience for your users. For example, you can ask your user what colors they like and what their name is. Using properties of the `Session` object, you can use ASP to create pages with the user's favorite colors and refer to him by name for the duration of his visit.

A new session object comes to life every time a new user comes to your Web site and gets destroyed when the user leaves your Web site or when there is a time of inactivity called the `Session` time-out. To refer to a `Session` object's custom property, you use the identical syntax as the `Application` object.

```
<%Session("propertyname")=value %>
```

After this property is set, you can refer to it from every page in your Web site.

Using the `Response` and `Request` Objects

The `Application` and `Session` objects outlined in the previous section had the capability to create custom properties that maintained state for you. Two more objects, `Response` and `Redirect`, have methods that enable you to, through server-side scripting, take certain actions or collect data.

The `Response` Object

To manage the interaction between the server and the browser, you will use the `Response` object. There are eight methods of the `Response` object available to you; however, for my discussion of ASP and Access 2000, I will be looking at the `Redirect` and `Write` methods.

Response.Redirect

When you want to display a certain page in the browser, you should use the `Redirect` method of the `Response` object from within your server-side script. For example, imagine you have a Web page where your user is brought to a sign-in form that will authenticate their user ID against an Access 2000 database. If the ID exists, they are brought to your main page; if not, they are brought to a new member sign-up page. You can use an `If...Then` construct along with the `Response.Redirect` method as shown here.

```
<%If fLogin=True then
        'User Passed login Test
        Response.Redirect "welcome.html"
Else
        'User not in system
        Response.Redirect "newmember.asp"
End if%>
```

Response.Write

When you are constructing an ASP file to output HTML to the Web browser, you will want to write text for the HTML. You can do this with the `Write` method of the `Response` object. `Response.Write` has a very simple syntax:

```
Response.Write("string value")
```

For example, you can conditionally create messages for your users based on information they provide. You might ask the user how old they are and might want to use the `Write` method to give them some feedback when constructing a new page. The code here will use the `Response.Write` method to give the user feedback:

```
<%If intAge < 21 Then
Response.Write("The Drinking Laws in New York")
Response.Write ("State that you cannot buy any")
 Response.Write("alcohol until you reach the age")
Response.Write(" of 21. Sorry!")
Else
Response.Redirect "buy.asp"
End If%>
```

The Request Object

You might have been wondering "How can you determine what a user typed into a text box on a particular HTML page?" Enter the `Request` object. The `Request` object is your link what the user typed into the Web browser. The `Request` object can pass the information from many different places on your user's Web page; however, I will only concern myself with the calling HTML form on your user's Web page. Each form that calls an ASP will have HTML controls like text boxes and combo boxes inside. If you name these controls and call an ASP file, the ASP file has access to the values inside these controls with the following syntax:

```
Request.Form("controlname")
```

You can use the `Request.Form` object to capture the user's information and insert it into an Access 2000 database or construct a SQL statement. You can also assign a variable to something the user typed, as seen here:

```
<% intAge=Request.Form("txtAge")%>
```

The Global.asa File

There is a special file used with Active Server Pages called the Global.asa file. This file is placed in the root of your virtual directory and manages the events of the `Application` and `Session` objects. Global.asa is also used to create `Application` and `Session` variables. The `Application` and `Session` objects have events that fire off on the start and end of the object's creation. They are

- `Application_OnStart`
- `Application_OnEnd`
- `Session_OnStart`
- `Session_OnEnd`

You can use these events to create variables, insert or look up records in a database, and make sure that the user logged on. The Global.asa is not like the default document in your virtual directory. Global.asa is accessed the first time your user enters any page in your virtual directory. Global.asa produces no HTML like ASP files; instead, Global.asa has code that will execute the events associated with the `Application` and `Session` objects. As ASP takes off and Microsoft adds a richer event model to ASP, Global.asa will be the location for these events' code handlers to be placed.

The code in Listing 27.6 is an example of the Global.asa using the `Session` and `Application OnStart` events. With the `Application` object, you set a global variable called `VisitorNum` to keep track of the number of concurrent visitors to the site as described in a previous section. Inside the `Session OnStart` event, you set a connection to the sample database, so each page can use the `Connection` object created here. (There is more on the database connection features in Chapters 6, "Introduction to ActiveX Data

Objects," and 7, "Advanced ADO.") Inside the `Session OnStart` event handler, you create five session-wide variables based on the database information.

LISTING 27.6 THE GLOBAL.ASA FILE FOR OUR VIRTUAL DIRECTORY

```
<SCRIPT LANGUAGE="VBScript" RUNAT="Server">
'Global ASA file for www.orcs.com/access2000
'Purpose: Set up Application and Session Properties
'Stephen Forte

</SCRIPT>
<SCRIPT LANGUAGE=VBScript RUNAT=Server>

Sub Application_OnStart
'Set up for Global
Application("VisitorNum")=0
Application("Start")=Now
End Sub

Sub Session_OnStart
'This is setting the database connection for the user
'Also This sets the connection time-out, etc
Session("Start")=Now
            Session("DataConn_ConnectionString") = _
                "provider=Microsoft.Jet.OLEDB.4.0;" & _
                "data source=C:/wwwroot/access2000/data/nyc.mdb"
            Session("DataConn_ConnectionTimeout") = 15
            Session("DataConn_CommandTimeout") = 30
            Session("DataConn_RuntimeUserName") = ""
            Session("DataConn_RuntimePassword") = ""
End Sub
</SCRIPT>
```

27

WEB PUBLISHING
WITH ACCESS
2000 AND ASP

Examples of Active Server Page Objects

The example at the end of this chapter will use ASP objects in action. Figure 27.6 also shows an example of ASP objects printed to HTML.

The sample Web page takes advantage of `Application` and `Session` custom variables. I created a `Start` and `VisitorNum` variables of the `Application` object and assign the current time to the start variable during the `Application OnStart` event. During the `OnStart` event of the current user's session, I also assigned the `Session`'s start property to the current time. A user's session start time might not be the current time because the `Session OnStart` event fires off when the user goes to any page in the /access2000 directory. Listing 27.7 shows how these variables are referred to in the sample Web page.

LISTING 27.7 APPLICATION AND SESSION VARIABLES

```
<hr>
<%Application("VisitorNum")=Application("VisitorNum")+1%>
<p align="left"><strong>Application &amp; Session Variables:</strong></p>
<p><strong>Application Started: <%=Application("Start")%> </strong></p>
<p><strong>Application Visitor Number:
        <%=Application("VisitorNum")%> </strong></p>
<p><strong>Your Session Started: <%=Session("Start")%> </strong></p>
<hr>
```

FIGURE 27.6

ASP objects.

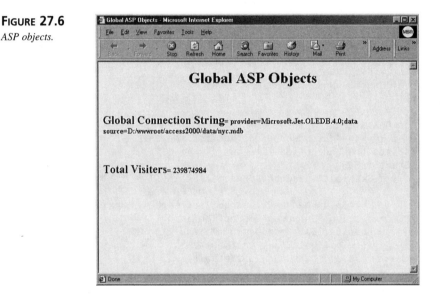

Using ADO in Your Active Server Page Applications

There are many properties and methods of the recordset object available to you. I will look at the EOF or End of File property in the next example. EOF will enable you to move through a recordset inside a loop from the first record to the last. Listing 27.8 opens a connection and a recordset, loops through all the records, and writes them to the HTML output of the ASP file.

LISTING 27.8 USING ADO IN AN ACTIVE SERVER PAGE

```
<!DOCTYPE HTML PUBLIC "-//IETF//DTD HTML//EN">
<html>
<head>
<title>Chapter 26: ADO Example</title>
</head>
<body>
<h2 align="center">Northwind Traders Customer Listing </h2>
<p align="center">Chapter 27 ADO Example</p>
<hr>
<% 'Begin VB Server-Side Script
Dim x
Dim dbconn
Dim rst
'Set up connection
Set dbconn=server.createobject("adodb.connection")

'Set up database
dbconn.open "provider=Microsoft.Jet.OLEDB.4.0;" & _
        "data source=D:\wwwroot\db\ch27.mdb"

'Set up the recordset
set rst=dbconn.execute ("Select * from Customers")

'Use for a counter
x=1
Do Until rst.eof
        response.write x & ". " & rst("CompanyName")%>
<br>
<%rst.movenext
x=x+1
loop
dbconn.close
'End All Server-Side Script%>
<hr>

</body>
</html>
```

Figure 27.7 demonstrates the result of the ASP file in Listing 27.8.

As you can see with the combination of ASP, VBScript, and ADO, you can create very powerful data-driven Web pages with Access 2000 databases as an engine. The next section of this chapter describes a real-life example.

27

WEB PUBLISHING
WITH ACCESS
2000 AND ASP

FIGURE 27.7

The results of the ADO-based ASP file.

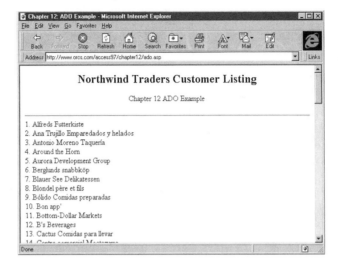

Real-Life Example: Establishing a Self Maintaining Membership-Based Web Page

If you run a Web site that needs to keep track of members and provide a login, Access 2000 and Active Server Pages are your answer. I run a local Access and Visual Basic Users Group in New York City. We have a Web site located at www.nycaccessvb.com that uses ASP to display a member listing, meeting finder, and a code library all created by ASP files. The ASP pages have a live connection to our Access 2000 member database. In addition, we want a member to be able to update their own information via a login and see some Web site content that is available to members only, like a job forum.

This application should only allow people with a valid UserId and correct password enter the system. After a user logs on, a session variable will be set to the UserId so the user will not have to type their name at every subsequent page in the system. Lastly, the system will write the current date to the database as the last login time.

The application starts when the user visits the NYC Access VB Web site with a prompt to login as shown in Figure 27.8.

The login page is just an HTML form that calls an ASP file as its action. Listing 27.9 show the HTML code to create the login form.

FIGURE 27.8

The login prompt.

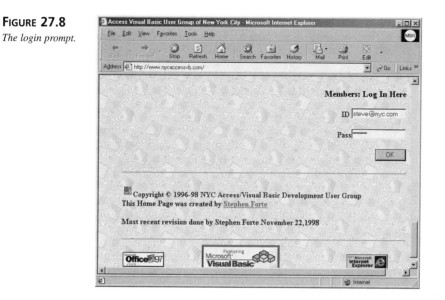

LISTING 27.9 HTML CODE TO CREATE A LOGIN CODE

```html
<form action="login.asp"
method="post" name="frmLogin">
    <p align="right">ID <input type="text" size="15" name="txtID"></p>
    <p align="right">Pass<input type="password" size="15"
    name="txtPass"></p>
    <p align="right"><input type="submit" name="cmdOK"
    value="    OK    "> </p>
</form>
```

When the user clicks the Submit button the ASP login.asp will run. Login.asp will look at the membership Access 2000 database. This table has a field for the UserID, password, last login date, and other fields. Listing 27.10 shows the contents of the login.asp file.

LISTING 27.10 ASP FILE LOGIN.ASP

```asp
<%@ LANGUAGE="VBSCRIPT" %>

<HTML>
<HEAD>
<META NAME="GENERATOR" Content="Microsoft Visual InterDev 6.0">
<META HTTP-EQUIV="Content-Type" content="text/html; charset=iso-8859-1">
<TITLE>Login Form</TITLE>
</HEAD>
```

continues

LISTING 27.10 CONTINUED

```
<BODY>
<BODY BGCOLOR=#FFFFFF>


<%
'Purpose: All users to login
'Will kick back if user did not enter a UserID or pwd
'Also will kick back if incorrect pwd

'Variables
Dim rst
Dim strUserID
Dim strPass
Dim strSQL
Dim strConnect

Dim ado_OpenKeyset
Dim ado_LockOptimistic

'For the recordset open arguments
ado_OpenKeyset=1
ado_LockOptimistic=3

'Assign a Connection String
strConnect="provider=Microsoft.Jet.OLEDB.4.0;" & _
        "data source=D:\wwwroot\db\ch27.mdb"

'Pass the form info into the variables
strPass=request.form("txtPass")
strUserID=request.form("txtID")

'Build SQL String
strSQL="SELECT FName, LName, Email, lastLogin, pass, " & _
    "Status FROM tblMembers WHERE (Email =" & "'" & strUserID & "'" & ")"

'set up rst
Set rst=server.createobject("ADODB.RECORDSET")

'Open rst
rst.open strSQL, _
        strConnect, ado_OpenKeyset,ado_LockOptimistic

'First test to See that the User Entered a UserID and a Password
If strUserID="" or strPass="" then
        Response.Write "You did not enter a User ID " & _
```

```
            "or a Password, please do."

else

'If rst is at the end of file (EOF) then there is no match
if rst.eof then
        response.write "Your User ID is not in the System!!!"

else
'OK a match, see if correct pass

        If rst("pass")= strPass Then
'Pass OK
'Begin to Build the WWW page

                Response.Write "Welcome " & rst("FName") & _
                    " " & rst("LName")
                Response.Write "<br>"
                Response.Write "You last logged on " & rst("lastLogin")
                Response.Write "<br><br>" & _
                "<a href=" & chr(34) & "admin.htm" & chr(34) & ">Update" & _
                    "</a>Account profile "
                Response.Write "<br> <a href=" & _
                chr(34) & "job.htm" & chr(34) & _
                 ">Members </a> Only Job Forum"

'Set the Last Update Time to Now

rst.update ("lastlogin"),Date()


'Set a "Global" or Session Variable
Session("User") = strUserID

Else
'Incorrect pass
        response.write "Your User ID: <strong>" & _
            strUserID & "</strong> is  OK, Wrong Password!!!"
end if


end if
end if
'Close rst
rst.close
%>
</BODY>
</HTML>
```

The Login.asp file shown in Listing 27.10 will first set up variables for use in the script. Then a SQL statement is built using the information the user input in the form as part of the `Where` clause. The variable `strUserId` is used to hold the user's ID. The SQL statement looks like.

```
strSQL="SELECT FName, LName, Email, lastLogin, pass, " & _
  "Status FROM tblMembers WHERE (Email =" & "'" & strUserID & "'" & ")"
```

As you can see, the primary key of tblMembers is the field email. A user's email address is also their UserID. If the user did not enter an UserId or password, a warning is returned with a `Response.Write` method, as shown in Figure 27.9.

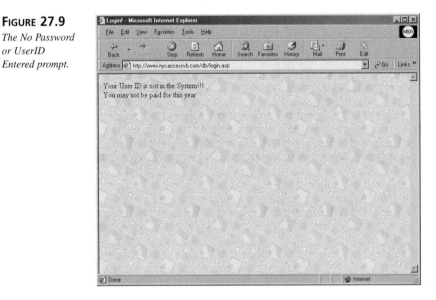

If the user did enter a password and a valid UserID, the script looks to see if the user entered the correct password. The VBScript code to determine if a password is correct is

```
If rst("pass")= strPass
```

If the password is incorrect they will be prompted with a `Response.Write`, as shown in Figure 27.10.

If the user enters the correct password, a session variable must be set to the UserID and the Access 2000 database field called lastlogin must be updated as shown here:

```
'Set the Last Update Time to Now
rst.update ("lastlogin"),Date()
'Set a "Global" or Session Variable
Session("User") = strUserID
```

FIGURE 27.10

The Incorrect Password prompt.

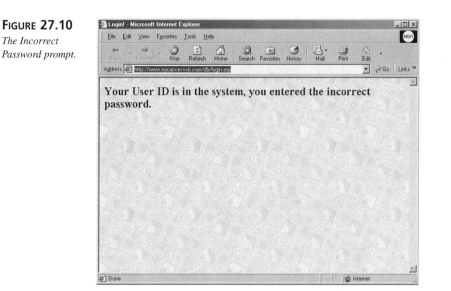

After the user is validated, we use the `Response.Write` to build the Members Only Web page. You can choose to use a `Response.Redirect` to show the user a completely different HTML Members Only page. The Members Only page is shown in Figure 27.11.

FIGURE 27.11

The Members Only page.

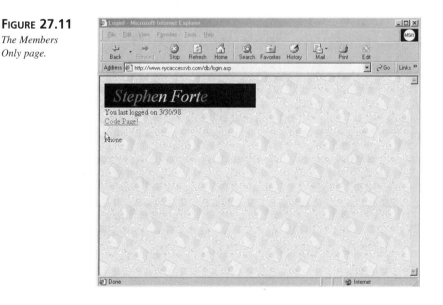

Now that the user is logged into the system, you will want to provide all the member-specific content here. In addition, one of the key selling points of Active Server Pages is that you can give users the ability to maintain their own account information. In this situation we are only concerned with giving the user the ability to change their own password. After the user logs into the Members Only site, there is an option to update his own account information as shown in Figure 27.12.

FIGURE 27.12

The Members Only change password page.

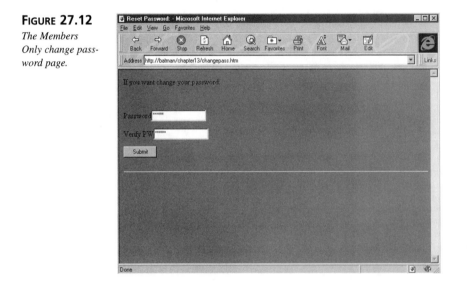

There is an HTML form available for the user to enter and verify a new password into the system. Listing 27.11 shows the HTML code needed to create this form.

LISTING 27.11 THE CHANGE PASSWORD FORM

```
<form action= "changepass.asp" form method="POST" name="frmNew">
    <p>Password<input type="password" size="20" name="txtPass"></p>
        <p>Verify PW<input type="password" size="20" name="txtVerify"></p>
    <p><input type="submit" name="cmdOK" value="Submit"></p>
</form>
```

The form in Listing 27.11 calls the changepass.asp file that will do the actual password change for the user and confirm it. Listing 27.12 shows the source code for the changepass.asp file.

LISTING 27.12 THE CHANGEPASS.ASP FILE

```
<%@ LANGUAGE="VBSCRIPT" %>

<HTML>
<HEAD>
<META NAME="GENERATOR" Content="Microsoft Visual InterDev 1.0">
<META HTTP-EQUIV="Content-Type" content="text/html; charset=iso-8859-1">
<TITLE>Document Title</TITLE>
</HEAD>
<BODY>

<%
'Purpose: Check for password confirmation and update database
'If the password is not the same in each box, abort

'Dims
Dim rst
Dim strPass
Dim strVerify
Dim strSQL
Dim strConnect

Dim ado_OpenKeyset
Dim ado_LockOptimistic

ado_OpenKeyset=1
ado_LockOptimistic=3

'Assign a Connection String
strConnect="provider=Microsoft.Jet.OLEDB.4.0;" & _
        "data source=D:\wwwroot\db\ch27.mdb"

'Get the values the user entered in the form
strPass=request.form("txtPass")
strVerify=request.form("txtVerify")

'Check to see if the text boxes match
If strpass <> strVerify then
        response.write "You did not enter" & _
            " the correct password in the verify box! <br>"
        response.write "Please do"

else

        strSQL="SELECT  pass, Status FROM tblMembers " & _
            "WHERE (Email =" & "'" & Session("User") & "'" & ")"
```

27

WEB PUBLISHING
WITH ACCESS
2000 AND ASP

continues

LISTING 27.12 CONTINUED

```
        'set up rst
        Set rst=server.createobject("ADODB.RECORDSET")

        rst.open strSQL, _
                strConnect,ado_OpenKeyset,ado_LockOptimistic

        If rst.eof then
                response.write "Your User ID is not in the System!!!"

        else

                rst.update ("pass"),strVerify
                Response.Write "Your password has been changed, " & _
                        "please remember it!!"

        end if
        rst.close
end if%>

</BODY>
</HTML>
```

The code in Listing 27.12 is not all that different than the code you mastered in Listing 27.10. In Listing 27.12 we first make sure that the user typed a matching password in the Confirmation box and only proceeds if they did. Then Listing 27.12 builds a SQL string using the global session variable User that we defined at login as the UserId in the Where clause. This is an example of maintaining state at a Web site. There is no need to ask the user to retype in her UserID or call a complex and server-intensive CGI-BIN program to maintain state.

After the recordset is opened, we use the Update method of the Recordset object to update the user's password in the database on the Web server. The next time the user logs in, the new password will be in effect. Figure 27.13 shows the Password Changed confirmation screen.

This concludes the real life example. You can go to the Web at http:\\www.nyc accessvb.com for a listing of all Web sites that are using Access 97 and 2000 as a data engine for some more ideas and examples.

I hope that this example and this chapter can get you started with building great Internet-based Access 2000 applications.

FIGURE 27.13

The Password Changed confirmation screen.

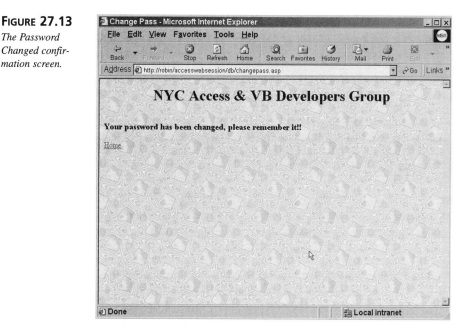

Access 2000 Web Publishing with XML

Chances are that you have heard of the latest buzzword on the Internet these days: XML or Extensible Markup Language. XML is a data-aware document mark-up standard developed by the W3C. As a database Web developer, you will want to harness the power of XML. Let's take a look at what it is and how we can put it to use in our applications.

Understanding the Basics of XML

XML is a set of rules for creating descriptive tags that identify the data that makes up a document. Although similar to HTML, XML is much more powerful because it is all about data. With XML, you create tags in your document that break the document into logical chunks. The "X" in XML actually stands for "Extensible," because as opposed to HTML, which has a fixed set of tags, XML has almost no fixed tags. You create the tags that you need to describe your data as you need them. Because we as database programmers work with data every day, XML will be very useful to us.

Let's create a simple XML document to describe the Customers table in Northwind. Because XML is Unicode-based, you can use an ASCII or Unicode text editor to create the XML file. To create an XML document, open Notepad or Visual InterDev and type the following line:

```
<?xml version="1.0"?>
```

This is the declaration line that tells the XML processor that this is an XML document. As your XML documents grow more sophisticated, you will include more information in your declaration, like what tags are legal in your document and where the formatting style sheet is. For now we will stick with the basics.

After the declaration, we need to define our root element. The root element is the entity that you are describing in your document, and you can have only one root element per document. Since this is a document of Customer data, our root element will be called `<Customers>`.

Next, we define our child nodes. The child nodes are the elements that make up our data. We will make a child node of the root called `<Customer>`. Inside each customer node, we will have child nodes that describe the contents of the data. These child nodes will map to our database fields in Northwind's Customer table. We will define our nodes with tags that we create and nest them in the `<Customer>` node. An example is shown in Listing 27.13.

LISTING 27.13 A BASIC XML DOCUMENT THAT REPRESENTS CUSTOMERS

```xml
<?xml version="1.0"?>

<Customers>
<Customer>
<CustomerID>ALFKI</CustomerID>
<CompanyName>Alfreds Futterkiste</CompanyName>
<ContactName>Maria Anders</ContactName>
<ContactTitle>Sales Representative</ContactTitle>

</Customer>
<Customer>
<CustomerID>ANATR</CustomerID>
<CompanyName>Ana Trujillo Emparedados y helados</CompanyName>
<ContactName>Ana Trujillo</ContactName>
<ContactTitle>Owner</ContactTitle>
</Customer>
<Customer>
<CustomerID>ANTON</CustomerID>
```

```
<CompanyName>Antonio Moreno Taqueria</CompanyName>
<ContactName>Antonio Moreno</ContactName>
<ContactTitle>Owner</ContactTitle>
</Customer>
</Customers>
```

Now that you are done, save the file as "Customers.xml".

Now we can keep the data and formatting separate by using XML and Dynamic HTML. We will fill an HTML table with XML data stored in your customers.xml file. You can use IE 4.0/5.0 data binding via a Java applet to bind XML data saved on disk to an HTML table as shown in Figure 27.14. To load the XML into your Web page, save the XML document to disk and then create a simple Web page as shown in Listing 27.14.

LISTING 27.14 DATABINDING XML IN IE 4 AND IE 5

```
<html>
<head>
<title>XML Databinding From XML on Disk</title>
<meta name="GENERATOR" content="Microsoft FrontPage 3.0">
</head>
<!—Java Applet—>
<APPLET code="com.ms.xml.dso.XMLDSO.class"
MAYSCRIPT id=xmldso WIDTH="100%" HEIGHT="20">
<PARAM NAME="URL" VALUE=" Customers.xml ">' +
</APPLET>

<p>XML Databinding From XML on Disk </p>

<table id="table" border="2" width="100%"
     datasrc="#xmldso" cellpadding="5">
<thead>
  <tr>
    <th>ID </th>
    <th>Name </th>
</thead>
  </tr>
  <tr>
    <td align="center" valign="top"><div datafld="CustomerId"></td>
    <td align="center" valign="top"><div datafld="CompanyName"></td>
  </tr>
</table>
</body>
</html>
```

FIGURE 27.14

Databinding XML to an HTML page.

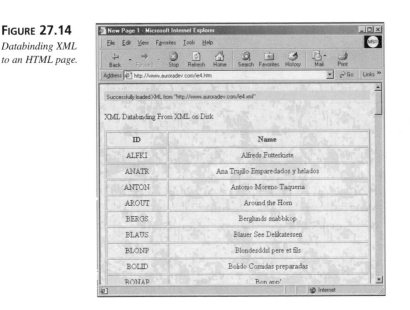

To parse the XML file, you have to use a Java applet that is a standard part of IE 4.0. (You can also download this applet's code from Microsoft's Web site.) Add the APPLET code shown in Listing 27.14 to your HTML file and set its "URL" property to the location or URL of the XML document. Then you can use simple Dynamic HTML data binding with the `datasrc="#xmldso"` tag in your Table declaration where `#xmldso` is the name of your Java applet object in your code. Lastly, just set the `datafld` property of each field in your table to an XML child node name. As you change the XML document, the Web page will change. It's that easy!

Creating XML Programmatically

Since XML is so easy to create and use in your applications, let's create a generic ActiveX DLL in VB to produce XML code. We can create XML files on-the-fly from our DLL that we can use in our Web and VB applications. The DLL can be used to power Web sites or client/server applications.

To begin, we are going to start VB 6 and create a new ActiveX DLL project called XML_TOOL with one class module called Database. Our class will have exactly one method, the CreateXML method. We must set a reference to ADO 2.0 under Tools, References. This method will use ADO to connect to a database, open a recordset, and return XML to the client. The method will accept three arguments, the root element you want to name, a connection string, and a SQL statement to execute. The method is shown in Listing 27.15.

LISTING 27.15 CREATING XML PROGRAMMATICALLY INSIDE A VB COMPONENT

```
Public Function CreateXML _
    (strEntity As String, strSQLStatement As String, _
        strConnectionString As String) As String

'Generic Function that will create XML from
'An ADO Recordset and return it to an application
'Return value can be put into an XML string or HTML doc

Dim rst As ADODB.Recordset
Dim fld As ADODB.Field
Dim strReturn As String

On Error GoTo Proc_Err

Set rst = New ADODB.Recordset

'Open the recordset based on the SQL Statement
'That was passed in along with the connection info
rst.Open strSQLStatement, strConnectionString

'Begin the start of the XML Document
'With the XML Version
strReturn = "<?XML version= '1.0'?>"

If rst.EOF And rst.BOF Then
    'Produce an Empty Element if no data
    strReturn = strReturn & vbNewLine & "<" & strEntity & "s/>"
Else
    'Open the First Entity Tag
    strReturn = strReturn & vbNewLine & "<" & strEntity & "s>"

    'Loop through the Records in the recordset and
    'output them to XML
    Do Until rst.EOF
        'Begin the Element
        strReturn = strReturn & vbNewLine & "<" & strEntity & ">"

        'Dump each field of the recordset
        'If you want less fields, restrict
        'them in your SQL Statement
        For Each fld In rst.Fields
            strReturn = strReturn & vbNewLine & "<" & fld.Name & ">"
            strReturn = strReturn & fld.Value
            strReturn = strReturn & "</" & fld.Name & ">"
        Next fld
```

continues

LISTING **27.15** CONTINUED

```
            'Close the Element
            strReturn = strReturn & vbNewLine & "</" & strEntity & ">"
            'Move the next record
            rst.MoveNext
        Loop
        'Close the Entity
        strReturn = strReturn & vbNewLine & "</" & strEntity & "s>"
End If

'Assign the Created text to the method
CreateXML = strReturn

'Clean up
rst.Close
Set rst = Nothing

Proc_Exit:
    Exit Function

Proc_Err:
    'Pass the Error Back to the Application
    Err.Raise Err, "XML DLL", Err.Description
    Resume Proc_Exit


End Function
```

Now let's put this ActiveX DLL to work. After compiling the DLL, let's start with another Visual Basic application and set a reference to our DLL. The code to instantiate the DLL and XML is shown in Listing 27.16, where Pubs is a DSN to the Pubs database in SQL Server.

LISTING **27.16** CALLING THE COMPONENT CREATED IN LISTING 27.15

```
Private Sub cmdPrintXML_Click()

Dim xml As XML_Tool.Database
Set xml = New XML_Tool.Database

Debug.Print xml.CreateXML("Publishers", "Select * From Publishers",
"Pubs")

End Sub
```

The results are shown here:

```
<?XML version= '1.0'?>
<Publishers>
<Publisher>
<pub_id>0736</pub_id>
<pub_name>New Moon Books</pub_name>
<city>Boston</city>
<state>MA</state>
<country>USA</country>
</Publisher>
<Publisher>
<pub_id>0877</pub_id>
<pub_name>Binnet & Hardley</pub_name>
<city>Washington</city>
<state>DC</state>
<country>USA</country>
</Publisher>
</Publishers>
```

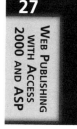

As you can see, our Visual Basic application prints only the XML to the debug window; however, you can create XML files by using simple File I/O or other techniques. Let's now use our DLL from an Active Server Page. Remember the last Web example where we loaded XML into the HTML table? That XML can also be inline XML inside of the Java Applet code. Well, now let's use this ActiveX DLL to dynamically create the in-line XML when the user requests the Web page. With a little bit of VBScript code, we can load our DLL from a Web page and dynamically create the XML used in our Web application. The following code creates the same Web page as before; however, now it is dynamic and creates the XML on-the-fly as the user requests the Web page. See Listing 27.17.

LISTING 27.17 CREATING XML INSIDE AN ASP

```
<%
Dim xml
Dim strSQL
Dim strConnect
Dim strXML

Set xml = Server.CreateObject("XML_Tool.Database")

strSQL="Select * from Customers "
strConnect="File Name=c:\jetweb.UDL;"
```

continues

LISTING 27.17 CONTINUED

```
strXML= xml.CreateXML("Customer", cstr(strSQL), cstr(strConnect))
%>
<APPLET code="com.ms.xml.dso.XMLDSO.class"
 MAYSCRIPT id=xmldso WIDTH="100%" HEIGHT="20">
<%=strXML%>
</APPLET>
```

Creating Charts with the Chart Control

Chapter 25 introduced us to the Office Web Components and how to use them in Access 2000 and Visual Basic. Chapter 26 showed us how to use them in Data Access Pages with Internet Explorer 5.0. What happens when you use a browser that does not support ActiveX Controls? The chart control can also use GIFs for Web browsers that do not support ActiveX Controls.

We are now going to use the simple CrossTab query from Northwind to create an unbound chart on our ASP. We are going to create a global.ASA file to keep track of some GIFs shown in Listing 27.18.

LISTING 27.18 CREATING A CHART GIF ON THE SERVER

```
<SCRIPT LANGUAGE="VBScript" RUNAT="Server">
Sub Session_OnStart
Session("nFiles") = 0
Set Session("FileSystem") = CreateObject("Scripting.FileSystemObject")
End Sub

Sub Session_OnEnd
Dim i

For i = 0 To Session("nFiles") - 1
Session("FileSystem").DeleteFile "D:\ntstuff\WebStuff\" & _
     Session("szFile" & i ), True
Next
End Sub
</SCRIPT>
```

In our ASP, we create two aHeaders arrays in which we fill in the values of our series headers, in this case the four Quarters of a fiscal year. Then we will open an ADO recordset based on the saved CrossTab query called qryQuarterlySales and then fill the aValues array with the values of the fields of the recordset. The full code is shown in Listing 27.19.

LISTING 27.19 WORKING WITH THE CHART OFFICE 2000 WEB COMPONENT

```
<%@ language="vbscript" %>
<html>
<body>
<%
Dim ChartSpace1, c, aHeaders(3), aValues(3)
Dim rst

'Create an array of items for the chart
aHeaders(0) = "Q1"
aHeaders(1) = "Q2"
aHeaders(2) = "Q3"
aHeaders(3) = "Q4"


'Open a recordset based on an XTAB query in Northwind
'and fill in the values for the chart bars
Set rst=Server.CreateObject("ADODB.Recordset")
rst.Open "qryQuarterlySales", "File Name=" & Server.MapPath("Jet.UDL")

aValues(0) = rst![Qtr 1]
aValues(1) = rst![Qtr 2]
aValues(2) = rst![Qtr 3]
aValues(3) = rst![Qtr 4]

'-- Create a non-visual version of the Chart CTL
Set ChartSpace1 = CreateObject("OWC.Chart")
Set c = ChartSpace1.Constants

ChartSpace1.Border.Color = c.chColorNone
ChartSpace1.Charts.Add
ChartSpace1.Charts(0).Type = _
      ChartSpace1.Constants.chChartTypeColumnClustered
ChartSpace1.Charts(0).SeriesCollection.Add
ChartSpace1.Charts(0).SeriesCollection(0).Caption = "Sales"
ChartSpace1.Charts(0).SeriesCollection(0).SetData _
      c.chDimCategories, c.chDataLiteral, aHeaders
```

continues

27

WEB PUBLISHING WITH ACCESS 2000 AND ASP

LISTING 27.19 CONTINUED

```
ChartSpace1.Charts(0).SeriesCollection(0).SetData _
        c.chDimValues, c.chDataLiteral, aValues
ChartSpace1.Charts(0).HasLegend = True

'-- Get a temporary filename from the file system from Global ASA

szFilename = Session("FileSystem").GetTempName & ".gif"

'-- Export a GIF of the current chart
ChartSpace1.ExportPicture "D:\ntstuff\WebStuff\" & _
        szFilename, "gif", 600, 512

'--Link to the Gif
Response.Write "<img src='" & szFilename & "'>"

'-- For later accounting / clean-up by the server,
'store this file and increment the count of the number of
'-- saved files. On Session_OnEnd these files will be deleted.
'----------------------------
Session("szFile" & Session("nFiles")) = szFilename
Session("nFiles") = Session("nFiles") + 1
%>
</body>
</html>
```

Summary

As you can see, you can create some very powerful Web sites with Access 2000. Using the knowledge you gained in prior chapters on ADO, you can do just about anything with Access 2000 and Active Server Pages, including e-commerce and charting. Lastly, the latest bleeding-edge technology, XML, is very operable with Access 2000 and ASP.

References for Further Reading

APPENDIX A

Recommended Books

Managing a Programming Project: People and Processes
Philip Metzger and John Boddie
Prentice Hall PTR, 1996

Successful Software Process Improvement
Robert B. Grady
Prentice Hall PTR, 1997

Project Management Made Simple
David King
PTR Prentice Hall, 1992

Managing the Software Process
Watts S. Humphrey
Addison Wesley Publishing Company, Inc., 1989

Software Metrics: Establishing a Company-Wide Program
Robert B. Grady and Deborah L. Caswell
Prentice Hall PTR, 1987

Exploring Requirements: Quality Before Design
Donald C. Gause and Gerald M. Weinberg
Dorset House Publishing Co., Inc., 1989

Quality Software Management: Systems Thinking (Volume 1)
Gerald M. Weinberg
Dorset House Publishing Co., Inc., 1992

Introduction to the Personal Software Process
Watts S. Humphrey
Addison Wesley Publishing Company, Inc., 1997

The Complete Guide to Software Testing
Bill Hetzel
John Wiley & Sons, Inc., 1988

The Art of Software Testing
Glenford Myers
John Wiley & Sons, Inc., 1979

Dynamics of Software Development
Jim McCarthy
Microsoft Press, 1995

Debugging the Development Process
Steve Maguire
Microsoft Press, 1994

Writing Solid Code
Steve Maguire
Microsoft Press, 1993

Code Complete
Steve McConnell
Microsoft Press, 1993

A

REFERENCES FOR
FURTHER READING

Rapid Development: Taming Wild Software Schedules
Steve McConnell
Microsoft Press, 1996

Software Project Survival Guide
Steve McConnell
Microsoft Press, 1998

How to Manage a Successful Software Project
Sanjiv Purba, David Sawh, and Bharat Shah
John Wiley & Sons, Inc., 1995

Software Inspection
Tom Gilb and Dorothy Graham
Addison Wesley, 1993

Principles of Software Engineering Management
Tom Gilb
Addison Wesley, 1988

Handbook of Team Design
Peter H. Jones
McGraw-Hill, 1998

Building the Right Things Right
Charles J. Nuese
Quality Resources, 1995

The Team Handbook—How to Use Teams to Improve Quality
Peter R. Scholtes
Joiner Associates, Inc., 1988

The Mythical Man-Month
Frederick P. Brooks, Jr.
Addison Wesley Longman, Inc., 1995

Peopleware: Productive Projects and Teams
Tom DeMarco & Timothy Lister
Dorset House Publishing Co., Inc., 1987

Software Engineering Economics
Barry W. Boehm
Prentice-Hall, Inc., 1981

Access 97 Expert Solutions
Stan Leszynski
Que Corporation, 1997

Online Resources

Analyzing Requirements and Defining Solution Architectures
Microsoft Certified Professional Exam 70-100

`http://www.microsoft.com/mcp/exam/stat/sp70-100.htm`

Institute of Electrical and Electronics Engineers, Inc. (IEEE)
Software Engineering Standards Catalog:

`http://standards.ieee.org/catalog/software1.html`

IEEE Recommended Practice for Software Requirements
Specifications #830-1998

IEEE Guide to Software Design Descriptions #1016.1-1993

IEEE Standard Classification for Software Anomalies #1044-1993

IEEE Standard for Software Project Management Plans #1058-1998

INDEX

F

X-Y-Z

Get **FREE** books and more...when you register this book online for our Personal Bookshelf Program

http://register.samspublishing.com/

SAMS

Register online and you can sign up for our *FREE Personal Bookshelf Program*...unlimited access to the electronic version of more than 200 complete computer books—immediately! That means you'll have 100,000 pages of valuable information onscreen, at your fingertips!

Plus, you can access product support, including complimentary downloads, technical support files, book-focused links, companion Web sites, author sites, and more!

And you'll be automatically registered to receive a *FREE subscription to a weekly email newsletter* to help you stay current with news, announcements, sample book chapters, and special events, including sweepstakes, contests, and various product giveaways!

We value your comments! Best of all, the entire registration process takes only a few minutes to complete, so go online and get the greatest value going—absolutely FREE!

Don't Miss Out On This Great Opportunity!

Sams is a brand of Macmillan Computer Publishing USA.

For more information, please visit *www.mcp.com*

This is a legal agreement between you, the end user, and 20/20 Software, Inc. ("20/20"). The enclosed 20/20 software programs (the "SOFTWARE") are licensed by 20/20 to the original customer and any subsequent transferee of the product for use only on the terms set forth here. Please read this license agreement. Opening this diskette package indicates that you accept these terms. If you do not agree to these terms, return the full, unopened product with proof of purchase to your place of purchase within 30 days for a full refund.

* GRANT OF LICENSE. 20/20 grants to you the right to use one copy of the enclosed SOFTWARE on a single computer (i.e. single CPU) not serving as a network server, OR if the enclosed SOFTWARE is designated a "Network Version", one copy of the SOFTWARE may be installed on a single computer serving as a network server and the SOFTWARE may be used concurrently on a single network by the number of users indicated on the system disk.

* COPYRIGHT. The SOFTWARE is owned by 20/20 or its suppliers and is protected by United States copyright laws and international treaty provisions. You may either (a) make two copies of the SOFTWARE solely for backup or archival purposes provided that you reproduce all copyright and other proprietary notices that are on the original copy of the SOFTWARE provided to you, or (b) transfer the SOFTWARE to a single hard disk provided you keep the original solely for backup or archival purposes. You may not copy the written materials accompanying the SOFTWARE.

* OTHER RESTRICTIONS. You may not rent or lease the SOFTWARE, but you may transfer the SOFTWARE and accompanying written materials on a permanent basis provided you retain no copies and the recipient agrees to the terms of this Agreement. You may not reverse engineer, decompile, disassemble, or create derivative works from the SOFTWARE.

* GOVERNMENT LICENSEE. If you are acquiring the SOFTWARE on behalf of any unit or agency of the United States Government, the following provisions apply:

The Government acknowledges 20/20's representation that the SOFTWARE and its documentation were developed at private expense and no part of them is in the public domain. The Government acknowledges 20/20's representation that the SOFTWARE is "Restricted Computer Software" as that term is defined in Clause 52.227-19 of the Federal Acquisition Regulations (FAR) and is "Commercial Computer Software" as that term is defined in Subpart 227.471 of the Department of Defense Federal Acquisition Regulation Supplement (DFARS). The Government agrees that:

(i) if the SOFTWARE is supplied to the Department of Defense (DoD), the SOFTWARE is classified as "Commercial Computer Software" and the Government is acquiring only "restricted rights" in the SOFTWARE and its documentation as that term is defined in Clause 252.227-7013 (c) (1) of the DFARS, and

(ii) if the SOFTWARE is supplied to any unit or agency of the United States Government other than DoD, the Government's rights in the SOFTWARE and its documentation will be as defined in Clause 52.227-19 (c) (2) of the FAR.

RESTRICTED RIGHTS LEGEND. Use, duplication, or disclosure by the Government is subject to restrictions as set forth in subparagraph (c) (1) (ii) of the Rights in Technical Data and Computer Software clause at DFARS 252.227-7013. 20/20 Software, Inc., 8196 SW Hall Blvd. #200, Beaverton, OR 97008.

* GENERAL. This Agreement will be governed by the laws of the State of Oregon, except for that body of law dealing with conflicts of law. Should you have any questions concerning this Agreement, or if you desire to contact 20/20 for any reason, please write: 20/20 Software, Inc., 8196 SW Hall Blvd. #200, Beaverton, OR 97008.

What's on the CD-ROM

CD-ROM Installation

Windows 95 Installation Instructions

1. Insert the CD-ROM disc into your CD-ROM drive.
2. From the Windows 95 desktop, double-click on the My Computer icon.
3. Double-click on the icon representing your CD-ROM drive.
4. Double-click on the icon titled START.EXE to run the CD-ROM interface.

> **NOTE**
>
> If Windows 95 is installed on your computer and you have the AutoPlay feature enabled, the START.EXE program starts automatically whenever you insert the disc into your CD-ROM drive.

Windows NT Installation Instructions

1. Insert the CD-ROM disc into your CD-ROM drive.
2. From File Manager or Program Manager, choose Run from the File menu.
3. Type `<drive>\START.EXE` and press Enter, where `<drive>` corresponds to the drive letter of your CD-ROM. For example, if your CD-ROM is drive D:, type
   `D:\START.EXE`